FERNS, SPIKEMOSSES, CLUBMOSSES, AND QUILLWORTS

OF EASTERN NORTH AMERICA

FERNS, SPIKEMOSSES, CLUBMOSSES, AND QUILLWORTS

OF EASTERN NORTH AMERICA

EMILY B. SESSA

Princeton University Press

Princeton and Oxford

This book is dedicated to fern and lycophyte enthusiasts everywhere,
and especially to the members of the American Fern Society, among whom
I have found both professional inspiration and many treasured friendships.

Special thanks to Alan Cressler; this book might not have been
possible without Alan, and it certainly would have been much less fun.

Requests for permission to reproduce
material from this work should be sent to
permissions@press.princeton.edu

Published by Princeton University Press
41 William Street, Princeton, New Jersey 08540
99 Banbury Road, Oxford OX2 6JX

press.princeton.edu

All Rights Reserved

ISBN (pbk.) 978-0-691-21945-5
ISBN (e-book) 978-0-691-22044-4

Library of Congress Control Number: 2023945152

British Library Cataloging-in-Publication Data is
available

Editorial: Robert Kirk and Megan Mendonça
Production Editorial: Kathleen Cioffi
Text Design: D & N Publishing, Wiltshire, UK
Cover Design: Benjamin Higgins
Production: Steven Sears
Publicity: Matthew Taylor and Caitlyn Robinson
Copyeditor: Laurel Anderton

Cover Credit: Emily B. Sessa

This book has been composed in Nexus Sans

Printed on acid-free paper. ∞

Printed in China

10 9 8 7 6 5 4 3 2 1

CONTENTS

INTRODUCTION 7
What Are Ferns, Spikemosses, Clubmosses, and Quillworts? 7
What's Included: Ferns, Spikemosses, Clubmosses, and Quillworts of Eastern North America 10
How to Use This Book 13

IDENTIFYING FERNS AND LYCOPHYTES 16
Lycophyte Morphology and Identification 16
Fern Morphology and Identification 22

GLOSSARY 27

KEY TO PTERIDOPHYTE GENERA OF EASTERN NORTH AMERICA 32

LYCOPHYTES—Descriptions of Genera and Species 41

Dendrolycopodium 42
Diphasiastrum 47
Huperzia 53

Isoetes 59
Lycopodiella 79
Lycopodium 86

Palhinhaea 90
Pseudolycopodiella 92
Selaginella 94

Spinulum 111

FERNS—Descriptions of Genera and Species 113

Acrostichum 114
Actinostachys 118
Adiantum 120
Amauropelta 130
Amblovenatum 134
Anchistea 136
Anemia 138
Arachniodes 142
Argyrochosma 144
Aspidotis 145
Asplenium 146
Astrolepis 180
Athyrium 183
Azolla 187
Blechnum 191
Botrychium 193
Botrypus 213
Campyloneurum 215
Ceratopteris 219
Cheiroglossa 223
Christella 225
Claytosmunda 228

Coryphopteris 230
Crepidomanes 232
Cryptogramma 234
Ctenitis 237
Cyclosorus 240
Cyrtomium 242
Cystopteris 245
Dennstaedtia 254
Deparia 257
Dicranopteris 260
Didymoglossum 262
Diplazium 266
Dryopteris 269
Equisetum 289
Goniopteris 303
Gymnocarpium 309
Homalosorus 315
Hymenophyllum 317
Hypolepis 320
Leptogramma 322
Lomariopsis 324
Lorinseria 326

Lygodium 328
Macrothelypteris 333
Marsilea 335
Matteuccia 343
Meniscium 345
Microgramma 348
Microsorum 350
Moranopteris 352
Myriopteris 353
Nephrolepis 361
Odontosoria 371
Onoclea 373
Ophioderma 375
Ophioglossum 377
Osmunda 386
Osmundastrum 388
Pecluma 390
Pelazoneuron 395
Pellaea 402
Phegopteris 408
Phlebodium 414
Physematium 416

Pilularia 421
Pityrogramma 423
Platycerium 427
Pleopeltis 429
Polypodium 432
Polystichum 435
Psilotum 440
Pteridium 442
Pteris 445
Rumohra 453
Salvinia 455
Sceptridium 458
Schizaea 467
Tectaria 469
Telmatoblechnum 473
Thelypteris 475
Trichomanes 477
Vandenboschia 479
Vittaria 481
Woodsia 486

CHECKLISTS OF FERN AND LYCOPHYTE SPECIES IN EASTERN NORTH AMERICA 491

ACKNOWLEDGMENTS 501

FURTHER READING AND REFERENCES 502

ISOETES IMAGE CREDITS 505

INDEX TO SCIENTIFIC NAMES 507

INDEX TO COMMON NAMES 519

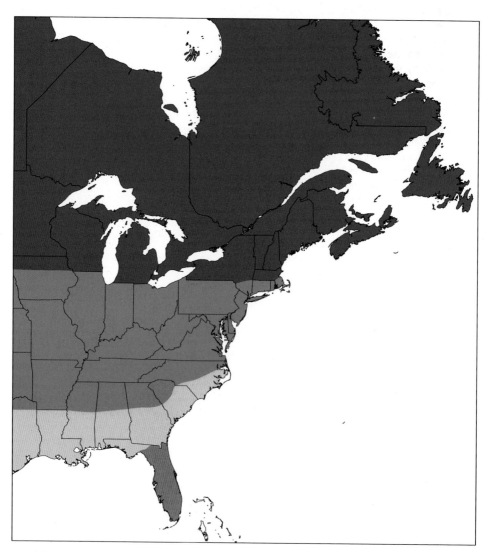

Map of the coverage area of this book. Eastern North America has been divided into subregions based loosely on geographic affinities of species: peninsular Florida (F-Florida; orange), the outer southern coastal plain (S-South; yellow), the central inland United States (C-Central; green), and the northern Midwest, Northeast, and Canada (N-North; blue). These colors are used throughout the book to indicate the presence of a genus or species in each of these regions.

INTRODUCTION
WHAT ARE FERNS, SPIKEMOSSES, CLUBMOSSES, AND QUILLWORTS?

Ferns, spikemosses, clubmosses, and quillworts are spore-bearing, vascular land plants, and they have existed for many millions of years. The earliest ancestors of these plants are known from the fossil record nearly 500 million years ago, and at various times during the history of our planet, members of these groups have been among the most diverse and abundant plants on Earth.

Historically, the ferns, spikemosses, clubmosses, and quillworts were lumped together and described collectively as "pteridophytes" or "ferns and fern allies." This grouping made sense given our understanding of these plants at the time: they are all vascular plants, meaning that they have internal plumbing (xylem and phloem) for moving water and nutrients, which sets them apart from the bryophytes, and they use spores rather than seeds for reproduction, which separates them from the seed plants (gymnosperms and flowering plants). It was therefore natural to assume that these plants were closely related to each other. However, DNA-based analyses in recent decades have clarified the relationships among all major plant lineages, resulting in quite a different understanding of how these particular groups are related to one another, and to all other land plants. The ferns, in fact, are most closely related to the seed plants, and the spikemosses, clubmosses, and quillworts together make up another large group called the lycophytes. The lycophytes as a whole are "sister" to, or equally related to, the group made up of the ferns and seed plants. This clarification of the relationships among the ferns, the three lycophyte lineages, and the seed plants has been one of the great advances in our scientific understanding of plant evolution in the last few decades. (Many lycophytes, however, still have common names that reflect their historical association with other plant groups, such as mosses or conifers; these common names, such as spikemoss, clubmoss, firmoss, ground-pine, and ground-cedar, were based on superficial similarity of appearance and are now recognized as not reflecting real relationships, but they are well established and persistent.)

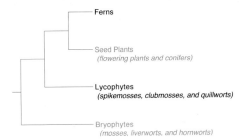

A phylogeny, or family tree, of land plants, showing the relationships between major groups. Ferns and seed plants are each other's closest relatives; the lycophytes, which include the spikemosses, clubmosses, and quillworts, are "sister" to the group composed of ferns and seed plants together. The bryophytes (mosses and their relatives) are sister to the lycophytes plus the ferns and seed plants. The ferns and lycophytes, in black font, are the subject of this book.

Today there are nearly 10,500 species of ferns and around 1,300 species of lycophytes. Within the lycophytes, the 3 groups—spikemosses, clubmosses, and quillworts—correspond, respectively, to the scientific groups recognized at the family level as Selaginellaceae, Lycopodiaceae, and Isoetaceae. The much larger fern lineage is divided into 48 families and includes plants traditionally recognized as ferns as well as several groups that were previously thought of as "fern allies" but are now recognized as belonging to the ferns, such as *Psilotum nudum*, the whisk fern, and the horsetails (members of the genus *Equisetum*).

The eastern North American flora includes species from all 3 lycophyte families, and 27 of the 48 fern families. The figure on p. 11 shows a complete phylogeny, or family tree, for all the fern and lycophyte families, with the circle sizes indicating how many species from each family are present in our region. The families without any eastern North American members are primarily tropical families, such as the tree ferns.

One unique natural history feature that ferns and lycophytes share is their life cycle. All land plants undergo an "alternation of generations" in their life cycle, which refers to their 2 life stages, both of which are multicellular and capable of living independently (unlike in humans and other animals, which have only 1 multicellular, independent life stage). The life stage that is analogous to humans is called the sporophyte, and it is the charismatic, often large, leafy, or fernlike entity that we are used to seeing and thinking of as a plant. The sporophyte is also, like us, diploid, meaning that it has 2 sets of chromosomes in each cell, 1 set inherited from each parent. The sporophyte's counterpart, which has no equivalent in animals, is called the gametophyte, and this

Representatives of the lycophyte lineages (from left to right): spikemosses (*Selaginella rupestris*, Selaginellaceae); clubmosses (*Lycopodiella inundata*, Lycopodiaceae); and quillworts (*Isoetes engelmanii*, Isoetaceae).

From left to right: a fern, *Pecluma dispersa*, and 2 former "fern allies" that are now recognized as ferns: *Equisetum fluviatile*, a horsetail, and *Psilotum nudum*, the whisk fern.

is a haploid entity with only 1 set of chromosomes per cell, and it is often quite small and difficult to find unless you are looking for it.

While humans are analogous to the fern or lycophyte sporophyte in terms of being relatively large and diploid, the similarities, such as they are, end there, especially when it comes to reproduction. We produce our gametes directly, via meiosis, and, depending on our sex, we typically produce either egg cells or sperm cells. Because adult humans are diploid, with 2 sets of chromosomes, and successful meiosis is a halving process, our gametes are therefore haploid, with only 1 set of chromosomes in each egg or sperm cell. At fertilization, these 2 chromosome sets come back together again, restoring the diploid state. Plants do things a bit differently: the sporophyte, rather than directly producing gametes via meiosis, instead adds an additional step. Meiosis in the sporophyte produces haploid spores, not haploid gametes, and these spores may be dispersed by wind, or by animals, especially birds, if they manage to lodge in or on fur, feet, or feathers. After landing in a suitable spot, a spore germinates to become a haploid gametophyte, and it is the gametophyte that then produces eggs and sperm. While the order of these steps is identical in all land plants, ferns and lycophytes are the only groups in which the gametophyte is capable of living on its own, nutritionally and ecologically independent from the sporophyte. Lycophyte gametophytes are typically subterranean and extremely difficult to find, but fern gametophytes can be easier to spot. A small handful of fern species have actually done away with the sporophyte altogether, and the plants persist entirely in the haploid gametophyte stage (see p. 26).

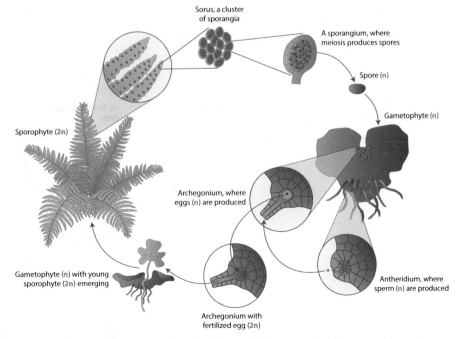

The fern life cycle. A diploid sporophyte (2n) produces haploid spores (n) by meiosis, and each spore germinates to become a gametophyte (n). The gametophyte produces gametes, eggs (n), and sperm (n) in structures called gametangia (the female archegonia and the male antheridia, respectively). When sperm are released from an antheridium, if they make their way to an egg inside an archegonium and fertilization occurs, the resulting zygote (2n) grows up to become a sporophyte (2n).

WHAT'S INCLUDED: FERNS, SPIKEMOSSES, CLUBMOSSES, AND QUILLWORTS OF EASTERN NORTH AMERICA

To determine which species are present in eastern North America, the first step is to define that region. This book takes as its coverage area the entire United States east of the Mississippi River (including the eastern parts of the states that border the river to the west) and contiguous Canada from Ontario eastward, but not extending into the extreme north and northeast of Canada (i.e., Newfoundland, Labrador, and northern Québec). Only a small handful of additional species are likely to occur in this area, including *Athyrium americanum*, *Diphasiastrum alpinum*, *Huperzia miyoshiana*, *Oreopteris quelpartensis*, *Polystichum scopulinum* (a mostly western North American species with disjunct populations in northeastern Canada), and possibly some *Botrychium* and *Isoetes* species of the far north.

Within the region of interest, the most obvious species to include are those that are native to that area. Native species are recognized via the historical record, primarily in the form of preserved herbarium specimens, as having been in the region prior to the modern era when the regular movement of plants by humans commenced, and these species form the great majority of our fern and lycophyte flora. In addition to this group, several other groups are also commonly encountered in natural habitats and should therefore be included for the sake of thoroughness: the many introduced species that are now present in the landscape, and hybrid taxa that have formed between native species, or between native and introduced species.

Introduced, Invasive, and Naturalized Species

Ferns and lycophytes are increasingly popular in the horticultural and gardening trades, and many species are now present in natural habitats that have escaped from cultivation or were introduced by other means. These nonnative species are included in the descriptions, keys, and checklists in this book if they have become naturalized, meaning that they have established populations that are persisting in otherwise natural habitats and are therefore likely to be encountered.

There are also a number of escapees from cultivation that have been recorded only once or were known historically but have not been seen in decades. This is particularly relevant in the southeastern U.S., and especially in Florida, where many nonnative species were recorded at one point and are sometimes still included in checklists. However, because they failed to establish and are no longer thought to be present in our region, they are not included in the species covered by this book. This group includes *Adiantum caudatum*, *Adiantum hispidulum*, *Adiantum trapeziforme*, *Adiantum villosum*, *Equisetum ramosissimum*, *Pteris grandifolia*, *Pteris plumula* (also known as *Pteris quadriaurita*), *Selaginella kraussiana*, *Stenochlaena tenuifolia*, and probably a few others.

Hybrids, Polyploids, and Reticulate Evolution

Hybrids are likely familiar to horticultural enthusiasts, and they occur in nearly all major groups of plants. Ferns and lycophytes are particularly prone to hybridization as well as polyploidy, a phenomenon that often accompanies hybridization and results in the doubling of the entire genome in an offspring organism relative to its parental species. When polyploidy occurs along with hybridization, it typically restores fertility to what would otherwise have been a sterile hybrid at the same ploidy level (i.e., homoploid, with the same genome size) as its parent taxa.

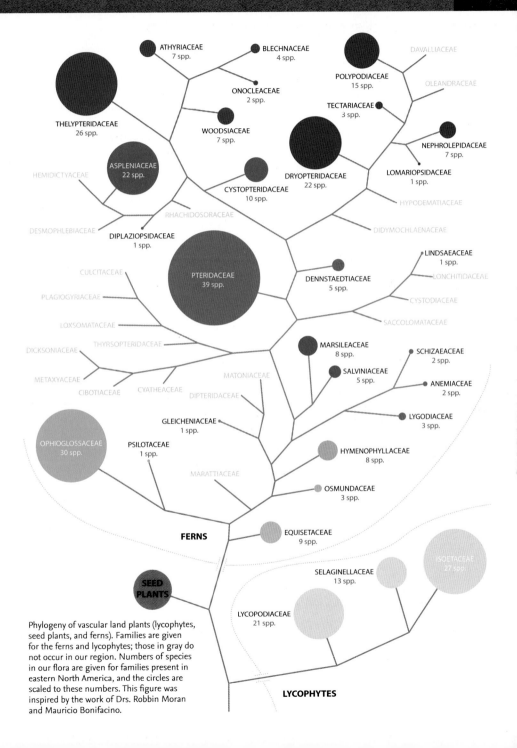

Phylogeny of vascular land plants (lycophytes, seed plants, and ferns). Families are given for the ferns and lycophytes; those in gray do not occur in our region. Numbers of species in our flora are given for families present in eastern North America, and the circles are scaled to these numbers. This figure was inspired by the work of Drs. Robbin Moran and Mauricio Bonifacino.

A number of our fern and lycophyte genera are famous in the botanical world for their extensive "reticulate" evolution, a term used to refer to situations in which hybridization and polyploidy have contributed to increasing species diversity via a complex web of relationships. These groups in eastern North America include *Asplenium*, *Dryopteris*, and *Isoetes*, among others. In the pages devoted to these genera, figures depict the relationships among species and indicate which taxa are fertile diploids, sterile hybrids, or various levels of polyploids. The determination of ploidy level is based on the number of chromosomes counted in a species, using the "base," or haploid number (denoted by "x"), as a guide. In this book, the base chromosome numbers are given for all genera at the end of each genus description, and at the end of each species description, that species' sporophytic (2n) chromosome count is given, if known, and the resultant ploidy level (diploid, triploid, tetraploid, etc.) is noted. All hybrids known to occur in eastern North America are either mentioned in the text or included in the figures depicting reticulate relationships, and they are listed in the indices. However, hybrids are not included in the total count of species in the book, and they are not given the complete descriptive treatment that nonhybrid species receive, because they are usually not nearly as common or likely to be encountered. However, in a few groups with hybrids that do occur frequently, those are included in the keys to the genera.

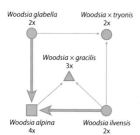

Woodsia glabella
2x

Woodsia × *tryonis*
2x

Woodsia × *gracilis*
3x

Woodsia alpina
4x

Woodsia ilvensis
2x

An example of a reticulogram figure, illustrating relationships in the genus *Woodsia*. In our region this genus includes two diploids (shown as blue circles), one allopolyploid (the green square), and two sterile hybrids: a diploid and triploid (gray circle and triangle, respectively). Arrows show the direction of genetic contribution from parental toward offspring taxa, with wide arrows where crosses have produced fertile hybrids, and narrow arrows for sterile hybrids. Ploidy level is given below each taxon's name, with 2x indicating diploid, 3x triploid, and so on.

Extinct and Extirpated Species

A number of species were considered to be native members of our flora historically but are now extinct or extirpated. The majority of these are tropical, typically Caribbean or Central American species that were found in Florida or elsewhere in the south. Most were likely natural occurrences of species that were at the extreme northern edge of their otherwise fully tropical ranges and have become extinct, either because populations naturally died out or because of extensive changes to land use (particularly in Florida) over the last century. Species that fit this profile include the following: *Didymoglossum lineolatum* (*Trichomanes lineolatum*), *Didymoglossum membranaceum* (*Trichomanes membranaceum*), *Maxonia apiifolia* var. *apiifolia*, *Phlegmariurus dichotomus*, *Pleopeltis astrolepis*, *Pleopeltis marginata*, *Serpocaulon triseriale* (*Polypodium triseriale*), and *Tectaria coriandrifolia*.

In total, this book provides full descriptions for 305 species (61 lycophytes and 244 ferns), belonging to 96 genera in 30 families. Checklists at the end of the book list each species by its occurrence in 4 subregions of eastern North America (p.491).

HOW TO USE THIS BOOK

A good starting point is to first familiarize yourself with the subregions, a map of which can be found on p. 6. To lessen the options available when you try to identify a plant, eastern North America has been divided into 4 subregions corresponding broadly to peninsular Florida (F-Florida), the outer southern coastal plain (S-South), the central inland United States (C-Central), and the northern Midwest, Northeast, and Canada (N-North). When you find a plant of interest, the keys and descriptions will use color codes to indicate which of these subregions that genus or species is present in.

Once you have found a plant and wish to identify it, start with the key to genera on p. 32, or if you know which genus your plant belongs to, you can skip to the descriptions of individual genera and species starting on p. 41. Each genus with more than 1 species includes a key to those species in the genus information. At each step in the keys, choose the option (either a or b) that matches your plant best, but be sure to read through both parts of the couplet thoroughly before making a decision. The only tool you might desire is a hand lens, which can be purchased for a few dollars online or at gem and mineral shops. A 10× lens will suffice for viewing most characters, but one with 20× or higher magnification will be needed in a few cases to make decisive identifications.

The keys will work best if you have mature adult plants with reproductive structures (spore-bearing sporangia). For many ferns and lycophytes, the arrangement of sporangia provides essential information for identification. The immature, young leaves of many ferns look identical to one another, as they have not yet grown into their diagnostic features, so using early-season or immature plants is not ideal for identification purposes. It is also important to remember that even with adult, reproductively mature leaves, keys are not infallible. Plants are variable by nature, and no 2 plants or even leaves on an individual plant will look exactly alike. A number of species and even genera in our flora look very much alike, and the possibility that you are handling a hybrid is a constant complicating factor for many of our ferns and lycophytes. The keys in this book are also intended to work only in eastern North America; elsewhere in the world and even in the western part of the continent, where other species and genera are present that are not covered here, the keys either will not work at all or will be missing vital information that will render them misleading. Finally, the key to genera assumes that you know ahead of time that you are handling a fern; this is an unavoidable failing of such a key, because many of our ferns are decidedly unfernlike in appearance (such as the water ferns). There are also many look-alikes among the ferns and lycophytes and the flowering plants, in both directions (e.g., the grasslike quillworts and the fernlike members of the carrot family, Apiaceae). An exhaustive key covering all the potential look-alikes is outside the scope of this book, and the numerous images provided should help rule them out.

The features needed to identify ferns and lycophytes can be observed without removing even a leaf, and every effort should be made to leave plants intact and undisturbed during identification. It is especially important to know that, while many of the species descriptions in this book include features of underground stems and/or roots, these are included for thoroughness only and should not be taken as an invitation to dig these parts up. Mature plants of many, and perhaps most, fern and lycophyte species can be decades old or even older, and they will not tolerate major disturbance, uprooting, or attempts at transplantation. Plants in the wild should *never* be dug or pulled up for identification or any other reason. If you are interested in growing ferns from spores, there are many excellent manuals and guides online, including the website of the American Fern Society (https://www.amerfernsoc.org).

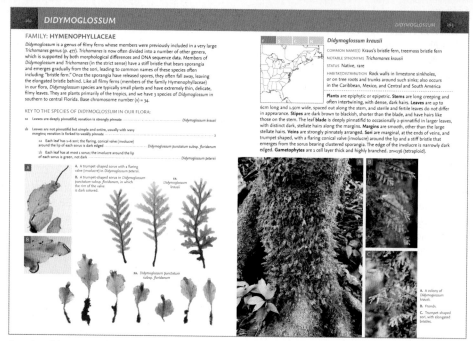

Examples of the genus and species descriptions in this book. Introductory text about each genus, including its base chromosome number, is followed by (in most cases) scans or herbarium specimens of one or more species (these images are not shown to scale). If applicable, a key is included for the species of the genus present in eastern North America. Additional figures and/or photographs illustrate interesting aspects of the genus. For each species, a range map is included, along with all common names, any notable scientific synonyms, an assessment of status (native or not native), and a description of habitat and distribution, followed by a complete description of the species, including its ploidy level, and illustrative photographs.

Range Maps

The range maps provided for each species were informed by several sources, including observation data from iNaturalist, herbarium specimen records (via the Global Biodiversity Information Facility, or GBIF), and maps from the Flora of North America project and the Biota of North America Program. Each range map started with a query to GBIF for all records of that species, and this was edited manually based on the other sources listed above. The goal was to be as inclusive as seemed reasonable, with a range limit extended anywhere that multiple sources indicated a broader range than was suggested by any one map. The final maps could be considered a consensus from the various sources, but range edges in particular should always be treated as provisional, with potential new populations yet to be discovered that may extend the range in the future. It is also possible that past populations have gone extinct, and species may no longer be present in areas where the maps indicate they should be. In some cases, a distribution may seem to follow an arbitrary political boundary, and this is likely artificial; the area may not have been thoroughly explored yet, or perhaps no one happens to have recorded the species from the other side of the border.

Status

The status of each species is indicated as either *native* or *not native*. Species that are *endemic*, to either North America or eastern North America, or that are considered noxious *invasives* in eastern North America, are noted. These designations are based on the historical record and governmental assessments of invasiveness (and not all nonnative species are invasive; this term is reserved for nonnative species that have been documented as displacing natives and altering ecosystem dynamics, or that are expected to do so in the future). This status is followed by a designation of the species as *common, somewhat common, uncommon,* or *rare*. These are subjective assessments of how likely you are to encounter the species within its range, and they consider the range size itself to some extent. Species indicated as common tend to have larger ranges, though some are smaller, and whether the range is large or small, common species occur frequently throughout that area. Species indicated as rare are known from only one or a small number of sites in our region (though it is important to note that these same species may be common elsewhere, if their range extends outside eastern North America). The intervening combinations of range size and lower occurrence are classified into the intermediate categories. These are meant to serve only as rough guides for how likely you are to find a particular species in eastern North America, and even species considered to be rare in the region as a whole can be locally abundant in the right habitat.

IDENTIFYING FERNS AND LYCOPHYTES

For both lycophytes and ferns, it is helpful to know some of the specialized terminology used to describe their appearance, or morphology. This book attempts to keep the jargon to a minimum, but it is often easiest to learn the appropriate descriptive words for these plants. The sections below first discuss the overall morphology of lycophyte and fern sporophytes, which are the large, charismatic, diploid plants one usually pictures when thinking about these plants or encountering them in the field. Next is a section on fern gametophytes, and then a glossary of terms used throughout the book to describe various morphological features and aspects of appearance.

LYCOPHYTE MORPHOLOGY AND IDENTIFICATION

The lycophyte lineage includes 3 families, or groups, of plants that are quite different from one another in appearance. These are the Lycopodiaceae (clubmosses), Selaginellaceae (spikemosses), and Isoetaceae (quillworts), and their identifying features are discussed separately below.

Lycopodiaceae

The basic morphology of a member of Lycopodiaceae starts with a **horizontal, creeping stem**, which is usually belowground but may also sit just on top of the ground surface. Both **roots** and **upright shoots** emerge from the stems, and the shoots may branch or not branch. In some groups the upright shoots may branch at the base in a forking manner, with all the subbranches pointing upward and essentially identical to each other, or there may be a **central shoot axis** (the stout, upright part) from which horizontal side branches emerge. The **leaves** emerge from the central axes of the shoots and/or side branches; they are typically very small and may be scalelike or needlelike. The leaves can be pressed against the shoot axis or may spread away from it. **Annual growth constrictions** may be present, which occur when leaves become noticeably shorter at the point where growth slowed and then paused over the winter, with distinctly larger leaves marking the resumption of growth in the spring. The abutment of the narrow and large leaves gives the appearance of a constriction along the stem. When plants are fertile, **sporangia** (which contain the **spores**) will be present, usually toward the tips of the shoot. Each sporangium sits on top of a leaf (a **sporophyll**), tucked in at the leaf base. The sporophylls may be similar in appearance to the other leaves, with the sporangia clearly visible, or they may be organized into distinct structures called **strobili** (plural; the singular is strobilus), which are somewhat similar in appearance to very small, green pinecones. The strobili either sit directly at the shoot tips, or they may each be elevated on a long stalk, a **peduncle**, with a strobilus at the tip. In some species the peduncle may fork one or more times, forming small candelabra-like arrangements of strobili. One genus of lycophytes in our flora (*Huperzia*) has an additional feature: vegetative propagules called **gemmae** (singular: gemma). Gemmae are small, highly compressed lateral shoots that can detach from the parent plant and regenerate new plants if they fall on suitable substrate. The spores of many Lycopodiaceae species are large and high in fat content, making them quite flammable. "*Lycopodium* powder," which consists of the dried spores of these plants, was used historically as flash powder for early cameras and continues to be employed today for special effects where a reasonably safe, small explosion is needed (or to impress undergraduates in introductory botany courses).

A.

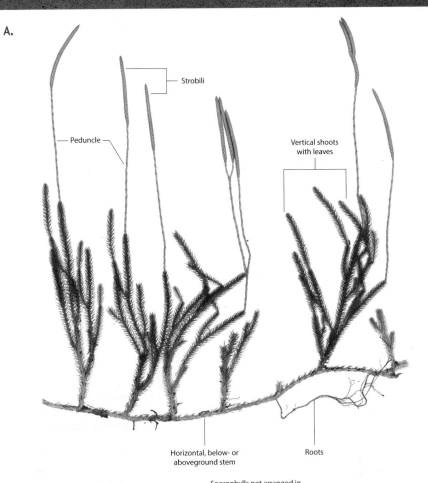

Strobili

Peduncle

Vertical shoots
with leaves

Horizontal, below- or
aboveground stem

Roots

Sporophylls not arranged in
strobili, and with sporangia visible

B.   C.

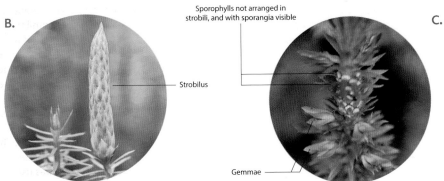

Strobilus

Gemmae

A. *Lycopodium clavatum* subsp. *clavatum*, showing the major morphological features of members of Lycopodiaceae.

B. Strobilus of *Spinulum annotinum*.

C. Shoot apex of *Huperzia porophila*, with sporangia and gemmae.

Diphasiastrum digitatum, with horizontal side branches.

Huperzia lucidula, with forking branch structure and all shoots/branches pointing upward.

Selaginellaceae

The basic morphology of members of Selaginellaceae is similar to that of Lycopodiaceae, starting with **horizontal stems** that are usually belowground, and **aboveground shoots** that are typically branching, erect, and pointing upward, or horizontally spreading. Some species have **rhizophores**, which are stemlike structures that can produce roots at their tips when they touch the soil surface. **Leaves** may be all alike and arranged spirally around the shoot axis, or they may be of 2 distinct types that differ in size and either run in a line along the top of the shoot axis or emerge laterally from the sides, giving the branches a horizontally flattened appearance. The leaves have a very small outgrowth called a **ligule** on the upper surface near the base; these are often difficult to see and may require a hand lens to locate. The **sporangia** are on the upper surfaces of specialized leaves called **sporophylls**, and the sporophylls are loosely arranged in **strobili** that may be flattened, cylindrical, or distinctly 4-sided. The strobili may not be particularly well distinguished from the leaves below.

A. *Selaginella acanthonota*, showing the major morphological features of members of Selaginellaceae.

B. Leaves of 1 kind arranged spirally around the shoot axis.

C. *Selaginella uncinata*, which has flattened branches with 2 distinct leaf types: median and lateral.

D. Ligules visible on median leaves of *S. willdenowii*.

E. Sporangia-bearing leaves (sporophylls) of *S. acanthonota*, with mature sporangia visible in the leaf axils.

Isoetaceae

The basic morphology of the quillworts, members of the genus *Isoetes* in the family Isoetaceae, is quite different from that of the other lycophytes. Each *Isoetes* plant has a central (usually round) **underground corm** with the **leaves** arranged around it. The base of each leaf is swollen (flared out) and contains **sporangial sacs** that house the spores, with a small flap of tissue (a **ligule**) just above the **sporangium**. The exposed sporangium wall is plain in some species and variously marked with short brown streaks or spots in others. A transparent or pale-colored membrane called the **velum** partially or completely covers the sporangium, with an uncovered "window" (the **fenestra**) creating an opening below the velum through which the mature spores can be released. The extent to which the velum covers the sporangium is often an important identifying character among species.

The spores are of 2 kinds, with separate male and female spores produced in separate sporangia. The female **megaspores** are highly variable in their surface ornamentation, and both their size and the nature of their surface pattern and ornamentation are extremely useful (often diagnostic) in telling species apart. While a 40–50x microscope is best for clearly seeing the details of these patterns, a 15–20x hand lens can be used to make out some of the basic differences. The male spores are rightly called "**microspores**," with individuals being literally the size of a speck of dust. Given their minute size, microspores are not practical for identification purposes, and their appearance is not described in the species descriptions.

A. *Isoetes georgiana*, showing the overall morphology of *Isoetes* plants.
B. Close-up of leaf bases of *I. flaccida*, with spores visible
through the transparent outer surface of the leaves.
C. *Isoetes butleri*, dissected to show the corm with leaves attached around it.

A leaf of *Isoetes engelmannii* with features of the leaf base and sporangium labeled. Identical images are shown in grayscale on the left and color on the right to make the features easier to see.

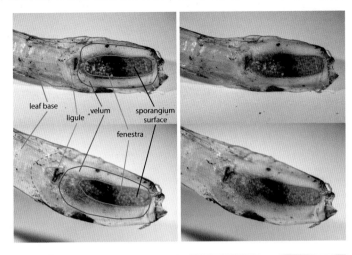

A. Megaspores of *Isoetes flaccida* on a napkin.

B. Megaspore features labeled on a megaspore from *I. tuckermanii*.

C–F. Examples of megaspore surface texture and patterns.

C. *I. echinospora*, spiny surface;
D. *I. butleri*, granular or finely low-tuberculate surface;
E. *I. tegetiformans*, unornamented to obscurely wrinkled surface;
F. *I. engelmannii*, evenly reticulate with even-height walls;
G. *I. melanopoda* subsp. *silvatica*, numerous low tubercles or walls;
H. *I. georgiana*, open pattern with thick walls.

PHOTOS B–H COURTESY OF DANIEL BRUNTON; ALL SCALE BARS ARE 100 μm

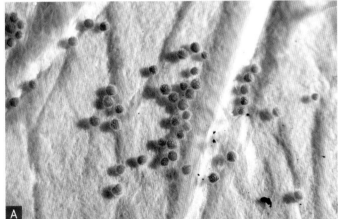

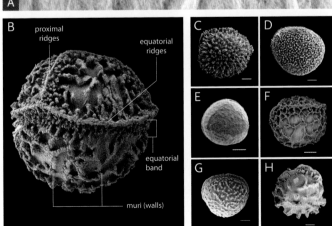

FERN MORPHOLOGY AND IDENTIFICATION

The majority of the fern species described in this book share major features of overall morphology, but there are a number of exceptions. For example, the horsetails (members of the genus *Equisetum*) are very different in their appearance and characteristics from the other ferns. The description and illustrations below apply to what could be considered a "typical" fern, and deviations found in specific genera are discussed in the sections devoted to those groups throughout the book.

Fern Sporophytes

Starting belowground, basic fern morphology begins with the **stem**, which is generally either horizontally elongated and creeping, with the plants forming diffuse colonies, or oriented upright (erect), in which case plants often form well-defined, somewhat vase-shaped clusters of leaves. **Roots** are attached to the stems, as are **leaves**, which are the major aboveground unit of the plant. Leaves can either be **monomorphic**, with the sterile and fertile leaves very similar to each other in overall appearance, or **dimorphic**, with the fertile leaves or leaf sections very different in appearance from the sterile leaves or leaf sections.

Each leaf is composed of a nonleafy, stalklike section called the **stipe** (or petiole) and a leafy **blade**. In some species the blade reaches all the way to ground level, with the stipe essentially nonexistent. The continuation of the stipe into the blade (i.e., the midrib of the blade) is called the **rachis**. The stipe, rachis, and blade frequently have **hairs** and/or **scales**, and these can vary in density, size, and color and are often very useful for identification. In many species, characteristics of the leaf or pinna **margins** are important; these are simply the edges of the leaves or leaflets. The pattern of **veins** is also a useful character for many ferns, and species descriptions may refer either to the main, central veins in the leaf segments, or to the lateral, side veins. The venation patterns, especially of the lateral veins, can often be seen best by holding a leaf up to the light (see the glossary on p. 27 for terms describing leaf venation).

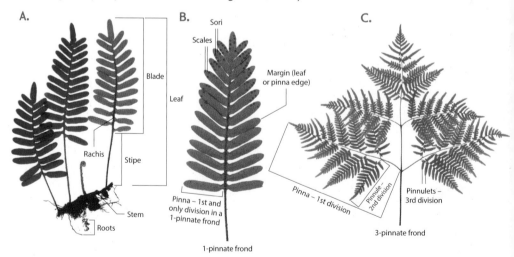

A & B. *Pleopeltis michauxiana* with the major features of a fern and a 1-pinnate frond labeled.

C. *Pteridium aquilinum* with features of a multiply divided frond labeled.

Botrypus virginianus, one of many ferns with dimorphic leaves, where the fertile and sterile parts of the leaf are very different in appearance from one another.

Fertile segment

Sterile segment

Examples of hairs, scales, margins, and venation patterns in ferns.

A. A stipe of *Arachniodes simplicior,* with relatively narrow scales;
B. Pinnae of *Pecluma plumula,* with fine, short hairs along the rachis and scattered on the pinna margins, which are slightly undulating;
C. A pinna of *Dryopteris cristata,* with serrate margins and free, forking lateral veins;
D. A stipe of *Cyrtomium falcatum* subsp. *falcatum,* with small, narrow scales mixed with large, wide ones;
E. Rachis and pinna bases of *Pelazoneuron kunthii,* with dense, long hairs on the rachis, pinna midveins, blade tissue, and margins;
F. A pinna of *Cyrtomium falcatum* subsp. *falcatum,* with smooth margins and anastomosing veins that form networks of shapes/polygons called areoles, some of which have free, "included" veinlets that end inside the areole.

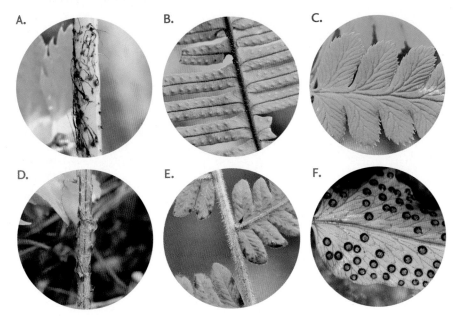

A.

B.

C.

D.

E.

F.

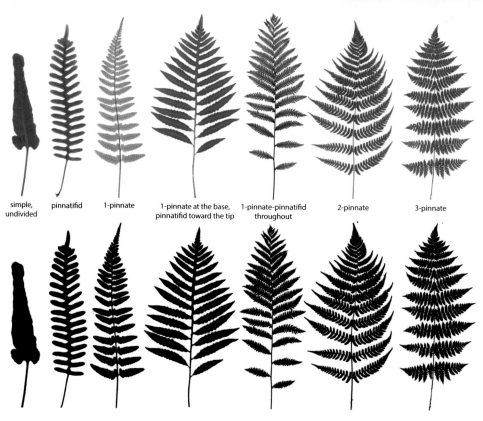

| simple, undivided | pinnatifid | 1-pinnate | 1-pinnate at the base, pinnatifid toward the tip | 1-pinnate-pinnatifid throughout | 2-pinnate | 3-pinnate |

Examples of leaf division in ferns, from simple and undivided through 3-pinnate.

Across ferns, there is huge variation in the overall leaf shape and the level of division of the blade. Leaves can be **undivided**, which is also referred to as simple or entire. Some leaves are deeply lobed but not fully divided, with the lobes or divisions not reaching all the way to the rachis; these are termed **pinnatifid**. Leaves that are fully divided, with the divisions reaching all the way to the rachis, are **pinnate or 1-pinnate**. When fern leaves are fully divided, the primary divisions are called **pinnae** (singular: pinna). The pinnae of 1-pinnate leaves can be further lobed, or fully further divided. If the pinnae are only deeply lobed, the leaf is described as **1-pinnate-pinnatifid**, because it has a full first division into pinnae, which are themselves pinnatifid. If the pinnae of a 1-pinnate leaf are completely divided a second time, with the divisions reaching all the way to the pinna midveins, the leaf is considered **bipinnate or 2-pinnate**, and the second-level divisions are called **pinnules**. Pinnules can be further pinnatifid (in a **2-pinnate-pinnatifid** leaf), or fully divided into third-level divisions called **pinnulets**, in a **tripinnate or 3-pinnate** leaf. Occasionally ferns have 4-pinnate or more divided leaves.

The primary dispersal and reproductive unit in ferns is the spore, and spores are produced and housed inside **sporangia**. In one group of species, called the eusporangiate ferns, the sporangia (termed eusporangia, singular: eusporangium) simply tear open and release spores passively into the air current for dispersal. The eusporangiate ferns in our flora include the

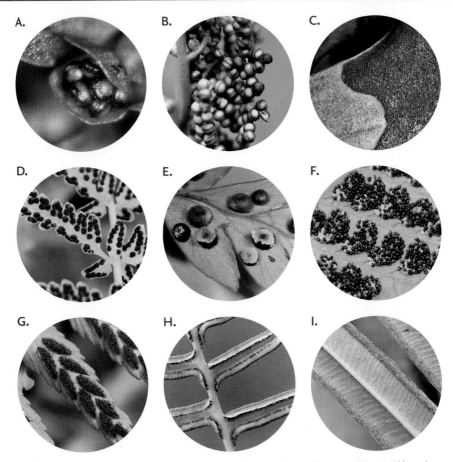

Examples of sporangia and sori in ferns. **A.** A sorus of a species of *Hymenophyllum*, with green sporangia visible, each of which has a ring of brown cells that make up the annulus; **B.** eusporangia of *Sceptridium dissectum*; **C.** acrostichoid sporangia in *Platycerium bifurcatum*; **D.** round sori with no indusia in *Amauropelta sancta*; **E.** round sori with indusia in *Cyrtomium falcatum* subsp. *falcatum*; **F.** oblong, curved sori in *Meniscium reticulatum*; **G.** linear sori in *Asplenium auritum*; **H.** marginal, linear sori with false indusia in *Pteridium caudatum*; **I.** marginal, linear sori in *Pteris vittata*, with false indusia present but hidden by the very mature sporangia.

horsetails (genus *Equisetum*), the whisk fern (*Psilotum nudum*), and members of the family Ophioglossaceae (the grape ferns, rattlesnake ferns, and their relatives). In the remaining ferns (the leptosporangiate ferns), which include the majority of species globally and in our flora, there is a more complex leptosporangium (plural: leptosporangia), with a set of specialized cells called the **annulus** that is involved in tearing the sporangium open to allow for more active spore dispersal. In the leptosporangiate ferns, sporangia can be spread across the surface of the leaf (termed **acrostichoid**), but more often they are clustered into structures called **sori** (singular: sorus), which take on various shapes, such as round or elongated, and which may be covered by a protective flap of tissue called an **indusium** (plural: indusia). Sporangia can also form lines, and in some groups they occur directly along the leaf margins; in some cases these are covered by a "false indusium" formed by an overrolling of the leaf margin that protects the sporangia.

young sporophyte emerging from the gametophyte

gametophyte

A. A colony of *Cystopteris tennesseensis* gametophytes.

B & C. Two examples of new sporophytes growing out of gametophytes.

Fern Gametophytes

Fern gametophytes are typically very small and resemble mosses, and they may grow intermixed with them. The best place to look for gametophytes is on exposed soil banks where there is less competition for space. In our flora, most gametophytes will be more or less **heart shaped** (**cordate**), and only a single cell layer thick, with no obvious midrib. These details can help set them apart from liverworts and hornworts, which usually have a thicker, tougher **thallus** (plant body), and most mosses, which usually appear to have small leaflets organized around a central axis or midrib. Small, rootlike structures called **rhizoids** may sometimes be present, and if gametophytes are fertile, you may be able to see **gametangia** (**archegonia** and **antheridia**), the structures in which eggs and sperm are produced, though this will require a strong hand lens or microscope. Given their small size and limited number of features, gametophytes often cannot be determined even to genus, so they have limited utility for identification, but they are critical and beautiful components of the fern life cycle (see p. 9), and searching for them can be very enjoyable and rewarding.

   Globally, 25 species of ferns are known to persist in at least part of their geographic range in only the gametophyte stage, never producing a sporophyte. In our flora we have 2 such species: *Crepidomanes intricatum* (p. 232) and *Vittaria appalachiana* (p. 483). Both of these species are gametophyte-only ferns that have never been known to produce mature, spore-producing sporophytes, even in laboratory conditions.

GLOSSARY

LEAF SHAPES

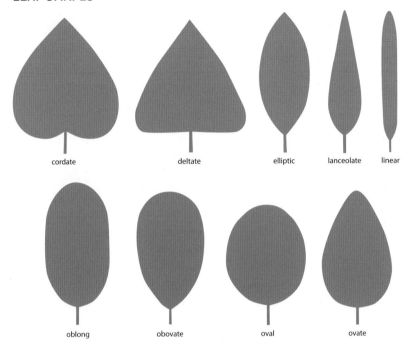

cordate   deltate   elliptic   lanceolate   linear

oblong   obovate   oval   ovate

TERMS

Acrostichoid: usually refers to sori that are densely spread across the leaf surface and closely packed together, such that individual sori are difficult to discern.

Alternate: describes structures such as leaves or pinnae that are not directly across from one another but are staggered and offset from one another on either side of a central axis (such as a stem, rachis, or midvein).

Amphibious: tolerant of fluctuating water levels.

Annual growth constriction: a point along the stem at which leaves become shorter where seasonal growth paused for winter in the previous year, with larger leaves immediately beside them, marking the resumption of growth the following spring.

Annulus: a specialized ring of cells that runs around the sporangium and typically tears in one place at maturity, to aid in spore dispersal.

Antheridium (plural antheridia): the structure on the gametophyte in which sperm are produced.

Apex: the tip of a structure, such as a shoot, leaf, or pinna.

Apogamous: a type of reproduction in which a new sporophyte forms from the tissue of the gametophyte, without the fusion of egg and sperm.

Appressed: pressed tightly against, such as leaves tightly pressed against a stem axis.

Archegonium (plural archegonia): the structure on the gametophyte in which eggs are produced.

Arching: usually refers to leaves that are held upright at the base but then gradually relax toward the tip to become nearly horizontal.

Areole: a shape (polygon) outlined by the lateral veins in a leaf with networking or anastomosing venation.

Articulate: having a distinct detachment point; usually describes stipes that have clear breakage points at their bases from which they will snap off at maturity or senescence.

Ascending: pointing toward the tip, often of a leaf or shoot.

Asymmetrical: describes structures on either side of a central axis that differ in size, shape, or orientation.

Auricle; auriculate: an ear-shaped lobe or projection, usually at the base of a leaf or pinna; having such a lobe or projection.

Axis: the main central line around which structures are arranged; usually a stem, stalk, midvein, or midrib.

Base: the lowest part of a structure; typically the end closest to the ground or the central axis.

Base chromosome number: the number of chromosomes in the haploid generation of the life cycle (including the spores, gametophyte, and egg and sperm cells) in a diploid organism. Typically denoted by "x."

Blade: the leafy, usually green, photosynthetic portion of the leaf; the blade is above the stipe, and the rachis runs down its center.

Bristle: a structure often found at the tip of a small leaf or pinnule that is typically long, pointed, and stiff.

Circumneutral: soils having a pH near 7 (neutral).

Clathrate scales: scales that resemble stained glass, with translucent "panes" embedded in a dark-colored lattice.

Cordate: heart shaped.

Corm: in the quillworts, the fleshy central stem around which leaves are arranged.

Determinate: growth that is not continuous.

Dichotomously branching: branching in 2, equally.

Dimorphic: a plant in which different parts of the plant body (usually leaves, parts of leaves, or entire stems) are sterile (without reproductive structures) or fertile (with reproductive structures), and the sterile and fertile plants or portions of the plant are distinctly different from one another in appearance. See also monomorphic, the opposite of dimorphic.

Diploid: may refer to 1) the sporophytic generation of the life cycle, which has 2 full sets of chromosomes in each cell, or 2) a diploid organism, whose chromosome count in the sporophytic generation is twice the base chromosome number of the genus (i.e., 2n = 2x).

Distal tooth: a small hooklike structure on the top side of a sporocarp (the reproductive structure in the genus *Marsilea*).

Emergent: rooted below the water level but with some portion of the plant emerging out of the water.

Entire: usually refers to a margin that is smooth and not toothed, or to a leaf that is simple and undivided.

Epipetric: growing directly on rock.

Epiphyte; epiphytic: a plant that grows on another plant, often a tree; growing on another plant.

Erect: growing vertically, upright.

Eusporangiate ferns: a set of fern lineages in which the sporangium develops from several initial cells on the leaf epidermis (as opposed to 1 cell in the leptosporangiate ferns).

Eusporangium (plural eusporangia): the sporangium in eusporangiate ferns, which develops from several initial cells and is different in form from the leptosporangium, most notably in lacking an annulus.

Falcate: curved or hooked up at the end (often used to describe pinna tips).

False indusium: a structure formed by the edge of the leaf margin rolling inward or underneath, creating a flap of tissue that typically covers sori located next to the margin.

Frond: another word for a leaf in ferns.

Furcate: with 2 projections (i.e., forked).

Gametangium (plural gametangia): the structure on the gametophyte in which either eggs or sperm are produced (archegonium and antheridium, respectively).

Gametophyte: the haploid, usually minuscule phase of the plant life cycle, where gametes (eggs and sperm) are produced.

Gemma (plural gemmae): vegetative propagule that can break off the parent plant and form a new plant, without sexual reproduction.

Hairs: typically microscopic, white or translucent structures that are 1 cell thick and may be glandular (with a rounded tip producing a sticky exudate), furcate (forking into 2 projections at the tip), or stellate (star shaped, with multiple projections at the tip).

Haploid: may refer to 1) an organism that has 1 set of chromosomes per cell, or 2) specifically the gametophytic generation of the plant life cycle, which has 1 set of chromosomes per cell.

Hastate: with downward-pointing lobes, like an arrowhead.

Heterosporous: plants that produce 2 types of spores, male and female, which become unisexual gametophytes that produce either eggs or sperm, but not both.

Hexaploid: an organism with 6 sets of chromosomes in each sporophytic cell.

Homosporous: plants that produce 1 type of spore, with each spore germinating into a gametophyte that can be bisexual (producing both eggs and sperm).

Hybrid: an organism produced during a mating event between members of 2 different species. In plants, hybrids are often sterile, but hybridization is sometimes accompanied by whole-genome duplication (polyploidy), which often restores fertility to the offspring.

Hydathode: a modified pore on the leaf surface, which often appears to be a slight widening of a vein at its very tip.

Indeterminate: growth that is continuous, allowing potentially indefinite elongation.

Indusium (plural indusia): a protective structure that covers a sorus; it may be variously shaped and attached to the leaf surface either at its center or side.

Lateral: going toward or emerging from the side.

Leaves: also called fronds in ferns; the main photosynthetic units of a fern or lycophyte.

Leptosporangiate ferns: a set of fern lineages in which the sporangium develops from 1 initial cell on the leaf epidermis (as opposed to several cells in the eusporangiate ferns).

Leptosporangium (plural leptosporangia): the sporangium in leptosporangiate ferns, which develops from 1 initial cell and has an annulus to aid in spore dispersal.

Margins: the edges of leaves or pinnae. Terms used to describe leaf margins include:

Biserrate: doubly toothed, each large tooth also having a smaller tooth.

Crenate: with smooth, bluntly rounded teeth.

Dentate: with teeth spreading outward (as opposed to pointing forward).

Entire: smooth, without teeth or lobes.

Serrate: with sharp, sawlike teeth that point forward (toward the leaf or leaflet tip).

Serrulate: with minutely fine, forward-pointing teeth.

Wavy: undulating, but not deeply enough to be considered lobed.

Megaspore: in heterosporous plants, the larger, female spore.

Microspore: in heterosporous plants, the smaller, male spore.

Monomorphic: a plant in which the sterile and fertile stems, leaves, or leaf sections are not different from one another in appearance. See also dimorphic, the opposite of monomorphic.

Opposite: describes structures such as leaves or pinnae that are directly across from one another, on either side of a central axis (such as a stem, rachis, or midvein).

Palmate: with lobes or projections emerging from a single, central point, usually near the base, and somewhat resembling a hand.

Paraphyses: sterile, hairlike filaments that are sometimes intermixed with sporangia. A hand lens is recommended to observe them.

Pectinate: pinnate but with very narrow, closely spaced pinnae that give the leaf a comblike appearance.

Pedate: palmately divided into 2 or more lobes.

Peltate: attached at the very center, like an umbrella (usually refers to an indusium).

Pinna: the first leaf segment, or level of division, in a fern with a divided blade.

Pinnate (1-pinnate): fully divided, with the divisions reaching all the way to the rachis and creating separate pinnae.

Pinnate-pinnatifid (1-pinnate-pinnatifid): with a full first-level division into pinnae, which are themselves deeply lobed but not fully divided further into pinnules.

Pinnatifid: deeply lobed but not fully divided, with the lobes or divisions not reaching all the way to the rachis.

Pinnule: a second-level division in a fern with a divided blade.

Pinnulet: a third-level division in a fern with a divided blade.

Ploidy level/ploidal level: the number of chromosome sets in the cells of an organism (typically the sporophyte generation). See also haploid, diploid, tetraploid, hexaploid.

Polyploid: an organism that has experienced whole-genome duplication and has more than 2 full sets of chromosomes in each cell.

Pseudopedate: fan shaped.

Pseudowhorl: a tightly packed arrangement of leaves that appears to be a true whorl (in which all leaves arise at the same level around the stem axis), but in which the leaves actually arise at slightly different levels relative to one another.

Pteridophyte: a term used historically to collectively describe the plants now recognized as ferns and lycophytes.

Rachis: the midrib of the leaf blade.

Reticulate: may refer to 1) reticulate evolution, in which a set of species are interrelated, usually because of hybridization and polyploidy, or 2) reticulate venation, in which the veins are networking or anastomosing rather than free or simply forking.

Rhizoid: rootlike structure on a fern gametophyte.

Rhizoid primordia: initial cells that will become rhizoids.

Rhizome: another word often used to describe the stem in ferns (but "stem" is used throughout this book).

Rhizophore: a stemlike structure that can produce roots at its tip when it touches the soil surface; occurs only in *Selaginella* (though not in all species).

Root: the part of the plant body that is typically underground, attached to the stem and anchoring the plant to the substrate, and involved in absorption of water and nutrients.

Scale: a thin, papery structure usually found at the base of the stipe or on the stipe, rachis, and/or blade tissue.

Simple: usually describes a leaf that is undivided; also referred to as "entire."

Smooth: without hairs or scales; usually refers to the stipe, rachis, or leaf surfaces.

Sorus (plural sori): a cluster or aggregation of sporangia that can be variously shaped and may be protected by an indusium.

Sporangiaster: a highly modified sporangium that looks like a tiny bulbous head studded with glandular hairs.

Sporangiophore: the sporangia-bearing structure that makes up the strobili of *Equisetum*.

Sporangium (plural sporangia): the structure in which spores are produced and held until maturity, at which point the sporangium will open and spores will be released.

Spores: the haploid, primary dispersal and reproductive units of ferns and lycophytes; they are housed inside sporangia.

Sporocarp: the spore-bearing structure in *Marsilea*.

Sporophore: the fertile, spore-bearing portion of the leaf in members of the family Ophioglossaceae.

Sporophyll: the specialized leaf that bears sporangia in lycophytes.

Sporophyte: the diploid, large, charismatic stage of the plant life cycle, where spores are produced.

Stellate: with multiple projections arising from a single point; starlike.

Stem: the portion of the plant that roots emerge from, and which in ferns and many lycophytes is underground. Terms used to describe stems include:

Ascending: pointing upward at the tip, but not completely vertical.

Erect: vertically oriented for all or most of its length.

Long creeping: growing horizontally and with leaves and roots spaced out, the stem growing outward for some distance through the soil.

Short creeping: growing horizontally but with leaves and roots relatively close together, the stem not extending out very far.

Stipe: the nonleafy, stalklike section at the base of the leaf, below the blade; equivalent to a petiole in flowering plants.

Strobilus (plural strobili): a reproductive structure made up of sporangia-bearing structures (such as sporophylls or sporangiophores) that are densely packed into a cone-like shape.

Submerged: describes plants that spend a significant part (or all) of their life entirely under water.

Symmetrical: describes structures on either side of a central axis that are alike in size, shape, or orientation.

Terrestrial: a plant growing on the ground, from various types of soil-based substrates (in contrast to epiphytes, which grow on trees, or epipetric plants, which grow directly on rocks).

Tetraploid: an organism with 4 sets of chromosomes in each sporophytic cell.

Thallus: the plant body; usually refers to a fern or bryophyte gametophyte.

Trophophore: the sterile portion of the leaf in members of the family Ophioglossaceae.

Veins: the vascular tissue that runs throughout the plant. In leaves and pinnae, the central midveins and lateral veins can be important for identification. Terms used to describe venation patterns include:

Anastomosing/networking: veins form a network of shapes or polygons (called areoles).

Evident: veins are visible and obvious.

Forked/forking: each vein branches in 2, either once or multiple times.

Free: veins do not form networks and stay separated after branching, running straight to the leaf margin.

Obscure: veins are not obvious on the leaf surface (sometimes holding the leaf up to the light will make them more apparent).

Simple: veins are unbranched and may be straight or curving.

KEY TO PTERIDOPHYTE GENERA OF EASTERN NORTH AMERICA

Presence/absence in subregions

Florida   South   Central   North

1a   Plants are floating, submerged, or emergent aquatics, for at least a substantial part of the year (some *Isoetes* species occur in ephemeral ponds and become terrestrial when the water recedes seasonally) ─────────────────────────────────── 2

  2a   Plants are floating on the surface and are not rooted ─────────────── 3

    3a   Individual leaf blades are mostly less than 1mm, but leaves are often tightly clustered into larger units ──────────────────────────── *Azolla* ▪▫▪▪

    3b   Individual leaf blades are mostly 5mm or more, and leaves typically occur singly, though they can form massive colonies ──────────── *Salvinia* ▪▫▪▪

  2b   Plants are rooted in the substrate ────────────────────────── 4

    4a   Leaves are distinctly grasslike or quill-like, with the blade not widely expanded; plants are submerged to emergent ───────────────── 5

      5a   Leaves are tightly clustered in a whorl around a fleshy central stem (a corm); sporangia are located on the upper surfaces of the swollen leaf bases ────── *Isoetes* ▪▫▪▪

      5b   Leaves are spaced out along a short-creeping stem; spores are enclosed in round, hardened structures (sporocarps) that emerge along the stem, near the leaf bases ────── *Pilularia* ▪▫▫▪

    4b   Leaves are not grasslike, and the blade is either deeply pinnately divided or resembles a four-leaf clover; leaves are emergent or may float on the surface (in *Marsilea*) ──────── 6

      6a   Leaves are deeply pinnately divided, and dimorphic, with sterile and fertile leaves looking somewhat to very different from one another; leaves are emergent ──────── *Ceratopteris* ▪▫▪▫

      6b   Leaves resemble four-leaf clover and have spores enclosed in round, hardened structures (sporocarps) that emerge along the stem, near the leaf bases; leaves are floating or emergent ──────── *Marsilea* ▪▫▪▪

1b   Plants are essentially terrestrial, growing on various substrates including soil, rocks, or other plants, or in wetland habitats (where plants may occasionally be in standing water, but not to the extent that they would be considered emergent aquatics) ──────── 7

  7a   Plants are known only as gametophytes; sporophytes are not known to occur ──────── 8

    8a   Gametophytes are filamentous and multiply branching; the filaments are uniformly 1 cell wide ──────────────── *Crepidomanes* ▫▫▪▪

    8b   Gametophytes are not filamentous and have a wide, multicelled body (thallus), often with tiny projections that may have gemmae (small vegetative bodies) at the tips ──────── *Vittaria appalachiana* ▫▫▪▪

  7b   Plants produce sporophytes (typical-looking plants larger than a few centimeters in size) ──────── 9

    9a   Plants lack obvious, aboveground leaves; the aboveground parts are green stems that may be branched or not ──────── 10

      10a   The aboveground stems are jointed and often hollow and have a sheath or whorl of highly reduced leaves around each of the joints; stems are typically topped with cone-shaped, spore-bearing strobili ──────── *Equisetum* ▪▫▪▪

      10b   The aboveground stems are dichotomously branched, often many times so, and have no obvious leaves; when fertile, yellow 2–3-lobed synangia (fused sporangia) are present along the branches ──────── *Psilotum* ▪▫▪▫

    9b   Plants have obvious, aboveground leaves of various sizes and appearances (some of which are not particularly leaflike) ──────── 11

      11a   Leaves are small (not more than ~1cm long and typically much shorter than this) and may be scalelike or needlelike; each leaf has only a single vein running through it; sporangia are either clustered into strobili at the tips of the stems, or occur in the leaf axils, on the upper surfaces of the leaves ──────── 12

12a Leaves have a small flap (a ligule) on the upper surface, near the leaf base; strobili are flattened, cylindrical, or 4-sided and are often not well differentiated from the shoot below ⋯⋯⋯⋯⋯⋯⋯⋯⋯⋯⋯⋯⋯⋯⋯⋯⋯ *Selaginella* ■■■■

12b Leaves do not have a ligule, and sporangia occur either in the axils of leaves toward the stem tips, or in well-defined, usually rounded strobili ⋯⋯⋯⋯⋯ 13

13a Sporangia-bearing leaves (sporophylls) are similar to the sterile leaves, with sporangia occurring in the leaf axils (at the base of the leaf, on the upper surface) ⋯⋯ *Huperzia* ■■■■

13b Sporangia-bearing leaves are organized into well-defined strobili that occur at the tips of shoots ⋯⋯⋯⋯⋯⋯⋯⋯⋯⋯⋯⋯⋯⋯⋯⋯⋯⋯⋯⋯⋯⋯⋯ 14

14a Strobili are nodding or pendent and occur at the tips of side branches; plants are typically found in wet habitats including depressions, ditches, streamsides, and moist pinelands ⋯⋯⋯⋯⋯⋯⋯⋯⋯⋯⋯ *Palhinhaea* ■■■■

14b Strobili are erect and occur at the tips of upright, main shoots; plants are either in wet habitats or drier uplands ⋯⋯⋯⋯⋯⋯⋯⋯⋯⋯⋯⋯⋯ 15

15a Upright shoots are unbranched; strobili sit at the tip of a long stalk (peduncle) that may have many or only a few small leaves; plants typically occur in wet habitats ⋯⋯⋯⋯⋯⋯⋯⋯⋯⋯⋯⋯⋯⋯⋯⋯ 16

16a Upright stalks leading to strobili have many small, densely packed leaves ⋯⋯⋯⋯⋯⋯⋯⋯⋯⋯⋯⋯⋯⋯⋯⋯⋯ *Lycopodiella* ■■■■

16b Upright stalks leading to strobili have very few, if any, small leaves, and these are scalelike ⋯⋯⋯⋯⋯ *Pseudolycopodiella* ■■■■

15b Upright shoots are occasionally or frequently branched (and branching may occur only near the base); strobili may have a stalk or not; plants typically occur in drier uplands ⋯⋯⋯⋯⋯⋯⋯⋯⋯ 17

17a Branches appear flattened in cross section (or quadrangular, in 1 species); leaves are scalelike and pressed to the stem surface; if strobilus stalks are branched, they always branch in 2 ⋯⋯ *Diphasiastrum* ■■■■

17b Branches appear rounded in cross section (or slightly flattened in 1 species of *Lycopodium*); leaves are not pressed against the stem surface; if strobilus stalks are branched, they appear to have a central axis plus side stalks ⋯⋯⋯ 18

18a Strobili occur at the ends of distinct stalks (peduncles) that are sparsely leafy ⋯⋯⋯⋯⋯⋯⋯⋯⋯⋯⋯⋯⋯ *Lycopodium* ■■■■

18b Strobili do not have distinct stalks but sit right above the leafy part of the upright stem ⋯⋯⋯⋯⋯⋯⋯⋯⋯ 19

19a Shoots have a main central axis from which numerous horizontally oriented, many-branched side branches emerge; shoots closely resemble small conifer trees ⋯⋯⋯⋯⋯⋯⋯⋯⋯ *Dendrolycopodium* ■■■■

19b Shoots are branched near the base and do not have a distinct central axis with side branches; all branches are oriented upright ⋯⋯⋯⋯⋯⋯⋯⋯⋯ *Spinulum* ■■■■

11b **Leaves are typically more than ~1cm long (with a few exceptions) and vary in appearance; leaves have multiple veins in the leaf blade; sporangia are located on the bottom surface of the leaf and are arranged in various patterns** ⋯⋯⋯⋯⋯⋯⋯⋯⋯⋯ 20

20a Leaves are not lobed or divided at all but are simple and entire (note that *Ophioglossum* technically has a 2-parted leaf and so is included in 20b) ⋯⋯⋯⋯⋯⋯⋯ 21

21a Leaves are not typically fernlike and instead appear grasslike or strap-like; plants are epiphytic, with hanging (pendent) leaves, or terrestrial, with upright leaves ⋯⋯⋯⋯ 22

22a Plants are epiphytic, with narrow, strap-like, hanging leaves; sori are linear and recessed, forming 2 long parallel lines that run along either side of the midrib and are sunken into the leaf surface ⋯⋯⋯⋯⋯⋯ *Vittaria* (remaining species) ■■■■

22b Plants are terrestrial, with upright leaves that are straight or curled;
fertile leaves terminate in a cluster of short, fingerlike projections or
"digits" that hold sporangia ⸺⸺⸺ 23

23a At least some leaves (the sterile ones) are curled and mostly within 5cm
of the ground; plants occur only in the northeastern United States and Canada ⸺⸺ *Schizaea* ■ ■ ■

23b All leaves are fertile and erect and are mostly around 5–20cm tall;
plants occur only in Florida ⸺⸺⸺ *Actinostachys* ■ ▨ ▨ ▨

21b Leaves are not grasslike, and at least some portion of the blade is clearly
expanded and leaflike ⸺⸺⸺ 24

24a Sori are linear and elongated, running parallel to one another and
at an angle from the midrib, forming parallel lines along the lateral veins ⸺⸺ *Asplenium* ■ ■ ■
(4 species: *A. rhizophyllum*,
A. scolopendrium, *A. septentrionale*, *A. serratum*)

24b Sori are round, oblong, or oval ⸺⸺⸺ 25

25a Leaves are dimorphic (the sterile and fertile leaves differ in appearance);
the leaves are spaced out along the stem and are not more than 17cm long
and 1.5cm wide; the lateral veins in the leaves are not parallel to one another ⸺⸺ *Microgramma* ■ ▨ ▨ ▨

25b Leaves are not dimorphic; the leaves are typically clustered along the
stem and are typically 50cm to 1.4m long and 1.5–12cm wide; the lateral
veins in the leaves run parallel to one another ⸺⸺⸺ *Campyloneurum* ■ ▨ ▨ ▨

20b Leaves are deeply lobed, forked, or up to several times divided, or each leaf is
divided at or near its base into a sterile and a fertile component (as in *Ophioglossum*
and other members of Ophioglossaceae, and some *Anemia* plants) ⸺⸺⸺ 26

26a Leaves are a single cell layer thick between the veins; sori occur at the leaf tips, within
sporangia at the base of small cuplike structures that are either conical or clamshell shaped ⸺⸺ 27

27a Sori are clamshell shaped, with 2 distinct valves ⸺⸺⸺ *Hymenophyllum* ▨ ▨ ■ ▨

27b Sori are conical or trumpet shaped ⸺⸺⸺ 28

28a Leaves are 1-pinnate to 2-pinnate-pinnatifid; plants occur in sheltered
rocky areas in temperate regions ⸺⸺⸺ *Vandenboschia* ▨ ▨ ■ ▨

28b Leaves are deeply and irregularly lobed, or clearly pinnatifid; plants are
typically associated with rocks or trees, mostly in more tropical areas (*Trichomanes*)
but also extending into the temperate region (*Didymoglossum*) ⸺⸺⸺ 29

29a Leaves are unlobed, with wavy margins, or are deeply pinnatifid
(to 2-pinnatifid in larger plants), with narrow lobes that are well separated
from one another ⸺⸺⸺ *Didymoglossum* ■ ■ ■ ▨

29b Leaves are lobed and lobes are wide, with undulating margins,
and neighboring lobes often overlap one another ⸺⸺⸺ *Trichomanes* ■ ▨ ▨ ▨

26b Leaves are more than a single cell layer thick between the veins ⸺⸺⸺ 30

30a Plants are either scrambling and shrublike, or climbing and vining ⸺⸺⸺ 31

31a Leaves branch frequently and dichotomously, forming shrubby, bushy,
scrambling plants ⸺⸺⸺ *Dicranopteris* ■ ▨ ▨ ▨

31b Leaves are vining or climbing, extending up and over other vegetation
and often reaching into the canopy ⸺⸺⸺ 32

32a Leaves are dimorphic, with separate fertile and sterile leaves, and
sterile leaves strongly resemble holly leaves ⸺⸺⸺ *Lomariopsis* ■ ▨ ▨ ▨

32b Leaves are not dimorphic, and sterile and fertile leaves are similar
in appearance overall ⸺⸺⸺ *Lygodium* ■ ■ ■ ▨

30b Plants are not scrambling, shrublike, climbing, or vining ⸺⸺⸺ 33

**33a Leaves are entirely dimorphic (with separate, morphologically distinct fertile and
sterile leaves) or partly dimorphic (with morphologically distinct fertile sections or segments)** ⸺⸺⸺ 34

34a Each leaf has 2 distinct components: a sterile, expanded, leaflike blade, and a fertile stalk with contracted pinnae that bear sporangia (these may separate from one another at or above ground level) ---------- 35

35a The sterile portion of the leaf is either: simple and ovate; deeply palmately lobed; or with extremely long, ribbonlike lobes ---------- 36

36a Plants are terrestrial; the sterile portion of the leaf is simple (undivided), ovate, and up to 10cm long and 5cm wide ---------- Ophioglossum ■■■■

36b Plants are epiphytic; the sterile portion of the leaf is deeply lobed and either hand to fan shaped or with elongated, ribbonlike lobes ---------- 37

37a Leaves are up to 45cm long and 35cm wide and are hand to fan shaped, with deeply palmate lobes ---------- Cheiroglossa ■■▨▨

37b Leaves are up to 80cm long, with numerous long, ribbonlike lobes that dangle and may fork or divide toward their tips ---------- Ophioderma ■■▨▨

35b The sterile portion of the leaf is pinnately lobed or divided, or is up to 4-pinnate ---------- 38

38a The sporangia are arranged into small round clusters surrounded by blade tissue that wraps around them ---------- Anemia ■■▨▨

38b The sporangia sit directly against the stalk and on pinnately arranged side branches of various lengths, with no blade tissue present ---------- 39

39a The sterile segment of the leaf is usually 2–4cm wide at maturity and lobed (pinnatifid) to 2-pinnate-pinnatifid ---------- Botrychium ▨▨■■

39b The sterile segment of the leaf is usually more than 7cm wide at maturity and up to 3–4-pinnate ---------- 40

40a When leaves are fertile, the sterile and fertile segment share a long common petiole, with the fertile stalk separating at the base of the blade, above ground level ---------- Botrypus ■■■■

40b When leaves are fertile, the fertile and sterile segments share a short common petiole and then quickly separate from one another near ground level ---------- Sceptridium ■■■■

34b Each leaf is either fertile or sterile; these leaves are entirely separate from one another ---------- 41

41a Fertile and sterile leaves are totally different in appearance: sterile leaves are typically fernlike while fertile leaves are reduced to upright stalks bearing sporangia ---------- 42

42a Plants are distinct from one another; each plant is vase shaped, with fertile leaves at the center, surrounded by sterile leaves ---------- 43

43a Fertile leaves are 2-pinnate and turn from light green to cinnamon brown over the summer; fertile pinnae have no blade tissue and consist only of sporangia ---------- Osmundastrum ■■■■

43b Fertile leaves are 1-pinnate and turn from green to dark brown or black over the summer; fertile pinnae are highly contracted and narrow, their margins wrapped around the sporangia ---------- Matteuccia ▨▨■■

42b Plants often form dense stands or colonies; plants are not vase shaped, and fertile and sterile leaves are intermixed ---------- 44

44a Sterile leaves are pinnatifid throughout or 1-pinnate-pinnatifid at the base and pinnatifid toward the tip ---------- 45

45a Sori are linear to oblong and deeply sunken into the surfaces of the highly contracted pinnae ---------- Lorinseria ■■▨▨

45b Sori are round and surrounded by the contracted pinna margins to form hard, globose structures ---------- Onoclea ■■▨▨

44b Sterile leaves are 1-pinnate-pinnatifid to 2-pinnate throughout ---------- 46

46a Sori are linear and run around the margins of the fertile pinnae, which are narrow and contracted relative to the sterile pinnae but still have blade tissue ---------- Cryptogramma ▨▨■■

46b Sori are round and grouped into small clusters at the tips of fertile pinnae, which are reduced to just the tissue that wraps around the sporangia ⸺ *Anemia wrightii* ■ ▫ ▫ ▫

41b Fertile and sterile leaves look more or less alike, but the fertile leaves have fertile pinnae that are very different in appearance from the sterile pinnae and may be clustered in 1 part of the leaf ⸺ 47

47a The fertile pinnae occur in the middle of an otherwise sterile blade, "interrupting" it ⸺ *Claytosmunda* ▫ ▫ ■ ■

47b The fertile pinnae occur toward the tip of the leaf ⸺ 48

48a Sterile pinnae are distinctly holly shaped (with spiny margins); plants are usually somewhat vining or climbing ⸺ *Lomariopsis* ■ ▫ ▫ ▫

48b Sterile pinnae are not holly shaped; plants are not vining or climbing ⸺ 49

49a Leaves are 2-pinnate; fertile pinnae are clustered at the leaf tip and are reduced to short, contracted stalks bearing globose sporangia ⸺ *Osmunda* ■ ▫ ■ ■

49b Leaves are 1-pinnate to 1-pinnate-pinnatifid; fertile pinnae occur in the tip-ward half of the leaf and are not reduced to stalks ⸺ 50

50a Pinnae have a distinct ear-shaped lobe at the base, on the upper edge ⸺ *Polystichum acrostichoides* ■ ■ ■ ■

50b Pinnae do not have an ear-shaped lobe at the base ⸺ *Dryopteris* ■ ■ ■ ■
(3 species: *D. clintoniana, D. cristata, D. ludoviciana*)

33b Leaves are not strongly dimorphic; overall, the sterile and fertile leaves and leaf segments resemble each other ⸺ 51

51a Sori are protected by cup-shaped or flap-like indusia; sori are located along the leaf margins, either at the very tips or near the bases of the leaf segments, pinnules, or pinna lobes ⸺ 52

52a Indusia are flap-like and sori are located at the tips of flared, somewhat wedge-shaped leaf segments ⸺ *Odontosoria* ■ ▫ ▫ ▫

52b Indusia are cup shaped or flap-like and sori are located toward the bases of the pinnules or pinna lobes ⸺ 53

53a Indusia are distinctly cup shaped or tubular, with sporangia sitting inside ⸺ *Dennstaedtia* ■ ▫ ■ ■

53b Indusia are flap-like, attached at the margin and arching or curving over the sporangia from the side ⸺ *Hypolepis* ■ ▫ ▫ ▫

51b Sori may have indusia or not, but if indusia are present they are not cup shaped or flap-like; sori are located on the lower surface of the leaf blade, along the margins or between the margins and midveins ⸺ 54

54a Sporangia are not organized into sori and instead are spread across the leaf surface (acrostichoid); sporangia may appear to follow veins or not ⸺ 55

55a Plants are epiphytic, growing on trees ⸺ *Platycerium* ■ ▫ ▫ ▫

55b Plants are terrestrial, growing on the ground ⸺ 56

56a Leaves are 2-pinnate to 2-pinnate-pinnatifid and have a distinct white to yellowish, waxy coating on the lower surface ⸺ *Pityrogramma* ■ ▫ ▫ ▫

56b Leaves are 1-pinnate and do not have a white or yellowish coating on the lower surface ⸺ *Acrostichum* ■ ▫ ▫ ▫

54b Sporangia are organized into discrete sori of various shapes, or form linear bands around the pinna margins ⸺ 57

57a Sporangia form continuous or nearly continuous lines or bands, very close and parallel to either the pinna midvein or the pinna margin ⸺ 58

58a Sporangia form linear sori that lie along the pinna midveins; true indusia are present and open toward the midveins ⸺ 59

59a Leaves are 1-pinnate toward the base but become pinnatifid toward the tip; pinna margins are mostly smooth and entire ——————— *Blechnum* ■■▨▨

59b Leaves are 1-pinnate throughout; pinna margins are distinctly toothy and serrate ————————————————— *Telmatoblechnum* ■■▨▨

58b Sporangia are located along the pinna margins; the margins are inrolled, forming false indusia that cover the sporangia ——————————— 60

60a Leaves are usually broadly triangular; plants are commonly found in acidic or sandy soils and/or disturbed areas ——————— *Pteridium* ■■■■

60b Leaves have various shapes other than triangular (i.e., linear, fan shaped, ovate, etc.) ————————————————————————— 61

61a The stipes and rachises have 2–3 distinct ridges or grooves that run longitudinally along their length ————————— *Pteris* ■■■▨

61b The stipes and rachises do not have 2–3 distinct grooves ————— 62

62a Leaves are 1-pinnate to 1-pinnate-pinnatifid throughout ——— *Astrolepis* ▨■■▨

62b Leaves are 2-pinnate to 4-pinnate at the base, becoming less divided farther up the leaf ————————————— 63

63a The lower leaf surfaces are distinctly, densely hairy and/or scaly ————————————————— *Myriopteris* ■■■■

63b The lower leaf surfaces are smooth or have only sparse, fine hairs ———————————————————————— 64

64a Ultimate segments are lanceolate to linear and pointy tipped; margins are widely dentate on the sterile leaves ——————————————— *Aspidotis* ▨▨▨■

64b Ultimate segments are elliptic and round tipped; margins are smooth to somewhat bluntly toothed ——————— 65

65a Whitish farina is present on the lower surface of the blade; ultimate segments are less than 4mm wide ————————— *Argyrochosma* ▨▨■▨

65b Whitish farina is not present on the leaf blade; ultimate segments are more than 4mm wide ——————— *Pellaea* ■■■■

57b Sporangia are organized into discrete sori of various shapes ——————— 66

66a Sori sit directly on the pinna margins and are usually entirely covered by a revolute (rolled under) pinna margin that forms a false indusium around each sorus —————————————————————— *Adiantum* ■■■■

66b Sori are not on the edges of the pinna margins, and the margins do not form false indusia; sori are located between the margin and the pinna midvein ——— 67

67a Sori are linear or elongated and may be slightly curved at 1 end (falcate) ——— 68

68a Sori are located immediately next to the pinna and pinnule midveins and open toward the midveins ——————— *Anchistea* ■■■■

68b Sori are not located next to the midveins but run along the secondary, lateral veins —————————————————— 69

69a Sori are typically on only 1 side of the vein and do not curve over it; scales on the stem and stipe are clathrate (resembling stained glass) ————————————— *Asplenium* (remaining species) ■■■■

69b Sori are often along both sides of a vein and may curve over the vein at the tip; scales on the stem and stipe are not clathrate ——— 70

70a Leaves are 2-pinnate to 3-pinnate ————————— 71

71a The leaf blade may gradually become pinnatifid toward the tip; sori are usually distinctly curved or hooked at 1 end —————————— *Athyrium* ■▨■■

71b   The leaf blade becomes abruptly pinnatifid at the tip; sori are straight, and not distinctly curved or hooked ⸺ *Diplazium esculentum* ■■□□

70b Leaves are 1-pinnate to 1-pinnate-pinnatifid ⸺ 72

72a The grooves on the upper surfaces of the pinna midveins are shallow, and not continuous with the groove on the rachis ⸺ *Deparia* ■■■■

72b The grooves on the upper surfaces of the pinna midveins are deep, and continuous with the groove on the rachis ⸺ 73

73a Leaves are 1-pinnate-pinnatifid; pinnae are deeply lobed ⸺ *Diplazium lonchophyllum* ■■□□

73b Leaves are 1-pinnate; pinnae are not lobed ⸺ *Homalosorus* ■■■□

67b Sori are more or less round, or strongly curved (sometimes almost into a circle) ⸺ 74

74a Sori have no indusia, indusia that are inconspicuous at maturity, or disorganized indusia that are separated into straps or filaments emerging from under the outside edges of each sorus ⸺ 75

75a The indusium emerges from under the outside edge of the sorus and surrounds it; indusia are often not obvious in mature plants and may appear to be absent ⸺ 76

76a The indusia attach at 1 edge and curl up and around each sorus; indusia are cuplike, with smooth edges that are not lobed or filamentous; hydathodes are not present ⸺ *Cystopteris* ■■■□

76b The indusia are saucer shaped, with edges that are deeply lobed or filamentous; hydathodes are often present ⸺ 77

77a Stipes are articulate, with a swollen abscission zone where old fronds will break off; the indusium edges are filamentous and resemble long hairs; hairs may be present on the rachis and/or blade but are not glandular ⸺ *Woodsia* ■■■□

77b Stipes are not articulate, and no abscission zone is present; the indusium edges are lobed or strap-like, and not filamentous; hairs are present on the rachis and/or blade, and glandular hairs are always present ⸺ *Physematium* ■■■□

75b Sori have no indusia, or indusia are minute at maturity ⸺ 78

78a Leaves are distinctly triangular and ternate (3-parted); leaves are 2-pinnate or more divided ⸺ *Gymnocarpium* ■■■□

78b Leaves are not triangular and are not 3-parted; leaves are mostly pinnatifid to 1-pinnate-pinnatifid (except in *Macrothelypteris*, which is more divided) ⸺ 79

79a Leaves are mostly pinnatifid and deeply lobed (they may be up to 1-pinnate in *Pleopeltis*) ⸺ 80

80a Leaves of plants in our region are no more than 3cm long; plants are usually sterile, though sori would be round; plants are known from only 1 location in North Carolina ⸺ *Moranopteris* ■■■□

80b Leaves are typically much longer than 3cm; plants are usually fertile; plants are relatively widespread, with much wider ranges than a single location ⸺ 8

81a The lower surface of the leaf blade has a dense covering of 2-colored scales with a darker brown center and lighter edges ⸺ *Pleopeltis* ■■■□

81b The lower surface of the leaf blade either lacks scales or has 1-colored, light brown scales ⸺ 82

82a The lateral veins in the leaf blade are free and forked; plants are widespread but do not range south into Florida ⸺ *Polypodium* ■■■■

82b The lateral veins in the leaf blade are reticulate and anastomosing, forming networks of small polygons; plants are mostly in Florida (though *Phlebodium* also occurs in southernmost Georgia and Alabama) ⸺ 83

83a Stems are more than 8mm in diameter and have a dense covering of bright reddish-brown to golden scales ⸺ *Phlebodium* ■■■□

83b Stems are less than 8mm in diameter and have dark brown
to black scales ··· *Microsorum* ■ ▪ ▪ ▪

79b Leaves are 1-pinnate or more divided ·· 84

84a Leaves are 2-pinnate to 3-pinnate ·· 85

85a Leaves are 2-pinnate to 3-pinnate; hairs are present on the lower
surfaces of the pinnae ··· *Macrothelypteris* ■ ▪ ■ ▪

85b Leaves are 2-pinnate to 3-pinnate-pinnatifid; no hairs are present
on the lower surfaces of the pinnae ······························· *Ctenitis sloanei* ■ ▪ ▪ ▪

84b Leaves are 1-pinnate to 1-pinnate-pinnatifid ·································· 86

86a No hairs are present on the stipe, rachis, or blade surfaces ········· *Ctenitis submarginalis* ■ ▪ ▪ ▪

86b Moderate to dense hairs are present on the stipe, rachis,
and/or blade surfaces ··· 87

87a Leaves are 1-pinnate and pectinate (with narrow, comblike
pinnae) ··· *Pecluma* ■ ▪ ▪ ▪

87b Leaves are 1-pinnate to 1-pinnate-pinnatifid and not pectinate
or comblike ··· 88

88a Leaves have distinctive furcate (forked) or stellate (star-shaped)
hairs on the stipe, rachis, and/or blade ··················· *Goniopteris* ■ ▪ ▪ ▪

88b Leaves have hairs but they are not forked or starlike ·············· 89

89a All or most pinnae are connected to one another by
a wing of tissue along the rachis; pinna midveins are not
grooved on the upper surface ······························· *Phegopteris* ▪ ▪ ■ ■

89b Pinnae are not connected by a wing of tissue along the
rachis; pinna midveins are grooved on the upper surface ········· 90

90a Leaves are no more than 45cm long at maturity,
and 1-pinnate at the base but pinnatifid farther up;
plants occur in sandstone rockhouses in Alabama ·········· *Leptogramma* ▪ ▪ ■ ▪

90b Leaves are around 2m long at maturity, and
1-pinnate throughout; plants occur in swampy
hammocks in southern Florida ··························· *Meniscium* ■ ▪ ▪ ▪

74b Sori have distinct indusia that are attached at the center or edge of each sorus ·················· 91

91a The pinnule midveins, lateral veins, and blade tissue have a sparse to dense
covering of transparent, needlelike or starlike hairs ·· 92

92a The lowest veins of adjacent pinnules do not come together but run
to their own pinnule margins, reaching the margin at or above the sinus ·············· 93

93a The lowest few pairs of pinnae are much shorter than those above,
giving the leaf blade a tapering appearance at the bottom ··············· *Amauropelta* ■ ■ ■ ■

93b The lowest few pairs of pinnae are not shorter than those above,
and the leaf does not taper strongly toward the base ························· 94

94a The lateral veins in the pinnae are strongly forked ················· *Thelypteris* ■ ■ ■ ■

94b The lateral veins in the pinnae are free and not forked ·············· *Coryphopteris* ▪ ▪ ■ ■

92b The lowest veins of adjacent pinnules come together, either right at the
margin at the base of the sinus, or up to a few millimeters below the sinus margin
and then join together to form a single (excurrent) vein that runs upward to the sinus ·············· 95

95a The lowest veins of adjacent pinnules always come together a few
millimeters below the sinus, forming an excurrent vein that runs to the sinus ·············· 96

96a No scales are present on the lower leaf surface; the upper leaf surface
is densely hairy, with hairs longer than 0.3mm ··· *Christella* ■ ▪ ▪ ▪

96b Tan scales are present on the lower leaf surface, along the pinna midveins; the upper leaf surface is smooth or sparsely hairy, with hairs shorter than 0.2mm ··· *Cyclosorus* ■■□□

95b The lowest veins of adjacent pinnules, in at least a few places, come together right at the sinus, or reach the margin above the sinus ············· 97

97a Yellowish glands are present on the lower surface of the leaf (especially along the veins and at the pinnule tips) ··················· *Amblovenatum* ■□□□

97b No yellowish glands are present on the lower surface of the leaf ··········· *Pelazoneuron* ■□■□

91b The pinnule midveins, lateral veins, and blade tissue do not have a sparse to dense covering of transparent, needlelike or starlike hairs ··· 98

98a Leaves are 1-pinnate and the leaf tip always remains curled in a tiny fiddlehead ·········· *Nephrolepis* ■□□□

98b Leaves are variously divided and the leaf tip unfurls completely, not remaining as a fiddlehead ·· 99

99a Lateral veins are distinctly reticulate and anastomosing, forming networks of small polygons ··· 100

100a Leaves are tough and leathery and strongly 1-pinnate; pinnae have long tips that usually curve upward toward the leaf tip ················· *Cyrtomium* ■■■□

100b Leaves are not particularly leathery and are lobed to pinnatifid or 1-pinnate; pinna tips are not long and drawn out ················· *Tectaria* ■□□□

99b Lateral veins are free or form networks only occasionally ··············· 101

101a Sori are round and indusia are attached at their center, like an umbrella (peltate) ··· 102

102a Leaves are 1-pinnate or 2-pinnate and form vaselike clusters ··· *Polystichum* (remaining species) □□□■

102b Leaves are 2-pinnate to 3-pinnate and spread out along long-creeping stems ··· *Rumohra* ■□□□

101b Sori are kidney shaped and indusia are attached at 1 edge ················· 103

103a Leaves are variegated in color, the pinnae yellow to light green at the center and darkening toward the margins; indusia may appear round or peltate but are attached along 1 edge ··············· *Arachniodes* ■□■□

103a Leaves are not variegated and are uniform in color; indusia are usually clearly attached along 1 edge and do not appear peltate ··· *Dryopteris* (remaining species) □□■□

LYCOPHYTES

DESCRIPTIONS OF
GENERA AND SPECIES

FAMILY: **LYCOPODIACEAE**

Dendrolycopodium is a genus of lycophytes known as the tree clubmosses, and this common name references an easily recognizable aspect of their appearance: they strongly resemble small pine trees. The members of this genus were historically included in *Lycopodium*, the clubmoss genus (p. 86), which explains the remainder of the common name. *Lycopodium* has been broken up in recent years into several smaller genera, and *Dendrolycopodium* is perhaps the most readily distinguishable of these, based on its unique miniature tree–like morphology. Globally there are 4 or 5 species in the genus, all in mountainous, temperate, and/or boreal regions of the Northern Hemisphere, and we have 3 species in our flora. The lateral branches of *Dendrolycopodium* usually have whorls of leaves in sets of 6, and the arrangement and relative size of these leaves are useful characters for distinguishing the 3 species (see figure below). Base chromosome number (x) = 34.

KEY TO THE SPECIES OF *DENDROLYCOPODIUM* IN OUR FLORA:

1a   The leaves on the main upright shoot axes are spaced widely apart and spread outward, sometimes nearly horizontally; the lateral shoots have 2 leaves on the top surface pointing upward, 2 on the lower surface pointing downward, and 1 on each side pointing outward ⋯⋯⋯⋯⋯ *Dendrolycopodium dendroideum*

1b   The leaves on the main upright shoot axes are close together and are pressed more or less against the axis, pointing strongly upward; the lateral shoots have 1 leaf on the top surface pointing upward, 1 leaf on the lower surface pointing downward, and 2 leaves on each side pointing outward ⋯⋯⋯⋯⋯ 2

     2a   The lateral shoots are round in cross section; the lateral leaves of the lateral shoots are not twisted and are all more or less the same length ⋯⋯⋯⋯⋯ *Dendrolycopodium hickeyi*

     2b   The lateral shoots are flat in cross section; the lateral leaves of the lateral shoots are somewhat twisted, so that the side of the leaf points upward; the leaves pointing downward from the lower surfaces of the lateral shoots are shorter than the other leaves ⋯⋯⋯⋯⋯ *Dendrolycopodium obscurum*

 Upper leaves   Lateral leaves   Lower leaves

Key 1a.	Key 2a.	Key 2b.

Dendrolycopodium dendroideum	***Dendrolycopodium hickeyi***	***Dendrolycopodium obscurum***
Two upper leaves, two lower leaves, one lateral leaf on each side; all leaves are the same size; the branch is round in cross section	One upper leaf, one lower leaf, two lateral leaves on each side; all leaves are the same size; the branch is round in cross section	One upper leaf, one lower leaf, two lateral leaves on each side; the lower leaf is shorter; the branch is flat in cross section

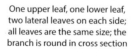

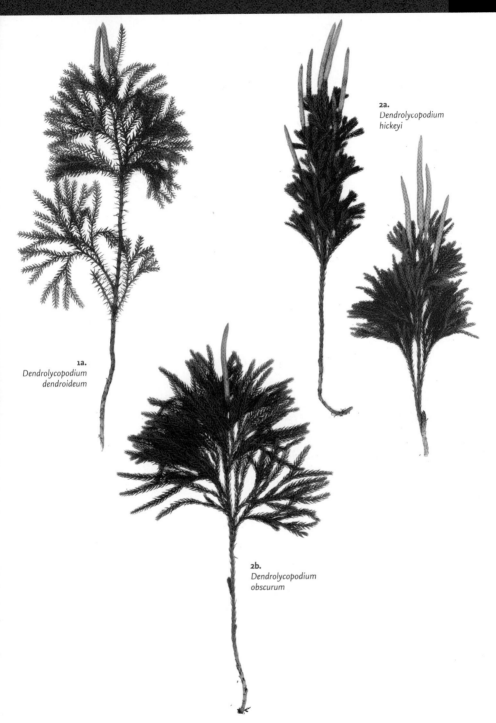

2a.
Dendrolycopodium hickeyi

1a.
Dendrolycopodium dendroideum

2b.
Dendrolycopodium obscurum

Dendrolycopodium dendroideum

COMMON NAME(S) Northern tree clubmoss, prickly tree clubmoss

NOTABLE SYNONYMS *Lycopodium dendroideum*

STATUS Native, somewhat common

HABITAT/DISTRIBUTION Dry forests and shrubby habitats; also occurs in western North America and Asia

Plants are terrestrial. **Stems** are belowground and long creeping. **Shoots** are erect and treelike, up to 26cm tall, with a central axis and numerous lateral side shoots that branch further. **Leaves** on the main upright shoot axes are up to 4mm long and 1mm wide, are spaced widely apart, and spread outward, sometimes nearly horizontally. The horizontal **branches** are round in cross section, with more or less obvious annual growth constrictions, and with leaves up to 3.5mm long and 1.2mm wide that spread slightly outward before pointing toward the shoot tip. The branches have 2 leaves on the top surface pointing upward, 2 on the lower surface pointing downward, and 1 lateral leaf on each side pointing outward. All leaves are roughly the same length, and none of the leaves are twisted. **Margins** are entire, and leaves are linear and pointed but do not have a hairlike tip. **Strobili** are up to 55mm long and sit directly atop the leaf portion of the upright shoots, with 1–7 strobili per shoot. 2n=68 (diploid).

A. Plants of *Dendrolycopodium dendroideum*.

B. Main shoot axis showing widely spaced, spreading leaves.

C. Lateral branches.

D. Strobili.

Dendrolycopodium hickeyi

COMMON NAME(S) Hickey's tree clubmoss

NOTABLE SYNONYMS *Lycopodium hickeyi*

STATUS Native (endemic to North America), somewhat common

HABITAT/DISTRIBUTION Forests and shrubby habitats; also occurs in western North America

Plants are terrestrial. **Stems** are belowground and long creeping. **Shoots** are erect and treelike, up to 16cm tall, with a central axis and numerous lateral side shoots that branch further. **Leaves** on the main upright shoot axes are up to 4.5mm long and 0.6mm wide and are close together and pressed more or less against the axis, pointing strongly upward. The horizontal **branches** are round in cross section, with more or less obvious annual growth constrictions, and with leaves up to 5mm long and 1mm wide that spread slightly outward before pointing toward the shoot tip. The branches have 1 leaf on the top surface pointing upward, 1 leaf on the lower surface pointing downward, and 2 lateral leaves on each side pointing outward. All leaves are roughly the same length, and none of the leaves are twisted. **Margins** are entire, and leaves are linear and pointed but do not have a hairlike tip. **Strobili** are up to 65mm long and sit directly atop the leaf portion of the upright shoots, with 1–7 strobili per shoot. 2n=68 (diploid).

A & B. Plants of *Dendrolycopodium hickeyi*.

C. Plants showing lateral branches that are round in crosssection.

D. Strobili.

Dendrolycopodium obscurum

COMMON NAME(S) Flat-branched tree clubmoss

NOTABLE SYNONYMS *Lycopodium obscurum*

STATUS Native (endemic to eastern North America), common

HABITAT/DISTRIBUTION Forests and shrubby habitats

Plants are terrestrial. **Stems** are belowground and long creeping. **Shoots** are erect and treelike, up to 21cm tall, with a central axis and numerous lateral side shoots that branch further. **Leaves** on the main upright shoot axes are up to 4.5mm long and 0.7mm wide and are close together and pressed more or less against the axis, pointing strongly upward. The horizontal **branches** are flat in cross section, with more or less obvious annual growth constrictions, and with leaves up to 5.5mm long and 1.2mm wide that spread slightly outward before pointing toward the shoot tip. The branches have 1 leaf on the top surface pointing upward, 1 leaf on the lower surface pointing downward, and 2 lateral leaves on each side pointing outward. The downward-pointing leaves on the lower surface are distinctly shorter and give the branch its flattened appearance. The outward-pointing lateral leaves are somewhat twisted, so that the top surfaces of the leaves point upward instead of outward. **Margins** are entire, and leaves are linear and pointed but do not have a hairlike tip. **Strobili** are up to 60mm long and sit directly atop the leaf portion of the upright shoots, with 1–6 strobili per shoot. 2n=68 (diploid).

B. Lateral branches appear flat in cross section.

C. Side view of flattened lateral branches.

A. Plants of *Dendrolycopodium obscurum*.

FAMILY: **LYCOPODIACEAE**

Diphasiastrum is a genus of lycophytes commonly known as ground-pines, ground-cedars, or running-pines for their resemblance to miniature conifer trees. They have minute, scalelike leaves and distinctive fan-shaped branches that set them apart from other, closely related and morphologically similar genera. Globally there are 16 species recognized in *Diphasiastrum*, and 4 occur in our flora. The group is known worldwide for its ability to produce hybrids, many of which are fertile and can be locally abundant (see figure below). Base chromosome number (x) = 23.

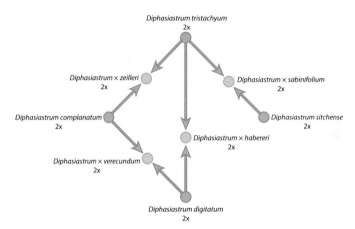

Relationships among *Diphasiastrum* species in eastern North America. Darker blue circles are diploid parental taxa (2x), and arrows show the direction of their parental contributions to fertile diploid (also 2x) hybrids (lighter blue circles). For more information about interpreting these figures, see p. 12.

KEY TO THE SPECIES OF *DIPHASIASTRUM* IN OUR FLORA:

1a The upright shoots are mostly less than 12cm tall; the strobili are mostly unstalked, sitting directly atop the leafy part of the shoot ⋯⋯⋯⋯ *Diphasiastrum sitchense*

1b The upright shoots are mostly more than 12cm tall; the strobili are mostly stalked, sitting atop long peduncles ⋯⋯ 2

2a The tip-most branchlets are 4-sided and nearly square in cross section; leaves and plants are usually somewhat bluish or grayish green; the leaves on the tops, sides, and bottoms of the branches are more or less all equal in size ⋯⋯ *Diphasiastrum tristachyum*

2b The tip-most branchlets are flat in cross section; leaves and plants are bright to dark green; the leaves on the bottoms of the branches are much smaller than those on the tops and sides ⋯⋯⋯⋯ 3

3a Branching is irregular; annual growth constrictions are usually apparent along the branches; strobili are mostly 10–25mm long and sit at the tips of relatively thin peduncles ⋯⋯⋯⋯ *Diphasiastrum complanatum* subsp. *complanatum*

3b Branching is regular and fanlike; annual growth constrictions are not present; strobili are mostly 20–40mm long and sit at the tips of relatively thick, stout peduncles ⋯⋯⋯⋯ *Diphasiastrum digitatum*

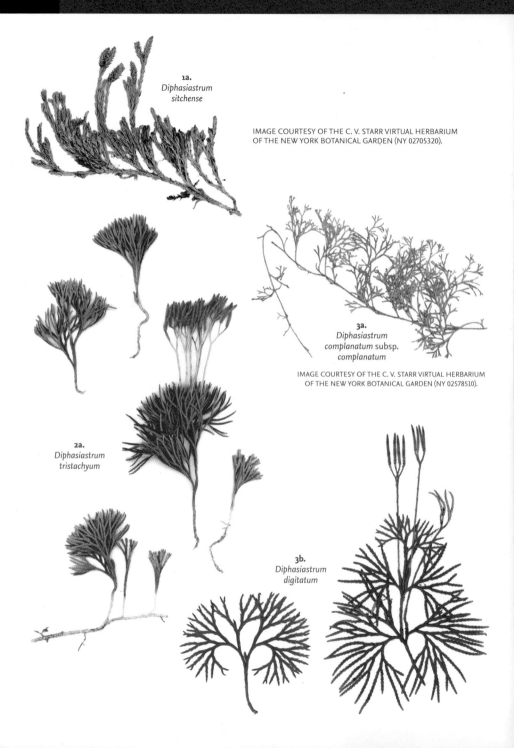

1a.
Diphasiastrum sitchense

IMAGE COURTESY OF THE C. V. STARR VIRTUAL HERBARIUM OF THE NEW YORK BOTANICAL GARDEN (NY 02705320).

3a.
Diphasiastrum complanatum subsp. *complanatum*

IMAGE COURTESY OF THE C. V. STARR VIRTUAL HERBARIUM OF THE NEW YORK BOTANICAL GARDEN (NY 02578510).

2a.
Diphasiastrum tristachyum

3b.
Diphasiastrum digitatum

Diphasiastrum complanatum subsp. complanatum

COMMON NAME(S) Northern ground-cedar, northern running-pine

NOTABLE SYNONYMS *Lycopodium complanatum*

STATUS Native, somewhat common

HABITAT/DISTRIBUTION Dry, open forests and slopes; also occurs in Greenland, Europe, and Asia (a second subspecies, *D. complanatum* subsp. *montellii*, has been described from Europe)

Plants are terrestrial and can form large colonies. **Stems** are horizontal and long creeping, sitting against the substrate or underneath litter, with small, linear, appressed leaves. **Upright shoots** are up to 44cm tall, with an erect central axis that has small, pointed, appressed leaves up to 3.2mm long and 1.1mm wide. Horizontal **branches** are up to 4.4mm wide including the leaves, bright to dark green, flat in cross section, and irregularly branched, with conspicuous annual growth constrictions. Leaves on the branches are pressed against the branch for at least half their length, making the branches themselves appear green. Leaves are linear to lanceolate, with pointed tips that spread away from the branch axis. The leaves on the upper surface of the branches are up to 2mm long and 1.2mm wide; the lateral leaves are up to 7.3mm long and 2.1mm wide; and the leaves on the underside of the branches are the smallest, up to 1.5mm long and 0.9mm wide. **Peduncles** are up to 8.5cm long and slender, with minute leaves, and 1 or 2 strobili per peduncle, at the ends of short stalks. **Strobili** are up to 25mm long and do not end in sterile tips. 2n=46 (diploid).

A. Plants of *Diphasiastrum complanatum* subsp. *complanatum*.

B. Branches with appressed leaves and annual growth constrictions.

C. Young plants with bright green new foliage.

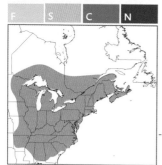

F | S | C | N

Diphasiastrum digitatum

COMMON NAME(S) Southern ground-cedar, southern running-pine

NOTABLE SYNONYMS *Lycopodium digitatum*

STATUS Native (endemic to eastern North America), common

HABITAT/DISTRIBUTION Forested and shrubby habitats, sometimes open meadows

Plants are terrestrial and can form large colonies. **Stems** are horizontal and long creeping, sitting against the substrate or underneath litter, with small, linear, appressed leaves. **Upright shoots** are up to 50cm tall, with an erect central axis that has small, pointed, appressed leaves up to 3.5mm long and 1mm wide. Horizontal **branches** are up to 3.9mm wide including the leaves, bright to dark green, flat in cross section, and irregularly branched, without conspicuous annual growth constrictions. Leaves on the branches are pressed against the branch for at least half their length, making the branches themselves appear green. Leaves are linear to lanceolate, with pointed tips that spread away from the branch axis. The leaves on the upper surface of the branches are up to 1.5mm long and 0.9mm wide; the lateral leaves are up to 5.5mm long and 2mm wide; and the leaves on the underside of the branches are the smallest, up to 1mm long and 0.7mm wide. **Peduncles** are up to 12.5cm long, thick and stout, with minute leaves, and 2–4 strobili per peduncle, at the ends of short, branched stalks. **Strobili** are up to 40mm long and may end in sterile tips up to 11mm long. 2n=46 (diploid).

A. A colony of *Diphasiastrum digitatum.*

B. Fertile plants.

C. Close-up of strobili.

D. Dichotomous branching.

E. Strobili that have released their spores.

Diphasiastrum sitchense

COMMON NAME(S) Sitka clubmoss

NOTABLE SYNONYMS *Lycopodium sitchense*

STATUS Native, uncommon

HABITAT/DISTRIBUTION Open meadows, conifer forests, rocky areas above tree line; also occurs in western North America and Asia

Plants are terrestrial and can form large colonies. **Stems** are horizontal and long creeping, sitting against the substrate or underneath litter, with small, linear, appressed leaves. **Upright shoots** are mostly 12cm tall or less but can be up to 17.5cm tall, branch near the base, do not have a clear central axis, and have small, linear, appressed leaves. Horizontal **branches** are up to 2.5mm wide including the leaves, bright to dark green, round in cross section, and irregularly branched, with annual growth constrictions, but these are not obvious. Leaves on the branches are pressed against the branch for less than half their length, with the tips spreading outward, and leaves are arranged in pseudowhorls of 2 and 3 leaves. Leaves are all alike in size, up to 5.6mm long and 0.9mm wide, with sharply pointed tips. **Peduncles** are absent, or if present are up to 1cm long at most. **Strobili** are up to 38mm long and do not have stalks, instead sitting directly atop the leafy portion of the shoot. 2n=46 (diploid).

A. A colony of *Diphasiastrum sitchense*.

B. Fertile plants.

C. Immature strobili.

D. Mature stems with dehisced strobili.

PHOTOGRAPHS A & C BY NOLAN EXE
PHOTOGRAPHS B & D BY GREG RAND

Diphasiastrum tristachyum

COMMON NAME(S Blue ground-cedar

NOTABLE SYNONYMS *Lycopodium tristachyum*

STATUS Native, uncommon

HABITAT/DISTRIBUTION Open forests and rocky areas, on acidic soils; also occurs in Europe and Asia

Plants are terrestrial and can form large colonies. **Stems** are horizontal and long creeping and are typically buried in the soil, with small, linear, appressed leaves. **Upright shoots** cluster together and are up to 36cm tall, with an erect central axis that has small, pointed, appressed leaves up to 3.4mm long and 1mm wide. Horizontal **branches** are up to 2.2mm wide including the leaves, bluish or grayish green, quadrangular in cross section, and irregularly branched, with conspicuous annual growth constrictions. Leaves on the branches are pressed against the branch for at least half their length, making the branches themselves appear green. Leaves are linear or needlelike, with pointed tips that spread away from the branch axis. The leaves on the upper surface of the branches are up to 1.7mm long and 0.9mm wide; the lateral leaves are up to 7.2mm long and 2mm wide; and the leaves on the underside of the branches are similar to those on top, up to 2mm long and 0.7mm wide. **Peduncles** are up to 15cm long, slender, with minute leaves, and 2–4 strobili per peduncle, at the ends of short, branched stalks. **Strobili** are up to 28mm long and do not end in sterile tips. 2n=46 (diploid).

A. A colony of *Diphasiastrum tristachyum.*

B. Plants with prominent central axis.

C. Branches with appressed leaves.

D. Strobili that have released their spores.

FAMILY: **LYCOPODIACEAE**

Huperzia is a lycophyte genus whose species can typically be found in the northern part of our region (though a few also occur in the south). The common name of the genus, temperate firmosses, refers to their similarity to miniature fir trees and their occurrence only in the temperate zone. The association with mosses predates our modern understanding of relationships among land plants (see p. 7). *Huperzia* species are similar in appearance to some other members of Lycopodiaceae, especially *Spinulum* (p. 111), but can easily be distinguished by not having well-defined strobili; their spore-bearing leaves are located at the tips of the shoots, but they resemble the sterile leaves and you must look closely to discern the sporangia tucked in at the leaf bases. Gemmae (small vegetative propagules) are common in some species and are unique to this genus of lycophytes. They may occur either throughout the shoots, or in 1 or more whorls near the shoot tip. Three of the *Huperzia* species in our eastern flora are diploids and 1 is a tetraploid, and several sterile hybrids are known to form from crosses between them (see figure below). Base chromosome number (x) = 67, 68.

RIGHT: Shoots of *Huperzia porophila* with gemmae (toward the bottom of the left shoot and the middle of the right one). PHOTOGRAPH BY ALAN CRESSLER

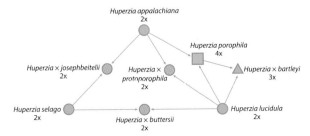

LEFT: Relationships among *Huperzia* species in eastern North America. Blue circles are fertile diploids (2x), the green square is a fertile allotetraploid (4x), and the gray circles and triangle are sterile diploid and triploid hybrids, respectively. Arrows show the direction of genetic contribution from parental toward offspring taxa. For more information about interpreting these figures, see p. 12.

KEY TO THE SPECIES OF *HUPERZIA* IN OUR FLORA:

1a Leaves are widest above the middle, with an obovate overall shape; leaves spread away from the shoot axis and have at least a few distinct teeth along the margins; annual growth constrictions are conspicuous ⋯⋯⋯⋯⋯⋯⋯⋯⋯⋯⋯⋯⋯⋯⋯⋯⋯⋯ *Huperzia lucidula*

1b Leaves are widest at the base, with a lancelike overall shape; leaves point upward and have no teeth or only a few small teeth; annual growth constrictions are indistinct or absent ⋯⋯⋯⋯ 2

    2a Leaves are lanceolate but the sides are parallel for most of the leaf length; stomata are present on both surfaces of the leaf (hand lens required for viewing), but fewer than 50 are present on the upper leaf surface ⋯⋯⋯⋯⋯⋯⋯⋯⋯⋯⋯⋯⋯⋯ *Huperzia porophila*

    2b Leaves are lanceolate to ovate or triangular; stomata are present on both surfaces of the leaf, but more than 60 are present on the upper surface ⋯⋯⋯⋯⋯⋯⋯⋯⋯ 3

        3a The sterile leaves are of 2 kinds, with those near the base of the shoots much longer and more spreading than those farther up; gemmae can be found throughout the shoots ⋯⋯⋯⋯⋯⋯⋯⋯⋯⋯⋯⋯ *Huperzia appalachiana*

        3b The sterile leaves are all alike; gemmae occur in only a single whorl near the shoot tip ⋯⋯⋯⋯⋯⋯⋯⋯⋯⋯⋯⋯⋯⋯⋯⋯ *Huperzia selago*

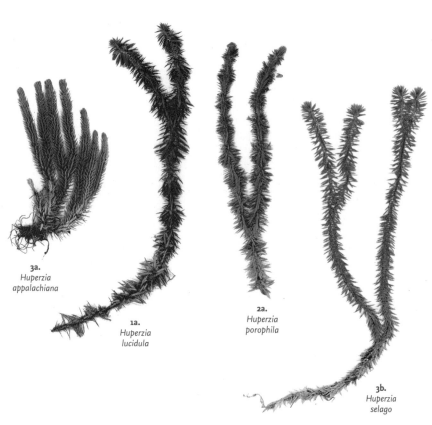

3a.
Huperzia appalachiana

1a.
Huperzia lucidula

2a.
Huperzia porophila

3b.
Huperzia selago

Huperzia appalachiana

COMMON NAME(S) Mountain firmoss

NOTABLE SYNONYMS *Huperzia appressa, Huperzia selago* subsp. *appressa, Lycopodium selago* subsp. *appressum*

STATUS Native, uncommon

HABITAT/DISTRIBUTION Typically on damp but exposed, rocky cliffs or talus slopes, occasionally on thin soils; also occurs in Greenland

- -

Plants are terrestrial. **Stems** are compact and erect. **Shoots** are erect, up to 10cm tall, and often form clusters. If shoots branch, they do so dichotomously. Annual growth constrictions are typically not distinct. **Leaves** at the base of the shoots are distinctly larger and more spreading than those farther up the shoot, which are more closely pressed against the shoot. Leaves are up to 6mm long and widest at their base (lanceolate in overall shape to ovate or even triangular) and have entire **margins** with no teeth. Stomata are present on both surfaces and are numerous (more than 60) on the upper surface. **Sporangia** occur on the upper surfaces of the tip-most leaves, tucked in at the leaf bases. **Gemmae** occur throughout the shoots. 2n=134 (diploid).

A. A colony of *Huperzia appalachiana*.

B. Plants.

C. Fertile leaves and gemmae.

Huperzia lucidula

COMMON NAME(S) Shining firmoss

NOTABLE SYNONYMS *Lycopodium lucidulum*

STATUS Native (endemic to North America), common

HABITAT/DISTRIBUTION Shady conifer or hardwood forests; also occurs sporadically farther west in the U.S. and Canada

Plants are terrestrial. **Stems** are compact and erect. **Shoots** are erect, up to 20cm tall, and often form clusters. If shoots branch, they do so dichotomously. Annual growth constrictions are distinct along the shoots. **Leaves** are similar in size and shape along the length of the shoot. Leaves are up to 12mm long and widest above the middle of the leaf (obovate in overall shape) and have distinctly toothy **margins**. Stomata are visible only on the bottom surface of the leaf. **Sporangia** occur on the upper surfaces of the tip-most leaves, tucked in at the leaf bases. **Gemmae** occur in a single whorl toward the shoot tip. 2n=134 (diploid).

A. Plants of *Huperzia lucidula*.

B. A shoot with dichotomous branching.

C. Fertile section of the stem.

D. Fertile leaves with sporangia.

E. Shoot tip with gemmae.

Huperzia porophila

COMMON NAME(S) Rock firmoss

NOTABLE SYNONYMS *Lycopodium porophilum*

STATUS Native (endemic to eastern North America), uncommon

HABITAT/DISTRIBUTION Typically in rocky woods on damp, shaded (or occasionally more exposed) sandstone substrates

---

Plants are terrestrial. **Stems** are compact and erect. **Shoots** are erect, up to 15cm tall, and often form clusters. If shoots branch, they do so dichotomously. Annual growth constrictions are typically not distinct. **Leaves** are similar in size and shape along the length of the shoot. Leaves are up to 8mm long and widest at their base (lanceolate in overall shape), but the sides are parallel for most of the leaf length. Leaves have nearly entire **margins** with no or only a few small teeth. Stomata are present on both surfaces but are sparse (fewer than 50) on the upper surface. **Sporangia** occur on the upper surfaces of the tip-most leaves, tucked in at the leaf bases. **Gemmae** occur in 1–3 whorls toward the tips of the shoots. 2n=268 (tetraploid).

A. Fertile plants of *Huperzia porophila*.

B. Fertile section of stem, with gemmae.

C. Lower surfaces of leaves, with stomata (small white dots)..

F S C N

Huperzia selago

COMMON NAME(S) Northern firmoss

NOTABLE SYNONYMS *Lycopodium selago*

STATUS Native, uncommon

HABITAT/DISTRIBUTION Damp habitats including swamps, conifer woods, and along streams, moist cliffs, and old trails; also occurs in western North America, Europe, and Asia

Plants are terrestrial. **Stems** are compact and erect. **Shoots** are erect, up to 15cm tall, and often form clusters. If shoots branch, they do so dichotomously. Annual growth constrictions are typically not distinct. **Leaves** are similar in size and shape along the length of the shoot. Leaves are up to 8mm long and are widest at their base (lanceolate in overall shape to ovate or even triangular). Leaves have nearly entire **margins** with no or only a few small teeth. Stomata are present on both surfaces and are numerous (more than 60) on the upper surface. **Sporangia** occur on the upper surfaces of the tip-most leaves, tucked in at the leaf bases. **Gemmae** occur in a single whorl toward the shoot tip. 2n=134 (diploid).

A

B

C

A. Plants of *Huperzia selago*.

B. Fertile section of stem, with gemmae.

C. Top-down view showing gemmae.

ALL PHOTOGRAPHS BY NATE MARTINEAU

FAMILY: **ISOETACEAE**

Isoetes is a genus of lycophytes commonly known as quillworts or Merlin's grasses. This is perhaps the most intriguing and enigmatic group of plants in our fern and lycophyte flora; the members of this genus are unique in their appearance and lifestyle, in ways that lead to their being easily overlooked in nature. All *Isoetes* species are perennials and associate closely with water. Many species are fully submerged aquatics, while others are emergent but rooted in permanent water, and still others are only seasonally inundated, occurring in ephemeral water bodies and becoming essentially terrestrial once these waters have receded or dried up. The vast majority of the 200+ quillwort species known worldwide require acidic or at least circumneutral substrates; very few can tolerate limy or nutrient-rich soils. The ability of most *Isoetes* to grow in these relatively sterile conditions may reduce competition from other plants, but it also greatly limits the possible geographic extent of their occurrence in eastern North America.

Quillworts in our region can be categorized within three distinct groupings of habitat and seasonality: 1) rock outcrop and ephemeral meadow species, which have the shortest growing season, appearing in late winter to early spring but becoming dormant and usually invisible aboveground by early summer; 2) woodland swamp species that develop in late spring and are evident aboveground into late summer or early fall; and 3) fully aquatic species that develop in mid to late summer, mature well into autumn, and often remain evident until freeze-up. Their aquatic nature makes it unlikely that you will encounter these plants on the average hike; often they will be found only by a targeted search. Despite an inconspicuous overall appearance (most quillworts look like a tuft of grass or an upright bundle of pine needles), the unique morphological features of their appearance and structure will become clear upon closer inspection (see the *Isoetes* section in the description of lycophyte morphology on p. 20).

In addition to their distinctive appearance and watery habit, *Isoetes* species are noteworthy for several additional reasons. First, unlike most plants, they absorb CO_2 through their roots and expel oxygen into the soil. A red color is often evident in the substrate around the roots of many aquatic quillworts, and it is literally rust, caused by oxidation. They also employ CAM photosynthesis, an alternative photosynthetic pathway to the one employed by most plants, which is particularly interesting in *Isoetes* because CAM photosynthesis is typically seen in plants adapted to arid and desert habitats. The CAM process is especially useful for plants growing where photosynthetic productivity is limited by environmental stress (e.g., in deserts) or sterility (e.g., nutrient-poor, aquatic habitats).

Quillworts are extremely prone to hybridization and polyploidy, and this has been the primary route for the formation of new species in our region. Ploidy—the number of sets of chromosomes in an organism—has provided critical insights into the classification, taxonomy, and relationships of quillworts. The genus may have the most complicated network of interspecies hybridization of any group in the North American pteridophyte flora (see figure below), and over a dozen sterile hybrids involving eastern North American species have been formally described. New hybrids continue to be identified regularly, as do sexual species, and it seems likely that significant diversity still remains to be discovered. The base number of chromosomes in the genus is 11, and all distinct North American species of *Isoetes* have even ploidal levels (e.g., a diploid will have 2n=22 chromosomes, a tetraploid 2n=44 chromosomes, etc.). Odd-numbered sets of chromosomes reflect hybrids between parents of different ploidal levels (e.g., a triploid with 2n=33 or a pentaploid with 2n=55), and these are always sterile (though even-numbered fertile hybrids, between parents at the same ploidal level, are also known). Hybrid plants are most often first detected by their aborted, sterile megaspores, which vary in appearance and size, with a mix of ornamentation features from both parental taxa. All members of the family Isoetaceae are heterosporous, with separate female megaspores and male microspores.

Finally, it is worth mentioning that the name of this genus can be spelled legitimately in two ways: *Isoetes* and *Isoëtes* are both technically correct and acceptable spellings. The former is used here for simplicity. Base chromosome number (x) = 11.

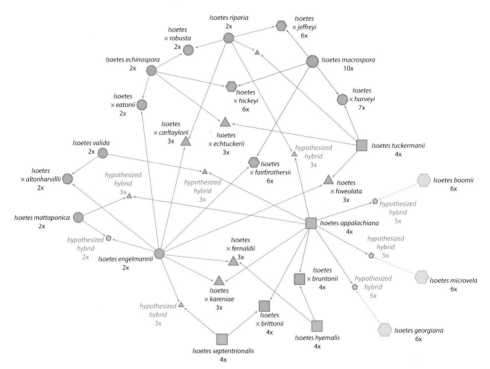

Relationships among *Isoetes* species in eastern North America. Blue circles are fertile diploids (2x), green squares are fertile allotetraploids (4x), yellow hexagons are fertile allohexaploids (6x), and the orange dodecagon is a fertile dodecaploid (10x). Gray circles, triangles, squares, and hexagons are sterile diploids, triploids, tetraploids, and hexaploids, respectively. Purple shapes are hypothesized hybrids that have not yet been found in nature. Large shapes are named taxa, and small shapes are as yet unnamed. Arrows show the direction of genetic contribution from parental toward offspring taxa. For more information about interpreting these figures, see p. 12.

OPPOSITE PAGE:

A. *Isoetes georgiana* growing in a slow-moving forest stream.

B. *Isoetes engelmannii* growing in a forest pool.

C. *Isoetes butleri* growing in a grassy swale that is seasonally flooded.

D. *Isoetes flaccida* growing in a cypress dome in the Everglades.

E. Leaves of *Isoetes flaccida*.

F. Outside of a leaf base of *Isoetes engelmannii*.

G. Sporangium of *Isoetes engelmannii*, with its outline visible (the velum has been removed).

H. Leaf base of *Isoetes flaccida* with ligule still attached.

KEY TO THE SPECIES OF *ISOETES* IN OUR FLORA:

A combination of features can be used to arrive at credible field identifications of quillworts, but most of them cannot be identified by the unaided eye. The examination of megaspore ornamentation at 15x (preferably 30x) magnification is usually essential, in concert with leaf features (especially velum coverage) and attributes such as plant form, phenology, and site ecology. In order to provide reliable information about ornamentation pattern and spore size, megaspores must be mature (appearing pure white in all but a few species, and never yellow and/or glassy). Spores retained in the soil around the roots from previous growing seasons can often provide the mature material needed for identification.

1a   **Megaspores from the same plant are variable in shape and size and/or exhibit more than one ornamentation pattern (i.e., they are abortive and not viable); individual plants are often substantially larger than associates (i.e., they display hybrid vigor)** ············ *various sterile hybrid species*

1b   **Megaspores from the same plant are uniform in shape, size, and ornamentation; all plants are approximately the same size** ·· **2**

    2a   Plants are terrestrial or occur in seasonally flooded or ephemeral soils, swales, or pools, or on and around rock outcrops (note that plants may be in flowing water early in the season but typically end up on soil later, when the water recedes) ··· **3**

        3a   The velum covers 70–100% of the sporangium; megaspores are gray to black; plants are tiny (< 7cm tall) and occur only on isolated granite outcrops (Georgia and South Carolina) ··········· **4**

            4a   Plants are up to 5–7cm tall and grow individually; corms are globose; megaspores are densely ornamented with tubercles ···························· *Isoetes melanospora*

            4b   Plants are up to 3–4cm tall and grow in dense mats; corms are elongated; megaspores are somewhat wrinkled or unornamented ························· *Isoetes tegetiformans*

        3b   The velum covers less than 70% of the sporangium; megaspores are white; plants are substantially larger (8–30cm tall) and variously distributed ······························· **5**

            5a   Plants occur on basic substrates (e.g., calcareous, limestone-derived soils); megaspores are generally more than 525µm in diameter ···························· *Isoetes butleri*

            5b   Plants occur on acidic or circumneutral substrates (e.g., noncalcareous soils); megaspores are mostly less than 500µm in diameter ····································· **6**

                6a   The velum covers approximately 40% of the sporangium; megaspore ornamentation is of low, broad walls forming a broken-reticulate pattern; plants are confined to the coastal plain (Georgia) ································· *Isoetes junciformis*

                6b   The velum covers less than 25% of the sporangium; megaspore ornamentation is of a granular to tubercular (rarely obscurely reticulate) pattern; plants are variously distributed ··········· **7**

                    7a   Leaves are loosely reflexed to sprawling; megaspores average more than 465µm in diameter, with a dense pattern of low, rugulate (wrinkled) ornamentation; plants are rare and found only in the eastern Piedmont ············· *Isoetes virginica*

                    7b   Leaves are stiffly erect to reflexed, or may be erect when immature but sprawling as they mature; megaspores average less than 450µm in diameter, with obscurely granular or tuberculate ornamentation ································· **8**

                        8a   Plants typically have 35–40 leaves; leaves are 1.5–2.0mm wide and 15–30cm long; the velum covers 5–20% of the sporangium; megaspore ornamentation is plain to densely low tuberculate; plants occur in shaded deciduous swamps ········· *Isoetes melanopoda*

                      8b   Plants typically have 20–30 leaves; leaves are 1.0–1.5mm wide and typically less than 15cm long; the velum covers less than 10% of the sporangium; megaspore ornamentation is tuberculate to wrinkled; plants occur in ephemeral pools on open bedrock outcrops ···························· **9**

                          9a   Mature megaspores average 455µm in diameter, and ornamentation is sparsely wrinkled to short walled or densely tuberculate; plants are found on granite (or rarely sandstone) outcrops ················· *Isoetes piedmontana*

9b   Mature megaspores average 475μm in diameter, and ornamentation is typically wrinkled to low tuberculate; plants are found on granite outcrops in the western Piedmont (Alabama) ·········· *Isoetes graniticola*

2b   Plants are aquatic, either submerged or emergent, in permanent water bodies or in persistently extremely wet soils ········· 10

10a   Plants are in tidal freshwater marsh habitats; megaspores are less than 350μm in diameter; plants occur on the coastal plain (eastern Virginia) ········· *Isoetes mattaponica*

10b   Plants are in various freshwater habitats; megaspores are more than 400μm in diameter; plants are variously distributed ········· 11

11a   Megaspore ornamentation is a dense, uniform pattern of thin, sharp spines ········· *Isoetes echinospora* subsp. *muricata*

11b   Megaspore ornamentation is of various patterns other than exclusively spiny ········· 12

12a   Megaspores average more than 575μm in diameter ········· 13

13a   Plants occur in deep lakes or fast-flowing rivers; the velum typically covers less than 30% of the sporangium; leaves are 6–20cm long ········· 14

14a   Plants occur in fast-flowing water; the walls of the megaspore ornamentation are thick and even in height, forming an uncongested, evenly reticulate pattern; plants occur in the southern Appalachian Mountains (Tennessee) ········· *Isoetes tennesseensis*

14b   Plants occur in deep or slow-flowing water; the walls of the megaspore ornamentation are thin to moderately thick and uneven in height, forming a congested, unevenly reticulate pattern; plants are widespread in northern lakes ········· *Isoetes macrospora*

13b   Plants occur in slow-moving stream channels in deciduous swamp forests; the velum covers more than 30% of the sporangium; leaves are 20–45cm long ········· 15

15a   The walls of the megaspore ornamentation are thick, and the pattern is open and uncongested; the velum covers ca. 60% of the sporangium; plants occur on the coastal plain (southern Georgia) ········· *Isoetes georgiana*

15b   The walls of the megaspore ornamentation are thin to somewhat thick, and the pattern is congested; the velum covers ca. 30% of the sporangium; plants are somewhat widespread but in localized populations in the southeast ········· *Isoetes boomii*

12b   Megaspores average less than 575μm in diameter ········· 16

16a   The velum covers more than 40% of the sporangium ········· 17

17a   The velum covers more than 80% (up to 100%) of the sporangium ········· 18

18a   The leaves are dark green and rigid; plants occur in northern New England and the Canadian Maritimes ········· *Isoetes prototypus*

18b   The leaves are bright green and flexible; plants occur in the extreme southeast ········· *Isoetes flaccida*

17b   The velum covers less than 70% (typically 50–60%) of the sporangium ········· 19

19a   Plants are large (20–35cm tall); leaves are broad and often distinctively yellow green; megaspore ornamentation is tall and ragged reticulate; plants are early emergent (May–June) in woodland seepage areas (rarely fully aquatic) and are widely distributed in the south and southeast ········· *Isoetes valida*

19b   Plants are small (ca. 10cm tall); leaves are narrow and uniformly green; megaspore ornamentation is obscurely wrinkled; plants are permanently aquatic and are known from a single lake in the northern Appalachian Mountains (Vermont) ········· *Isoetes viridimontana*

16b   The velum covers less than 40% of the sporangium ········· 20

20a   The megaspores are typically less than 500μm in diameter ········· 21

21a Leaves are bright green and flexible; megaspore ornamentation is evenly, uniformly reticulate; plants are widely distributed in the eastern U.S .... *Isoetes engelmannii*

21b Leaves are dull gray green and mostly erect; megaspore ornamentation is densely broken reticulate to almost spiny; plants are confined to freshwater tidal marshes in eastern Canada (Québec) .... *Isoetes laurentiana*

20b The megaspores are typically more than 525µm in diameter 22

22a Leaves are narrow (mostly less than 2mm wide) and typically dark green to olive green (or reddish); megaspore walls form a moderately to densely congested or almost spiny ornamentation pattern, usually with a distinct, densely spiny band below the equatorial ridge (except in *I. septentrionalis*) 23

23a Leaves are olive green to reddish brown; megaspore ornamentation is reticulate, with walls either tall and narrow or low and broad, and an equatorial band that is either densely papillate (with numerous very small, smooth projections) or broad and plain ...... *Isoetes tuckermanii*

23b Leaves are dark green to olive green; megaspore ornamentation is moderately to densely congested, with walls typically in a cristate or almost spiny pattern, and an equatorial band that is narrow and spiny, or absent 24

24a The vellum covers 10–20% of the sporangium; leaves are relatively narrow (1–1.5mm wide) and 20–45cm long; megaspore walls are in a uniformly, moderately congested, almost spiny pattern .... *Isoetes hyemalis*

24b The velum covers 25–40% of the sporangium; leaves are relatively broad (1.5–2mm wide) and 10–25cm long; megaspore walls are short and branching, in a dense to open, cristate pattern 25

25a Megaspore walls are in a densely crowded, congested ornamentation pattern, with an equatorial band of obscure to conspicuous spines; plants occur in the coastal plain, often in emergent, tidal beach habitats .... *Isoetes riparia*

25b Megaspore walls are in a dispersed, somewhat broken, network-forming ornamentation pattern, with no equatorial band; plants occur in freshwater habitats ...... *Isoetes septentrionalis*

22b Leaves are broad (ca. 2mm wide or sometimes wider) and bright to dark green; megaspore ornamentation is a moderately reticulate pattern of walls with no or a few short, stand-alone tubercles; the equatorial band is absent or only obscurely spiny below the equatorial ridge 26

26a The megaspore ornamentation pattern is of irregularly reticulate, long, interconnected and short, stand-alone walls; the velum covers ca. 30% of the sporangium; plants are usually deeply rooted, growing in clay or clayey sand; plants occur in the southern coastal plain .... *Isoetes louisianensis*

26b The megaspore ornamentation pattern is typically of regularly reticulate, mostly interconnected walls and only a few or no isolated, shorter walls; the velum usually covers 10–25% of the sporangium; plants are usually shallowly rooted, growing in sandy or silty-sandy soils 27

27a The velum covers 20–25% of the sporangium; megaspores are 525–550µm in diameter, with a broadly reticulate ornamentation pattern; plants are widespread .... *Isoetes appalachiana*

27b The velum covers ca. 10% of the sporangium; megaspores are 530–590µm in diameter, with a congested and densely reticulate ornamentation pattern; plants occur in the coastal plain (North Carolina) .... *Isoetes microvela*

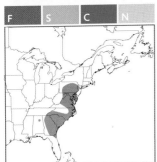

Isoetes appalachiana

COMMON NAME(S) Appalachian quillwort

NOTABLE SYNONYM(S) *Isoetes engelmannii* var. *georgiana*

STATUS Native (endemic to eastern North America), somewhat common

HABITAT/DISTRIBUTION A variety of aquatic and seasonally emergent habitats, including swampy forests and the shores of clear, flowing rivers and pools; widespread in the eastern and southeastern U.S.

Plants are submerged and amphibious (tolerant of fluctuating water levels). **Leaves** are erect to reflexed, 25–30cm long, 1–2mm wide, and dull olive green, with bases that are whitish green to pale brownish green. The **velum** covers 20% (rarely up to 40%) of the sporangium. **Megaspores** are 525–550 (average 535) µm in diameter. Ornamentation is in a ragged-reticulate pattern with variably tall and irregularly connected walls; a dense but obscure equatorial band of short spines is often present. 2n=44 (tetraploid).

Isoetes boomii

COMMON NAME(S) Boom's quillwort, swamp quillwort

STATUS Native (endemic to eastern North America), rare

HABITAT/DISTRIBUTION Shallow, permanently flowing streams in swamps; known from only a handful of locations in the southern U.S.

Plants are submerged to uncommonly emergent. **Leaves** are flexible and pliant, up to 45cm long, and bright green, with pale bases. The **velum** covers ca. 30% of the sporangium. **Megaspores** are 460–610µm in diameter. Ornamentation is in a congested, cristate to reticulate pattern with moderately thick, interconnecting walls. 2n=66 (hexaploid).

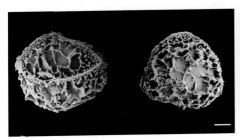

Megaspores of *Isoetes appalachiana*. Left: lateral view; right: distal view. Scale bar 100µm.

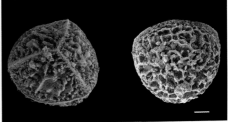

Megaspores of *Isoetes boomii*. Left: proximal view; right: distal view.

Isoetes butleri

COMMON NAME(S) Butler's quillwort, limestone quillwort

STATUS Native (endemic to eastern North America), locally uncommon

HABITAT/DISTRIBUTION The only North American quillwort known from calcareous substrates, in seasonally wet glades and wet prairies; scattered in the central-southern U.S.

Plants are emergent to terrestrial, in seasonally damp soils in early spring, but become fully terrestrial as water recedes. **Leaves** are erect but flexible, up to 15cm long (sometimes longer), and dull gray green to green, with pale bases. The **velum** covers less than 25% of the sporangium. **Megaspores** are 480–650µm in diameter. Ornamentation is obscurely tuberculate on a fibrose surface, with an obscure equatorial ridge. 2n=22 (diploid).

Isoetes echinospora subsp. muricata

COMMON NAME(S) Spiny-spored quillwort

STATUS Native, somewhat common

HABITAT/DISTRIBUTION Cool, noncalcareous, oligotrophic (i.e., oxygen-rich) lakes and ponds; also occurs in the western U.S. and Canada, and Greenland (a second subspecies, *I. echinospora* subsp. *echinospora*, occurs in Europe and Asia)

Plants are submerged to occasionally emergent late in the season. **Leaves** are pliant, up to 15cm long (rarely 25cm or longer), and bright green to brownish green, with pale bases. The **velum** covers less than 50% of the sporangium. **Megaspores** are 450–500µm in diameter (rarely up to 550µm). Ornamentation is uniformly of thin, sharp spines. 2n=22 (diploid).

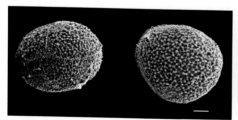

Megaspores of *Isoetes butleri*. Left: lateral view; right: distal view. Scale bar 100µm.

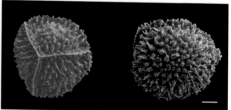

Megaspores of *Isoetes echinospora* subsp. *muricata*. Left: proximal view; right: distal view. Scale bar 100µm.

Isoetes engelmannii

COMMON NAME(S) Engelmann's quillwort

STATUS Native (endemic to eastern North America), formerly common but much reduced in recent decades, especially in New England, because of habitat degradation

HABITAT/DISTRIBUTION Shallow, cool, freshwater streams, lakes, ponds, and ditches; widely distributed in the east

Plants are submerged to emergent. **Leaves** are pliant, up to 25cm long (rarely up to 40cm), and bright green, with pale bases. The **velum** typically covers 5–10% (rarely up to 20%) of the sporangium. **Megaspores** are 400–480µm (rarely up to 500µm) in diameter. Ornamentation pattern is of tall, connected, evenly reticulate walls that are continuous to the equatorial ridge. 2n=22 (diploid).

Isoetes flaccida, including varieties flaccida and chapmanii

COMMON NAME(S) Florida quillwort

STATUS Native (endemic to eastern North America), rare

HABITAT/DISTRIBUTION Shallow waters, usually at the edges of marshes, ponds, lakes, streams, and ditches; *I. flaccida* var. *chapmanii* is known only from Jackson County, Florida, while *I. flaccida* var. *flaccida* is more widely distributed, throughout the Florida peninsula and into southernmost Georgia and Alabama

Isoetes flaccida var. chapmanii
Isoetes flaccida var. flaccida

Plants are submerged to emergent. **Leaves** are pliant, up to 60cm long, bright green, and 1.25–1.5mm (var. *chapmanii*) or ca. 1mm (var. *flaccida*) wide. The **velum** covers the entire sporangium. **Megaspores** are ca. 500µm (var. *chapmanii*) or less than 450µm (var. *flaccida*) in diameter. Ornamentation is dense with small tubercles (var. *chapmanii*) or more dispersed with broad tubercles and/or loosely interconnected mounds (var. *flaccida*). 2n=22 (diploid).

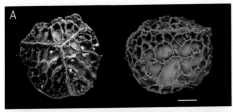

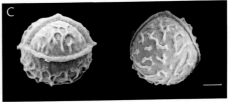

A. Megaspores of *Isoetes engelmannii*. Left: proximal view (note microspores on the megaspore surface); right: distal view. Scale bar 100µm.

B. Megaspores of *Isoetes flaccida* var. *chapmanii*. Left: lateral view; right: distal view. Scale bar 100µm.

C. Megaspores of *Isoetes flaccida* var. *flaccida*. Left: lateral view; right: distal view. Scale bar 100µm.

Isoetes georgiana

COMMON NAME(S) Georgia quillwort

STATUS Native (endemic to eastern North America), rare

HABITAT/DISTRIBUTION Ephemeral streams in deciduous swamp forests; known only from several small watersheds on the Gulf of Mexico coastal plain in Georgia

Plants are submerged to emergent. Leaves are pliant, up to 40cm long, and olive green, with pale bases. The velum covers 55–60% of the sporangium. Megaspores are 450–650 (average 625) µm in diameter. Ornamentation pattern is open and uncongested, with thick, loosely connected or isolated walls. 2n=66 (hexaploid).

Isoetes graniticola

COMMON NAME(S) Flat rock quillwort

NOTABLE SYNONYMS Isoetes piedmontana, in part

STATUS Native (endemic to eastern North America), rare

HABITAT/DISTRIBUTION Shallow, ephemeral pools on flat granite outcrops; known from only a few locations in east-central Alabama

Plants are emergent to terrestrial, in seasonally damp soils, but become fully terrestrial as water recedes. Leaves are stiffly erect to broadly arching, up to 10cm long and 1.0–1.5mm wide, and dull brownish green, with whitish-green to blackish-brown bases. The velum covers less than 10% of the sporangium. Megaspores are 450–525 (average 475) µm in diameter. Ornamentation pattern is smooth or wrinkled to low tuberculate, with low, wide walls, and no distinct equatorial band. 2n=44 (tetraploid).

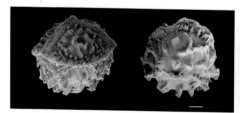

Megaspores of Isoetes georgiana. Left: lateral view; right: distal view. Scale bar 100µm.

Megaspores of Isoetes graniticola. Left: lateral view; right: distal view. Scale bar 100µm.

IMAGES COURTESY OF DANIEL BRUNTON; SEE P. 505 FOR SPECIMEN SOURCE INFORMATION

Isoetes hyemalis

COMMON NAME(S) Winter quillwort

STATUS Native (endemic to eastern North America), uncommon and local

HABITAT/DISTRIBUTION Shaded forest streams; widely scattered from the lower Piedmont of Virginia and North Carolina to the Gulf of Mexico coastal plain in southern Georgia and Alabama

Plants are submerged and amphibious (tolerant of seasonally fluctuating water levels). **Leaves** are wiry, 20–45cm long at maturity and 1–1.5mm wide, bright green when young but becoming dark green to dark brownish green with age, with pale bases. The **velum** covers 10–20% of the sporangium. **Megaspores** are 400–580 (average 525) μm in diameter. Ornamentation is of tall walls with irregular crests in a congested, somewhat reticulate pattern, with thin tubercles and a spiny equatorial band. 2n=44 (tetraploid).

Isoetes junciformis

COMMON NAME(S) Rush quillwort

STATUS Native (endemic to eastern North America), rare

HABITAT/DISTRIBUTION Open swales along the margins of deciduous swamp forest; known from only a few locations (some of which have been lost, either to human activity or natural successional processes) on the Gulf of Mexico coastal plain in Georgia

Plants are seasonally flooded and then emergent in saturated soils, becoming fully terrestrial as water recedes. **Leaves** are erect, 35–40cm long at maturity, and dull, pale green to grayish green, with pale to white bases that may have a light pinkish-purple cast, especially in young leaves. The **velum** covers ca. 40% of the sporangium, and the surface of the sporangium is whitish with brown streaks. **Megaspores** average 460μm in diameter. Ornamentation is in a prominent, ragged-reticulate pattern of low, broad, smooth-topped walls. 2n=44 (tetraploid).

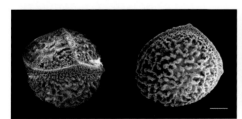

Megaspores of *Isoetes hyemalis*. Left: lateral view; right: distal view. Scale bar 100μm.

Megaspores of *Isoetes junciformis*. Left: lateral view; right: distal view. Scale bar 100μm.

Isoetes laurentiana

COMMON NAME(S) St. Lawrence quillwort

NOTABLE SYNONYM(S) *Isoetes tuckermanii*, in part

STATUS Native (endemic to eastern North America), rare but locally abundant

HABITAT/DISTRIBUTION Known only from freshwater tidal marshes along the St. Lawrence River in Québec

----

Plants are amphibious (tolerant of twice-daily emergence from tidally fluctuating fresh water). **Leaves** are erect to arching, up to 12cm long, and dull gray green, with paler bases that have a brownish cast. The **velum** covers up to 25% of the sporangium. **Megaspores** average 460µm in diameter. Ornamentation is of densely broken-reticulate to almost spiny and ragged-crested walls, with a very narrow equatorial band of fine spines. 2n=44 (tetraploid).

Isoetes louisianensis

COMMON NAME(S) Louisiana quillwort

STATUS Native (endemic to eastern North America), rare

HABITAT/DISTRIBUTION Forest creeks with clay or clayey sand; on the Gulf of Mexico coastal plain between Alabama and Louisiana

----

Plants are submerged to emergent and typically deeply rooted. **Leaves** are pliant, up to 40cm long, and bright green, with paler bases. The **velum** covers ca. 30% of the sporangium (sometimes more). **Megaspores** average 500–550µm in diameter (rarely up to 600µm). Ornamentation pattern is irregularly reticulate, with both long, interconnected and short, stand-alone walls; the lower side of the equatorial ridge is typically obscurely, coarsely spiny. 2n=44 (tetraploid).

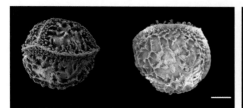

Megaspores of *Isoetes laurentiana*. Left: lateral view; right: distal view. Scale bar 100µm.

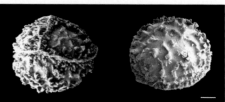

Megaspores of *Isoetes louisianensis*. Left: lateral view; right: distal view. Scale bar 100µm.

Isoetes macrospora

COMMON NAME(S) Lake quillwort

NOTABLE SYNONYMS *Isoetes lacustris*, in part

STATUS Native (endemic to North America), common

HABITAT/DISTRIBUTION Cool lakes or flowing rivers 0.5–1.5m (occasionally up to 10m) deep, with nutrient-poor, acidic, sandy, or silty-sandy soils, or gravel; widespread across the northeastern U.S. and eastern Canada; also occurs in central Canada

----

Plants are permanently submerged. **Leaves** are firm and persistent to evergreen, erect to upright and arching or strongly reflexed, 6–15cm long (sometimes longer in flowing water), 1–1.5mm wide, and dull olive green to dark blackish green, with paler bases. The **velum** covers 20–35% of the sporangium. **Megaspores** are 650–725μm in diameter (occasionally up to 850μm). Ornamentation is of uneven-height walls that form a congested, unevenly reticulate (coarse to dispersed) pattern, with a conspicuous equatorial band of coarse spines. 2n=110 (decaploid).

Isoetes mattaponica

COMMON NAME(S) Chesapeake quillwort

STATUS Native (endemic to eastern North America), rare

HABITAT/DISTRIBUTION Tidally influenced freshwater river marshes; known only from the Chesapeake Bay area of Virginia

----

Plants are submerged to emergent and amphibious (tolerant of daily fluctuating water levels). **Leaves** are pliant and flexible, up to 25cm long and 1mm wide, and bright green with paler bases, but typically appearing duller in color because of tidal sediment buildup. The **velum** covers 30% of the sporangium, on average (occasionally up to 55%). **Megaspores** are tiny (350–360μm in diameter). Ornamentation is in a moderately dense pattern of low, obscure, irregularly elongated mounds on a granular surface, with a wide, typically unornamented equatorial band. 2n=22 (diploid).

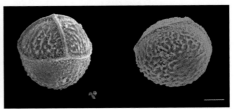

Megaspores of *Isoetes macrospora*. Left: lateral view; right: distal view. Scale bar 100μm.

Megaspores of *Isoetes mattaponica*. Left: lateral view (note the cluster of microspores at lower right); right: distal view. Scale bar 100μm.

IMAGES COURTESY OF DANIEL BRUNTON; SEE P. 505 FOR SPECIMEN SOURCE INFORMATION

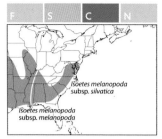

Isoetes melanopoda, including subspecies melanopoda and silvatica

COMMON NAME(S) Eastern black-footed quillwort, woodland quillwort

STATUS Native (endemic to eastern North America), somewhat common

HABITAT/DISTRIBUTION Shallow depressions and drainage channels in wooded (typically oak) swamps; *I. melanopoda* subsp. *melanopoda* occurs widely west of the Mississippi River, while *I. melanopoda* subsp. *silvatica* occurs in the southeast

---

Plants are submerged to emergent in seasonally damp soils but become fully terrestrial as water recedes (leaves wither and plants become dormant and invisible aboveground by early summer). **Leaves** are pliant and flexible, 15–30cm long (rarely up to 60cm) and 1.5–2.0mm wide, and green to gray green, with lighter green or whitish bases. The **velum** covers 5–20% of the sporangium. **Megaspores** are 290–380 μm (subsp. *melanopoda*) or 350–500 (average 420) μm (subsp. *silvatica*) in diameter. Ornamentation is plain to obscurely wrinkled (subsp. *melanopoda*), or densely low tuberculate or in a dense pattern of short, broad walls and mounds (subsp. *silvatica*). 2n=22 (diploid).

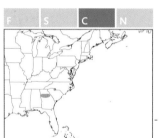

Isoetes melanospora

COMMON NAME(S) Black-spored quillwort

STATUS Native (endemic to eastern North America), rare

HABITAT/DISTRIBUTION Shallow, ephemeral pools on open granite outcrops; known only from the Piedmont of Georgia and South Carolina

---

Plants are emergent to terrestrial in seasonally damp soils but become fully terrestrial as water recedes (leaves wither and plants become dormant and invisible aboveground by early summer). **Leaves** are pliant and flexible, up to 7cm long, and bright green, with paler bases. The **velum** covers 70–100% of the sporangium. **Megaspores** are 350–480μm in

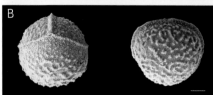

A. Megaspores of *Isoetes melanopoda* subsp. *melanopoda*. Left: lateral view; right: distal view. Scale bar 100μm.

B. Megaspores of *Isoetes melanopoda* subsp. *silvatica*. Left: lateral view; right: distal view. Scale bar 100μm.

C. Megaspores of *Isoetes melanospora*. Left: lateral view; right: distal view (note microspore at bottom right edge). Scale bar 100μm.

diameter and gray to black. Ornamentation is low, in a densely tuberculate pattern with short, irregular walls and a thin, obscure equatorial ridge. 2n=22 (diploid).

Isoetes microvela

COMMON NAME(S) Short-veiled quillwort

STATUS Native (endemic to eastern North America), rare

HABITAT/DISTRIBUTION Permanent, often-flooded waterways within swamp forests; known from only a handful of locations in the Atlantic coastal plain in North Carolina

Plants are submerged to emergent. Leaves are pliant and flexible or strongly reflexed, up to 35cm long or sometimes longer, and dark, dull olive green, with paler bases. The velum covers ca. 10% of the sporangium. Megaspores are 530–580 (rarely up to 650) µm in diameter. The ornamentation pattern is congested and densely reticulate (coral-like). 2n=66 (hexaploid).

Isoetes piedmontana

COMMON NAME(S) Piedmont quillwort

NOTABLE SYNONYMS Isoetes virginica var. piedmontana

STATUS Native (endemic to eastern North America), uncommon and local

HABITAT/DISTRIBUTION Shallow, ephemeral pools on granite or (in one area) sandstone outcrops; widespread and locally abundant in numerous isolated locations along a narrow region of the southeastern Piedmont and rarely on the upper Atlantic coastal plain

Plants are emergent to terrestrial, in seasonally damp soils, but become fully terrestrial as water recedes. Leaves are pliant and flexible, 10–15cm long (occasionally up to 30cm in deeper water), 1.0–1.5mm wide, and dull green, with pale to dark brown bases. The velum covers 5–15% (usually less than 10% but occasionally up to 25%) of the sporangium. Megaspores are 375–525 (average 455) µm in diameter. The ornamentation pattern varies from sparsely wrinkled to short walled or densely tuberculate. 2n=22 (diploid); also reported as 2n=44 (tetraploid) in Virginia.

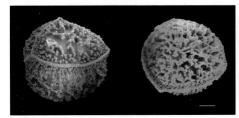

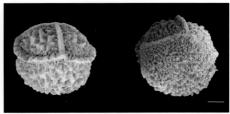

Megaspores of Isoetes microvela. Left: lateral view; right: distal view. Scale bar 100µm.

Megaspores of Isoetes piedmontana (both are lateral views). Scale bar 100µm.

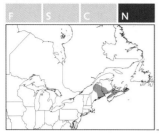

Isoetes prototypus

COMMON NAME(S) Prototype quillwort

STATUS Native (endemic to eastern North America), rare

HABITAT/DISTRIBUTION Deep, cold, spring-fed ponds and lakes; known only from widely dispersed locations in the Canadian Maritimes (New Brunswick and Nova Scotia) and New England (Maine)

Plants are permanently submerged. Leaves are straight and stiff, up to 12.5cm long, and dark green, with reddish or chestnut-brown bases. The velum covers 100% of the sporangium. Megaspores average 500μm in diameter. The ornamentation pattern is obscurely reticulate, with low, broad, mound-like markings on an otherwise smooth surface. 2n=22 (diploid).

Isoetes riparia, including varieties riparia and reticulata

COMMON NAME(S) Shore quillwort

NOTABLE SYNONYMS Isoetes saccharata

STATUS Native (endemic to eastern North America), formerly common but significantly reduced from its historical abundance by extensive habitat destruction

HABITAT/DISTRIBUTION Emergent tidal shores as well as coastal plain ponds, lakes, and streams; I. riparia var. riparia occurs from New Jersey to Virginia, while I. riparia var. reticulata is largely confined to the Chesapeake Bay area of Virginia

Plants can be submerged in freshwater lakes and emergent in fresh and brackish water along tidal shores. Leaves are pliant and flexible, up to 20cm long and 1.25–2.0mm wide, and bright to dark olive green, with paler bases. The velum covers 25–30% of the sporangium. Megaspores average ca. 540μm in diameter. Ornamentation is densely congested, with an obscure to typically conspicuous equatorial band of spines, and either with tubercles and moderately tall, narrow walls (var. riparia) or with low, evenly reticulate, relatively wide walls with few tubercles (var. reticulata). 2n=44 (tetraploid).

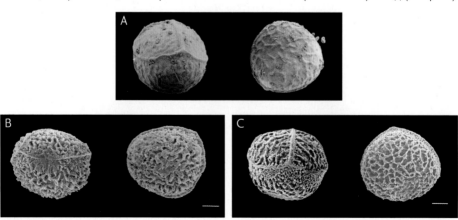

Isoetes septentrionalis

COMMON NAME(S) Northern quillwort

NOTABLE SYNONYMS *Isoetes riparia*, in part

STATUS Native (endemic to eastern North America), uncommon

HABITAT/DISTRIBUTION Along river and lake shores; northeastern U.S. and southeastern Canada (Ontario and Québec)

Plants are submerged to emergent. **Leaves** are erect to reflexed, up to 25cm long, and dull olive green, with whitish-green to white bases. The **velum** covers 25–40% of the sporangium. **Megaspores** average 545μm in diameter. The ornamentation pattern is open, with short, broken, or somewhat network-forming walls, and no equatorial band. 2n=44 (tetraploid).

Isoetes tegetiformans

COMMON NAME(S) Mat-forming quillwort

STATUS Native (endemic to eastern North America), rare

HABITAT/DISTRIBUTION Shallow, ephemeral pools on granite outcrops; known from only a handful of sites in northeastern Georgia (several of which have been destroyed)

Plants are rhizomatous and form dense, uniquely lawn-like mats in seasonally damp soils; initially emergent but become fully terrestrial as water recedes (leaves wither and plants become dormant and invisible aboveground by early summer). **Leaves** are erect and flexible, up to 4cm long, and bright green, with paler bases. The **velum** covers 70–100% of the sporangium. **Megaspores** are 275–370μm in diameter, and gray to black. The ornamentation pattern is plain, obscurely wrinkled, or low tuberculate. 2n=22 (diploid).

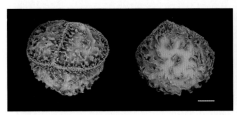

Megaspores of *Isoetes septentrionalis*. Left: lateral view; right: distal view. Scale bar 100μm.

Megaspores of *Isoetes tegetiformans*. Left: lateral view; right: distal view. Scale bar 100μm.

OPPOSITE PAGE:

A. Megaspores of *Isoetes prototypus*. Left: lateral view; right: distal view (note the cluster of microspores on the top right edge). Scale bar 100μm.

B. Megaspores of *Isoetes riparia* var. *riparia*. Left: lateral view; right: distal view. Scale bar 100μm.

C. Megaspores of *Isoetes riparia* var. *reticulata*. Left: lateral view; right: distal view. Scale bar 100μm.

Isoetes tennesseensis

COMMON NAME(S) Tennessee quillwort

NOTABLE SYNONYMS *Isoetes macrospora*, in part

STATUS Native (endemic to eastern North America), rare

HABITAT/DISTRIBUTION Fast-flowing water; known only from the Hiwassee River region of Tennessee (possibly also disjunct in eastern Virginia)

Plants are permanently submerged. **Leaves** are erect and rigid, up to 11cm long and 1.5mm wide, and dark olive green, with paler bases. The **velum** covers less than 20% of the sporangium. **Megaspores** are 615–950 (average 725) µm in diameter. Ornamentation is coarse and evenly reticulate, with tall, even-height walls. 2n=88 (octoploid).

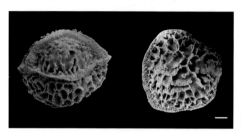

Megaspores of *Isoetes tennesseensis.*
Left: lateral view; right: distal view.
Scale bar 100µm.
IMAGE COURTESY OF DANIEL BRUNTON; SEE P. 505 FOR SPECIMEN SOURCE INFORMATION

Isoetes tuckermanii, including subspecies acadiensis and tuckermanii

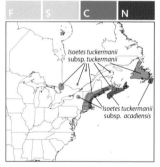

COMMON NAME(S) Tuckerman's quillwort

STATUS Native (endemic to eastern North America), somewhat common

HABITAT/DISTRIBUTION Shallow margins of lakes and rivers, usually in acidic, sandy or gravelly soils; *I. tuckermanii* subsp. *tuckermanii* occupies a larger range, reaching far inland, while *I. tuckermanii* subsp. *acadiensis* is confined to the outer Atlantic coastal plain

Plants are submerged but sometimes become emergent in late summer. **Leaves** are upright to strongly arching, up to 25cm long and 1mm wide, and olive green to reddish brown (subsp. *tuckermanii*) or predominantly reddish green (subsp. *acadiensis*), with paler bases. The **velum** covers 25–35% of the sporangium. **Megaspores** average 540µm in diameter. The ornamentation pattern is boldly reticulate, either with relatively tall, ragged-topped walls and an equatorial band that is smooth to densely papillate (subsp. *tuckermanii*) or with low, broad walls and a smooth equatorial band (subsp. *acadiensis*). 2n=44 (tetraploid).

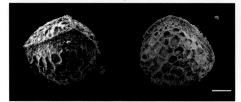

Megaspores of *Isoetes tuckermanii* subsp. *tuckermanii*. Left: lateral view; right: distal view. Note microspores to the right of both megaspores. Scale bar 100μm.

Megaspores of *Isoetes tuckermanii* subsp. *acadiensis*. Left: lateral view; right: distal view. Scale bar 100μm

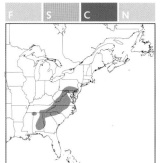

Isoetes valida

COMMON NAME(S) Carolina quillwort, strong quillwort, true quillwort

NOTABLE SYNONYMS *Isoetes caroliniana*

STATUS Native (endemic to eastern North America), somewhat common

HABITAT/DISTRIBUTION Rich, acidic soils in wooded streams and (especially) seepage areas; widely distributed in the southern Appalachian Mountains, upper Piedmont, and southeastern coastal plain

Plants are submerged to emergent or amphibious (tolerant of seasonally fluctuating water levels), and large (20–35cm tall). **Leaves** are broad (up to 2.5mm wide), upright and erect to broadly arching, up to 60cm long, and grass green to distinctly yellow green (especially when young), with white bases. The **velum** coverage averages 50% (ranging up to 60%) of the sporangium. **Megaspores** average 450μm in diameter (rarely up to 500μm). The ornamentation pattern is irregularly ragged reticulate, with short, thick walls that are dramatically uneven in height. 2n=22 (diploid).

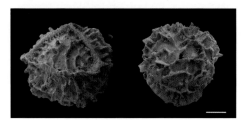

Megaspores of *Isoetes valida*. Left: lateral view (note microspore at upper right); right: distal view. Scale bar 100μm.

Isoetes virginica

COMMON NAME(S) Virginia quillwort

STATUS Native (endemic to eastern North America), rare

HABITAT/DISTRIBUTION Ephemeral stream channels and ponds in swamp forest; known from only a few highland populations in central Virginia and the Piedmont of North Carolina

---

Plants are submerged early in the season but typically become terrestrial as waters recede or dry up (leaves wither and plants become dormant and invisible aboveground by early summer). **Leaves** are stiffly erect to sprawling, up to 25cm long and 0.75–1.5mm wide (or occasionally wider), and dull gray green, with paler bases. The **velum** covers ca. 10% of the sporangium. **Megaspores** average 465µm in diameter. The ornamentation pattern is of broad, irregularly connected, round-topped walls of variable height and in a low cristate pattern on a granular surface; equatorial band ornamentation is subdued. 2n=44 (tetraploid).

Isoetes viridimontana

COMMON NAME(S) Green Mountain quillwort

STATUS Native (endemic to eastern North America), rare

HABITAT/DISTRIBUTION Known from 1 freshwater pond in the northern Appalachian Mountains (Vermont)

Plants are submerged and small (ca. 10cm tall). **Leaves** are stiffly erect, up to 5cm long and 1mm wide, and light green, with paler brownish to white bases. The **velum** covers ca. 50% of the sporangium. **Megaspores** are 335–400 (average 365) µm in diameter. The ornamentation pattern is of very low, obscure, irregularly connected, round-topped walls in a cristate pattern. 2n=22 (diploid).

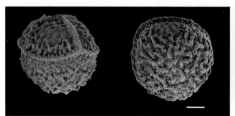

Megaspores of *Isoetes virginica*. Left: lateral view; right: distal view. Scale bar 100µm.

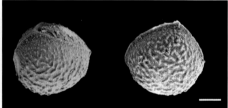

Megaspores of *Isoetes viridimontana*. Left: lateral view; right: distal view. Scale bar 100µm.

IMAGES COURTESY OF DANIEL BRUNTON; SEE P. 505 FOR SPECIMEN SOURCE INFORMATION

FAMILY: **LYCOPODIACEAE**

Lycopodiella is a genus of lycophytes commonly known as bog clubmosses. Globally there are 12–15 species in the genus, and they are found throughout temperate and tropical regions, with the highest species diversity in the Americas. *Lycopodiella* species are most similar in appearance to their relatives in the genus *Lycopodium* (p. 86) but are distinct in having upright shoots that are never branched, and only a single strobilus at the end of each upright shoot or peduncle. Their common name refers to their preference for extremely damp, wetland habitats, and this can also help distinguish them from *Lycopodium* species, which prefer drier, more upland locations. In addition to the 5 species described below, a sixth has been described from the Midwest—*L. margueritae*—but its taxonomic status is uncertain and thus it is not included here. A number of hybrids are also known to form in our region, some of which are fertile (see figure below), but none are common. Base chromosome number (x) = 78.

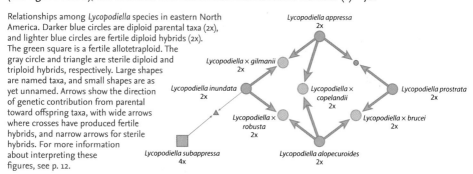

Relationships among *Lycopodiella* species in eastern North America. Darker blue circles are diploid parental taxa (2x), and lighter blue circles are fertile diploid hybrids (2x). The green square is a fertile allotetraploid. The gray circle and triangle are sterile diploid and triploid hybrids, respectively. Large shapes are named taxa, and small shapes are as yet unnamed. Arrows show the direction of genetic contribution from parental toward offspring taxa, with wide arrows where crosses have produced fertile hybrids, and narrow arrows for sterile hybrids. For more information about interpreting these figures, see p. 12.

Lycopodiella appressa 2x
Lycopodiella × *gilmanii* 2x
Lycopodiella inundata 2x
Lycopodiella × *copelandii* 2x
Lycopodiella prostrata 2x
Lycopodiella × *robusta* 2x
Lycopodiella × *brucei* 2x
Lycopodiella subappressa 4x
Lycopodiella alopecuroides 2x

KEY TO THE SPECIES OF *LYCOPODIELLA* IN OUR FLORA:

1a **Fertile shoots are mostly less than 6cm tall; the spore-bearing leaves spread outward from the stem axis; the horizontal stems (excluding leaves) are extremely slender, 1mm or less in diameter** ⋯⋯⋯⋯⋯⋯⋯⋯⋯⋯ *Lycopodiella inundata*

1b **Fertile shoots are mostly more than 10cm tall; the spore-bearing leaves are spreading or ascending; the horizontal stems (excluding leaves) are more than 1mm in diameter** ⋯⋯ **2**

    2a The leaves on the horizontal stems have smooth margins or sparse marginal teeth; the strobili are 0–2mm thicker than the upright shoot they attach to ⋯⋯⋯⋯⋯ **3**

        3a Fertile shoots are 15–40cm tall; the leaves on the horizontal stems have scattered marginal teeth ⋯⋯⋯⋯⋯⋯⋯⋯ *Lycopodiella appressa*

        3b Fertile shoots are 9–15cm tall; the leaves on the horizontal stems are smooth, without teeth ⋯⋯⋯⋯⋯⋯⋯⋯ *Lycopodiella subappressa*

    2b The leaves on the horizontal stems have dense marginal teeth; the strobili are 3–6mm thicker than the upright shoot they attach to ⋯⋯⋯⋯⋯⋯ **4**

        4a The horizontal stems (excluding leaves) are 2–4mm in diameter and arch strongly off the ground surface; the largest leaves are 0.5–0.7mm wide ⋯⋯ *Lycopodiella alopecuroides*

        4b The horizontal stems (excluding leaves) are mostly less than 2mm in diameter and lie flat against the ground surface; the largest leaves are 0.8–1.8mm wide ⋯⋯ *Lycopodiella prostrata*

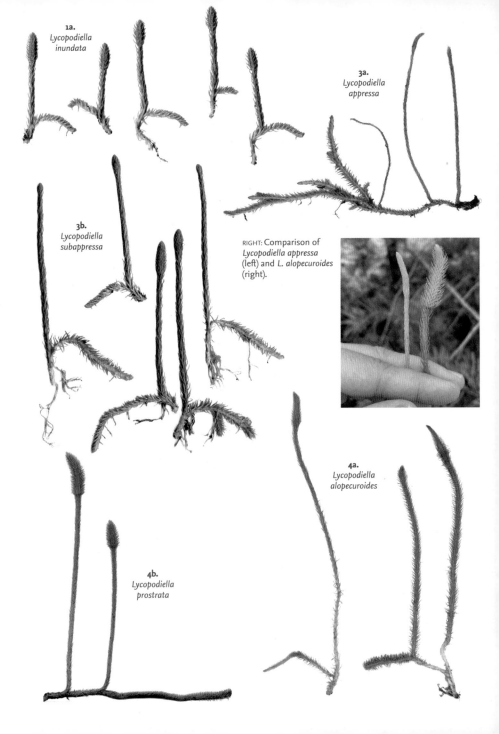

1a.
*Lycopodiella
inundata*

3a.
*Lycopodiella
appressa*

3b.
*Lycopodiella
subappressa*

RIGHT: Comparison of
Lycopodiella appressa
(left) and *L. alopecuroides*
(right).

4a.
*Lycopodiella
alopecuroides*

4b.
*Lycopodiella
prostrata*

Lycopodiella alopecuroides

COMMON NAME(S) Foxtail bog clubmoss

NOTABLE SYNONYMS *Lycopodium alopecuroides*

STATUS Native, somewhat common

HABITAT/DISTRIBUTION Wet habitats including marshes, damp meadows, bogs, ditches, and pond edges; also occurs in the Caribbean and Central and South America

- -

Plants are terrestrial. **Horizontal stems** arch strongly over the substrate and are up to 40cm long and 2–4mm in diameter (excluding the leaves), often rooting at the tips and with roots emerging from the underside. Leaves on the horizontal stems are up to 7mm long and 0.7mm wide, spreading, and with 1–7 teeth along the margins on each side. **Upright shoots** or peduncles are up to 30cm tall, with leaves spreading to pointing upward, up to 7mm long and 0.5mm wide, and with 1–10 teeth along the margins on each side. **Strobili** are solitary, up to 6cm long, at least 3–6mm thicker than the peduncle, and with spore-bearing leaves that are widely spreading and up to 7mm long and 1mm wide, with 1–5 teeth along the margins on each side, but only in the lower part of the strobilus (leaves in the upper part have entire margins). 2n=156 (diploid).

A. Plants of *Lycopodiella alopecuroides*

B. Horizontal stem arching off the ground.

C. Leafy, unbranched upright shoots.

D. Strobili, and leaves with marginal teeth on upright shoots.

E. Leaves with marginal teeth on horizontal shoot.

Lycopodiella appressa

COMMON NAME(S) Appressed bog clubmoss

NOTABLE SYNONYMS *Lycopodium appressum, Lycopodium inundatum* var. *appressum*

STATUS Native, somewhat common

HABITAT/DISTRIBUTION Wet habitats including marshes, damp meadows, bogs, ditches, and pond edges; also occurs in the Caribbean

Plants are terrestrial. **Horizontal stems** lie flat on the ground and are up to 45cm long and 1.5–2mm in diameter (excluding the leaves), often rooting at the tips and with roots emerging from the underside. Leaves on the horizontal stems are up to 7mm long and 1mm wide, pressed against the stem or spreading, and have smooth margins or may have very few, scattered teeth. **Upright shoots** or peduncles are up to 40cm tall, with leaves pressed against the shoot axis and up to 5.5mm long and 0.5mm wide, with no or only a few teeth along the margins on each side. **Strobili** are solitary, up to 6cm long, usually not thicker or only very slightly thicker than the peduncle, with spore-bearing leaves appressed, curved inward, and up to 5mm long and 0.3mm wide, with no marginal teeth. 2n=156 (diploid).

A. Plants of Lycopodiella appressa.

B. Creeping horizontal stems.

C. Leaves with toothed margins on the horizontal stems.

D. Strobilus.

Lycopodiella inundata

COMMON NAME(S) Northern bog clubmoss

NOTABLE SYNONYMS *Lycopodium inundatum*

STATUS Native, somewhat common

HABITAT/DISTRIBUTION A variety of damp to wet habitats including lake and pond edges, bogs, marshes, damp meadows, and ditches; also occurs in western North America, Europe, and Asia

Plants are terrestrial. **Horizontal stems** lie flat on the ground and are up to 12cm long and less than 1mm in diameter (excluding the leaves), often rooting at the tips and with roots emerging from the underside. Leaves on the horizontal stems are up to 6mm long and 0.7mm wide, spread outward from the stem, and have smooth margins with no teeth. **Upright shoots** or peduncles are up to 6cm tall, with leaves that spread away from the shoot axis and are up to 6mm long and 0.8mm wide, occasionally with a few scattered teeth along the margins. **Strobili** are solitary, up to 2cm long, usually slightly thicker than the peduncle, with spore-bearing leaves spreading outward and somewhat upward, and up to 5mm long and 0.9mm wide, rarely with a few marginal teeth. 2n=156 (diploid).

A. Plants of *Lycopodiella inundata*.

B. A mixed population of *Lycopodiella inundata* (shorter, yellowish-green shoots) and *L. subappressa* (taller, darker green shoots).

Lycopodiella prostrata

COMMON NAME(S) Prostrate bog clubmoss

NOTABLE SYNONYMS *Lycopodium prostratum*

STATUS Native (endemic to North America), uncommon

HABITAT/DISTRIBUTION Typically in pine barrens or along roadsides; range extends into Texas

Plants are terrestrial. **Horizontal stems** lie flat on the ground and are up to 45cm long and 1–1.5mm in diameter (excluding the leaves), often rooting at the tips and with roots emerging from the underside. Leaves on the upper side of the horizontal stems are up to 5mm long and 0.6mm wide and point upward; leaves on the sides of the horizontal stem are up to 8mm long and 1.8mm wide, point outward, and have 1–10 teeth along the margins on each side, with most of the teeth in the lower half of the leaf. **Upright shoots** or peduncles are up to 35cm tall, with leaves that are pressed against the shoot axis or point upward and are up to 8mm long and 0.6mm wide, with 1–4 teeth along the margins on each side. **Strobili** are solitary, up to 8cm long, at least 3–6mm thicker than the peduncle, and spore-bearing leaves are widely spreading to somewhat upward pointing and are up to 9mm long and 0.5mm wide, with 1–5 teeth along the margins on each side. 2n=156 (diploid).

A. Plants of *Lycopodiella prostrata*.

B. A strobilus.

C. Leaves with marginal teeth on upright shoots.

Lycopodiella subappressa

COMMON NAME(S) Northern appressed clubmoss

STATUS Native (endemic to North America), rare

HABITAT/DISTRIBUTION Wet ditches, meadows, and borrow pits; known only from a relatively small area of the upper Midwest of the U.S.

Plants are terrestrial. **Horizontal stems** lie flat on the ground and are up to 17cm long and 1–1.5mm in diameter (excluding the leaves), often rooting at the tips and with roots emerging from the underside. Leaves on the horizontal stems are up to 6mm long and 1mm wide, point somewhat outward and upward (even more so when dry), and have smooth margins. **Upright shoots** or peduncles are up to 13cm tall, with leaves that are pressed against the shoot axis and are up to 6mm long and 0.8mm wide, with smooth margins and no teeth. **Strobili** are solitary, up to 4cm long, usually not thicker or only very slightly thicker than the peduncle, and with spore-bearing leaves that are appressed and up to 4mm long and 0.5mm wide, with no marginal teeth. 2n=312 (tetraploid).

A. Plants of *Lycopodiella subappressa*.

B. Plants with horizontal stems and upright shoots.

FAMILY: **LYCOPODIACEAE**

Lycopodium is a genus of lycophytes commonly known as clubmosses. Historically, this was a genus of about 50 species, but recent research has led to the division of this formerly large *Lycopodium* into several smaller genera, leaving *Lycopodium* itself with about 15 species. In our flora, we previously had 6 *Lycopodium* species; we now have 2. The other 4 species are now included in the genera *Spinulum* (1 species, p. 111) and *Dendrolycopodium* (3 species, p. 42). *Lycopodium* in the strict, more limited sense can be distinguished from these other genera by its strobili, which are held away from the leafy parts of the shoots, sitting at the tips of long peduncles. In *Spinulum* and *Dendrolycopodium*, the strobili are sessile, sitting directly atop the leafy part of the shoot, without a long peduncle. *Dendrolycopodium* also has distinctly treelike, spreading horizontal branches, which the other 2 genera do not. Base chromosome number (x) = 34.

KEY TO THE SPECIES OF *LYCOPODIUM* IN OUR FLORA:

1a   Strobili are in clusters of 2–5, and each strobilus has a distinct short stalk connecting it to the peduncle; branches spread outward from the central plant axis; leaves are 4–6mm long and their bases point outward from the shoot axis (the tips usually curl upward) ·· *Lycopodium clavatum* subsp. *clavatum*

1b   Strobili are singular or in pairs, and if paired, no stalk is present that is distinct from the peduncle; branches are mostly oriented upright; leaves are 3–5mm long and their bases point upward, with the tips continuing to point upward ·· *Lycopodium lagopus*

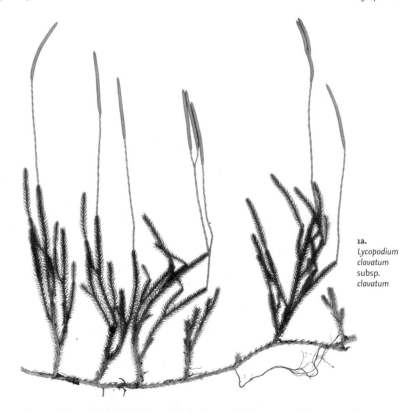

1a.
Lycopodium clavatum subsp. *clavatum*

1b.
*Lycopodium
lagopus*

Shoots (**A**) and strobili (**B**) of *Lycopodium clavatum* subsp. *clavatum* (left) and
L. lagopus (right).

Lycopodium clavatum subsp. *clavatum*

COMMON NAME(S) Common clubmoss, stag's horn clubmoss

STATUS Native, common

HABITAT/DISTRIBUTION Forests, forest edges, and grassy habitats; also occurs in western North America, Europe, Asia, and Africa (a second subspecies, *L. clavatum* subsp. *contiguum*, has been described from Central and South America)

Plants are terrestrial. **Stems** are horizontal and long creeping. **Shoots** are erect and branching, usually with a main shoot and 3–6 short branches that spread outward. Annual growth constrictions are distinct along the shoots. **Leaves** are up to 6mm long and 0.8mm wide and linear, with an elongated, hairlike tip. Leaves spread away from the shoot axis and their tips often curve to point upward toward the shoot tip. **Margins** are smooth. **Strobili** are held at the tips of **peduncles** up to 12.5cm long. Peduncles have appressed, scalelike leaves and often branch at the tips, with up to 5 strobili. Strobili are up to 25mm long and 6mm in diameter, and each strobilus has a small, distinct stalk that connects it to the peduncle. 2n=68 (diploid).

A. A colony of *Lycopodium clavatum* subsp. *clavatum*.

B. Sterile branches.

C. Long-creeping stems.

D. Strobili at the tops of long peduncles.

E. A cluster of strobili.

Lycopodium lagopus

COMMON NAME(S) One-cone clubmoss

STATUS Native, somewhat common

HABITAT/DISTRIBUTION Open forests and grassy habitats; also occurs in Greenland, Europe, and Asia

Plants are terrestrial. **Stems** are horizontal and long creeping. **Shoots** are erect and branching, usually with a main shoot and 2–3 equally long branches that point upward. Annual growth constrictions are distinct along the shoots. **Leaves** are up to 5mm long and 0.7mm wide and linear, each with an elongated, hairlike tip. Leaves point upward and can be somewhat pressed against the shoot axis. **Margins** are smooth. **Strobili** are held at the tips of **peduncles** up to 12.5cm long. Peduncles have appressed, scalelike leaves and do not branch. Strobili are up to 55mm long and 5mm in diameter; strobili may be solitary or in pairs, but if they are paired, no stalk connects them to the peduncle. 2n=68 (diploid).

A. Long-creeping stems of *Lycopodium lagopus*.

B. Plants with strobili atop long peduncles.

C. Paired strobili.

D. Close-up of immature fertile leaves on strobili.

FAMILY: **LYCOPODIACEAE**

Palhinhea is a lycophyte genus with 25 species globally, and 1 in our flora, which was previously treated in the genus *Lycopodiella* (p. 79). *Palhinhaea cernua* plants are very distinctive and resemble small trees, with erect main stems and slim, horizontal side branches that end in pendent (hanging) strobili. In our region, the species occurs in Florida and its range extends somewhat northward into the southeast. It can typically be found in wet habitats, including roadside ditches and pinelands. Base chromosome number (x) = 78.

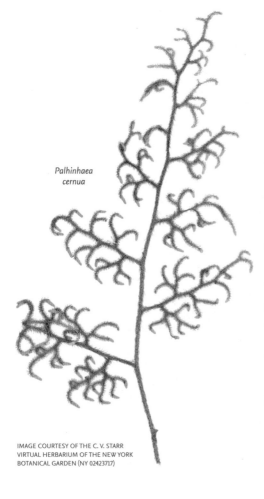

Palhinhaea cernua

A. A colony of *Palhinhaea cernua* at the edge of a sandy path.

B. Tip of a branching shoot.

Palhinhaea cernua

COMMON NAME(S) Nodding clubmoss, staghorn clubmoss

NOTABLE SYNONYMS *Lycopodiella cernua*

STATUS Native, common

HABITAT/DISTRIBUTION Wet habitats including depressions, ditches, streamsides, and moist pinelands; occurs in tropical and subtropical regions worldwide

---

Plants are terrestrial. **Stems** are horizontal, creeping, and may appear rootlike. Upright **shoots** are up to 80cm tall, with lateral **branches** that are spreading and themselves multiply branching; the branches droop somewhat at the tips, ending in downward-pointing, well-defined **strobili** up to 1cm long at maturity. **Leaves** are up to 5mm long and needlelike, spreading away from the stem, often curving downward at the base of the stem and branches, and upward toward the tips. 2n=312 (tetraploid).

A. A colony of *Palhinhaea cernua*.

B. Plants.

C. Downward-pointing strobili.

D. Spreading leaves.

FAMILY: **LYCOPODIACEAE**

We have a single species of *Pseudolycopodiella* in our flora; as the name of the genus suggests, these plants are similar in appearance to members of *Lycopodiella* (p. 79), to which they are closely related. The 2 genera can be distinguished most easily by their peduncles, the upright stalks that lead to the strobili. In *Lycopodiella*, these stalks have a relatively dense coating of tiny leaves, but in *Pseudolycopodiella*, the stalks are bare or have only a few small, scattered, scalelike leaves. Base chromosome number (x) = 35.

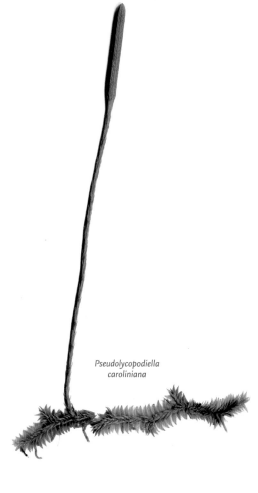

*Pseudolycopodiella
caroliniana*

A. Horizontal stems of *Pseudolycopodiella caroliniana*, with leaves oriented in multiple directions.

B. Closeup of a strobilus.

Pseudolycopodiella caroliniana

COMMON NAME(S) Slender clubmoss, bog clubmoss

NOTABLE SYNONYMS *Lycopodiella caroliniana, Lycopodium carolinianum*

STATUS Native, somewhat common

HABITAT/DISTRIBUTION Moist and often sandy habitats, including wetlands, pinelands, flatwoods, and roadside ditches; also occurs in the Caribbean, Asia, and some Pacific islands

Plants are terrestrial. **Horizontal stems** are long creeping and anchored tightly against the ground by the roots. Leaves on the horizontal stems are up to 6mm long and 2mm wide and occur in multiple sets that point either strongly upward or outward. **Upright shoots** or peduncles are up to 30cm tall and slender, with sparse, almost scalelike **leaves** up to 3mm long and less than 1mm wide that are pressed tightly against the shoot axis. **Strobili** are up to 8cm long, with the spore-bearing leaves organized in whorls. 2n=70, 140 (both diploid and tetraploid cytotypes are known).

A. Plants of *Pseudolycopodiella caroliniana*.

B. Upright shoots.

C. Leaves on horizontal stems.

D. Peduncle with scalelike leaves.

FAMILY: **SELAGINELLACEAE**

Selaginella is a genus of lycophytes commonly known as spikemosses. The family Selaginellaceae has had a complicated taxonomic history, with multiple different naming systems suggested over the years. Historically, all ca. 750 members of the family belonged to a single large genus, *Selaginella*, which was further divided into a number of subgenera and sections. This scheme is still the most widely used today, with the various alternative naming systems differing in whether some of the subgeneric groups are elevated and recognized at the genus level. Phylogenetically, the type species of the genus, *Selaginella selaginoides*, which we have in our flora, is in a 2-species cluster that is sister to all the other species in the genus, and it always retains the genus name *Selaginella*. Under one of the other naming systems that is sometimes used in North America, our remaining "*Selaginella*" species belong to the genera *Bryodesma* and *Lycopodioides*. The appropriate alternative names for our species in these 2 genera are given below, and the morphological distinctions between the groups are noted in the key, but for simplicity, all species in the family in our flora are treated here as *Selaginella*.

No matter how they are divided into genera, all members of the family Selaginellaceae are alike morphologically in having small, often scalelike leaves that have a small flap of tissue (a ligule) on the upper surface near the leaf base, and by having their spore-bearing leaves arranged into strobili that are flattened, cylindrical, or quadrangular and are usually not well differentiated from the leafy shoot below. The spore-bearing structures (sporangia) are on the upper surfaces of the leaves, tucked into the leaf bases where they meet the shoot axis. Most of the *Selaginella* species in our flora also have rhizophores; these stemlike structures, found only in this family, can produce roots at their tips when they touch the soil surface. All members of Selaginellaceae are heterosporous, meaning that the plants produce 2 distinct types of spores: larger, female megaspores, and smaller, male microspores. Base chromosome number $(x) = 7, 8, 9, 10, 11, 12$.

KEY TO THE SPECIES OF *SELAGINELLA* IN OUR FLORA:

1a. Stems and branches are rounded or quadrangular; sterile leaves are all alike in size and shape and are spirally arranged around the stem axis; rhizophores, if present, typically emerge from the upper surface of the stems ⸻ 2

    2a   The strobili are cylindrical, and the spore-bearing leaves in the strobili spread away from the central shoot axis; rhizophores are not present ⸻ *Selaginella selaginoides*

    2b   The strobili are distinctly 4-sided (quadrangular), and the spore-bearing leaves in the strobili are pressed against the central stem; rhizophores are present ⸻ 3 (group of species sometimes treated in the genus *Bryodesma*)

        3a   Each leaf ends in an elongated tip that is twisted and contorted; strobili are less than 6mm long, and 1.5–2mm wide; leaf margins are mostly smooth, or with minute teeth ⸻ *Selaginella tortipila*

        3b   Each leaf ends in an elongated tip that is straight, not twisted or contorted; strobili are mostly more than 10mm long, and 1–1.5mm wide; leaf margins are variously toothed or fringed ⸻ 4

            4a   Rhizomatous (belowground) stems are not present; aboveground stems are mostly horizontally creeping, turning up at the tips, with plants forming spreading mats; rhizophores can be produced along the whole length of the stems ⸻ *Selaginella rupestris*

            4b   Both rhizomatous and aboveground stems are present; aboveground stems are mostly erect or upward pointing, with plants forming clusters or clumps; rhizophores are produced on rhizomatous stems or at the bases of aboveground stems ⸻ 5

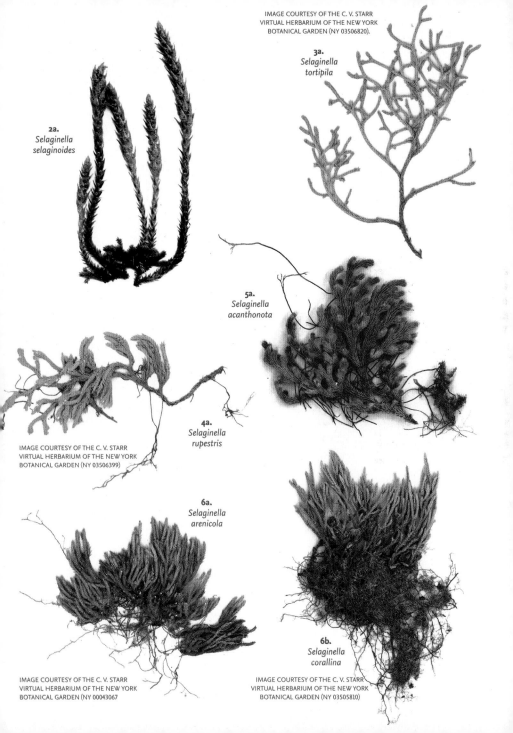

3a.
Selaginella tortipila

2a.
Selaginella selaginoides

5a.
Selaginella acanthonota

4a.
Selaginella rupestris

6a.
Selaginella arenicola

6b.
Selaginella corallina

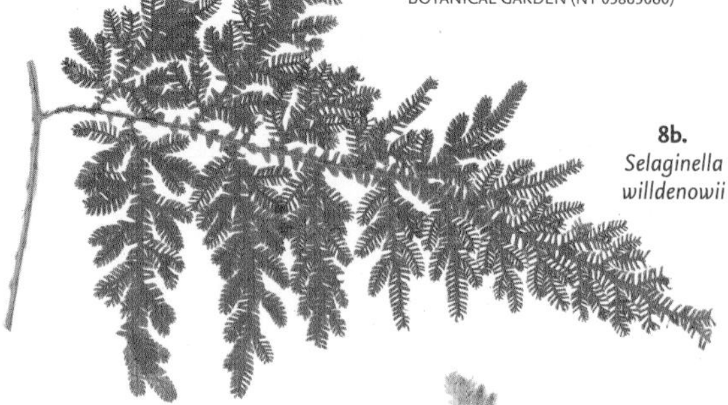

IMAGE COURTESY OF THE C. V. STARR VIRTUAL HERBARIUM OF THE NEW YORK BOTANICAL GARDEN (NY 03865060)

8b. *Selaginella willdenowii*

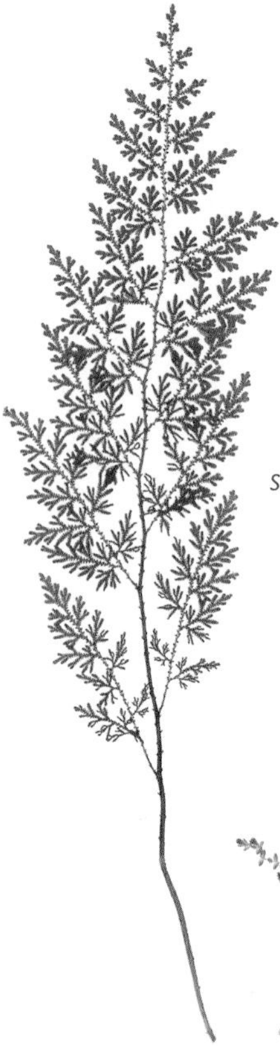

8a. *Selaginella braunii*

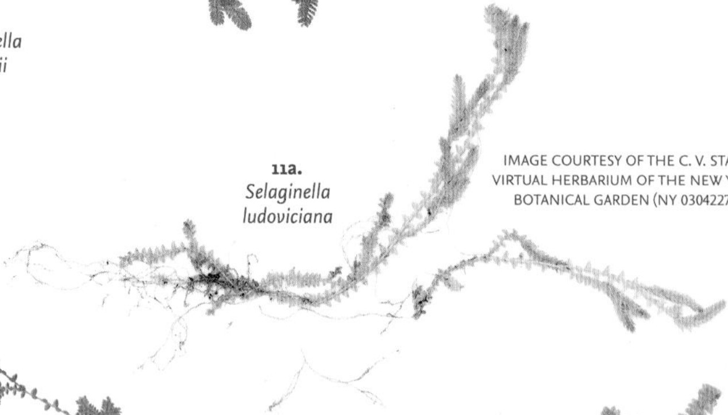

11a. *Selaginella ludoviciana*

IMAGE COURTESY OF THE C. V. STARR VIRTUAL HERBARIUM OF THE NEW YORK BOTANICAL GARDEN (NY 03042274)

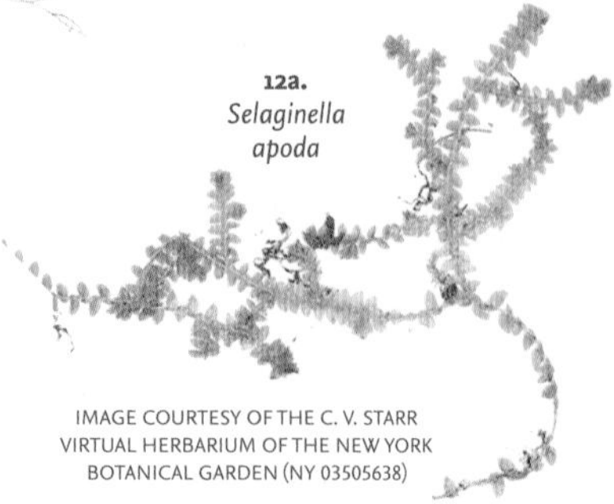

12a. *Selaginella apoda*

IMAGE COURTESY OF THE C. V. STARR VIRTUAL HERBARIUM OF THE NEW YORK BOTANICAL GARDEN (NY 03505638)

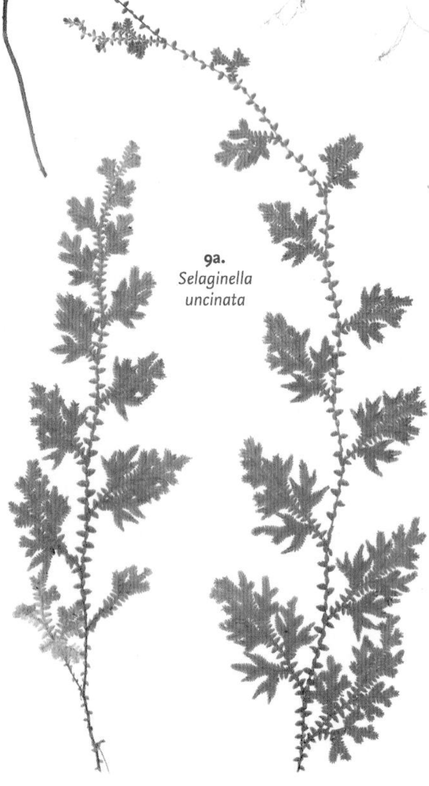

9a. *Selaginella uncinata*

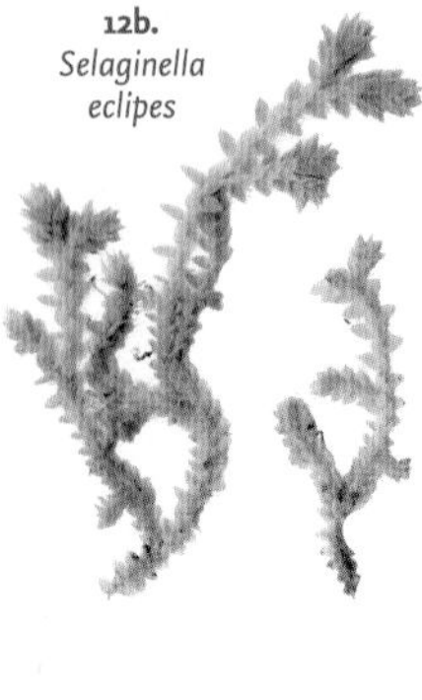

12b. *Selaginella eclipes*

5a   The fertile leaves are hairy at the base; both the fertile and sterile leaves are hairy toward the leaf tip; rhizophores are produced both on rhizomatous stems and at the bases of aboveground stems ⸻ *Selaginella acanthonota*

5b   The fertile leaves are smooth at the base; both the fertile and sterile leaves are smooth toward the leaf tip; rhizophores are produced only on belowground stems ⸻ 6

    6a   The sterile leaves are mostly tightly pressed against the shoot axis and are minutely hairy at the base; the fertile leaves often curve or bend inward at the tip; the strobili are distinctly larger in diameter than the leafy shoot below ⸻ *Selaginella arenicola*

    6b   The sterile leaves are only loosely pressed against the shoot axis and a re usually smooth at the base; the fertile leaves are usually straight at the tip; the strobili are not distinctly larger in diameter than the leafy shoot below ⸻ *Selaginella corallina*

1b   Stems and branches appear flattened, in a plane; sterile leaves are 2 distinct sizes and orientations, with 2 larger leaves on the sides that spread outward from the stem axis (lateral leaves), and 2 smaller leaves that press against the axis and point toward the stem tip (median leaves); rhizophores are usually present and typically emerge from the lower surface or sides of the stems ⸻ 7 (group of species sometimes treated in the genus *Lycopodioides*)

   7a   Plants are shrublike or vinelike; the main stems are erect ⸻ 8

    8a   Plants are shrublike; stems are densely covered with short, stiff hairs ⸻ *Selaginella braunii*

    8b   Plants are vinelike and may climb or scramble over surrounding vegetation; stems are smooth ⸻ *Selaginella willdenowii*

   7b   Plants are short and are not shrublike or vinelike; the main stems are horizontally creeping to somewhat ascending but are not erect ⸻ 9

    9a   The lateral leaves have margins that are smooth and entire; the side branches of the shoots branch another 2–3 times ⸻ *Selaginella uncinata*

    9b   The lateral leaves have margins that are toothed, with teeth of varying sizes; the side branches of the shoots branch another 1–2 times ⸻ 10

     10a   The median leaves are up to 1.2mm long and have a long-bristled tip; plants form mats less than 6cm in diameter ⸻ *Selaginella eatonii*

     10b   The median leaves are more than 1.25mm long and are pointed at the tip but lack a bristle; plants form loose mats more than 6cm in diameter ⸻ 11

      11a   The margins of the leaves have 3–5 rows of transparent cells, giving the leaf a white-ringed appearance; the lateral leaves have stomata only on the upper surface and only near the midrib ⸻ *Selaginella ludoviciana*

      11b.   The margins of the leaves have no transparent cells (or rarely 1–2 rows of paler cells), and the leaves are essentially uniform in color; the lateral leaves have stomata only on the upper surface, but across the entire leaf surface ⸻ 12

       12a   The median leaves have short-pointed tips ⸻ *Selaginella apoda*

       12b   The median leaves have long, drawn-out, or even bristled tips ⸻ *Selaginella eclipes*

Selaginella acanthonota

COMMON NAME(S) Spiny spikemoss, sandy spikemoss

NOTABLE SYNONYMS *Bryodesma acanthonota*, *Bryodesma arenicola* subsp. *acanthonota*

STATUS Native (endemic to eastern North America), uncommon

HABITAT/DISTRIBUTION Sandy habitats such as scrubs, pine barrens, dunes, or even open sandy soils

- -

Plants are terrestrial and form clumps or clusters. Main **stems** are aboveground and mostly erect or upward pointing. Rhizomatous, belowground stems are also present. Stems and branches appear rounded or quadrangular in cross section. **Rhizophores** are present and are produced both on rhizomatous stems and at the bases of aboveground stems. **Leaves** are all alike, narrowly lanceolate and up to 3.25mm long and 0.7mm wide, arranged in pseudowhorls and pressed tightly against the shoot axis, pointing upward. Leaves have a somewhat rounded base, a white to transparent tip, and hairy margins and surfaces. There are ridges on the lower surfaces of the leaves, and hairs that run lengthwise along their sides; these ridges are less prominent in the fertile leaves that make up the strobili. **Strobili** are 4-sided (quadrangular) and are up to 3.5cm long and 1–1.5mm wide. 2n=unknown.

A. Plants of *Selaginella acanthonota*.

B. Leaves with white to transparent tips.

C. Strobili

Selaginella apoda

COMMON NAME(S) Meadow spikemoss

NOTABLE SYNONYMS *Lycopodioides apodum*

STATUS Native, somewhat common

HABITAT/DISTRIBUTION A variety of damp, often grassy habitats, including meadows and lawns, swamps and marshes, moist, open woods, and streamsides; also occurs in Mexico and Central America

Plants are terrestrial and form somewhat compact to more often very loose clumps, which are typically more than 6cm in diameter. Main **stems** are aboveground, short creeping, prostrate against the ground surface, and have side branches that branch only once more. Stems and branches appear flattened in cross section. **Rhizophores** are present and typically emerge from the sides of the stems, either throughout the stem length or clustered toward the base. **Leaves** are 2 distinct sizes and orientations: the larger **lateral leaves** spread outward from the stem axis, are up to 2.25mm long and 1.35mm wide, ovate to lanceolate with a somewhat heart-shaped base, and have sharply toothed margins, pointed tips that lack a bristle, and stomata across the entire upper leaf surface; the smaller **median leaves** press against the axis and point toward the stem tip, are up to 1.6mm long and 0.7mm wide, ovate to lanceolate, and have sharply toothed margins and short- to long-pointed tips. Both leaf types are either uniform in color or have at most 1 row of transparent cells around the leaf margin. **Strobili** are flattened, up to about 2cm long, and can be solitary or in pairs. 2n=18 (diploid).

A. A colony of *Selaginella apoda.*

B. Creeping stems.

C. Stems with lateral and median leaves.

Selaginella arenicola

COMMON NAME(S) Sand spikemoss

NOTABLE SYNONYMS *Bryodesma arenicola*

STATUS Native (endemic to eastern North America), rare

HABITAT/DISTRIBUTION Exposed sandy soils and dunes

Plants are terrestrial and form clumps or clusters. Main **stems** are aboveground and mostly erect or upward pointing. Rhizomatous, belowground stems are also present. Stems and branches appear rounded or quadrangular in cross section. **Rhizophores** are present and are produced only on rhizomatous stems. **Leaves** are all similar, narrowly triangular to narrowly lanceolate and up to 3mm long and 0.5mm wide, arranged in pseudowhorls and pressed tightly against the shoot axis, pointing upward. Leaves have a somewhat triangular base, a white to whitish, straight tip, and hairy margins. The sterile leaves are hairy at the base and smooth toward the tip. There are ridges on the lower surfaces of the leaves, and these are less prominent on the fertile leaves that make up the strobili. **Strobili** are 4-sided (quadrangular), up to 3.5cm long and 1–1.5mm wide, and distinctly wider in diameter than the leafy shoot below; the fertile leaves are smooth throughout and often curve or bend inward at the tip. 2n=unknown.

A. Plants of *Selaginella arenicola.*

B. Plants growing on sand.

C. Leaves with white tips.

D. Strobili.

Selaginella braunii

COMMON NAME(S) Braun's spikemoss

NOTABLE SYNONYMS *Lycopodioides braunii*

STATUS Not native, uncommon

HABITAT/DISTRIBUTION Escapes from cultivation in the south, where it can become established in shady, damp forests and disturbed areas; native to Asia

Plants are terrestrial and shrublike or tree shaped. Main **stems** are aboveground, erect, have a dense covering of short hairs, and branch frequently, forking up to 4 times toward their tips. Stems and branches appear flattened in cross section. **Rhizophores** are present and typically emerge from the sides of the stems, either throughout the stem length or clustered toward the base. **Leaves** are of 2 distinct sizes and orientations: the larger **lateral leaves** spread outward from the stem axis, are up to 2.5mm long and 1mm wide, ovate to oblong, with a squared-off base that may be slightly winged, and have wavy margins and rounded tips; the smaller **median leaves** press against the axis and point toward the stem tip, are up to 3mm long and 1mm wide, lanceolate to oblong, and have wavy margins and long-pointed tips. Both leaf types typically have somewhat transparent margins that are often revolute (curling under). **Strobili** are round, up to about 8mm long, and solitary. 2n=20 (diploid).

A. Plants of *Selaginella braunii*.

B. Branching shoots.

C. Branches with median and lateral leaves.

Selaginella corallina

COMMON NAME(S) Riddell's spikemoss

NOTABLE SYNONYMS *Bryodesma arenicola* subsp. *riddellii*, *Selaginella arenicola* subsp. *riddellii*, *Selaginella arenicola* var. *riddellii*

STATUS Native (endemic to eastern North America), rare

HABITAT/DISTRIBUTION Typically on rocky outcrops of granite, or sandy soils

- -

Plants are terrestrial and form clumps or clusters. Main **stems** are aboveground and mostly erect or upward pointing. Rhizomatous, belowground stems are also present. Stems and branches appear rounded or quadrangular in cross section. **Rhizophores** are present and are produced only on rhizomatous stems. **Leaves** are all similar, narrowly triangular to narrowly lanceolate and up to 3mm long and 0.5mm wide, arranged in pseudowhorls and pressed only loosely against the shoot axis, pointing upward. Leaves have a somewhat triangular base, a white to whitish, straight tip, and hairy margins. The sterile leaves are usually smooth throughout. There are ridges on the lower surfaces of the leaves, and these are less prominent on the fertile leaves that make up the strobili. **Strobili** are 4-sided (quadrangular), up to 3.5cm long and 1–1.5mm wide, and similar in diameter to the leafy shoot below; the fertile leaves are smooth throughout and straight at the tip. 2n=unknown.

A. Plants of *Selaginella corallina*

B. Plants, with quadrangular strobili in the foreground.

Selaginella eatonii

COMMON NAME(S) Eaton's spikemoss

NOTABLE SYNONYMS *Selaginella armata* var. *eatonii*, *Lycopodioides eatonii*

STATUS Native, rare

HABITAT/DISTRIBUTION Limestone hammocks and sinkholes in Florida; also occurs in the Caribbean

----

Plants are terrestrial and form small clumps that are typically less than 6cm in diameter. Main **stems** are aboveground, short creeping, prostrate against the ground to ascending, and branch infrequently. Stems and branches appear flattened in cross section. **Rhizophores** are present and typically emerge from the sides of the stems, throughout the stem length. **Leaves** are of 2 distinct sizes and orientations: the larger **lateral leaves** spread outward from the stem axis, are up to 1.5mm long and 0.9mm wide, ovate to oblong with a rounded base, and have sharply toothed margins and pointed tips; the smaller **median leaves** press against the axis and point toward the stem tip, are up to 1.2mm long and 0.35mm wide, lanceolate, and have sharply toothed margins and long-pointed, distinctly bristled tips. Both leaf types typically have several rows of transparent cells around the leaf margin and may be somewhat iridescent. **Strobili** are flattened, up to about 3mm long, and solitary. 2n=unknown.

A. Plants of *Selaginella eatonii.*

B. Creeping stems.

C. Plants with strobili.

Selaginella eclipes

COMMON NAME(S) Buck's meadow spikemoss, hidden spikemoss

NOTABLE SYNONYMS *Lycopodioides eclipes*

STATUS Native (endemic to eastern North America), rare

HABITAT/DISTRIBUTION A variety of moist habitats, including swamps, fens, damp pastures and meadows, occasionally open forests

Plants are terrestrial and form somewhat compact to more often very loose clumps, which are typically more than 6cm in diameter. Main **stems** are aboveground, short creeping and prostrate against the ground, and somewhat regularly branched, with the side branches branching another 1–2 times. Stems and branches appear flattened in cross section. **Rhizophores** are present and typically emerge from the sides of the stems, throughout the stem length. **Leaves** are of 2 distinct sizes and orientations: the larger **lateral leaves** spread outward from the stem axis, are up to 2mm long and 1.3mm wide, ovate to ovate lanceolate, with a somewhat heart-shaped base, and have sharply toothed margins, pointed tips that lack a bristle, and stomata across the entire upper leaf surface; the smaller **median leaves** press against the axis and point toward the stem tip, are up to 1.8mm long and 0.8mm wide, ovate to lanceolate, and have sharply toothed margins and long-pointed tips that may end in a bristle. Both leaf types are either uniform in color or frequently have a single row of transparent cells around the leaf margin. **Strobili** are flattened, up to about 4cm long, and can be solitary or in pairs. 2n=unknown.

A. Plants of *Selaginella eclipes*.
B. Median and lateral leaves.

Selaginella ludoviciana

COMMON NAME(S) Gulf spikemoss, Louisiana spikemoss

NOTABLE SYNONYMS *Lycopodioides ludovicianum, Selaginella apoda* var. *ludoviciana*

STATUS Native (endemic to eastern North America), uncommon

HABITAT/DISTRIBUTION Damp to wet soils such as streamsides, swamps, open forests, ditches

----

Plants are terrestrial and form diffuse mats that are typically more than 6cm in diameter. Main **stems** are aboveground, long creeping, prostrate against the ground to ascending, infrequently branched, and with side branches that branch only once more. Stems and branches appear flattened in cross section. **Rhizophores** are present and typically emerge from the sides of the stems, throughout the stem length. **Leaves** are of 2 distinct sizes and orientations: the larger **lateral leaves** spread outward from the stem axis, are up to 2.65mm long and 1.64mm wide, ovate to ovate lanceolate, with a somewhat heart-shaped base, and have sharply toothed margins, pointed tips that lack a bristle but are distinctly toothed, and stomata on the upper leaf surface but only near the midrib; the smaller **median leaves** press against the axis and point toward the stem tip, are up to 2mm long and 0.8mm wide, ovate to lanceolate, and have sharply toothed margins and long-pointed tips that may end in a bristle. Both leaf types typically have 3–5 rows of transparent cells around the leaf margin, giving the leaf a distinctly white-edged appearance. **Strobili** are flattened, up to about 4cm long, and can be solitary or in pairs. 2n=unknown.

A. Plants of *Selaginella ludoviciana*.

B. Long-creeping stems with strobili.

C. Branches with median and lateral leaves, and strobili.

Selaginella rupestris

COMMON NAME(S) Rock spikemoss, dwarf spikemoss

NOTABLE SYNONYMS *Bryodesma rupestre*

STATUS Native, somewhat common

HABITAT/DISTRIBUTION A variety of rocky habitats and sandy soils, occasionally in grassy meadows; also occurs in Greenland and ranges into western North America

Plants are terrestrial and form spreading mats or sometimes large, cushion-like clumps. Main **stems** are aboveground, mostly horizontally creeping, and turn upward at the tips; rhizomatous, belowground stems are not present. Stems and branches appear rounded or quadrangular in cross section. **Rhizophores** are present and can be produced along the whole length of the stem. **Leaves** are all alike, linear to narrowly lanceolate and up to 4mm long and 0.6mm wide, arranged in pseudowhorls and pressed tightly against the shoot axis, pointing upward. Leaves have a somewhat triangular base, a white to whitish, straight tip, hairy margins, and surfaces that are variously smooth or hairy. There are ridges on the lower surfaces of the leaves, and these are equally prominent on the fertile leaves that make up the strobili. **Strobili** are 4-sided (quadrangular) and up to 3.5cm long and 1–1.5mm wide. 2n=unknown.

A. A colony of *Selaginella rupestris*.

B. Plants with horizontally spreading stems, and strobili.

C. Close-up of strobili.

Selaginella selaginoides

COMMON NAME(S) Northern spikemoss, prickly mountain-moss

STATUS Native, uncommon

HABITAT/DISTRIBUTION Damp to wet habitats including various types of wetlands, stream banks, and damp talus slopes; also occurs in western North America, Greenland, Europe, and Asia

---

Plants are terrestrial and form dense to loose clumps or mats. Main **stems** are aboveground, long creeping, and dichotomously branched, with side branches that are erect and do not branch further, standing up to 10cm tall and ending in strobili. Stems and branches appear rounded or quadrangular in cross section. **Rhizophores** are not present. **Leaves** are all alike (though the leaves on the horizontal stems are smaller than those on the upright stems), lanceolate, and up to 4.5mm long and 1.2mm wide, arranged spirally around the shoot axis, with large, soft, spiny projections along the margins. **Strobili** are cylindrical and up to 6mm long and 1.5mm wide; the spore-bearing leaves (sporophylls) spread away from the central shoot axis. Strobili may have the female megasporophylls toward the base and the male microsporophylls toward the tip. 2n=18 (diploid).

A. Plants of *Selaginella selaginoides.*

B. Plants with strobili.

C. Strobilus leaves with spiny margins and sporangia at the base.

Selaginella tortipila

COMMON NAME(S) Twisted-hair spikemoss

NOTABLE SYNONYMS *Bryodesma tortipilum*

STATUS Native (endemic to eastern North America), rare

HABITAT/DISTRIBUTION Rocky outcrops, typically at higher elevations

Plants are terrestrial and form compact clumps. Main **stems** are aboveground, mostly erect or upward pointing, and tend to fork irregularly at the tips, with only 1 branch ending in a strobilus. Rhizomatous, belowground stems are also present. Stems and branches appear rounded or quadrangular in cross section. **Rhizophores** are present and are produced both on rhizomatous stems and at the bases of aboveground stems. **Leaves** are all similar, linear to narrowly lanceolate and up to 4.5mm long and 0.7mm wide, arranged in pseudowhorls and pressed tightly against the shoot axis, pointing upward. Leaves have a somewhat triangular base, hairy margins, and smooth surfaces and end in an elongated bristle tip that is distinctly twisted and contorted. There are inconspicuous ridges on the lower surfaces of the leaves, and these are more prominent on the fertile leaves that make up the strobili. **Strobili** are 4-sided (quadrangular) and up to 6mm long and 1.5–2mm wide. 2n=unknown.

A. Plants of *Selaginella tortipila.*

B. Leaves with twisted bristle tips.

C. Main stems and bristle-tipped leaves.

D. Strobilus.

Selaginella uncinata

COMMON NAME(S) Blue spikemoss, peacock spikemoss

NOTABLE SYNONYMS *Lycopodioides uncinatum*

STATUS Not native, uncommon

HABITAT/DISTRIBUTION Escapes from cultivation in the south, where it can become established in hammocks and shady, damp forests; native to Asia

Plants are terrestrial and form diffuse clusters. Main **stems** are aboveground, long creeping, prostrate against the ground to ascending, and branch frequently, with side branches that branch another 2–3 times. Stems and branches appear flattened in cross section. **Rhizophores** are present and typically emerge from the sides of the stems, mostly near its base. **Leaves** are of 2 distinct sizes and orientations: the larger **lateral leaves** spread outward from the stem axis, are iridescent, up to 4.2mm long and 2.5mm wide, ovate to oblong with a somewhat ear-shaped base, and have smooth margins and pointed to rounded tips; smaller **median leaves** press against the axis and point toward the stem tip, are up to 3.5mm long and 1.8mm wide, ovate to lanceolate, and have smooth margins and long-pointed tips. Both leaf types typically have several rows of transparent cells around the leaf margin. **Strobili** are rounded, up to about 1.5cm long, and solitary. 2n=18 (diploid).

A. Plants of *Selaginella uncinata*.

B. Branches with median and lateral leaves.

C. A long-creeping branch.

Selaginella willdenowii

COMMON NAME(S) Vine spikemoss

NOTABLE SYNONYMS *Lycopodioides willdenowii*

STATUS Not native, uncommon

HABITAT/DISTRIBUTION Escapes from cultivation in Florida, where it can become established in hammocks and shady, damp forests; native to Asia

Plants are terrestrial and vinelike or shrublike. Main **stems** are smooth, long creeping to climbing, and branch frequently, with the branches forking up to 5 times toward their tips. Stems and branches appear flattened in cross section. **Rhizophores** are present and emerge from the stems and shoots throughout their length. **Leaves** are of 2 distinct sizes and orientations: the larger **lateral leaves** spread outward from the stem axis, are distinctly iridescent, up to 4mm long and 2mm wide, ovate to oblong with a rounded base that has an ear-shaped wing on one side, and have smooth margins and rounded tips; smaller **median leaves** press against the axis and point toward the stem tip, are up to 2.7mm long and 1.3mm wide, lanceolate to somewhat ovate with an ear-shaped base, and have smooth margins and rounded tips. Both leaf types typically have somewhat transparent margins. **Strobili** are rounded, up to about 2cm long, and solitary. 2n=18 (diploid).

A. Plants of *Selaginella willdenowii*.

B. Long-creeping branches.

C. Branches with strobili and iridescent leaves.

D. Median and lateral leaves.

FAMILY: **LYCOPODIACEAE**

Spinulum is a lycophyte genus that was formerly included in the genus *Lycopodium* and includes 2 or 3 species globally and 1 in our flora: *Spinulum annotinum*, which is found throughout the Northern Hemisphere in temperate and boreal regions. *Spinulum* species are most similar in appearance to *Huperzia* (p. 53), but *Huperzia* does not have well-defined strobili, while *Spinulum* does. *Spinulum* can be distinguished from other, closely related genera (e.g., *Lycopodium*, p. 86; and *Dendrolycopodium*, p. 42) by having sessile strobili that sit directly atop the leafy part of the shoot (compared to strobili in *Lycopodium*, which are stalked), and by its shoots branching only once or twice, near the base, as opposed to branching many times and resembling small trees (as in *Dendrolycopodium*). In North America, *S. annotinum* can be quite variable morphologically, which has led to recognition of subspecies; one of these is sometimes treated as a separate full species (*S. canadense*). Base chromosome number (x) = 34.

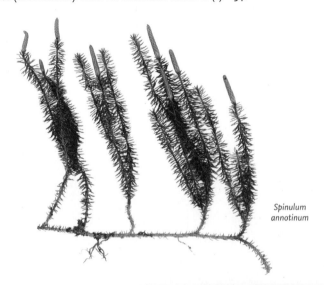

Spinulum annotinum

A colony of *Spinulum annotinum*.

Spinulum annotinum

COMMON NAME(S) Bristly clubmoss

NOTABLE SYNONYMS *Lycopodium annotinum*

STATUS Native, common

HABITAT/DISTRIBUTION Wet forests and wetland edges; also occurs in western North America, Greenland, Europe, and Asia

Plants are terrestrial. **Stems** are horizontal and creeping. **Shoots** are erect, up to 30cm tall, and often form clusters. Annual growth constrictions are distinct along the shoots. Shoots do not branch often, but when they do, branching occurs mostly near the shoot base. **Leaves** spread away from the shoot axis and may be reflexed downward. Leaves are up to 8mm long and linear to lanceolate, with a pointed tip. **Margins** have shallow teeth, mostly toward the leaf tip. Spore-bearing leaves have sporangia at their bases and are organized into well-defined **strobili** that sit directly atop the leafy part of the shoot and do not have stalks or peduncles. 2n=68 (diploid)

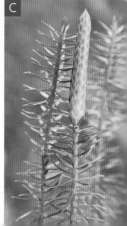

A. A colony of *Spinulum annotinum*.

B. Plants branching near the shoot base.

C. A fertile shoot with a strobilus.

FERNS

DESCRIPTIONS OF GENERA AND SPECIES

FAMILY: **PTERIDACEAE**

Members of the genus *Acrostichum* are some of the largest ferns in the eastern North American flora, with the leaves of *A. danaeifolium* reaching up to 4 meters in length at maturity. The members of this genus are often called mangrove or swamp ferns, in reference to their preference for damp, swampy, coastal or marine environments, or leather ferns, for the very tough, leathery texture of their leaves. *Acrostichum* species are unique in their ability to grow in salt water and can often be found in brackish habitats such as mangrove swamps, though they cannot tolerate having their roots submerged for long periods. The 2 species of *Acrostichum* in our flora can be distinguished from one another by a number of features, including the shapes formed by the reticulate (netted) veins on either side of the pinna midveins (see illustrations below). Base chromosome number (x) = 30.

KEY TO THE SPECIES OF *ACROSTICHUM* IN OUR FLORA:

1a On fertile leaves, fertile pinnae are found only toward the tip of the leaf; pinnae are spaced relatively far apart and adjacent pinnae rarely overlap one another; in the leaf venation network, the shapes (areoles) formed by the veins immediately beside the pinna midveins are elongated parallel to the midvein and are at least 3 times as long as they are wide ⋯⋯⋯⋯⋯⋯⋯⋯⋯⋯⋯⋯⋯⋯⋯⋯⋯⋯⋯⋯ *Acrostichum aureum*

1b On fertile leaves, fertile pinnae are found throughout the leaf; pinnae are spaced relatively close together, and adjacent pinnae frequently overlap one another; in the leaf venation network, the shapes formed by the veins immediately beside the pinna midveins are not elongated parallel to the midvein and are less than 3 times as long as they are wide ⋯⋯⋯⋯⋯⋯⋯⋯⋯⋯⋯⋯⋯⋯⋯⋯⋯⋯⋯ *Acrostichum danaeifolium*

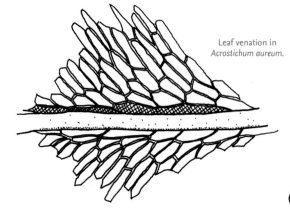

Leaf venation in
Acrostichum aureum.

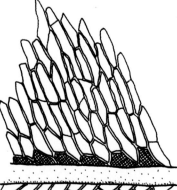

Leaf venation in
Acrostichum danaeifolium.

Close-up of the lower surface of a fertile pinna after sporangia have dehisced (released spores). Each elongated structure is an extended annulus from a single sporangium.

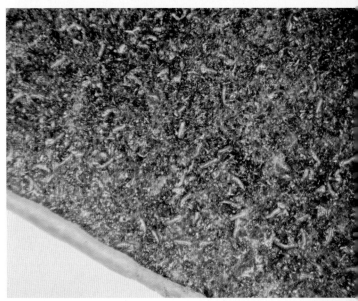

A small population of *Acrostichum aureum*.

A population of *Acrostichum danaeifolium* along a canal.

Acrostichum aureum

COMMON NAME(S) Leather fern, coast leather fern, golden leather fern

STATUS Native, uncommon

HABITAT/DISTRIBUTION Various freshwater, saline, or saltwater-associated habitats, including coastal swamps, hammocks, salt marshes, and canal and lake margins; prefers shaded habitats; occurs in tropical and subtropical regions worldwide

Plants are terrestrial. **Stems** are long creeping or ascending and branch frequently, with uniformly dark-colored scales. **Leaves** are up to 3m long and 50cm wide, arching or ascending to erect, somewhat dimorphic, and clustered, forming dense stands. **Stipes** are brown and smooth, with a groove running along the upper surface that may continue into the rachis. The **rachis** is rounded on the lower surface and grooved on the upper surface. The leaf **blade** is 1-pinnate, leathery, smooth, and lanceolate. **Pinnae** arise alternately along the rachis, have small stalks, are 10–30cm long and 1–7cm wide, narrowly oblong to lanceolate, and typically occur in 12–20 alternate pairs spaced well apart. Only the tip-most 5 to 6 sets of pinnae are fertile, and these may be slightly smaller than the lower, sterile pinnae and have somewhat inrolled margins. The lower pinnae in this species can have stalks up to 3cm long. **Margins** are smooth. **Veins** are conspicuous and anastomosing; areoles immediately beside the midveins of the pinnae are 3 or more times longer than they are wide. **Sporangia** are acrostichoid and intermixed with paraphyses. 2n = 60 (diploid).

A. Leaves of *Acrostichum aureum*; note the widely spaced pinnae.

B. Fertile leaves; note that only a few sets of pinnae toward the leaf tip are fertile, while the lower pinnae are sterile.

C. Close-up of venation on a sterile pinna; note that the areoles immediately beside the midveins of the pinnae are 3 or more times longer than they are wide.

Acrostichum danaeifolium

COMMON NAME(S) Giant leather fern, inland leather fern

STATUS Native, common

HABITAT/DISTRIBUTION Various freshwater, saline, or saltwater-associated habitats including coastal swamps, hammocks, salt marshes, and canal and lake margins; grows well in full sun; also occurs in Mexico and Central and South America

Plants are terrestrial. **Stems** are erect and typically unbranched, with uniformly dark-colored scales. **Leaves** are up to 4m long and 60cm wide, arching or ascending to erect, somewhat dimorphic, and clustered, forming dense stands. **Stipes** are brown and smooth, with a groove running along the upper surface that may continue into the rachis. The **rachis** is shallowly but distinctly grooved on the lower surface and flat or shallowly grooved on the upper surface. The leaf **blade** is 1-pinnate, leathery, smooth, and lanceolate. **Pinnae** arise alternately along the rachis, have small stalks, are narrowly oblong to lanceolate, up to 7–30cm long and 2–5cm wide, and typically occur in ca. 30 alternate pairs that are often close enough together for the pinna bases to overlap. All pinnae are typically fertile on the fertile leaves. The lower pinnae typically have stalks less than 2cm long. **Margins** are smooth. **Veins** are conspicuous and anastomosing; areoles immediately beside the midveins of the pinnae are less than 3 times as long as they are wide. **Sporangia** are acrostichoid and intermixed with paraphyses. 2n = 60 (diploid).

A. Leaves of *Acrostichum danaeifolium*.

B. Closely spaced pinnae, with overlapping bases.

C. Lower surface of a fertile pinna with acrostichoid sporangia (brown) intermixed with paraphyses (whitish, translucent).

FAMILY: **SCHIZAEACEAE**

Actinostachys is a member of the "curly grass" family, the Schizaeaceae, which has only 2 species in North America: *A. pennula* and *Schizaea pusilla* (p. 467). Both of these species have very unfernlike leaves that are narrow, elongated, and grasslike in appearance. In *Schizaea* the sterile leaves become distinctly curly close to the ground, while in *Actinostachys* they remain straight and erect. Both species are rare and very restricted in their ranges, with *Actinostachys* occurring only in Florida and *Schizaea* scattered in the northeast. Base chromosome number (x) = 134.

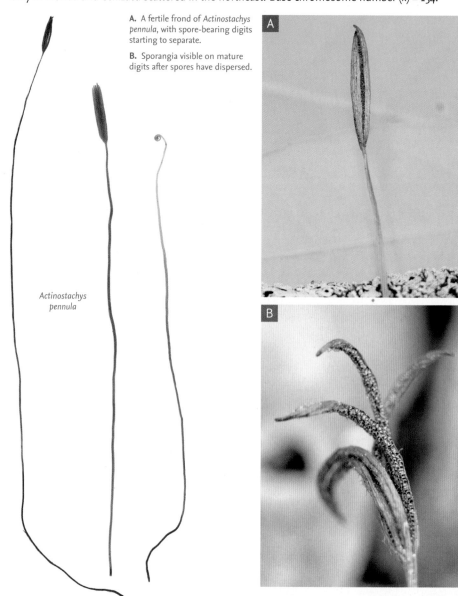

A. A fertile frond of *Actinostachys pennula*, with spore-bearing digits starting to separate.

B. Sporangia visible on mature digits after spores have dispersed.

Actinostachys pennula

Actinostachys pennula

COMMON NAME(S) Ray fern, ray spiked fern, tropical curly-grass fern

STATUS Native, rare

HABITAT/DISTRIBUTION Damp forests and hammocks, often among peat mosses; also occurs in Mexico and Central and South America

Plants are terrestrial. **Stems** are erect and covered in minute hairs. **Leaves** are undivided, extremely narrow, elongated, and grasslike and are up to 12cm long and 1–2mm wide. The **stipe** and **blade** are not clearly distinguished from one another. The leaf terminates in an expanded section where the blade appears to flatten out into several well-defined vertical "digits" or rays that may appear to either lie in a plane or be somewhat whorled. These rays bear **sporangia** in several rows. When the spores are mature, the digits will dry out and turn brown and may flare apart from one another to aid spore dispersal. The lower, grasslike portion of the leaf typically remains green. 2n = 268 (diploid).

A. *Actinostachys pennula* growing among leaves.

B. Fertile fronds.

C. Spore-bearing digits or rays.

D. A mature fertile leaf that has released its spores.

E. Close-up of fertile digits with sporangia visible.

FAMILY: PTERIDACEAE

Adiantum is a large genus of ferns, with about 250 species worldwide. Members of the genus are commonly called maidenhair ferns, in reference to their delicately divided fronds that often hang downward. Members of the family Pteridaceae, *Adiantum* species have the marginal sori characteristic of that group. The sporangia are covered by a false indusium that is formed by the leaf margin curling inward and carrying the sporangia that sit upon it along, enfolding them within the recurved marginal flap. The pattern of leaf division in many *Adiantum* species is different from the typical fern morphology of a central rachis with pinnae emerging at right angles from the rachis (see p. 22). Instead, in *Adiantum* the rachis tends to fork regularly, muddling the distinction between pinnae and pinnules (the text below refers to "leaflets" for the ultimate divisions of the blade, in order to avoid confusion). The term *pseudopedate* has been used to describe the leaf architecture in several species of *Adiantum*, where pinnae fork palmately at the base, producing a fan-shaped leaf with a central division and additional divisions to the sides that curve outward and backward. In our flora, these species include *A. pedatum*, *A. aleuticum*, and their allotetraploid offspring *A. viridimontanum*. Globally, *Adiantum* is most diverse in the tropics, and in eastern North America we have a mix of native species that occur in the temperate part of the continent, and a few tropical species found only in the south or in southernmost Florida. Base chromosome number (x) = 29, 30.

| *Adiantum aleuticum*
2x | *Adiantum viridimontanum*
4x | *Adiantum pedatum*
2x |

Relationships among *Adiantum* species in eastern North America. Blue circles are fertile diploids (2x), and the green square is a fertile allotetraploid (4x).

Marginal sori with false indusium in *Adiantum viridimontanum*.

Adiantum pedatum, with fan-shaped, pseudopedate leaf architecture.

KEY TO THE SPECIES OF *ADIANTUM* IN OUR FLORA:

1a   The petiole and rachises are hairy, with short, stiff hairs pressed close against the
shoot surface ⋯⋯⋯⋯⋯⋯⋯⋯⋯⋯⋯⋯⋯⋯⋯⋯⋯⋯⋯⋯⋯⋯⋯⋯⋯⋯⋯ *Adiantum melanoleucum*

1b   The petiole and rachises are smooth, without hairs ⋯⋯⋯⋯⋯⋯⋯⋯⋯⋯⋯⋯⋯⋯ 2

    2a   The overall leaf shape is not fanlike; the leaflets are about as wide as they are long
and are squarish, rhombic (diamond-like), ovate, or nearly round ⋯⋯⋯⋯⋯⋯⋯⋯ 3

        3a   Leaflets are 5–8cm long and 2.5–7cm wide ⋯⋯⋯⋯⋯⋯⋯⋯⋯⋯ *Adiantum anceps*

        3b   Leaflets are 0.5–3cm long and 0.5–3cm wide ⋯⋯⋯⋯⋯⋯⋯⋯⋯⋯⋯⋯ 4

            4a   The dark blackish-brown color of the rachis and leaflet stalks extends into
the base of the leaflets and branches once or twice before fading to green ⋯⋯⋯ *Adiantum capillus-veneris*

            4b   The dark color of the rachis and leaflet stalks ends immediately at the base
of the leaflet blade, in a small cuplike swelling ⋯⋯⋯⋯⋯⋯⋯⋯⋯⋯⋯⋯ *Adiantum tenerum*

3a.
*Adiantum
anceps*

4a.
*Adiantum
capillus-veneris*

1a.
*Adiantum
melanoleucum*

2b   The overall leaf shape is fanlike; leaflets are longer than they are wide and are oblong or elongate rectangular ·· 5

    5a   Plants are bright to dark green; leaves are fan shaped overall and arching or relaxed to somewhat flat; the ultimate leaflets are oblong and flat ·· *Adiantum pedatum*

    5b   Plants are green to dull grayish green or bluish in the sun; leaves are fan shaped to funnel shaped and arching to stiffly erect; the ultimate leaflets are oblong to somewhat triangular, and flat to funnel-like ··· 6

        6a   The leaflets toward the middle of the leaf are oblong triangular, with nearly parallel margins; the tips of the leaflets are rounded; the false indusia on the leaflets farthest from the stalk are mostly less than 3.5mm long; the sinuses between the false indusia are deeper on average than in *A. viridimontanum* ························· *Adiantum aleuticum*

        6b   The leaflets toward the middle of the leaf are more triangular than oblong (margins are not parallel); the tips of the segments are pointed; the false indusia on the leaflets farthest from the stalk are mostly more than 3.5mm long; the sinuses between the false indusia are shallower on average than in *A. aleuticum* ······························· *Adiantum viridimontanum*

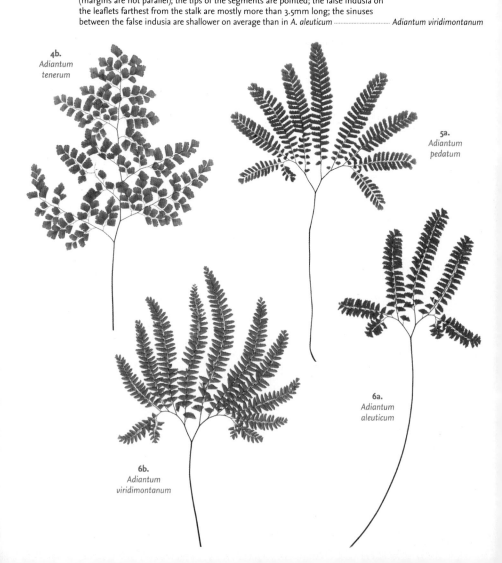

4b.
Adiantum
tenerum

5a.
Adiantum
pedatum

6a.
Adiantum
aleuticum

6b.
Adiantum
viridimontanum

Adiantum aleuticum

COMMON NAME(S) Aleutian maidenhair, western maidenhair

STATUS Native (endemic to North America), rare

HABITAT/DISTRIBUTION Serpentine or serpentine-derived soils, including on shaded slopes, banks, barrens, and wooded ravines; also occurs in western North America (where it is more common than in the east) and in Mexico

Plants are terrestrial. Stems are short creeping to somewhat erect, with bronze to golden scales. Leaves are up to 1.1m tall, green to dull grayish green or bluish in the sun, and arching to stiffly erect. Fertile and sterile leaves do not differ in appearance. Stipes and rachises are purplish to dark brown, smooth and hairless, or with a somewhat waxy or grayish bloom. The leaf blade is fan shaped to somewhat funnel shaped in the sun, and up to 45cm long and 45cm wide. The major divisions are 1-pinnate. The leaflets are flat to funnel-like, 2.5 to 4 times longer than wide, oblong to somewhat triangular, with nearly parallel margins and rounded tips, and with lobes separated by narrow sinuses up to 4mm deep; the edges of the lobes are pointed. Stalks leading to the leaflets are up to 0.9mm long or sometimes longer, their dark color either entering slightly into the base of the leaflet or not. Veins are free and forking. Sori are oblong to crescent shaped, up to 3.5mm long or occasionally longer, smooth, and each with a false indusium created by the pinna margin rolling under. 2n = 58 (diploid).

A. Plants of *Adiantum aleuticum*.

B. Fan-shaped frond.

C. Upper surface of a leaf.

D. Upper surfaces of leaflets.

E. Lower surfaces of leaflets, with sori covered by false indusia.

Adiantum anceps

COMMON NAME(S) Double-edge maidenhair

STATUS Not native, uncommon

HABITAT/DISTRIBUTION Escapes from cultivation in Florida, where it can become established in hammocks; native to South America

Plants are terrestrial. **Stems** are short creeping, with golden-brown to brown scales. **Leaves** are up to 60cm tall, bright to dark green, and arching to pendent. Fertile and sterile leaves do not differ in appearance. **Stipes and rachises** are dark brown to black, smooth and hairless, or occasionally with a somewhat waxy or grayish bloom. The leaf **blade** is ovate to trowel shaped, 2-pinnate, and up to 60cm long and 40cm wide. The **leaflets** are flat, 5–8cm long and 2.5–7cm wide, and squarish to ovate or quadrangular. Stalks leading to the leaflets are up to 1cm long, their dark color ending at the base of the leaflets. **Veins** are free and forking. **Sori** are oblong or somewhat crescent shaped, up to 5mm long or sometimes longer, smooth, and each with a false indusium created by the pinna margin rolling under. 2n = 60 (diploid).

A. Plants of *Adiantum anceps*.
B. Leaflets with stalks.
C. Lower surface of a leaflet, with sori.

Adiantum capillus-veneris

COMMON NAME(S) Common maidenhair, southern maidenhair, Venus's hair fern

STATUS Native, somewhat common

HABITAT/DISTRIBUTION Damp, shaded habitats along streams and rivers, on cliff and sink walls, and on masonry; also in the southwestern U.S. and in tropical to warm-temperate regions worldwide

Plants are terrestrial or epipetric. **Stems** are short creeping, with golden-brown to brown scales. **Leaves** are up to 75cm tall, bright to dark green, and arching to pendent. Fertile and sterile leaves do not differ in appearance. **Stipes and rachises** are dark brown to black, smooth and hairless, or occasionally with a somewhat waxy or grayish bloom. The leaf **blade** is lance shaped to trowel shaped, 3–4-pinnate, and up to 45cm long and 15cm wide. The **leaflets** are flat, about as long as wide (0.5–3cm in both directions), and fan shaped to rhombic (diamond shaped) or almost round, with lobes separated by narrow to wide, deep sinuses. Stalks leading to the leaflets are 0.5–3.5mm long, their dark color extending into the base of the leaflets and branching once or twice before fading to green. **Veins** are free and forking. **Sori** are oblong or somewhat crescent shaped, up to 3mm long or sometimes longer, smooth, and each with a false indusium created by the pinna margin rolling under. 2n = 120 (tetraploid).

A. A colony of *Adiantum capillus-veneris* growing on a rock wall over a stream.

B. Plants.

C. Upper surface of leaflets.

D. Lower surface of leaflets, with sori.

Adiantum melanoleucum

COMMON NAME(S) Fragrant maidenhair

STATUS Native, rare

HABITAT/DISTRIBUTION Limestone sinks and hammocks; also occurs in the Caribbean

Plants are terrestrial. **Stems** are short creeping, with dark reddish-brown scales. **Leaves** are up to 80cm tall, bright to dark green, and erect to arching. Fertile and sterile leaves do not differ in appearance. **Stipes and rachises** are dark brown to black and minutely hairy, with short, stiff hairs pressed against the surface. The leaf **blade** is ovate and up to 35cm long and 15cm wide; small leaves are 1-pinnate throughout, while larger leaves are 2- to sometimes 3-pinnate. The **leaflets** are flat, about 2 times as long as wide, up to 8mm long and 5mm wide, oblong and with bluntly to sharply pointed tips and shallow lobes separated by narrow sinuses. Stalks leading to the leaflets are up to 0.8mm long, their dark color extending slightly into the base of the leaflets. **Veins** are free and forking. **Sori** are crescent shaped, up to 4.5mm long, smooth, and each with a false indusium created by the pinna margin rolling under. 2n = 60 (diploid).

A. A colony of *Adiantum melanoleucum*.

B. Plants growing on limestone.

C. Lower surface of fertile leaflets.

D. Close-up of sori.

Adiantum pedatum

COMMON NAME(S) Northern maidenhair

STATUS Native, common

HABITAT/DISTRIBUTION Rich forests and often limy soils and talus slopes; range extends into western North America, also occurs in Asia

Plants are terrestrial. **Stems** are short creeping, with bronze to golden scales. **Leaves** are up to 75cm tall, bright to dark green (reddish when young), and arching to relaxed or sometimes flat. Fertile and sterile leaves do not differ in appearance. **Stipes and rachises** are dark brown to black, smooth and hairless, or with a somewhat waxy or grayish bloom. The leaf **blade** is fan shaped and up to 30cm long and 35cm wide. The major divisions are 1-pinnate. The **leaflets** are flat, about 3 times as long as wide, oblong or elongate rectangular, with rounded tips, and with lobes separated by narrow sinuses 2–3mm deep; the edges of the lobes are rounded to bluntly pointed. Stalks leading to the leaflets are up to 1.5mm long, their dark color usually entering slightly into the base of the leaflet. **Veins** are free and forking. **Sori** are oblong, usually 1–3mm long, smooth, and each with a false indusium created by the pinna margin rolling under. 2n = 58 (diploid).

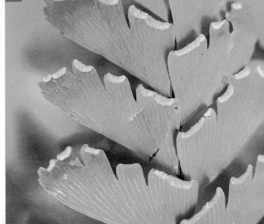

A. A large frond of *Adiantum pedatum*.

B. A smaller frond.

C. Upper surface of pinnae.

D. Close-up of sori.

F   S   C   N

Adiantum tenerum

COMMON NAME(S) Brittle maidenhair

STATUS Native, rare

HABITAT/DISTRIBUTION Limestone sinks, hammocks, and grottoes; also occurs in the Caribbean, Mexico, and Central and South America

Plants are terrestrial. **Stems** are short creeping, with scales that are dark reddish brown in the center, with pale margins. **Leaves** are up to 1.1m tall, bright green (reddish to bronze when young), and arching to pendent. Fertile and sterile leaves do not differ in appearance. **Stipes and rachises** are dark brown to black, smooth and hairless, or with a somewhat waxy or grayish bloom. The leaf **blade** is trowel shaped, 3-pinnate, and up to 60cm long and 60cm wide. The **leaflets** are flat, about as long as wide (0.5–3cm in both directions), and fan shaped to rhombic (diamond shaped), with lobes separated by narrow sinuses. Stalks leading to the leaflets are 1–5mm long, their dark color ending abruptly at the base of the leaflet, in a small cuplike swelling that is unique in this species. **Veins** are free and forking. **Sori** are oblong or somewhat crescent shaped, up to 2mm long, smooth, and each with a false indusium created by the pinna margin rolling under. 2n = 60 (diploid).

A. Fronds of *Adiantum tenerum*.
B. Reddish young fronds.
C. Lower surface of leaflets, with sori.

Adiantum viridimontanum

COMMON NAME(S) Green Mountain maidenhair

STATUS Native (endemic to eastern North America), rare

HABITAT/DISTRIBUTION Serpentine soils; known from only a few locations in the northeastern U.S. and Québec

Plants are terrestrial. **Stems** are short creeping, with bronze to golden scales. **Leaves** are up to 90cm tall, green to dull grayish green or bluish in the sun, and arching to stiffly erect. Fertile and sterile leaves do not differ in appearance. **Stipes and rachises** are dark brown to black, smooth and hairless, or with a somewhat waxy or grayish bloom. The leaf **blade** is fan shaped to somewhat funnel shaped in the sun, and up to 35cm long and 45cm wide. The major divisions are 1-pinnate. The **leaflets** are flat to funnel-like, about 2.5 times as long as wide, long triangular, with pointed tips, and with lobes separated by narrow sinuses less than 1mm deep; the edges of the lobes are rounded to pointed. Stalks leading to the leaflets are up to 1.5mm long or sometimes longer, their dark color usually entering slightly into the base of the leaflet. **Veins** are free and forking. **Sori** are oblong, usually ca. 3.5mm long or occasionally up to 10mm long, smooth, and each with a false indusium created by the pinna margin rolling under. 2n = 116 (tetraploid).

A. *Adiantum viridimontanum* growing in the shade.

B. *Adiantum viridimontanum* growing in the sun.

C. Upper surface of leaflets.

D. Lower surface of leaflets, with sori.

FAMILY: **THELYPTERIDACEAE**

Amauropelta is a large genus, with about 230 species worldwide, and it is one of several genera that used to be included in *Thelypteris* (p. 475). We have 3 species of *Amauropelta* in our flora, 2 of which have small ranges in Florida and are more widely distributed in the Caribbean and American tropics, while the third species has a very large range in eastern North America but does not reach as far south as Florida. The members of *Amauropelta* can be recognized relatively easily by their strongly tapering leaf bases: the lowest few sets of pinnae are gradually very reduced toward the ground. Base chromosome number (x) = 27, 29, 31.

KEY TO THE SPECIES OF *AMAUROPELTA* IN OUR FLORA:

1a   Stems are creeping; leaves are deciduous (dying back in winter); plants are found
     north of Florida ⸻ *Amauropelta noveboracensis*

1b   Stems are erect and form short trunks; leaves are evergreen; plants are found in Florida ⸻ 2

    2a   Fronds are no more than 40cm long at maturity; plants are known only from
    southeast Florida ⸻ *Amauropelta sancta*

    2b   Fronds are up to 1.3m long at maturity; plants are known only from west-central
    Florida ⸻ *Amauropelta resinifera*

1a.
*Amauropelta
noveboracensis*

2a.
*Amauropelta
sancta*

2b.
*Amauropelta
resinifera*

| F | S | C | N |

Amauropelta noveboracensis

COMMON NAME(S) New York fern

NOTABLE SYNONYMS *Parathelypteris noveboracensis,*
Thelypteris noveboracensis

STATUS Native (endemic to North America), common

HABITAT/DISTRIBUTION Damp woods and seepy areas,
especially along streams and other waterways; range
extends somewhat west of the Mississippi

Plants are terrestrial and often form large colonies. **Stems** are long creeping, with no scales or a few scattered scales. **Leaves** are up to 85cm long and clustered into tufts that are spaced out along the stem, and sterile and fertile leaves are similar in appearance, with the fertile leaves somewhat taller, narrower, and more erect than the sterile leaves. **Stipes** are up to 25cm long, yellowish to greenish, becoming green toward the blade, with tan to reddish-brown scales at the base. The **rachis** is similar to the stipe, with fine white hairs. The leaf **blade** is up to 60cm long and 15cm wide, 1-pinnate-pinnatifid (becoming pinnatifid toward the tip), and elliptic in overall shape, with the lowest 4–10 pairs of pinnae gradually becoming smaller and shorter, giving the blade a tapered appearance at the base. The blade surfaces have a moderate to dense covering of hairs, especially along the veins on the lower side. **Pinnae** are up to 13cm long and 2.5cm wide, oblong to linear, and usually in 20–24 pairs. The pinna midvein has a distinct narrow groove in the upper surface. **Margins** are smooth or may have slightly rounded, broad teeth. **Veins** are free and may be forked though usually are not; the lowest veins of adjacent pinnules reach the pinnule margins above the sinus. **Sori** are round and located midway between the pinnule midvein and the margin. **Indusia** are tan and may be hairy. 2n = 54 (diploid).

A. A colony of *Amauropelta noveboracensis.*

B. A frond.

C. Tapering base of leaf blade.

D. Lower surface of fertile leaf.

E. Sori on fertile pinnae.

F   S   C   N

Amauropelta resinifera

COMMON NAME(S) Glandular maiden fern, wax-dot maiden fern

NOTABLE SYNONYMS *Thelypteris resinifera*

STATUS Native, rare

HABITAT/DISTRIBUTION Damp woods, swamps, or along waterways; also occurs in the Caribbean, Mexico, and Central and South America

----

Plants are terrestrial. **Stems** are erect and can form short trunks. **Leaves** are up to 1.3m long and clustered toward the tips of the erect stems. Sterile and fertile leaves do not differ in appearance. **Stipes** are up to 25cm long but usually much shorter, with lowest sets of pinnae continuing almost to the ground, brownish toward the base and yellowish above, and with scattered brown scales, especially around the base. The **rachis** is similar to the stipe, and minutely hairy. The leaf **blade** is up to 1.1m long and 40cm wide, 1-pinnate-pinnatifid (becoming pinnatifid toward the tip), and elongate elliptic, with the lowest 6–12 pairs of pinnae gradually becoming smaller and shorter, giving the blade a tapered appearance at the base. The lower blade surface has minute hairs along the veins and sometimes the blade tissue, and scattered round, reddish to yellowish glands (requires magnification to see). The upper surface is smooth or may be sparsely hairy. **Pinnae** are up to 20cm long and 2.5cm wide, narrowly oblong to linear, and in at least 20 pairs. The pinna midvein has a distinct narrow groove in the upper surface. **Margins** are smooth or somewhat rough. **Veins** are free; the lowest veins of adjacent pinnules reach the pinnule margins above the sinus. **Sori** are round and located midway between the pinnule midvein and the margin, or closer to the margin. **Indusia** are tan and sparsely hairy. 2n = 58 (diploid).

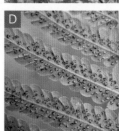

A. Plants of *Amauropelta resinifera*.

B. Tip of a frond.

C. Tapering leaf base.

D. Lower surface of fertile pinna.

E. Upper surface of pinna showing needlelike hairs.

Amauropelta sancta

COMMON NAME(S) Caribbean maiden fern

NOTABLE SYNONYMS *Thelypteris sancta*

STATUS Native, rare

HABITAT/DISTRIBUTION In and around solution holes in rocky hammocks; also occurs in the Caribbean, Mexico, and Central and South America

Plants are terrestrial. **Stems** are erect and can form short trunks. **Leaves** are usually around 25cm long (but can be longer) and clustered toward the tips of the erect stems. Sterile and fertile leaves do not differ in appearance. **Stipes** are up to 5cm long, darker toward the base and yellowish to pale greenish above, with scattered brown scales, especially at the base. The **rachis** is similar to the stipe, and minutely hairy. The leaf **blade** is usually up to 20cm long (or a bit longer) and 9cm wide, 1-pinnate-pinnatifid (becoming pinnatifid toward the tip), and oblanceolate, with the lowest 3–7 pairs of pinnae gradually becoming smaller and shorter, giving the blade a tapered appearance at the base. The lower blade surface may be smooth or have sparse, minute hairs along the veins and sometimes the blade tissue. Scattered round, reddish to yellowish glands may be present (requires magnification to see). The upper surface is smooth or may be sparsely hairy. **Pinnae** are up to 5cm long and 1.2cm wide, and narrowly and asymmetrically triangular. The pinna midvein has a distinct narrow groove in the upper surface. The lowest pinnules on each pinna may be free, with a gap between them and their neighboring pinnules. **Margins** are smooth or bluntly toothed. **Veins** are free; the lowest veins of adjacent pinnules reach the pinnule margins above the sinus. **Sori** are round and located midway between the pinnule midvein and the margin, or closer to the margin. **Indusia** are small, tan, and may be hairy. 2n = unknown.

A. Plants of *Amauropelta sancta*.

B. Fronds.

C. Plant with short trunk.

D. Lower surface of fertile leaf.

FAMILY: THELYPTERIDACEAE

Amblovenatum is a small genus of ferns with only 6 species worldwide, and it is one of several genera that were previously included in *Thelypteris* (p. 475). We have a single species of *Amblovenatum* in our flora: *A. opulentum*, a nonnative that is found only in southernmost Florida. This species is widespread in the tropics, and its native range is thought to be in Asia and the Austral-Pacific region. While it is not yet particularly common in Florida, elsewhere in its introduced range it is known to be an aggressive weed, so it is considered a noxious invasive here as well. Base chromosome number (x) = 36.

*Amblovenatum
opulentum*

Section of a pinna of *Amblovenatum opulentum* showing 2 adjacent pinnules and their venation pattern.

Upper surface of a fertile frond of *Amblovenatum opulentum*, with sori impressed into the leaf from the lower surface.

Amblovenatum opulentum

COMMON NAME(S) Jeweled maiden fern

NOTABLE SYNONYMS *Thelypteris opulenta, Amphineuron opulentum*

STATUS Not native, uncommon

HABITAT/DISTRIBUTION Shaded limestone hammocks in Miami-Dade County, Florida; native to Asia and the Austral-Pacific region

Plants are terrestrial. **Stems** are short creeping, with dark brown scales. **Leaves** are up to about 1.5m tall, and sterile and fertile leaves differ slightly in appearance, with the fertile leaves somewhat larger, and with pinnae that appear somewhat contracted because their margins roll inward. **Stipes** are up to 70cm long, dark brown or purplish brown at the base and becoming lighter toward the blade, with minute hairs (these require a 20× hand lens to see). The **rachis** is similar to the stipe in color but becomes lighter green toward the leaf tip. The leaf **blade** is up to 90cm long and 50cm wide, 1-pinnate-pinnatifid, broadly ovate in overall shape, and widest toward the base, with an abruptly tapering tip (which becomes pinnatifid). The surface of the blade is covered with tiny hairs that require 20× or higher magnification to see. **Pinnae** are up to 30cm long and 2.5cm wide, elongate lanceolate, and typically have numerous minute yellow glands on the lower surface, especially along the pinnule midveins and lateral veins and at the pinnule tips. The pinna midvein has a distinct narrow groove in the upper surface. **Margins** are smooth but often hairy, and the margins may roll inward toward the sori on the fertile pinnae. **Veins** are free; the lowest veins of adjacent pinnules may meet at the base of the sinus or below the sinus, joining into a single vein that runs into the sinus. **Sori** are round and sit near the margins. **Indusia** are present, attached at the center of the sorus, and often have small glandular hairs. 2n = 72 (tetraploid).

A. Frond of *Amblovenatum opulentum.*

B. Abruptly tapering, pinnatifid leaf tip.

C. Upper surface of fertile pinnae.

D. Lower leaf surface, with sori and yellow glands visible.

FAMILY: **BLECHNACEAE**

Anchistea is a monotypic genus, meaning that it includes only 1 species: *A. virginica*. Commonly known as the Virginia chain fern, *A. virginica* is readily identifiable by the unique, chain-like arrangement of elongated sori that run along the midveins of its pinnules. This feature, combined with its distinct venation pattern and very dark, almost black stipe bases, will help distinguish this species from other, similar-looking ferns. This species was previously included in the genus *Woodwardia* (as *W. virginica*). As in other members of the family Blechnaceae, young leaves of *A. virginica* often have a reddish color that is useful in identifying the species before the leaves reach maturity. Base chromosome number (x) = 35.

Anchistea
virginica

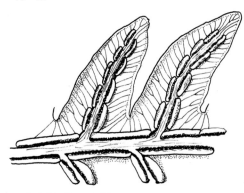

Sori of *Anchistea virginica*

Lower leaf surface of *Anchistea virginica* showing the distinct venation pattern.

Anchistea virginica

COMMON NAME(S) Virginia chain fern

NOTABLE SYNONYMS *Woodwardia virginica*

STATUS Native (endemic to North America), common

HABITAT/DISTRIBUTION Moist habitats, including swamps, bogs, fens, marshes, and other wetlands, as well as shaded forest edges and roadside ditches; range extends into Texas

Plants are terrestrial. **Stems** are long creeping and ropy, with scattered dark brown to black scales. **Leaves** are up to 1.1m long and often spread apart from one another along the stem. Fertile and sterile leaves do not differ in appearance. **Stipes** are up to 50cm long, swollen and dark at the base, purplish to black but becoming lighter and yellowish to green toward the blade. The **rachis** is dark purplish brown to green, smooth but scaly, and grooved. The leaf **blade** is 1-pinnate-pinnatifid, up to 60cm long, and narrowly ovate and widest toward the middle, with a mix of hairs and scales, though typically only the hairs persist into maturity. **Pinnae** are 6–16cm long and 1–3.5cm wide, linear to narrowly lanceolate and deeply lobed (pinnatifid). **Margins** are dentate to serrate. **Pinna midveins** may be somewhat scaly. **Pinnule midveins** may be more or less prominent, and the **lateral veins** of the pinnules are netted toward the pinnule center but then become free and forked toward the pinnule margins. **Sori** are elongated and linear, running in distinct chain-like rows along the pinna and pinnule midveins, and open toward the midveins. **Indusia** are present and open toward the midvein. 2n = 70 (diploid).

A. A colony of *Anchistea virginica*.

B. Reddish young leaves.

C. Sterile pinnae with the characteristic venation pattern of this species.

D. Immature fertile pinna.

E. Mature fertile pinna, with sori opening toward the midveins.

FAMILY: **ANEMIACEAE**

Members of *Anemia* and related genera are sometimes referred to as the flowering ferns because of the somewhat showy sporangia-bearing segments of their leaves. The 2 species in our flora can usually be readily distinguished from one another by their level of leaf dimorphism: *A. adiantifolia* is only partly dimorphic, with the fertile leaves having both a long-stalked, fertile segment and an expanded, sterile blade segment, while *A. wrightii* is usually entirely dimorphic, with completely separate sterile and fertile leaves. However, *A. wrightii* can occasionally be found with a partially dimorphic form like that of *A. adiantifolia*; in this case, the smaller overall size and much more delicate texture of *A. wrightii* can help distinguish it. Base chromosome number (x) = 38.

The large, central frond pointing to the right is *Anemia adiantifolia*, and smaller fronds of *A. wrightii* are around its base, several of them pointing to the left.

Fertile leaf segment
of *Anemia adiantifolia*.

KEY TO THE SPECIES OF *ANEMIA* IN OUR FLORA:

1a   Plants are always partly dimorphic, with the stipe separating just below the blade into 2 segments, one a sterile, expanded blade and the other an upright stalk with contracted, fertile pinnae; the sterile leaf blade is coarse or leathery, with bluntly lobed pinnules, and is typically 3-pinnate; the fertile segment of the leaf can bring the total leaf height up to 85cm ·· *Anemia adiantifolia*

1b   Plants are usually entirely dimorphic, with separate sterile and fertile leaves, though occasionally a single leaf will have both a sterile and a fertile segment, as in *A. adiantifolia* above; the sterile leaf blade is finely textured, with long, deeply toothed pinnules, and is 1-pinnate-pinnatifid to 2-pinnate; the fertile segment of the leaf can bring the total leaf height up to 25cm ·· *Anemia wrightii*

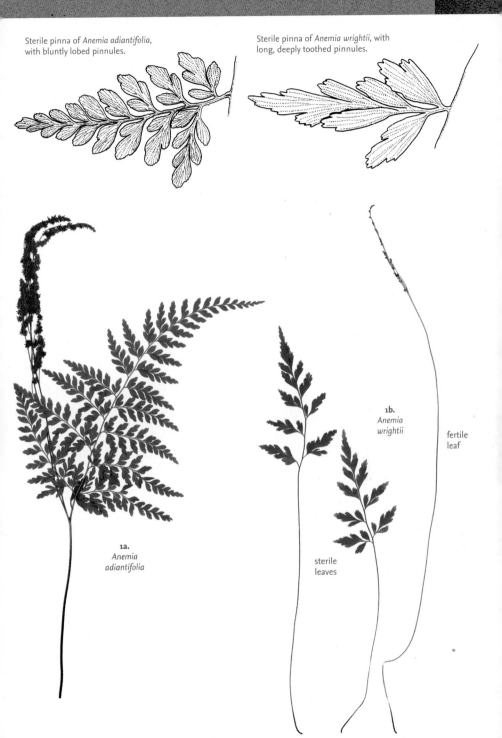

Sterile pinna of *Anemia adiantifolia*, with bluntly lobed pinnules.

Sterile pinna of *Anemia wrightii*, with long, deeply toothed pinnules.

1a.
Anemia adiantifolia

1b.
Anemia wrightii

sterile leaves

fertile leaf

Anemia adiantifolia

COMMON NAME(S) Pine fern, maidenhair pineland fern

STATUS Native, somewhat common

HABITAT/DISTRIBUTION Rocky hammocks and pinelands, typically on limestone; also occurs in the Caribbean, Mexico, and Central and South America

Plants are terrestrial and often epipetric. **Stems** are slender and short creeping, with dark, narrow hairs. **Stipes** are yellowish to brown or black, and smooth to hairy, with hairs similar to those on the stem. The **rachis** is green and smooth, or with scattered hairs. **Leaves** are partly dimorphic and erect, but with the sterile blade portion spreading while the fertile stalk remains upright. The **stipe** is up to 40cm long (typically ½–⅔ the total length of the leaf) and separates at the top into 2 segments, one a sterile, expanded blade and the other a slender stalk with several fertile sporangia-bearing pinnae that lack obvious, expanded blade tissue. The **sterile segment** is up to 60cm tall, while the erect **fertile segment** can bring the leaf to a total height of 85cm. The **blade** is narrowly to broadly triangular, 3-pinnate, up to 35cm wide, and coarse to leathery and may have small, stiff white hairs on the pinnules that disappear with age; sterile **pinnae** are in 10–18 pairs, alternate to nearly opposite, and oblanceolate to narrowly triangular, with lobed pinnules. **Fertile pinnae** are present only in the upper half of the fertile segment and are reduced to fingerlike projections bearing clusters of globose sporangia that are green when young and become orange brown at maturity. **Margins** are minutely toothed. **Veins** are free. 2n = 76, 114, 152 (i.e., diploid, triploid, and tetraploid cytotypes are known).

A. Frond of *Anemia adiantifolia*.

B. Fertile leaf tip.

C. Dark scales on the stipe.

D. Fertile leaf segment with open sporangia.

F S C N

Anemia wrightii

COMMON NAME(S) Wright's pineland fern

STATUS Native, rare

HABITAT/DISTRIBUTION Solution holes and pinelands in Miami-Dade County, Florida, typically on limestone; also occurs in the Caribbean

Plants are terrestrial and often epipetric. **Stems** are slender and short creeping, with dark, narrow hairs. **Leaves** are entirely dimorphic, the sterile leaves spreading outward while the fertile stalks are erect (much less commonly, this species can have a single leaf type similar to that of *A. adiantifolia*, with the stipe separating just below the blade into a sterile blade segment and a fertile stalk). **Stipes** are yellowish to brown or black, and smooth to hairy, with hairs similar to those on the stem. The **rachis** is green and smooth, or with scattered hairs. **Sterile leaves** are up to 10cm long, 1-pinnate-pinnatifid to 2-pinnate, and narrowly to broadly triangular, with the blade up to 6cm long and 4cm wide and finely textured, and may have small, stiff white hairs on the pinnules that disappear with age; **sterile pinnae** are in 2–4 pairs, alternate to nearly opposite, and narrowly triangular to oblanceolate, with smooth-sided pinnules that are long toothed at the tips. **Fertile leaves** are up to 25cm long and 2.5cm wide, with widely spaced **fertile pinnae** that are reduced to fingerlike projections bearing clusters of globose sporangia that are present only in the tip-most few centimeters of the leaf. **Margins** are minutely toothed. **Veins** are free. 2n = unknown.

A

B

C

A. Frond of *Anemia wrightii*.

B. Fronds.

C. Fertile pinnae with sporangia visible.

FAMILY: DRYOPTERIDACEAE

Arachniodes is a genus of ferns native to the global tropics, and we have 1 introduced species in North America, *A. simplicior*. This species was originally introduced to South Carolina but has since spread in the southeast because of its popularity as a horticultural plant; it can often be found in gardens, or as an escapee that has naturalized. The species is easily recognized by 2 features: 1) the distinct variegated coloration of the pinnae, which are yellow to light greenish at the center, along the midvein, but become significantly darker toward the margins, giving the leaves a somewhat striped appearance overall; and 2) the lowermost pinnae, which have an exaggerated innermost lower pinnule that is greatly elongated and is itself further divided. Base chromosome number (x) = 41.

*Arachniodes
simplicior*

A. A colony of *Arachniodes simplicior*.

B. Plants of *Arachniodes simplicior*.

C. Upper leaf surface showing color variegation.

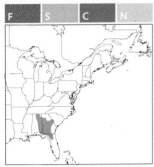

Arachniodes simplicior

COMMON NAME(S) East Indian holly fern

STATUS Not native, uncommon

HABITAT/DISTRIBUTION Escapes from cultivation in the south (where it may be planted in landscaping) and can become established in damp woods; native to Asia

Plants are terrestrial. **Stems** are short creeping to somewhat long creeping, with dense light to dark brown or blackish scales. **Leaves** are up to 85cm long and 40cm wide, typically evergreen, and distinctly variegated in color, with yellow to light green pinna centers that darken toward the margins. Fertile and sterile leaves do not differ in appearance. **Stipes** are light yellow to light brown, with tan to orange-brown or dark brown scales, and are up to 46cm long. **Rachises** are similar to stipes. The leaf **blade** is 2–3-pinnate: typically strongly 3-pinnate at the base, where the lower innermost pinnule is itself further divided, and then becoming 2-pinnate through the rest of the blade until the very tip, which becomes pinnatifid. The blade is broadly triangular to somewhat pentagonal (5-sided), up to 40cm wide, and often has scattered fine scales on the lower surface. **Pinnae** are usually in 3–5 pairs and are up to 18cm long and 4cm wide (though the lowest, innermost pinnule may be longer). **Margins** are spiny to finely toothed. The pinna **midveins** may be grooved on the lower surface, and if so, this groove continues into the rachis; the lateral veins are free and forked. **Sori** are round. **Indusia** are round reniform (kidney bean shaped but curved essentially into a circle) and attached at 1 side, though they may appear to be attached at the center. 2n = 164 (tetraploid).

A. Plants of *Arachniodes simplicior*.

B. Lower surface of fertile pinnae, showing mature sori, some of which have lost their papery indusia.

C. Mature sori that have dispersed their spores.

D. Stipe base with dense covering of brown scales.

FAMILY: PTERIDACEAE

Argyrochosma is a genus with about 20 species globally, most of which occur in the Americas, though 1 species is endemic to China. We also have a single species in eastern North America, but its range extends only slightly into this region. *Argyrochosma dealbata* is most similar in appearance to members of *Pellaea*, but they can easily be separated by the presence of a waxy farina on the lower surface of the leaves in *Argyrochosma* and its absence in *Pellaea*, and by the size of the ultimate leaf segments (pinnules): these are less than 4mm wide in *Argyrochosma* and more than 4mm wide in *Pellaea*. Base chromosome number (x) = 27.

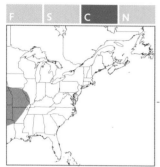

Argyrochosma dealbata

COMMON NAME(S) Powdery false cloak fern

STATUS Native (endemic to North America), uncommon

HABITAT/DISTRIBUTION Rocky cliffs and ledges, on calcareous substrates; range extends into western North America

----

Plants are terrestrial and epipetric. **Stems** are compact and erect, with brown scales. **Leaves** are up to 15cm long, and fertile and sterile leaves do not differ in appearance. **Stipes** are up to 10cm long and reddish brown, with brown scales near the base but otherwise smooth. **Rachises** are similar to stipes. The leaf **blade** is 3–5-pinnate at the base, broadly lanceolate to triangular, up to 7cm long and 5cm wide, smooth on the upper surface (or with a few glands), and with a dense coating of whitish farina on the lower surface. **Pinnae** are up to 2.5cm long and 2cm wide, with stalks similar to the rachis, and pinnules or ultimate segments that are elliptic, with rounded tips, and less than 4mm wide. **Margins** are smooth and strongly inrolled, forming a **false indusium** that covers the **sporangia**. **Veins** are free and pinnately branched. 2n = 54 (diploid).

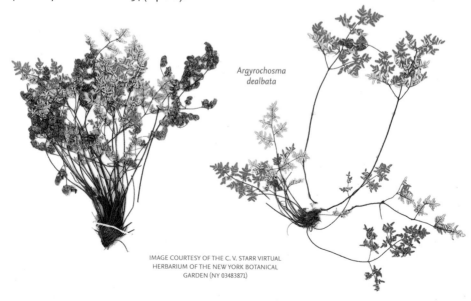

Argyrochosma dealbata

IMAGE COURTESY OF THE C. V. STARR VIRTUAL HERBARIUM OF THE NEW YORK BOTANICAL GARDEN (NY 03483871)

FAMILY: **PTERIDACEAE**

Aspidotis is a small genus of dry-adapted ferns endemic to North America, with its 4 species found predominantly in the western part of the continent and into Mexico. One of these species has a disjunct distribution, with several small populations known in the east, in Québec. *Aspidotis densa* is unlikely to be confused with any other eastern species, except perhaps for close relatives in the Pteridaceae; its smooth stipe and blade surfaces, linear leaf segments, and dentate margins on the sterile pinnules will help distinguish it from these. Base chromosome number (x) = 30.

Aspidotis densa

COMMON NAME(S) Dense lace fern, serpentine fern

STATUS Native (endemic to North America), rare

HABITAT/DISTRIBUTION Rocky slopes and outcrops, especially on serpentine; also occurs in western North America

Plants are terrestrial and epipetric. **Stems** are short creeping and ascending at the tips, with dark brown scales that may have lighter edges. **Leaves** are up to 25cm long; fertile leaves may be longer and more erect than sterile leaves and have narrower, more upward-pointing pinnules. **Stipes** are up to 15cm long, dark reddish brown, grooved on the upper surface, and smooth. **Rachises** are similar to stipes. The leaf **blade** is 3–4-pinnate, triangular to elongate triangular, up to 10cm long and 6cm wide, smooth, and somewhat leathery. **Pinnae** are up to 3cm long and 2cm wide, with short green stalks, and pinnules or ultimate segments are lanceolate to linear, with pointed tips, and up to 8mm wide. **Margins** are widely dentate on sterile pinnae; on fertile pinnae, margins are wavy to shallowly toothed and are strongly inrolled, forming a **false indusium** that covers the **sporangia**. **Veins** are free and unbranched. 2n = 60 (diploid).

sterile leaves

fertile leaves

Aspidotis densa

FAMILY: **ASPLENIACEAE**

Asplenium is the largest genus of ferns in eastern North America, with more than 30 species in the flora. This number includes fertile diploids and tetraploids as well as numerous sterile hybrids. Globally, *Asplenium* is also one of the largest fern genera, with at least 700 species described worldwide. The genus gets its common name, spleenworts, from early herbalist practices that used it to treat ailments of the spleen (the suffix "-wort" simply refers to "plant," or specifically to a plant's presumed medicinal properties). The *Asplenium* species in our flora vary considerably in some of their most obvious features, such as size and level of leaf division, but in general they are easy to distinguish from other eastern North American ferns. Most of our *Asplenium* species are quite small in stature, and they all have linear, indusiate sori that occur on only 1 side of a vein. A handful of taxa in *Athyrium* (p. 183), *Deparia* (p. 257), *Diplazium* (p. 266), and *Homalosorus* (p. 315) also have linear sori that look somewhat similar to those in *Asplenium*, but the overall plant size and examination of additional characters (see the key to genera, p. 32) should enable *Asplenium* species to be fairly easily distinguished from all other ferns. In particular, *Asplenium* species have clathrate scales on their stems and stipe bases, which you may need a 10–20x hand lens to see well. These scales resemble stained-glass windows, with transparent panes between brown scaffolding.

The North American *Asplenium* flora has long been of interest to avocational and professional botanists because of the complex reticulate relationships among these species, and there are several distinct hybrid complexes in our region (see figure below). *Asplenium* taxa are notorious for their tendency to form hybrids, and to undergo whole genome duplication to form fertile polyploid species. Some *Asplenium* hybrids are relatively common, as they are able to persist perennially via vegetative growth despite their inability to reproduce via spores, while others are extremely rare and are found only occasionally. Hybrids and polyploids may look somewhat intermediate between their parental taxa, or they may closely resemble one or the other of their parents. A cross between 2 species may yield a sterile hybrid, a fertile polyploid, or both, and distinguishing these from one another and from the progenitor species can provide either an enjoyable afternoon of botanical entertainment or hours of torment, depending on one's perspective. Several of the common hybrids are named below and are included in the key, but all are capable of variability in their morphology, and individual plants of the same hybrid taxon can look different from one another, in addition to being more or less similar to either parent. The key can be used as a guide, but if you have a suspected hybrid, it is worth consulting the descriptions for all species that could potentially be its progenitors. Base chromosome number (x) = 36.

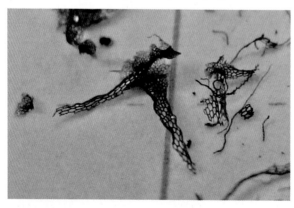

Clathrate scales.

Appalachian _Asplenium_ complex:

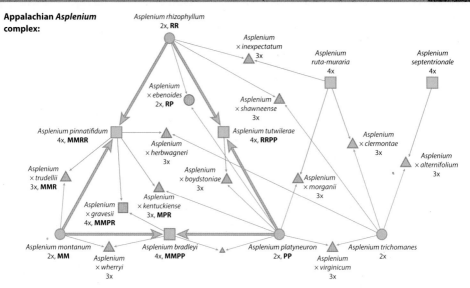

Florida _Asplenium_ complexes:

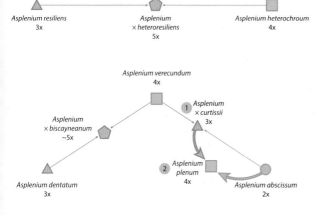

Relationships among _Asplenium_ species in eastern North America. Blue circles are fertile diploids (2x), and green squares are fertile allotetraploids (4x). Some of the diploids have traditionally been assigned letters to indicate their genomic contributions to hybrids, and these are given in bold text. Gray circles, triangles, squares, and pentagons are sterile diploids, triploids, tetraploids, and pentaploids, respectively. Arrows show the direction of genetic contribution from parental toward offspring taxa, with wide arrows where crosses have produced fertile hybrids, and narrow arrows for sterile hybrids. For more information about interpreting these figures, see p. 12.

Asplenium hybrids in Eastern North America

1. _A._ × _alternifolium_ (alternate-leaved spleenwort; 3x) = _A. septentrionale_ subsp. _septentrionale_ (4x) × _A. trichomanes_ (2x)

2. _A._ × _biscayneanum_ (Biscayne spleenwort; 5x) = _A. verecundum_ (4x) × _A. dentatum_ subsp. _dentatum_ (3x)

3. _A._ × _curtissii_ (Curtiss's spleenwort; 3x) = _A. verecundum_ (4x) × _A. abscissum_ (2x)

4. _A._ × _ebenoides_ (Scott's spleenwort; 2x) = _A. rhizophyllum_ (2x) × _A. platyneuron_ (2x)

5. _A._ × _gravesii_ (Graves's spleenwort; 4x) = _A. pinnatifidum_ (4x) × _A. bradleyi_ (4x)

6. _A._ × _heteroresiliens_ (Morzenti's spleenwort; 5x) = _A. resiliens_ (3x) × _A. heterochroum_ (4x)

7. _A._ × _kentuckiense_ (Kentucky spleenwort; 3x) = _A. pinnatifidum_ (4x) × _A. platyneuron_ (2x)

8. _A._ × _trudellii_ (Trudell's spleenwort; 3x) = _A. pinnatifidum_ (4x) × _A. montanum_ (2x)

A & B. *Asplenium* × *alternifolium.*

C & D. *Asplenium* × *biscayneanum.*

E & F. *Asplenium* × *curtissii.*

G. *Asplenium* × *ebenoides.*

H & I. *Asplenium* × *gravesii.*

BOTH PHOTOGRAPHS BY ALAN CRESSLER

J & K. *Asplenium* × *heteroresiliens.*

L. *Asplenium* × *kentuckiense*.
PHOTOGRAPH BY ALAN CRESSLER.

M & N. *Asplenium* × *trudellii*.

KEY TO THE SPECIES OF *ASPLENIUM* IN OUR FLORA
(including some of the more common hybrids):

1a **The leaf blade is simple and undivided, or extremely narrow and forked near the tip** ⋯⋯⋯⋯⋯⋯ 2

  2a The leaf blade is narrow and linear, only 2–3mm wide, and forked
near the tip; plants have a somewhat grasslike appearance overall ⋯⋯⋯⋯ *Asplenium septentrionale* subsp. *septentrionale*

  2b The leaf blade is lanceolate, more than 10mm wide, and not forked; plants are not
at all grasslike in appearance ⋯⋯⋯⋯⋯⋯⋯⋯⋯⋯⋯⋯⋯⋯⋯⋯⋯⋯⋯⋯⋯⋯⋯⋯ 3

    3a The leaf blade is widest at the base and elongate triangular, often with a dramatically
elongated, narrowing tip; the leaves are typically held prostrate or spreading against the
substrate; the leaf tip often forms a new plantlet where it touches the substrate ⋯⋯⋯⋯ *Asplenium rhizophyllum*

    3b The leaf blade is widest toward the middle and linear to somewhat lanceolate,
without an elongated tip; the leaves are held erect and may be spreading but do
not rest against the substrate; plantlets do not form at the leaf tips ⋯⋯⋯⋯⋯⋯⋯⋯⋯⋯⋯ 4

      4a The leaf blade is squared off or heart shaped at the base, or the
base may take the shape of 2 curling lobes; plants are known only
from Alabama and New York ⋯⋯⋯⋯⋯⋯⋯⋯⋯⋯⋯⋯⋯ *Asplenium scolopendrium* var. *americanum*

      4b The leaf blade tapers gradually at the base; plants are known
only from southern Florida ⋯⋯⋯⋯⋯⋯⋯⋯⋯⋯⋯⋯⋯⋯⋯⋯⋯⋯⋯⋯ *Asplenium serratum*

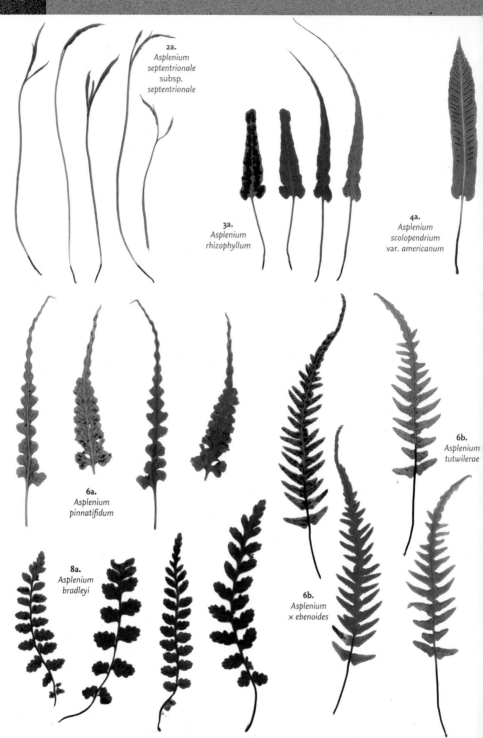

2a.
*Asplenium
septentrionale*
subsp.
septentrionale

3a.
*Asplenium
rhizophyllum*

4a.
*Asplenium
scolopendrium*
var. *americanum*

6a.
*Asplenium
pinnatifidum*

6b.
*Asplenium
tutwilerae*

8a.
*Asplenium
bradleyi*

6b.
*Asplenium
× ebenoides*

1b   The leaf blade is pinnatifid or up to 4-pinnate 5

   5a   The leaf blade is lobed or strongly pinnatifid at the base, with a long pinnatifid
tip that is up to ca. ⅓ the length of the entire blade 6

      6a   The stipe is dark brown at the base but becomes green farther up; the blade
is narrowly triangular .... *Asplenium pinnatifidum*

      6b   The stipe is dark brown to black along its whole length;
thc blade is oblong to lanceolate .... *Asplenium × ebenoides* and *Asplenium tutwilerae*

   5b   The leaf blade is 1-pinnate or more divided 7

      7a   The leaf blade is 1- or 2-pinnate only at the base, becoming strongly
pinnatifid in at least the tip-most ¼ of the blade 8

         8a   The leaf blade is 2-pinnate at the base .... *Asplenium bradleyi*

         8b   The leaf blade is 1-pinnate at the base 9

            9a   The leaf blade is broadest at the base; the stipe is brown at the
very base and then quickly becomes green .... *Asplenium × trudellii*

            9b   The leaf blade is broadest at or just below the middle; the stipe is brown
at the base and becomes green closer to the blade, or the brown extends into
the rachis 10

               10a The stipe is brown at the base and becomes green somewhat
close to the blade; the rachis is green throughout and is distinctly
flattened .... *Asplenium × kentuckiense*

               10b The stipe is brown throughout, and the brown sometimes extends
into the rachis .... *Asplenium × gravesii*

      7b   The leaf blade is 1-pinnate or more throughout (the very tip may be pinnatifid
in some species, but this does not make up a substantial portion of the blade) 11

         11a The leaf blade is only 1-pinnate; pinnae may be variously lobed or toothed 12

            12a The leaf blade has fewer than 4 pairs of pinnae; the leaf blade is
strongly triangular .... *Asplenium pumilum*

            12b The leaf blade is divided into more than 5 pairs of pinnae; the blade
is lanceolate tow oblong 13

9a.
*Asplenium
× trudellii*

12a.
*Asplenium
pumilium*

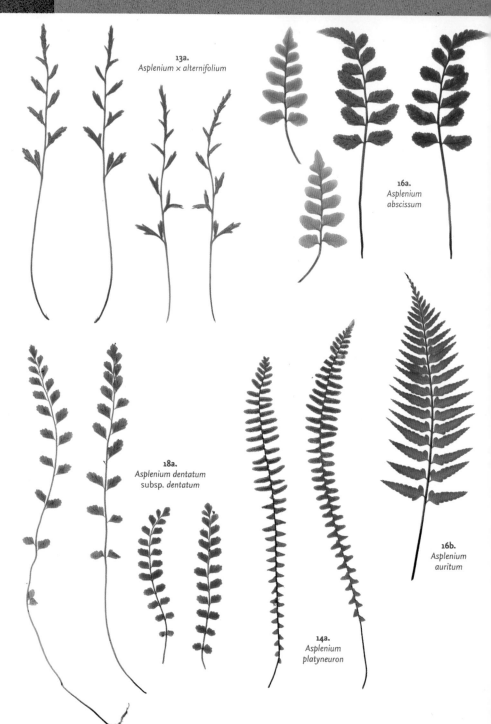

13a.
Asplenium × alternifolium

16a.
Asplenium abscissum

18a.
Asplenium dentatum subsp. dentatum

14a.
Asplenium platyneuron

16b.
Asplenium auritum

13a The pinnae are strongly alternate and spread apart along the rachis; pinnae are very narrow (less than 5mm wide) and elongated and have lobes only at the tip and not along the sides ⸺ *Asplenium × alternifolium*

13b The pinnae are opposite to somewhat alternate but are close together along the rachis; pinnae are generally more than 5mm wide and variously shaped, and if teeth or lobes are present, they are along the entire pinna margin ⸺ 14

14a Each pinna has a distinct auricle at its base, and these strongly overlap the rachis; plants are slightly dimorphic, with the fertile leaves taller and held more erect and the sterile leaves shorter and spreading outward ⸺ *Asplenium platyneuron*

14b Pinnae may or may not have auricles at the base, but if so, the auricles do not overlap the rachis; plants are not dimorphic; leaves are all alike ⸺ 15

15a The leaf blade is more than 4cm wide at maturity ⸺ 16

16a Plants are terrestrial, on damp limestone or rarely on the bases of old live oaks; the leaf blade has fewer than 10 pairs of pinnae ⸺ *Asplenium abscissum*

16b Plants are epiphytic on a variety of trees; the leaf blade has more than 10 pairs of pinnae ⸺ *Asplenium auritum*

15b The leaf blade is less than 4cm wide at maturity ⸺ 17

17a The rachis is green throughout its length ⸺ 18

18a Plants are found in Florida ⸺ *Asplenium dentatum* subsp. *dentatum*

18b Plants are found in the northern U.S. or southern Canada ⸺ *Asplenium viride*

17b The rachis is brown or black throughout its length ⸺ 19

18b.
Asplenium viride

19a Pinnae typically have fewer than 3 sori, which are located along and parallel to the lower margin of the pinna ⸺ *Asplenium monanthes*

19b Pinnae typically have more than 3 sori, which are located along and parallel to the lateral veins ⸺ 20

20a Pinnae are round to somewhat egg shaped ⸺ *Asplenium trichomanes* (both subspecies)

20b Pinnae are oblong or elongate rectangular ⸺ 21

21a Pinna margins are entire or have only a few teeth or lobes; pinnae often point backward/downward; pinnae are generally opposite for the whole length of the blade ⸺ *Asplenium resiliens*

21b Pinna margins are toothed, either all the way around or at least along the upper margin; pinnae point straight outward or slightly upward; pinnae are opposite toward the base of the blade but may become alternate toward the tip ⸺ 22

22a Pinna margins are distinctly toothed all the way around; an auricle may or may not be present at the pinna base; veins in the pinnae are distinct ⸺ *Asplenium heterochroum*

22b Pinna margins are shallowly or bluntly toothed, often only on the upper margin, with the lower margin smooth; an auricle is typically present at the pinna base; veins in the pinnae are obscure ⸺ *Asplenium × heteroresiliens*

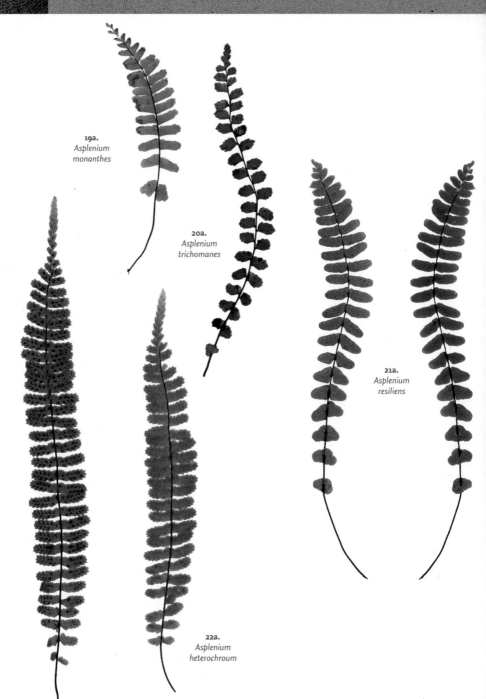

19a.
*Asplenium
monanthes*

20a.
*Asplenium
trichomanes*

21a.
*Asplenium
resiliens*

22a.
*Asplenium
heterochroum*

11b The leaf blade is 2–4-pinnate 23

    23a Plants are found north of northern Georgia and Alabama 24

        24a The leaf blade is 2-pinnate and has 2–5 pairs of pinnae; the stipe is green throughout its length; the leaf is broadly triangular .... *Asplenium ruta-muraria* var. *cryptolepis*

        24b The leaf blade is 2–3-pinnate and has more than 5 pairs of pinnae; the stipe is dark at the base; the leaf is broadly lanceolate .... *Asplenium montanum*

    23b Plants are found in Florida 25

        25a The leaf blade is linear in outline, with the sides nearly parallel .... *Asplenium* × *biscayneanum*

        25b The leaf blade is lanceolate to narrowly ovate or triangular 26

            26a The lower portion of the rachis is dark 27

                27a The blade is widest at the base; the leaf blade is 2-pinnate, and the pinnules are wide and lobed .... *Asplenium* × *curtissii*

                27b The blade is widest toward the middle; the leaf blade is 2–3-pinnate, and the ultimate pinnules are very narrow .... *Asplenium verecundum*

            26b The rachis is green throughout its length 28

                28a The leaf blade becomes pinnatifid toward the tip; the pinnae are divided completely into pinnules only at the pinna base; the rest of the pinna is merely lobed .... *Asplenium plenum*

                28b The leaf blade is 2-pinnate throughout; the pinnae are divided into pinnules along the entire length of the pinna .... *Asplenium cristatum*

22b.
Asplenium ×
heteroresiliens

24a.
*Asplenium
ruta-muraria*
var. *cryptolepis*

24b.
Asplenium montanum

25a.
Asplenium × biscayneum

27a.
Asplenium × curtissii

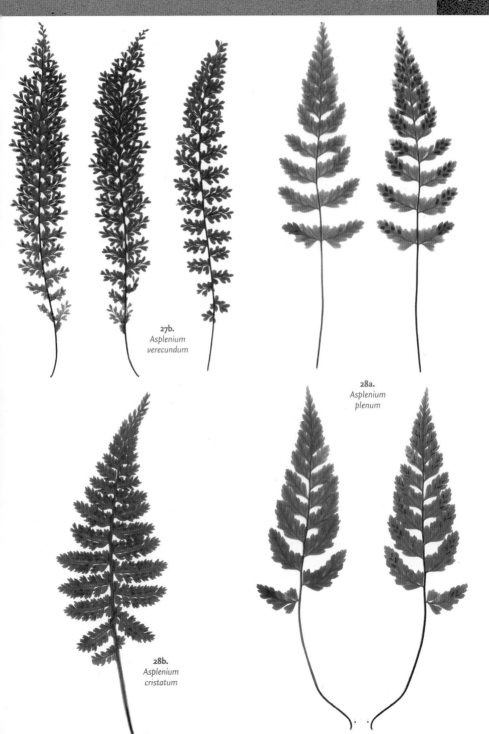

27b.
*Asplenium
verecundum*

28a.
*Asplenium
plenum*

28b.
*Asplenium
cristatum*

F   S   C   N

Asplenium abscissum

COMMON NAME(S) Abscised spleenwort, cutleaf spleenwort

STATUS Native, rare

HABITAT/DISTRIBUTION Limestone substrates such as sinkholes, boulders, and ledges; also occurs in the Caribbean, Mexico, and Central and South America

Plants are terrestrial or epipetric. **Stems** are erect and unbranched, with brown, clathrate scales. **Leaves** are arching to pendent; plants often cling to the sides of rocky surfaces, with the leaves hanging downward. Sterile and fertile leaves do not differ in appearance. **Stipes** are smooth, green to gray, and up to 20cm long, with a groove along the upper surface. The **rachis** is green and smooth. **Blades** are 1-pinnate (becoming pinnatifid at the tip) and broadly triangular in overall shape, up to 20cm long and 9cm wide and tapering gradually at the tip but not at the base (the base is truncate). **Pinnae** are linear to lanceolate, up to 8cm long and 1.5cm wide, typically occurring in 4–8 pairs per leaf, and may have a small auricle at the base of each pinna, on the upper edge. **Margins** are entire to coarsely toothed. Lateral **veins** are free and obscure. **Sori** are linear, with indusia, and usually occur in 2–9 pairs per pinna, with each pair having 1 sorus on either side of the pinna midrib, located midway between the midrib and pinna margin and at an acute angle to the midrib, pointing toward the pinna tip. 2n = 72 (diploid).

A. Plants of *Asplenium abscissum*.

B. Upper leaf surface.

C. Lower leaf surface with sori.

D. Close-up of sori.

Asplenium auritum

COMMON NAME(S) Eared spleenwort, auricled spleenwort

NOTABLE SYNONYMS *Asplenium erosum* was previously treated as a synonym of *A. auritum* but is now usually recognized as a separate species endemic to the Caribbean.

STATUS Native, rare

HABITAT/DISTRIBUTION Shaded forests and hammocks, on older tree trunks and occasionally on mossy, dead stumps; also occurs in the Caribbean, Mexico, and Central and South America

Plants are epiphytic. **Stems** are erect and unbranched, with brown, clathrate scales. **Leaves** are erect, and sterile and fertile leaves do not differ in appearance. **Stipes** are green to purplish black, up to 12cm long, and smooth, though sometimes with a few scattered scales toward the base. The **rachis** is green to black, and smooth. The leaf **blade** is 1–2-pinnate and narrowly triangular, tapering gradually at the tip but not at the base (the base is truncate), and up to 35cm long and 18cm wide. **Pinnae** are linear to narrowly lanceolate, up to 9cm long and 2.5cm wide, typically occurring in 10–22 pairs per leaf, and with a conspicuous auricle at the base of each pinna, on the upper edge. This lobe may be so deeply cut that it effectively becomes a separate pinnule rather than an auricle. **Margins** are usually highly toothed. Lateral **veins** are free and conspicuous. **Sori** are linear, with indusia, and lie almost parallel to the pinna midrib, usually in 4–10 pairs per pinna, with each pair having 1 sorus on either side of the midrib. 2n = unknown.

A. Plant of *Asplenium auritum* hanging from a tree.

B. Upper leaf surface.

C. Lower leaf surface.

D. Fertile pinnae with sori.

E. Mature sori that have released their spores.

Asplenium bradleyi

COMMON NAME(S) Bradley's spleenwort

STATUS Native (endemic to eastern North America), rare

HABITAT/DISTRIBUTION Acidic rocks (such as granite and sandstone) throughout the Appalachian region, often wedged into tiny crevices

---

Plants are terrestrial and epipetric. **Stems** are short creeping to erect, usually unbranched, and with dark reddish-brown to brown, clathrate scales. **Leaves** are arching to somewhat pendent and form a small cluster. Sterile and fertile leaves do not differ in appearance. **Stipes** are up to 13cm long, dark reddish brown or purplish brown, and with scales at the base that gradually grade into hairs. The **rachis** is dark reddish brown or purplish brown at the base and becomes green toward the tip; it may be sparsely hairy. The **blade** is 1-pinnate-pinnatifid to 2-pinnate, up to 20cm long and 6cm wide, and is narrowly lanceolate, tapering acutely at the tip but not at the base (the base is truncate). **Pinnae** are ovate to lanceolate (or may be deltate toward the base of the leaf), up to 4cm long and 1cm wide, with acute or rounded tips, occurring in 5–15 pairs. **Margins** may be toothed to lobed. Lateral **veins** are free and obscure. **Sori** are linear, with indusia, and with 3 to many pairs per pinna, on either side of the pinna midrib, following the lateral veins. 2n = 144 (tetraploid).

A. Plants of *Asplenium bradleyi*.

B. Upper leaf surface.

C. & D. Lower leaf surfaces, with sori.

Asplenium cristatum

COMMON NAME(S) Hemlock spleenwort, crested spleenwort, parsley spleenwort

STATUS Native, rare

HABITAT/DISTRIBUTION Limestone boulders, ledges, and outcrops; also occurs in the Caribbean and Central and South America

Plants are terrestrial and epipetric. **Stems** are erect or ascending and unbranched, with black, clathrate scales (these may sometimes have lighter margins). **Leaves** are arching to somewhat pendent, forming a small cluster, and sterile and fertile leaves do not differ in appearance. **Stipes** are brown to black or green, smooth except for a few scattered scales toward the base, and up to 17cm long. The **rachis** is smooth and green, usually with distinct wings. The **blade** is 2–3-pinnate, oblong to lanceolate, thin and fine in texture and noticeably bright green, and up to 18cm long and 10cm wide, narrowing gradually at the tip and the base. **Pinnae** are also oblong to lanceolate, up to 5cm long and 1cm wide, and typically occur in 7–20 pairs; pinnae are further divided, with pinnules that are themselves deeply lobed or even fully divided again, bringing the blade to 3-pinnate. The lowermost pinnae are reflexed, pointing down toward the base of the leaf. The leaves have a distinctly lacy look that gives the plant several of its common names. **Margins** are toothed. **Veins** are free to once forked, and prominent. **Sori** are linear, with indusia, usually with 1–4 sori per pinnule, these occurring on both sides of the pinna midrib. 2n = 72 (diploid).

A. Plants of *Asplenium cristatum*.

B. Fronds.

C. Upper leaf surface and wing along the rachis.

D. Lower leaf surface with sori.

F | S | C | N

Asplenium dentatum subsp. *dentatum*

COMMON NAME(S) Toothed spleenwort

NOTABLE SYNONYMS *Asplenium trichomanes-dentatum*

STATUS Native, rare

HABITAT/DISTRIBUTION Limestone substrates, including hammocks, on rocks and sinkhole walls; also occurs in the Caribbean, Mexico, and Central and South America (a second subspecies, *A. dentatum* subsp. *barbadense*, occurs only in the Caribbean)

Plants are terrestrial and epipetric and often form large stands or colonies. **Stems** are erect and unbranched, with black, clathrate scales. **Leaves** are up to 20cm long, and fertile and sterile leaves can be somewhat different in appearance, with fertile leaves longer, held more erect, and with more widely spaced pinnae. **Stipes** are typically up to 6cm long, smooth, and dark at the very base before becoming dull green. The **rachis** is dull green and smooth for its entire length. The leaf **blade** is 1-pinnate, linear, with an elongated pinna at the tip, delicate in texture, and up to 15cm long and 2.5cm wide. **Pinnae** are asymmetrical and ovate, with a narrow base, up to 12mm long and 6mm wide, and typically occur in 5–8 pairs. **Margins** are bluntly toothed. **Veins** are free and may be obvious. **Sori** are linear, with indusia, and there are usually 2–5 sori per pinna, these occurring in the upper half of the pinna. 2n = 108 (triploid).

A. A dense colony of *Asplenium dentatum* subsp. *dentatum* growing on a limestone wall.

B. Fronds.

C. Upper leaf surface.

D. Lower leaf surface with sori.

Asplenium heterochroum

COMMON NAME(S) Varicolored spleenwort

STATUS Native, rare

HABITAT/DISTRIBUTION Limestone substrates, especially in sinkholes, caves, hammocks, and rock walls; also occurs in the Caribbean, Mexico, and Central and South America

Plants are terrestrial and epipetric. **Stems** are ascending to erect and typically unbranched, with black, clathrate scales. **Leaves** are spreading or arching to erect, and sterile and fertile leaves do not differ in appearance. **Stipes** are shiny, dark brown to purplish to black, and up to 5cm long, with black scales toward the base. The **rachis** is smooth and black and may become brownish toward the leaf tip. The **blade** is 1-pinnate, linear to narrowly oblanceolate, and up to 35cm long and 3cm wide, tapering gradually at the base and more acutely at the tip. **Pinnae** are oblong or elliptic and up to 1.5cm long and 0.5cm wide, sometimes with an auricle at the pinna base, on the upper edge; pinnae typically occur in 15–40 pairs, with members of a pair nearly opposite one another across the rachis. **Margins** are crenate to more often serrate. **Veins** are free and prominent. **Sori** are linear, with indusia, and in 3–6 pairs per pinna, with 1 member of each pair on either side of the midrib. 2n = 144 (tetraploid).

A. Plants of *Asplenium heterochroum*.

B. Fronds with elongated tip.

C. Upper leaf surfaces.

D. Lower leaf surfaces with sori.

F	S	C	N

Asplenium monanthes

COMMON NAME(S) Single-sorus fern

STATUS Native, rare

HABITAT/DISTRIBUTION Rocks in damp habitats, especially around seeps and waterfalls; common throughout the tropics worldwide

Plants are terrestrial and epipetric. Stems are erect and unbranched, with black, clathrate scales that lighten toward their margins. Leaves are spreading and up to 35cm long, and sterile and fertile leaves do not differ in appearance. Stipes are bright reddish brown and up to 12cm long, with black scales. The rachis is similar to the stipe, but smooth and without scales. The blade is 1-pinnate, linear, and up to 25cm long and 3cm wide, tapering gradually at the base and more acutely at the tip. Pinnae are oblong or quadrangular and up to 1.5cm long and 0.5cm wide; pinnae typically occur in 10–40 pairs, with members of a pair ranging from nearly opposite to alternate across the rachis. Margins are crenate, with teeth often only on the upper margin, while the lower margin has fewer or no teeth. Veins are free and obscure. Sori are linear, with indusia, typically with only 1 (or at most 3) per pinna; the sori occur on the lower margin, parallel to the margin. 2n = 108 (triploid).

A. A plant of *Asplenium monanthes*.

B. Upper leaf surface (top) and lower leaf surface with sori (bottom).

C. Upper surfaces of leaves.

PHOTOGRAPHS BY ALAN CRESSLER

Asplenium montanum

COMMON NAME(S) Mountain spleenwort

STATUS Native (endemic to eastern North America), somewhat common

HABITAT/DISTRIBUTION Acidic rocks throughout the Appalachian region, including sandstones, especially those with high silica content

---

Plants are terrestrial and epipetric. **Stems** are short creeping and unbranched, with dark brown, clathrate scales. **Leaves** are erect to spreading and up to 22cm long, and sterile and fertile leaves do not differ in appearance. **Stipes** are up to 11cm long and dark brown to black for most of their length but becoming green toward the blade, with black scales at the base and minute hairs throughout. The **rachis** is green, with scattered minute hairs. The **blade** is 1–2-pinnate-pinnatifid, triangular to lanceolate, up to 11cm long and 7cm wide, squared off at the base, and tapering gradually or acutely pointed at the tip. **Pinnae** are triangular to lanceolate and up to 3.5cm long and 2cm wide; pinnae typically occur in 4–10 pairs. **Margins** are coarsely cut and somewhat lacy in appearance. **Veins** are free and obscure. **Sori** are linear, with indusia, typically with 1–15 sori per pinna, running along lateral veins but not in pairs. 2n = 72 (diploid).

A. Plants of *Asplenium montanum*.

B. Fronds.

C. Plants with mature sori.

D. Lower leaf surface with immature sori.

Asplenium pinnatifidum

COMMON NAME(S) Lobed spleenwort

STATUS Native (endemic to North America), somewhat common

HABITAT/DISTRIBUTION Cliffs, ledges, and crevices of acidic rocks such as sandstones; range extends somewhat west of the Mississippi

Plants are terrestrial and epipetric. **Stems** are short creeping to erect, frequently branched, and with dark brown to reddish-brown, clathrate scales. **Leaves** are erect to spreading and up to 27cm long, and sterile and fertile leaves do not differ in appearance. **Stipes** are up to 10cm long and dark brown and shiny toward the base but becoming green toward the blade, with dark brown to reddish-brown scales at the base that grade into small hairs. The **rachis** is green, with scattered minute hairs on only the lower surface. The **blade** is up to 17cm long and 4cm wide and pinnatifid, or may have a single fully cut lobe at the very base but then become pinnatifid. The blade is narrowly triangular, with deeply cut lobes, an elongated tip, and hairs only on the lower surface. **Margins** are bluntly lobed to somewhat toothed. **Veins** are free and obscure. **Sori** are linear, with indusia, typically with 1–6 sori per lobe, running along lateral veins but not in pairs. 2n = 144 (tetraploid).

A. A plant of Asplenium pinnatifidum.

B. Lower leaf surface with sori.

C. Sori that have released their spores.

Asplenium platyneuron

COMMON NAME(S) Ebony spleenwort

STATUS Native, common

HABITAT/DISTRIBUTION Grows on soil (as opposed to rock, like most of our *Asplenium* species), in a variety of forested and disturbed habitats; ranges farther west in North America and also occurs in South Africa, one of the most intriguing disjunct distributions known in ferns

Plants are terrestrial and grow on soil. **Stems** are short creeping and unbranched, with dark brown or black, clathrate scales. **Leaves** are erect to spreading and up to 60cm long, and sterile and fertile leaves differ somewhat in appearance, with fertile leaves longer and held more erect than sterile leaves and having somewhat larger pinnae. **Stipes** are up to 10cm long and shiny, dark brown to reddish brown, with dark brown to black scales at the base. The **rachis** is similar to the stipe, and smooth, without hairs or scales. The **blade** is 1-pinnate, up to 50cm long and 5cm wide, and linear to narrowly lanceolate, with a gradually tapering base. **Pinnae** are up to 2.5cm long and 0.5cm wide and oblong to quadrangular, with a distinct auricle at the pinna base, on the upper edge and sometimes also the lower edge; these auricles overlap the rachis. Pinnae typically occur in 15–45 pairs. **Margins** are roundly to sharply toothed. **Veins** are free and obvious. **Sori** are linear, with indusia, typically with 1–12 pairs of sori per pinna, on both sides of the pinna midvein. 2n = 72 (diploid).

D. Mature sori.
E. Sori that have released their spores.

A. A plant of *Asplenium platyneuron*.
B. The base of the blade, with increasingly small pinnae.
C. Lower leaf surface with immature sori.

Asplenium plenum

COMMON NAME(S) Ruffled spleenwort

STATUS Native (endemic to eastern North America), rare

HABITAT/DISTRIBUTION Known only from scattered hammock forests in Florida, where it occurs on limestone boulders

Plants are terrestrial and epipetric. Stems are erect and unbranched, with black, clathrate scales. Leaves are spreading and up to 20cm long, and sterile and fertile leaves do not differ in appearance. Stipes are up to 6cm, dark brown to black, and smooth. The rachis is dark at the base but quickly becomes green and is smooth, often with wings of tissue. The blade is 1–2-pinnate, up to 14cm long and 5cm wide, and lanceolate. Pinnae are up to 3.5cm long and 1.8cm wide, oblong triangular, and typically occur in 10–20 pairs. The ultimate divisions (pinnules) are often notched at their tips. Margins are smooth. Veins are free and obscure. Sori are linear, with indusia, typically with 1 sorus per ultimate segment or lobe. 2n = 144 (tetraploid).

A. Fronds of *Asplenium plenum*.

B. Upper leaf surface.

C. Lower leaf surface with mature sori.

Asplenium pumilum

COMMON NAME(S) Hairy spleenwort, triangle spleenwort

STATUS Native, rare

HABITAT/DISTRIBUTION Limestone boulders in hammocks; also occurs in the Caribbean, Mexico, and Central and South America

Plants are terrestrial and epipetric. **Stems** are erect and unbranched, with black, clathrate scales that get lighter toward their margins. **Leaves** are held erect and are up to 15cm long, and sterile and fertile leaves do not differ in appearance. **Stipes** are up to 7cm long and green on both sides in small leaves, or darker on the lower surface in larger leaves, with very fine hairs. The **rachis** is green and smooth. The **blade** is strongly triangular and up to 8cm long and 6cm wide, with small hairs on both the upper and lower surfaces. The blade may be a single undivided triangle but more often is divided into up to 5 pinna pairs (most frequently 1–2 pairs plus a triangular terminal segment); the **pinnae** are triangular to ovate, up to 6cm long and 3.5cm wide, with the lowest pair largest and subsequent pairs gradually getting smaller. **Margins** are bluntly lobed to irregularly, roundly toothed. **Veins** are free and obvious. **Sori** are linear, with indusia, typically with 1–15 sori per pinna, on both sides of the pinna midvein but not in obvious pairs. 2n = 72 (diploid).

A. A plant of *Asplenium pumilum.*

B. Lower leaf surface with sori.

C. Close-up of sori.

PHOTOGRAPHS B & C BY ALAN CRESSLER

Asplenium resiliens

COMMON NAME(S) Black-stemmed spleenwort

STATUS Native, uncommon

HABITAT/DISTRIBUTION Cliffs, ledges, and boulders of basic rocks, especially limestones; also occurs in the Caribbean, Mexico, and Central and South America

Plants are terrestrial and epipetric. **Stems** are erect and unbranched, with black, clathrate scales. **Leaves** are erect to spreading and up to 23cm long, and sterile and fertile leaves do not differ in appearance. **Stipes** are up to 3cm long and shiny, dark brown or black, with blackish-brown scales. The **rachis** is similar to the stipe but smooth, without hairs or scales. The **blade** is 1-pinnate, up to 20cm long and 2cm wide, and linear to narrowly oblanceolate, with a gradually tapering base. **Pinnae** are up to 20mm long and 5mm wide and oblong, usually with a distinct auricle at the pinna base, on the upper edge. Pinnae typically occur in 20–40 pairs. **Margins** are smooth to shallowly, roundly toothed. **Veins** are free and obscure. **Sori** are linear, with indusia, typically with 2–5 pairs of sori per pinna, on both sides of the pinna midvein. 2n = 108 (triploid).

A. Plants of *Asplenium resiliens.*

B. Fronds.

C. Leaf bases.

D. Upper (left) and lower (right) leaf surfaces.

Asplenium rhizophyllum

COMMON NAME(S) Walking fern

STATUS Native (endemic to North America), common

HABITAT/DISTRIBUTION Mossy rocks in moist pockets of shaded forests, seepy cliff faces, or damp boulders along streamsides; prefers basic rocks (like limestone) but may also occur on acidic rocks; range extends somewhat west of the Mississippi

----

Plants are terrestrial and epipetric. **Stems** are erect and typically unbranched, with dark brown, clathrate scales. **Leaves** are prostrate and spreading and may appear somewhat flattened against the substrate; sterile and fertile leaves may differ somewhat in appearance, with the fertile leaves larger, longer, and held more erect than the sterile ones. **Stipes** are up to 12cm long and reddish brown to brown toward the base, becoming greener toward the blade. The **rachis** is usually green. The leaf **blade** is undivided and may be somewhat hairy on both surfaces, up to 30cm long and 5cm wide, and deltate to linear-lanceolate in overall shape; the base of the blade is cordate to auriculate or hastate. The **leaf tip** tapers gradually, often to a very long, narrow, drawn-out point, and the apex can be proliferating, with small plantlets forming that take root when the leaf tip contacts the substrate (this gives the leaves the appearance of "walking" along, setting down new plants as they go, which is the source of the species' common name). The leaf **margins** may be slightly wavy and are generally smooth. **Veins** are obscure but often form networks near the midrib and base of the blade. **Sori** are linear and scattered irregularly across the underside of the blade. 2n = 72 (diploid).

A. A colony of *Asplenium rhizophyllum*.

B. Plants.

C. Lower leaf surface with mature sori.

D. Mature sori that have released their spores.

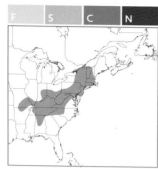

F   S   C   N

Asplenium ruta-muraria var. *cryptolepis*

COMMON NAME(S) Wall rue

STATUS Native (this variety is endemic to North America), uncommon

HABITAT/DISTRIBUTION Cliffs, ledges, boulders, and shale fields, typically on limestone; range extends somewhat west of the Mississippi (additional varieties are described from Europe and Asia)

Plants are terrestrial and epipetric. **Stems** are short creeping to erect and usually branched, with dark brown, clathrate scales. **Leaves** are spreading to erect, and sterile and fertile leaves do not differ in appearance. **Stipes** are up to 9cm long and reddish brown to brown toward the base, becoming greener toward the blade, with dark brown scales at the base that grade into scattered hairs. The **rachis** is green and smooth except for a few scattered minute hairs. The leaf **blade** is 2-pinnate to 2-pinnate-pinnatifid, or occasionally up to 3-pinnate, up to 6cm long and 4cm wide, and deltate ovate to oblanceolate in overall shape. **Pinnae** are up to 30mm long and 20mm wide, deltate ovate, and typically occur in 2–4 pairs. **Margins** are finely toothed. **Veins** are free and obvious. **Sori** are linear, with indusia, typically with up to 5 sori per ultimate segment, on both sides of the pinna midvein. 2n = 144 (tetraploid).

A. Plants of *Asplenium ruta-muraria* var. *cryptolepis*.

B. Fronds.

C. Lower leaf surface with sori.

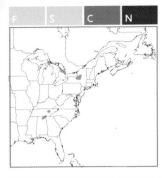

Asplenium scolopendrium var. americanum

COMMON NAME(S) American hart's-tongue fern

NOTABLE SYNONYMS *Phyllitis scolopendrium* var. *americanum*

STATUS Native (this variety endemic to North America), rare

HABITAT/DISTRIBUTION Basic, calcareous rocks, including sinkholes, talus slopes, and cave openings, in deeply shaded forests; disjunct populations occur in New York, Alabama, the southwestern U.S., and Mexico; this variety (*A. scolopendrium* var. *americanum*) is a tetraploid, and a diploid variety (*A. scolopendrium* var. *scolopendrium*) occurs in Europe

Plants are terrestrial, on rock or soil. Stems are erect and unbranched, with brown, narrow, clathrate scales. Leaves are erect to pendent and may form a vase-shaped cluster. Stipes are up to 10cm long, brown to yellowish, and scaly. The rachis is brown to yellowish. The leaf blade is up to 60cm long and 6cm wide, simple and undivided, cordate (heart shaped), and often curling at the base, pointed at the tip, and linear in overall shape, with a tough, smooth texture. Margins are smooth and entire. Lateral veins are free and obscure and occur at right angles to the midrib, or nearly so. Sori are linear, oriented along the lateral veins, and typically present only in the upper half of the leaf blade. 2n = 144 (tetraploid).

A. A colony of *Asplenium scolopendrium* var. *americanum*.

B. Plants.

C. Lower leaf surface with sori.

D. Leaf bases.

E. Mature sori.

Asplenium septentrionale subsp. *septentrionale*

COMMON NAME(S) Forked spleenwort

STATUS Native, rare

HABITAT/DISTRIBUTION Rocky cliff faces of a variety of substrates; also occurs in western North America and Europe (2 additional subspecies, *A. septentrionale* subsp. *caucasicum* and subsp. *rehmanii*, are described from the Middle East and Asia)

Plants are terrestrial and epipetric. **Stems** are erect and branching, with clathrate scales that are dark reddish brown to black. **Leaves** are somewhat stiff and erect, forming clumps or mats with numerous leaves emerging in a dense cluster that will spread gradually outward. **Stipes** are smooth, lacking hairs or scales, up to 13cm long, and dark brown to reddish brown at the base, becoming greener toward the blade. The **rachis** is green and smooth. The leaf **blade** is leathery and smooth, linear, and up to 4cm long and 5mm wide. The blade may appear undivided, but it splits 1 or more times into small forklike divisions near the leaf tip. **Margins** are smooth. **Veins** are free and obscure. **Sori** are linear, with indusia, and run parallel to the leaf margins in the blade. 2n = 144 (tetraploid).

A. A clump of *Asplenium septentrionale* subsp. *septentrionale*.

B. Plants growing on rock.

C. Lower leaf surface with sori.

D. Plants with many fertile leaves.

F S C N

Asplenium serratum

COMMON NAME(S) American bird's-nest fern; this species resembles the popular houseplant known as the bird's-nest fern, *A. nidus*, which is native to Southeast Asia and the Austral-Pacific region, but the 2 species are not particularly closely related

STATUS Native, rare

HABITAT/DISTRIBUTION Hammocks and swamps, on tree bases, old logs, and stumps; also occurs in the Caribbean, Mexico, and Central and South America

Plants are epiphytic. **Stems** are erect and unbranched, with narrow, brown, clathrate scales. **Leaves** are ascending or arching, forming a distinct vase-shaped cluster. **Stipes** are up to 8cm long if present, but often a wing of blade tissue continues down the rachis to the very base of the leaf, making a distinct stipe essentially absent. The **rachis** is green and smooth. The **blade** is thick and smooth, up to 70cm long and 12cm wide, and broadly linear to oblanceolate, tapering gradually at the base and quickly at the tip. **Margins** are serrulate to serrate. **Veins** are free and obvious, and at right angles to the midrib (or nearly so). **Sori** are linear, with indusia, and oriented along the lateral veins, typically only in the upper half of the blade. 2n = 144 (tetraploid).

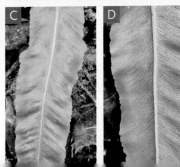

A. Plant of *Asplenium serratum*.

B. Lower leaf surface.

C. Upper leaf surface; note the distinctly serrate margins.

D. Lower leaf surface with mature sori and serrate margins.

F   S   C   N

Asplenium trichomanes, including subsp. trichomanes and quadrivalens

COMMON NAME(S) Maidenhair spleenwort

NOTABLE SYNONYMS *Asplenium trichomanes* subsp. *quadrivalens* is tetraploid and is sometimes treated as a separate species, *Asplenium quadrivalens*

STATUS Native, common

HABITAT/DISTRIBUTION The 2 subspecies have different substrate preferences: *A. trichomanes* subsp. *quadrivalens* prefers calcareous rocks (e.g., limestones), while *A. trichomanes* subsp. *trichomanes* occurs on noncalcareous, acidic rocks (e.g., sandstones and granites); both subspecies occur essentially worldwide

----

Description: The 2 subspecies are nearly identical in appearance, differing only in their substrate preference and spore size (which requires a high-powered microscope to observe). **Plants** are terrestrial and epipetric. **Stems** are short creeping and branched, with black, clathrate scales that may be brown at the edges. **Leaves** are erect to spreading and up to 26cm long, and sterile and fertile leaves do not differ in appearance. **Stipes** are up to 4cm long, shiny, blackish to reddish brown, and smooth or with black scales at the base. The **rachis** is similar to the stipe, and smooth, without hairs or scales. The **blade** is 1-pinnate, up to 22cm long and 1.5cm wide, and linear, with a gradually tapering base. The blade is smooth or may have scattered minute hairs. **Pinnae** are up to 8mm long and 4mm wide, oval to oblong, sometimes with a small lobe at the pinna base, on the upper edge. Pinnae typically occur in 15–35 pairs. **Margins** are shallowly, roundly to sharply toothed. **Veins** are free and obvious. **Sori** are linear, with indusia, typically with 2–4 pairs of sori per pinna, on both sides of the pinna midvein. 2n = 72 (diploid; subsp. *trichomanes*) or 144 (tetraploid; subsp. *quadrivalens*).

A

B

C

A & B. Plants of *Asplenium trichomanes*.

C. Lower leaf surface with sori.

Asplenium tutwilerae

COMMON NAME(S) Tutwiler's spleenwort, Scott's fertile spleenwort

STATUS Native (endemic to eastern North America), rare

HABITAT/DISTRIBUTION Known from only a single county in Alabama, where it grows on boulders

Plants are terrestrial and epipetric. **Stems** are ascending to erect and unbranched, with dark brown to black, clathrate scales. **Leaves** are erect to spreading and up to 30cm long, and sterile and fertile leaves differ somewhat in appearance, with fertile leaves longer and held more erect than sterile ones. **Stipes** are up to 10cm long, shiny, and purplish or reddish brown, with dark brown or black scales at the base that grade into hairs farther up. The **rachis** is similar to the stipe but becomes green toward the tip and is smooth, without hairs or scales. The **blade** is pinnatifid to 1-pinnate, up to 20cm long and 6cm wide, and oblanceolate, with a squared-off base and long-tapering tip. The blade has sparse hairs on the upper surface but is smooth on the lower surface. **Pinnae** are up to 3cm long and 1cm wide, and narrowly triangular to oblong, with small lobes at the pinna base, on both edges. **Margins** are entire to finely toothed. **Veins** are free and somewhat obvious. **Sori** are linear, with indusia, typically with 1–10 pairs of sori per pinna, on both sides of the pinna midvein. 2n = 144 (tetraploid).

A. Plants of *Asplenium tutwilerae.*

B. Upper surfaces of leaves.

C. Lower leaf surface with sori.

PHOTOGRAPHS BY ALAN CRESSLER

Asplenium verecundum

COMMON NAME(S) Delicate spleenwort, modest spleenwort

STATUS Native, uncommon

HABITAT/DISTRIBUTION Boulders and rock faces in limestone hammocks, outcrops, and sinks; also occurs in the Caribbean

Plants are terrestrial and epipetric. **Stems** are erect and unbranched, with black, clathrate scales. **Leaves** are erect to spreading and up to 23cm long, and sterile and fertile leaves do not differ in appearance. **Stipes** are up to 3cm long and brownish black, with black scales at the base. The **rachis** is similar to the stipe but smooth, without hairs or scales. The **blade** is 2–3-pinnate, up to 20cm long and 5cm wide, and narrowly lanceolate, with both the base and tip somewhat tapering. **Pinnae** are up to 2.5cm long and 1cm wide, oblong, and further divided into 1–5 ultimate segments that are rounded at their tips. **Margins** are entire. **Veins** are free and obvious. **Sori** are linear, with indusia, typically with 1 sorus per ultimate segment. 2n = 144 (tetraploid).

A. A colony of *Asplenium verecundum*.

B. Plants.

C. Upper surfaces of leaves.

D. Lower leaf surface with mature sori.

Asplenium viride

COMMON NAME(S) Green spleenwort

NOTABLE SYNONYMS *Asplenium trichomanes-ramosum*

STATUS Native, uncommon

HABITAT/DISTRIBUTION Boulders and cliffs of calcareous rocks, especially limestones; also occurs in Greenland, Europe, and Asia

Plants are terrestrial and epipetric. **Stems** are short creeping to ascending and branched, with dark brown to black, clathrate scales. **Leaves** are erect to spreading and up to 18cm long, and sterile and fertile leaves do not differ in appearance. **Stipes** are up to 5cm long and dark reddish brown toward the base, becoming green farther up, with dark brown to black scales at the base that grade into hairs. The **rachis** is green and has scattered hairs. The **blade** is 1-pinnate, up to 13cm long and 1.2cm wide, and linear, with the base tapering but the tip pointed, and either smooth or with minute scattered hairs. **Pinnae** are up to 1cm long and 0.6cm wide, quadrangular and somewhat asymmetrical, and occur in 6–21 pairs. **Margins** are shallowly, bluntly toothed. **Veins** are free and obvious. **Sori** are linear, with indusia, typically with 2–4 pairs of sori per pinna, on both sides of the pinna midvein. 2n = 72 (diploid).

A. Plants of *Asplenium viride*.

B. Upper leaf surfaces.

C. Lower leaf surface with sori.

D. Mature sori.

FAMILY: **PTERIDACEAE**

Astrolepis is one of several ferns that have extremely limited ranges in eastern North America but are widespread elsewhere. This genus is common in the southwestern U.S. but is essentially unknown in the east, except for 2 species; these desert-adapted ferns have apparently dispersed from their natural range in the arid regions of Texas, Arizona, New Mexico, and Mexico to a few locations in the southeast. One species, *A. sinuata*, has formed several stable populations in the east but does not appear to be expanding its range in this part of the continent. A second species, *A. integerrima*, has been reported only from Bibb County, Alabama, and likewise does not seem to be spreading. The 2 species differ in the shapes of their pinnae (*A. integerrima* has pinnae that are less lobed, *A. sinuata* more lobed) and in the density of scales on the upper surface of the pinnae. These scales are described as "stellate" for their starlike appearance. *Astrolepis integerrima* is thought to be a hybrid between *A. sinuata* and *A. cochisensis*, a species that occurs only in the western U.S. Base chromosome number (x) = 29.

KEY TO THE SPECIES OF *ASTROLEPIS* IN OUR FLORA:

1a The upper surface of the leaf is densely covered with white, star-shaped scales; the pinnae are unlobed to somewhat lobed, often asymmetrically so ⋯⋯⋯ *Astrolepis integerrima*

1b The upper surface of the leaf is sparsely to moderately densely covered with white, star-shaped scales; the pinnae are distinctly, symmetrically lobed ⋯⋯⋯ *Astrolepis sinuata*

1a.
Astrolepis integerrima

1b.
Astrolepis sinuata

Astrolepis integerrima

COMMON NAME(S) Hybrid cloak fern

NOTABLE SYNONYMS *Cheilanthes integerrima, Notholaena integerrima*

STATUS Native, rare

HABITAT/DISTRIBUTION Exposed cliffs or rocky slopes; known only from Bibb County, Alabama, in the east; also occurs in the southwestern U.S., Mexico, and the Caribbean

Plants are terrestrial. **Stems** are compact and short creeping, with tan or golden scales. **Leaves** are clustered and can be up to 45cm long. Fertile and sterile leaves do not differ in appearance. **Stipes** and **rachises** are yellowish to reddish brown and scaly, with a distinct stipe up to 10cm long. The leaf **blade** is 1-pinnate to 1-pinnate-pinnatifid, up to 30cm long, linear, and somewhat leathery. The lower surface of the blade is densely covered with scales that are lanceolate, have toothed margins, and are light in color when immature but gradually become darker toward maturity. The upper surface of the blade has a dense covering of stellate scales that are white or translucent. **Pinnae** are up to 1.5cm long and 1cm wide, with a very short stalk, or they sit against the rachis; they usually occur in 20–45 pairs and are oblong to ovate. Pinnae are entire to shallowly, asymmetrically lobed, especially near the base. **Margins** are smooth and may be slightly rolled under. **Pinna veins** are obscured by the dense covering of scales but are branched or forked. **Sori** are not well formed, and **sporangia** are instead scattered around the pinna margins, usually concentrated near vein endings, and they often appear to form a continuous line around the margin. There is not a true **false indusium**, but the pinna margin is usually somewhat folded over. 2n = 87 (triploid).

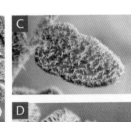

A. Plants of *Astrolepis integerrima*.

B. Upper leaf surface with stellate scales.

C. Close-up of stellate scales.

D. Lower leaf surface with dense scales and sporangia around the margins.

E. Golden stem scales.

Astrolepis sinuata

COMMON NAME(S) Wavy cloak fern, wavy scaly cloak fern

NOTABLE SYNONYMS *Cheilanthes sinuata, Notholaena sinuata*

STATUS Native, rare

HABITAT/DISTRIBUTION Exposed rock outcroppings, cliffs, slopes, occasionally concrete structures; known from only a handful of locations in South Carolina, Georgia, and Louisiana in the east, but more common in the southwestern U.S.; also occurs in the Caribbean, Mexico, and Central and South America

Plants are terrestrial. **Stems** are compact and short creeping, with brown or reddish-brown scales. **Leaves** are clustered and can be up to 1.3m long but are typically much shorter than this in the east; usually not more than 50cm. Fertile and sterile leaves do not differ in appearance. **Stipes** and **rachises** are yellowish to reddish brown and scaly, and the pinnae continue almost to the base of the leaf, so the stipe portion may be quite short. The leaf **blade** is 1-pinnate-pinnatifid, up to 1.25m long (though usually much shorter), linear, and somewhat leathery. The lower surface of the blade is densely covered with scales that are lanceolate to ovate, have toothed margins, and are white when immature but gradually become chestnut brown with a dark central patch at maturity. The upper surface of the blade has scattered stellate scales that are white or translucent. **Pinnae** are up to 3.5cm long and 1.5–2cm wide, with a small stalk, usually occur in 30–60 pairs along the rachis, and are deltate to ovate, deeply lobed, and typically symmetrically lobed (i.e., with matching lobes on both sides of the pinna). **Margins** are smooth and may be slightly rolled. **Pinna veins** are obscured by the dense covering of scales but are branched or forked. **Sori** are not well formed, and **sporangia** are instead scattered around the pinna margins, usually concentrated near vein endings, and they often appear to form a continuous line around the margin. There is not a true **false indusium**, but the pinna margin is usually somewhat folded over. 2n = 87 (triploid).

A. Plants growing on a rocky cliff.

B. Upper leaf surface of *Astrolepis sinuata*, with stellate scales visible as white dots on the pinnae.

C. Lower surfaces of immature pinnae, with dense covering of white scales.

D. Lower surfaces of more mature pinnae, with brown scales.

E. Mature pinnae with sori.

FAMILY: **ATHYRIACEAE**

We have 3 species of *Athyrium* in our flora: the widespread, native northern and southern lady ferns—*A. angustum* and *A. asplenioides*, respectively—and the introduced, exotic Japanese painted fern, *A. niponicum*. The first 2 were long considered to be a single species (*A. filix-femina*) with regional forms, but these are now routinely recognized as distinct species (though they can still be quite difficult to tell apart, especially as both tend to be variable in appearance). The native lady ferns are some of the most widespread and common ferns in eastern North America and can be most easily distinguished from other, similar-appearing ferns by their sori, which are elongated and curved at the tip, giving them a hooked or J-shaped appearance. Base chromosome number (x) = 40.

KEY TO THE SPECIES OF *ATHYRIUM* IN OUR FLORA:

1a The leaf blade is variegated in color, with pinnules distinctly lighter toward the base; overall the leaf blade may have a silvery-greenish or gray cast ················· *Athyrium niponicum*

1b. The leaf blade is uniformly green, not variegated ·· 2

    2a The leaf blade is widest at or just below the middle and narrows toward the base; pinnae sit directly against the rachis or have short stalks; the scales at the base of the stipe are brown to black ··············· *Athyrium angustum*

    2b The leaf blade is widest below the middle and narrows slightly toward the base; the pinnae have distinct stalks; the scales at the base of the stipe are light brown to brown ······*Athyrium asplenioides*

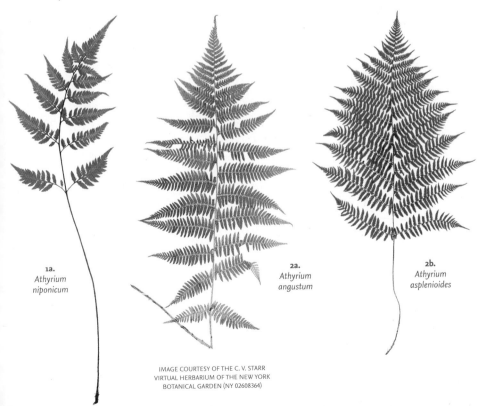

1a.
*Athyrium
niponicum*

2a.
*Athyrium
angustum*

2b.
*Athyrium
asplenioides*

IMAGE COURTESY OF THE C. V. STARR
VIRTUAL HERBARIUM OF THE NEW YORK
BOTANICAL GARDEN (NY 02608364)

Athyrium angustum

COMMON NAME(S) Northern lady fern, narrow lady fern

NOTABLE SYNONYMS *Athyrium filix-femina* var. *angustum*

STATUS Native (endemic to North America), common

HABITAT/DISTRIBUTION Wet woods, meadows, swamps, and stream banks; range extends somewhat west of the Mississippi; also occurs in Greenland

Plants are terrestrial. **Stems** are short creeping to ascending, with brown to black scales toward the base that become sparser toward the blade. **Leaves** are erect to arching, up to 1.3m long, and form irregular clusters. Fertile and sterile leaves do not differ in appearance. **Stipes** are up to 55cm long, greenish or yellowish to reddish, and smooth but with scattered light brown scales. The leaf **blade** is up to 75cm long and 35cm wide, elliptic and widest at or just below the middle, narrowing toward the base, and 2-pinnate to 2-pinnate-pinnatifid. The **rachis** is smooth or may have scattered glands and is typically grooved on the upper surface; this groove is continuous with the pinna midveins. **Pinnae** are oblong lanceolate to lanceolate, up to 18cm long and 10cm wide, and either sit against the rachis or have short stalks. **Pinnules** are linear to oblong and bluntly to sharply lobed. **Margins** are serrate. **Lateral veins** are free and may be forked. **Sori** are linear elongate but are typically hooked or curved at the tip and occasionally become almost horseshoe shaped. At least some sori curve across the lateral veins rather than running straight along them. **Indusia** are present, finely toothed at the margins, and may or may not have glandular hairs. 2n = 80 (diploid).

A. A colony of *Athyrium angustum*.

B. Fronds.

C. Sori.

Athyrium asplenioides

COMMON NAME(S) Southern lady fern, lowland lady fern

NOTABLE SYNONYMS *Athyrium filix-femina* var. *asplenioides*

STATUS Native (endemic to North America), common

HABITAT/DISTRIBUTION Woods, meadows, swamps, and stream banks; widespread but becoming more common farther south; range extends somewhat west of the Mississippi

Plants are terrestrial. **Stems** are short creeping to ascending, with light brown to brown scales toward the base that become sparser toward the blade. **Leaves** are erect to arching, up to 1.2m long, and form irregular clusters. Fertile and sterile leaves do not differ in appearance. **Stipes** are up to 55cm long, greenish or yellowish to reddish, and smooth but with scattered light brown scales. The leaf **blade** is up to 60cm long and 30cm wide, ovate lanceolate to lanceolate and widest below the middle, narrowing only slightly toward the base, and 2-pinnate to 2-pinnate-pinnatifid. The **rachis** is smooth or may have scattered glands and is typically grooved on the upper surface; this groove is continuous with the pinna midveins. **Pinnae** are oblong lanceolate to lanceolate, up to 15cm long and 10cm wide, and typically have distinct stalks. **Pinnules** are oblong lanceolate or narrowly triangular, and bluntly to sharply lobed. **Margins** are serrate. **Lateral veins** are free and may be forked. **Sori** are linear elongate but are typically hooked or curved at the tip and occasionally become almost horseshoe shaped. At least some sori curve across the lateral veins rather than running straight along them. **Indusia** are present, finely toothed at the margins, and may or may not have glandular hairs. 2n = 80 (diploid).

A. Plants of *Athyrium asplenioides*. PHOTOGRAPH BY ALAN CRESSLER

B. Upper part of a frond.

C. Lower leaf surface with immature sori.

Athyrium niponicum

COMMON NAME(S) Japanese painted fern

NOTABLE SYNONYMS *Anisocampium niponicum*

STATUS Not native, uncommon

HABITAT/DISTRIBUTION Escapes from cultivation and becomes naturalized, preferring forests, streamsides, and other shady areas; native to Asia

Plants are terrestrial. **Stems** are short creeping to ascending, with brown to dark brown or purplish scales. **Leaves** are erect to arching, up to 75cm long, and form irregular clusters. Fertile and sterile leaves do not differ in appearance. **Stipes** are up to 35cm long and dark red to reddish brown or black at the base, becoming yellowish or green toward the blade or remaining reddish, and smooth but with scattered light brown scales. The **rachis** is smooth or with a few scattered glandular hairs, yellowish to reddish or green. The leaf **blade** is up to 40cm long and 25cm wide, narrowly triangular, rounded toward the base, and 2–3-pinnate. The blade is somewhat variegated in color, with the pinnules often lighter colored toward the base, and overall the blade may have a grayish or silverish cast. **Pinnae** are oblong lanceolate, up to 25cm long and 12cm wide, and have short stalks. **Pinnules** are lanceolate to oblong lanceolate or narrowly triangular, and sharply lobed. Pinna **midveins** may be greenish to distinctly reddish, depending on the horticultural variety. **Margins** are serrate. **Lateral veins** are free and may be forked. **Sori** are linear elongate but are typically hooked or curved at the tip and occasionally become almost horseshoe shaped. At least some sori curve across the lateral veins rather than running straight along them. **Indusia** are present, finely toothed at the margins, and may or may not have glandular hairs. 2n = 80 (diploid).

A. Plants of *Athyrium niponicum*.

B. Frond with grayish color.

C. Lower surface of a young leaf showing the reddish color of the stipe and rachis, and sori.

D. Lower surface of a young, unfurling leaf, showing the reddish color of the stipe and rachis, and strongly curved sori.

FAMILY: **SALVINIACEAE**

Azolla is a genus of aquatic ferns whose species live entirely in association with water, though they can become stranded if water levels drop, and they may be able to persist for some time on damp soil or mud. *Azolla* is closely related to *Salvinia* (p. 455), as well as the members of Marsileaceae (*Marsilea*, p. 335; *Pilularia*, p. 421; and *Regnellidium*, the last of which does not occur in our flora). Together these groups make up the true water ferns, which are all heterosporous, meaning that they produce separate male and female spores that are distinctly different in size, with larger female megaspores and smaller male microspores. The spores are produced inside structures called sporocarps that hang in the water column. A megasporocarp will contain a single large megaspore, while a microsporocarp will contain many smaller microspores. Unlike their close relatives in *Salvinia*, *Azolla* species have true roots, which either dangle in the water column or occasionally attach to soil. *Azolla* species are also of interest because internal chambers in the leaves harbor a nitrogen-fixing bacterial symbiont that makes the plants an excellent green manure; *Azolla* has been used this way in Southeast Asia for centuries. The individual leaves of *Azolla* are quite small and packed closely together, and multiple plants often aggregate together, sometimes forming dense colonies. Each leaf has 2 lobes: a large upper lobe that is emergent, photosynthetic, and may be various shades of green, blue, or red; and a smaller lower lobe that is submerged, typically colorless or light brown, and somewhat translucent. Each leaf fits into the curve of the adjacent leaf's lobes, giving the leaves overall a stacked or nested appearance. The leaves typically have wide, stout hairs on the upper surfaces that are water repellent, giving the leaves a velvety appearance, which is reflected in some of the common names of *Azolla* species (e.g., water velvet).

The number and taxonomy of *Azolla* species in North America have been unclear historically, and the group needs further study. Three species are included here, 1 native (*A. cristata*), 1 definitely introduced (*A. pinnata* subsp. *pinnata*), and another very likely introduced (*A. mexicana*). *Azolla cristata* and *A. mexicana* strongly resemble one another, and this has contributed to the uncertainty about the status of *Azolla* species in our flora; these species can be distinguished from one another only by observing their megaspores (with a hand lens or microscope). The megaspores of *A. cristata* have a relatively smooth surface with a dense covering of tangled hairs/filaments, while the megaspores of *A. mexicana* have a distinctly pitted surface with only a few sparse filaments. A fourth species, *A. filiculoides*, may also be present; it has previously been considered to occur only in western North America, but it is extremely similar in appearance to *A. cristata*, and the 2 are almost certain to be confused with one another. The only way to distinguish them is to observe, with a hand lens, the hairs (trichomes) on the upper leaf lobe. In *A. filiculoides* these hairs have only a single cell, while in *A. cristata* they have 2 or more cells. Base chromosome number (x) = 22.

KEY TO THE SPECIES OF *AZOLLA* IN OUR FLORA:

1a   Plants are triangular, often resembling small pine trees; branching is pinnate,
giving the appearance of strong bilateral symmetry and a triangular shape ⸻ *Azolla pinnata* subsp. *pinnata*

1b   Plants are loosely circular or ovate; branching is unequal, giving the clusters
of leaves a loose, asymmetrical, roughly circular shape ⸻ 2

        2a Megaspores have a dense covering of hairy filaments, and an otherwise
relatively smooth surface ⸻ *Azolla cristata*

        2b Megaspores have only a few sparse filaments, and a distinctly pitted surface ⸻ *Azolla mexicana*

A. *Azolla cristata* plants on mud.

B. Plants with sporocarps visible.

C. Nested leaves.

Azolla cristata

COMMON NAME(S) Mosquito fern, Carolina mosquito fern, crested mosquito fern, eastern mosquito fern, water velvet

NOTABLE SYNONYMS *Azolla caroliniana.* In North America this species has frequently been called *A. caroliniana,* but *A. cristata* technically has taxonomic precedence. Note that because of the extreme similarity in appearance between this species and *A. mexicana,* the range maps for both species are almost certainly based on at least some incorrectly identified specimens, so both maps should be considered preliminary.

STATUS Native, uncommon

HABITAT/DISTRIBUTION Slow-moving or still bodies of water; also occurs in western North America, the Caribbean, Mexico, and Central and South America

Plants are aquatic. Fine, hairlike **roots** hang down into the water column. **Stems** are largely obscured by the leaves, branching regularly but unequally. Individual **leaves** are up to 2mm wide; the upper lobe is green or bluish green to red when in full sun. The **aggregations** or clusters of leaves can be up to several centimeters long and wide, and multiple clusters form large floating mats. **Hairs** on the upper surface of the upper leaf lobes consist of 2 or more cells. **Sporocarps** emerge from the leaf axils, but plants are not often fertile. **Megaspores** have a dense covering of hairy filaments, and an otherwise relatively smooth (unpitted) surface. 2n = 44 (diploid).

Azolla mexicana

COMMON NAME(S) Mexican mosquito fern

NOTABLE SYNONYMS *Azolla microphylla*

STATUS Unclear, but likely not native; uncommon

HABITAT/DISTRIBUTION Occurs along the Mississippi River from Wisconsin to Tennessee but is likely native to Mexico. Note that because of the extreme similarity in appearance between this species and *A. cristata,* the range maps for both are almost certainly based on incorrectly identified specimens, so both maps should be considered provisional.

Plants are aquatic. Fine, hairlike **roots** hang down into the water column. **Stems** are largely obscured by the leaves, branching regularly but unequally. Individual **leaves** are up to 2mm wide; the upper lobe is green or bluish green to red when in full sun. The **aggregations** or clusters of leaves can be up to several centimeters long and wide, and multiple clusters form large floating mats. **Hairs** on the upper surface of the upper leaf lobes consist of 2 or more cells. **Sporocarps** emerge from the leaf axils, and plants are often fertile. **Megaspores** have only a few sparse filaments, and a distinctly pitted surface. 2n = 44 (diploid).

F   S   C   N

Azolla pinnata subsp. pinnata

COMMON NAME(S) Feathered mosquito fern

STATUS Not native, uncommon

HABITAT/DISTRIBUTION Slow-moving or still bodies of water, especially along canal edges; native to the Austral-Pacific region (2 other subspecies are described from Africa and Asia: *A. pinnata* subsp. *africana* and *A. pinnata* subsp. *asiatica*, respectively)

Plants are aquatic. Fine, hairlike **roots** hang down into the water column. **Stems** are largely obscured by the leaves, branching pinnately, giving plants the appearance of small pine trees. Individual **leaves** are up to 2mm wide; the upper lobe is green or more often light to dark red. The **aggregations** or clusters of leaves can be up to several centimeters long and wide. **Hairs** on the upper surface of the upper leaf lobes consist of only 1 cell. **Sporocarps** emerge from the leaf axils, but plants are not often fertile. **Megaspores** have hairy filaments, and small protuberances across the spore surface. 2n = 44 (diploid).

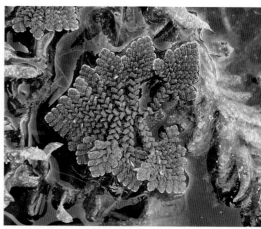

Plants of *Azolla pinnata* subsp. *pinnata*.

FAMILY: **BLECHNACEAE**

Blechnum is a large genus of temperate and tropical ferns, but we have only 1 species in our flora: *B. appendiculatum*. This primarily tropical species occurs in a handful of locations in Florida and the south. The fern now known as *Telmatoblechnum serrulatum* (p. 473) was previously treated in the genus *Blechnum* and is quite similar in appearance to *B. appendiculatum*; they can be most easily distinguished by the smooth pinna margins of *B. appendiculatum*, and the obviously serrate and sharply toothed margins of *T. serrulatum*. All members of the family Blechnaceae, which also includes *Anchistea* (p. 136) and *Lorinseria* (p. 326) in our flora, tend to have immature leaves that are distinctly red or reddish brown, a feature that *B. appendiculatum* regularly displays. Base chromosome number (x) = 31.

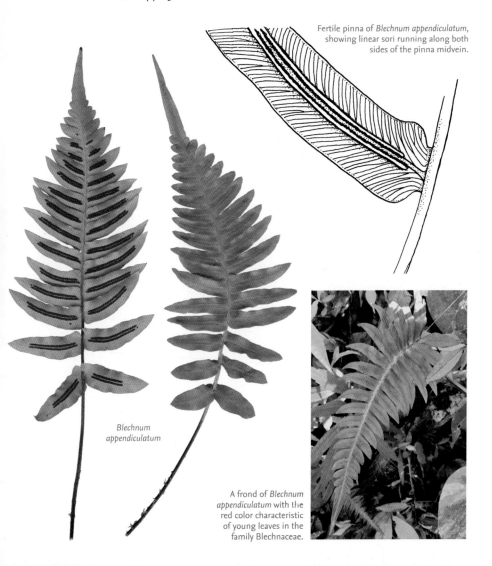

Fertile pinna of *Blechnum appendiculatum*, showing linear sori running along both sides of the pinna midvein.

Blechnum appendiculatum

A frond of *Blechnum appendiculatum* with the red color characteristic of young leaves in the family Blechnaceae.

F S C N

Blechnum appendiculatum

COMMON NAME(S) Hammock fern, sinkhole fern, New World midsorus fern

SYNONYMS *Blechnum occidentale* var. *minus*

STATUS Native, rare

HABITAT/DISTRIBUTION Moist, open or shady woods, near creeks or seasonally dry streams; also occurs in the Caribbean, Mexico, and Central and South America

Plants are terrestrial or occasionally epipetric on limestone. **Stems** are long creeping and branched, becoming erect at the tips, with brown to black scales. This species often spreads vigorously via stolons. **Leaves** are up to 50cm long and erect to arching, and young leaves may be distinctly reddish. Fertile leaves may be longer than sterile ones. **Stipes** are up to 34cm long and yellowish to light reddish brown, with reddish scales near the base, becoming somewhat hairy near the base of the blade. The **rachis** is yellowish to light reddish brown and hairy, especially on the lower surface, and hairs may be tipped with small glands. The leaf **blade** is up to 30cm long and 12cm wide, lanceolate to broadly lanceolate or triangular and widest somewhat below or at the midpoint, and 1-pinnate toward the base but pinnatifid toward the tip (though the entire blade can occasionally be pinnatifid). The lower surface of the blade is typically hairy, especially along the midveins of the pinnae. Individual **pinnae** are 2–7cm long and 0.5–1.5cm wide, lanceolate to oblong, and may be somewhat falcate. The fertile pinnae are often somewhat contracted, and the lower pinnae have bluntly tapered tips while the upper pinnae have long-tapering tips. Pinna bases are generally free of the rachis in the lower pinnae but become joined to the rachis in the upper pinnae as the blade gradually becomes pinnatifid. **Margins** are smooth to serrulate. **Veins** are free and forked. **Sori** are linear, running in 2 continuous lines on either side of the pinna midveins. **Indusia** are present, have minutely toothed margins, and open toward the midvein. 2n = 124 (tetraploid).

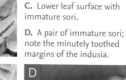

A. Fronds of *Blechnum appendiculatum*.

B. Lower leaf surface with mature sori.

C. Lower leaf surface with immature sori.

D. A pair of immature sori; note the minutely toothed margins of the indusia.

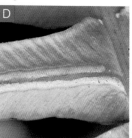

FAMILY: OPHIOGLOSSACEAE

The genus *Botrychium*, whose members are commonly called moonworts (a reference to the crescent-shaped pinnae or pinna lobes of many species), contributes significantly to the diversity of our northernmost fern flora. Members of this group occur nearly worldwide but strongly prefer cooler habitats at high latitudes and high elevations, and the genus is most diverse in the temperate and boreal regions of North America. *Botrychium* species are notoriously difficult to find when you are looking for them; the plants of most species are less than 10cm tall and ephemeral, emerging in early summer, producing and releasing spores, and then typically dying back by late summer or early fall. Most moonwort species also have fairly specific preferences for soil type, moisture level, and degree of habitat disturbance, and all species are entirely dependent on mycorrhizal fungi to help them absorb nutrients from the soil. These fungi have their own habitat preferences, further contributing to the rarity and patchiness of *Botrychium* distributions. This group is also known for its many morphologically cryptic species, which are extremely similar to one another in appearance despite being recognized as separate species. Frequent hybridization and polyploidy have contributed to the number of species (see figure below) and can make identification of individual *Botrychium* plants to species quite challenging.

Botrychium species share several morphological characteristics with the other members of the family Ophioglossaceae, in the genera *Botrypus* (p. 213), *Cheiroglossa* (p. 223), *Ophioderma* (p. 375), *Ophioglossum* (p. 377), and *Sceptridium* (p. 458). The leaves of all these plants are divided into 2 distinct parts: a fertile spore-bearing segment (the sporophore), and a sterile segment (the trophophore). There is only 1 leaf, but it looks very much like 2 separate leaves, or even 2 separate plants, if the segments diverge belowground and their stalks emerge a few millimeters apart. Members of the family also lack the well-defined annulus apparatus that is present in most other ferns to facilitate spore dispersal. Instead, their sporangia simply split open and drop spores into the air current. *Botrychium* is most similar in appearance to species of *Sceptridium* and the single species in the genus *Botrypus*, *B. virginianus*. The members of both of these latter genera were previously included in *Botrychium* and have only recently been treated regularly in their own genera, on the basis of morphological differences as well as analyses of DNA sequence data. *Botrychium* differs from them both in overall size and shape, especially that of its sterile trophophore. In most *Botrychium* species, this part of the leaf is ovate to oblong or narrowly triangular in overall shape, usually not more than 4cm wide, and at most 2-pinnate-pinnatifid. In both *Sceptridium* and *Botrypus*, the sterile trophophore is broadly triangular, usually more than 4cm wide, and typically 3–4-pinnate. The key below to the *Botrychium* species in our flora relies heavily on features of the sterile trophophore, including the shape, division, and other features of the sterile pinnae, as well as the relative lengths of the sporophore and trophophore stalks and the shared, common stalk at the base of the plant. It is important to note that the key assumes one is working with mature plants; these 3 different stalk sections will not reach their final lengths, and therefore the relative lengths between them that the key references, until the plants are fully mature (with yellow or brown sporangia apparent). Base chromosome number (x) = 45.

Plants of *Botrychium pallidum*.
PHOTOGRAPH BY DONALD FARRAR

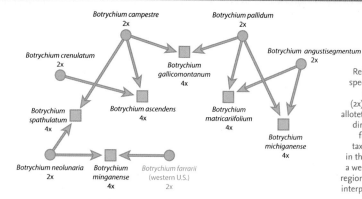

Relationships among *Botrychium* species in eastern North America. Blue circles are fertile diploids (2x), and green squares are fertile allotetraploids (4x). Arrows show the direction of genetic contribution from parental toward offspring taxa. One of the species involved in these relationships, *B. farrarii*, is a western species not found in our region. For more information about interpreting these figures, see p. 12.

KEY TO THE SPECIES OF *BOTRYCHIUM* IN OUR FLORA:

1a   On the sterile trophophore, the pinnae in the second pair from the bottom have pinnate venation, with a clear midrib; each pinna is broadest at its middle, and the ultimate divisions of the pinnae are lobes with more or less pointed ends ⋯⋯⋯⋯ 2

    2a   The pinnae in the lowest pair are divided into narrow lobes with parallel sides and pointed tips; the sporophore has a short stalk or is sessile, and is divided at the base into 3 more or less equal-length branches; at maturity the sporangia are bright yellow ⋯⋯ *Botrychium angustisegmentum*

    2b   The pinnae in the lowest pair are divided into wide lobes that get broader toward the pinna tip, with relatively rounded tips; the sporophore has a distinct stalk, and the side branches are rarely as long as the central rachis; at maturity the sporangia are brown or dull yellow ⋯⋯⋯⋯ 3

       3a   The trophophore has a very small stalk or is sessile; the lowest pair of pinnae are narrowly ovate to oblong; the lowest pinnae are distinctly larger than the ones above; the divisions on the upper edge of the pinnae are generally shallower than those on the lower edge; the common stalk is uniformly green or has only a light reddish stripe below the trophophore ⋯⋯⋯⋯ *Botrychium michiganense*

       3b   The trophophore has a distinct stalk; the lowest pair of pinnae are narrowly triangular to ovate or oblong; the lowest pinnae are the largest, but pinnae gradually become smaller farther up the blade; the divisions on both upper and lower edges of the pinnae are equally deep; the common stalk often has a distinct reddish stripe below the trophophore ⋯⋯⋯⋯ *Botrychium matricariifolium*

1b   On the sterile trophophore, the pinnae in the second pair from the bottom have palmate venation, without a clear midrib; pinnae are either simple or may be split into lobes; pinnae are more or less fan shaped and widest at the tip ⋯⋯⋯⋯ 4

    4a   The pinnae in the lowest pair are simple and elongated, or divided into more or less rounded pinnules that are each similar to the pinnae farther up; above the lowest pair, the pinnae bases are broad where they attach to the rachis (usually more than ⅓ of the pinna width) ⋯⋯⋯⋯ 5

       5a   The pinnae on the trophophore are sessile and somewhat blocky; the sporangia on the sporophore are partially embedded in the rachis ⋯⋯⋯⋯ *Botrychium mormo*

       5b   The pinnae on the trophophore have either long stalks or short, distinct stalks; the sporangia on the sporophore have short stalks or sit against the rachis but are not embedded in it ⋯⋯⋯⋯ 6

          6a   The sporophore and trophophore join near the ground; the sporophore's stalk is longer than the entire trophophore; the sporophore is often flexible, bending over at maturity ⋯⋯⋯⋯ *Botrychium simplex* var. *simplex*

          6b   The sporophore and trophophore join well above the ground; the sporophore's stalk is shorter than or equal to the length of the trophophore; the sporophore is upright and erect ⋯⋯⋯⋯ *Botrychium tenebrosum*

2a.
*Botrychium
angustisegmentum*

3a.
*Botrychium
michiganense*

3b.
*Botrychium
matricariifolium*

5a.
*Botrychium
mormo*

6a.
*Botrychium simplex
var. simplex*

ALL IMAGES (EXCEPT *BOTRYCHIUM MATRICARIIFOLIUM*)
COURTESY OF DONALD FARRAR

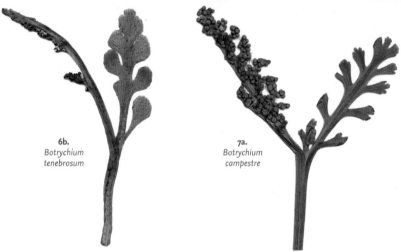

6b.
*Botrychium
tenebrosum*

7a.
*Botrychium
campestre*

4b The pinnae in the lowest pair are simple and entire, or palmately divided; above the lowest pair, the pinnae bases are narrow where they attach to the rachis (usually less than ⅓ of the pinna width) ··· 7

7a The lowest pinnae or their segments, if divided, are narrow, their outer margin spanning an arc less than 60°; at maturity, the sporophore stalk is about 25% the length of the trophophore ··· *Botrychium campestre*

7b The lowest pinnae are broad, their outer margins spanning an arc more than 60°; at maturity, the sporophore stalk is 33% to more than 50% the length of the trophophore ········· 8

8a The lowest pinnae are broadly crescent shaped, spanning more than 150° ················· 9

9a The trophophore and its pinnae are sessile or have only short stalks; the lowest pinnae span ca. 180°; the spaces between the pinnae decrease gradually from the basal pair upward; the sporophore stalk is longer than the entire trophophore; the sporangia-bearing part of the sporophore takes up the tip-most ⅓, and the branches are densely clustered ··················· *Botrychium neolunaria*

9b The trophophore and its pinnae have distinct stalks; the lowest pinnae span less than 180°; the space between the lowest pinna and the second pinna is disproportionately larger than the spaces between pinnae farther up; the sporophore stalk is shorter than or equal to the length of the trophophore; the sporangia-bearing part of the sporophore takes up ca. ½ its length, and the branches are spaced apart ··· *Botrychium crenulatum*

8b The lowest pinnae are narrowly fan shaped to somewhat spatula shaped, spanning 60–120° ··· 10

10a Plants are bluish green; on the trophophore, if the lowest pinnae are divided, the lobes are unequal in size, with the lobe(s) on the upper margin larger than the lobe(s) on the lower margin ····································· 11

11a The sporophore stalk is ca. ½ or more as long as, but not longer than, the trophophore; the branches and branchlets on the sporophore have distinct stalks and are not crowded ···················· *Botrychium pallidum*

11b The sporophore stalk is ⅓–½ the length of the trophophore; the branches on the sporophore are sessile or short stalked and crowded, obscuring the central rachis ······················ *Botrychium gallicomontanum*

10b Plants are green; if the lowest pinnae are divided, the lobes on the upper and lower margins are more or less equal in size ································ 12

9a.
*Botrychium
neolunaria*

9b.
*Botrychium
crenulatum*

11a.
*Botrychium
pallidum*

11b.
*Botrychium
gallicomontanum*

12a.
*Botrychium
minganense*

ALL IMAGES (EXCEPT *BOTRYCHIUM MINGANENSE*)
COURTESY OF DONALD FARRAR

12a The trophophore has a distinct stalk; if the lowest pinnae are divided, they are shallowly divided into 3–5 lobes; the sporophore stalk is longer than the entire trophophore ·········· *Botrychium minganense*

12b The trophophore has no stalk or only a short stalk; if the lowest pinnae are divided, they are deeply divided into 2–4 lobes; the sporophore stalk is shorter than the trophophore ········· 13

13a The pinnae on the trophophore are entire or only shallowly lobed, with rounded gaps between the lobes; the tip-most margins of the pinnae or pinna lobes are smooth, shallowly scalloped, or wavy ·········· *Botrychium spathulatum*

13b The pinnae on the trophophore are usually deeply cut into lobes, with sharp gaps between the lobes; the tip-most margins of the pinnae or pinna lobes are coarsely toothed ·········· *Botrychium ascendens*

13a.
Botrychium spathulatum

13b.
Botrychium ascendens

Botrychium angustisegmentum

COMMON NAME(S) Narrow triangle moonwort

NOTABLE SYNONYMS *Botrychium lanceolatum* subsp. *angustisegmentum*

STATUS Native (endemic to North America), uncommon

HABITAT/DISTRIBUTION Shaded forests, forest edges, and cedar swamps; also occurs in western North America

Plants are terrestrial and inconspicuous, usually less than 7cm tall. **Stems** are upright. **Leaves** are green to dark green, lustrous, and divided into a sterile bladelike trophophore and a fertile sporophore that join well above the ground. The shared common stalk may be green or dark brownish green with a reddish stripe below the trophophore. The **trophophore** is 1–2-pinnate, broadly to narrowly triangular, sessile or with a very short stalk, and with up to 5 pairs of pinnae. The **pinnae** are ovate to lanceolate and broadest at the middle, and the ultimate divisions of the pinnae are lobes with more or less pointed ends. The pinnae above the lowest pair have pinnate venation, with a clear midrib. **Veins** in the trophophore pinnae are free and forked. The **sporophore** has a short stalk or is sessile and is divided at the base into 3 more or less equal-length branches (the only *Botrychium* species in our flora with even-length sporophore branches). **Sporangia** are bright yellow at maturity. 2n = 90 (diploid).

Plants of *Botrychium angustisegmentum.*

PHOTOGRAPHS BY MALCOLM MACFARLANE

Botrychium ascendens

COMMON NAME(S) Upswept moonwort

STATUS Native (endemic to North America), uncommon

HABITAT/DISTRIBUTION Grassy meadows, disturbed areas such as quarry edges, occasionally in forests; also occurs in western North America

Plants are terrestrial and inconspicuous, usually less than 10cm tall. **Stems** are upright. **Leaves** are yellow green to dark green, may be somewhat lustrous, and are divided into a sterile bladelike trophophore and a fertile sporophore that join well above the ground. The **trophophore** is 1-pinnate, oblong to oblong lanceolate, sessile or with a short stalk, and with up to 5 well-spaced pairs of pinnae. The **pinnae** are strongly ascending (angled upward), and the pinnae in the lowest pair are often somewhat larger than those above, fan shaped, spanning an arc of 60–120°, and entire or with 2–4 narrow, deep lobes that are more or less equal in size, separated by sharp gaps between the lobes. The tip-most margins of the pinnae or pinna lobes are coarsely toothed. The pinnae above the lowest pair are similar in shape and have palmate venation and no clear midrib, and the pinna bases are narrow where they attach to the rachis (usually less than 1/3 of the pinna width). **Veins** in the trophophore pinnae are free and forked. The **sporophore** is erect, with a stalk ca. 50% the length of the trophophore, and a central rachis with sessile or short-stalked side branches that are crowded and may obscure the rachis. **Sporangia** are yellowish brown at maturity and are sessile but not sunken into the stalks. 2n = 180 (tetraploid).

Plants of *Botrychium ascendens*.

PHOTOGRAPHS BY DONALD FARRAR

Botrychium campestre

COMMON NAME(S) Prairie moonwort

STATUS Native (endemic to North America), rare

HABITAT/DISTRIBUTION Drier grassy habitats including dune meadows and prairies, and disturbed areas including quarries and mine tailings; also occurs in western North America

Plants are terrestrial and inconspicuous, usually 4cm tall or less. **Stems** are upright. **Leaves** are grayish green to green, fleshy, may be somewhat glaucous (i.e., somewhat waxy but not shiny), and are divided into a sterile bladelike trophophore and a fertile sporophore that join well above the ground. The **trophophore** is 1-pinnate, obovate to oblong, with no stalk, and up to 5 (rarely more) pairs of well-defined, widely separated lobes or pinnae. The **pinnae** are narrowly spatula shaped to fan or wedge shaped and widest at their tips. The pinnae in the lowest pair are about the same size as the other pinnae or are frequently smaller than the more tip-ward pinnae. The lowest pinnae, or their segments if they are divided, are relatively narrow, their outer margin spanning an arc less than 60°, often less than 45°. Above the lowest pair, the pinnae have palmate venation and no clear midrib, and the pinna bases are narrow where they attach to the rachis (usually less than ⅓ of the pinna width). **Veins** in the trophophore pinnae are free and forked. The **sporophore** stalk is ca. 25% the length of the trophophore, and the fertile section has a central rachis with side branches that are often crowded, obscuring the rachis. **Sporangia** are yellowish brown at maturity. 2n=90 (diploid).

Plants of *Botrychium campestre*.

PHOTOGRAPHS BY DONALD FARRAR

Botrychium crenulatum

COMMON NAME(S) Dainty moonwort

NOTABLE SYNONYMS *Botrychium lunaria* var. *crenulatum*

STATUS Native (endemic to North America), rare

HABITAT/DISTRIBUTION Marshy or saturated soils of forests and in moist, open meadows; also occurs in western North America

Plants are terrestrial and inconspicuous, usually 6cm tall or less. **Stems** are upright. **Leaves** are light yellowish green to green, lustrous, and divided into a sterile bladelike trophophore and a fertile sporophore that join well above the ground. The **trophophore** is 1-pinnate, oblong, with a distinct short stalk, and up to 5 pairs of widely separated lobes or pinnae. The **pinnae** are short stalked, crescent to fan shaped and widest at their tips, undivided, and gradually reduced in size from the bottom of the blade to the tip. The distance between the lowest pinnae and second pinnae is disproportionately long compared to the spacing of pinnae farther up. The lowest pinnae are very broad, spanning an arc more than 150° (but less than 180°), and they have distinctly minutely toothed margins. Above the lowest pair, the pinnae have palmate venation and no clear midrib, and the pinna bases are narrow where they attach to the rachis (usually less than ⅓ of the pinna width). **Veins** in the trophophore pinnae are free and forked. The **sporophore** stalk is 75–100% the length of the trophophore and has a central rachis with widely spaced side branches. The fertile section takes up ca. ½ the total length of the sporophore. **Sporangia** are yellowish brown at maturity. 2n=90 (diploid).

A plant of *Botrychium crenulatum*.

Botrychium gallicomontanum

COMMON NAME(S) Frenchman's Bluff moonwort (a reference to the type locality of this species)

STATUS Native (endemic to North America), rare

HABITAT/DISTRIBUTION Prairies; also occurs in western North America

Plants are terrestrial and can be up to ca. 10cm tall. **Stems** are upright. **Leaves** are yellow green to green, glaucous, and divided into a sterile bladelike trophophore and a fertile sporophore that join above ground level. The **trophophore** is 1-pinnate, narrowly ovate to oblong, either sessile or with a distinct short stalk, with up to 6 well-spaced pairs of lobes or pinnae. The **pinnae** are short stalked, usually undivided, asymmetrically fan shaped to somewhat spatula shaped, and widest at their tips, with the upper portion larger than the lower. The pinnae gradually reduce in size from the bottom of the blade to the tip. The lowest pinnae span an arc of 60–120°. Above the lowest pair, the pinnae have palmate venation and no clear midrib, and the pinna bases are narrow where they attach to the rachis (usually less than ⅓ of the pinna width). **Veins** in the trophophore pinnae are free and forked. The **sporophore** stalk is 33–50% (sometimes more) the length of the trophophore, with a central rachis with short-stalked or sessile side branches that are crowded and partially obscure the rachis. **Sporangia** are yellowish brown at maturity. 2n=180 (tetraploid).

Plants of *Botrychium gallicomontanum*.

PHOTOGRAPHS BY MALCOLM MACFARLANE

F S C N

Botrychium matricariifolium

COMMON NAME(S) Daisy-leaf moonwort

NOTABLE SYNONYMS *Botrychium lunaria* var. *matricariifolium*, *Botrychium acuminatum* (*B. acuminatum* has been shown to be genetically identical to *B. matricariifolium*)

STATUS Native, uncommon

HABITAT/DISTRIBUTION Old fields, meadows, disturbed habitats including roadsides, and forest edges and open woods; also occurs in Europe

Plants are terrestrial and inconspicuous, usually less than 10cm tall. **Stems** are upright. **Leaves** are pale to yellow green to bright green, dull to slightly glaucous, and divided into a sterile bladelike trophophore and a fertile sporophore that join well above the ground. The mostly green shared common stalk often has a reddish stripe below the trophophore. The **trophophore** is 1–3-pinnate, narrowly ovate to oblong, with a distinct stalk (up to 2cm long) and up to 7 pairs of pinnae. The **pinnae** are oblong and broadest at the middle, and the ultimate divisions of the pinnae are lobes with more or less pointed ends. The divisions on both the upper and lower edges of the pinnae are equally deep. The pinnae in the lowest pair are narrowly triangular to ovate or oblong and are the largest of the pinnae, with the remaining pinnae becoming gradually smaller toward the tip of the blade. The pinnae above the lowest pair have pinnate venation, with a clear midrib. **Veins** in the trophophore pinnae are free and forked. The **sporophore** stalk is 50–100% as long as the entire trophophore, and the fertile section has a central rachis with side branches. **Sporangia** are dull yellow or brown at maturity. 2n=180 (tetraploid).

Plants of *Botrychium matricariifolium*.

Botrychium michiganense

COMMON NAME(S) Michigan moonwort

STATUS Native (endemic to North America), rare

HABITAT/DISTRIBUTION Meadows and forest edges; also occurs in western North America

Plants are terrestrial and inconspicuous, usually less than 10cm tall but can be up to 20cm. **Stems** are upright. **Leaves** are bluish green to dark green, slightly waxy, and divided into a sterile bladelike trophophore and a fertile sporophore that join well above the ground. The mostly greenish-yellow shared common stalk may have a very light reddish stripe below the trophophore. The **trophophore** is 2-pinnate, ovate to triangular, with no stalk or only a very short stalk, and up to 7 pairs of pinnae. The **pinnae** are narrowly ovate to oblong and broadest at the middle, and the ultimate divisions of the pinnae are lobes with more or less pointed ends. The divisions on the upper edges of the pinnae are generally shallower than those on the lower edges. The pinnae in the lowest pair are narrowly triangular to ovate or oblong and are distinctly larger than the remaining pinnae toward the tip of the blade. The pinnae in the second pair from the bottom are abruptly reduced in size compared to the lowest pinnae, and all subsequent pinnae have pinnate venation, with a clear midrib. **Veins** in the trophophore pinnae are free and forked. The **sporophore** stalk is 50–100% as long as the entire trophophore, and the fertile section has a central rachis with side branches. **Sporangia** are dull yellow or brown at maturity. 2n=180 (tetraploid).

Plants of *Botrychium michiganense*.
PHOTOGRAPH (RIGHT) BY MALCOLM MACFARLANE

Botrychium minganense

COMMON NAME(S) Mingan moonwort
(in reference to Mingan Archipelago, Québec)

NOTABLE SYNONYMS *Botrychium lunaria* var. *minganense*

STATUS Native, uncommon

HABITAT/DISTRIBUTION Meadows, open forests, and grassy dunes;
also occurs in western North America, Mexico, and Iceland

Plants are terrestrial and inconspicuous, usually less than 10cm tall. **Stems** are upright. **Leaves** are yellow green to green, lustrous, and divided into a sterile bladelike trophophore and a fertile sporophore that join well above the ground. The **trophophore** is 1-pinnate, oblong to narrowly ovate, with a distinct short stalk, and up to 10 well-spaced pairs of pinnae. The **pinnae** are short stalked, usually undivided, symmetrical, and narrowly fan shaped. The pinnae gradually reduce in size from the bottom of the blade to the tip. The lowest pinnae span an arc of 60–120° and may be somewhat smaller than the second set of pinnae. Above the lowest pair, the pinnae are entire or with 3–5 lobes, have palmate venation and no clear midrib, and the pinna bases are narrow where they attach to the rachis (usually less than 1/3 of the pinna width). **Veins** in the trophophore pinnae are free and forked. The **sporophore** is sprawling and flexible, has a stalk that is longer than the trophophore, and has a central rachis with long-stalked side branches spaced apart. **Sporangia** are yellowish brown at maturity. 2n=180 (tetraploid).

Plants of *Botrychium minganense*.

Botrychium mormo

COMMON NAME(S) Little goblin moonwort

STATUS Native (endemic to eastern North America), rare

HABITAT/DISTRIBUTION Dense forests with moist soils in the upper Midwest of the U.S.

Plants are terrestrial and inconspicuous, usually 5cm tall or less. **Stems** are upright. **Leaves** are yellowish white to pale green, lustrous, fleshy to somewhat succulent, and divided into a sterile bladelike trophophore and a fertile sporophore that join well above the ground. The shared common stalk is pale whitish. The **trophophore** is 1-pinnate, linear to narrowly oblong, with a stalk up to 2.5cm long and up to 3 pairs of pinnae spaced widely apart. The **pinnae** are variable in shape, mostly rectangular to fan shaped and widest at the tip, simple or split into lobes, and sessile, with a broad base where the pinna attaches to the rachis (usually more than ⅓ of the pinna width). The pinnae in the lowest pair are simple and elongated, or divided into rounded pinnules that are each similar to the pinnae farther up. The pinnae above the lowest pair have palmate venation, without a clear midrib. **Veins** in the trophophore pinnae are free and forked. The **sporophore** stalk is about as long as the entire trophophore or somewhat longer, and the fertile section has a central rachis with side branches. **Sporangia** are dull yellow or brown at maturity and are partly embedded in the rachis (a distinctive feature of *B. mormo*). 2n=90 (diploid).

Plants of *Botrychium mormo*.

PHOTOGRAPHS BY MALCOLM MACFARLANE

F S C **N**

Botrychium neolunaria

COMMON NAME(S) American moonwort

NOTABLE SYNONYMS *Botrychium lunaria*. Historically, *B. lunaria* was considered a single species with a circumboreal distribution in the Northern Hemisphere, but a recent study showed that this taxon includes multiple species that can be differentiated genetically and morphologically. In our region, we have *B. neolunaria* but not *B. lunaria*.

STATUS Native (endemic to North America), uncommon

HABITAT/DISTRIBUTION Rich, open meadows and woods; also occurs in western North America

Plants are terrestrial and inconspicuous, usually 7cm tall or less. **Stems** are upright. **Leaves** are deep green, lustrous, and divided into a sterile bladelike trophophore and a fertile sporophore that join well above the ground. The **trophophore** is 1-pinnate, oblong, sessile or with a distinct short stalk, and up to 5 widely separated pairs of pinnae. The **pinnae** in the lowest pair are fan shaped, short stalked, undivided or palmately divided, very broad, spanning an arc of 160–180°, and are not as strongly ascending as the other pinnae. Pinnae, and the spaces between them, gradually reduce in size from the bottom of the blade to the tip. Above the lowest pair, the span of the pinnae is narrower than in the lowest pair (only 90–120°), the pinnae angle upward, have palmate venation and no clear midrib, and their bases are narrow where they attach to the rachis (usually less than ⅓ of the pinna width). **Veins** in the trophophore pinnae are free and forked. The **sporophore** stalk is longer than the trophophore and has a central rachis with side branches crowded together. The fertile section takes up the tip-most ⅓ of the sporophore. **Sporangia** are yellowish brown at maturity. 2n=90 (diploid).

Plants of *Botrychium neolunaria*.

PHOTOGRAPH (LEFT) BY DONALD FARRAR

Botrychium pallidum

COMMON NAME(S) Pale moonwort

STATUS Native (endemic to North America), rare

HABITAT/DISTRIBUTION Open fields, meadows, and woods; also occurs in western North America

Plants are terrestrial and inconspicuous, usually 7cm tall or less. **Stems** are upright. **Leaves** are pale whitish green to bluish green, glaucous, and divided into a sterile bladelike trophophore and a fertile sporophore that join above ground level. The **trophophore** is 1-pinnate, narrowly ovate to oblong, with a distinct short stalk, and up to 5 pairs of closely spaced lobes or pinnae. The **pinnae** are short stalked, usually undivided, asymmetrically fan shaped to somewhat spatula shaped, and widest at their tips, with the upper portion larger than the lower. The pinnae gradually reduce in size from the bottom of the blade to the tip. The lowest pinnae span an arc of 60–120°. Above the lowest pair, the pinnae have palmate venation and no clear midrib, and the pinna bases are narrow where they attach to the rachis (usually less than ⅓ of the pinna width). **Veins** in the trophophore pinnae are free and forked. The **sporophore** stalk is ca. 50% the length of the trophophore and has a central rachis with long-stalked side branches spaced apart. **Sporangia** are yellowish brown at maturity. $2n=90$ (diploid).

Plants of *Botrychium pallidum*.
PHOTOGRAPH (CENTER) BY DONALD FARRAR

Botrychium simplex var. *simplex*

COMMON NAME(S) **Least moonwort**

STATUS **Native, uncommon**

HABITAT/DISTRIBUTION **Moist fields, meadows, ski slopes, occasionally edges of marshes and other wetlands (although in these habitats, most plants that appear to be *B. simplex* var. *simplex* are instead etiolated individuals of *B. tenebrosum*, p. 212); also occurs in Europe and Greenland (a second variety, *B. simplex* var. *compositum*, occurs in western North America)**

Plants are terrestrial and inconspicuous, usually 7cm tall or less. **Stems** are upright. **Leaves** are yellowish green to green, lustrous or not, and divided into a sterile bladelike trophophore and a fertile sporophore that join at or near ground level. The **trophophore** is undivided (in very small plants) to 1–2-pinnate, linear to oblong or somewhat triangular, with a stalk up to 3cm long and up to 7 pairs of well-defined pinnae. In large plants, the **pinnae** in the lowest pair are disproportionately larger, long stalked, and more dissected than the pinnae farther toward the tip, but with rounded pinnules that are each similar to the tip-ward pinnae. The tip-ward pinnae are asymmetrically fan shaped and widest at the tip, with palmate venation and no clear midrib. The pinnae are simple and sessile, with a broad base where the pinna attaches to the rachis (usually more than ⅓ of the pinna width). **Veins** in the trophophore pinnae are free and forked. The **sporophore** stalk is longer than the entire trophophore, and the fertile section has a central rachis with side branches. The sporophore is often sprawling and flexible, bending over at maturity. **Sporangia** are yellowish brown at maturity. 2n=90 (diploid).

Plants of *Botrychium simplex* var. *simplex*. The photo on the right shows the exaggerated lowest pinnae that sometimes occur in this species.

Botrychium spathulatum

COMMON NAME(S) Spatulate moonwort

STATUS Native (endemic to North America), rare

HABITAT/DISTRIBUTION Meadows, fields, coastal dunes, and disturbed grassy habitats; also occurs in western North America

Plants are terrestrial and inconspicuous, usually less than 8cm tall. **Stems** are upright. **Leaves** are green to dark green and divided into a sterile bladelike trophophore and a fertile sporophore that join well above the ground. The **trophophore** is 1-pinnate, oblong to narrowly triangular, sessile or with a minuscule stalk, and with up to 8 well-spaced pairs of lobes or pinnae. The **pinnae** in the lowest pair are usually larger than those above, fan shaped to spatula shaped, spanning an arc of 60–120°, and entire or with 2–4 shallow lobes that are more or less equal in size, with rounded gaps between the lobes. The tip-most margins of the pinnae or pinna lobes are smooth or may be shallowly scalloped or wavy. The pinnae above the lowest pair are more spatula shaped and may have bluntly pointed tips, palmate venation, and no clear midrib, and the pinna bases are narrow where they attach to the rachis (usually less than ⅓ of the pinna width). **Veins** in the trophophore pinnae are free and forked. The **sporophore** is stiffly erect and has a stalk that is 50–75% the length of the trophophore, with a central rachis and long-stalked side branches spaced apart. **Sporangia** are yellowish brown at maturity. 2n=180 (tetraploid).

Plants of *Botrychium spathulatum*.

PHOTOGRAPHS BY MALCOLM MACFARLANE

F　S　C　N

Botrychium tenebrosum

COMMON NAME(S) Mischievous moonwort

NOTABLE SYNONYMS *Botrychium simplex* var. *tenebrosum*

STATUS Native, rare

HABITAT/DISTRIBUTION Moist meadows, swales, occasionally marsh edges; also occurs in western North America and Switzerland

Plants are terrestrial and inconspicuous, usually 7cm tall or less. **Stems** are upright. **Leaves** are yellowish green to green, lustrous or not, and divided into a sterile bladelike trophophore and a fertile sporophore that join well above the ground. The **trophophore** is lobed to 2–3-pinnate, ovate to somewhat triangular, with a stalk up to 3cm long and up to 7 pairs of well-defined pinnae. The **pinnae** in the lowest pair are somewhat larger than those above and are pinnately divided, with fan-shaped or squarish pinnules that are each similar to the tip-ward pinnae. The tip-ward pinnae are smaller, fan shaped, and widest at their tips, with palmate venation and no clear midrib, and with a broad base where the pinna attaches to the rachis (usually more than ⅓ of the pinna width). The lowest pinnae of the trophophore may occasionally have some sporangia along the margins. **Veins** in the trophophore pinnae are free and forked. The **sporophore** stalk is shorter than or equal to the length of the trophophore, and the fertile section has a central rachis with side branches. The sporophore is upright and erect. **Sporangia** are yellowish brown at maturity. 2n=90 (diploid).

Plants of *Botrychium tenebrosum*.
PHOTOGRAPHS BY DONALD FARRAR

FAMILY: OPHIOGLOSSACEAE

Botrypus virginianus is perhaps the most common and widespread member of the botrychioid group of ferns in eastern North America. This group includes approximately 23 species in our flora that were all formerly included in a large *Botrychium* genus but have now been separated into 3 genera: *Botrypus* (with a single species, *B. virginianus*), *Sceptridium* (with 7 species, p. 458), and a smaller *Botrychium* (now with 15 species, p. 193). Evolutionarily, *Botrychium* and *Sceptridium* are sister genera, meaning that they are each other's closest relatives, and the single species *Botrypus virginianus* is sister to them both. *Botrypus* is typically now treated as a monotypic genus (i.e., it includes only a single species). Plants of *B. virginianus* tend to be quite a bit bigger than members of *Botrychium* and *Sceptridium*, and the sterile portion of its blade often persists after the fertile portion has released spores and withered. Base chromosome number (x) = 46.

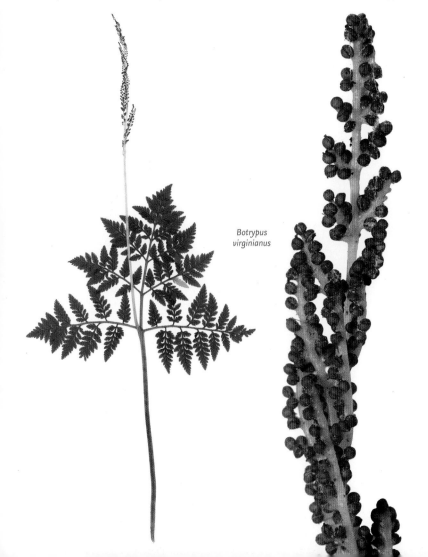

Botrypus virginianus

Botrypus virginianus

COMMON NAME(S) Rattlesnake fern, common grape fern

NOTABLE SYNONYMS *Botrychium virginianum*

STATUS Native, common

HABITAT/DISTRIBUTION Shady forests throughout eastern North America; also occurs in western North America, Mexico, Central and South America, Europe, and Asia

Plants are terrestrial. **Stems** are erect. **Leaves** are up to about 50cm tall and divided into a sterile blade portion (trophophore) and a fertile portion (sporophore) that separate from one another well above ground level, above a common stalk. The **stalk** is fleshy, erect, and pinkish to green. The **trophophore** is broadly triangular, 3–4-pinnate, not stalked, up to 30cm wide at maturity, and oriented horizontally. The **pinnae** of the trophophore are lanceolate and typically have serrate margins. The **sporophore** has a long, erect stalk that emerges directly below the base of the trophophore and ends in a cluster of yellowish to green **sporangia** that are pinnately arranged. 2n=184 (tetraploid).

A. A plant of *Botrypus virginianus.*

B. Trophophore (sterile portion of the leaf).

C. Sporophore (fertile portion of the leaf).

D. The connection point between the sterile trophophore blade and the sporophore stalk.

FAMILY: **POLYPODIACEAE**

Campyloneurum is one of the relatively few fern genera in our flora with undivided, simple fronds; the genus as a whole has the common name strap ferns because of these long, strap-like leaves. As with several other members of the family Polypodiaceae (e.g., *Moranopteris*, p. 352; *Microgramma*, p. 348; and *Phlebodium*, p. 414), *Campyloneurum* is a genus primarily of the Neotropics that enters the North American flora only in southernmost Florida. One species, *C. phyllitidis*, is somewhat common in southern Florida, while the other 2 species are extremely rare and are probably now restricted to Big Cypress and the Fakahatchee Strand. All 3 are epiphytes. Base chromosome number (x) = 37.

KEY TO THE SPECIES OF *CAMPYLONEURUM* IN OUR FLORA:

1a Mature leaves are typically more than 6cm wide; lateral veins are parallel and prominent, and straight to slightly curved ⋯⋯⋯⋯⋯ *Campyloneurum phyllitidis*

1b Mature leaves are less than 6cm wide; lateral veins are obscure and not prominent, and slightly to strongly curved ⋯⋯⋯⋯⋯ 2

  2a Leaves are up to 2cm wide; the petiole is very short, or frequently absent ⋯⋯⋯ *Campyloneurum angustifolium*

  2b Leaves are 2–6cm wide; the petiole is distinct and always present ⋯⋯⋯ *Campyloneurum costatum*

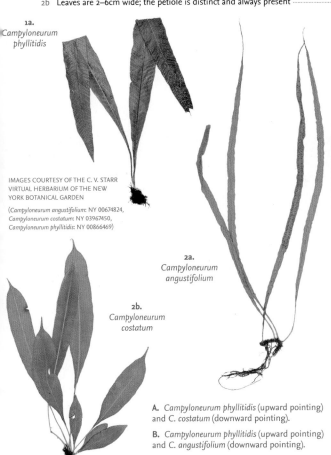

1a.
Campyloneurum phyllitidis

IMAGES COURTESY OF THE C. V. STARR
VIRTUAL HERBARIUM OF THE NEW
YORK BOTANICAL GARDEN

(*Campyloneurum angustifolium*: NY 00674824,
Campyloneurum costatum: NY 03967450,
Campyloneurum phyllitidis: NY 00866469)

2a.
Campyloneurum angustifolium

2b.
Campyloneurum costatum

A. *Campyloneurum phyllitidis* (upward pointing)
and *C. costatum* (downward pointing).

B. *Campyloneurum phyllitidis* (upward pointing)
and *C. angustifolium* (downward pointing).

Campyloneurum angustifolium

COMMON NAME(S) Narrow strap fern

STATUS Native, rare

HABITAT/DISTRIBUTION Wet hammocks, swamps, and sloughs (especially the Fakahatchee Strand and Big Cypress), on the bases of rough-barked tree species (e.g., oaks, magnolias); also occurs in the Caribbean, Mexico, and Central and South America

Plants are epiphytes. **Stems** are short creeping and 3–7mm wide, with brown scales. **Leaves** are up to 60cm long, arching or pendent and often clustered along the stem, with a **stipe** that is typically very short or absent; if present, it is up to 8cm long. The leaf **blade** is undivided, yellowish green to dark green, up to 1.5cm wide, and linear, tapering gradually at both ends. Sterile and fertile leaves do not differ in appearance. Leaf **margins** may be somewhat rolled under. The lateral **veins** are not prominent but are parallel and distinctly curved. **Sori** are round, without indusia, and occur in 1–2 rows on either side of the midrib. 2n=74 (diploid).

A

B

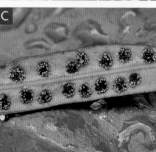
C

D

A. Fertile (left) and sterile (right) leaves of *Campyloneurum angustifolium.*

B. Hanging leaves.

C. Close-up of sori.

D. Sterile leaf; note that lateral veins are not prominent.

Campyloneurum costatum

COMMON NAME(S) Tailed strap fern

STATUS Native, rare

HABITAT/DISTRIBUTION Wet hammocks, swamps, and sloughs (especially the Fakahatchee Strand and Big Cypress), on the bases of rough-barked tree species (e.g., oaks, magnolias); also occurs in the Caribbean, Mexico, and Central and South America

Plants are epiphytes. **Stems** are short creeping and 2–5mm wide, with brown scales. **Leaves** are up to 50cm long, arching or pendent and often clustered along the stem, with a distinct **stipe** up to 15cm long. The leaf **blade** is dark green, undivided, somewhat stiff and leathery, up to 6cm wide, and narrowly elliptic, tapering gradually at the base and quickly at the tip. Sterile and fertile leaves do not differ in appearance. The **leaf tip** may be somewhat long tapering, and the leaf **margins** are often wavy or undulating. The lateral **veins** are not prominent but are parallel and distinctly curved. **Sori** are round, without indusia, and form 1 to several poorly defined rows on either side of the midrib. 2n=74 (diploid).

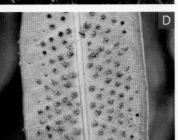

A. Plants of *Campyloneurum costatum.*

B. Young leaves.

C. Older leaves.

D. Sori.

Campyloneurum phyllitidis

COMMON NAME(S) Long strap fern

STATUS Native, somewhat common

HABITAT/DISTRIBUTION Wet hammocks, swamps, and sloughs, occasionally on the walls of limestone sinkholes; also occurs in the Caribbean, Mexico, and Central and South America

Plants are epiphytes or occasionally epipetric (plants are smaller when growing on rock). **Stems** are short creeping and 4–10mm wide, with brown scales. **Leaves** are up to 1.4m long, erect to somewhat arching, often clustered along the stem, and forming a vase shape, usually with no stipe, though if a stipe is present, it can be up to 9cm long. The leaf **blade** is yellowish green, undivided, leathery, up to 12cm wide, and linear to narrowly elliptic, tapering gradually at both ends. Sterile and fertile leaves do not differ in appearance. The leaf **margins** are often slightly wavy or undulating. The lateral **veins** are prominent, parallel to one another and generally straight; if curved, they are only slightly so. **Sori** are round, without indusia, and form 2 well-defined, parallel rows between each pair of lateral veins. 2n=148 (tetraploid).

A. *Campyloneurum phyllitidis* plant.

B. Lower surface of a fertile leaf.

C. Lower leaf surface with prominent lateral veins.

FAMILY: **PTERIDACEAE**

The genus *Ceratopteris* is unique in our flora in being partially to entirely aquatic and having strongly dimorphic leaves. A member of the Pteridaceae, it shares that family's distinguishing characteristic of marginal, linear sori and strongly inrolled pinna margins that form false indusia around the sporangia. All 3 of the *Ceratopteris* species in eastern North America are narrowly distributed in the southeast and Florida and can be found in a variety of natural aquatic habitats, including ponds, lakes, swamps, marshes, and slow-moving streams and rivers, as well as roadside ditches and canals. They are sometimes referred to as "water ferns" because of their strong association with these habitats and their occasional ability to forgo rooting and become entirely floating aquatics, but they are not closely related to the "true" water ferns in the genera *Azolla* (p. 187), *Marsilea* (p. 335), *Pilularia* (p. 421), and *Salvinia* (p. 455). The single native species in our flora, C. *pteridoides*, can be distinguished by its frequently inflated petiole bases, but the other 2 species, both of which are introduced, are essentially indistinguishable from one another morphologically and can be told apart only by counting the number of spores in a sporangium: C. *richardii* is diploid and will have 16 spores, while C. *thalictroides* subsp. *thalictroides* is tetraploid and will have 32. Base chromosome number (x) = 39.

KEY TO THE SPECIES OF *CERATOPTERIS* IN OUR FLORA:

1a Sterile leaves are simple to deeply palmately or pinnately lobed (occasionally more divided) and triangular to heart shaped or ovate; lowest pinnae or lobes of sterile leaves are opposite; petioles are often distinctly inflated ⋯⋯⋯⋯⋯⋯⋯⋯⋯ *Ceratopteris pteridoides*

1b Sterile leaves are 2–3-pinnate and lance shaped to elongate ovate; lowest pinnae of sterile lobes are alternate; petioles are not inflated ⋯⋯⋯⋯⋯⋯⋯⋯⋯⋯⋯⋯⋯⋯⋯⋯ 2

    2a Sporangia contain 32 spores ⋯⋯⋯⋯⋯⋯⋯⋯⋯ *Ceratopteris thalictroides* subsp. *thalictroides*

    2b Sporangia contain 16 spores ⋯⋯⋯⋯⋯⋯⋯⋯⋯⋯⋯⋯⋯⋯⋯⋯⋯⋯⋯⋯ *Ceratopteris richardii*

A colony of *Ceratopteris thalictroides* subsp. *thalictroides*.

F   S   C   N

Ceratopteris pteridoides

COMMON NAME(S) Floating water fern, floating antler fern

STATUS Native, rare (historically much more common)

HABITAT/DISTRIBUTION Semiaquatic to fully aquatic habitats such as canals, swamps, ponds, and marshes; also occurs in the Caribbean, Mexico, Central and South America, and Asia

Plants are floating or sometimes rooted in mud. **Stems** are short, fleshy, and horizontal, becoming erect at the tips. **Leaves** are strongly dimorphic, with sterile leaves arching to spreading and fertile leaves erect, taller, and narrower than the sterile ones. **Stipes** and **rachises** are smooth, green, ridged, and furrowed along their length. **Sterile leaves: Stipes** are up to 19cm long, spongy and usually distinctly inflated, and up to 2cm in diameter. The leaf **blade** is undivided to deeply pinnatifid or palmately 3-lobed, or occasionally up to 4- or 5-pinnate, ovate to heart shaped (cordate) or triangular, and up to 33cm long and 29cm wide. **Pinnae** are typically opposite, with lobes ovate to oblong and tips blunt or sharp. **Fertile leaves: Stipes** are similar to those of sterile leaves but slightly longer, up to 25cm. The leaf **blade** is 1–4-pinnate, heart shaped (cordate) to broadly triangular, and up to 25cm long and 50cm wide. **Pinnae** are typically alternate, with linear, narrow terminal segments. **Veins** form networks. **Margins** are smooth and strongly inrolled on the fertile pinnae, forming a **false indusium** that covers the sporangia. 2n=78 (diploid).

Plants of *Ceratopteris pteridoides* with sterile (left) and fertile (right) leaves. Note the inflated stipe bases.

Ceratopteris richardii

COMMON NAME(S) Triangle water fern, "C-Fern" (when used for educational and scientific purposes)

STATUS Unclear but likely introduced; uncommon

HABITAT/DISTRIBUTION Ponds or other still to slow-moving bodies of water; known from only 1 or 2 locations each in Alabama and Louisiana; native to the Caribbean and West Africa

Plants are floating or sometimes rooted in mud. **Stems** are short, fleshy, and horizontal, becoming erect at the tips. **Leaves** are strongly dimorphic, with sterile leaves arching to spreading and fertile leaves erect, taller, and narrower than the sterile ones. **Stipes** and **rachises** are smooth, green, ridged, and furrowed along their length. **Sterile leaves: Stipes** are up to 11cm long and spongy but not inflated. The leaf **blade** on small leaves is deeply lobed to 1-pinnate, but on bigger leaves is up to 2-pinnate-pinnatifid, lanceolate to ovate or broadly triangular, and up to 16cm long and 17cm wide. **Pinnae** are typically alternate, with ovate to triangular lobes and blunt or sharp tips. **Fertile leaves: Stipes** are up to 9cm long and spongy but not inflated. The leaf **blade** is 2–3-pinnate, lanceolate to ovate or broadly triangular, and up to 19cm long and 12cm wide. **Pinnae** are typically alternate, with linear, narrow terminal segments. **Veins** form networks. **Margins** are smooth and strongly inrolled on the fertile pinnae, forming a **false indusium** that covers the sporangia. 2n=78 (diploid).

A. Sterile leaves of *Ceratopteris richardii*.

B. Sterile leaves with vegetative plantlets.

C. Lower surfaces of fertile pinnae.

D. Fertile pinnae.

F S C N

Ceratopteris thalictroides subsp. *thalictroides*

COMMON NAME(S) Water sprite, water hornfern

STATUS Unclear but may be native; somewhat common

HABITAT/DISTRIBUTION Semiaquatic to fully aquatic habitats such as canals, swamps, ponds, and marshes; occurs worldwide in the tropics, except for Africa (additional, cryptic subspecies are suspected to be present in Asia and the Austral-Pacific region)

- -

Plants are usually rooted in mud or soil. **Stems** are short, fleshy, and horizontal, becoming erect at the tips. **Leaves** are strongly dimorphic, with sterile leaves arching to spreading and fertile leaves erect, taller, and narrower than the sterile ones. **Stipes** and **rachises** are smooth, green, ridged, and furrowed along their length. **Sterile leaves: Stipes** are up to 31cm long and spongy but not inflated. The leaf **blade** is 1–3-pinnate, ovate to heart shaped (cordate) to broadly triangular, and up to 41cm long and 20cm wide. **Pinnae** are more or less alternate, and ultimate segments are ovate lanceolate. **Fertile leaves: Stipes** are up to 46cm long and spongy but not inflated. The leaf **blade** is 2-, 3-, or 4-pinnate toward the base but 2-pinnate toward the tip, lanceolate to ovate or broadly triangular, and up to 71cm long and 48cm wide. **Pinnae** are typically alternate, with linear, narrow terminal segments. **Veins** form networks. **Margins** are smooth and strongly inrolled on the fertile pinnae, forming a **false indusium** that covers the sporangia. 2n=156 (tetraploid).

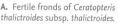

A. Fertile fronds of *Ceratopteris thalictroides* subsp. *thalictroides*.

B. A sterile frond.

C. Lower surface of a fertile frond.

FAMILY: **OPHIOGLOSSACEAE**

The genus *Cheiroglossa* has only 1 (or possibly 2) species known worldwide, and *C. palmata*, the hand fern, occurs in our flora in Florida. Historically this taxon has been included in the genera *Ophioderma* and *Ophioglossum*, but it is now stably recognized as belonging to its own genus, *Cheiroglossa*. This species differs from all other members of the family Ophioglossaceae in eastern North America, except for *Ophioderma pendulum* (p. 375), in being epiphytic. These 2 species can easily be distinguished from one another by the broad, fan-shaped, deeply palmately lobed leaves of *C. palmata* versus the elongated, ribbon-like leaves of *O. pendulum*. Base chromosome number (x) = 30.

*Cheiroglossa
palmata*

Fertile fronds of *Cheiroglossa palmata*.

IMAGE COURTESY OF THE C. V. STARR
VIRTUAL HERBARIUM OF THE NEW YORK
BOTANICAL GARDEN (NY 03865972)

Cheiroglossa palmata

COMMON NAME(S) Hand fern, dwarf staghorn, hand tongue

NOTABLE SYNONYMS *Ophioglossum palmatum, Ophioderma palmatum*

STATUS Native, rare

HABITAT/DISTRIBUTION Wet hammocks and swamps, often growing on sabal palms (*Sabal palmetto*); also occurs in the Caribbean, Mexico, and Central and South America

Plants are epiphytic, with dichotomously branching **roots** that proliferate under and around humus and old leaf bases. **Stems** are tan to yellow, with light brown to brown hairs near the stem apex. **Leaves** are pendent, hanging down from the attachment point on the tree, and have a stalk up to 17cm long. The **sterile segment of the leaf** (trophophore) is firm, may be somewhat leathery, and is up to 45cm long and 35 wide, fan shaped, and deeply palmately lobed, dividing into several elongated lobes (each up to 15cm or so long) that hang down straight or at an angle from the center of the leaf. The **fertile segments of the leaf** (sporophores) emerge from the stalk before the trophophore blade begins, with each sporophore consisting of a small stalked unit up to 7cm long that bears **sporangia** in 2 rows. **Margins** are entire. **Veins** are anastomosing, forming networks with large areoles, up to 8 × 35mm. 2n=unknown.

A. A sabal palm with several *Cheiroglossa palmata* plants growing on it.

B. Two leaves, one with a fertile sporophore at the base of the blade.

C. Close-up of a sporophore.

D. Fertile leaves with multiple sporophores.

FAMILY: **THELYPTERIDACEAE**

Christella was previously included in *Thelypteris* (p. 475) but is now considered to be separate based on morphological and DNA-sequence evidence. Historically, 1 native species of *Christella*, *C. hispidula*, was present throughout the south, but a second species, *C. dentata*, was introduced several decades ago from Asia and seems to have displaced *C. hispidula* almost completely. The latter is now extremely difficult to find. The 2 are quite similar in appearance but can be distinguished by their stipe color (yellowish in *C. hispidula* vs. purplish in *C. dentata*), and by the venation of the pinnules in the pinnae. The lowest veins of 2 adjacent pinnules typically join each other below the sinus, or gap, between the pinnules, to form a single "excurrent" vein that then runs up to reach the leaf margin at the base of the sinus. In *C. dentata*, this excurrent vein is 2–4mm long, and in *C. hispidula* it is less than 2mm long (and sometimes absent, with the lowest veins running straight to the margin rather than forming an excurrent vein). Base chromosome number (x) = 36.

KEY TO THE SPECIES OF *CHRISTELLA* IN OUR FLORA:

1a Stipes are pale yellow or straw colored; lowest veins in adjacent pinnules either come together right at the sinus, or form an excurrent vein that is less than 2mm long and continues to the sinus ⋯⋯⋯⋯⋯⋯⋯⋯⋯⋯⋯⋯⋯⋯⋯⋯ *Christella hispidula*

1b Stipes are dark green-purple to purple; lowest veins in adjacent pinnules join to form an excurrent vein that is 2–4mm long and continues to the sinus ⋯⋯⋯⋯⋯⋯ *Christella dentata*

Pinnae of *Christella dentata* (top) and *C. hispidula* (bottom) showing adjacent pinnules and their venation pattern; the lengths of the excurrent veins are labeled.

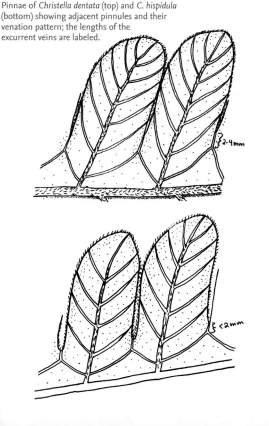

1b.
Christella dentata

F   S   C   N

Christella dentata

COMMON NAME(S) Downy maiden fern, downy shield fern, tapering tri-vein fern

NOTABLE SYNONYMS *Thelypteris dentata*

STATUS Not native, common

HABITAT/DISTRIBUTION Woods, hammocks, floodplains, and disturbed habitats; native to Asia and Africa

Plants are terrestrial. **Stems** are short creeping. **Leaves** are up to 1.5m long and close together along the stem. Sterile and fertile leaves are similar in appearance, though fertile leaves are often more erect and have a longer stipe, with somewhat contracted pinnae. **Stipes** are dark, usually purplish brown, up to 50cm long, with hairs and hairy brown scales, both of which are denser toward the base. The **rachis** is similar to the stipe. The leaf **blade** is up to 1m long and 25cm wide, 1-pinnate-pinnatifid and becoming pinnatifid toward the tip, and ovate lanceolate but with the lowest few pairs of pinnae gradually shortening in length. Minute hairs are present on the lower surface of the leaf and along the veins, and slightly larger hairs are present along the veins on the upper surface. **Pinnae** are up to 17cm long and 3cm wide, with blunt, rounded to squarish lobes. **Margins** are smooth. **Veins** are free, and the lowest veins in adjacent pinnules come together in an excurrent vein that continues to the sinus between the pinnules and is 2–4mm long. **Sori** are round or slightly kidney shaped and located midway between the pinnule midvein and the margin. Tan **indusia** are present and may be hairy. 2n=144 (tetraploid).

A. Fronds of *Christella dentata*.

B. Note the dark stipe and rachis.

C. Lowest pinnae gradually tapering in length.

D. Fertile pinnae with sori.

Christella hispidula

COMMON NAME(S) Variable maiden fern, rough hairy maiden fern, St. John's shield fern

NOTABLE SYNONYMS *Thelypteris hispidula* var. *versicolor* (the equivalent varietal name has not yet been published for this taxon in *Christella*, but the American plants will likely eventually be known as *Christella hispidula* var. *versicolor*)

STATUS Native, rare (historically much more common)

HABITAT/DISTRIBUTION Damp soils, especially in moist woodlands and around limestone sinks; also occurs in Mexico, Central America, Africa, and the Austral-Pacific region (though the American plants are considered to be their own variety; see above)

Plants are terrestrial. **Stems** are short creeping. **Leaves** are up to 95cm long and close together along the stem. Sterile and fertile leaves are similar in appearance. **Stipes** are pale yellow or straw colored, up to 40cm long, with hairs and hairy brown scales, both of which are denser toward the base. The **rachis** is similar to the stipe. The leaf **blade** is up to 55cm long and 28cm wide, 1-pinnate-pinnatifid and gradually becoming pinnatifid toward the tip, and ovate lanceolate but with the lowest few pairs of pinnae somewhat to much shorter than those farther up. Minute hairs are present on both surfaces of the blade, especially along the veins, and minute, yellow, stalked glands may be present. **Pinnae** are up to 14cm long and 2cm wide, with blunt, rounded lobes. **Margins** are smooth. **Veins** are free, and the lowest veins in adjacent pinnules either meet right at or beneath the sinus or join to form an excurrent vein that continues to the sinus and is no more than 2mm long. **Sori** are round or slightly kidney shaped, located midway between the pinnule midvein and the margin. Tan **indusia** are present and may be hairy. 2n=72 (diploid).

1a.
*Christella
hispidula*

FAMILY: **OSMUNDACEAE**

The interrupted fern, *Claytosmunda claytoniana*, is a large, distinctive plant whose common name derives from one of its most obvious features: the dimorphic fertile leaves, in which only the middle sets of pinnae are fertile and highly reduced, "interrupting" the otherwise sterile and leafy blade. This feature is emphasized later in the season, as the fertile pinnae tend to release their spores early and then wither away, leaving a gap in the leaf blade. The only other species the interrupted fern might be confused with is its close relative the cinnamon fern, *Osmundastrum cinnamomeum* subsp. *cinnamomeum* (p. 388), but the latter can be distinguished by the distinctive tufts of cinnamon-colored hairs at the bases of its pinnae, on the lower surfaces of the leaves. The interrupted fern does not have these tufts of hairs. This species forms a hybrid with another close relative, the royal fern (*Osmunda spectabilis*, p. 386) to form Rugg's osmunda (see p. 386), now recognized as the intergeneric hybrid ×*Osmunimunda ruggii*. Base chromosome number (x) = 22.

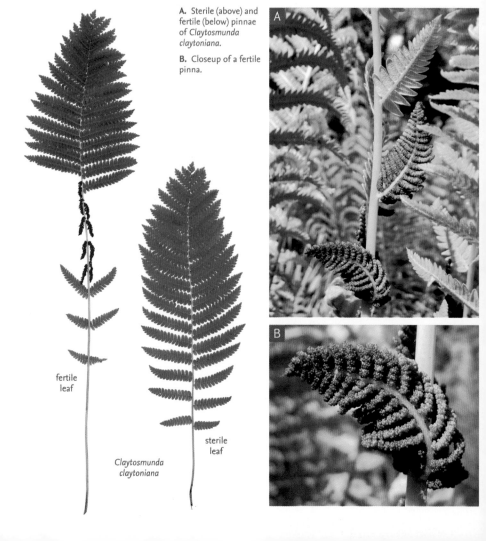

A. Sterile (above) and fertile (below) pinnae of *Claytosmunda claytoniana*.

B. Closeup of a fertile pinna.

A

B

fertile leaf

sterile leaf

Claytosmunda claytoniana

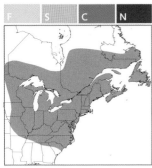

Claytosmunda claytoniana

COMMON NAME(S) Interrupted fern

NOTABLE SYNONYMS *Osmunda claytoniana*

STATUS Native (endemic to eastern North America), common

HABITAT/DISTRIBUTION Moist to wet forests, roadsides, and other somewhat damp habitats, in shade to partial shade

Plants are terrestrial. **Stems** lack scales and are creeping but become erect at the tips, forming small trunks or tussocks. Old persistent stipe bases and black fibrous roots are often apparent around the leaf bases. **Leaves** form vaselike clumps and are partly dimorphic. The fertile leaves are in the center of the plant and are upright, erect, and longer than the sterile leaves, which surround them and are arching to spreading. On the fertile leaves, the fertile pinnae "interrupt" the blade in the middle, while the pinnae above and below the fertile section are identical to those on the sterile leaves. **Sterile leaves:** up to 1m long; **stipes** are up to 30cm, often winged, yellow to green, with light brown hairs when young but becoming smooth at maturity; **rachis** is grooved on the upper surface, green, often winged, and covered in cinnamon-colored hairs only when young; leaf **blade** is elliptic to oblong, up to 70cm long and 30cm wide, 1-pinnate-pinnatifid at the base and becoming pinnatifid toward the very tip; **pinnae** are typically in 20–30 pairs, broadly oblong, without tufts of cinnamon hair at the bases; **margins** are smooth and lobed (pinnatifid); **veins** are free and forked, reaching to the margins. **Fertile leaves:** similar to the sterile leaves overall, but shorter and more erect; **fertile pinnae** are in 2–7 pairs toward the middle of the blade, while the remaining pinnae above and below are sterile; these fertile pinnae are reduced to short, contracted stalks bearing globose sporangia. 2n=44 (diploid).

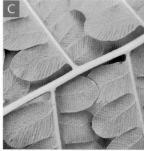

A. Sterile leaves of *Claytosmunda claytoniana*.

B. Fertile leaves.

C. Lower surface of the leaf, without distinct tufts of hair where the pinnae meet the rachis (for comparison with *Osmundastrum cinnamomeum*).

D. Wing of tissue along the rachis.

FAMILY: **THELYPTERIDACEAE**

Coryphopteris simulata, the Massachusetts fern, was previously treated in the genus *Thelypteris* and is a fairly common inhabitant of wetlands and damp forests in the northeastern U.S. and into southeastern Canada. It also has a disjunct distribution in the unglaciated portion of southern Wisconsin that is known as the Driftless Area. *Coryphopteris simulata* is most likely to be confused with the 2 other thelypteroid ferns found in the northern parts of eastern North America: *Thelypteris palustris*, the marsh fern (p. 475), and *Amauropelta noveboracensis*, the New York fern (p. 131). In *Coryphopteris*, the pinnae do not continue all the way to the ground, getting shorter as they go (which they do in *A. noveboracensis*), and the lateral veins of the pinnae in *Coryphopteris* do not fork, while *T. palustris* typically has strongly forked lateral pinna veins. Base chromosome number (x) = 31, 32, 33.

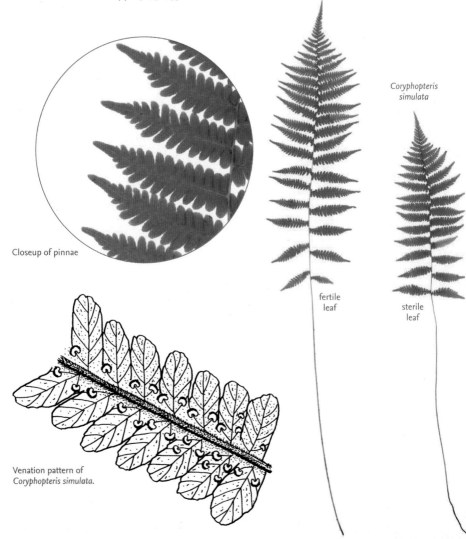

Closeup of pinnae

Coryphopteris simulata

fertile leaf

sterile leaf

Venation pattern of *Coryphopteris simulata*.

F | S | C | N

Coryphopteris simulata

COMMON NAME(S) Massachusetts fern, bog fern

NOTABLE SYNONYMS *Thelypteris simulata, Parathelypteris simulata*

STATUS Native (endemic to eastern North America), somewhat common

HABITAT/DISTRIBUTION Shady swamps, bogs, and other damp, acidic soils

----

Plants are terrestrial. **Stems** are long creeping, with scattered, pale brown scales. **Leaves** are up to 80cm long, and sterile and fertile fronds are similar, though fertile ones may be taller and more erect while sterile fronds are more arching. **Stipes** are up to 45cm long and brown to yellowish green toward the base, becoming greener toward the blade, with scattered tan scales at the base. The **rachis** is yellowish green to green, and often somewhat hairy on the upper surface but not the lower. The leaf **blade** is up to 35cm long and 15cm wide, 1-pinnate-pinnatifid (becoming pinnatifid at the tip), lanceolate, and widest at or just above the base of the blade. The lower surface of the blade may have scattered hairs, especially along the pinna midveins, often mixed with minute, yellowish-reddish glands, while the upper surface will have scattered hairs primarily along the veins. **Pinnae** are up to 10cm long and 2cm wide and lanceolate to linear; the lowest pinnae may be slightly smaller than the higher pairs, may narrow somewhat toward the rachis, and may reflex outward toward the base of the leaf. The pinna midvein has a distinct narrow groove in the upper surface. **Margins** are entire but may be somewhat crenulate or uneven. Lateral **veins** are free and never forked, and the pinna midveins may be grooved on the upper surface. **Sori** are round and located midway between the pinnule midvein and the margin. **Indusia** are present and kidney bean shaped and often have small glandular hairs. 2n=128 (tetraploid).

A. A colony of *Coryphopteris simulata.*

B. Frond with reflexed lowest pinnae.

C. Lower leaf surface with sori.

D. Close-up of fertile pinnae.

FAMILY: HYMENOPHYLLACEAE

Crepidomanes intricatum is 1 of only 2 fern species in eastern North America that is truly gametophyte only, meaning that the plants never produce sporophytes (the other such species is *Vittaria appalachiana*, p. 483). Several additional species in our flora (e.g., *Hymenophyllum tayloriae*, p. 318; *Moranopteris nimbata*, p. 352; and *Lomariopsis kunzeana*, p. 324) are most commonly encountered in the gametophyte stage but do in fact produce sporophytes when conditions are suitable (and are known to do so in our region). *Crepidomanes intricatum* and *V. appalachiana* both belong to primarily tropical genera and are presumed to have lost the ability to produce sporophytes after the last ice age. Unlike other members of these genera, which would have retreated to more tropical climates in the south during the ice age, these species apparently remained in the temperate region of eastern North American where today they are essentially stranded. Their continued survival outside the tropics relies on the availability of suitable habitat, primarily crevices and rockhouses in sandstone where temperature and humidity are buffered compared to the outside air. Even in these habitats, although the plants can persist vegetatively as gametophytes, they are unable to reproduce sexually and produce new sporophytes. Base chromosome number (x) = 34.

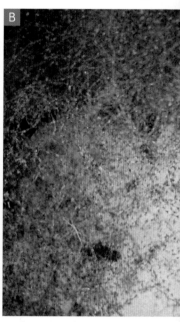

A. A large colony of *Crepidomanes intricatum* growing on the wall of a cave.

B. Gametophyte filaments under the microscope.

Crepidomanes intricatum

COMMON NAME(S) Weft fern

NOTABLE SYNONYMS *Trichomanes intricatum*

STATUS Native (endemic to eastern North America), rare

HABITAT/DISTRIBUTION Sandstone and other noncalcareous rocks, in caves, crevices, rockhouses, and grottoes throughout the inner uplands of the eastern U.S.

Plants are terrestrial and epipetric but may very occasionally be epiphytic. **Sporophytes** are not known. **Gametophytes** are filamentous, forming branching chains of elongated single cells that interweave to produce densely entangled mats. They somewhat resemble roughened felt, or a very fine moss. Vegetative reproduction occurs via **gemmae**, which are short sets of undifferentiated cells capable of regenerating a new gametophyte. 2n=136 (tetraploid).

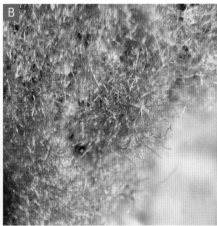

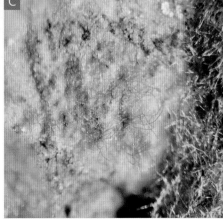

A. A colony of *Crepidomanes intricatum*.

B. Gametophyte filaments.

C. Close-up of gametophyte filaments.

FAMILY: **PTERIDACEAE**

The genus *Cryptogramma* is more common in western than eastern North America, and we have only 2 species in the eastern flora: *C. acrostichoides* and *C. stelleri*. Both species are strongly dimorphic, with the fertile leaves generally taller and having distinctly pointed pinna lobes, while the sterile leaves are shorter and have more rounded lobes. Both species also have distinctive inrolled leaf margins that form false indusia characteristic of the family Pteridaceae. These *Cryptogramma* species and the members of *Ceratopteris* (p. 219) are the only strongly dimorphic members of this family in our flora, but they do not resemble one another and their ranges do not overlap, so there is little danger of confusing them. Base chromosome number (x) = 30.

KEY TO THE SPECIES OF *CRYPTOGRAMMA* IN OUR FLORA:

1a   Stems are 10–20mm wide and branch regularly; stem scales are 2-colored, with
      a dark central stripe and lighter margins; leaves are firm in texture and densely
      clustered along the stem ·· *Cryptogramma acrostichoides*

1b   Stems are 1–1.5mm wide and branch infrequently; stem scales are uniformly
      pale brown; leaves are delicate in texture and scattered along the stem ····································· *Cryptogramma stelleri*

IMAGE COURTESY OF THE C. V. STARR VIRTUAL HERBARIUM OF THE NEW YORK BOTANICAL GARDEN (NY 02633725)

1a.
Cryptogramma acrostichoides

fertile leaf

sterile leaf

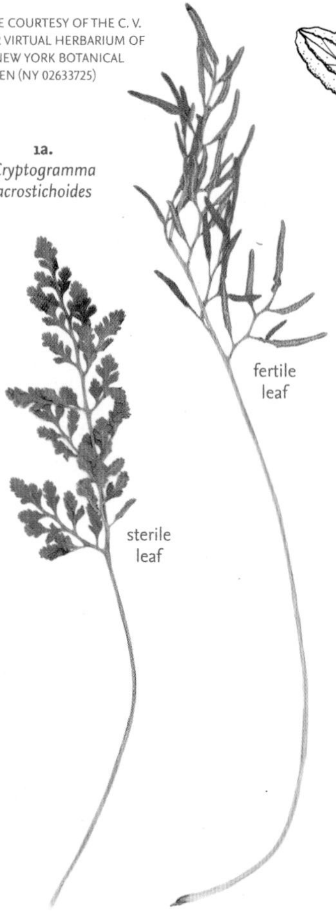

Lower leaf surface of *Cryptogramma stelleri*, showing sori and false indusium around the edges.

1b.
Cryptogramma stelleri

fertile leaves

sterile leaf

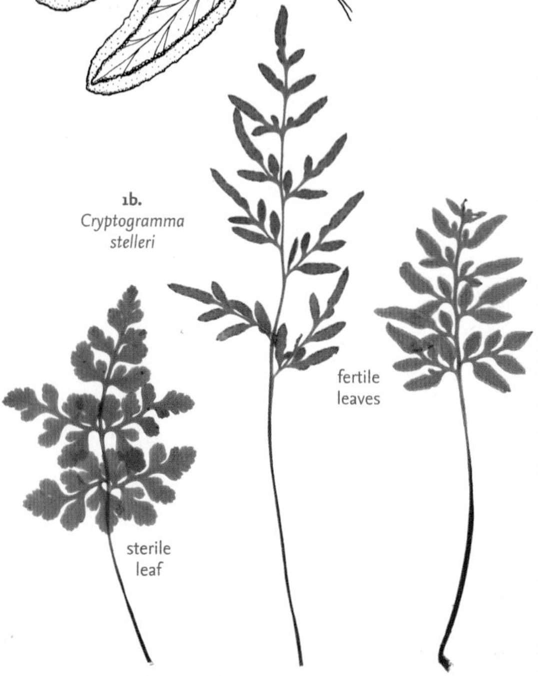

Cryptogramma acrostichoides

COMMON NAME(S) American parsley fern, American rockbrake

STATUS Native, rare

HABITAT/DISTRIBUTION Noncalcareous rocks; also occurs in western North America and Asia

Plants are terrestrial and epipetric. **Stems** are stout (10–20mm wide), long creeping, regularly branched, with many old petiole bases still attached, and with hairs and 2-colored scales (these are dark at the center with lighter brown margins). **Leaves** are firm in texture, densely clustered along the stem, may remain green over winter, and are strongly dimorphic, with the fertile leaves longer and wider than the sterile leaves. **Stipes** are smooth, roughly half the total length of the leaf, dark brown to black for a few centimeters near the base but then becoming green, and sometimes have a shallow groove on the upper surface. The **rachis** is green, with small scattered hairs, and occasionally some scattered brown scales. **Sterile leaves** are up to 17cm long and 6cm wide, with the **blade** deltate to ovate lanceolate and 2–3-pinnate. **Sterile pinnae** are oblong to ovate lanceolate and shallowly, bluntly lobed. **Fertile leaves** are up to 25cm long and 8cm wide, with the **blade** broadly lanceolate to elongate triangular and 2-pinnate at the base to 1-pinnate toward the tip. **Fertile pinnae** are linear. **Margins** are bluntly toothed on sterile pinnae, and smooth but strongly inrolled on fertile pinnae, forming a **false indusium** that covers the **sporangia**. **Veins** are free and forked. 2n=120 (tetraploid).

A. A plant of Cryptogramma acrostichoides.
PHOTOGRAPH BY ALAN CRESSLER

B. A young plant with fertile pinnae still unfurling.

C. Close-up of a fertile frond.

F   S   C   N

Cryptogramma stelleri

COMMON NAME(S) Slender parsley fern, fragile rockbrake, Steller's rockbrake, slender rockbrake, slender cliffbrake

STATUS Native, uncommon

HABITAT/DISTRIBUTION Rocky, typically calcareous habitats including ledges and cliffs, often in shaded, moist, seepy crevices; also occurs in western North America and Asia

Plants are terrestrial and epipetric. **Stems** are long creeping and narrow (1–1.5mm wide), branching only seldomly, with hairs and scattered, light brown scales. **Leaves** are finely textured, typically die back by late summer, and are strongly dimorphic, with the fertile leaves longer and wider than the sterile leaves. **Stipes** are smooth, roughly half the total length of the leaf, dark brown to black in the lower half but becoming green toward the blade, and sometimes have a shallow groove on the upper surface. The **rachis** is smooth and green. **Sterile leaves** are up to 15cm long and 6cm wide, with the **blade** ovate lanceolate and 1-pinnate-pinnatifid to 2-pinnate. **Sterile pinnae** are ovate lanceolate and shallowly, bluntly lobed. **Fertile leaves** are up to 20cm long and 7.5cm wide, with the **blade** broadly lanceolate to elongate triangular and 2-pinnate at the base to 1-pinnate toward the tip. **Fertile pinnae** are lanceolate to linear, with long-tapering tips; lower, 2-pinnate fertile pinnae have lance-shaped pinnules. **Margins** are shallowly toothed to wavy on sterile pinnae, and smooth but strongly inrolled on fertile pinnae, forming a **false indusium** that covers the **sporangia**. **Veins** are free and forked. 2n=60 (diploid).

A. A population of *Cryptogramma stelleri* on a rock ledge.

B. Fertile leaves.

C. Sterile leaves, with fertile leaves to the left and behind.

D. Lower surface of a fertile leaf, with false indusium running around the margins.

FAMILY: **DRYOPTERIDACEAE**

The 2 species of *Ctenitis* in our flora occur primarily in southern Florida, though 1 (*C. submarginalis*) has also been found in Louisiana, and other populations may be present in the Gulf Coast region. Both are currently listed as endangered in Florida and are very rare. The 2 species are quite dissimilar in appearance and are more likely to be confused with members of other genera: *C. sloanei* perhaps with *Macrothelypteris torresiana* (which has dense hairs on its lower leaf surface, while *C. sloanei* does not; p. 333), and *C. submarginalis* with *Christella dentata* (p. 226), which it is strikingly similar to. The latter 2 can be distinguished by their sori (*Ctenitis submarginalis* loses its indusia by maturity while *Christella dentata* retains them) and by their pinna bases: the pinnae in *Ctenitis submarginalis* may have a short stalk, and whether they are stalked or not, there is usually a gap between the rachis and the first pinnule on the tip-most side of the pinna; *Christella dentata* lacks this feature, with its first, upper pinnules typically touching the rachis. Both *Ctenitis* species include "comb fern" in their common names, a reference to the comblike nature of the pinnae in some members of this genus. *Ctenitis sloanei* is often referred to as the "Florida tree fern" because of its tendency to develop a short trunk; however, it is not a member of the true tree ferns (which are in the order Cyatheales), and this is therefore a rather misleading common name. Base chromosome number (x) = 41.

KEY TO THE SPECIES OF *CTENITIS* IN OUR FLORA:

1a   The leaf blade is 2–4-pinnate-pinnatifid and broadly ovate to triangular ⋯⋯⋯⋯⋯⋯⋯⋯⋯⋯⋯⋯⋯ *Ctenitis sloanei*

1b   The leaf blade is 1-pinnate-pinnatifid and narrowly ovate or lanceolate ⋯⋯⋯⋯⋯⋯⋯⋯⋯⋯⋯⋯ *Ctenitis submarginalis*

1a.
*Ctenitis
sloanei*

1b.
*Ctenitis
submarginalis*

Ctenitis sloanei

F S C N

COMMON NAME(S) Florida tree fern, red-hair comb fern

STATUS Native, rare

HABITAT/DISTRIBUTION Wooded hammocks and cypress swamps; also occurs in the Caribbean, Mexico, and Central and South America

----

Plants are terrestrial. **Stems** are erect to ascending and may form short trunks covered in orange-brown to golden scales. **Leaves** are arching and up to about 1.6m long. Sterile and fertile leaves do not differ in appearance. **Stipes** are greenish to pale brown and up to 1m long, with a dense covering of reddish-brown to orange scales, especially at the base. The **rachis** is similar in color to the stipe, with narrow, pale brown to yellowish scales. The leaf **blade** is up to 1m long and 80cm wide, broadly ovate to triangular, and 2–3-pinnate-pinnatifid or occasionally even more divided. Narrow, pale-colored scales are usually present on the lower surface, especially along the main veins. **Pinnae** are up to 50cm long and 23cm wide, with the lowest pair of pinnae noticeably longer and wider than those higher up the blade. The ultimate divisions (pinnulets) are bluntly lobed. **Margins** are smooth or slightly wavy and may have hairs. Lateral **veins** are either unbranched or once forked. **Sori** form 1 row midway between the pinnule margin and midrib and are round, with **indusia** that are round to kidney bean shaped, but these are present only when immature; mature sori typically appear not to have indusia. 2n=82 (diploid).

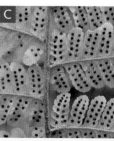

A. A plant of *Ctenitis sloanei.*

B. Lower surface of a fertile pinna.

C. Lower surface of a pinnule further divided into pinnulets, with sori and pale, narrow scales.

D. A plant with a short trunk.

Ctenitis submarginalis

COMMON NAME(S) **Brown-hair comb fern**

STATUS **Native, rare**

HABITAT/DISTRIBUTION **Wooded hammocks and cypress swamps; also occurs in the Caribbean, Mexico, and Central and South America**

Plants are terrestrial. **Stems** are short creeping to erect and may form short trunks covered in reddish-brown scales. **Leaves** are arching and up to about 1m long. Sterile and fertile leaves do not differ in appearance. **Stipes** are yellowish brown and up to 45cm long, with a dense covering of reddish-brown to brown scales, especially at the base. The **rachis** is similar in color to the stipe, with scattered narrow, pale brown scales. The leaf **blade** is up to 60cm long and 35cm wide, narrowly ovate to lanceolate, and 1-pinnate-pinnatifid. Glandular hairs and/or narrow, pale-colored scales may be present on the blade, especially on the lower surface and along the main veins. **Pinnae** are up to 18cm long and 3cm wide and may have a short stalk. **Margins** are smooth or slightly wavy and may have hairs. Lateral **veins** are unbranched. **Sori** form 1 row between the pinnule margin and midvein, often closer to the margin (the source of the specific epithet *submarginalis*), and are round, with **indusia** that are round to kidney bean shaped, but these are present only when immature; mature sori typically appear not to have indusia. 2n=unknown.

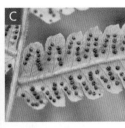

A. A plant of *Ctenitis submarginalis.*

B. Pinnatifid leaf tip.

C. Lower surface of pinnae with sori.

D. Pinna bases with a distinct gap between the upper, innermost pinnules and the rachis.

FAMILY: **THELYPTERIDACEAE**

Cyclosorus is another genus that was previously included in a large *Thelypteris* genus (which now has only 1 species in our flora; p. 475). We also have only 1 species of *Cyclosorus* in eastern North America, *C. interruptus*, which is a common fern of wet habitats in Florida. This fern is easily recognized by its shiny, hairless leaves that are often tough or leathery, and its sori, which are round but very close together, so that they appear to form a bumpy line that runs parallel to the leaf margins. Base chromosome number (x) = 36.

*Cyclosorus
interruptus*

A. Plants of *Cyclosorus interruptus*.

B. Lower leaf surface with immature sori.

Cyclosorus interruptus

COMMON NAME(S) Swamp shield fern, spready tri-vein fern, Willdenow's fern

NOTABLE SYNONYMS *Thelypteris interrupta*

STATUS Native, common

HABITAT/DISTRIBUTION Wet habitats including swamps, hammocks, marshes, open wet woods, and roadside ditches; also occurs in the Caribbean, Mexico, Central and South America, Africa, and the Austral-Pacific region

Plants are terrestrial. **Stems** are long creeping and black. **Leaves** are up to 2m tall, spaced out (every 3–6cm) along the stem and forming diffuse colonies; sterile and fertile leaves do not differ in appearance. **Stipes** are yellowish to tan and up to 1.2m long, without hairs or scales. The **rachis** is similar to the stipe in color, or darker. The leaf **blade** is up to 1.25m long and 30cm wide, 1-pinnate-pinnatifid, narrowly ovate, and widest toward the base and tapering toward the tip (which becomes pinnatifid). **Pinnae** are up to 30cm long and 2cm wide, narrowly triangular, and shiny and smooth on the upper surface but with tan scales on the lower surface; very short (0.1–0.3mm long) hairs may be scattered on the lower surface, especially along the veins. The pinna midvein has a distinct narrow groove in the upper surface. **Margins** are smooth but may be somewhat inrolled toward the sori on fertile pinnae. **Veins** are free; the lowest veins of adjacent pinnules typically meet below the sinus, joining into a single vein 2–4mm long that runs into the sinus. **Sori** are round and sit midway between the margin and the pinnule midvein. **Indusia** are present, attached at the center of the sorus, and may be smooth or have small glandular hairs. 2n=144 (tetraploid).

A. A colony of *Cyclosorus interruptus*.

B. Upper leaf surface.

C. Lower leaf surface with sori.

D. Sori with immature (light green) and mature (black) sporangia.

E. Sori with mature sporangia and tan indusia.

FAMILY: **DRYOPTERIDACEAE**

Cyrtomium is a fern genus native to Asia, Africa, and the Pacific region, but we have 2 introduced and widely distributed species that have escaped from cultivation and naturalized in eastern North America. Both species are relatively large and have 1-pinnate fronds, a feature that makes them fairly easy to distinguish from other, similarly sized ferns in our region. The common name "holly ferns" comes from the rough similarity of the pinnae to the leaves of the hollies (flowering plants in the genus *Ilex*). Both species in our flora are popular as houseplants and ornamentals and are reasonably hardy despite being native to primarily tropical areas. Their cold tolerance has allowed them to spread farther north than other introduced tropical species, which are often restricted to Florida or the southeast. Base chromosome number (x) = 41.

KEY TO THE SPECIES OF *CYRTOMIUM* IN OUR FLORA:

1a Leaves have 4–12 pairs of pinnae; pinnae are roughly ovate but have a
    long, tapering tip; margins are wavy to toothed, with large, irregular teeth ············ *Cyrtomium falcatum* subsp. *falcatum*

1b Leaves have 10–25 pairs of pinnae; pinnae are lanceolate and have an
    elongated tip; margins have small, pointed to minutely rounded teeth ································ *Cyrtomium fortunei*

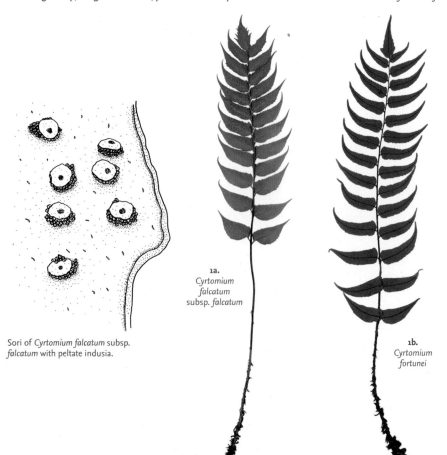

1a.
Cyrtomium
falcatum
subsp. *falcatum*

Sori of *Cyrtomium falcatum* subsp.
falcatum with peltate indusia.

1b.
Cyrtomium
fortunei

Cyrtomium falcatum subsp. falcatum

COMMON NAME(S) Holly fern, Asian holly fern

STATUS Not native, somewhat common

HABITAT/DISTRIBUTION Moist forests and ravines, and rocky areas including rock walls; native to Asia (2 other subspecies, *C. falcatum* subsp. *australe* and *littorale*, have been described from Asia)

Plants are terrestrial. Stems are erect to ascending, with large, dense, orange-brown scales. Leaves are erect to arching, evergreen, and up to 1m long and 18cm wide. Fertile and sterile leaves do not differ in appearance. Stipes are green, with dense scales similar to those on the stem, which become smaller and sparser toward the blade. The rachis is smooth or somewhat hairy, especially near the pinna attachment points. The leaf blade is up to 30cm long, 1-pinnate, and ovate to oblong or lanceolate, often with a long, tapering tip. Pinnae are leathery, up to 8.5cm long, and roughly ovate in overall shape but with an asymmetrical base and an elongated, usually falcate tip. Usually 4–12 pairs of pinnae are present. Margins are wavy to toothed, though the teeth are quite large and irregular. Veins are anastomosing, forming networks of small polygons (areoles). Sori are round and often scattered irregularly, though they may also form lines. Indusia are present, peltate (umbrellalike), and brown, sometimes with a darker brown or blackish dot at the center. 2n=123 (triploid).

A. Plants of *Cyrtomium falcatum* subsp. *falcatum*.

B. Upper surface of a leaf.

C. Lower surface of a fertile leaf, with irregularly arranged sori.

D. Lower surface of a fertile pinna.

E. Large, dense, orange-brown scales at the base of the stipe.

F   S   C   N*

Cyrtomium fortunei

COMMON NAME(S) Fortune's holly fern

STATUS Not native, uncommon

HABITAT/DISTRIBUTION Moist forests and ravines, rocky areas including rock walls; native to Asia

Plants are terrestrial. **Stems** are erect to ascending, with large, dense scales that are brown to dark brown or blackish. **Leaves** are erect to arching, evergreen, and up to 90cm long and 18cm wide. Fertile and sterile leaves do not differ in appearance. **Stipes** are green, with dense scales similar to those on the stem, which become smaller and sparser toward the blade. The **rachis** is smooth or somewhat hairy, especially near the pinna attachment points. The leaf **blade** is up to 30cm long, 1-pinnate, and ovate to oblong or lanceolate, often with a long, tapering tip. **Pinnae** are not leathery and are up to 9cm long and lanceolate, often with a slightly asymmetrical base and an elongated tip that may be falcate. Usually 10–25 pairs of pinnae are present. **Margins** have very small, pointed to rounded teeth; some forms of this species may have smooth but distinctly rounded, wavy margins. **Veins** are anastomosing, forming networks of small polygons (areoles). **Sori** are round and often scattered irregularly, though they may also form lines. **Indusia** are present, peltate (umbrellalike), light brown to tan, and usually dried and shriveled at maturity. 2n=123 (triploid).

A. A plant of *Cyrtomium fortunei*.

B. Fertile pinnae with minutely toothed margins.

C. Fertile pinnae with wavy margins.

D. Large, dense, dark brown scales at the base of the stipe.

E. Scales are smaller and scattered near the blade and up the rachis.

FAMILY: **CYSTOPTERIDACEAE**

There are 6 species of *Cystopteris* in eastern North America. The most widespread and common of these, *C. bulbifera*, is relatively easy to identify by the presence of small vegetative bulblets on the undersides of its leaves. The remaining species can be challenging to separate from one another, largely because of their high degree of interrelatedness, which results in much similarity in appearance. Two of our eastern species, *C. bulbifera* and *C. protrusa*, are diploids, and they plus an additional 2 diploids have hybridized in various combinations to produce the remaining 4 eastern species, all of which are also polyploids with duplicated genomes (see figure below). Three are allotetraploids (with 4 genomic copies), and 1 is an allohexaploid (with 6 genomic copies). This polyploid complex also undoubtedly includes multiple origins of the various polyploid hybrid species, as well as backcrosses between these and their parental taxa. Several additional sterile hybrids are also known to form between members of this group (2 of these have been named, as indicated in the figure). Individual plants of the same hybrid species may have various combinations of the parental characters; this is especially true for *C. fragilis* and *C. tenuis*, which are notoriously difficult to distinguish from one another. In addition to the hybrids within the genus, *C. fragilis* also forms one of the only intergeneric hybrids known in ferns: it crosses with *Gymnocarpium dryopteris* (p. 313) to produce ×*Cystocarpium roskamianum*, which has been found only in Europe. Base chromosome number (x) = 42.

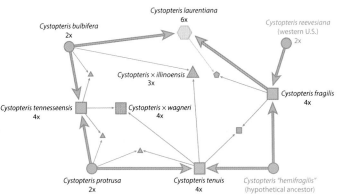

Relationships among *Cystopteris* species in eastern North America. Blue circles are fertile diploids (2x), green squares are fertile allotetraploids (4x), and the yellow hexagon is a fertile allohexaploid (6x). Gray triangles, squares, and pentagons are sterile triploids, tetraploids, and pentaploids, respectively. Large shapes are named taxa, and small shapes are as yet unnamed. Arrows show the direction of genetic contribution from parental toward offspring taxa, with wide arrows where crosses have produced fertile hybrids, and narrow arrows for sterile hybrids. Two of the species involved in these relationships are not found in the east; one is a western species (*C. reevesiana*) and the other is a hypothetical ancestral species that has never been identified in nature (*C. "hemifragilis"*). For more information about interpreting these figures, see p. 12.

One sorus of *Cystopteris bulbifera* showing the hood-shaped indusium characteristic of the genus.

KEY TO THE SPECIES OF *CYSTOPTERIS* IN OUR FLORA:

1a **The leaf blade is widest at or near the base; glandular hairs are present on the rachises, indusia, and pinna midveins; bulblets are often present** ⸱⸱⸱⸱⸱⸱⸱⸱⸱⸱⸱⸱⸱⸱⸱⸱⸱⸱⸱⸱⸱⸱⸱⸱⸱⸱ **2**

    2a Glandular hairs are typically dense; the blade is widest at the base and long tapering; bulblets are almost always present and well formed; stipes are reddish when immature ⸱⸱⸱⸱⸱⸱ *Cystopteris bulbifera*

    2b Glandular hairs are typically sparse; the blade is widest at the base but not long tapering; bulblets are sometimes present but misshapen; stipes are not reddish when immature, but brown to green or yellow ⸱⸱⸱⸱⸱⸱⸱⸱⸱⸱⸱⸱⸱⸱⸱⸱⸱⸱⸱⸱⸱⸱⸱⸱⸱⸱ **3**

        3a The leaf blade is ovate to narrowly ovate and widest slightly above the base ⸱⸱⸱⸱⸱⸱⸱⸱⸱⸱⸱⸱⸱⸱⸱⸱⸱⸱⸱⸱⸱⸱⸱⸱ *Cystopteris laurentiana*

        3b The leaf blade is triangular to narrowly triangular and widest right at the base ⸱⸱⸱⸱⸱⸱⸱⸱⸱⸱⸱⸱⸱⸱⸱⸱⸱⸱⸱⸱⸱⸱⸱⸱ *Cystopteris tennesseensis*

1a **The leaf blade is widest at or just below the middle; glandular hairs are not present; bulblets are not present** ⸱⸱⸱⸱⸱⸱⸱⸱⸱⸱⸱⸱⸱⸱⸱⸱⸱⸱⸱⸱⸱⸱⸱⸱⸱⸱⸱⸱⸱ **4**

    4a The stem extends 2–3cm beyond the attachment point of the current year's leaves; yellowish hairs are present on the stem ⸱⸱⸱⸱⸱⸱⸱⸱⸱⸱⸱⸱⸱⸱⸱⸱ *Cystopteris protrusa*

    4b The stem does not extend beyond the attachment point of the current year's leaves (these leaves are attached right at the tip of the stem); the stem is not hairy ⸱⸱⸱⸱⸱⸱⸱⸱⸱⸱ **5**

        5a Pinnae are usually oriented at an acute angle to the rachis; pinna tips often curve upward toward the leaf tip; margins typically have rounded teeth ⸱⸱⸱⸱⸱⸱⸱⸱⸱⸱⸱⸱⸱⸱ *Cystopteris tenuis*

        5b Pinnae are usually oriented perpendicular to the rachis; pinna tips do not curve toward the leaf tip; margins typically have sharp teeth ⸱⸱⸱⸱⸱⸱⸱⸱⸱⸱⸱⸱⸱⸱ *Cystopteris fragilis*

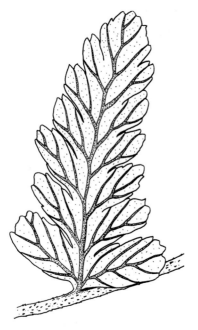

Pinnae of *Cystopteris protrusa*; note that the lateral veins end at the tips of the teeth along the margins.

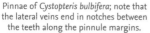

Pinnae of *Cystopteris bulbifera*; note that the lateral veins end in notches between the teeth along the pinnule margins.

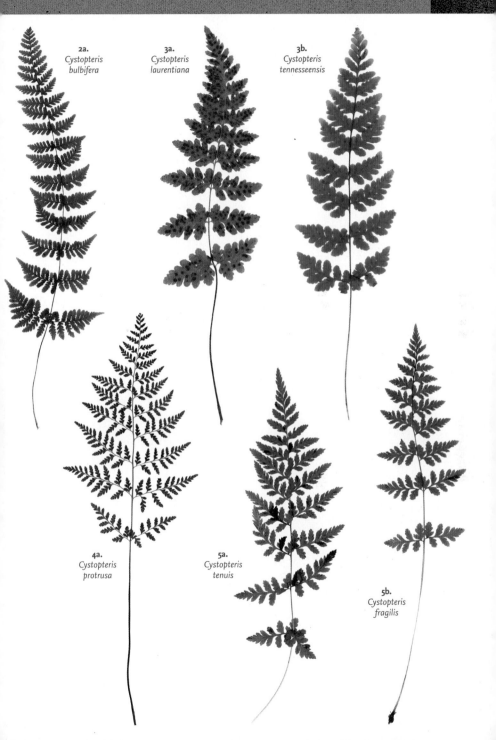

2a.
Cystopteris bulbifera

3a.
Cystopteris laurentiana

3b.
Cystopteris tennesseensis

4a.
Cystopteris protrusa

5a.
Cystopteris tenuis

5b.
Cystopteris fragilis

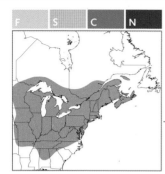

Cystopteris bulbifera

COMMON NAME(S) Bulblet bladder fern

STATUS Native (endemic to North America), common

HABITAT/DISTRIBUTION Rocks, especially moist cracks and cliff ledges, though very rarely it may be found on extremely damp wetland soils; also occurs in western North America

------

Plants are terrestrial and usually epipetric. **Stems** are short creeping, typically with numerous old petiole bases remaining attached. Stem scales are brown and scattered. **Leaves** emerge in a cluster at the tip of the stem and are up to 75cm long and 15cm wide; sterile and fertile leaves do not differ in appearance. **Stipes** are reddish when immature and become green or yellowish as they mature; sparse scales are present at the base. The **rachis** is the same color as the stipe and is densely covered in glandular hairs. Small pea-shaped bulblets are usually present on the underside of the rachis at the intersections of the pinnae, in the upper 1/3 to 1/2 of the blade; these can produce new plants if they fall off and land in suitable habitat. The leaf **blade** is 2-pinnate to 2-pinnate-pinnatifid, broadly to narrowly triangular, and widest at the base, with a long-tapering tip. **Pinnae** are lanceolate, typically oriented perpendicular to the rachis, and do not curve upward. On the lowest pinna pair, the innermost, lower pinnules are not enlarged, and they are either sessile or have short stalks. **Margins** are serrate. Pinnae **midveins** typically have a dense covering of hairs and are grooved on the upper surface, with this groove continuing onto the rachis. **Lateral veins** are free and simple or forked and end in the notches between teeth on the pinnule margins. **Sori** are round and form 1 row between pinnule midveins and margins. **Indusia** typically have scattered glandular hairs and are ovate to hooded or cup shaped, attached at 1 edge, curling over the sorus. 2n=84 (diploid).

A. Plants of *Cystopteris bulbifera*.

B. Lower leaf surface with a bulblet attached.

C. Lower leaf surface with hooded indusia around the sori.

D. Fronds are widest at the base, with a long-tapering tip.

Cystopteris fragilis

COMMON NAME(S) Fragile fern, brittle fern, brittle bladder fern

STATUS Native, somewhat common

HABITAT/DISTRIBUTION Rocks and cliff faces, may occasionally grow on soil; occurs essentially worldwide

Plants are terrestrial and usually epipetric. **Stems** are short creeping, typically with numerous old petiole bases remaining attached. Stem scales are tan to brown and scattered. **Leaves** emerge in a cluster at the tip of the stem and are up to 40cm long and 10cm wide. Sterile and fertile leaves do not differ in appearance. **Stipes** are dark brown or blackish toward the base and become yellowish or greenish toward the blade, with scattered scales near the base like those on the stem. The **rachis** is greenish to yellowish, and smooth, without hairs or scales. Bulblets are not present. The leaf **blade** is 2-pinnate to 2-pinnate-pinnatifid, lanceolate to narrowly ovate, and widest at or just below the middle of the blade. **Pinnae** are lanceolate, typically oriented perpendicular to the rachis, and do not curve upward. On the lowest pinna pair, the innermost, lower pinnules are not enlarged, and they are sessile. **Margins** are serrate. Pinna **midveins** are not hairy but are grooved on the upper surface, with this groove continuing onto the rachis. **Lateral veins** are free and simple or forked and end mostly in the tips of the teeth on the pinnule margins. **Sori** are round and form 1 row between pinnule midveins and margins. **Indusia** are ovate to hooded or cup shaped, attached at 1 edge, curling over the sorus; indusia lack hairs. 2n=168 (tetraploid).

A. A small colony of *Cystopteris fragilis*.

B. Upper leaf surface.

C. Underside of a frond showing immature sori.

D. Stipe base with scattered scales.

F   S   C   N

Cystopteris laurentiana

COMMON NAME(S) Laurentian bladder fern, St. Lawrence bladder fern

STATUS Native (endemic to eastern North America), rare

HABITAT/DISTRIBUTION Rocks, especially moist cracks and cliff ledges

Plants are terrestrial and usually epipetric. **Stems** are short creeping, typically with numerous old petiole bases remaining attached. Stem scales are brown and scattered. **Leaves** emerge in a cluster at the tip of the stem and are up to 45cm long and 12cm wide. Sterile and fertile leaves do not differ in appearance. **Stipes** are dark brown or blackish toward the base and become yellowish or greenish toward the blade, with scattered scales near the base like those on the stem. The **rachis** is greenish to yellowish green, with sparse glandular hairs. Small bulblets may be present where the pinnae intersect the rachis, but they are small and misshapen. The leaf **blade** is 2-pinnate to 2-pinnate-pinnatifid, ovate to narrowly ovate, widest slightly above the base, and not long tapering. **Pinnae** are lanceolate, typically oriented perpendicular to the rachis, and do not curve upward. On the lowest pinna pair, the innermost, lower pinnules are not enlarged, and they are either sessile or have short stalks. **Margins** are serrate. Pinna **midveins** are grooved on the upper surface, with this groove continuing onto the rachis, and they typically have a sparse covering of hairs. **Lateral veins** are free and simple or forked and end in both the marginal teeth and the notches between the teeth. **Sori** are round and form 1 row between pinnule midveins and margins. **Indusia** are ovate to hooded or cup shaped, attached at 1 edge, curling over the sorus, and typically have scattered glandular hairs. 2n=252 (hexaploid).

A. Plants of *Cystopteris laurentiana*.

B. Upper leaf surface.

C. Lower leaf surface with mature sori.

D. Close-up of mature sori.

Cystopteris protrusa

COMMON NAME(S) Southern bladder fern, lowland bladder fern

STATUS Native (endemic to North America), somewhat common

HABITAT/DISTRIBUTION Moist forests; range extends somewhat west of the Mississippi

Plants are terrestrial, growing on soil. **Stems** are short creeping, typically with numerous old petiole bases remaining attached; the stem protrudes 2–3cm beyond the point where the current year's leaves attach, giving the species its specific epithet, *protrusa*. The stem has scattered tan to light brown scales, and golden hairs. **Leaves** emerge behind the stem tip and are up to 45cm long and 10cm wide. Sterile and fertile leaves do not differ in appearance. **Stipes** are dark brown or blackish toward the base and become yellowish or greenish toward the blade, with scattered scales near the base like those on the stem. The **rachis** is greenish to yellowish, and smooth, without hairs or scales. Bulblets are not present. The leaf **blade** is 2-pinnate to 2-pinnate-pinnatifid, narrowly ovate to lanceolate, and widest at or just below the middle. **Pinnae** are lanceolate, typically oriented perpendicular to the rachis, and do not curve upward; the lowest pair often curve downward. On the lowest pinna pair, the innermost, lower pinnules are not enlarged, and they have short stalks. **Margins** are dentate to serrate. Pinna **midveins** are not hairy but are grooved on the upper surface, with this groove continuing onto the rachis. **Lateral veins** are free and simple or forked and end mostly in the tips of the teeth on the pinnule margins. **Sori** are round and form 1 row between pinnule midveins and margins. **Indusia** are ovate to hooded or cup shaped, lack hairs, and are attached at 1 edge, curling over the sorus. 2n=84 (diploid).

A. Fronds of Cystopteris protrusa.

B. Underside of a leaf with mature sori.

C. Close-up of sori.

Cystopteris tennesseensis

COMMON NAME(S) Tennessee bladder fern

STATUS Native (endemic to North America), uncommon

HABITAT/DISTRIBUTION Rocks, especially moist cracks and cliff ledges, and frequently human-made rock surfaces (e.g., walls, foundations); very rarely it may grow on soil; range extends somewhat west of the Mississippi

Plants are terrestrial and usually epipetric. **Stems** are short creeping, typically with numerous old petiole bases remaining attached. Stem scales are tan to brown and scattered. **Leaves** emerge in a cluster at the tip of the stem and are up to 45cm long and 12cm wide. Sterile and fertile leaves do not differ in appearance. **Stipes** are dark brown or blackish toward the base and become yellowish or greenish toward the blade, with scattered scales near the base like those on the stem. The **rachis** is greenish to yellowish green, with sparse glandular hairs. Small bulblets may be present where the pinnae intersect the rachis, but they are small and misshapen. The leaf **blade** is 2-pinnate to 2-pinnate-pinnatifid, triangular to narrowly triangular, widest at the base, and not long tapering. **Pinnae** are narrowly triangular, typically oriented perpendicular to the rachis, and do not curve upward. On the lowest pinna pair, the innermost, lower pinnules are not enlarged, and they either are sessile or have short stalks. **Margins** are serrate. Pinnae **midveins** are grooved on the upper surface, with this groove continuing onto the rachis, and typically have a sparse covering of hairs. **Lateral veins** are free and simple or forked and end in both the marginal teeth and the notches between the teeth. **Sori** are round and form 1 row between pinnule midveins and margins. **Indusia** are ovate to hooded or cup shaped, attached at 1 edge, curling over the sorus, and typically have scattered glandular hairs. 2n=168 (tetraploid).

A. A population of *Cystopteris tennesseensis*.

B. Fronds.

C. Lower surface of a leaf with sori, and bulblet attachment points where the pinnae intersect the rachis.

D. Close-up of a bulblet.

Cystopteris tenuis

COMMON NAME(S) Mackay's brittle fern,
upland brittle bladder fern

STATUS Native (endemic to North America), somewhat common

HABITAT/DISTRIBUTION Rocks in shaded, moist cracks and ledges,
occasionally may grow on soil; also occurs in western North
America

- -

Plants are terrestrial and usually epipetric. **Stems** are short creeping, typically with numerous old petiole bases remaining attached. Stem scales are tan to light brown and scattered. **Leaves** emerge in a cluster at the tip of the stem and are up to 40cm long and 10cm wide. Sterile and fertile leaves do not differ in appearance. **Stipes** are dark brown or blackish toward the base and become yellowish or greenish toward the blade, with scattered scales near the base like those on the stem. The **rachis** is greenish to yellowish and smooth, without hairs or scales. Bulblets are not present. The leaf **blade** is 2-pinnate to 2-pinnate-pinnatifid, lanceolate to ovate, and widest at or just below the middle. **Pinnae** are lanceolate and oriented at an acute angle to the rachis, with the tips of the pinnae curving upward toward the leaf tip. On the lowest pinna pair, the innermost, lower pinnules are not enlarged, and they are sessile. **Margins** have rounded teeth. Pinna **midveins** are not hairy but are grooved on the upper surface, with this groove continuing onto the rachis. **Lateral veins** are free and simple or forked and end in both the marginal teeth and the notches between the teeth. **Sori** are round and form 1 row between pinnule midveins and margins. **Indusia** are ovate to hooded or cup shaped, lack hairs, and are attached at 1 edge, curling over the sorus. 2n=168 (tetraploid).

Plants of *Cystopteris tenuis*.

FAMILY: **DENNSTAEDTIACEAE**

The genus *Dennstaedtia* belongs to the family Dennstaedtiaceae, which is often referred to as the bracken fern family, but it is also called the cuplet fern family because members of some genera have distinctive, cup-shaped indusia around their sori. These indusia may be cylindrical to almost spherical (as is often the case in the common species *D. punctilobula*), or they may appear somewhat flattened toward the top (as in the rare species *D. bipinnata*). In our flora, these species might be confused with *Hypolepis barringtonii* (p. 322), which is a close relative that occurs only in Florida, but in *Hypolepis* the indusium is more flap-like and curves over the sorus, as opposed to holding the sorus like a cup as in *Dennstaedtia*. A recent DNA-based analysis of relationships in part of the family Dennstaedtiaceae has moved these 2 species into other genera; they are treated here as *Dennstaedtia* because this is still the name most commonly used for them, but the synonyms given below may become the accepted names for these species in coming years. Base chromosome number (x) = 34, 46, 47.

KEY TO THE SPECIES OF *DENNSTAEDTIA* IN OUR FLORA:

1a   Leaves are typically more than 1m long; leaf blades are medium to dark green and 3–4-pinnate; stipes, rachises, and pinna midveins have only scattered hairs or may be hairless ··· *Dennstaedtia bipinnata*

1b   Leaves are typically less than 1m long; leaf blades are light green or yellowish and 2-pinnate-pinnatifid; stipes, rachises, and pinna midveins are covered in long, jointed, translucent hairs ··· *Dennstaedtia punctilobula*

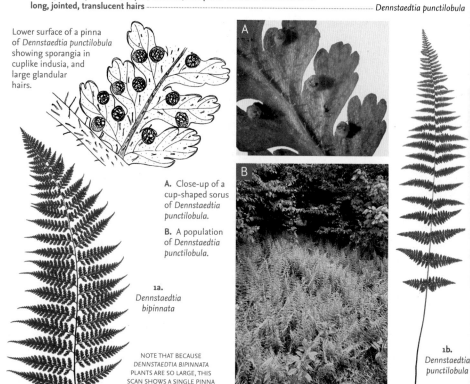

Lower surface of a pinna of *Dennstaedtia punctilobula* showing sporangia in cuplike indusia, and large glandular hairs.

A. Close-up of a cup-shaped sorus of *Dennstaedtia punctilobula*.

B. A population of *Dennstaedtia punctilobula*.

1a.
Dennstaedtia bipinnata

NOTE THAT BECAUSE *DENNSTAEDTIA BIPINNATA* PLANTS ARE SO LARGE, THIS SCAN SHOWS A SINGLE PINNA RATHER THAN A WHOLE FROND

1b.
Dennstaedtia punctilobula

Dennstaedtia bipinnata

COMMON NAME(S) Cuplet fern, bipinnate cuplet fern

NOTABLE SYNONYMS *Mucura bipinnata*

STATUS Native, rare

HABITAT/DISTRIBUTION Damp to muddy, shaded forests with acidic soils; also occurs in the Caribbean and Central and South America

Plants are terrestrial and may form large colonies. **Stems** are long creeping and contribute to colony formation. **Leaves** are erect to arching and up to 2.5m long, typically clustered closely together, and sterile and fertile leaves do not differ in appearance. **Stipes** are up to ca. 1m long, dark brown or blackish toward the base but becoming lighter and more yellow or light green toward the blade, with sparse hairs around the base when young that are typically lost as the leaf matures. The **rachis** is similar in color to the stipe. Hairs may be sparse along both the stipe and rachis. The leaf **blade** is up to 1.25m long and 1m wide, green to dark green, typically 3–4-pinnate and widest toward the middle, and only sparsely hairy on either surface. **Pinnae** are spaced widely apart and are lanceolate in overall shape. The pinna segments (pinnules) are nearly opposite at the base of the pinna but become alternate toward the tip. **Margins** are lobed to bluntly toothed. Fronds may release a smell similar to hay or grass when crushed, though this scent is typically not as strong as in the hay-scented fern, *D. punctilobula*. **Veins** are free and forked, usually ending in the tips of teeth along the pinna margins. **Sori** occur along the margins, at the tips of veins. **Indusia** are present and cup shaped, either rounded and cylindrical to spherical, or somewhat flattened. 2n=188 (tetraploid).

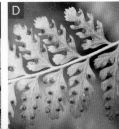

A. A frond of *Dennstaedtia bipinnata*, with 2 large pinnae in the center.

B. Several pinnules from a single pinna; each pinnule is divided even further.

C. Immature sori.

D. Mature sori with brown sporangia inside cup-shaped indusia.

Dennstaedtia punctilobula

COMMON NAME(S) Hay-scented fern

NOTABLE SYNONYMS *Sitobolium punctilobulum*

STATUS Native (endemic to eastern North America), common

HABITAT/DISTRIBUTION Meadows, stream and forest edges, roadsides, and open woods, in acidic soils

Plants are terrestrial and may form large colonies. **Stems** are long creeping and contribute to colony formation. **Leaves** are erect and up to 1.3m long (though typically 1m or less), usually clustered closely together, and sterile and fertile leaves do not differ in appearance. **Stipes** are 30–45cm long, dark brown or blackish toward the base but becoming lighter and more yellow or light green toward the blade, and typically densely covered with soft, translucent glandular hairs. The **rachis** is similar in color to the stipe. Hairs may be dense along both the stipe and rachis. The leaf **blade** is up to 90cm long and 30cm wide, yellowish to pale or light green, 2-pinnate-pinnatifid, widest at or somewhat above the base, and hairy on both surfaces, especially along the pinna midveins and lateral veins. **Pinnae** are narrowly lanceolate. **Margins** are deeply lobed to bluntly toothed. Fronds smell strongly of hay or grass, especially when crushed or drying out, giving the species its common name. **Veins** are free and forked, usually ending in the tips of teeth along the pinna margins. **Sori** occur along the margins, at the tips of veins. **Indusia** are present and cup shaped, either rounded and cylindrical to spherical, or somewhat flattened. 2n=68 (diploid).

A. Plants of *Dennstaedtia punctilobula.*

B. Lower leaf surface, with hairs and cup-shaped indusia around sori.

C. Lower leaf surface with a mix of immature and mature sporangia in the sori.

D. Stipes bases; note that they are very hairy and are darker toward the base, becoming lighter farther up.

FAMILY: **ATHYRIACEAE**

We have 2 species of *Deparia* in our flora, 1 of which is native (*D. acrostichoides*), while the other (*D. petersenii*) is an Australasian species that has become naturalized in eastern North America and is considered a noxious invasive. The ranges of the 2 species in our region are largely nonoverlapping, with *D. acrostichoides* common farther north and *D. petersenii* preferring the warmer south, but where they might occur together, they can be distinguished most easily by 2 features: size—leaves of *D. acrostichoides* can be almost double the length of those of *D. petersenii*—and the lengths of the pinnae toward the leaf base, which are very short in *D. acrostichoides*, causing the overall shape of the blade to narrow substantially toward the base. The blade of *D. petersenii* does not narrow toward the base. Base chromosome number (x) = 40.

KEY TO THE SPECIES OF *DEPARIA* IN OUR FLORA:

1a   The leaf blade narrows conspicuously toward the base ·············· *Deparia acrostichoides*

1b   The leaf blade does not narrow conspicuously toward the base ·············· *Deparia petersenii*

A. Fronds of *Deparia acrostichoides*.
B. Fronds of *Deparia petersenii*.

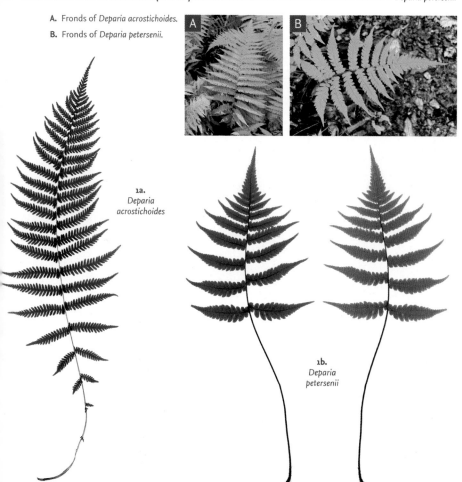

1a.
*Deparia
acrostichoides*

1b.
*Deparia
petersenii*

Deparia acrostichoides

COMMON NAME(S) Silvery spleenwort, silvery glade fern

STATUS Native (endemic to eastern North America), common

HABITAT/DISTRIBUTION Shaded habitats including moist deciduous or conifer-hardwood forests, and along streams and swamp edges

Plants are terrestrial. **Stems** are short creeping, with light brown scales. **Leaves** are erect to spreading, up to 1.2m long, and fertile and sterile leaves do not differ significantly in appearance, though fertile fronds may be slightly taller and narrower. **Stipes** are up to 45cm long, have swollen bases, and are dark reddish brown at the base to yellowish or green toward the blade, with light brown scales that grade into pale hairs. The **rachis** is light green, very hairy, may be lightly scaly, and is shallowly grooved, but this groove is not continuous with the grooves on the pinna midveins. The leaf **blade** is 1-pinnate-pinnatifid, up to 80cm long and 25cm wide, elliptic to oblong lanceolate, and distinctly narrowed at the base and gradually tapering at the tip, with hairs along the pinna midveins. **Pinnae** are well separated along the rachis and linear oblong, with squared-off bases that may be somewhat lobed, and gradually tapering tips. Pinna lobes have slightly pointed tips. **Margins** are smooth or finely toothed. **Lateral veins** are simple or once forked. **Sori** are elongated to slightly curved and follow the pinnule lateral veins in a herringbone pattern on either side of the pinnule midvein. **Indusia** are present, may be thick or thin, and are typically white or silvery when immature, giving the species its common name. 2n=80 (diploid).

A. A frond of *Deparia acrostichoides*.

B. Lower leaf surface with immature sori.

C. Lower leaf surface with mature sori.

D. Close-up of mature sori.

Deparia petersenii

COMMON NAME(S) Japanese lady fern, Japanese false spleenwort

STATUS Not native (invasive), somewhat common

HABITAT/DISTRIBUTION Escapes from cultivation in the south, where it can become established in moist, rich woods, ravines, and lowlands; native to Asia and the Austral-Pacific region

Plants are terrestrial. **Stems** are short creeping, with light brown scales. **Leaves** are erect to spreading, up to 70cm long, and fertile and sterile leaves do not differ significantly in appearance, though fertile fronds may be slightly taller and narrower. **Stipes** are up to 30cm long, do not have swollen bases, and are dark brown to blackish at the base and yellowish toward the blade, with pale brown scales. The **rachis** is light brown to green, with pale to light brown scales, and is shallowly grooved, but this groove is not continuous with the grooves on the pinna midveins. The leaf **blade** is 1-pinnate-pinnatifid but becomes pinnatifid at the tip, is up to 40cm long and 28cm wide, and ovate lanceolate to triangular. The blade may be somewhat narrowed toward the base but not strongly so. The leaf tip may be long tapering or short tapering. Hairlike scales may be present, and hairs are typically present, especially along the pinna midveins. **Pinnae** are oblong to linear lanceolate, with bases squared to somewhat triangularly tapering; tips are gradually tapering and may be distinctly elongated. The lowermost pinna pair is often strongly reflexed, pointed downward toward the base of the plant. Pinna lobes have blunt tips. **Margins** are smooth or serrate. **Lateral veins** are simple but may become forked in larger leaves. **Sori** are typically straight, or very rarely curved, and follow the pinnule lateral veins in a herringbone pattern on either side of the pinnule midvein. **Indusia** are present, thin, and papery. 2n=80 (diploid).

A. Fronds of *Deparia petersenii*.

B. Lower leaf surface with sori.

C. Close-up of mature sori.

D. Upper leaf surface with hairs on rachis, pinna midveins, and blade tissue.

FAMILY: **GLEICHENIACEAE**

Gleicheniaceae is a tropical fern family whose members typically do not occur in North America, with one exception: *Dicranopteris flexuosa*, the forked fern, which is known from a few locations in Florida and Alabama. Members of this family are all known as "forked" or "forking" ferns because of their leaves, which grow indeterminately and regularly fork, or branch dichotomously, into 2 equal subunits. These new subdivisions continue to fork repeatedly. The result is a scrambling habit that allows the plants to become shrublike as the leaves continuously branch, using other vegetation or themselves for support and forming dense thickets. Because they are ferns, the initial leaf division is technically into a pair of pinnae, and it is these pinnae that continue to branch and fork, making it difficult to describe the leaf in total as 1-pinnate, 2-pinnate, and so forth. However, at each branching point (fork), the subdivisions produced appear 1-pinnate. A resting bud can be found at the base of each fork, which will eventually resume upward growth. Base chromosome number (x) = 34.

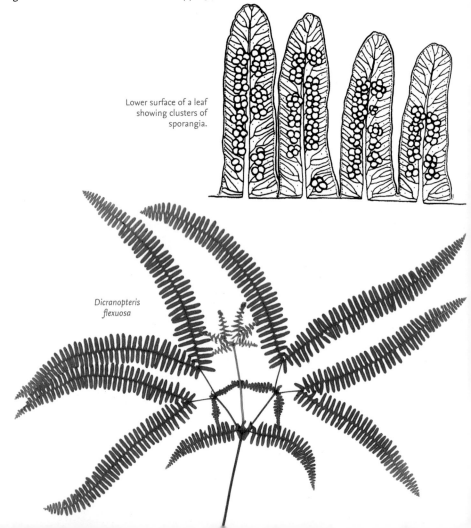

Lower surface of a leaf showing clusters of sporangia.

Dicranopteris flexuosa

Dicranopteris flexuosa

COMMON NAME(S) Forked fern

STATUS Native, rare

HABITAT/DISTRIBUTION Open or partly shaded slopes, ditches, or embankments; also occurs in the Caribbean, Mexico, and Central and South America

Plants are terrestrial, scrambling and forming dense thicket-like patches. Stems are long creeping and may be hairy. Leaves are erect, stiff and leathery, and up to 1m or more long. Stipes and rachises are green to yellow or reddish brown, and smooth (except for the base of the stipe, where some hairs may be present). The blade forks repeatedly, into 2 opposite segments with a resting bud at the apex or forking point. The frond-like side segments are lanceolate, up to 30cm long and 6cm wide, pectinate or deeply pinnatifid, often with a waxy or whitish cast to the lower surface; the blade lacks hairs or scales (except on the resting buds, which often have blackish hairs). Margins are smooth and usually strongly inrolled. Veins are free and forked. Sori are clusters of 4–12 yellowish sporangia, with no indusia. 2n=68 (diploid).

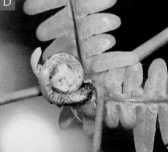

A. A colony of *Dicranopteris flexuosa.*

B. Leaves with dichotomously branching pinnae.

C. Two new fiddleheads growing upward from resting buds.

D. Close-up of a resting bud.

E. Lower leaf surface with sori.

FAMILY: **HYMENOPHYLLACEAE**

Didymoglossum is a genus of filmy ferns whose members were previously included in a very large *Trichomanes* genus (p. 477). *Trichomanes* is now often divided into a number of other genera, which is supported by both morphological differences and DNA sequence data. Members of *Didymoglossum* and *Trichomanes* (in the strict sense) have a stiff bristle that bears sporangia and emerges gradually from the sori, leading to common names of these species often including "bristle fern." Once the sporangia have released spores, they often fall away, leaving the elongated bristle behind. Like all filmy ferns (members of the family Hymenophyllaceae) in our flora, *Didymoglossum* species are typically small plants and have extremely thin, delicate, filmy leaves. They are plants primarily of the tropics, and we have 3 species of *Didymoglossum* in southern to central Florida. Base chromosome number (x) = 34.

KEY TO THE SPECIES OF *DIDYMOGLOSSUM* IN OUR FLORA:

1a   Leaves are deeply pinnatifid; venation is strongly pinnate ··· *Didymoglossum krausii*

1b   Leaves are not pinnatifid but simple and entire, usually with wavy
    margins; venation is forked to weakly pinnate ·· 2

      2a   Each leaf has 1–6 sori; the flaring, conical valve (involucre)
      around the lip of each sorus is dark edged ·············· *Didymoglossum punctatum* subsp. *floridanum*

      2b   Each leaf has at most 1 sorus; the involucre around the lip
      of each sorus is green, not dark ·· *Didymoglossum petersii*

A. A trumpet-shaped sorus with a flaring valve (involucre) in *Didymoglossum petersii*.

B. A trumpet-shaped sorus in *Didymoglossum punctatum* subsp. *floridanum*, in which the rim of the valve is dark colored.

1a. *Didymoglossum krausii*

2a. *Didymoglossum punctatum* subsp. *floridanum*

Didymoglossum krausii

F S C N

COMMON NAME(S) Kraus's bristle fern, treemoss bristle fern

NOTABLE SYNONYMS *Trichomanes krausii*

STATUS Native, rare

HABITAT/DISTRIBUTION Rock walls in limestone sinkholes, or on tree roots and trunks around such sinks; also occurs in the Caribbean, Mexico, and Central and South America

----

Plants are epiphytic or epipetric. **Stems** are long creeping and often intertwining, with dense, dark hairs. **Leaves** are up to 6cm long and 1.5cm wide, spaced out along the stem, and sterile and fertile leaves do not differ in appearance. **Stipes** are dark brown to blackish, shorter than the blade, and have hairs like those on the stem. The leaf **blade** is deeply pinnatifid to occasionally 2-pinnatifid in larger leaves, with distinct dark, stellate hairs along the margins. **Margins** are smooth, other than the large stellate hairs. **Veins** are strongly pinnately arranged. **Sori** are marginal, at the ends of veins, and trumpet shaped, with a flaring conical valve (involucre) around the lip and a stiff bristle that emerges from the sorus bearing clustered sporangia. The edge of the involucre is narrowly dark edged. **Gametophytes** are 1 cell layer thick and highly branched. 2n=136 (tetraploid).

A. A colony of *Didymoglossum krausii.*

B. Fronds.

C. Trumpet-shaped sori, with elongated bristles.

Didymoglossum petersii

COMMON NAME(S) Dwarf bristle fern, Peters's bristle fern

NOTABLE SYNONYMS *Trichomanes petersii*

STATUS Native, uncommon

HABITAT/DISTRIBUTION Tree trunks or rock walls, including limestone boulders and sinkhole walls, often in narrow gorges or slots where humidity remains high year-round; also occurs in Mexico and Central America

Plants are epiphytic or epipetric, forming large mat-like colonies by vegetative spread. **Stems** are long creeping and often intertwining, with dense, dark hairs. **Leaves** are up to 2cm long and 0.5cm wide, spaced out along the stem, and sterile and fertile leaves do not differ in appearance. **Stipes** are dark brown to blackish and only a few millimeters long, with hairs like those on the stem. The leaf **blade** is simple and entire, and elliptic to obovate, with large, distinct, branched hairs along the margins. **Margins** are smooth to wavy. **Veins** are weakly pinnately arranged. **Sori** are marginal, at the ends of veins, typically 1 per leaf, and trumpet shaped, with a flaring conical valve (involucre) around the lip and a stiff bristle that emerges from the sorus bearing clustered sporangia. The edge of the involucre is *not* dark edged. **Gametophytes** are 1 cell layer thick and highly branched. 2n=ca. 102 (triploid).

A. A colony of *Didymoglossum petersii.*

B. A fertile frond, with an elongated bristle.

C. & D. Fertile fronds with large, branched hairs.

Didymoglossum punctatum subsp. floridanum

COMMON NAME(S) Florida bristle fern

NOTABLE SYNONYMS *Trichomanes punctatum* subsp. *floridanum*

STATUS Native (endemic to eastern North America), rare

HABITAT/DISTRIBUTION Limestone boulders or sinkhole walls, or very rarely on tree roots and trunks around limestone sinks; known from only a few hammocks each in central and southern Florida (several other subspecies are present in the Caribbean)

Plants are epiphytic or epipetric, forming large mat-like colonies by vegetative spread. **Stems** are long creeping and often intertwining, with dense, dark hairs. **Leaves** are up to 1.5cm long and 9mm wide, spaced out along the stem, and sterile and fertile leaves do not differ in appearance. **Stipes** are dark brown to blackish and only a few millimeters long, with hairs like those on the stem. The leaf **blade** is simple and entire or with some lobing, and oblong to elliptic to diamond shaped, with distinct dark, stellate hairs along the margins. **Margins** are smooth to wavy. **Veins** are forked to weakly pinnately arranged. **Sori** are marginal, at the ends of veins, typically 1–6 per leaf, and trumpet shaped, with a flaring conical valve (involucre) around the lip and a stiff bristle that emerges from the sorus bearing clustered sporangia. The edge of the involucre is distinctly dark edged. **Gametophytes** are 1 cell layer thick and highly branched. 2n=68 (diploid).

A. A large colony of *Didymoglossum punctatum* subsp. *floridanum*.

B. Fertile fronds.

C. Fertile fronds with elongated bristles

FAMILY: **ATHYRIACEAE**

Diplazium is a fern genus whose members are distributed worldwide, especially in the tropics. In North America, 2 species are known to occur, 1 of which (*D. esculentum*) is native to Asia and Africa and occurs on this continent only as a sporadic escape from cultivation (typically in Florida). The other species, *D. lonchophyllum*, may be a native member of our flora; there is no record of its having been introduced, and it has been known from a handful of locations in Louisiana since the early 1900s. Elsewhere it is widely distributed in central and northern South America. Base chromosome number (x) = 40, 41.

KEY TO THE SPECIES OF *DIPLAZIUM* IN OUR FLORA:

1a   Mature leaves are 2-pinnate to 2-pinnate-pinnatifid at the base,
becoming gradually 1-pinnate and then pinnatifid at the very tip ················· *Diplazium esculentum*

1b   Mature leaves are 1-pinnate-pinnatifid and deeply lobed,
becoming pinnatifid at the tip ················· *Diplazium lonchophyllum*

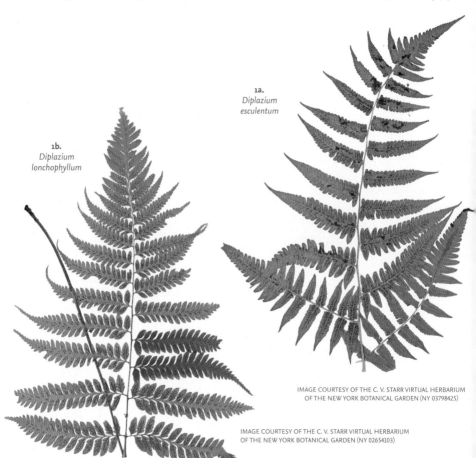

1a.
Diplazium esculentum

1b.
Diplazium lonchophyllum

IMAGE COURTESY OF THE C. V. STARR VIRTUAL HERBARIUM
OF THE NEW YORK BOTANICAL GARDEN (NY 03798425)

IMAGE COURTESY OF THE C. V. STARR VIRTUAL HERBARIUM
OF THE NEW YORK BOTANICAL GARDEN (NY 02654103)

Diplazium esculentum

COMMON NAME(S) Vegetable fern

STATUS Not native, uncommon

HABITAT/DISTRIBUTION Moist, wooded lowlands
and along stream banks; native to Asia and Africa

Plants are terrestrial. **Stems** are erect, with brown scales.
Leaves are erect to spreading, up to 1.6m long (or occasionally
longer), and fertile and sterile leaves do not differ in appearance.
Stipes are up to 60cm long, yellowish to dark brown, scaly
toward the base, and hairy throughout. The **rachis** is similar to the stipe and somewhat grooved
on the upper surface; this groove continues into the pinna base. The leaf **blade** is 2-pinnate to
2-pinnate-pinnatifid at the base, becoming gradually 1-pinnate and then abruptly pinnatifid at
the tip. The blade is up to 1m long and 50cm wide, ovate to ovate triangular, and smooth. **Pinnae**
are lanceolate oblong, tapering gradually at the tips, with oblong pinnules that may be deeply
lobed and/or auriculate at the base. Vegetative buds or small plantlets may be present at the
bases of the lower pinnae. **Margins** are smooth to serrate. **Lateral veins** are anastomosing. **Sori**
are indusiate, elongated, and usually single, though they may be paired back to back across a
lateral vein. Sori follow the pinna lateral veins in a herringbone pattern on either side of the
pinna midvein and open away from the vein. 2n=82 (diploid).

A. Fronds
of *Diplazium
esculentum*.

B. Frond tips
reducing from
2-pinnate to
1-pinnate to
pinnatifid.

C. Lower leaf
surface with sori.

PHOTOGRAPHS A & C
BY ALAN CRESSLER

Diplazium lonchophyllum

COMMON NAME(S) Lance-leaf twin-sorus fern

STATUS Unclear, possibly native; rare

HABITAT/DISTRIBUTION Moist, wooded lowlands and along stream banks; also occurs in the Caribbean, Mexico, and Central and South America

Plants are terrestrial. **Stems** are ascending to erect, with dark brown scales. **Leaves** are erect to spreading, up to 80m long, and fertile and sterile leaves do not differ in appearance. **Stipes** are up to 45cm long and green to purplish. The **rachis** is grooved, and this groove is continuous with those on the pinna midveins. The leaf **blade** is 1-pinnate-pinnatifid and deeply lobed but becomes pinnatifid at the tip. The blade is up to 35cm long and 22cm wide, deltate lanceolate, broadest at or slightly above the base, with a gradually tapering tip, and is smooth but can be lightly scaly on the lower surface. **Pinnae** are lanceolate oblong, tapering gradually at the tips, with the lower corner of the pinna base wedge shaped and the upper corner more square. Pinnae are deeply lobed, especially toward their bases. Vegetative buds or small plantlets may be present at the bases of the lower pinnae. **Margins** are serrate. **Lateral veins** are free and forked. **Sori** are indusiate, elongated, and usually single, though they may be paired back to back across a lateral vein. Sori follow the pinna lateral veins in a herringbone pattern on either side of the pinna midvein and open away from the vein. 2n=82 (diploid).

Lower leaf surface of *Diplazium lonchophyllum*, with sori.

Vegetative bulblets.

PHOTOGRAPHS BY ROBBIN MORAN

FAMILY: **DRYOPTERIDACEAE**

The wood fern genus, *Dryopteris*, includes several of the most frequently encountered and beautiful ferns in our flora, and various members of the genus can be found throughout our region. As their common name suggests, these plants are found most often in forests and woodlands, though individual species differ in their preferences; some favor extremely damp, swampy forest habitats (like *D. cristata* and *D. clintoniana*), while others prefer relatively dry, open or rocky woods (like *D. intermedia* and *D. marginalis*). The most unique member of the group is probably *D. fragrans*, a petite species that can grow directly on open, exposed rock cliff faces. Globally, *Dryopteris* is one of the largest fern genera, with roughly 400 species, and it is especially diverse in temperate regions worldwide. Several of our species have circumboreal distributions and grow throughout Europe and northern Asia (e.g., *D. carthusiana* and *D. fragrans*), while others are North American endemics (e.g., *D. ludoviciana*).

A plant of *Dryopteris marginalis*.

The *Dryopteris* species in eastern North America represent one of the classic scenarios of reticulate evolution in plants (see figure below); the 6 diploid species native to our flora have hybridized with one another, with an additional extinct diploid species (*D. "semicristata"*), and with various offspring of the initial crosses, to produce more than 30 additional entities. Five of these are stable, fertile allopolyploids recognized at the species level. Another 17 are sterile hybrids that have been named as such, while at least another 11 are known to exist but have not been formally named. The named hybrids are numbered below, and their parentage, ploidy, and genomic makeup are given. Only 2 of these—*D. × boottii* and *D. × triploidea*—can be considered common; the rest are typically quite rare, though some (such as *D. × australis* and *D. × uliginosa*) may become locally abundant, especially where the parental species co-occur or are both close by. Morphologically, *Dryopteris* hybrids are usually more or less intermediate between their parental species, but individual hybrid plants will vary from one to the next and can resemble one or the other parent more strongly. In addition to these hybrids within the genus, *D. goldiana* also forms one of the only intergeneric hybrids known in ferns: it crosses with *Polystichum lonchitis* (p. 439) to produce ×*Dryostichum singulare*, which is known from only a couple of sites in Ontario. Base chromosome number (x) = 41.

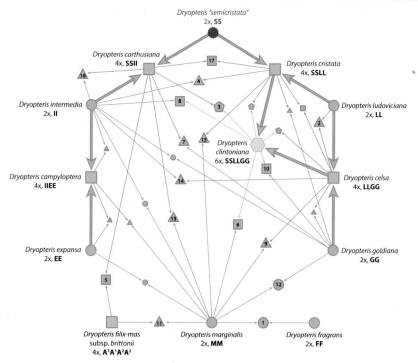

Relationships among *Dryopteris* species in eastern North America. Blue circles are fertile diploids (2x), green squares are fertile allotetraploids (4x), and the yellow hexagon is a fertile allohexaploid (6x). The darker blue circle at the top is a hypothetical ancestor that is thought to now be extinct, *Dryopteris* "semicristata." The diploids have traditionally been assigned letters to indicate their genomic contributions to hybrids, and these are given in bold text (note that the genomic contributions to *D. filix-mas* subsp. *brittonii* are not yet known with certainty, so its genomes are given as A^1 and A^2). Gray circles, triangles, squares, and pentagons are sterile diploids, triploids, tetraploids, and pentaploids, respectively. Large shapes are named taxa, and small shapes are as yet unnamed. The sterile hybrids with names are numbered, and their names are given in the text. Arrows show the direction of genetic contribution from parental toward offspring taxa, with wide arrows where crosses have produced fertile hybrids, and narrow arrows for sterile hybrids. For more information about interpreting these figures, see p. 12.

Dryopteris hybrids in Eastern North America

1. *D.* × *algonquinensis* (Algonquin wood fern; 2x, FM) = *D. fragrans* (2x) × *marginalis* (2x)

2. *D.* × *australis* (Dixie wood fern; 3x, LLG) = *D. celsa* (4x) × *ludoviciana* (2x)

3. *D.* × *benedictii* (Benedict's wood fern; 5x, ISSLG) = *D. carthusiana* (4x) × *clintoniana* (6x)

4. *D.* × *boottii* (Boott's wood fern; 3x, SLI) = *D. cristata* (4x) × *intermedia* subsp. *intermedia* (2x)

5. *D.* × *brathaica* (Brathay wood fern; 4x, A^1A^2SI) = *D. filix-mas* subsp. *brittonii* (4x) × *carthusiana* (4x)

6. *D.* × *burgessii* (Burgess's wood fern; 4x, SLGM) = *D. clintoniana* (6x) × *marginalis* (2x)

7. *D.* × *correllii* (Correll's hybrid wood fern; 3x, SIG) = *D. carthusiana* (4x) × *goldiana* (2x)

8. *D.* × *dowellii* (Dowell's wood fern; 4x, SLGI) = *D. clintoniana* (6x) × *intermedia* subsp. *intermedia* (2x)

9. *D.* × *leedsii* (Leeds's wood fern; 3x, LGM) = *D. celsa* (4x) × *marginalis* (2x)

10. *D.* × *mickelii* (Mickel's wood fern; 4x, SLGG) = *D. clintoniana* (6x) × *goldiana* (2x)

11. *D.* × *montgomereyi* (Montgomery's wood fern; 3x, A^1A^2M) = *D. filix-mas* subsp. *brittonii* (4x) × *marginalis* (2x)

12. *D.* × *neowherryi* (Wherry's wood fern; 2x, GM) = *D. goldiana* (2x) × *marginalis* (2x)

13. *D.* × *pittsfordensis* (Pittsford's wood fern; 3x, SIM) = *D. carthusiana* (4x) × *marginalis* (2x)

14. *D.* × *separabilis* (separate wood fern; 3x, LGI) = *D. celsa* (4x) × *intermedia* subsp. *intermedia* (2x)

15. *D.* × *slossoniae* (Slosson's wood fern; 3x, SLM) = *D. cristata* (4x) × *marginalis* (2x)

16. *D.* × *triploidea* (triploid wood fern; 3x, SII) = *D. carthusiana* (4x) × *intermedia* subsp. *intermedia* (2x)

17. *D.* × *uliginosa* (marsh wood fern; 4x, ISSL) = *D. carthusiana* (4x) × *cristata* (4x)

A–C. *Dryopteris* × *australis.*
D–E. *Dryopteris* × *boottii.*
F–G. *Dryopteris* × *separabilis.*
H–J. *Dryopteris* × *leedsii.*
K–M. *Dryopteris* × *neowherryi.*

KEY TO THE SPECIES OF *DRYOPTERIS* IN OUR FLORA (including 2 common hybrids):

1a   Leaves at maturity are usually not longer than 25cm (though they can sometimes be a bit longer); the lower surface of the blade is very densely scaly, and the entire blade has a dense covering of aromatic glandular hairs; old leaves remain attached and form a dense, rounded, gray or brown clump around the plant base ·································· *Dryopteris fragrans*

1b   Leaves at maturity are longer than 25cm; the lower surface of the blade is only sparsely scaly, and if glandular hairs are present on the blade, they are not aromatic; old leaves may persist or not but do not form a conspicuous, more or less rounded clump around the plant base ·· 2

     2a   The leaf blade is 2-pinnate to 3-pinnate-pinnatifid (occasionally up to 4-pinnate) at the base ·································· 3

         3a   The leaf blade is widely linear, with parallel sides; glandular hairs are present, especially on the rachis, pinna midveins, and indusia; on the lowest pinnae, the first pinnules on the lower side are shorter than the second pinnules; leaves are evergreen ································· *Dryopteris intermedia* subsp. *intermedia*

         3b   The leaf blade is triangular in overall shape; glandular hairs are not present or are very sparse and concentrated on the indusia (or glandular hairs are present as in *D. intermedia* subsp. *intermedia*, in *D.* × *triploidea*); on the lowest pinnae, the first pinnules on the lower side are longer than the second pinnules; leaves die back in the winter ················· 4

             4a   On the lowest pinnae, the innermost pinnules (on the upper and lower side of the pinna) are nearly opposite; the first pinnule on the lower side is not much wider and is ca. 2–3 times longer than the first pinnule on the upper side ················· 5

                 5a   Glandular hairs are not present or are very sparse and concentrated on the indusia ·· *Dryopteris carthusiana*

                 5b   Glandular hairs are present as in *D. intermedia*, but plants otherwise resemble *D. carthusiana* ·· *Dryopteris* × *triploidea*

             4b   On the lowest pinnae, the innermost pinnules are widely offset to alternate; the first pinnule on the lower side is ca. twice as wide as, and usually 3–5 times longer than, the first pinnule on the upper side ·································· 6

                 6a   Leaves are erect to somewhat spreading or arching; the scales on the stipe are tan, with a dark central stripe; plants are found in the upper Midwest of the U.S. through northeastern Canada ·································· *Dryopteris expansa*

                 6b   Leaves are widely spreading; the scales on the stipe are tan to dark brown, but without a central stripe; plants are found in the Appalachians, the northeastern U.S., and eastern Canada ······················ *Dryopteris campyloptera*

     2b   The leaf blade is 1-pinnate-pinnatifid to 2-pinnate at the base ··· 7

         7a   Sori are located at or near the margins of the pinna divisions; scales at the base of the petiole are densely packed and pale to light brown ·································· *Dryopteris marginalis*

         7b   Sori are located midway between the margin and midrib of the pinna divisions, or close to the midribs; scales at the base of the petiole are scattered and tan to dark brown ·· 8

             8a   Two distinct types of scales are present on the stipe, rachis, and pinna midribs (broad vs. narrow and hairlike); the stipe is less than ¼ of the total length of the leaf ·································· *Dryopteris filix-mas* subsp. *brittonii*

             8b   Only 1 type of scale is present on the stipe, rachis, and pinna midribs (broad, not narrow or hairlike); the stipe is ¼–⅓ of the total length of the leaf ··············· 9

                 9a   Leaves are partly dimorphic; the fertile leaves are upright, erect, and longer than the sterile leaves, which are arching to spreading ·································· 10

                     10a   The fertile pinnae are only in the tip-most half of the blade and are much narrower and more widely spaced than the sterile pinnae toward the base; plants are found in the southeast and Florida ·································· *Dryopteris ludoviciana*

                     10b   The fertile pinnae are located throughout nearly the whole blade and are not noticeably narrower than the sterile pinnae; plants are

1a.
Dryopteris fragrans

3a.
Dryopteris intermedia
subsp. *intermedia*

5a.
Dryopteris carthusiana

6b.
Dryopteris campyloptera

6a.
Dryopteris expansa

7a.
Dryopteris marginalis

found in the northeastern U.S. and into Canada (though *D. cristata* can be found as far south as North Carolina) ··· 11

11a The pinnae on the fertile leaves are twisted out of the plane of the leaf axis, often at or nearly at right angles, giving the pinnae a "venetian blind" appearance; the pinnae, especially the lowest ones, are widely triangular ··· 12

12a Pinnules are not further divided; margins are toothed but not distinctly lobed ··· *Dryopteris cristata*

12b Pinnules are distinctly lobed, especially toward the pinnule base, somewhat resembling *D. intermedia* subsp. *intermedia* ·············· *Dryopteris × boottii*

11b The pinnae on the fertile leaves are nearly in the plane of the leaf axis, or twisted out of it but not far enough to be at right angles; the pinnae, especially the lowest ones, are narrowly elongate triangular ·············· *Dryopteris clintoniana*

9b Leaves are not dimorphic; all leaves are arching to spreading and more or less the same length ··· 13

13a Leaves have rounded, somewhat blister-like scales on the lower surface of the blade; leaves are often somewhat reddish green to golden red, especially when young, or in the fall ·························· *Dryopteris erythrosora*

13b Leaves do not have rounded, blister-like scales; all scales are long and papery; leaves are not reddish green, but bright to dark green ······················ 14

14a Sori are located closer to the midvein than the margin on pinna divisions; the leaf blade is ovate, with an abruptly tapering tip; scales at the base of the stipe are dark brown to black, with narrow, pale margins ·············· *Dryopteris goldiana*

14b Sori are located midway between the midvein and margin of pinna segments; the leaf blade is ovate to lanceolate, with a gradually narrowing tip; scales at the base of the stipe are medium to dark brown, with a black central stripe ··· *Dryopteris celsa*

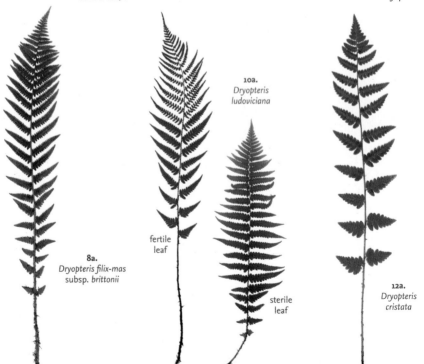

10a.
Dryopteris ludoviciana

fertile leaf

8a.
Dryopteris filix-mas subsp. brittonii

sterile leaf

12a.
Dryopteris cristata

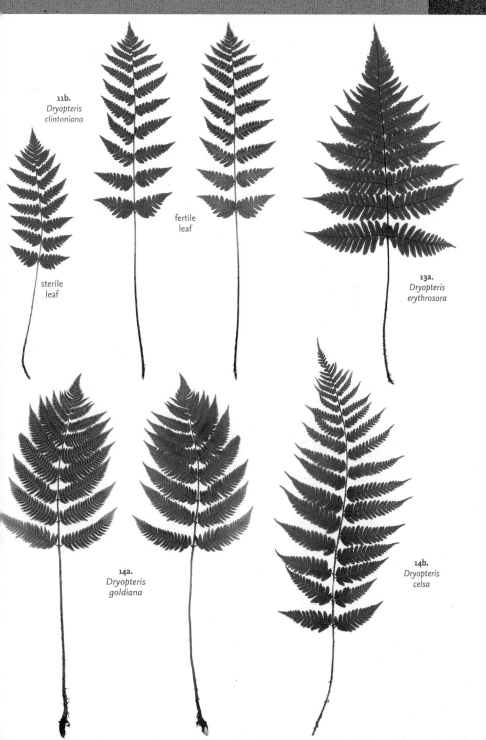

11b.
*Dryopteris
clintoniana*

fertile
leaf

sterile
leaf

13a.
*Dryopteris
erythrosora*

14a.
*Dryopteris
goldiana*

14b.
*Dryopteris
celsa*

Dryopteris campyloptera

COMMON NAME(S) Mountain wood fern

STATUS Native (endemic to eastern North America), somewhat common

HABITAT/DISTRIBUTION Cool, moist forests at high elevations

Plants are terrestrial. **Stems** are short creeping to erect. **Leaves** are up to 90cm long and 30cm wide and die back in winter. Fertile and sterile leaves do not differ in appearance. **Stipes** are roughly ⅓ the length of the leaf (up to 30cm long), green, with a groove in the upper surface, and with scattered tan to brown scales at the base. The **rachis** is similar to the stipe. The leaf **blade** is light green, triangular to narrowly ovate, 3-pinnate to 3-pinnate-pinnatifid, and without glandular hairs, or occasionally with a few scattered hairs, mostly on the indusia. The **pinnae** are triangular to lanceolate and lie in the plane of the blade. On the lowest pinnae, the innermost pinnules are widely offset to alternate; the first pinnules on the lower side are longer than the second pinnules, and the first pinnule on the lower side is ca. twice as wide as, and usually 3–5 times longer than, the first pinnule on the upper side. **Margins** are toothed, with spiny teeth. **Veins** are free and forked. **Sori** are in 1 row, midway between the pinnule midvein and margin. **Indusia** are present, round to kidney shaped, attached at a narrow point on 1 side of the sorus, and may have a few scattered glandular hairs. 2n=164 (tetraploid).

A. A frond of *Dryopteris campyloptera.*

B. Lowest pinnae.

C. Lower leaf surface with sori.

D. Stipe scales.

Dryopteris carthusiana

F S C N

COMMON NAME(S) Spinulose wood fern, toothed wood fern

STATUS Native, common

HABITAT/DISTRIBUTION A variety of damp forests and woods; also occurs in western North America, Europe, and Asia

Plants are terrestrial. **Stems** are short creeping to erect. **Leaves** are up to 75cm long and 30cm wide and die back in winter. Fertile and sterile leaves do not differ in appearance. **Stipes** are ¼–⅓ the length of the leaf (up to 25cm long), green, with a groove in the upper surface, and with scattered tan scales, especially at the base. The **rachis** is similar to the stipe. The leaf **blade** is light to dark green, narrowly ovate, 2–3-pinnate-pinnatifid, and without glandular hairs. The **pinnae** are narrowly triangular to lanceolate and lie in the plane of the blade. On the lowest pinnae, the innermost pinnules (on the upper and lower side of the pinna) are nearly opposite; the first pinnules on the lower side are longer than the second pinnules, and the first pinnule on the lower side is not much wider and is ca. 2–3 times longer than the first pinnule on the upper side. **Margins** are toothed, with forward-pointing, spiny teeth. **Veins** are free and forked. **Sori** are in 1 row, midway between the pinnule midvein and margin. **Indusia** are present, round to kidney shaped, and attached at a narrow point on 1 side of the sorus. 2n=164 (tetraploid).

A. *Dryopteris carthusiana* plants.

B. A frond.

C. Lowest pinnae.

D. Lower leaf surface with sori.

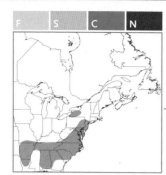

F S C N

Dryopteris celsa

COMMON NAME(S) Log fern

STATUS Native (endemic to North America), uncommon

HABITAT/DISTRIBUTION Seepy forested areas and swamps;
range extends somewhat west of the Mississippi

Plants are terrestrial. **Stems** are short creeping to erect. **Leaves**
are up to 1.2m long and 30cm wide and die back in winter. Fertile
and sterile leaves do not differ in appearance. **Stipes** are roughly
⅓ the length of the leaf (up to 40cm long), green, with a groove
in the upper surface, and with scattered scales, especially at the base. Scales are medium to dark
brown, with a black central stripe. The **rachis** is similar to the stipe. The leaf **blade** is green to dark
green, ovate to lanceolate, tapering gradually to the tip, 1-pinnate-pinnatifid, and without glandular
hairs. The **pinnae** are lanceolate to ovate and lie in the plane of the blade. The lowest pinnae are
shorter than those farther up the blade. **Margins** are scalloped to shallowly toothed. **Veins** are
free and forked. **Sori** are in 1 row, midway between the pinnule midvein and margin. **Indusia**
are present, round to kidney shaped, and attached at a narrow point on 1 side of the sorus.
2n=164 (tetraploid).

A. Fronds of
Dryopteris celsa.

B. A fertile frond.

C. Lower leaf surface
with immature sori.

Dryopteris clintoniana

COMMON NAME(S) Clinton's wood fern

STATUS Native (endemic to eastern North America), uncommon

HABITAT/DISTRIBUTION Swamps and swampy woods

Plants are terrestrial. **Stems** are short creeping to erect. **Leaves** are up to 1m long and 20cm wide. Leaves are partly dimorphic; the fertile leaves are in the center of the plant and are upright, erect, and longer than the sterile leaves, which surround them and are arching to spreading. Fertile leaves die back in the winter while sterile leaves may remain green. **Stipes** are ¼–⅓ the length of the leaf (up to 35cm long), dark at the base but becoming bright green toward the blade, with a groove in the upper surface, and with scattered tan scales (sometimes with a darker center), especially at the base. The **rachis** is similar to the stipe. The leaf **blade** is green, lanceolate with nearly parallel sides, 1-pinnate-pinnatifid, and without glandular hairs. The **pinnae**, especially the lowest ones, are narrowly elongate triangular. **Fertile pinnae** are located throughout the blade and are somewhat but not substantially narrower than the **sterile pinnae**; fertile pinnae are twisted out of the plane of the blade but not so far as to be at right angles with it, while the sterile pinnae lie more or less within the plane of the blade. On both leaf types, the lowest pinnae are smaller than those farther up the blade. **Margins** are distinctly toothed and may be doubly toothed, with spiny teeth. **Veins** are free and forked. **Sori** are in 1 row, midway between the pinnule midvein and margin. **Indusia** are present, round to kidney shaped, and attached at a narrow point on 1 side of the sorus. 2n=246 (hexaploid).

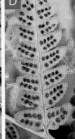

A. A plant of *Dryopteris clintoniana*.

B. Sterile fronds.

C. Lowest pinnae.

D. Lower leaf surface with sori.

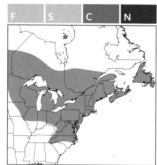

Dryopteris cristata

COMMON NAME(S) Crested wood fern

STATUS Native, somewhat common

HABITAT/DISTRIBUTION Swampy forests and various types of wetlands; also occurs in western North America and Europe

Plants are terrestrial. **Stems** are short creeping to erect. **Leaves** are up to 70cm long and 12cm wide. Leaves are partly dimorphic; the fertile leaves are in the center of the plant and are upright, erect, and longer than the sterile leaves, which surround them and are arching to spreading. Fertile leaves die back in the winter while sterile leaves may remain green. **Stipes** are ¼–⅓ the length of the leaf (up to 35cm long), green, with a groove in the upper surface, and with scattered tan scales, especially at the base. The **rachis** is similar to the stipe. The leaf **blade** is green, narrowly lanceolate and often with nearly parallel sides, 1-pinnate-pinnatifid (to 2-pinnate at the base), and without glandular hairs. The **pinnae**, especially the lowest ones, are widely triangular to elongate triangular. **Fertile pinnae** are located throughout the blade and are somewhat but not substantially narrower than the **sterile pinnae**; fertile pinnae are twisted out of the plane of the blade far enough to be at right angles to it, giving the pinnae a "venetian blind" effect in their orientation. On both leaf types, the lowest pinnae are smaller than those farther up the blade. **Margins** are serrulate and spiny. **Veins** are free and forked. **Sori** are in 1 row, midway between the pinnule midvein and margin. **Indusia** are present, round to kidney shaped, and attached at a narrow point on 1 side of the sorus. 2n=164 (tetraploid).

A. A plant of *Dryopteris cristata*.

B. Fertile fronds with "venetian blind" pinnae.

C. Fronds with "venetian blind" pinnae and serrulate margins.

D. Lower leaf surface with sori.

Dryopteris erythrosora

COMMON NAME(S) Autumn fern

STATUS Not native, uncommon (but spreading in the south)

HABITAT/DISTRIBUTION Escapes from cultivation in the south, where it can become established in damp, open forests and along streamsides; native to Asia

Plants are terrestrial. **Stems** are short creeping to erect. **Leaves** are up to 90cm long and 25cm wide and may die back in winter or not. Fertile and sterile leaves do not differ in appearance. **Stipes** are roughly ⅓ the length of the leaf (up to 30cm long), light yellowish green to reddish brown, with a groove in the upper surface, and with dense brown scales, especially at the base. The **rachis** is similar to the stipe. The leaf **blade** is shiny and bright green to golden, bronze, or reddish brown, oblong to lanceolate, 2-pinnate at the base, and without glandular hairs. The **pinnae** are lanceolate and lie in the plane of the blade or are angled slightly upward. On the lower surface of the leaf are small, rounded, somewhat blister-like scales. **Margins** are toothed to lobed. **Veins** are free and forked. **Sori** are in 1 row, a bit closer to the pinnule midvein than to the margin. **Indusia** are present, round to kidney shaped, and attached at a narrow point on 1 side of the sorus. 2n=82 (diploid).

A. Plants of *Dryopteris erythrosora*.

B. Upper surface of leaves.

C. Lower leaf surface with sori and small, blister-like scales.

D. Stipe scales.

Dryopteris expansa

COMMON NAME(S) Northern wood fern, spreading wood fern

STATUS Native, common

HABITAT/DISTRIBUTION Cool, moist woods; also occurs in western North America, Greenland, Europe, and Asia

Plants are terrestrial. **Stems** are short creeping to erect. **Leaves** are up to 90cm long and 30cm wide and die back slowly in winter. Fertile and sterile leaves do not differ in appearance. **Stipes** are roughly ⅓ the length of the leaf (up to 30cm long), green, with a groove in the upper surface, and with scattered scales, especially at the base. Scales are tan, with a dark central stripe. The **rachis** is similar to the stipe. The leaf **blade** is green, triangular, 3-pinnate-pinnatifid, and without glandular hairs, or occasionally with a few scattered hairs. The **pinnae** are lanceolate to oblong and lie in the plane of the blade. On the lowest pinnae, the innermost pinnules are widely offset to alternate; the first pinnules on the lower side are longer than the second pinnules, and the first pinnule on the lower side is ca. twice as wide as, and usually 3–5 times longer than, the first pinnule on the upper side. **Margins** are toothed. **Veins** are free and forked. **Sori** are in 1 row, midway between the pinnule midvein and margin. **Indusia** are present, round to kidney shaped, attached at a narrow point on 1 side of the sorus, and may have a few scattered glandular hairs. 2n=82 (diploid).

A. Fronds of *Dryopteris expansa*.

B. Lowest pinnae.

C. Lower leaf surface with sori.

Dryopteris filix-mas subsp. brittonii

COMMON NAME(S) Male fern

STATUS Native, uncommon

HABITAT/DISTRIBUTION Dense forests or talus (limestone) slopes; also occurs in Greenland (a second subspecies, *D. filix-mas* subsp. *filix-mas*, occurs in western North America, Mexico, and Eurasia)

Plants are terrestrial. Stems are short creeping to erect. Leaves are up to 1.2m long and 30cm wide and die back in winter. Fertile and sterile leaves do not differ in appearance. Stipes are less than ¼ the length of the leaf (up to 40cm long), green, with a groove in the upper surface, and with scattered tan to brown scales, especially at the base. Scales are of 2 distinct types, one large and broad and the other small, narrow, and hairlike. The rachis is similar to the stipe. The leaf blade is dark green, ovate to lanceolate, 1-pinnate-pinnatifid to 2-pinnate at the base, firm in texture, and without glandular hairs. The pinnae are lanceolate and lie in the plane of the blade. The lowest pinnae are shorter than those farther up the blade. Margins are toothed to lobed. Veins are free and forked. Sori are in 1 row, midway between the pinnule midvein and margin. Indusia are present, round to kidney shaped, and attached at a narrow point on 1 side of the sorus. 2n=164 (tetraploid).

A. Plants of *Dryopteris filix-mas* subsp. *brittonii*.

B. Lowest pinnae.

C. Lower leaf surface with sori.

D. Stipe with 2 types of scales.

Dryopteris fragrans

COMMON NAME(S) Fragrant wood fern

STATUS Native, uncommon

HABITAT/DISTRIBUTION Shaded cliffs and rocky areas, often on limestone; also occurs in western North America, Europe, and Asia

Plants are terrestrial and epipetric. **Stems** are short creeping to erect. **Leaves** are usually not more than 25cm long (though they can be longer) and 6cm wide and remain green through the winter, with old leaves remaining attached to the plant and forming a dense, rounded, gray or brown clump around the plant base. Fertile and sterile leaves do not differ in appearance. **Stipes** are roughly ⅓ the length of the leaf (up to 12cm long), dark at the base but becoming green toward the blade, with a groove in the upper surface, dense brown to reddish-brown scales throughout, and a dense covering of aromatic glandular hairs. Scales are tan, with a dark central stripe. The **rachis** is similar to the stipe. The leaf **blade** is bright to dark green, linear lanceolate, and 1-pinnate-pinnatifid to 2-pinnate. The lower surface of the blade is densely scaly and has a dense covering of hairs like those on the stipe and rachis. The **pinnae** are linear oblong and lie in the plane of the blade. The lowest pinnae are shorter than those farther up. **Margins** are round toothed. **Veins** are free and forked. **Sori** are in 1 row, midway between the pinnule midvein and margin. **Indusia** are present, round to kidney shaped, attached at a narrow point on 1 side of the sorus, and covered in glandular hairs similar to those on the rest of the leaf. 2n=82 (diploid).

A. Plants of *Dryopteris fragrans.*

B. Upper leaf surfaces.

C. Lower leaf surface with mature sori.

D. Lower leaf surfaces with immature sori and numerous glands and scales.

E. Stipe scales.

Dryopteris goldiana

COMMON NAME(S) Goldie's wood fern

SYNONYMS This species was named for botanist John Goldie and according to the rules of taxonomy, the correct spelling of its name is *D. goldieana*. However, *D. goldiana*, without the "e," is much more commonly used.

STATUS Native (endemic to eastern North America), somewhat common

HABITAT/DISTRIBUTION Dense, wet woods, seepy areas, or wetland edges

Plants are terrestrial. **Stems** are short creeping to erect. **Leaves** are up to 1.2cm long and 40cm wide and die back in winter. Fertile and sterile leaves do not differ in appearance. **Stipes** are roughly ⅓ the length of the leaf (up to 40cm long), dark toward the base but becoming green toward the blade, with a groove in the upper surface, and with scattered scales, especially at the base. Scales are dark brown to black, with narrow, pale margins. The **rachis** is similar to the stipe. The leaf **blade** is green to dark green, widely ovate and tapering quickly at the tip, 1-pinnate-pinnatifid to 2-pinnate at the base, and without glandular hairs. The **pinnae** are ovate to lanceolate and lie in the plane of the blade. The lowest pinnae are slightly shorter than those farther up the blade. **Margins** are shallowly wavy to toothed. **Veins** are free and forked. **Sori** are in 1 row, a bit closer to the pinnule midvein than to the margin. **Indusia** are present, round to kidney shaped, and attached at a narrow point on 1 side of the sorus. 2n=82 (diploid).

A. Plants of *Dryopteris goldiana*.

B. Upper leaf surface.

C. Lower leaf surface with mature sori.

D. Stipe scales.

Dryopteris intermedia subsp. *intermedia*

COMMON NAME(S) Evergreen wood fern

STATUS Native (endemic to eastern North America), common

HABITAT/DISTRIBUTION A variety of forest and wetland habitats (2 other subspecies, *D. intermedia* subsp. *azorica* and subsp. *maderensis*, occur in Europe)

Plants are terrestrial. **Stems** are short creeping to erect. **Leaves** are up to 90cm long and 20cm wide and remain green through the winter (often collapsing under the weight of snow). Fertile and sterile leaves do not differ in appearance. **Stipes** are roughly ⅓ the length of the leaf (up to 30cm long), green, with a groove in the upper surface, and with scattered tan scales, especially at the base, and moderately dense, glandular hairs. The **rachis** is similar to the stipe. The leaf **blade** is bright to dark green, widely linear to slightly ovate, with parallel sides, and 3-pinnate to 3-pinnate-pinnatifid. Glandular hairs are present and similar to those on the stipe and rachis. The **pinnae** are lanceolate to oblong and lie in the plane of the blade. On the lowest pinnae, the first pinnules on the lower side are shorter than the second pinnules. **Margins** are serrate, with minutely spiny teeth. **Veins** are free and forked. **Sori** are in 1 row, midway between the pinnule midvein and margin. **Indusia** are present, round to kidney shaped, attached at a narrow point on 1 side of the sorus, and with glandular hairs similar to those on the rest of the leaf. 2n=82 (diploid).

A. A plant of *Dryopteris intermedia* subsp. *intermedia*.

B. Lowest pinnae.

C. Lower leaf surface with mature sori.

D. Stipe scales.

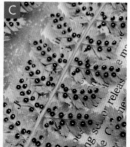

Dryopteris ludoviciana

COMMON NAME(S) Southern wood fern, southern shield fern

STATUS Native (endemic to eastern North America), common

HABITAT/DISTRIBUTION Swamps and wet forests

Plants are terrestrial. **Stems** are short creeping to erect. **Leaves** are up to 1.2m long and 30cm wide. Leaves are partly dimorphic; the fertile leaves are in the center of the plant and are upright, erect, and longer than the sterile leaves, which surround them and are arching to spreading. All leaves generally remain green through the winter. **Stipes** are roughly ¼ the length of the leaf (up to 30cm long), green, with a groove in the upper surface, and with scattered brown scales, especially at the base. The **rachis** is similar to the stipe. The leaf **blade** is dark green, lanceolate, 1-pinnate-pinnatifid, and without glandular hairs. The **pinnae** are lanceolate to oblong and lie almost in the plane of the blade. **Fertile pinnae** are located in the tip-most half of the fertile leaves and are more widely spaced and distinctly narrow and contracted compared to the **sterile pinnae.** On both leaf types, the lowest pinnae are smaller than those farther up the blade. **Margins** are distinctly toothed. **Veins** are free and forked. **Sori** are in 1 row, midway between the pinnule midvein and margin. **Indusia** are present, round to kidney shaped, and attached at a narrow point on 1 side of the sorus. 2n=82 (diploid).

A. Sterile fronds of *Dryopteris ludoviciana.*

B. Fertile fronds.

C. Sterile pinnae below and fertile pinnae farther up.

D. Lower leaf surface with mature sori.

F   S   C   N

Dryopteris marginalis

COMMON NAME(S) Marginal wood fern

STATUS Native, common

HABITAT/DISTRIBUTION Rocky woods and slopes, on boulders, and along streams; range extends somewhat west of the Mississippi; also occurs in Greenland

Plants are terrestrial. **Stems** are short creeping to erect. **Leaves** are up to 1m long and 25cm wide and remain green through winter, either remaining erect or collapsing. Fertile and sterile leaves do not differ in appearance. **Stipes** are ¼–⅓ the length of the leaf (up to 33cm long), green, with a groove in the upper surface, and a dense tuft of pale to light brown scales at the base. The **rachis** is similar to the stipe. The leaf **blade** is bluish to grayish or bright green, ovate to lanceolate, 1-pinnate-pinnatifid to 2-pinnate at the base, and without glandular hairs. The **pinnae** are lanceolate and lie in the plane of the blade. The lowest pinnae are slightly smaller than those farther up the blade. **Margins** are shallowly scalloped or wavy to smooth. **Veins** are free and forked. **Sori** are in 1 row, very close to the margin. **Indusia** are present, round to kidney shaped, and attached at a narrow point on 1 side of the sorus. 2n=82 (diploid).

A. A plant of *Dryopteris marginalis.*

B. Upper leaf surface.

C. Lower leaf surface with mature sori.

D. Stipe scales.

FAMILY: **EQUISETACEAE**

Equisetum is an easily recognized genus whose species are commonly called horsetails or scouring rushes. Globally there are about 15 species in the genus, and we have 9 in our flora. Historically it was unclear exactly how *Equisetum* was related to the other pteridophyte groups and it was long considered a "fern ally," but DNA sequence studies have confirmed repeatedly that *Equisetum* is sister to all the other extant ferns, and it is thus now routinely treated as a member of the fern lineage. *Equisetum* species are quite distinct in their appearance, with robust, stalklike green stems that may or may not have whorls of branches. Although they appear leafless, they in fact have highly reduced leaves that are fused into short sheaths that surround the stems and branches at the nodes; the individual leaves in the sheath are described as the "teeth." The reproductive structures are cone-like strobili at the tips of the stems. Each strobilus is made up of structures called *sporangiophores*, which resemble tiny armored umbrellas that are shield-like and pressed side by side until the spores reach maturity, at which point the sporangiophores retract and spread apart to allow the sporangia, which are tucked underneath the wings of the sporangiophores, to release spores.

The *Equisetum* species in our region belong to 2 of the 3 subgenera in the genus. The species in subgenus *Equisetum* are commonly known as horsetails, and those in subgenus *Hippochaete* are called scouring rushes. The latter name notes the resemblance of these species to members of the flowering plant family Juncaceae (the rush family), and the silica crystals often present in their stems, which make them useful for scrubbing and polishing. The 2 subgenera can be distinguished primarily by whether the stems are evergreen and last multiple years, or are deciduous and last less than a year; this feature is where the key below begins. Within the subgenus *Equisetum*, plants can be either branched or unbranched, and the key provides options for this. A number of sterile hybrids are known in *Equisetum*, and several occur in our region (see figure below), but all are extremely rare and thus not included in the key. Base chromosome number (x) = 108.

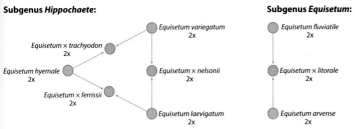

Subgenus *Hippochaete*:

Equisetum × trachyodon
2x

Equisetum variegatum
2x

Equisetum hyemale
2x

Equisetum × nelsonii
2x

Equisetum × ferrissii
2x

Equisetum laevigatum
2x

Subgenus *Equisetum*:

Equisetum fluviatile
2x

Equisetum × litorale
2x

Equisetum arvense
2x

Relationships among *Equisetum* species in eastern North America. Blue circles are diploid parental taxa (2x), and arrows show the direction of their parental contributions to sterile diploid (also 2x) hybrids (gray circles). For more information about interpreting these figures, see p. 12.

KEY TO THE SPECIES OF *EQUISETUM* IN OUR FLORA:

1a   Stems are deciduous, lasting only a year or even less; plants are usually branched
but can be unbranched, or (in 3 species) can have separate fertile stems that
are brown and unbranched; when branches are present, they are in
regular whorls; the tips of the strobili are rounded ⋯⋯⋯⋯⋯⋯⋯⋯⋯ 2 *Equisetum* subgen. *Equisetum*, the horsetails

      2a   Stems have regular whorls of branches ⋯⋯⋯⋯⋯⋯⋯⋯⋯⋯⋯⋯⋯⋯⋯⋯⋯⋯⋯⋯⋯⋯⋯⋯⋯⋯⋯⋯⋯⋯⋯⋯⋯⋯ 3

            3a   At the base of each branch, the first internode on the branch
(the distance between the tips of subsequent sheaths of leaves)
is shorter than the sheath of leaves around the main stem just
above where the branch attaches ⋯⋯⋯⋯⋯⋯⋯⋯⋯⋯⋯⋯⋯⋯⋯⋯⋯⋯⋯⋯⋯⋯⋯⋯⋯⋯⋯⋯⋯⋯⋯⋯⋯⋯⋯⋯ 4

4a   The leaf sheaths have more than 11 teeth; the teeth
are dark but may have a very narrow white margin ································· *Equisetum fluviatile*

4b   The leaf sheaths have fewer than 11 teeth; the teeth are
dark with white margins (the leaf teeth right below a strobilus
may have alternating bands of dark and light colors) ·········· *Equisetum palustre*

3b   At the base of each branch, the first internode on the branch is as long
as or longer than the sheath of leaves around the main stem just above
where the branch attaches ··· 5

5a   The branches are themselves further branched; the leaf sheath
teeth are reddish brown at the tips and around the margins ··············· *Equisetum sylvaticum*

5b   The branches are not further branched; the leaf sheath teeth
are dark brown or black at the tips and around the margins ················· 6

6a   The branches point upward; the teeth of the leaf
sheaths are long tapering, coming gradually to a
pointed tip ·· *Equisetum arvense* subsp. *arvense*

6b   The branches spread outward or downward; the
teeth of the leaf sheaths are broadly triangular ················· *Equisetum pratense*

2b   Stems are unbranched ··· 7

7a   Stems are green ·· 8

8a   The leaf sheaths have more than 11 teeth; the teeth are dark
but may have a very narrow white margin ··················· *Equisetum fluviatile*

8b   The leaf sheaths have fewer than 11 teeth; the teeth are dark
with white margins (the leaf teeth right below a strobilus may have
alternating bands of dark and light colors) ··················· *Equisetum palustre*

7b   Stems are brownish (these are the fertile stems of the next 3 species) ················· 9

9a   The leaf sheath teeth are reddish brown at the tips and around
the margins ·· *Equisetum sylvaticum*

9b   The leaf sheath teeth are dark brown or black at the tips and around the margins ············ 10

10a   The stems do not have stomata and die back
after spores are released ································ *Equisetum arvense* subsp. *arvense*

10b   The stems do have stomata and persist after
spores are released, becoming green and branching ··············· *Equisetum pratense*

1b   Stems are evergreen, typically overwintering and lasting more than a year
(though *E. laevigatum* can be an annual); plants are usually unbranched but
if branches are present they are not in regular whorls; all stems are alike
(fertile and sterile stems are not different in appearance); the tips of the
strobili are pointed (but may be bluntly rounded in *E. laevigatum*) ··············· 11 *Equisetum* subgen. *Hippochaete*,
the scouring rushes

11a   Stems are up to about 20cm high at maturity, usually curving and
bending, and solid, with no central cavity ································· *Equisetum scirpoides*

11b   Stems are usually more than 20cm high at maturity, straight and erect,
and hollow, with a central cavity ··· 12

12a   The leaf sheaths usually have a dark band, both at the tips and
around the base ··· *Equisetum hyemale* subsp. *affine*

12b   The leaf sheaths are usually dark only at the tips, not at the base ·············· 13

13a   Strobili are rounded or have a bluntly pointed tip; the
teeth of the leaf sheaths often break off and are shed ············· *Equisetum laevigatum*

13b   Strobili have a distinctly, sharply pointed tip; the
teeth of the leaf sheaths usually persist and do not
break off ··· *Equisetum variegatum* subsp. *variegatum*

A. *Equisetum arvense*

B. *Equisetum fluviatile*

C. *Equisetum hyemale*

D. *Equisetum laevigatum*

E. *Equisetum palustre*

F. *Equisetum pratense*

G. *Equisetum scirpoides*

H. *Equisetum sylvaticum*

I. *Equisetum variegatum*

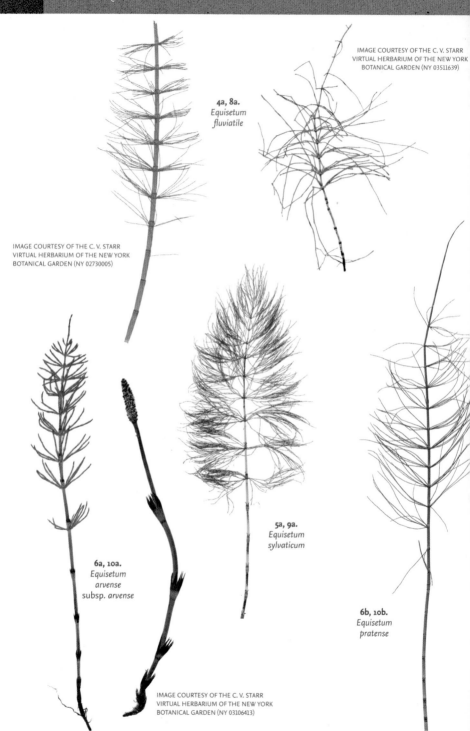

4a, 8a.
*Equisetum
fluviatile*

6a, 10a.
*Equisetum
arvense*
subsp. *arvense*

5a, 9a.
*Equisetum
sylvaticum*

6b, 10b.
*Equisetum
pratense*

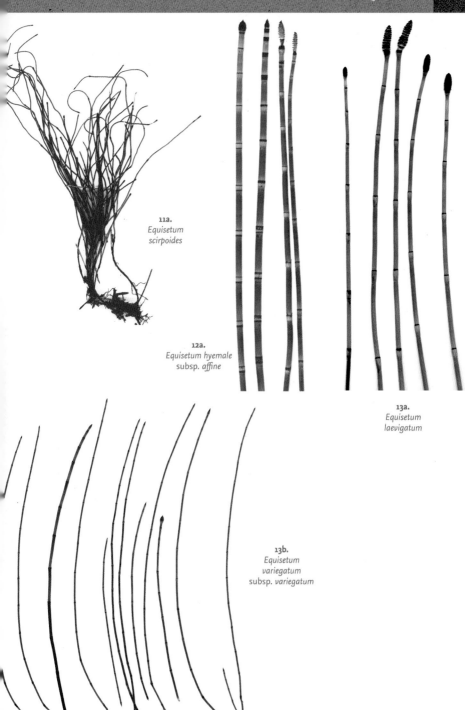

11a.
*Equisetum
scirpoides*

12a.
Equisetum hyemale
subsp. *affine*

13a.
*Equisetum
laevigatum*

13b.
*Equisetum
variegatum*
subsp. *variegatum*

Equisetum arvense subsp. arvense

COMMON NAME(S) Common horsetail, field horsetail

STATUS Native, common

HABITAT/DISTRIBUTION A variety of (usually damp) habitats, including fields, wetlands, wet woods, ditches, and tundra; also occurs in western North America, Greenland, Europe, and Asia (additional subspecies are also described from Europe and Asia)

Plants are terrestrial. **Stems** are dimorphic and deciduous, typically lasting less than a year. **Sterile stems** are green, branched, up to 60cm tall or sometimes taller, and with a hollow center, the cavity taking up ⅓–⅔ the diameter of the stem. A ring of small cavities surrounds this, alternating with the ridges on the outside of the stem. There are typically 4–14 ridges, with silica forming dots along the ridges. The leaf sheaths are up to 5mm long, with 4–14 teeth that are narrow and dark, with long-tapering tips. **Branches** occur in regular whorls, are not branched any further, and point somewhat upward. At the base of each branch, the first internode on the branch (the distance between the tips of subsequent sheaths of leaves) is typically longer than the sheath of leaves around the main stem just above where the branch attaches. **Fertile stems** are pinkish to brown, unbranched, with no stomata, and are shorter than the sterile stems, dying back after spores are released. **Strobili** mature early in the spring, and the tips of the strobili are rounded. 2n=216 (diploid).

A. Sterile, branched stems of *Equisetum arvense* subsp. *arvense*.

B. A young sterile stem.

C. Stem node showing leaf sheaths and branch bases.

D. A fertile stem, early in spring.

PHOTOGRAPH BY BRANDON CORDER

Equisetum fluviatile

COMMON NAME(S) River horsetail

STATUS Native, somewhat common

HABITAT/DISTRIBUTION Wet habitats, including ditches, marshes, grassy swales, and pond edges; also occurs in western North America, Europe, and Asia

Plants are terrestrial, often standing in water. **Stems** are all alike and deciduous, typically lasting less than a year. Stems are green, branched or unbranched, up to 115cm tall or sometimes even taller, and with a hollow center, the cavity taking up ⅘ or more of the diameter of the stem. There are typically no smaller cavities around the central one, or there may be a ring of very, very small cavities. There are typically 10–30 ridges around the outside of the stem. The leaf sheaths are up to 10mm long, with 12–24 teeth that are narrow and black, but with a narrow white border around the margin. **Branches** are produced at the nodes toward the middle of the stem, occur in regular whorls, are not branched any further, and spread outward. At the base of each branch, the first internode on the branch (the distance between the tips of subsequent sheaths of leaves) is shorter than the sheath of leaves around the main stem just above where the branch attaches. **Strobili** mature in the summer, and the tips of the strobili are rounded. 2n=216 (diploid).

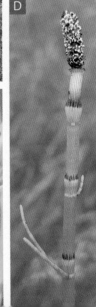

A. A colony of *Equisetum fluviatile.*

B. Branched stems.

C. A node where branches meet the stem.

D. Close-up of a strobilus.

F S C **N**

Equisetum hyemale subsp. *affine*

COMMON NAME(S) Common scouring rush

STATUS Native, common

HABITAT/DISTRIBUTION A variety of damp habitats, including roadsides, along lakes and rivers, and in wet woods; also occurs in western North America, Greenland, Mexico, and Central America (a second subspecies, *E. hyemale* subsp. *hyemale*, occurs in Eurasia)

- -

Plants are terrestrial. **Stems** are all alike and evergreen, typically overwintering and lasting more than a year. Stems are almost always unbranched and are up to 1.2m tall or even taller, with a hollow center, the cavity taking up at least ⅔ the diameter of the stem. There may be a ring of much smaller cavities around the central cavity, these smaller ones alternating with the ridges around the outside of the stem. There are typically 14–50 ridges. The leaf sheaths are up to 17mm long and constricted at the base, with 14–50 long-tapering teeth that are usually shed or lost early on. When stems are young, the leaf sheaths are uniformly green, but they gradually develop darker bands at the base and tips that become black by maturity. **Strobili** mature in the summer, and the tips of the strobili are pointed. 2n=216 (diploid).

A. A colony of *Equisetum hyemale* subsp. *affine*.
PHOTOGRAPH BY ALAN CRESSLER

B. A leaf sheath that has lost its teeth.

C. Close-up of a strobilus.

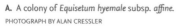

Equisetum laevigatum

COMMON NAME(S) Smooth scouring rush

STATUS Native, uncommon

HABITAT/DISTRIBUTION Disturbed or successional habitats, including ditches, waterways, and damp grassy areas; also occurs in western North America and Mexico

Plants are terrestrial. **Stems** are all alike and can be evergreen, though in our region they typically last less than a year. Stems are almost always unbranched and are up to 1m tall or even taller, with a hollow center, the cavity taking up $^2/_3$–$^3/_4$ of the diameter of the stem. There may be a ring of much smaller cavities around the central cavity, these smaller ones alternating with the ridges around the outside of the stem. There are typically 14–26 ridges. The leaf sheaths are up to 15mm long and constricted at the base, with 10–32 long-tapering teeth that are usually shed or lost early on. The leaf sheaths are green, with a dark ring around the top edge where the teeth detach. **Strobili** mature in late spring to early summer, and the tips of the strobili have a small sharp point or may be bluntly pointed. 2n=216 (diploid).

A. Stems of *Equisetum laevigatum*.

B. Close-up of strobili.

C. A mature strobilus.

F | S | C | N

Equisetum palustre

COMMON NAME(S) Marsh horsetail

STATUS Native, uncommon

HABITAT/DISTRIBUTION Wetland habitats including marshes, swamps, wet woods, and the shores of waterways; also occurs in western North America, Europe, and Asia

Plants are terrestrial and often standing in shallow water. **Stems** are all alike and deciduous, typically lasting less than a year. Stems are green, branched or unbranched, and up to 80cm tall, with a hollow center, the cavity taking up less than ⅓ of the diameter of the stem. A ring of cavities surrounds this, each of which is nearly as large as the central cavity, alternating with the ridges on the outside of the stem. There are typically 5–10 ridges. The leaf sheaths are up to 9mm long, with 5–10 teeth that are narrow and dark, but with a narrow white border around the margin. **Branches** are produced at the nodes toward the middle of the stem, occur in regular whorls, are not branched any further, and spread outward or upward. At the base of each branch, the first internode on the branch (the distance between the tips of subsequent sheaths of leaves) is shorter than the sheath of leaves around the main stem just above where the branch attaches. **Strobili** mature in the summer, and the tips of the strobili are rounded. 2n=216 (diploid).

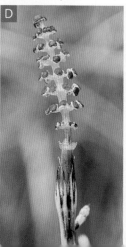

A. Plants of *Equisetum palustre.*

B. Nodes where branches meet the stem.

C. Close-up of a strobilus.

D. A strobilus that has fully dehisced and released its spores.

Equisetum pratense

COMMON NAME(S) Meadow horsetail

STATUS Native, somewhat common

HABITAT/DISTRIBUTION Wet meadows and woods; also occurs in western North America, Europe, and Asia

Plants are terrestrial. **Stems** are dimorphic and deciduous, typically lasting less than a year. **Sterile stems** are green, branched, and up to 60cm tall, with a hollow center, the cavity taking up ⅙–⅓ of the diameter of the stem. A ring of smaller cavities surrounds this, alternating with the ridges on the outside of the stem. There are typically 8–18 ridges, and silica dots may be present along the ridges toward the middle and upper portion of the stem. The leaf sheaths are up to 5mm long, with 8–18 teeth that are triangular and dark, but with white margins. **Branches** occur in regular whorls, are not branched any further, and are spreading to somewhat drooping. At the base of each branch, the first internode on the branch (the distance between the tips of subsequent sheaths of leaves) is as long as or longer than the sheath of leaves around the main stem just above where the branch attaches. **Fertile stems** are not produced often, but when present they are pinkish to brown, unbranched, with stomata, but after spore release they persist and become branched and green. **Strobili** mature late in the spring, and the tips of the strobili are rounded. 2n=216 (diploid).

A. A stem of *Equisetum pratense*.

B. Nodes where branches meet the stem.

C. An unbranched stem section with leaf sheath.

D. Close-up of a node.

Equisetum scirpoides

COMMON NAME(S) Dwarf scouring rush

STATUS Native, rare

HABITAT/DISTRIBUTION Wet woods and swamps, usually in shade; also occurs in western North America, Greenland, Europe, and Asia

Plants are terrestrial. **Stems** are all alike and evergreen, typically overwintering and lasting more than a year. Stems are unbranched, slender, curving and bending, and up to only about 20cm tall or sometimes a bit taller. Stems do not have a central cavity and are solid except for 3–4 narrow cavities that alternate irregularly with the ridges on the outside of the stem; there are usually 6 ridges. The leaf sheaths are up to 2.5mm long, blackish, with 3–4 triangular black teeth with white margins. **Strobili** mature in the summer (or may persist and release spores the following spring), and the tips of the strobili have a small sharp point that often breaks off. 2n=216 (diploid).

A. Plants of *Equisetum scirpoides*.

B. Stems with unbranched nodes.

C. Nodes and leaf sheaths.

D. A strobilus.

Equisetum sylvaticum

COMMON NAME(S) Woodland horsetail

STATUS Native, somewhat common

HABITAT/DISTRIBUTION Damp forests and wetland edges; also occurs in western North America, Europe, and Asia

Plants are terrestrial. **Stems** are dimorphic and deciduous, typically lasting less than a year. **Sterile stems** are brownish to green, branched, and up to 70cm tall, with a hollow center, the cavity taking up ⅓–½ of the diameter of the stem. A ring of smaller cavities surrounds this, alternating with the ridges on the outside of the stem. There are typically 10–18 ridges, and silica dots may be present along the ridges. The leaf sheaths are up to 6mm long, with 8–18 teeth that are narrow, long tapering, distinctly reddish, and papery around the margins. **Branches** occur in regular whorls, branching even further, and are spreading to somewhat drooping. At the base of each branch, the first internode on the branch (the distance between the tips of subsequent sheaths of leaves) is longer than the sheath of leaves around the main stem just above where the branch attaches. **Fertile stems** are pinkish to brown, unbranched, with stomata, but after spore release they persist and become branched and green. **Strobili** mature late in the spring, and the tips of the strobili are rounded. 2n=216 (diploid).

A. Sterile stems of *Equisetum sylvaticum*.

B. Whorls of branches.

C. Leaf sheaths with reddish, papery teeth.

F S C N

Equisetum variegatum subsp. *variegatum*

COMMON NAME(S) Variegated scouring rush

STATUS Native, uncommon

HABITAT/DISTRIBUTION Wet ditches or meadows, damp woods, and along waterways; also occurs in western North America, Greenland, Europe, and Asia (a second subspecies, *E. variegatum* subsp. *alaskanum*, is also known from parts of western North America and Asia)

Plants are terrestrial. **Stems** are all alike and evergreen, typically overwintering and lasting more than a year. Stems are almost always unbranched and are up to 55cm tall, with a hollow center, the cavity taking up ⅓–⅔ of the diameter of the stem. A ring of small cavities surrounds this, alternating with the ridges on the outside of the stem; there are typically 3–12 ridges. The leaf sheaths are up to 6mm long, with a black band around the top and 3–14 long-tapering teeth that are brown in the center with white margins. **Strobili** mature in the summer (or may persist and release spores the following spring), and the tips of the strobili have a sharply pointed tip. 2n=216 (diploid).

A. A colony of *Equisetum variegatum* subsp. *variegatum*.

B. Stems.

C. A fertile stem with a young strobilus.

FAMILY: **THELYPTERIDACEAE**

Goniopteris is a genus of around 140 species, and its members are found only in the American tropics, from Florida southward throughout Central America, the Caribbean, and as far south as Argentina and Bolivia. We have 4 species in our flora, all of which have relatively small ranges, as they are at the northern limits of their tropical distributions even in the southernmost part of our region. Members of this genus can be distinguished relatively easily by the presence of stellate or furcate hairs, which require a 10–20x hand lens to see well. These hairs typically have a stalk topped with additional projections. If there are 2 of these projections, the hairs are furcate; if there are more, they are stellate, or starlike. *Goniopteris* is one of the genera previously included in *Thelypteris* (p. 475), and its species are most similar to other members of Thelypteridaceae, but these hairs should easily separate them. Base chromosome number (x) = 36.

KEY TO THE SPECIES OF *GONIOPTERIS* IN OUR FLORA:

1a The leaf blade is only lobed or pinnatifid throughout or is 1-pinnate just at the base, with 1–3 pairs of free pinnae, but becomes pinnatifid farther up ⋯⋯⋯ *Goniopteris domingensis*

1b The leaf blade is at least 1-pinnate throughout (though it may become pinnatifid toward the tip) ⋯⋯⋯ 2

  2a The leaf blade is either 1-pinnate to 1-pinnate-pinnatifid at the base and pinnatifid farther up, or 1-pinnate throughout but with an elongated, vinelike tip that produces new plantlets ⋯⋯⋯ *Goniopteris reptans*

  2b The leaf blade is 1-pinnate-pinnatifid throughout, becoming pinnatifid at the tip ⋯⋯⋯ 3

    3a The leaf blade is usually less than 10cm wide; the pinna lobes (pinnules) are generally pointed; the lowest few sets of pinnae narrow gradually toward the leaf base; the tip of the blade becomes gradually pinnatifid ⋯⋯⋯ *Goniopteris sclerophylla*

    3b The leaf blade is usually more than 15cm wide; the pinna lobes (pinnules) are rounded; the lowest few sets of pinnae do not narrow, and the leaf is often widest at the base; the tip of the blade resembles a pinnatifid terminal pinna that is separated from the lateral pinnae just below it ⋯⋯⋯ *Goniopteris tetragona*

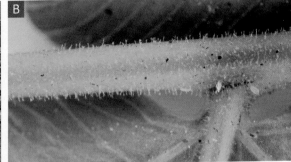
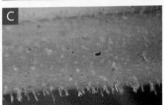

A. Plants of *Goniopteris reptans* growing on limestone.

B & C. Magnified images showing stellate and furcate hairs of *Goniopteris tetragona*.

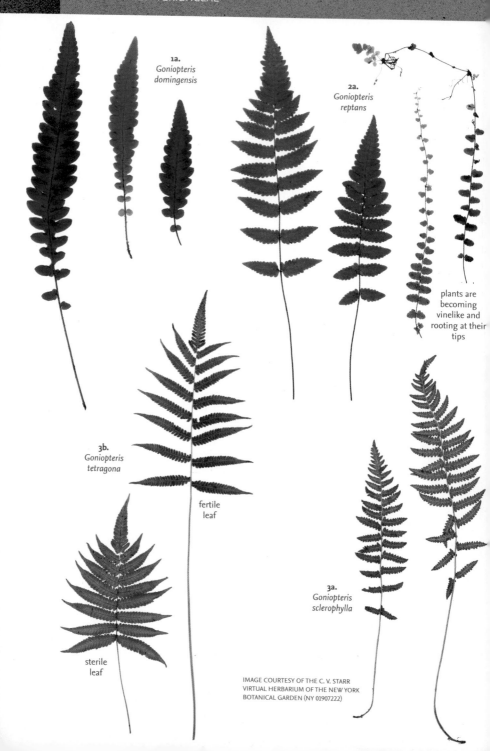

1a.
Goniopteris domingensis

2a.
Goniopteris reptans

plants are becoming vinelike and rooting at their tips

3b.
Goniopteris tetragona

fertile leaf

sterile leaf

3a.
Goniopteris sclerophylla

IMAGE COURTESY OF THE C. V. STARR
VIRTUAL HERBARIUM OF THE NEW YORK
BOTANICAL GARDEN (NY 01907222)

Goniopteris domingensis

COMMON NAME(S) Guadeloupe maiden fern

NOTABLE SYNONYMS *Thelypteris guadalupensis*

STATUS Native, rare

HABITAT/DISTRIBUTION Rocky hammocks, on limestone, in crevices or thin soil over rock; also occurs in the Caribbean, Mexico, and Central America

Plants are terrestrial and epipetric. **Stems** are short creeping to somewhat erect, with pale brown scales clustered toward the tip. **Leaves** are up to 55cm long, and sterile and fertile leaves are similar in appearance, with fertile leaves somewhat longer and more erect, and with longer stipes. **Stipes** are up to 15cm long and brownish green, with minute stellate hairs. The **rachis** is similar to the stipe. The leaf **blade** is lanceolate to linear, up to 40cm long and 9cm wide, and 1-pinnate at the base, where there are 1–3 pairs of free, small pinnae, but then becoming pinnatifid. Stellate hairs are present on the lower surface of the blade, especially along the veins and margins, with some scattered on the blade surface. The upper surface is smooth except for a few scattered hairs on the midveins. **Margins** are smooth to shallowly lobed or with rounded teeth. **Veins** are free toward the tips of the lobes but may form networks toward the bases of the lobes. **Sori** are round. **Indusia** are minute, often appearing absent. 2n= unknown.

A. Fronds of *Goniopteris domingensis.*

B. Plants growing on limestone.

C. Lower leaf surface with maturing sori.

D. Stellate hairs along the leaf margin.

Goniopteris reptans

COMMON NAME(S) Creeping star-hair fern

NOTABLE SYNONYMS *Thelypteris reptans*

STATUS Native, uncommon

HABITAT/DISTRIBUTION Rocky hammocks and around sinks and solution holes, often growing on limestone walls or thin soils over rock; also occurs in the Caribbean, Mexico, and Central America

Plants are terrestrial and epipetric, often hanging down from where they have rooted in vertical rock walls. **Stems** are creeping to slightly erect. **Leaves** are up to 55cm long, and sterile and fertile leaves are similar in appearance, with fertile leaves held more erect, while sterile leaves are spreading and often produce new roots along the rachis or at the tips, or the tips become elongated and vinelike, producing new plantlets. **Stipes** are up to 25cm long, and green, with brown scales at the base and minute stellate hairs throughout. The **rachis** is similar to the stipe. The leaf **blade** is broadly lanceolate, up to 32cm long and 10cm wide, and 1-pinnate to shallowly 1-pinnate-pinnatifid, but typically becoming pinnatifid toward the tip (though vining sterile leaves often remain 1-pinnate throughout). Minute hairs are present on both surfaces of the blade, especially along veins but also on the blade tissue; stellate, furcate, unbranched, needlelike hairs are present. **Pinnae** are up to 5cm long and 2.5cm wide and are spaced out at the bottom of the blade but gradually get closer together until the blade becomes pinnatifid. **Margins** are smooth to shallowly lobed or with rounded teeth. **Veins** are free and may be forked; the lowest veins in adjacent pinnules may join to form networks. **Sori** are round. **Indusia** are minute, often appearing absent. 2n=144 (tetraploid).

A. A colony of *Goniopteris reptans* on a limestone wall.

B. Fronds.

C. Lower leaf surface with hairs.

D. Lower leaf surface with mature sori.

Goniopteris sclerophylla

COMMON NAME(S) Stiff star-hair fern

NOTABLE SYNONYMS *Thelypteris sclerophylla*

STATUS Native, rare

HABITAT/DISTRIBUTION Limestone hammocks; also occurs in the Caribbean

Plants are terrestrial and epipetric. **Stems** are short creeping to erect, with brown scales clustered toward the tip. **Leaves** are up to 55cm long, and sterile and fertile leaves do not differ in appearance. **Stipes** are up to 25cm long, reddish brown at the base and yellowish to greenish above, with brown scales at the base and minute stellate hairs throughout. The **rachis** is similar to the upper part of the stipe. The leaf **blade** is up to 50cm long and 10cm wide, tough in texture, elongate elliptic and tapering at both ends, and 1-pinnate-pinnatifid but typically becoming pinnatifid toward the tip. Minute stellate hairs are present on both surfaces of the blade, especially along veins but also on the blade tissue. **Pinnae** are up to 8cm long and 2cm wide and are spaced out at the bottom of the blade but gradually get closer together until the blade becomes pinnatifid. Pinnule lobes are generally pointed rather than rounded. The pinna midvein has a distinct narrow groove in the upper surface. **Margins** are smooth or with rounded teeth. **Veins** are free; the lowest veins in adjacent pinnules may join to form networks. **Sori** are round. **Indusia** are minute, often appearing absent. 2n=144 (tetraploid).

A. Fronds of *Goniopteris sclerophylla*.

B. Upper leaf surface.

C. Lowest pinnae, with stellate hairs on the rachis.

D. Lower leaf surface with mature sori.

F | S | C | N

Goniopteris tetragona

COMMON NAME(S) Free-tip star-hair fern

NOTABLE SYNONYMS *Thelypteris tetragona*

STATUS Native, rare

HABITAT/DISTRIBUTION Wet, rocky woods; also occurs in the Caribbean, Mexico, and Central and South America

Plants are terrestrial. **Stems** are short creeping, with brown scales. **Leaves** are up to 1.1m long, and sterile and fertile leaves are similar in appearance, but fertile leaves are longer, have longer stipes, and are held erect, while sterile leaves are shorter and more spreading. **Stipes** are up to 60cm long, darker toward the base and becoming yellowish or light greenish above, with minute hairs throughout, at least some of which are stellate or furcate. The **rachis** is similar to the upper part of the stipe. The leaf **blade** is up to 45cm long and 30cm wide, tough in texture, broadly lanceolate, widest at the base, and 1-pinnate-pinnatifid throughout. The tip of the blade resembles a pinnatifid terminal pinna that is separated from the lateral pinnae just below it. Minute hairs are present on both surfaces of the blade, along the midveins but not the lateral veins or blade tissue, which are smooth. A mixture of stellate, furcate, and unbranched, needlelike hairs is present. **Pinnae** are up to 18cm long and 3cm wide and are spaced out, especially in the fertile leaves. Pinnule lobes are bluntly rounded to slightly pointed. The pinna midvein has a distinct narrow groove in the upper surface. The lowest pinna pair may be reflexed and pointed downward. **Margins** are smooth or wavy. **Veins** are free; the lowest veins in adjacent pinnules may join to form networks. **Sori** are round. **Indusia** are absent. 2n=144 (tetraploid).

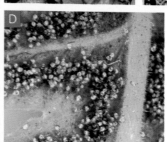

A. Plant of *Goniopteris tetragona*.

B. Leaf with pinnatifid tip that resembles a separate pinna.

C. Lower leaf surface with sori.

D. Magnified image of sori with mature sporangia; note the many dehisced spores, especially on the midribs.

FAMILY: **CYSTOPTERIDACEAE**

Gymnocarpium is a genus of small, delicate ferns that are unique in having ternate (3-parted) fronds that are strongly triangular in overall shape. This makes them readily distinguishable from all other ferns in our flora. Globally, *Gymnocarpium* is a genus of temperate and mountainous regions in the Northern Hemisphere; in eastern North America, 3 species are found in the northern temperate and boreal zones, with an additional species occurring at high elevations in the Appalachian region. These species cross to produce several sterile hybrid intermediates (see figure below). Of these, 3 have been reported from our region (*G.* × *intermedium*, *G.* × *brittonianum*, and an unnamed hybrid), and 2 others have not (*G.* × *heterosporum* was previously known from 1 location in Pennsylvania but is presumed to have been extirpated, and *G.* × *achriosporum* has been reported only in Europe). None of the hybrids are included in the key below, as even the ones known from our region are extremely rare. In addition to these hybrids within the genus, *G. dryopteris* also forms one of the only intergeneric hybrids known in ferns: it crosses with *Cystopteris fragilis* (p. 249) to produce ×*Cystocarpium roskamianum*, which has also been found only in Europe. Base chromosome number (x) = 40.

Relationships among *Gymnocarpium* species in eastern North America. The blue circles are fertile diploids (2x), green squares are fertile allotetraploids (4x), and gray triangles and squares are sterile triploids and tetraploids, respectively. Large shapes are named taxa, and small shapes are as yet unnamed. Arrows show the direction of genetic contribution from parental toward offspring taxa. For more information about interpreting these figures, see p. 12.

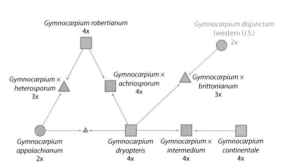

KEY TO THE SPECIES OF *GYMNOCARPIUM* IN OUR FLORA:

1a   Both the upper and lower surfaces of the leaf blade and the rachis are smooth, with no glandular hairs (or very few hairs); the blade is widely triangular and can be as wide as or wider than it is long 2

    2a   On the lowest pair of pinnae, and the first pinnule pointing downward, the first lobe (pinnulet) is shorter than the second lobe; on the second pair of pinnae, there is a short stalk where the pinna connects to the rachis .... *Gymnocarpium appalachianum*

    2b   On the lowest pair of pinnae, and the first pinnule pointing downward, the first lobe (pinnulet) is roughly equal in length to the second lobe; on the second pair of pinnae, there is usually no stalk where the pinna connects to the rachis, and the first lobe sits directly against the rachis .... *Gymnocarpium dryopteris*

1b   The upper surfaces of the leaf blade and rachis are smooth or have glandular hairs; the lower leaf surfaces have a moderate to dense covering of glandular hairs; the blade is usually longer than it is wide 3

    3a   The leaf blade is smooth on the upper surface; the lowest pinnae point distinctly upward; on the second pair of pinnae, there is no stalk where the pinna connects to the rachis, and the first lobe sits directly against the rachis .... *Gymnocarpium continentale*

    3b   The leaf blade is moderately to densely glandular on the upper surface; the lowest pinnae point outward, at a right angle from the rachis; on the second pair of pinnae, there is usually a short stalk where the pinna connects to the rachis .... *Gymnocarpium robertianum*

2a.
*Gymnocarpium
appalachianum*

2b.
*Gymnocarpium
dryopteris*

3a.
*Gymnocarpium
continentale*

3b.
*Gymnocarpium
robertianum*

Gymnocarpium appalachianum

COMMON NAME(S) Appalachian oak fern

STATUS Native (endemic to eastern North America), rare

HABITAT/DISTRIBUTION Mixed hemlock-hardwood forests and slopes at high elevations in the Appalachians

Plants are terrestrial. **Stems** are long creeping, with small scales. **Leaves** are up to 32cm tall. Fertile and sterile leaves do not differ in appearance. **Stipes** are up to 20cm long, green to brownish and darker toward the base, with small scales and sparse glandular hairs toward the blade. The **rachis** is similar to the stipe but is smooth and without hairs. The leaf **blade** is 2–3-pinnate-pinnatifid, broadly deltate, and up to 12cm long and 20cm wide. The leaf is delicate in texture, and both surfaces are smooth and without glandular hairs (though a very few may be present on the lower surface). The lowest **pinnae** are up to 10cm long, and on the first pinnule pointing downward, the first lobe (pinnulet) is shorter than the second lobe; on the second pair of pinnae, there is usually a short stalk where the pinna connects to the rachis. The tips of the pinnae are rounded rather than pointed. **Margins** are entire to shallowly lobed. **Veins** are free and simple or forked. **Sori** are round and form a single row between the midvein and margin of the pinnulet. **Indusia** are absent. 2n=80 (diploid).

A. Plants of Gymnocarpium appalachianum.

B. Upper leaf surface.

C. On the lowest pair of pinnae, and the first pinnule pointing downward, the first lobe (white arrow) is shorter than the second lobe (black arrow).

D On the second pair of pinnae, there is a short stalk where the pinna connects to the rachis (gray arrow).

Gymnocarpium continentale

COMMON NAME(S) Nahanni oak fern, Asian oak fern

NOTABLE SYNONYMS *Gymnocarpium jessoense* subsp. *parvulum*

STATUS Native, rare

HABITAT/DISTRIBUTION Cool woods, talus slopes, and rocky outcrops, usually on acid or neutral substrates; also occurs in western North America, Europe, and Asia

Plants are terrestrial. **Stems** are long creeping, with small scales. **Leaves** are up to 39cm tall. Fertile and sterile leaves do not differ in appearance. **Stipes** are up to 25cm long, green to brownish and darker toward the base, with small scales and moderately dense glandular hairs toward the blade. The **rachis** is similar to the stipe. The leaf **blade** is 2-pinnate-pinnatifid, narrowly deltate to deltate, and up to 14cm long and 18cm wide. The leaf is firm in texture, and the upper surface is smooth, while the lower surface is moderately glandular. The lowest **pinnae** are up to 9cm long and point distinctly upward. On the second pair of pinnae, there is no stalk where the pinna connects to the rachis, and the first lobe sits directly against the rachis. The tips of the pinnae are pointed. **Margins** are entire to shallowly lobed. **Veins** are free and simple or forked. **Sori** are round and form a single row between the midvein and margin of the pinnulet. **Indusia** are absent. 2n=160 (tetraploid).

A. Plants of *Gymnocarpium continentale*.

B. Upper leaf surface.

C. Close-up of rachis showing small glandular hairs.

PHOTOGRAPHS BY NATE MARTINEAU

Gymnocarpium dryopteris

COMMON NAME(S) Northern oak fern

STATUS Native, common

HABITAT/DISTRIBUTION Cool, moist forests and talus slopes; also occurs in western North America, Greenland, Europe, and Asia

Plants are terrestrial. **Stems** are long creeping, with small scales. **Leaves** are up to 42cm tall. Fertile and sterile leaves do not differ in appearance. **Stipes** are up to 28cm long, green to yellowish and darker toward the base, with small scales and sparse glandular hairs toward the blade. The **rachis** is similar to the stipe but is smooth and without hairs (or only a few sparse hairs), and bends so that the blade is almost horizontal to the ground. The leaf **blade** is 2-pinnate-pinnatifid, broadly deltate, and up to 14cm long and 24cm wide. The leaf is delicate in texture, and both surfaces are smooth and without glandular hairs (though a very few may be present on the lower surface). The lowest **pinnae** are up to 12cm long, and on the lowest pair of pinnae, on the first pinnule pointing downward, the first lobe (pinnulet) is roughly equal in length to the second lobe. On the second pair of pinnae, there is no stalk where the pinna connects to the rachis, and the first lobe sits directly against the rachis. The tips of the pinnae are rounded to somewhat pointed. **Margins** are entire to shallowly lobed. **Veins** are free and simple or forked. **Sori** are round and form a single row between the midvein and margin of the pinnulet. **Indusia** are absent. 2n=160 (tetraploid).

A. Plants of Gymnocarpium dryopteris.

B. On the lowest pair of pinnae, and the first pinnule pointing downward, the first lobe (pinnulet) is roughly equal in length to the second lobe (white arrows), and on the second pair of pinnae, there is no stalk where the pinna connects to the rachis, and the first lobe sits directly against the rachis (black arrow).

C. Lower leaf surface with sori.

Gymnocarpium robertianum

COMMON NAME(S) Limestone oak fern

STATUS Native, uncommon

HABITAT/DISTRIBUTION Woods and wetland habitats, including cedar swamps, on calcareous substrates; also occurs in Europe and Asia

Plants are terrestrial. **Stems** are long creeping, with small scales. **Leaves** are up to 50cm tall. Fertile and sterile leaves do not differ in appearance. **Stipes** are up to 33cm long, green to brownish and darker toward the base, with small scales and moderately dense glandular hairs toward the blade. The **rachis** is similar to the stipe, with dense glandular hairs. The leaf **blade** is 2–3-pinnate-pinnatifid, narrowly deltate to deltate, and up to 19cm long and 26cm wide. The leaf is firm in texture, and both surfaces are moderately to densely glandular. The lowest **pinnae** are up to 13cm long and point outward, at a right angle from the rachis. On the second pair of pinnae, there is usually a short stalk where the pinna connects to the rachis. The tips of the pinnae are pointed. **Margins** are entire to shallowly lobed. **Veins** are free and simple or forked. **Sori** are round and form a single row between the midvein and margin of the pinnulet. **Indusia** are absent. 2n=160 (tetraploid).

A. Plants of *Gymnocarpium robertianum.*

B. Upper leaf surface with glandular hairs.

C. Lower leaf surface with glandular hairs and sori.

FAMILY: **DIPLAZIOPSIDACEAE**

Homalosorus is a genus with only 1 species, and we have that species in our flora: *H. pycnocarpos.* This taxon, which is now placed in the family Diplaziopsidaceae, is somewhat similar morphologically to members of the families Aspleniaceae and Athyriaceae, which are not particularly closely related to each other, and this has led to confusion in its naming. Analyses of DNA sequences in recent years have shown Diplaziopsidaceae and therefore *Homalosorus* to be more closely related to Aspleniaceae than to Athyriaceae, which makes one of the species' common names (narrow-leaved spleenwort) somewhat appropriate but also likely to confuse, as *Homalosorus* is not actually in the spleenwort family but is merely a close relative. Another confusing name is the synonym *Diplazium pycnocarpon*, which was the widely accepted and long-used former name for this species; *Diplazium* is recognized as belonging to the family Athyriaceae, and the old name *D. pycnocarpon* for the plant we now call *H. pycnocarpos* is a relic of its former treatment in that genus and family. Base chromosome number (x) = 40.

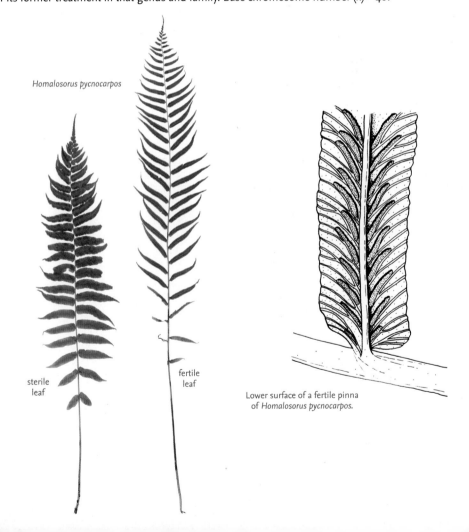

Homalosorus pycnocarpos

sterile
leaf

fertile
leaf

Lower surface of a fertile pinna
of *Homalosorus pycnocarpos.*

Homalosorus pycnocarpos

COMMON NAME(S) Glade fern, narrow-leaved glade fern, narrow-leaved spleenwort

NOTABLE SYNONYMS *Diplazium pycnocarpon, Diplaziopsis pycnocarpa*

STATUS Native (endemic to eastern North America), common

HABITAT/DISTRIBUTION Moist woods and meadows in primarily neutral soils, in sunny or partially shaded areas

Plants are terrestrial. **Stems** are short creeping, with brown, broadly lanceolate scales. **Leaves** are up to 1m long, with fertile fronds slightly taller and more erect, while sterile fronds are shorter and arching or spreading. Leaves arise one at a time or in clusters. **Stipes** are up to 40 or sometimes 50cm long, reddish brown or brown at the base and becoming green toward the blade, hairy, and with scales at the base similar to those on the stem. The **rachis** is green to yellowish, may be hairy on the lower surface, and has a distinct groove on the upper surface that is continuous with the grooves on the pinna midveins. The leaf **blade** is smooth, up to 75cm long and 25cm wide, 1-pinnate, oblong lanceolate to lanceolate, and widest in the lower half of the blade. The tip of the leaf tapers somewhat abruptly. **Pinnae** arise alternately along the rachis, are up to 12cm long and 1cm wide, linear, and taper gradually to an acute tip. Pinna bases are rounded or lobed, and the lower pinnae may have short stalks. Fertile pinnae may be somewhat contracted, narrower, and stiff compared to the sterile ones. **Margins** are smooth to crenate. **Veins** are free and forked, usually once forked on fertile pinnae and twice or more forked on sterile pinnae, with the forks ending in the sinuses between the crenations (rounded teeth). **Sori** are linear or slightly curved and lie along the lateral veins of the pinnae. **Indusia** are present and attached along the lower side of the sori, opening toward the pinna tip. 2n=80 (diploid).

A. A large population of *Homalosorus pycnocarpos.*

B. A mix of erect, fertile fronds and arched, spreading sterile fronds.

C. Sterile fronds.

D. Fertile fronds with deeply impressed veins.

E. Fertile pinnae with immature sori.

FAMILY: **HYMENOPHYLLACEAE**

Members of *Hymenophyllum* are commonly called filmy ferns, a reference to their thin, delicate leaves that may be only 1 to a few cell layers thick. All members of the family Hymenophyllaceae share this characteristic and tend to be restricted to warmer, wetter regions; as a rule, they are not cold tolerant. However, the 2 species of *Hymenophyllum* in our flora occur in the southeast, in areas where frosts and even snow are not uncommon in the colder months. The plants persist by occupying microhabitats that are climatically buffered, such as deep, narrow gorges, rockhouses, or small crevices in rock walls that maintain higher humidity (and thus warmer temperatures) than their surroundings. *Hymenophyllum* can be distinguished from the other eastern North American members of Hymenophyllaceae (in the genera *Crepidomanes*, p. 232; *Didymoglossum*, p. 262; *Trichomanes*, p. 477; and *Vandenboschia*, p. 479) by its 2-valved, clamshell-shaped sori; sori in the other genera are conical or trumpet shaped. Base chromosome number (x) = 13.

KEY TO THE SPECIES OF *HYMENOPHYLLUM* IN OUR FLORA:

1a   **Leaves are typically 1–2cm long; the leaf blade has numerous large, stellate hairs** .... *Hymenophyllum tayloriae*

1b   **Leaves are typically 2–6cm long; the leaf blade is smooth (some glandular hairs may be present, but these are small)** .... *Hymenophyllum tunbrigense*

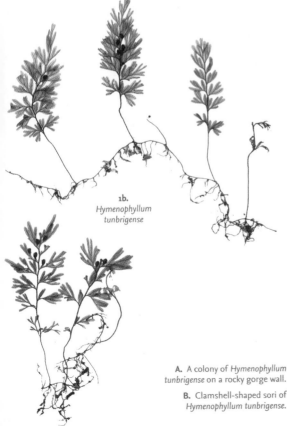

1b.
Hymenophyllum tunbrigense

A. A colony of *Hymenophyllum tunbrigense* on a rocky gorge wall.

B. Clamshell-shaped sori of *Hymenophyllum tunbrigense*.

Hymenophyllum tayloriae

COMMON NAME(S) Taylor's filmy fern

STATUS Native (endemic to eastern North America), rare

HABITAT/DISTRIBUTION Gorges and sandstone rockhouses where temperature and humidity remain relatively constant and high; known from 30 or so locations across the southeastern U.S., including in Alabama, Georgia, North Carolina, South Carolina, and Tennessee.

Plants are terrestrial. **Stems** are long creeping, with scattered brown hairs. **Leaves** are up to 2cm long and 1.5cm wide, deeply lobed, and irregularly branched, and sterile and fertile **leaves** do not differ in appearance. **Stipes and rachises** are brown to black, and smooth. The leaf **blade** is usually 1 cell layer thick between the veins, and deeply lobed to pinnatifid. Numerous dense, star-shaped (stellate) hairs are present on the blade, mostly along the veins and margins. **Veins** are free, typically with 1 prominent midvein leading into each division of the blade. **Sori** are marginal, at the ends of veins, and clamshell shaped, with 2 distinct rounded valves that surround a cluster of sporangia. **Sporophytes** are uncommon, and it occurs most often as **gametophytes**, which are ribbonlike and branched. 2n=unknown.

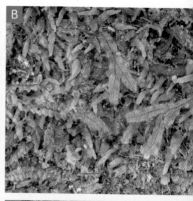

A. A large sporophyte of *Hymenophyllum tayloriae*.

B. Several sporophytes surrounded by gametophytes and mosses.

C. Gametophytes of *Hymenophyllum tayloriae*, with a sporophyte near the bottom.

PHOTOGRAPHS BY ALAN CRESSLER

Hymenophyllum tunbrigense

COMMON NAME(S) Tunbridge filmy fern

STATUS Native, rare

HABITAT/DISTRIBUTION In North America, this species is known only from a single river gorge system in South Carolina; also occurs in tropical and warm-temperate areas of the Caribbean, Mexico, Central America, Europe, Africa, and Asia

Plants are terrestrial and form dense colonies. **Stems** are long creeping, with scattered brown hairs. **Leaves** are up to 6cm long and 1.5cm wide, 2–3-pinnatifid, and sterile and fertile leaves do not differ in appearance. **Stipes and rachises** are brown to black, and smooth. The leaf **blade** is usually 1 cell layer thick between the veins, and deeply lobed to pinnatifid. Minute glandular hairs may be present on the leaf blade, along the veins. **Margins** have distinct, minute, well-spaced teeth. **Veins** are free, typically with 1 prominent midvein leading into each division of the blade. **Sori** are marginal, at the ends of veins, and clamshell shaped, with 2 distinct rounded valves that surround a cluster of sporangia. **Gametophytes** are often present and are ribbonlike and branched. 2n=26 (diploid).

A. A population of *Hymenophyllum tunbrigense* intermixed with bryophytes.

B. Fronds intermixed with bryophytes.

C. A fertile frond.

FAMILY: **DENNSTAEDTIACEAE**

Hypolepis is a genus primarily of tropical regions, and *H. repens* was treated historically as the only member of the genus found in North America, where it occurs only in Florida. However, in 2018 it was determined that the taxon present in Florida is actually a distinct species that is endemic to the state, and it was therefore given its own name. *Hypolepis barringtonii* can be distinguished from *H. repens*, which is widespread in the Caribbean, Mexico, and Central and northern South America, by the following traits: leaves of *H. barringtonii* are a maximum of 1.5m long, in contrast to those of *H. repens*, which can be up to 4m long; the stipes and rachises of *H. barringtonii* are only sparsely prickly, whereas in *H. repens* they are densely prickly; and the leaf texture in *H. barringtonii* is thin and delicate, while leaves of *H. repens* are papery. Base chromosome number (x) = 26, 29.

*Hypolepis
barringtonii*

Hypolepis barringtonii

COMMON NAME(S) Creeping bramble fern, flakelet fern

NOTABLE SYNONYMS *Hypolepis repens*

STATUS Native (endemic to eastern North America), somewhat common

HABITAT/DISTRIBUTION Swamps and other wet woods and hammocks, on mildly acidic to circumneutral soils

Plants are terrestrial and often form large colonies or thickets. **Stems** are long creeping, with brown hairs. **Leaves** are arching and up to 1.5m long. **Stipes** are up to 60cm long, reddish brown toward the base but becoming lighter toward the blade, and smooth except for scattered small prickles (2–3mm long). The **rachis** is similar to the stipe. The leaf **blade** is up to 1m long and 80cm wide, 3-pinnate-pinnatifid (or occasionally 4-pinnate), triangular in overall shape, and delicate in texture. **Pinnae** are lanceolate to narrowly triangular, up to 40cm long and 20cm wide, and may have hairs similar to those on the stipe and rachis but shorter (not more than 1mm), these mostly along the midveins. **Margins** are lobed. **Veins** are simple or once forked and do not quite reach the margins. **Sori** are curved and tucked in at the bases of the pinnule lobes, right at the margin, and typically sit atop the tips of veins. **Indusia** are formed by small flaps of blade tissue that curve back over each sorus. 2n=208 (octoploid).

A. A colony of *Hypolepis barringtonii*.

B. Fronds.

C. Lower leaf surface with sori.

FAMILY: **THELYPTERIDACEAE**

Leptogramma is one of several fern genera whose species used to be included in a large *Thelypteris* genus (p. 475). We have 1 species of *Leptogramma* in our flora, the very rare *L. burksiorum*, which is known from only a small area in Alabama. The species most closely related to it occurs only in Mexico, and the other members of the genus (ca. 27 species) are located primarily in Asia, with a couple occurring in Africa and Europe. *Leptogramma* can be distinguished from other former members of *Thelypteris* by its elongated sori that do not have indusia, and by the long, thin, multicellular hairs on the upper leaf surface, between the veins, and on the rachis. *Leptogramma burksiorum* occurs only in sandstone "rockhouses," cave-like recesses that are carved into cliff walls, often along waterways, where humidity and temperature are buffered year-round. This may explain why this species, most of whose relatives are found in the tropics, is able to occur in North America, but apparently only within this sheltered, climatically moderated habitat. Base chromosome number (x) = 36.

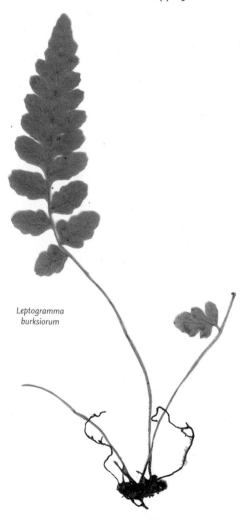

*Leptogramma
burksiorum*

Leptogramma burksiorum

COMMON NAME(S) Alabama streak-sorus fern, Alabama maiden fern

NOTABLE SYNONYMS *Stegnogramma burksiorum*, *Thelypteris pilosa* var. *alabamensis*

STATUS Native (endemic to eastern North America), rare

HABITAT/DISTRIBUTION Shaded sandstone cliffs along waterways

Plants are terrestrial and epipetric. **Stems** are short creeping. **Leaves** are up to 45cm long and clustered along the stem. Sterile and fertile leaves do not differ in appearance. **Stipes** are yellowish and up to 20cm long, with sparse scales toward the base. The **rachis** is similar to the stipe. The leaf **blade** is up to 35cm long and 6cm wide, 1-pinnate to 1-pinnate-pinnatifid but becoming pinnatifid toward the tip, and linear to lanceolate and narrowing toward the base. Both surfaces of the blade have small (up to 1.5mm long) hairs on the blade tissue and along the veins. **Pinnae** are up to 3cm long and 1.5cm wide, and the lower pinnae have short stalks while those farther up gradually loose the stalk and grade into the pinnatifid leaf tip. Pinnae are deeply lobed, especially the lower ones. **Margins** are smooth to wavy. **Veins** are free, and the pinna midveins have a narrow groove that runs along the vein on the upper leaf surface. **Sori** are slightly elongated and run along the veins. **Indusia** are absent. 2n=72 (diploid).

A. A colony of *Leptogramma burksiorum*.

B. Plants.

C. Lower leaf surface with sori.

PHOTOGRAPHS BY ALAN CRESSLER

FAMILY: **LOMARIOPSIDACEAE**

Lomariopsis is one of several primarily tropical fern genera that are part of the eastern North American flora only because of their presence in southernmost Florida. *Lomariopsis kunzeana* is rare in the state, as well as in the rest of its range in the Caribbean. It often grows only as a gametophyte, forming sizable colonies on the walls of limestone sinks and solution holes, and sporophytes are only rarely encountered. The common names of the species reference its hollylike pinnae, and also the tendency of sporophytes to become elongated and somewhat vinelike, enabling them to climb up into trees (though they rarely do this in Florida). Base chromosome number $(x) = 41$.

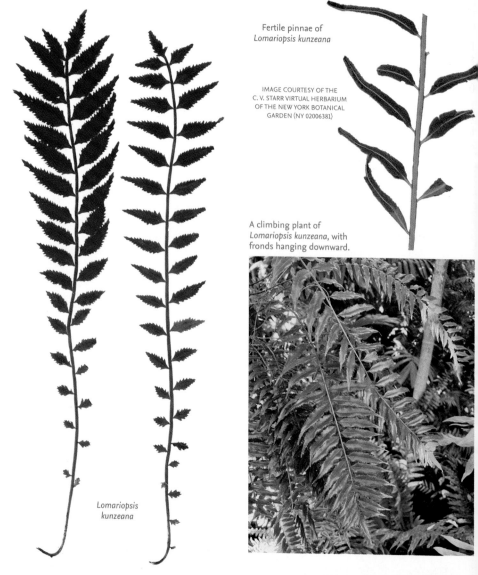

Fertile pinnae of
Lomariopsis kunzeana

IMAGE COURTESY OF THE
C. V. STARR VIRTUAL HERBARIUM
OF THE NEW YORK BOTANICAL
GARDEN (NY 02006381)

A climbing plant of
Lomariopsis kunzeana, with
fronds hanging downward.

*Lomariopsis
kunzeana*

Lomariopsis kunzeana

COMMON NAME(S) Climbing holly fern, holly vine fern, holly fern

STATUS Native, rare

HABITAT/DISTRIBUTION Limestone hammocks and sinkholes; also occurs in the Caribbean

Plants are terrestrial and epipetric and may climb trees via their long-creeping stems. Leaves are evergreen, up to 60cm long, and strongly dimorphic. The sterile leaves are longer and their pinnae are wider than on the fertile leaves. Stipes are yellowish to green and up to 12cm long, with scales toward the base. The rachis is yellowish to green, with a narrow wing or flap of tissue running up each side, on the upper surface. The blade is oblanceolate, 1-pinnate, typically up to 25cm long (though can be longer) and 6cm wide, tapering toward the base, and ending in a single terminal pinna. Sterile pinnae are ovate, up to 6cm long and 1.5cm wide, and resemble holly leaves, while fertile pinnae are much narrower, contracted, and linear elongate. Margins are serrate, with large, coarse, sharp teeth. Veins are free and simple or forked. Sporangia are acrostichoid, completely covering the lower surfaces of the fertile pinnae. Indusia are absent. 2n=unknown.

A. Plants of *Lomariopsis kunzeana*.

B. A frond.

C. Pinnae and winged rachis.

D. Gametophytes (with intermixed bryophytes).

PHOTOGRAPHS A & D BY ALAN CRESSLER

FAMILY: **BLECHNACEAE**

Lorinseria is a monotypic genus (it includes only 1 species), and it is one of 2 genera in our flora whose species were formerly treated as part of the larger genus *Woodwardia* (the other is *Anchistea virginica*, p. 136). The netted chain fern, *L. areolata*, is readily identified by its dimorphic leaves that have strongly contracted fertile pinnae, persistent indusia, and sunken sori. The other dimorphic ferns in our flora are typically larger than *Lorinseria* and/or have their fertile fronds reduced to sporangia-bearing stalks only, with very little or no expanded blade tissue. Base chromosome number (x) = 35.

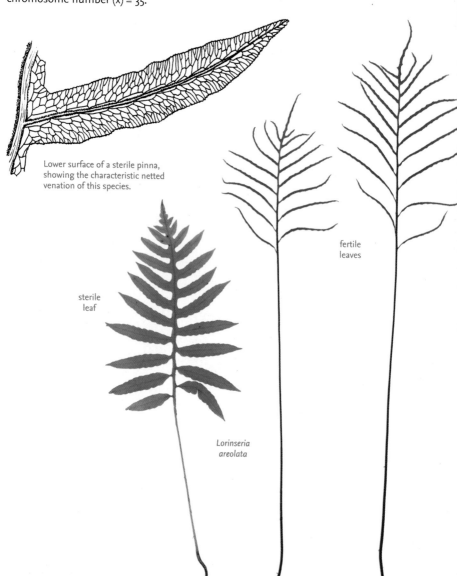

Lower surface of a sterile pinna, showing the characteristic netted venation of this species.

sterile leaf

fertile leaves

Lorinseria areolata

Lorinseria areolata

COMMON NAME(S) Netted chain fern

NOTABLE SYNONYMS *Woodwardia areolata*

STATUS Native (endemic to eastern North America), common

HABITAT/DISTRIBUTION Moist habitats, including shaded woods, seeps, and acidic wetlands such as bogs and fens

Plants are terrestrial or occasionally epipetric in the northern parts of their range. **Stems** are long creeping and narrow, with numerous brown scales. **Leaves** are up to 70cm long, arise one at a time from the stem but may appear to form clusters, and are entirely dimorphic. Sterile leaves have an expanded blade and are arching or spreading, while fertile leaves lack an expanded blade and are taller, stiffer, and more erect. **Stipes** are up to 35cm long, reddish brown or dark purplish brown toward the base and yellowish to greenish toward the blade, with scattered brown scales. The **rachis** is dark green to yellowish, smooth but with a few scattered scales on the lower surface. **Sterile leaves** are up to 60cm long, pinnatifid, with the blade bright green and lanceolate. In both leaf types, the blade is often hairy and scaly when young but becomes smooth by maturity. **Sterile pinnae** are lanceolate, up to 11cm long and 2.5cm wide, and alternate. **Margins** of sterile pinnae are serrate and often wavy. **Veins** form networks with 2 or more rows of areoles on either side of the midvein, with veins becoming free toward the pinna margins. **Fertile leaves** are up to 70cm long, 1-pinnate, and with the blade highly contracted, broadly lanceolate, and up to 27cm long. Fertile leaves are green when immature but brown and crispy when mature and after spores have been released. **Fertile pinnae** are linear, up to 11cm long and 5mm wide, and nearly but not quite opposite. **Sori** are linear to oblong and deeply sunken into the blade surface, in chain-like rows on either side of the midvein. They may take up all the space between the midvein and the pinna margin, and the margins may be somewhat inrolled around the sori. **Indusia** are present and open toward the midvein. 2n=70 (diploid).

A. A colony of *Lorinseria areolata*.

B. Sterile fronds.

C. Fertile fronds.

D. Lower surface of an immature fertile pinna, with elongated sori tucked between the midvein and the leaf margin.

E. Mature fertile pinnae, brown and ready to release spores.

FAMILY: LYGODIACEAE

Lygodium is a unique genus whose members are the only ferns with a true vining habit, complete with a twining rachis, or petiole, that can wrap around supporting vegetation, allowing the plants to climb. These ferns are found throughout the tropics, with a few species occurring in temperate regions. One such species, *L. palmatum*, is native to eastern North America, and 2 others, *L. microphyllum* and *L. japonicum*, are nonnative species that have become naturalized in parts of the southeastern U.S. These latter 2 are among the few ferns considered to be truly invasive species, with the capacity to significantly (and negatively) alter native plant communities and ecosystems. Increasingly, resources are being expended by states in the southeast, especially Florida, to control these noxious pest plants, but their enormous capacity to reproduce and spread via spore dispersal makes management extremely difficult. Base chromosome number $(x) = 29, 30$.

Magnified image of a fertile leaf tip of *Lygodium japonicum*.

Fertile pinnae of *Lygodium microphyllum*.

KEY TO THE SPECIES OF *LYGODIUM* IN OUR FLORA:

1a   Sterile pinnae are palmately lobed; fertile pinnae have almost no blade tissue ·········· *Lygodium palmatum*

1b   Sterile pinnae are 1–3-pinnate; fertile pinnae have blade tissue toward the center, with sporangia clustered on lobes around the pinna margins ········· 2

    2a   Fertile pinnae are 1-pinnate; the lower surface of the blade is hairless ··········· *Lygodium microphyllum*

    2b   Fertile pinnae are at least 2-pinnate and often 3-pinnate; the lower surface of the blade is hairy ········· *Lygodium japonicum*

1a.
Lygodium palmatum
(sterile pinnae)

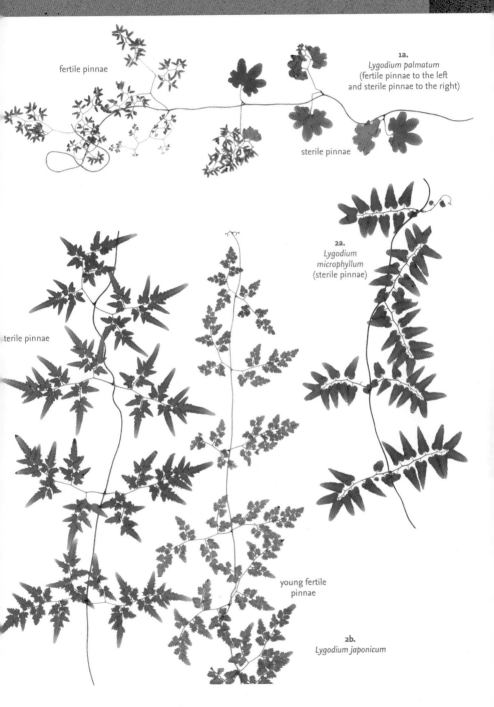

fertile pinnae

1a.
Lygodium palmatum
(fertile pinnae to the left
and sterile pinnae to the right)

sterile pinnae

2a.
*Lygodium
microphyllum*
(sterile pinnae)

sterile pinnae

young fertile
pinnae

2b.
Lygodium japonicum

F S C N

Lygodium japonicum

COMMON NAME(S) Japanese climbing fern

STATUS Not native (invasive), common

HABITAT/DISTRIBUTION Damp habitats including forests, wetlands, roadside ditches, and disturbed habitats; native to Asia

Plants are terrestrial (not epiphytic; although they regularly grow on trees, they are rooted in the ground). **Stems** are creeping, with dark hairs. **Leaves** have indeterminate growth and are up to 6m long, sometimes longer. The **rachis** is long and twining and often wiry, up to 35cm long, and yellowish to greenish. The leaf **blade** consists of **pinnae** that emerge alternately along the rachis; sterile and fertile pinnae differ strongly in appearance, and fertile pinnae are located closer to the leaf tip. **Sterile pinnae** are triangular to lanceolate in overall shape, broadest toward the base, and up to 15cm long and 13cm wide. Pinnae have short stalks up to 3.5cm long, and each pinna is divided, appearing 2–3-pinnate, with the ultimate segments often elongated and pointy. The lower surface may have scattered hairs. **Fertile pinnae** have stalks up to 2cm long and are up to 18cm long and 14cm wide. They otherwise resemble the sterile pinnae, but with small, contracted lobes along the margins that bear the sporangia and give the pinnae a lacy or delicate appearance. **Margins** are entire. **Veins** are inconspicuous. **Sporangia** occur on narrow, elongated lobes along the margins of fertile pinnae and form 2 rows, with each sporangium covered by a flap-like **indusium**. 2n=116 (tetraploid).

A

B

C

D

A. Climbing fronds of *Lygodium japonicum.*

B. Young fertile pinnae.

C. Mature fertile pinnae.

D. Sterile pinnae.

Lygodium microphyllum

COMMON NAME(S) Old World climbing fern, small-leaved climbing fern

STATUS Not native (invasive), common

HABITAT/DISTRIBUTION Wet habitats including swamps, riverbanks, ditches, wet hammocks, and pinelands; native to Asia

Plants are terrestrial (not epiphytic; although they regularly grow on trees, they are rooted in the ground). Stems are creeping, with dark hairs. Leaves have indeterminate growth and are up to 10m long. The rachis is long and twining and often wiry, up to 25cm long and yellowish to brownish. The leaf blade consists of pinnae that emerge alternately along the rachis; sterile and fertile pinnae differ strongly in appearance, and fertile pinnae are located closer to the leaf tip. Sterile pinnae are narrowly oblong in overall shape and up to 14cm long and 6cm wide. Pinnae have short stalks up to 1.5cm long, and each pinna is 1-pinnate, with triangular pinnule segments with blunted to pointed tips. No hairs are present. Fertile pinnae have stalks up to 1cm long and are up to 14cm long and 6cm wide. They otherwise resemble the sterile pinnae, but with small, contracted lobes along the margins that bear the sporangia and give the pinnae a lacy or delicate appearance. Margins are entire. Veins are inconspicuous. Sporangia occur on narrow, elongated lobes along the margins of fertile pinnae and form 2 rows, with each sporangium covered by a flap-like indusium. 2n=60 (diploid).

A. Vining leaves of *Lygodium microphyllum*.

B. Sterile pinnae.

C. Sterile and fertile pinnae.

D. Fertile pinna.

E. A colony of *Lygodium microphyllum* that has been treated for invasive species management. The vines have died back where they were clipped; the vine mass is several feet thick around the supporting tree, whose base is just visible toward the center of the photo.

Lygodium palmatum

COMMON NAME(S) American climbing fern, Hartford fern

STATUS Native (endemic to eastern North America), uncommon

HABITAT/DISTRIBUTION Woods and wetland margins with acidic soils

Plants are terrestrial (not epiphytic; although they regularly grow on trees, they are rooted in the ground). **Stems** are creeping, with dark hairs. **Leaves** have indeterminate growth and are up to 3m long. The **rachis** is long and twining and often wiry, up to 15cm long and yellowish to greenish. The leaf **blade** consists of **pinnae** that emerge alternately along the rachis; sterile and fertile pinnae differ strongly in appearance, and fertile pinnae are located closer to the leaf tip. **Sterile pinnae** are broadly ovate in overall shape, up to 4cm long and 6cm wide, and deeply palmately lobed, with lobes bluntly to acutely tipped. Pinnae have short stalks up to 2cm long. Scattered hairs may be present on the lower surface. **Fertile pinnae** are highly reduced, with almost no blade tissue; they are irregularly forked or lobed, with sporangia at the tips of the ultimate divisions. **Margins** are entire. **Veins** are inconspicuous. **Sporangia** occur on narrow, elongated lobes along the margins of fertile pinnae and form 2 rows, with each sporangium covered by a flap-like **indusium**. 2n=60 (dipoid).

A. Vining fronds of *Lygodium palmatum*.

B. Sterile pinnae.

C. Fertile pinnae.

D. Close-up of fertile pinnae.

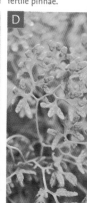

FAMILY: **THELYPTERIDACEAE**

Macrothelypteris torresiana is a large, lacy fern that is native to tropical Africa and Asia and was introduced to the southeastern United States in the 1900s as an ornamental species. It has since become naturalized in Florida and nearby states and is one of the larger ferns to be encountered in the region. Its native range includes the Mariana Islands, hence its common name "Mariana maiden fern." One of these islands is Guam, and the other common name for the species, "Torres's fern," honors Luís de Torres, an administrator in Guam in the early 1800s. Base chromosome number (x) = 31.

Macrothelypteris torresiana

Macrothelypteris torresiana growing in a limestone hammock.

F S C N

Macrothelypteris torresiana

COMMON NAME(S) Mariana maiden fern, Torres's fern

STATUS Not native, common

HABITAT/DISTRIBUTION Wet forests and along streams and waterways; native to Asia and Africa

Plants are terrestrial. **Stems** are short creeping and up to 1cm in diameter. **Leaves** are erect to arching and up to 1.5m long. Sterile and fertile leaves do not differ in appearance. **Stipes** are up to 75cm long and whitish to light green, often with a few dark scales near the base. The **rachis** is similar in color to the stipe. The leaf **blade** is up to 85cm long and 50cm wide, and 2–3-pinnate. The **pinnae** are up to 35cm long and 10cm wide, with pinnules up to 8cm long and 2.5cm wide, and dense hairs on the lower surface; hairs may be 1–2mm long on pinna midveins, and typically less than half a millimeter on the blade surface. **Margins** are toothed. **Veins** may be forked or simple. **Sori** are round and may have small **indusia**, but these are often missing. 2n=124 (tetraploid).

A. A frond of *Macrothelypteris torresiana.*

B. Upper surfaces of pinnae.

C & D. Lower surfaces of fertile pinnae.

FAMILY: **MARSILEACEAE**

Marsilea is a genus of water ferns whose members are distinct in their strong resemblance to "four-leaf clover." They live entirely in association with fresh water, most often along the banks of ponds, lakes, and slow-moving bodies of water (or occasionally in extremely wet, frequently mown lawns). Unlike the floating water ferns in the genera *Salvinia* (p. 455) and *Azolla* (p. 187), *Marsilea* and its relatives (*Pilularia*, p. 421; and *Regnellidium*, the latter not present in our flora) are anchored to the soil substrate by their roots. They have horizontal stems and 2 types of upright leaves, which either float on the water surface or are emergent above it (sometimes called "land leaves," as they persist when water levels drop). None of the *Marsilea* taxa in our region are particularly common, but they can be locally abundant. Seven species are included here, none of which are technically native to eastern North America: 3 have been introduced from the western part of the continent (*M. macropoda, M. oligospora, and M. vestita*), 3 from Australia, Asia, and Africa (*M. hirsuta, M. minuta, and M. mutica*), and 1 from Europe (*M. quadrifolia*). The first 6 species are restricted to the south in our region, while *M. quadrifolia* occurs in the north. Historically, *M. ancylopoda* was listed as occurring in Florida, but those plants have since been determined to be *M. oligospora* instead. Identification of *Marsilea* species can be challenging because they tend to be quite similar to one another in appearance, and in several cases, the characters needed to distinguish species are features of their spore-bearing structures, called sporocarps, which are produced for only a short time during the year. One such feature is a small hooklike structure on the top side of the sporocarp, at the end where the peduncle attaches, called the *distal tooth*. Base chromosome number (x) = 20.

KEY TO THE SPECIES OF *MARSILEA* IN OUR FLORA:

1a Pinnae are distinctly 2-colored, usually with a brighter shade of green toward the center of the pinna circle, and a darker band toward the pinna tips ·········· *Marsilea mutica*

1b Pinnae are not 2-colored; each pinna is a solid shade of green from base to tip ········· 2

    2a Roots emerge from the stem both at nodes (where leaves attach) and between nodes (in the internodes) ········· 3

        3a Sporocarps are 4–5.6mm long and up to 3mm thick; the pinnae of the emergent land leaves have entire margins ········· *Marsilea quadrifolia*

        3b Sporocarps are 3.5–5mm long and up to 1.7mm thick; the pinnae of the emergent land leaves have widely, bluntly toothed margins ········· *Marsilea minuta*

    2b Roots emerge from the stem only at nodes ········· 4

        4a The distal tooth on the sporocarp is up to 1.2mm long, sharply pointed, and often hooked or angled backward at its tip ········· *Marsilea vestita*

        4b The distal tooth on the sporocarp is absent or up to 0.4mm long, not sharply pointed, and not hooked or angled backward at its tip ········· 5

            5a Distal tooth is present; sporocarps are spherical to elliptic ········· *Marsilea oligospora*

            5b Distal tooth is absent or minute; sporocarps are elliptic to 4-sided ········· 6

                6a Sporocarps are up to 9mm long; peduncles are up to 17mm long and often branched ········· *Marsilea macropoda*

                6b Sporocarps are up to 5mm long; peduncles are up to 6mm long and not branched ········· *Marsilea hirsuta*

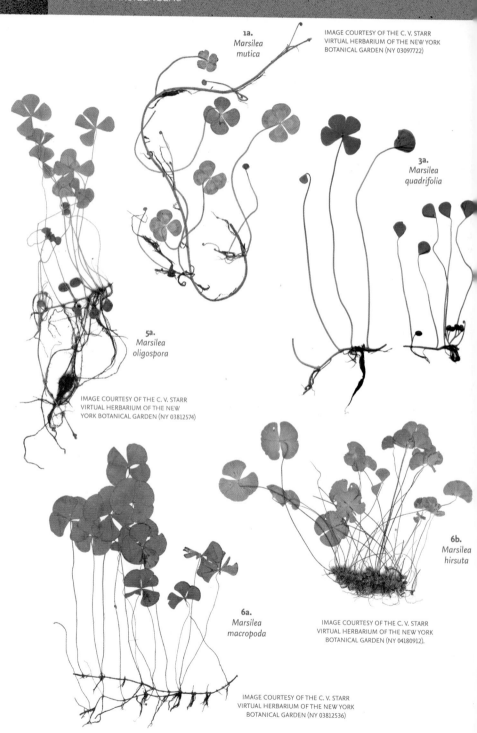

1a.
*Marsilea
mutica*

IMAGE COURTESY OF THE C. V. STARR
VIRTUAL HERBARIUM OF THE NEW YORK
BOTANICAL GARDEN (NY 03097722)

3a.
*Marsilea
quadrifolia*

5a.
*Marsilea
oligospora*

IMAGE COURTESY OF THE C. V. STARR
VIRTUAL HERBARIUM OF THE NEW
YORK BOTANICAL GARDEN (NY 03812574)

6b.
*Marsilea
hirsuta*

6a.
*Marsilea
macropoda*

IMAGE COURTESY OF THE C. V. STARR
VIRTUAL HERBARIUM OF THE NEW YORK
BOTANICAL GARDEN (NY 04180912).

IMAGE COURTESY OF THE C. V. STARR
VIRTUAL HERBARIUM OF THE NEW YORK
BOTANICAL GARDEN (NY 03812536)

Marsilea hirsuta

COMMON NAME(S) Bristly water clover, short-fruit nardoo

STATUS Not native, uncommon

HABITAT/DISTRIBUTION Known from a handful of locations in Florida, where it has escaped from cultivation; native to Australia

Plants are emergent aquatics and form dense colonies. **Roots** emerge from the stem only at nodes. **Stipes** are up to 25cm long and are smooth or have small, scattered hairs. **Pinnae** are up to 22mm long and 25mm wide. The lower surface is hairy, with hairs becoming denser near the **margins**, which are entire and somewhat flared. Together the pinnae form a circle up to 5cm in diameter. **Sporocarp stalks** are up to 6mm long, unbranched, and attached at the base of a stipe. **Sporocarps** are up to 4.5mm long and 3.5mm wide, elliptic to distinctly 4-sided, held horizontally or pointing downward, and may be smooth or have a covering of shaggy hairs. The distal tooth is either absent or up to 0.25mm long. 2n=unknown.

Marsilea macropoda

COMMON NAME(S) Bigfoot water clover

STATUS Native (endemic to North America), uncommon

HABITAT/DISTRIBUTION Sporadically distributed in coastal Florida, Alabama, and Louisiana; also occurs in Texas, New Mexico, and Mexico

Plants are emergent aquatics and form dense colonies. **Roots** emerge from the stem only at nodes. **Stipes** are up to 39cm long and hairy. **Pinnae** are up to 35mm long and 39mm wide. The upper surface is moderately hairy, while the lower surface is densely hairy, with hairs becoming denser near the **margins**, which are entire. Together the pinnae form a circle up to 8cm in diameter. **Sporocarp stalks** are up to 17mm long, often branched, and attached up to 4.5mm above the base of a stipe. **Sporocarps** are up to 9mm long and 5.5mm wide, elliptic to distinctly 4-sided, held horizontally or pointing upward, and usually covered in dense, matted hairs. The distal tooth is either absent or is a small, raised bump. 2n=40 (diploid).

Marsilea minuta

COMMON NAME(S) Small water clover

STATUS Not native, uncommon

HABITAT/DISTRIBUTION Sporadically distributed in the southeast and central Tennessee; native to Africa, Asia, and the Austral-Pacific region

Plants are emergent aquatics and form dense colonies. **Roots** emerge from the stem at both nodes and internodes. **Stipes** are up to 22cm long and are smooth or have scattered hairs. **Pinnae** are up to 18mm long and 17mm wide. Both surfaces are smooth or have a few scattered hairs. **Margins** are widely, bluntly toothed. Together the pinnae form a circle up to 4cm in diameter. **Sporocarp stalks** are up to 11mm long, unbranched, smooth to sparsely hairy, and attached at the base of a stipe. **Sporocarps** are up to 5mm long and 4.5mm wide, oval to oblong or bean shaped, held horizontally or pointing slightly upward, and may be somewhat hairy or have a pattern of indentations at maturity. The distal tooth is prominent, pointed, and up to 0.4mm long. 2n=40 (diploid).

A. Sporocarps of *Marsilea minuta*.

PHOTOGRAPH BY ALAN CRESSLER

B. A colony of *Marsilea minuta*.

Marsilea mutica

COMMON NAME(S) Nardoo

STATUS Not native, uncommon

HABITAT/DISTRIBUTION Sporadically distributed over a large portion of the southeast and Florida; native to Australia and New Caledonia

Plants are emergent aquatics and form dense colonies. **Roots** emerge from the stem at both nodes and internodes. **Stipes** are up to 18cm long (or much longer if plants are in deeper water) and smooth. **Pinnae** are up to 18mm long and 17mm wide and are distinctly 2-colored, usually with a lighter, brighter shade of green toward the center of the pinna circle, and a darker band toward the pinna tips. Both surfaces are smooth, but a few hairs may be present where the pinnae come together. **Margins** are smooth. Together the pinnae form a circle up to 3.5cm in diameter. **Sporocarp stalks** are up to 21mm long, unbranched or once branched, smooth, and attached at the base of a stipe or very slightly above it. **Sporocarps** are up to 6mm long and 4.5mm wide, oval, with a groove on the upper surface, held horizontally or pointing upward, and with thick, short, densely tangled hairs. The distal tooth is absent. 2n=unknown.

Variegated leaves of *Marsilea mutica*.

PHOTOGRAPH BY ALAN CRESSLER

Marsilea oligospora

COMMON NAME(S) Tropical water clover

STATUS Native, uncommon

HABITAT/DISTRIBUTION Known only from Lake and Seminole Counties in Florida; also occurs in western North America.

Plants are emergent aquatics and form dense colonies. Roots emerge from the stem at nodes and occasionally at internodes. Stipes are up to 26cm long (or sometimes a bit longer), and smooth to sparsely hairy. Pinnae are up to 15mm long and 14mm wide. Both surfaces are finely hairy, the lower surface more so than the upper. Margins are entire but may be somewhat wavy, and the pinnae may be ruffly toward the margins. Together the pinnae form a circle up to 4cm in diameter. Sporocarp stalks are up to 10mm long, unbranched, smooth to slightly hairy, and attached at the base of a stipe. Sporocarps are up to 6mm long and 5mm wide, spherical to elliptic or discoid, and are held pointing slightly upward or downward. Sporocarps have a dense covering of long, fine brown hairs when immature but have a pattern of indentations at maturity. The distal tooth is up to 0.25mm long. 2n=unknown.

Marsilea quadrifolia

COMMON NAME(S) European water clover

STATUS Not native, somewhat common

HABITAT/DISTRIBUTION Sporadically distributed across a wide area of the U.S. and extending slightly into Canada; native to Europe and Asia

Plants are emergent aquatics and form diffuse colonies. Roots emerge from the stem at both nodes and internodes. Stipes are up to 16.5cm long, and smooth to sparsely hairy. Pinnae are up to 21mm long and 19mm wide. Both surfaces are smooth to very sparsely hairy. Margins are entire. Together the pinnae form a circle up to 4.5cm in diameter. Sporocarp stalks are up to 16mm long, frequently branched, smooth to slightly hairy, and attached up to 12mm above the base of a stipe. Sporocarps are up to 5.6mm long and 4mm wide, spherical to elliptic or oval, and held horizontally or pointing slightly upward. Sporocarps have a covering of fine hairs when immature but become smooth at maturity. The distal tooth is up to 0.2mm long. 2n=40 (diploid).

OPPOSITE PAGE:

A. A colony of *Marsilea quadrifolia*.

B. Leaves of *Marsilea quadrifolia*.

Marsilea vestita

COMMON NAME(S) Hairy water clover

STATUS Native, uncommon

HABITAT/DISTRIBUTION Known from several locations in Florida and coastal Louisiana; also occurs in western North America, the Caribbean, Mexico, and Central and South America

Plants are emergent aquatics and form diffuse or dense colonies. **Roots** emerge from the stem only at nodes. **Stipes** are up to 20cm long and sparsely hairy. **Pinnae** are up to 19mm long and 16mm wide. Both surfaces are smooth to somewhat hairy. **Margins** are entire. Together the pinnae form a circle up to 4cm in diameter. **Sporocarp stalks** are up to 25mm long, unbranched, smooth to slightly hairy, and attached at the base of a stipe or sometimes up to 3mm above the base. **Sporocarps** are up to 7.6mm long and 6.5mm wide, spherical to elliptic, and held horizontally or pointing slightly downward. Sporocarps have a covering of fine hairs when immature but become smooth at maturity. The distal tooth is up to 1.2mm long, sharply pointed, and often hooked or angled backward at its tip. 2n=40 (diploid).

Leaves of *Marsilea vestita*.
PHOTOGRAPH BY ALAN CRESSLER

FAMILY: **ONOCLEACEAE**

Matteuccia is a genus with only 1 species, *M. struthiopteris*, which has several subspecies and varieties. One of these occurs in our region and is quite common in the northeast and Midwest of the U.S. This species gets its common name, ostrich fern, from its sterile fronds, which are large and plumelike, resembling ostrich feathers. The fiddleheads of this species are edible and can be collected in early spring, though care should be taken not to confuse them with those of other species; the distinct deep groove in the upper surface of the rachis and the covering of golden-brown scales can help identify the fiddleheads of *Matteuccia*. As in *Onoclea sensibilis*, the sensitive fern (p. 373), the fertile leaves of *Matteuccia* persist through the winter while the sterile leaves die back, opening in early spring to release spores before the next year's crop of leaves emerges. Base chromosome number (x) = 40.

A. A plumelike frond of *Matteuccia struthiopteris*.

B. Young fiddleheads.

*Matteuccia
struthiopteris
var. pensylvanica*

F S C N

Matteuccia struthiopteris var. pensylvanica

COMMON NAME(S) Ostrich fern

NOTABLE SYNONYMS *Matteuccia pensylvanica*

STATUS Native (endemic to North America), common

HABITAT/DISTRIBUTION Rich woods and wetlands; also occurs in western North America (a second variety, *M. struthiopteris* var. *struthiopteris*, occurs in Eurasia)

Plants are terrestrial and often form large colonies. **Stems** are ascending to erect and spreading, with brown to golden-brown or orange scales (these often cover the fiddleheads quite densely). **Leaves** are up to 1.75m long, form vase-shaped clusters, and are entirely dimorphic. Sterile leaves have an expanded blade and are arching or spreading, while fertile leaves lack an expanded blade and are stiff and erect. **Sterile leaves: stipes** are up to 45cm, bright green when young and becoming darker at maturity, with a deep groove on the upper surface, pale orange to golden-brown scales, with or without hairs (if present, these often don't persist); the **rachis** is deeply grooved, this groove not continuous with grooves on pinna midveins; the leaf **blade** is elliptic to oblanceolate, up to 85cm long and 25cm wide, 1-pinnate-pinnatifid at the base and becoming pinnatifid toward the tip, and smooth or lightly hairy on the lower surface; **pinnae** are typically in 20–60 pairs, linear, and up to 13.5cm long but gradually shortening toward the bottom of the leaf and continuing almost to the base of the stipe; **margins** are smooth and lobed; **veins** are free and reach the margins. **Fertile leaves: stipes** are up to 24cm, dark brown to black, with the base somewhat swollen and scaly; the leaf **blade** is 1-pinnate, narrowly oblong to oblanceolate in overall shape, up to 40cm long and 6.5cm wide, green early in the season but becoming brown to black at maturity and over winter; **pinnae** are typically in 30–45 pairs, linear, highly contracted and narrow, up to 6cm long, and angled upward, nearly parallel with the stipe and rachis; **margins** are strongly revolute and wrapped around sporangia to form hardened, globose, bead-like structures. 2n=80 (diploid).

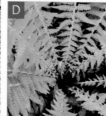

A. Plants of *Matteuccia struthiopteris* var. *pensylvanica*.

B. Rachises with deep grooves on the upper surface.

C. Fertile fronds in front of sterile fronds.

D. Leaf bases, with pinnae continuing almost to the ground.

E. Fertile frond after spores have been released.

FAMILY: **THELYPTERIDACEAE**

We have 2 species of *Meniscium* in eastern North America, both of which are found only in central and southern Florida. These are quite large ferns, with 1-pinnate leaves that can be up to about 2m long, which makes them distinct in our flora; because of their size, they are likely to be confused only with *Acrostichum* (p. 114), but members of the 2 genera are easily distinguished by their fertile pinnae: species of *Acrostichum* do not have well-defined sori, and their sporangia are instead spread out across the lower leaf surface, while *Meniscium* species have distinct, somewhat curved sori set closely together in lines between the lateral veins. *Meniscium* belongs to the family Thelypteridaceae and is one of the genera that used to be included in *Thelypteris* (p. 475). Base chromosome number (x) = 36.

KEY TO THE SPECIES OF *MENISCIUM* IN OUR FLORA:

1a   Pinna margins are undulating to widely, bluntly toothed ⸱⸱⸱⸱⸱⸱⸱⸱⸱⸱⸱⸱⸱⸱⸱⸱⸱⸱⸱⸱⸱⸱⸱⸱⸱⸱⸱⸱⸱ *Meniscium reticulatum*

1b   Pinna margins have distinctly hooked teeth or points ⸱⸱⸱⸱⸱⸱⸱⸱⸱⸱⸱⸱⸱⸱⸱⸱⸱⸱⸱⸱⸱⸱⸱⸱⸱⸱⸱⸱⸱⸱⸱⸱⸱⸱⸱⸱ *Meniscium serratum*

A. Pinnae of *Meniscium reticulatum* with undulating margins but no teeth.

B. Pinnae of *Meniscium serratum* with distinct teeth along the margins.

Meniscium reticulatum

COMMON NAME(S) Lattice-vein fern

NOTABLE SYNONYMS *Thelypteris reticulata*

STATUS Native, uncommon

HABITAT/DISTRIBUTION Swampy hammocks; also occurs in the Caribbean, Mexico, and Central and South America

Plants are terrestrial. Stems are short creeping. Leaves are up to about 2m long or sometimes longer, and fertile and sterile leaves are similar in appearance, though fertile leaves can be somewhat longer and have pinnae that are narrower and spaced farther apart. Stipes are up to about 1m long and tan, with only a few scales toward the base and no scales or hairs farther up. The rachis is similar to the stipe. The leaf blade is up to 1.2m long and 60cm wide, 1-pinnate, and narrowly to broadly ovate. The surface is smooth except for minute hairs on the lower surface only, along the pinna midveins. Pinnae are up to 30cm long and 6cm wide, in 20 or more pairs spaced out along the rachis. The terminal pinna is similar to the lateral pinnae. Proliferous vegetative plantlets are often present at the bases of the pinnae. The pinna midvein has a distinct narrow groove in the upper surface. Margins are entire to rough and undulating, sometimes with wide, blunt teeth but not sharp teeth or points. Veins form networks with 12–20 rows of areoles between the pinna midvein and the margin. Sori are oblong and curved and form lines between the lateral veins. Indusia are not present. 2n=144 (tetraploid).

A. Leaves of *Meniscium reticulatum*.

B. Lower surface of a sterile pinna showing areoles.

C. A proliferous bud emerging from the rachis.

D. Close-up of sori.

Meniscium serratum

COMMON NAME(S) Dentate lattice-vein fern, toothed lattice-vein fern

NOTABLE SYNONYMS *Thelypteris serrata*

STATUS Native, rare

HABITAT/DISTRIBUTION Swampy hammocks, sloughs, and along rivers; also occurs in the Caribbean, Mexico, and Central and South America

Plants are terrestrial. Stems are short creeping. Leaves are up to about 2m long or sometimes longer, and fertile and sterile leaves are similar in appearance, though fertile leaves can be somewhat longer and have pinnae that are narrower and spaced farther apart. Stipes are up to about 1.2m long and tan, with only a few scales toward the base and no scales or hairs farther up. The rachis is similar to the stipe. The leaf blade is up to 1m long, sometimes longer, and 50cm wide, 1-pinnate, and broadly lanceolate. The surface is smooth except for minute hairs along the pinna midveins, on the lower surface, and sometimes on the upper surface. The blade itself is smooth. Pinnae are up to 25cm long and 4.5cm wide, in 15–25 pairs spaced out along the rachis. The terminal pinna is similar to the lateral pinnae. Proliferous vegetative plantlets are sometimes present at the bases of the pinnae. The pinna midvein has a distinct narrow groove in the upper surface. Margins are serrate, with small hooked teeth or points. Veins form networks with 10–18 rows of areoles between the pinna midvein and the margin. Sori are oblong and curved and form lines between the lateral veins. Indusia are absent. 2n=72 (diploid).

A. Plants of *Meniscium serratum*.

B. Fronds.

C. Proliferous buds emerging from the rachis.

D. Close-up of sori.

FAMILY: **POLYPODIACEAE**

Microgramma is a fern genus restricted mostly to the African and American tropics, but we have 1 species in our flora: *M. heterophylla*. This species gets its common name, climbing vine fern, from the long-creeping stem that frequently gives the plants the appearance of climbing up trees. As with many common names, however, this one may be a source of confusion, as the genus *Microgramma* is not closely related to the group typically referred to as the climbing ferns (the genus *Lygodium*, p. 328). The specific epithet of *M. heterophylla* is Greek and means "different" (*hetero-*) "leaves" (*phyll-*). It refers to the dimorphic sterile and fertile leaves that are a distinctive feature of the species. Base chromosome number (x) = 37.

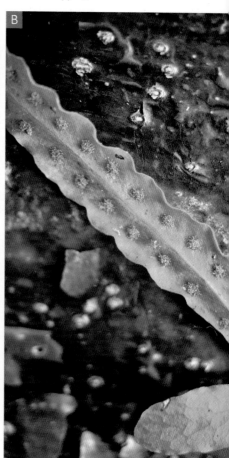

A. Vining plants of *Microgramma heterophylla*.

B. Closeup of sori.

Microgramma heterophylla

COMMON NAME(S) Climbing vine fern

STATUS Native, uncommon

HABITAT/DISTRIBUTION On logs and smooth-barked trees in hammocks, occasionally on neutral to acidic rocks (it is fond of limestone); also occurs in the Caribbean

Plants are epiphytic or occasionally epipetric. **Stems** are 0.5–1.5mm wide, long creeping, branched, and pressed to the substrate, with reddish to dark brown scales. **Leaves** are spaced out along the stem and are up to 17cm long, with somewhat flattened **stipes** and a leaf **blade** that is undivided, smooth, and with wavy margins. **Fertile** leaves have short but distinct stipes (up to 2cm long) and a linear to narrowly lanceolate blade up to 11cm long and 1cm wide. **Sterile** leaves generally do not have well defined stipes, and the blade is elliptic to oblanceolate and up to 4cm long and 1.5cm wide. **Sori** are round to oval and lack indusia, occurring in a single row between the midrib and margin of the leaf. Lateral **veins** form a network of areoles. 2n=unknown.

A. *Microgramma heterophylla* growing on a tree trunk, with sterile leaves toward the top of the photo and fertile leaves toward the bottom.

B. Sterile leaves.

C. Mostly fertile leaves, sticking out from the tree trunk.

D. Lower surfaces of fertile leaves with sori.

FAMILY: **POLYPODIACEAE**

We have 1 species of this genus in our flora—*Microsorum grossum*—and it occurs only in Florida, where it is considered to be a Category 1 invasive species. This determination, from the Florida Exotic Pest Plant Council (FLEPPC), is given to the most damaging invasive exotics that are displacing and/or hybridizing with native species and changing the structure or function of native plant communities. *Microsorum grossum* is easily confused with *Phlebodium aureum* (p. 414), a native species that it resembles closely, but both have unique, easily observed features that give them their common names: *M. grossum*, the wart fern, has large, deeply impressed sori that stick out of the upper surface of the leaf, creating a warty look, while *P. aureum*, the goldfoot fern, has a dense covering of long, reddish-brown to golden scales on its stem and lower stipe. *Phlebodium* can occasionally also have impressed sori, but they are typically not as large or pronounced as those of *Microsorum*. It is always best to check the stem scales to be sure; if they are golden brown, the plant is *P. aureum* and not *M. grossum*. Base chromosome number (x) = 36, 37.

A. *Microsorum grossum* growing in a hammock in Florida.

B. Upper surface of a fertile frond, showing "warts" from deeply impressed sori.

Microsorum grossum

Microsorum grossum

COMMON NAME(S) Serpent fern, wart fern

NOTABLE SYNONYMS *Phymatosorus grossus, Polypodium grossum.*
Microsorum in Florida has also historically been misidentified
as *M. scolopendria* rather than *M. grossum*. However, *M. grossum*
is the correct name for the plants present in Florida.

STATUS Not native (invasive), common

HABITAT/DISTRIBUTION Hammocks and rocky woods;
native to Africa, Asia, and the Austral-Pacific region

Plants are epiphytic or terrestrial. **Stems** are long creeping and branched, less than 8mm in diameter, and with a sparse covering of dark brown to blackish scales. **Leaves** are up to 1.3m long, and sterile and fertile leaves do not differ in appearance. **Stipes** are up to 90cm long, light brown or straw colored, and smooth except for scattered scales at the base. The leaf **blade** is up to 50cm wide, pinnatifid and deeply lobed, with rounded sinuses, and broadly ovate to elliptic, often with slightly wavy margins and a somewhat leathery, smooth feel. Individual **pinna** segments are lanceolate to oblanceolate, each 3–20cm long and 1–4cm wide, with a long terminal segment. **Margins** are entire. The **midvein** is thick and prominent on both surfaces of the leaf. **Sori** are round to oblong and large (up to 5mm in diameter), lack indusia, and occur in 1 to 2 irregular rows on either side of the midrib and pinna midveins. Sori are deeply impressed into the leaf, sunken in on the lower surface and raised on the upper side, giving the species its common name "wart fern." 2n=unknown.

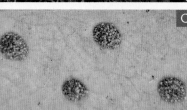

A. Fertile and sterile fronds of *Microsorum grossum.*

B. Lower surface of a fertile frond.

C. Close-up of sori on the lower surface.

D. A leaf base and section of stem, with scattered dark brown scales.

FAMILY: **POLYPODIACEAE**

We have 1 species of this genus in our flora: *Moranopteris nimbata*. *Moranopteris* is primarily
a tropical genus, occurring throughout Mexico and Central and northern South America, and
M. nimbata is primarily a Caribbean species. It is known in North America from a single location
in North Carolina, which is the only known occurrence of any member of the genus outside the
tropics. It occurs primarily as a gametophyte in North Carolina; sporophytes have been found in
some years, but these are always sterile. It likely persists at this location because of the high humidity
and protection afforded by the waterfalls and surrounding rocky areas. Base chromosome number
(x) = 37.

Moranopteris nimbata

COMMON NAME(S) Dwarf polypody, West Indian dwarf polypody

NOTABLE SYNONYMS *Grammitis nimbata, Micropolypodium nimbatum*

STATUS Native, rare

HABITAT/DISTRIBUTION Moist cliff walls, often associated
with waterfalls; also occurs in the Caribbean

Plants are terrestrial. **Gametophytes** are green, thin, elongated,
and ribbonlike and may have minute propagules (gemmae) along
the margins. If sporophytes are present, these have erect **stems** with yellow to brownish scales.
Leaves can be up to 7cm long, though in North America they have been found to reach a maximum
length of only 3cm. Sterile and fertile leaves do not differ in appearance. **Stipes** as well as the leaf
surface are moderately to densely hairy, with brown or red-brown hairs. The leaf **blade** is pinnatifid,
up to 5mm wide, and linear, with **pinna** lobes ovate to oblong. **Sori**, if present, are round and lack
indusia, with only 1 sorus per pinna; in North America this species is typically sterile. 2n=unknown.

Fronds of *Moranopteris nimbata*, growing among mosses.
PHOTOGRAPHS BY ALAN CRESSLER

FAMILY: **PTERIDACEAE**

Myriopteris is a genus of arid-adapted ferns that are often found growing on and around rocky outcrops. The species in this genus were all formerly included in *Cheilanthes*, and the latter may be a name more familiar to readers; however, recent DNA sequencing work showed that *Cheilanthes* in the broad sense contained many species that are not each other's closest relatives. To make the names more accurately match evolutionary relationships, many species formerly treated in *Cheilanthes* are now named in *Myriopteris*, including all the species in eastern North America. The eastern *Myriopteris* include a mixture of somewhat widespread species (e.g., *M. alabamensis*, *M. lanosa*, and *M. tomentosa*) and highly restricted species that are known from only a few locations (e.g., *M. gracilis*, *M. microphylla*, and *M. rufa*). Base chromosome number (x) = 29, 30.

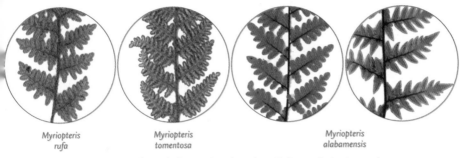

| Myriopteris rufa | Myriopteris tomentosa | Myriopteris alabamensis |

Fertile pinnae of several of our *Myriopteris* species, with the marginal sori covered by false indusia that are typical in the family Pteridaceae (not shown to scale).

KEY TO THE SPECIES OF *MYRIOPTERIS* IN OUR FLORA:

1a The lower leaf surfaces have only a few hairs, mostly along the pinna midveins, with some scattered hairs across the blade surface ⋯⋯⋯⋯⋯⋯⋯⋯⋯⋯⋯⋯⋯⋯⋯ 2

    2a The upper surface of the pinna midvein is green for most of its length; the stems are compact or short creeping ⋯⋯⋯⋯⋯⋯⋯ *Myriopteris alabamensis*

    2b The upper surface of the pinna midvein is black for most of its length; the stems are long creeping ⋯⋯⋯⋯⋯⋯⋯⋯⋯⋯ *Myriopteris microphylla*

1b The lower leaf surfaces are densely hairy, on both the pinna midveins and the blade surface ⋯⋯⋯⋯⋯⋯ **3**

    3a The stipe and rachis have only hairs, not scales, and these may be somewhat scattered rather than forming a dense covering; the leaf margins are somewhat curled over but do not completely cover the sporangia ⋯⋯⋯⋯⋯⋯⋯⋯⋯⋯ 4

        4a The ultimate leaf divisions are rounded and bead-like on the upper surface; the leaf blade is 3-pinnate toward the base ⋯⋯⋯⋯⋯ *Myriopteris gracilis*

        4b The ultimate leaf divisions are not rounded, but flattened and typically bladelike; the leaf base is 2-pinnate or 2-pinnate-pinnatifid toward the base ⋯⋯⋯⋯ *Myriopteris lanosa*

    3b The stipe and rachis have both hairs and scales, and these often form a dense covering, especially on the rachis; the leaf margins are fully folded over the sporangia and form obvious false indusia ⋯⋯⋯⋯⋯⋯⋯⋯⋯⋯⋯⋯⋯⋯ 5

        5a The scales along the pinna midveins on the lower leaf surface are narrow and hairlike; the upper leaf surface has a moderate to dense covering of white hairs ⋯⋯⋯⋯⋯⋯⋯⋯⋯⋯⋯⋯⋯ *Myriopteris tomentosa*

        5b The scales along the pinna midveins on the lower leaf surface are wide and typically scalelike; the upper leaf surface has a sparse covering of white hairs ⋯⋯⋯⋯⋯⋯⋯⋯⋯⋯⋯⋯⋯⋯⋯ *Myriopteris rufa*

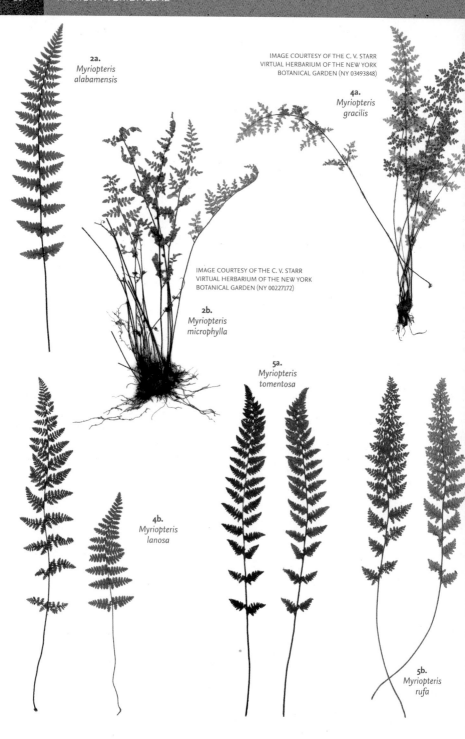

2a.
*Myriopteris
alabamensis*

IMAGE COURTESY OF THE C. V. STARR
VIRTUAL HERBARIUM OF THE NEW YORK
BOTANICAL GARDEN (NY 03493848)

4a.
*Myriopteris
gracilis*

IMAGE COURTESY OF THE C. V. STARR
VIRTUAL HERBARIUM OF THE NEW YORK
BOTANICAL GARDEN (NY 00227172)

2b.
*Myriopteris
microphylla*

5a.
*Myriopteris
tomentosa*

4b.
*Myriopteris
lanosa*

5b.
*Myriopteris
rufa*

Myriopteris alabamensis

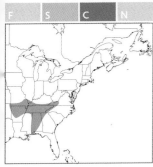

COMMON NAME(S) Alabama lip fern, smooth lip fern

NOTABLE SYNONYMS *Cheilanthes alabamensis*

STATUS Native, uncommon

HABITAT/DISTRIBUTION Limestone, especially outcrops, ledges, cliff faces, and rocky slopes; also occurs in the southwestern U.S., Mexico, and the Caribbean

----

Plants are terrestrial and epipetric. **Stems** are compact or short creeping, with scales that are uniformly dark brown or may be darker toward the base. **Leaves** are up to 50cm long and clustered along the stem, and sterile and fertile leaves do not differ in appearance. **Stipes** are up to 23cm long, and black, with sparse brown or whitish to yellowish hairs. The **rachis** is similar to the stipe and sparsely hairy on the lower surface but more densely hairy on the upper surface. The leaf **blade** is up to 31cm long and 7cm wide, 2-pinnate to 2-pinnate-pinnatifid toward the base, and narrowly elliptic to narrowly lanceolate. **Pinnae** are lanceolate to oblong, the ultimate segments bluntly to sharply pointed, and smooth or with only scattered hairs on both surfaces. The pinna midveins are green on the upper surface throughout their length, but the black color of the rachis continues into the midveins on the lower surface. Lateral **veins** are free and inconspicuous. **Sori** form a continuous band around the margins of the ultimate segments, and a **false indusium** is formed by the margin rolling inward over the sporangia. 2n=87 (triploid).

A. A colony of *Myriopteris alabamensis.*

B. Fronds.

C. Lower leaf surface with marginal sori and false indusia.

D. Close-up of a fertile pinna.

Myriopteris gracilis

COMMON NAME(S) Slender lip fern

NOTABLE SYNONYMS *Cheilanthes feei*

STATUS Native (endemic to North America), rare

HABITAT/DISTRIBUTION Limestone or sandstone substrates including ledges and cliff faces; also occurs in western North America and Mexico (in North America this is a primarily western species known in the east from a few populations in Wisconsin, Illinois, Indiana, Kentucky, and Virginia)

Plants are terrestrial and epipetric. **Stems** are compact or short creeping, with scales that are either uniformly dark brown or have a dark central stripe and become paler toward the margins. **Leaves** are up to 20cm long and clustered along the stem, and sterile and fertile leaves do not differ in appearance. **Stipes** are up to 10cm long, dark brown to black, with sparse whitish hairs (but not scales). The **rachis** is similar to the stipe but more densely hairy. The leaf **blade** is up to 10cm long and 3cm wide, 2-pinnate-pinnatifid to 3-pinnate toward the base, and lanceolate. **Pinnae** are lanceolate, and the ultimate leaf divisions are rounded and bead-like on the upper surface. The upper surface is sparsely hairy to almost hairless, but the lower surface is densely hairy; hairs are whitish when young but become brown or orangish toward maturity. The dark color of the rachis continues into the pinna midveins (though this is often obscured and difficult to see). Lateral **veins** are free. **Sori** form a more or less continuous band around the margins of the ultimate segments; the leaf margins are somewhat curled over to form a false indusium, but this is not strongly formed and usually does not completely cover the sporangia. 2n=90 (triploid).

A. A population of *Myriopteris gracilis.*

B. Fronds.

C. Upper and lower leaf surfaces.

D. Lower leaf surface with sporangia and dense hairs.

E. Close-up of lower leaf surface.

Myriopteris lanosa

COMMON NAME(S) Hairy lip fern

NOTABLE SYNONYMS *Cheilanthes lanosa*

STATUS Native (endemic to North America), somewhat common

HABITAT/DISTRIBUTION Rocky slopes, cliff faces, and ledges of a variety of substrates; range extends somewhat west of the Mississippi

Plants are terrestrial and epipetric. **Stems** are compact or short creeping, with scales that are either uniformly dark brown or have a weakly defined dark central stripe and become paler toward the margins. **Leaves** are up to 40cm long and clustered along the stem, and sterile and fertile leaves do not differ in appearance. **Stipes** are up to 13cm long and chestnut brown to dark brown, with sparse whitish to grayish hairs (but not scales). The **rachis** is similar to the stipe but more densely hairy. The leaf **blade** is up to 27cm long and 5cm wide, 2-pinnate-pinnatifid toward the base, and linear-oblong to lanceolate. **Pinnae** are narrowly lanceolate to ovate, and sparsely to densely hairy on both surfaces. The dark color of the rachis continues into the pinna midveins (though this is often obscured and difficult to see). Lateral **veins** are free and forked. **Sori** are discontinuous and concentrated toward the tips of lateral lobes; the leaf margins are somewhat curled over to form a false indusium, but this is not strongly formed and usually does not completely cover the sporangia. 2n=60 (diploid).

A. Plants of *Myriopteris lanosa*.

B. Fronds.

C. Lower leaf surface with dense hairs.

D. Lower leaf surface with sori around the lobe edges.

Myriopteris microphylla

COMMON NAME(S) Southern lip fern

NOTABLE SYNONYMS *Cheilanthes microphylla*

STATUS Native, rare

HABITAT/DISTRIBUTION Limestone outcrops and calcareous shell mounds; also occurs in the Caribbean, Mexico, and Central and South America

- -

Plants are terrestrial and epipetric. **Stems** are long creeping, with scales that are brown to orange and may be darker toward the base. **Leaves** are up to 40cm long and scattered along the stem, and sterile and fertile leaves do not differ in appearance. **Stipes** are up to 21cm long, and black, with sparse white to yellowish or orangish hairs. The **rachis** is similar to the stipe and sparsely hairy on the lower surface but more densely hairy on the upper surface. The leaf **blade** is up to 27cm long and 6cm wide, 2-pinnate-pinnatifid to 3-pinnate toward the base, and oblong to narrowly lanceolate. **Pinnae** are lanceolate to oblong, the ultimate segments bluntly to sharply pointed, and smooth or with only scattered hairs on both surfaces. The pinna midveins are black on the upper surface for at least part of their length, and the black color of the rachis continues into the midveins on the lower surface. Lateral **veins** are free and inconspicuous. **Sori** form a continuous to somewhat discontinuous band around the margins of the ultimate segments, and a **false indusium** is formed by the margin rolling inward over the sporangia. 2n=116 (tetraploid).

A. Plants of *Myriopteris microphylla.*

B. Sterile fronds.

C. Close-up of sterile frond with dark pinna midveins.

D. Fertile pinnae with marginal sori.

PHOTOGRAPHS BY KEITH BRADLEY

Myriopteris rufa

COMMON NAME(S) Eaton's lip fern

NOTABLE SYNONYMS *Cheilanthes eatonii*

STATUS Native, rare

HABITAT/DISTRIBUTION Rocky slopes, cliff faces, and ledges of a variety of substrates; also occurs in the southwestern U.S., Mexico, and Central America (in North America this is a primarily western species known in the east from a few populations in West Virginia and Virginia)

Plants are terrestrial and epipetric. **Stems** are compact, with scales that are mostly 2-colored, with a dark central stripe that becomes paler toward the margins. **Leaves** are up to 35cm long and clustered along the stem, and sterile and fertile leaves do not differ in appearance. **Stipes** are up to 12cm long and dark brown, with both hairs and scales, these often forming a dense covering. The **rachis** is similar to the stipe but often more densely hairy and scaly. The leaf **blade** is up to 23cm long and 5cm wide, 3–4-pinnate toward the base, and oblong lanceolate. **Pinnae** are narrowly lanceolate to ovate, and sparsely hairy on the upper surface and densely hairy on the lower surface. Wide scales are present along the pinna midveins on the lower surface. The dark color of the rachis continues into the pinna midveins on the lower surface (though this is often obscured and difficult to see), and the midveins are green on the upper surface. The ultimate leaf divisions are somewhat rounded or bead-like on the upper surface, but not as strongly as in *M. gracilis*. Lateral **veins** are free and forked. **Sori** are more or less continuous around the margins of the ultimate segments; the leaf margins are fully folded over the sporangia and form obvious **false indusia**. 2n=90, 120 (triploid and tetraploid cytotypes are known).

A. Plants of *Myriopteris rufa* on a cliff face.

B. Upper leaf surface.

C. Lower leaf surface, with dense hairs and scales.

D. Close-up of lower leaf surface, with sporangia visible under marginal false indusia.

Myriopteris tomentosa

COMMON NAME(S) Woolly lip fern

NOTABLE SYNONYMS *Cheilanthes tomentosa*

STATUS Native (endemic to North America), somewhat common

HABITAT/DISTRIBUTION Rocky slopes, cliff faces, and ledges of a variety of substrates; also occurs in the southwestern U.S. and Mexico

Plants are terrestrial and epipetric. **Stems** are compact, with scales that are mostly 2-colored, with a dark central stripe that becomes paler toward the margins. **Leaves** are up to 45cm long and clustered along the stem, and sterile and fertile leaves do not differ in appearance. **Stipes** are up to 15cm long and dark brown, with both hairs and scales, these often forming a dense covering. The **rachis** is similar to the stipe but often more densely hairy and scaly. The leaf **blade** is up to 30cm long and 8cm wide, up to 4-pinnate toward the base, and oblong lanceolate. **Pinnae** are lanceolate, moderately to densely hairy on the upper surface, and densely hairy on the lower surface. Narrow, hairlike scales are present along the pinna midveins on the lower surface. The dark color of the rachis continues into the pinna midveins on the lower surface (though this is often obscured and difficult to see), and the midveins are green on the upper surface. The ultimate leaf divisions are somewhat rounded or bead-like on the upper surface, but not as strongly as in *M. gracilis*. Lateral **veins** are free and forked. **Sori** are more or less continuous around the margins of the ultimate segments; the leaf margins are fully folded over the sporangia and form obvious **false indusia**. 2n=90 (triploid).

A. Plants of *Myriopteris tomentosa*.

B. Upper leaf surface.

C. Dense hairs along the rachis.

D. Lower leaf surface with dense hairs, scales, and marginal false indusia.

FAMILY: **NEPHROLEPIDACEAE**

Nephrolepis species are some of the most common ferns in Florida, and the 7 species in our flora include 4 introduced species, 2 native species, and a hybrid between a native and an introduced species (*N.* × *averyi*, which receives full treatment here because it is so common in southern Florida). The 4 nonnative species include 2 that are among the most noxious invasive plants in Florida; *N. cordifolia* and *N. brownii* are listed by the Florida Exotic Pest Plant Council (FLEPPC) as Category 1 invasives, the most damaging designation in terms of a species' impact on native plant communities. Many cultivars of the native species *N. exaltata* are sold as "Boston ferns," and these often escape cultivation in Florida. A distinctive feature of the genus is that the leaf tip typically remains curled in a tiny fiddlehead, even at maturity and on large leaves. In addition, the veins of the pinnae often end in *hydathodes*, tiny pores on the upper surface of the leaf that secrete minute amounts of water in which dissolved salts are often present, giving the hydathodes the appearance of tiny white dots.

It is important to distinguish between hairs and scales in the species descriptions and keys for *Nephrolepis*; if a leaf blade is described as "smooth," for example, that refers to an absence of hairs, but not necessarily of scales. Also note that descriptions of pinnae refer to the longer pinnae toward the midpoint of the leaf. Pinnae toward the leaf base and tip will be reduced in size and generally more ovate, oblong, or strongly triangular than the longer central pinnae, and they may not show features such as lobing or forking as strongly as the midpoint pinnae. Base chromosome number (x) = 41.

Persistent fiddleheads at the leaf tips in
(A) *Nephrolepis brownii*, (B) *N. cordifolia*,
and (C) *N. exaltata*.

KEY TO THE SPECIES OF *NEPHROLEPIS* IN OUR FLORA:

1a Leaves are not strictly 1-pinnate: the pinnae either have distinct lobes along
the sides (becoming almost pinnatifid) or become forked at the tips ·· 2

 2a Pinnae are obviously, deeply forked at the tips ·· *Nephrolepis falcata*

 2b Pinna margins are deeply wavy to actually lobed, or even pinnatifid, giving
the leaves a distinctly ruffly appearance from a distance ·································· *Nephrolepis hirsutula*

1b Leaves are strictly 1-pinnate throughout, with no lobing or forking of the pinnae
(though pinnae may have auricles at their bases) ··· 3

 3a Scales on the rachis are distinctly 2-colored, either with a dark central stripe
and lighter margins, or with a dark circular area at the point of attachment on
an otherwise light-colored scale; stem tubers may be present ·· 4

  4a Scales on the rachis have a very dark central stripe and much lighter,
almost translucent margins that are somewhat fringed and frayed; stem
tubers are not present ·· *Nephrolepis brownii*

  4b Scales on the rachis are pale except for a distinctly darker circular
patch where they attach; stem tubers are frequently present ························ *Nephrolepis cordifolia*

 3b Scales on the rachis are uniform in color or may be very weakly 2-colored ······················ 5

  5a The pinna midveins are smooth and hairless on the upper surface ···························· 6

   6a Pinnae have a distinct auricle at the pinna base, on the tip-ward
side ·· *Nephrolepis exaltata*

   6b Pinnae usually do not have a distinct auricle at the base ················ *Nephrolepis biserrata*

  5b The pinna midveins are sparsely to densely hairy on the upper surface ·················· 7

   7a The pinna midveins are only sparsely hairy on the upper surface;
the pinna tips mostly point upward toward the tip of the leaf ················ *Nephrolepis × averyi*

   7b The pinna midveins are densely hairy on the upper surface;
the pinna tips do not point upward toward the tip of the leaf ················ *Nephrolepis biserrata*

2a.
*Nephrolepis
falcata*

2b.
*Nephrolepis
hirsutula*

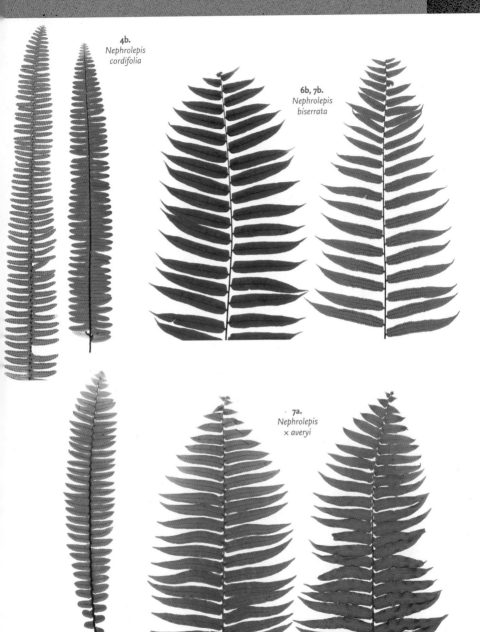

4b.
*Nephrolepis
cordifolia*

6b, 7b.
*Nephrolepis
biserrata*

7a.
*Nephrolepis
× averyi*

6a.
*Nephrolepis
exaltata*

F   S   C   N

Nephrolepis × averyi

COMMON NAME(S) Avery's sword fern

STATUS A hybrid between a native and a nonnative species (*N. biserrata* and *N. exaltata*, respectively); common

HABITAT/DISTRIBUTION Moist habitats such as swamps and wet hammocks, and disturbed habitats, including trails or roadsides; occurs only in Florida

Plants are terrestrial and frequently form dense stands or thickets. **Stems** are ascending to erect, with scales that are uniformly reddish to light brown, and somewhat pressed against the surface of the stem. **Leaves** are up to 3m long, and sterile and fertile leaves do not differ in appearance. **Stipes** are pale to dark brown, up to 50cm long, and moderately to densely scaly, with scales similar to those on the stem. The **rachis** is smooth but has scattered scales that are uniformly brown. The leaf **blade** is up to 2.5m long (or occasionally longer) and 35cm wide, 1-pinnate, and narrowly elliptic to linear lanceolate. The blade surface may be moderately scaly; the lower surface is smooth to lightly hairy, while the upper surface is generally smooth with a few scattered, fine hairs. **Pinnae** are up to 9cm long and 2cm wide, spaced 1–2.5cm apart, and narrowly triangular to oblong triangular. Pinna bases are truncate (not tapered) and may be squared off to somewhat rounded at the corners. Both corners of the pinna base are lobed, with the lobes broad to sharp or somewhat auriculate, especially on the upper edge. Pinna tips are gradually tapered and usually slightly falcate. **Margins** are serrulate. The midveins of the pinnae are sparsely hairy on the upper surface. **Veins** are free and forked. **Sori** are inset somewhat from the pinna margins and are either horseshoe shaped, with **indusia** attached along 1 side, or peltate (umbrellalike). 2n=164 (tetraploid).

A. A stand of *Nephrolepis × averyi* along a trail.

B. Upper surface of a sterile leaf.

C. Lower surface of a fertile leaf, with narrow scales and immature sori.

D. Upper surface of a fertile leaf, with narrow scales and hydathodes

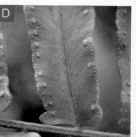

Nephrolepis biserrata

COMMON NAME(S) Giant sword fern

STATUS Native, somewhat common

HABITAT/DISTRIBUTION Moist habitats such as swamps or wet hammocks, occasionally in disturbed habitats or on roadsides; occurs in tropical and subtropical areas essentially worldwide

Plants are usually terrestrial, forming large clumps or stands. **Stems** are ascending to erect, with scales that are uniformly reddish to light brown, rarely with pale margins, and somewhat pressed against the surface of the stem. **Leaves** are up to 2.5m long, and sterile and fertile leaves do not differ in appearance. **Stipes** are brown to dark brown or purplish, up to 55cm long, and sparsely to moderately scaly, with scales similar to those on the stem. The **rachis** is smooth but has evenly spaced scales that are uniformly pale brown. The **blade** is up to 2m long and 35cm wide, 1-pinnate, and narrowly elliptic to linear lanceolate. The blade tissue is sparsely to densely scaly, and smooth to (more often) densely hairy, especially on the lower surface and along the veins on both surfaces. **Pinnae** are up to 23cm long and 2cm wide, spaced 7.5mm–3.5cm apart (wider than in other *Nephrolepis* species), and narrowly triangular to elliptic lanceolate. Pinnae bases are tapered to truncate (not tapering) and rounded at both corners, with the upper edge occasionally lobed or auriculate. Pinna tips are gradually tapered and not falcate. **Margins** are serrulate and may be doubly so (biserrate). **Veins** are free and forked. **Sori** are inset somewhat from the pinna margins and are either horseshoe shaped, with **indusia** attached along 1 side, or peltate (umbrellalike). The persistent fiddleheads are light green to grayish, and often densely hairy. 2n=82 (diploid).

A. Plants of *Nephrolepis biserrata*.

B. Upper surface of a fertile leaf.

C. Lower surface of a fertile leaf.

D. Close-up of sori and pinna margin.

F   S   C   N

Nephrolepis brownii

COMMON NAME(S) Asian sword fern

NOTABLE SYNONYMS *Nephrolepis multiflora*

STATUS Not native (invasive), common

HABITAT/DISTRIBUTION Roadsides and other open, well-lit, and/or disturbed habitats; native to Asia and the Austral-Pacific region

Plants are terrestrial and often form dense stands. **Stems** are ascending to erect, with scales pressed against the stem and distinctly 2-colored: darker brown in the center with pale brown or transparent edges. **Leaves** are up to 2.5m long, and sterile and fertile leaves do not differ in appearance. **Stipes** are up to 45cm long and green to brown, but this can be difficult to see through the dense covering of scales. The **rachis** is light yellowish green to pale or dark brown, with a scattered to dense covering of hairs and pale brown to whitish scales that are narrower than those on the stem and stipe. Hairs and scales may be denser on the lower surface of the rachis, especially where the pinnae attach. The leaf **blade** is up to 1m long and 20cm wide, 1-pinnate, and linear to lanceolate. The blade tissue is sparsely to moderately hairy and scaly, especially on the lower surface. The midveins of the pinnae are usually densely hairy on both surfaces. **Pinnae** are up to 12cm long and 2cm wide, spaced 8–24mm apart, and linear oblong to narrowly triangular. Pinna bases are rounded on the lower corner and have a distinct auricle along the upper edge. Pinna tips are long tapered and may be slightly falcate. **Margins** are biserrate to once serrate or serrulate. **Veins** are free and forked. **Sori** are marginal and either horseshoe shaped, with **indusia** attached along 1 side, or peltate (umbrellalike). The persistent fiddleheads are usually brownish. 2n=82 (diploid).

A. A colony of *Nephrolepis brownii.*

B. Upper surface of a leaf.

C. Fiddlehead covered with 2-colored scales.

D. Lower leaf surface with sori and scales.

Nephrolepis cordifolia

COMMON NAME(S) Tuberous sword fern

STATUS Not native (invasive), common

HABITAT/DISTRIBUTION Shady, usually moist habitats, roadsides, and disturbed areas; native to Asia and the Austral-Pacific region

Plants are terrestrial or sometimes epiphytic and often form dense stands. **Stems** are ascending to erect, with spreading scales that are uniformly pale brown. **Tubers** are frequently attached to the stems, a unique feature of this species that gives it its common name. Tubers are up to 1.5cm in diameter and are often densely scaly. **Leaves** are up to 1m long, and sterile and fertile leaves do not differ in appearance. **Stipes** are up to 20cm long and green to light brown, with dense scales similar to those on the stem. The **rachis** is light to dark brown and usually densely scaly, with distinct 2-colored scales on the upper surface. These scales are pale to yellowish or light brown, but with a distinctly darker, almost black, attachment point. The leaf **blade** is up to 90cm long and 7cm wide, 1-pinnate, and linear to lanceolate. The blade tissue is smooth and typically without scales, and if hairs are present, they are scattered on the lower surface only. **Pinnae** are up to 5cm long and 1cm wide, spaced 5mm–1cm apart, and oblong to lanceolate. Pinna bases have a distinct auricle along the upper edge; this lobe often overlaps the rachis, obscuring it from below. Pinna tips are pointed to bluntly lobed and may be slightly falcate. **Margins** are smooth to serrulate or crenate. **Veins** are free and forked. **Sori** are inset somewhat from the margins and kidney to crescent shaped or rounded, with the indusium attached at the sinus (inner edge). The persistent fiddleheads are pale green. 2n=82 (diploid).

A. A colony of *Nephrolepis cordifolia*.

B. Upper leaf surfaces with 2-colored scales, each with a darker area at the point of attachment.

C. Lower leaf surface with sori.

D. Close-up of a tuber.

E. Lower leaf surface with overlapping pinna auricles.

Nephrolepis exaltata

COMMON NAME(S) Sword fern, wild Boston fern

STATUS Native, common

HABITAT/DISTRIBUTION Closed forests to more open habitats, and moist areas like swamps and hammocks; also occurs in the Caribbean, Mexico, and Central and South America

Plants are usually terrestrial but can also be epiphytic, especially on palms and oaks. **Stems** are ascending to erect, with spreading scales that are uniformly pale brown to reddish brown. **Leaves** are up to 1.5m long, and sterile and fertile leaves do not differ in appearance. **Stipes** are up to 40cm long and pale green to brown, with a scattered to moderate covering of scales similar to those on the stem. The **rachis** is pale green to brown, with scattered scales that are pale to dark brown. The **blade** is up to 1m long and 12cm wide, 1-pinnate, and linear to lanceolate. The blade tissue is smooth but can be somewhat scaly, especially near the pinna midveins. **Pinnae** are up to 7.4cm long and 1.8cm wide, spaced 7–21mm apart, and oblong triangular to lanceolate. Pinna bases are truncate (not tapered) and have a distinct auricle along the upper edge; this lobe often overlaps the rachis on the lower surface. Pinna tips are sharply tapered to more triangular, and pinnae curve slightly or more often distinctly at the tip, giving a strongly falcate appearance. **Margins** are serrulate. **Veins** are free and forked. **Sori** are marginal and kidney to horseshoe shaped, with the indusium attached at the sinus (inner edge). The persistent fiddleheads are light green. 2n=82 (diploid).

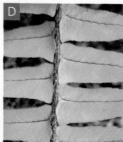

A. A sterile frond of *Nephrolepis exaltata*.

B. Upper surface of a fertile leaf.

C. Lower surface of a fertile leaf.

D. Lower leaf surface showing narrow scales on the rachis.

Nephrolepis falcata

COMMON NAME(S) Fishtail sword fern

STATUS Not native, uncommon

HABITAT/DISTRIBUTION Disturbed sunny areas near human activity; native to Asia

----

Plants are usually terrestrial but can also be epiphytic. **Stems** are ascending to erect, with dark brown scales. **Leaves** are up to 1.45m long, and sterile and fertile leaves do not differ in appearance. **Stipes** are up to 25cm long and pale green to brown, with scattered scales similar to those on the stem. The **rachis** is pale green to brown, with no scales or a sparse covering of narrow, pale scales. The leaf **blade** is up to 1.2m long and 11cm wide, 1-pinnate, and broadly lanceolate. The blade tissue is smooth on both surfaces. **Pinnae** are up to 6cm long and 1.8cm wide, and broadly lanceolate. Pinna bases are truncate (not tapered) and have a small auricle along the upper edge. Pinna tips are distinctly forked. **Margins** are distinctly, bluntly toothed. **Sori** are round to horseshoe shaped and inset somewhat from the pinna margin, with the indusium attached at the sinus (inner edge). The persistent fiddleheads are light green. 2n=164 (tetraploid).

A. A colony of *Nephrolepis falcata*.

B. Upper surface of a leaf, with hydathodes.

C. Lower surface of a fertile leaf.

D. Close-up of sori.

| F | S | C | N |

Nephrolepis hirsutula

COMMON NAME(S) Scaly sword fern, rough sword fern

STATUS Not native, uncommon

HABITAT/DISTRIBUTION Open habitats such as roadsides or trailsides; native to Asia and the Austral-Pacific region

Plants are terrestrial, forming dense stands or thickets. **Stems** are ascending to erect, with brown to dark brown scales. **Leaves** are up to 85cm long, and sterile and fertile leaves do not differ in appearance. **Stipes** are up to 22cm long and grayish brown, with dense scales similar to those on the stem. The **rachis** is pale green to grayish brown, with a dense covering of small, narrow brown scales. The leaf **blade** is up to 60m long and 15cm wide, 1-pinnate, and ovate lanceolate. The blade tissue is scaly on both surfaces, especially along the pinna midveins, with scales similar to those on the rachis. **Pinnae** are up to 8cm long and 3cm wide, and broadly lanceolate. Pinna bases are truncate (not tapered). **Margins** are deeply wavy to lobed, even approaching pinnatifid, giving the frond a distinctly ruffled appearance from a distance. **Sori** are usually not present. The persistent fiddleheads are light green to white scaly. 2n=82 (diploid).

A. Fronds of *Nephrolepis hirsutula.*

B. Upper surface of a leaf.

C. Scales on the upper leaf surface.

D. Scales on the lower leaf surface.

FAMILY: **LINDSAEACEAE**

We have only 1 species of this genus in our flora: *Odontosoria clavata*. While other members of *Odontosoria* look more or less like typical divided-leaved ferns, *O. clavata* much more closely resembles the whisk fern, *Psilotum nudum* (p. 440), in that its green, aboveground parts are dichotomously branched, lack expanded leaf blades, and, if fertile, end in terminal spore-bearing structures that are unlike the sori of most ferns. In *Psilotum*, however, there are no leaves at all, and the plants are composed entirely of green stems, while *O. clavata* does have distinct stems, and it is the leaves that are divided but are simply not expanded into fernlike leaf blades. Base chromosome number (x) = 38, 47.

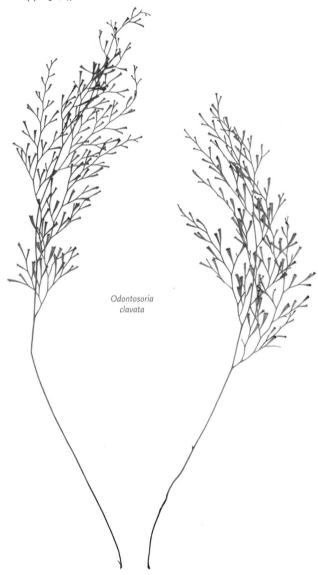

*Odontosoria
clavata*

Odontosoria clavata

COMMON NAME(S) Wedgelet fern

NOTABLE SYNONYMS *Sphenomeris clavata*

STATUS Native, rare

HABITAT/DISTRIBUTION Limestone substrates, including pinelands, hammocks, and sinkholes, in Miami-Dade County and the Florida Keys; also occurs in Mexico and the Caribbean

Plants are terrestrial or epipetric. **Stems** are short creeping, with brown hairs that grade into narrow, dark brown scales. **Leaves** are closely spaced along the stem, erect to arching, and up to 50cm long. **Stipes** are smooth and up to 20cm long, dark brown to purplish at the base and becoming pale green to yellowish farther up. The **rachis** is pale green to yellowish. The **blade** is narrowly oblong to ovate or somewhat triangular in overall shape, up to 25cm long and 10cm wide, and divides repeatedly, somewhat dichotomously, into narrow linear segments; the ultimate segments are tapered toward the base but flare out toward the tip, creating a distinctly wedge-like shape that gives the species its common name. **Margins** are entire, and **veins** are free and simple or forked. **Sori** are borne in horizontally flattened, cuplike structures with rough-edged indusial flaps, at the ends of veins on the wide tips of the wedge-shaped leaf segments. 2n=76 (diploid).

A. A population of *Odontosoria clavata*.

B. Frond.

C. Wedge-shaped pinna segments.

D. Cuplike sori.

FAMILY: **ONOCLEACEAE**

Onoclea is a monotypic genus (it includes only 1 species), and its single member is one of the most commonly encountered ferns in eastern North America: *O. sensibilis*, the sensitive fern. This species gets its common name from its low tolerance for even the lightest of frosts, which will readily damage the expanded sterile leaves. The upright fertile leaves of these dimorphic ferns are reduced to little more than stiff stalks bearing sporangia, with no expanded blade tissue. These fertile leaves persist through the winter while the sterile leaves die back, opening in early spring to release spores before the next year's crop of leaves emerges. Base chromosome number (x) = 37.

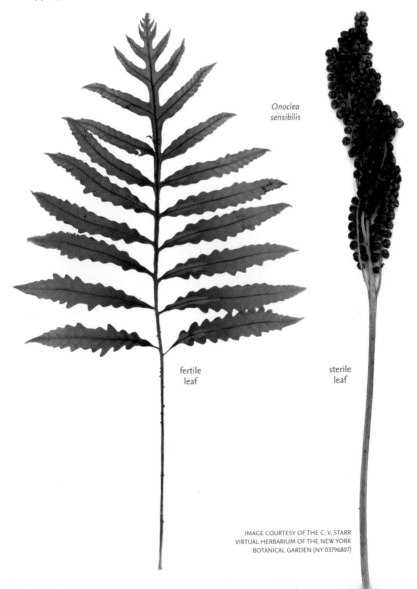

*Onoclea
sensibilis*

fertile
leaf

sterile
leaf

F S C N

Onoclea sensibilis

COMMON NAME(S) Sensitive fern

STATUS Native (endemic to North America), common

HABITAT/DISTRIBUTION A variety of shaded to sunny habitats, including woods, meadows, swamps, and other wetlands; range extends into western North America

Plants are terrestrial. **Stems** are smooth and long creeping, forming extensive mats or colonies. **Leaves** arise irregularly along the stem and are entirely dimorphic. Sterile leaves have an expanded blade and are arching or spreading, while fertile leaves lack an expanded blade and are stiff and erect. **Sterile leaves: stipes** are up to 58cm, dark brown to black, smooth, swollen at the base, and often with scattered light brown scales; the **rachis** is often winged; the leaf **blade** is triangular, up to 40cm long and 30cm wide, 1-pinnate-pinnatifid at the base and becoming pinnatifid toward the tip, and lightly hairy and scaly on both surfaces, especially along the rachis and pinna midveins; **pinnae** are opposite to subopposite, typically in 5–10 pairs, lanceolate, and up to 18cm long; **margins** are smooth but shallowly to deeply wavy (sinuate); **veins** form networks. **Fertile leaves: stipes** are up to 40cm long, light to dark brown or black, and smooth, often with scattered light brown scales at the base; the leaf **blade** is linear oblong in overall shape, without expanded blade tissue, up to 17cm long and 4cm wide, and green early in the season but becoming brown to black at maturity and over winter; **pinnae** are opposite to subopposite, typically in 5–10 pairs, linear, and up to 5cm long; **margins** are strongly revolute and wrapped around sporangia to form hardened, globose, bead-like structures that contain greenish **spores**. 2n=74 (diploid).

A. Plants of *Onoclea sensibilis*.

B. Sterile fronds.

C. A fertile frond.

D. Immature sporangia.

E. Mature sporangia.

FAMILY: **OPHIOGLOSSACEAE**

Ophioderma pendulum, the ribbon fern, is one of 2 epiphytic members of Ophioglossaceae in our flora (the other is *Cheiroglossa palmata*, the hand fern, p. 223). The ribbon fern is native to tropical regions of Asia and the Pacific and has been introduced to southernmost peninsular Florida, where it is maintained via the horticultural trade and seems to be encountered more and more frequently in the wild, though (so far) only in Miami-Dade County. The only species that *O. pendulum* is likely to be confused with is *Cheiroglossa palmata*, and the 2 species can easily be distinguished by the elongated, ribbonlike leaves of *O. pendula* versus the deeply palmately lobed, fan-shaped leaves of *C. palmata*. Base chromosome number (x) = 30.

Ophioderma pendulum

Ophioderma pendulum plants growing on sabal palm trees.

Ophioderma pendulum

COMMON NAME(S) Ribbon fern, Old World adder's tongue

NOTABLE SYNONYMS *Ophioglossum pendulum*

STATUS Not native, uncommon

HABITAT/DISTRIBUTION Escapes from cultivation in Florida, typically around human activity or disturbed areas; native to Asia and the Austral-Pacific region

Plants are epiphytic. **Stems** are short, up to 2.5cm long. **Leaves** are pendent, hanging down from the attachment point on the tree, with a narrow stalk up to 10cm long that widens into the **sterile leaf blade** (trophophore), which is ribbonlike, elongated, and up to 80cm long and 3cm wide. The blade may fork or divide once or more. The **fertile segment** (sporophore) of the leaf emerges from the upper surface of the blade and is a stalked unit up to 12cm long that bears sporangia in 2 rows. **Margins** are entire. **Veins** are anastomosing. 2n=960.

A. Fronds of *Ophioderma pendulum* growing with *Vittaria lineata* (at lower left and right) on a sabal palm tree.

B. Leaves, one with a sporophore.

C. Close-up of sporangia along the margins of a sporophore.

D. Leaf bases.

FAMILY: **OPHIOGLOSSACEAE**

Ophioglossum species, commonly known as adder's-tongue ferns, are unique morphologically in our fern flora and are quite easy to recognize—if you can find them. The plants are typically fairly small and ephemeral, like other members of the family Ophioglossaceae (especially *Botrychium*, p. 193), emerging from underground storage structures early in spring and often senescing once they have released their spores. In general, these plants favor open, grassy habitats and do well in disturbed areas (including those that are frequently mown, such as cemeteries and roadsides), but they are usually quite rare. The aboveground portion of an *Ophioglossum* plant has 2 distinct components that are actually part of a single leaf: a fertile sporophore that consists of an erect stalk with a series of sporangia in 2 parallel rows near its tip, and a sterile, ovate, leaflike trophophore that is undivided and roughly resembles the leaf of a lily or a plantain. *Ophioglossum* trophophores can be distinguished from these flowering plant look-alikes by not having a midrib, and by having exclusively netlike venation. This netted venation outlines shapes called *areoles*, and whether the main areoles have additional smaller, secondary areoles and/or free, unconnected veinlets within them is a key character for distinguishing between *Ophioglossum* species. Base chromosome number (x) = 30 (and note the extraordinarily high chromosome numbers given for the species below; this genus has some of the highest chromosome numbers known for any multicellular life form).

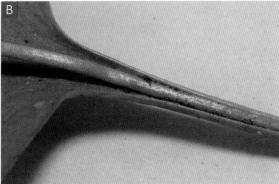

A. Close-up of the fused sporangia that make up the fertile portion of the sporophore; the yellowish powdery substance is spores that have already dropped out of the slightly open sporangia.

B. The base of the leaf where the sporophore stalk and leafy trophophore come together, fusing near the ground surface (which would be toward the right-hand side of the picture).

KEY TO THE SPECIES OF *OPHIOGLOSSUM* IN OUR FLORA:

1a The trophophore blade is oriented horizontally, lies flat on the ground,
and is ovate triangular to heart shaped ·· *Ophioglossum crotalophoroides*

1b The trophophore blade is oriented horizontally or points upward, is usually
elevated off the ground, and is ovate to lanceolate ··· 2

    2a The trophophore blade is usually no more than 1.5cm long and 1cm
wide at maturity (though occasionally larger); venation is netted but usually
without secondary areoles, except in larger leaves, which may have them ·············· *Ophioglossum nudicaule*

    2b The trophophore blade is more than 1.5cm long and 1cm wide at maturity;
venation is netted, and secondary areoles and/or free veinlets are present inside
the main areoles ··· 3

        3a The main areoles have secondary areoles within them, and free
veinlets may also be present ·· *Ophioglossum engelmannii*

        3b The main areoles are not further divided into secondary areoles,
but free veinlets may be present ·· 4

            4a The trophophore blade is pointed at the tip; the main areoles
are mostly more than 2mm wide, with only a few free veinlets ·············· *Ophioglossum petiolatum*

            4b The trophophore blade is rounded at the tip; the main areoles
are mostly less than 2mm wide, with many included free veinlets ·· 5

                5a The trophophore blade is widest near the middle
and tapers gradually to the base ·· *Ophioglossum pusillum*

                5b The trophophore blade is widest at the base and
tapers abruptly below this widest part ·· *Ophioglossum pycnostichum*

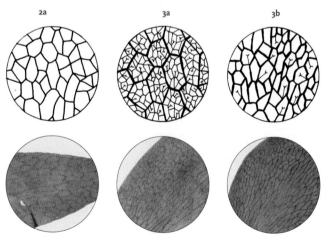

2a   3a   3b

Examples of leaf venation mentioned in the key.

Key choice 2a Netted venation without secondary areoles.
Key choice 3a Netted venation with secondary areoles and free veinlets.
Key choice 3b Netted venation without secondary areoles, but with free veinlets.

1a.
Ophioglossum
crotalophoroides

IMAGE COURTESY OF THE
C. V. STARR VIRTUAL HERBARIUM
OF THE NEW YORK BOTANICAL
GARDEN (NY 03538418)

2a.
Ophioglossum
nudicaule

IMAGE COURTESY OF THE
C. V. STARR VIRTUAL HERBARIUM
OF THE NEW YORK BOTANICAL
GARDEN (NY 03866113)

3a.
Ophioglossum
engelmannii

IMAGE COURTESY OF THE
C. V. STARR VIRTUAL HERBARIUM
OF THE NEW YORK BOTANICAL
GARDEN (NY 03538755)

4a.
Ophioglossum
petiolatum

5a.
Ophioglossum
pusillum

IMAGE COURTESY OF THE
C. V. STARR VIRTUAL HERBARIUM
OF THE NEW YORK BOTANICAL
GARDEN (NY 03538793)

5b.
Ophioglossum
pycnostichum

F S C N

Ophioglossum crotalophoroides

COMMON NAME(S) Bulbous adder's-tongue

STATUS Native, uncommon

HABITAT/DISTRIBUTION Fields, lawns, and disturbed habitats such as roadside ditches and abandoned lots; range extends into Texas; also occurs in the Caribbean, Mexico, and Central and South America

Plants are terrestrial. **Stems** are spherical, corm-like, and up to 1.2cm in diameter. Leaves emerge from a depression in the top of the stem. **Leaves** are 2-parted, with a short common stalk that separates into a sterile trophophore and fertile sporophore. The **trophophore** has a short stalk up to 0.6cm long and a blade that is up to 3cm long and 2cm wide, ovate triangular to heart shaped, and lies almost flat against the ground. **Venation** is netted, with free veinlets inside the areoles. The **sporophore** is up to 5 times as long as the trophophore (up to 15cm), with the fertile section of fused sporangia less than 1cm long, and a pointed tip (apiculum) above the sporangia that is up to 1.5mm long. 2n=570.

A B

C

A. A plant of *Ophioglossum crotalophoroides.*

B. Close-up of mature sporangia.

C. Senescent sporangia that have released their spores.

Ophioglossum engelmannii

COMMON NAME(S) Limestone adder's-tongue

STATUS Native, somewhat common

HABITAT/DISTRIBUTION Usually in fields, meadows, and lawns over limestone substrates; range extends into the southwestern U.S.; also occurs in Mexico and Central America

Plants are terrestrial. **Stems** are elongated and cylindrical, and up to 1.5cm long and 4mm wide. Leaves emerge from the top of the stem. **Leaves** are 2-parted, with a long common stalk that separates into a sterile trophophore and fertile sporophore. The **trophophore** has a very short stalk up to 0.1cm long and a blade that is up to 10cm long and 4.5cm wide, ovate to ovate lanceolate and often somewhat folded, and held erect or spreading outward. **Venation** is netted, with small secondary areoles inside the main ones; free veinlets may also be present. The **sporophore** is up to 2.5 times as long as the trophophore (up to 25cm), with the fertile section of fused sporangia 2–4cm long, and a pointed tip (apiculum) above the sporangia that is up to 1.3mm long. 2n=unknown.

A. A fertile plant of *Ophioglossum engelmannii*.

B. Two sterile trophophores.

C. Fertile section of a sporophore, with pointed tip (apiculum).

Ophioglossum nudicaule

COMMON NAME(S) Slender adder's-tongue

STATUS Native, uncommon

HABITAT/DISTRIBUTION Fields, lawns, and disturbed habitats such as roadside ditches and abandoned lots; also occurs in the Caribbean, Mexico, and Central and South America

Plants are terrestrial. **Stems** are elongated and cylindrical, and up to 1.2cm long and 5mm wide. Leaves emerge from the top of the stem. **Leaves** are 2-parted, with a long common stalk that separates into a sterile trophophore and fertile sporophore. The **trophophore** has a short stalk up to 0.8cm long and a blade that is usually up to 1.5cm long and 1cm wide (but some plants in a colony may be larger), ovate to lanceolate, and spreading outward. **Venation** is finely netted, with free veinlets inside the areoles on small leaves, and secondary areoles also present but only on larger leaves. The **sporophore** is up to 6 times as long as the trophophore (up to ca. 20cm), with the fertile section of fused sporangia 0.5–1.5cm long, and a pointed tip (apiculum) above the sporangia that is up to 1mm long. 2n=480.

A. A fertile plant of *Ophioglossum nudicaule.*

B. Young plants with immature sporophores.

C. Mature plants whose sporangia have dehisced and released their spores.

PHOTOGRAPHS
BY ALAN CRESSLER

Ophioglossum petiolatum

COMMON NAME(S) Stalked adder's-tongue

NOTABLE SYNONYMS *Ophioglossum reticulatum*

STATUS Native, uncommon

HABITAT/DISTRIBUTION Fields, lawns, ditches, and disturbed habitats; also occurs in the Caribbean, Mexico, Asia, and the Austral-Pacific region

Plants are terrestrial. **Stems** are elongated and cylindrical, and up to 1cm long and 2.5mm wide. Leaves emerge from the top of the stem. **Leaves** are 2-parted, with a long common stalk that separates into a sterile trophophore and fertile sporophore. The **trophophore** has a short stalk up to 3mm long and a blade that is usually up to 6cm long and 3cm wide, ovate to elongate heart shaped and pointed at the tip, and held erect or spreading outward. **Venation** is coarsely netted, with most of the main areoles more than 2mm wide, and with only a few free veinlets and no secondary areoles inside them. The **sporophore** is up to 7 times as long as the trophophore (up to ca. 40cm), with the fertile section of fused sporangia up to 4cm long, and a pointed tip (apiculum) above the sporangia that is up to 1.2mm long. 2n=960.

A & B. Plants of *Ophioglossum petiolatum*.

C. Fertile section of a sporophore.

PHOTOGRAPH A BY ALAN CRESSLER

Ophioglossum pusillum

COMMON NAME(S) Northern adder's-tongue

STATUS Native (endemic to North America), somewhat common

HABITAT/DISTRIBUTION Damp fields and pastures, wetland edges, roadside ditches; also occurs in western North America

Plants are terrestrial. **Stems** are elongated and cylindrical, and up to 2cm long and 3mm wide. Leaves emerge from the top of the stem. **Leaves** are 2-parted, with a long common stalk that separates into a sterile trophophore and fertile sporophore. The **trophophore** has a poorly defined stalk and a blade that is up to 10cm long and 3.5cm wide, ovate to obovate, widest near the middle, rounded at the tip, tapering gradually to the base, and held erect or spreading outward. Venation is finely netted, with most of the main areoles less than 2mm wide, and with many free veinlets but no secondary areoles inside them. The **sporophore** is up to 4.5 times as long as the trophophore (up to ca. 40cm), with the fertile section of fused sporangia 2–4.5cm long, and a pointed tip (apiculum) above the sporangia that is up to 2mm long. 2n=960.

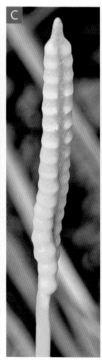

A. A plant of *Ophioglossum pusillum*.

B. A trophophore blade.

C. Fertile section of a sporophore.

PHOTOGRAPHS BY NATE MARTINEAU

Ophioglossum pycnostichum

COMMON NAME(S) Southern adder's-tongue

NOTABLE SYNONYMS *Ophioglossum vulgatum, Ophioglossum vulgatum* var. *pycnostichum*. In North America this taxon is now usually recognized as being separate from *O. vulgatum*, which, defined narrowly, occurs only in Europe.

STATUS Native, somewhat common

HABITAT/DISTRIBUTION Shady forests and floodplain woods; range extends into Texas and Oklahoma; also occurs in Mexico, Europe, and Asia

Plants are terrestrial. **Stems** are elongated and cylindrical, and up to 1cm long and 3mm wide. Leaves emerge from the top of the stem. **Leaves** are 2-parted, with a long common stalk that separates into a sterile trophophore and fertile sporophore. The **trophophore** has a very short stalk up to 5mm long and a blade that is up to 10cm long and 4cm wide, trowel shaped, widest at the base and pointed at the tip, and held erect or spreading outward. Venation is finely netted, with most of the main areoles less than 2mm wide, and with many free veinlets but no secondary areoles inside them. The **sporophore** is up to 4 times as long as the trophophore (up to ca. 40cm), with the fertile section of fused sporangia 2–4cm long, and a pointed tip (apiculum) above the sporangia that is up to 1.5mm long. 2n=ca. 1320.

A. Plants of *Ophioglossum pycnostichum*.

B. Sterile trophophore blade.

C. Fertile section of a sporophore, with sporangia open to release spores.

FAMILY: **OSMUNDACEAE**

The royal fern, *Osmunda spectabilis*, is one of the most distinctive ferns in our flora because of its large size and obviously 2-pinnate leaves, whose tip-most pinnae, when fertile, become reduced to sporangia-bearing stalks with no blade tissue. *Osmunda spectabilis* is now typically considered to be the only species of *Osmunda* in our flora; its close relatives the cinnamon fern (*Osmundastrum cinnamomeum*, p. 388) and the interrupted fern (*Claytosmunda claytoniana*, p. 228) were both included in this genus in the past but are now recognized as belonging to separate genera. This species was long referred to as *O. regalis* var. *spectabilis*, but DNA analyses have shown that the royal ferns in Europe and North America are separate species that are not each other's closest relatives, and each therefore needs its own name. Under the rules of taxonomy, the European taxon takes priority for the name *O. regalis*, and the North American plants are properly called *O. spectabilis*. This species forms a hybrid with its former genus mate *Claytosmunda claytoniana* to form Rugg's osmunda, now recognized as the intergeneric hybrid ×*Osmunimunda ruggii*. This hybrid is quite rare despite the commonness of its parents, and today only a single natural population is known, in western Virginia, though it can also be found in cultivation elsewhere in the eastern U.S. ×*Osmunimunda* is 2-pinnate, like *O. spectabiliis*, but its pinnules are sessile, sitting directly against the pinna midvein (as opposed to having short stalks as in *O. spectabiliis*), and its fertile pinnae can be at the tip of the leaf, in the middle of the blade, or both. Base chromosome number (x) = 22.

Osmunda spectabilis

Osmunda spectabilis growing along a swamp edge.

Osmunda spectabilis

COMMON NAME(S) American royal fern, royal fern

NOTABLE SYNONYM *Osmunda regalis* var. *spectabilis*

STATUS Native (endemic to North America), common

HABITAT/DISTRIBUTION Wetlands and wet woods; range extends into Oklahoma and Texas

Plants are terrestrial. **Stems** lack scales and are creeping but become erect at the tips, forming small trunks or tussocks. Old persistent stipe bases and black fibrous roots are often apparent around the leaf bases. **Leaves** form vaselike clumps and are partly dimorphic. The fertile leaves are in the center of the plant and are upright, erect, and taller than the sterile leaves, which surround them and are arching to spreading. On the fertile leaves, the fertile pinnae occur at the tips of leaves. **Sterile leaves:** up to 1.8m long; **stipes** are up to 80cm, winged, and greenish blue to pinkish, with light brown hairs when young but becoming smooth at maturity; **rachis** is grooved on the upper surface, greenish blue to pinkish, and covered in cinnamon-colored hairs only when young; leaf **blade** is broadly ovate, up to 1m long and 60cm wide, and 2-pinnate; **pinnae** are up to 28cm long and 14cm wide, typically in 5–9 pairs, broadly lanceolate, and without tufts of cinnamon hair at the bases; pinnules have short stalks, rounded to squared-off bases, and rounded to pointed tips; **margins** are smooth to serrate; **veins** are free and forked, reaching to the margins. **Fertile leaves:** similar to the sterile leaves overall, but taller and more erect; **fertile pinnae** occur at the tips of these leaves, with only the tip-most 3–5 pairs of pinnae becoming fertile; these fertile pinnae are reduced to short, contracted stalks bearing globose sporangia. 2n=44 (diploid).

A. A plant of *Osmunda spectabilis*.

B. Fertile pinnae.

C. Close-up of mature fertile pinnae and sporangia.

D. Close-up of immature fertile pinnae and sporangia.

FAMILY: **OSMUNDACEAE**

The cinnamon fern is the only member of the genus *Osmundastrum* and is an easily recognized species that is extremely common throughout eastern North America. This species was long treated in the genus *Osmunda*, to which it is closely related, and it resembles sterile fronds of the interrupted fern, *Claytosmunda claytoniana* (p. 228). Two easy-to-see features that can distinguish the two include the following: 1) when fertile, *C. claytoniana* has a set of fertile pinnae in the middle of an otherwise sterile leaf, "interrupting" the leaf blade, while *O. cinnamomeum* subsp. *cinnamomeum* has entirely separate fertile and sterile leaves, and 2) *O. cinnamomeum* subsp. *cinnamomeum* has distinctive tufts of cinnamon-colored hairs at the bases of the pinnae, where they meet the rachis on the lower surface of the leaf. The cinnamon fern also somewhat resembles *Matteuccia struthiopteris*, the ostrich fern (p. 343), and both have entirely dimorphic leaves, but their sterile fronds differ in overall shape, and those of *Matteuccia* have pinnae that continue almost all the way down the stipe base to the ground, becoming shorter as they go, while *Osmundastrum*'s leaves have well-defined stipes free of pinnae. Base chromosome number (x) = 22.

Osmundastrum cinnamomeum subsp. *cinnamomeum*

Osmundastrum cinnamomeum subsp. *cinnamomeum* with sterile and fertile leaves.

OPPOSITE PAGE:

A. Lower surface of a sterile frond, with tufts of hairs at pinna bases.

B. Tip of a fertile frond.

C. Close-up of a fertile pinna.

Osmundastrum cinnamomeum subsp. *cinnamomeum*

COMMON NAME(S) Cinnamon fern

NOTABLE SYNONYM *Osmunda cinnamomea*. This species was previously included in the genus *Osmunda* and is still widely referred to by its name in that genus.

STATUS Native, common

HABITAT/DISTRIBUTION Moist, partially shaded habitats, including forests and swamps, in acidic soils; range extends west of the Mississippi; also occurs in the Caribbean, Mexico, and Central and South America (a second subspecies, *O. cinnamomeum* subsp. *asiaticum*, occurs in Asia)

Plants are terrestrial. **Stems** lack scales and are large and erect, forming tussocks. Old persistent stipe bases and black fibrous roots are often apparent around the leaf bases. **Fiddleheads** are typically covered in a dense mat of whitish hairs that gradually become cinnamon colored as the leaf expands. **Leaves** form vase-shaped clusters and are entirely dimorphic. The outer leaves are sterile and arching to spreading, while the innermost leaves are fertile, shorter, narrower, and stiffly erect. **Sterile leaves: stipes** are up to 30cm, not winged, and yellow to green, with rust-colored hairs when young but becoming smooth at maturity; the **rachis** is grooved on the upper surface, green, and covered in cinnamon-colored hairs when young, but at maturity these are found only in distinctive tufts at the pinna bases; the leaf **blade** is elliptic to oblong or ovate lanceolate, up to 120cm long and 30cm wide, 1-pinnate-pinnatifid at the base and becoming pinnatifid toward the very tip; **pinnae** are typically in 20–25 pairs, linear, and with tufts of cinnamon hairs at the bases, on the lower surface; **margins** are smooth and lobed; **veins** are free, forked, and reach the margins. **Fertile leaves: stipes** are up to 45cm and yellow to green, with hairs similar to those on the sterile leaves; the leaf **blade** is 2-pinnate, narrowly lanceolate in overall shape, without expanded tissue, up to 45cm long and 6cm wide, and green early in the season but becoming brown later in the season; **pinnae** are reduced to short, contracted stalks bearing globose sporangia. 2n=44 (diploid).

FAMILY: **POLYPODIACEAE**

Pecluma is a genus in the Polypodiaceae family whose members in eastern North America occur only in Florida. *Pecluma* species are easily distinguished from other once-pinnate ferns by their pectinate leaf division: the leaf blade is divided into numerous narrow, linear, closely spaced segments that give an overall featherlike or comblike appearance. The bases of these pinna segments generally touch one another side to side along the rachis, leaving no space exposed between the separate pinna bases. Whether or not the leaf blade tapers gradually at the base is a helpful character for distinguishing the 3 species of *Pecluma* in our flora; another is venation pattern, but this usually requires a 20x hand lens to observe (while holding the leaf up to a light source so that the veins will be illuminated). Many species of *Pecluma* can behave as resurrection plants, drying out completely when water is scarce and rehydrating quickly when watered. Base chromosome number $(x) = 37$.

LEFT: *Pecluma dispersa* demonstrating the side-by-side pinnae typical in this genus.

BELOW:
A. Venation pattern in *Pecluma bourgeauana* (1a).

B. Venation pattern in *Pecluma plumula* (2a).

C. Venation pattern in *Pecluma dispersa* (2b).

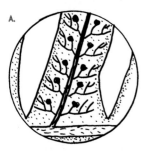
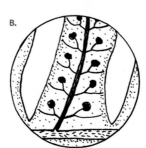

A.   B.   C.

KEY TO THE SPECIES OF *PECLUMA* IN OUR FLORA:

1a   Plants are terrestrial or occasionally grow on tree bases; the base of the leaf blade tapers
conspicuously to narrow auricles; veins are 2–4 times forked ·· *Pecluma bourgeauana*

1b   Plants are epiphytic and/or epipetric (growing on rocks); the base of the leaf blade is truncate or
narrows gradually; veins are 1–2 times forked ··· 2

   2a   Plants are usually epiphytic; leaves are linear and narrowly elongated, tapering gradually at
both ends; veins are 1-forked ·· *Pecluma plumula*

   2b   Plants are usually epipetric; leaves are lance shaped and typically truncate at the base, not
tapering gradually; veins are 2-forked ··· *Pecluma dispersa*

1a.
*Pecluma
bourgeauana*

2a.
*Pecluma
plumula*

2b.
*Pecluma
dispersa*

Pecluma bourgeauana

COMMON NAME(S) Comb polypody, swamp plume polypody

NOTABLE SYNONYMS This species has had several scientific names, and variations of spellings of names, that are still widely encountered in the literature, including *Pecluma ptilota* var. *bourgeauana*, *Pecluma ptilota* var. *caespitosa*, *Pecluma ptilodon* var. *caespitosa*, *Pecluma ptilotos* var. *bourgeauana*, and *Polypodium ptilodon*.

STATUS Native, rare

HABITAT/DISTRIBUTION Hammocks, wet woods, and swamps; also occurs in the Caribbean, Mexico, and Central America

Plants are usually terrestrial or occasionally grow on old logs or tree stumps. **Stems** are short creeping, with black scales. **Leaves** are erect to arching, and fertile and sterile leaves do not differ in appearance. **Stipes** are dark brown to reddish brown, rounded, and up to 15cm long, with sparse scales and/or scattered hairs. The **rachis** is similar to the stipe. The leaf **blade** is 1-pinnate and pectinate, up to 90cm long and 18cm wide, and long elliptic to narrowly ovate, tapering conspicuously at the base to a series of narrow auricles. **Pinnae** are up to 8mm wide and sparsely hairy, though more so around the sori. **Margins** are smooth to slightly undulating and may be sparsely hairy. **Veins** fork 2–4 times. **Sori** are oval and without indusia. 2n=148 (tetraploid).

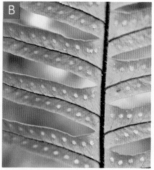

A. *Pecluma bourgeauana* growing on a rock.

B. Close-up of sori.

C. A leaf blade tapering to auricles.

D. Upper surface of a leaf showing very sparse hairs.

Pecluma dispersa

COMMON NAME(S) Widespread polypody

STATUS Native, rare

HABITAT/DISTRIBUTION Limestone hammocks and outcrops; also occurs in the Caribbean, Mexico, and Central America

Plants are epipetric or occasionally epiphytic. **Stems** are short creeping. **Leaves** are erect to arching, and fertile and sterile leaves do not differ in appearance. **Stipes** are black, rounded, and up to 21cm long, with dense brown scales and/or whitish hairs. The **rachis** is similar to the stipe. The leaf **blade** is 1-pinnate and pectinate, up to 70cm long and 11cm wide, and lanceolate, tapering gradually at the tip but squared off at the base (truncate). **Pinnae** are up to 5mm wide and finely hairy. **Margins** are smooth to slightly undulating and may be hairy. **Veins** fork twice. **Sori** are round to oval and without indusia. 2n=111 (triploid).

A. A frond of *Pecluma dispersa.*

B. Squared-off (truncate) leaf base.

C. Close-up of sori.

D. Upper surface of a leaf with hairs.

F S C N

Pecluma plumula

COMMON NAME(S) Plume polypody

STATUS Native, rare

HABITAT/DISTRIBUTION Hammocks and wet woods, along riverbanks, and in limestone sinkholes; also occurs in the Caribbean, Mexico, and Central America

Plants are epiphytic or occasionally epipetric. **Stems** are short creeping, with brown scales. **Leaves** are pendent or arching, and fertile and sterile leaves do not differ in appearance. **Stipes** are black, rounded, and up to 15cm long, with brown scales and/or scattered whitish hairs. The **rachis** is similar to the stipe. The leaf **blade** is 1-pinnate and pectinate, up to 50cm long and 7cm wide, and linear and narrowly elongated, tapering gradually at both ends. **Pinnae** are up to 3mm wide and finely hairy. **Margins** are smooth to slightly undulating, and finely hairy. **Veins** fork once. **Sori** are round to oval and without indusia. 2n=148 (tetraploid).

A. *Pecluma plumula* growing on a tree trunk.

B. Fronds.

C. Close-up of sori.

D. Upper surfaces of leaves with small, scattered hairs.

FAMILY: **THELYPTERIDACEAE**

We have 5 species of *Pelazoneuron* in eastern North America, 3 of which are found only in southernmost Florida, while 2 also range northward into the southeastern U.S. This genus is one of several that used to be included in *Thelypteris* (p. 475). Species of *Pelazoneuron* can be quite difficult to distinguish from one another and are also suspected to hybridize with at least 1 other genus in the family Thelypteridaceae (*Christella*; p. 225). *Pelazoneuron kunthii* is a particularly confusing taxon morphologically, as it is thought to be a hybrid between *P. ovatum* and *Christella hispidula* and thus often has a perplexing mix of characters from these 2 genera. Important characters for distinguishing the 2 genera include the lowest veins in adjacent pinnules: in *Christella*, these will typically come together below the sinus, joining to form an "excurrent" vein that runs into the sinus. In *Pelazoneuron*, these veins curve upward and come together right at the sinus, or they reach the pinnule margins above the sinus on either side. In addition, in *Christella*, the upper surface of the leaf has hairs along the veins as well as on the blade surface between the veins, while in *Pelazoneuron*, if hairs are present on the upper surface, they occur only along the veins and not between them (except in *P. kunthii*). Careful observation of these characters requires a hand lens or other magnification. Base chromosome number (x) = 36.

KEY TO THE SPECIES OF *PELAZONEURON* IN OUR FLORA:

1a On at least some pinnae, the lowest, innermost pinnules are noticeably reduced in size, giving the pinna base a bluntly tapered appearance ·········· *Pelazoneuron abruptum* var. *grande*

1b The innermost pinnules are not reduced in size but are equal to or longer than neighboring pinnules ··· 2

    2a The scales at the base of the stipe are ovate and not hairy; the stem is somewhat erect to erect ·· *Pelazoneuron patens*

    2b The scales at the base of the stipe are elongated and hairy; the stem is short or long creeping ·········· 3

        3a The upper surface of the leaf is hairy, including on the blade tissue as well as along the veins, with hairs at least 0.3mm long ·········· *Pelazoneuron kunthii*

        3b The upper surface of the leaf is smooth or has only a few minute hairs that are only on the veins and not on the blade tissue ·········· 4

            4a The blade is broad and tapers abruptly to a very narrow tip that is similar to one of the lateral pinnae ·········· *Pelazoneuron augescens*

            4b The blade is not particularly broad and tapers gradually toward the tip, which is pinnatifid but wider and with more widely spaced lobes than on the lateral pinnae ·········· *Pelazoneuron ovatum*

Fertile pinnae of
Pelazoneuron kunthii.

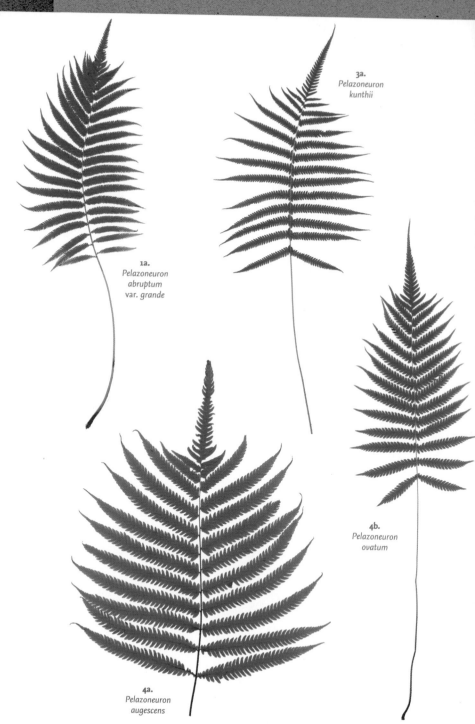

3a.
*Pelazoneuron
kunthii*

1a.
*Pelazoneuron
abruptum
var. grande*

4b.
*Pelazoneuron
ovatum*

4a.
*Pelazoneuron
augescens*

F   S   C   N

Pelazoneuron abruptum var. grande

COMMON NAME(S) Stately maiden fern

NOTABLE SYNONYMS *Thelypteris grandis* var. *grandis*

STATUS Native, rare

HABITAT/DISTRIBUTION Cypress swamps in the Fakahatchee Strand; also occurs in the Caribbean, Mexico, and Central America (a second variety, *P. abruptum* var. *pallescens*, occurs in the Caribbean, Central, and South America)

Plants are terrestrial. **Stems** are long creeping and scaly. **Leaves** can be up to 3m tall but in our flora are usually no more than 1.5m. Sterile and fertile leaves do not differ in appearance. **Stipes** are up to 1m long and brownish toward the base and yellowish farther up, with sparse, hairy, elongated scales. The **rachis** is yellowish, with minute hairs. The leaf **blade** is 1-pinnate-pinnatifid but becomes pinnatifid toward the tip, can be up to 2m long and 90cm wide, and is broadly lanceolate and widest at or near the base. **Pinnae** are up to 45cm long and 4.8cm wide and often angle upward. The pinnules may be somewhat curved toward the pinna tips, and the innermost pinnules are noticeably reduced in size, giving the pinna base a bluntly tapered appearance. The pinna midvein has a distinct narrow groove in the upper surface. Hairs ca. 0.1mm long are present on the veins on the lower leaf surface, but not between the veins, and the leaf is smooth on the upper surface. Small brown scales may also be present on the pinna midveins. **Margins** are smooth to slightly wavy. **Veins** are free; the lowest veins of adjacent pinnules curve strongly inward and upward but do not join until right at the base of the sinus. **Sori** are round and midway between the pinnule midvein and margin. **Indusia** are present. 2n=72 (diploid).

A. Plants of *Pelazoneuron abruptum* var. *grande*.

B. Fronds.

C. Leaf tip that becomes pinnatifid.

D. Lower leaf surface with sori.

Pelazoneuron augescens

COMMON NAME(S) Abrupt-tip maiden fern

NOTABLE SYNONYMS *Thelypteris augescens*

STATUS Native, uncommon

HABITAT/DISTRIBUTION Limestone hammocks; also occurs in the Caribbean, Mexico, and Central America

Plants are terrestrial. **Stems** are long creeping and scaly. **Leaves** are up to 1.4m long, and sterile and fertile leaves do not differ in appearance. **Stipes** are up to 70cm long, brownish toward the base and yellowish farther up, with scales at the base that are elongated, brown or tan, and hairy. The **rachis** is yellowish, with minute hairs. The leaf **blade** is up to 70cm long and 44cm wide, and 1-pinnate-pinnatifid but becoming pinnatifid toward the tip. The blade is broadly ovate and widest toward the base, with a markedly, abruptly narrow tip. **Pinnae** are up to 22cm long and 1.5cm wide and often angle upward. The pinnules may be somewhat curved toward the pinna tips, and the innermost pinnules are often elongated, especially on the tip-ward side of the pinna. The pinna midvein has a distinct narrow groove in the upper surface. The terminal pinna is similar to the lateral ones. Hairs ca. 0.2–0.4mm long are present on the veins and blade tissue on the lower leaf surface, and the leaf is smooth on the upper surface. Small brown scales may also be present on the pinna midveins. **Margins** are smooth to slightly wavy and may be slightly inrolled. **Veins** are free; the lowest veins of adjacent pinnules curve strongly inward and upward but do not join until right at the base of the sinus. **Sori** are round and midway between the pinnule midvein and margin. **Indusia** are present and tan at maturity, with hairs 0.2–0.4mm long. 2n=144 (tetraploid).

A. A frond of *Pelazoneuron augescens.*

B. Narrow, elongated leaf tip.

C. Lower leaf surface with sori and hairs.

Pelazoneuron kunthii

COMMON NAME(S) Widespread maiden fern, southern maiden fern

NOTABLE SYNONYMS *Thelypteris kunthii*

STATUS Native, common

HABITAT/DISTRIBUTION Woodlands and wet and/or disturbed habitats including riverbanks, streamsides, trailsides, ditches, and around limestone sinks and solution holes; also occurs in the Caribbean, Mexico, and Central America

Plants are terrestrial. **Stems** are short to long creeping. **Leaves** are up to 1.6m long, and sterile and fertile leaves do not differ in appearance. **Stipes** are up to 80cm long, dark reddish brown toward the base and yellowish farther up, with scales at the base that are elongated, brown, and hairy. The **rachis** is yellowish and hairy. The leaf **blade** is up to 80cm long and 40cm wide, 1-pinnate-pinnatifid but becoming pinnatifid toward the tip, triangular to broadly lanceolate, and widest at the base. **Pinnae** are up to 20cm long and 2.5cm wide. The pinnules may be somewhat curved toward the pinna tips. The pinna midvein has a distinct narrow groove in the upper surface. Hairs ca. 0.3–1mm long are present on the veins and blade tissue on the lower leaf surface, along the veins on the upper surface, and also on the blade tissue of the upper surface, though they may be sparse. Scattered yellow glands may also be present. **Margins** are smooth but hairy. **Veins** are free; the lowest veins of adjacent pinnules either join right at the base of the sinus or meet the pinnule margins above the sinus. **Sori** are round and midway between the pinnule midvein and margin, or closer to the margin. **Indusia** are present, kidney shaped, and tan at maturity, with hairs 0.2–0.4mm long. 2n=144 (tetraploid).

A. Fronds of *Pelazoneuron kunthii*.

B. Fertile pinnae with sori.

C. Upper leaf surface with hairs.

D. Lower leaf surface with sori and hairs.

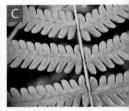

F S C N

Pelazoneuron ovatum

COMMON NAME(S) Ovate marsh fern

NOTABLE SYNONYMS *Thelypteris ovata*

STATUS Native, somewhat common

HABITAT/DISTRIBUTION Moist woods and limestone habitats including hammocks, outcrops, and sinks; also occurs in the Caribbean

Plants are terrestrial. **Stems** are long creeping. **Leaves** are up to 1.65m long, and sterile and fertile leaves do not differ in appearance. **Stipes** are up to 80cm long, dark reddish brown toward the base and yellowish farther up, with scales at the base that are elongated, tan to brownish, and hairy. The **rachis** is yellowish and sparsely to densely hairy. The leaf **blade** is up to 74cm long and 40cm wide, 1-pinnate-pinnatifid but becoming pinnatifid toward the tip, ovate and widest at the base, but tapering somewhat abruptly at the tip. **Pinnae** are up to 22cm long and 2.2cm wide. The pinnules may be somewhat curved toward the pinna tips. The pinna midvein has a distinct narrow groove in the upper surface. On the pinnae toward the middle of the blade, the lowest, innermost pinnules may be elongated and enlarged. Hairs ca. 0.2–0.5mm long are present on the veins and blade tissue on the lower leaf surface, and a few tan scales may also be present. The upper surface of the leaf has similar hairs along the pinna midveins but is otherwise smooth. **Margins** are smooth and may be inrolled. **Veins** are free; the lowest veins of adjacent pinnules either join right at the base of the sinus or meet the pinnule margins above the sinus. **Sori** are round and closer to the margin than to the pinnule midvein. **Indusia** are present, kidney shaped, and tan at maturity, with hairs 0.2–0.4mm long. 2n=72 (diploid).

A. Fronds of *Pelazoneuron ovatum*.

B. Leaf tip of a large frond.

C. Lower leaf surface with inrolled margins and sori.

D. Lower leaf surface and hairy rachis.

Pelazoneuron patens

COMMON NAME(S) Grid-scale maiden fern

NOTABLE SYNONYMS *Thelypteris patens* var. *patens*

STATUS Native, uncommon

HABITAT/DISTRIBUTION Rocky limestone hammocks; also occurs in the Caribbean, Mexico, and Central America

Plants are terrestrial. **Stems** are stout and somewhat erect to fully erect and trunk-like. **Leaves** are up to 2m long, and sterile and fertile leaves do not differ in appearance. **Stipes** are up to 50cm long (or occasionally twice as long, on really large leaves), darker toward the base and light greenish or yellowish farther up, with tan scales at the base that are ovate and smooth. The **rachis** is yellowish and densely hairy. The leaf **blade** is up to 1m long and 64cm wide, 1-pinnate-pinnatifid but becoming pinnatifid toward the tip, and widest at the base. **Pinnae** are up to 32cm long and 4cm wide. The pinnules may be somewhat curved toward the pinna tips. The pinna midvein has a distinct narrow groove in the upper surface. On the pinnae toward the middle of the blade, the lowest, innermost pinnules may be elongated and enlarged. Hairs ca. 0.2–0.8mm long are present on the veins and blade tissue on the lower leaf surface. The upper surface is smooth. **Margins** are smooth. **Veins** are free; the lowest veins of adjacent pinnules either join right at the sinus or meet the pinnule margins just above the sinus. **Sori** are round and midway between the margin and the pinnule midvein. **Indusia** are present, tan, and usually hairy. 2n=144 (tetraploid).

A. Plants of *Pelazoneuron patens*.

B. Lowest pinnae.

C. Upper leaf surface and hairy rachis.

D. Lower leaf surface with sori.

E. Scales at stipe bases.

FAMILY: **PTERIDACEAE**

Pellaea is a genus in the predominantly arid-adapted fern family Pteridaceae, and the 4 species in eastern North America are typically found on exposed cliff faces and dry, rocky hillsides and slopes. One of these species, *P. wrightiana*, is known in the east from only 1 location in South Carolina, though it is widespread in the western U.S. It almost certainly reached the west-facing cliff face where it resides in South Carolina by long-distance dispersal, highlighting the remarkable ability of fern spores to undertake long, wind-driven journeys. *Pellaea atropurpurea*, the member of the genus with the widest range in the east, is thought to be an autotriploid species that is capable of reproducing only apogamously—that is, without sexual reproduction. *Pellaea* species can be distinguished from relatives in closely related genera (such as *Argyrochosma*, p. 144) by their absence of farina and their large pinnules, which are more than 4mm wide. Base chromosome number $(x) = 29$.

KEY TO THE SPECIES OF *PELLAEA* IN OUR FLORA:

1a   Some stem scales are bicolored, with a dark central stripe but becoming light brown toward the margins ·· 2

    2a   The leaf blade is lanceolate to ovate or triangular, and more than 5cm wide; plants are naturalized in only a few locations in Georgia and Florida ···················· *Pellaea viridis*

    2b   The leaf blade is linear oblong and elongated, and no more than 5cm wide; plants are known in eastern North America only from Jocassee Gorges in South Carolina ·· *Pellaea wrightiana*

1b   All stem scales are uniformly colored and reddish brown to tan; plants have broad ranges in the east ·· 3

    3a   The stipe and rachis have short, curled hairs on the upper surface; the pinnules have sparse hairs or hairlike scales on the lower surface ···················· *Pellaea atropurpurea*

    3b   The stipe and rachis are smooth, without hairs on the upper surface; the pinnules have only a few scattered, hairlike scales on the lower surface ···················· *Pellaea glabella* subsp. *glabella*

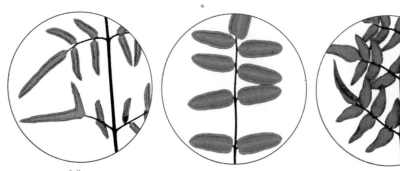

Pellaea
atropurpurea

Pellaea glabella
subsp. *glabella*

Pellaea
viridis

Fertile pinnae of several of our *Pellaea* species, with the marginal sori covered by false indusia that are typical in the family Pteridaceae (not shown to scale).

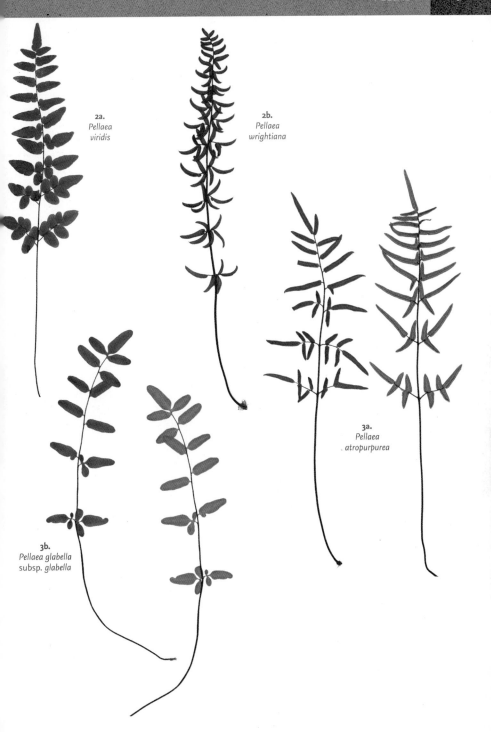

2a.
*Pellaea
viridis*

2b.
*Pellaea
wrightiana*

3a.
*Pellaea
atropurpurea*

3b.
*Pellaea glabella
subsp. glabella*

Pellaea atropurpurea

COMMON NAME(S) Purple-stem cliff brake

STATUS Native, common

HABITAT/DISTRIBUTION Drier habitats, including rocky outcrops, slopes, and ledges, usually on limestone; also occurs in western North America, Mexico, and Central America

Plants are terrestrial and epipetric. **Stems** are compact and ascending, with uniformly reddish-brown or golden-brown scales. **Leaves** are up to 50cm long, clustered along the stem, and somewhat dimorphic, with the fertile fronds a bit longer and more divided than the sterile ones. **Stipes** are reddish purple to black, smooth and shiny but with scattered curved hairs, and reddish-brown scales toward the base. The **rachis** is reddish to purplish brown throughout, up to 15cm long, and densely covered on the upper surface with short, curly hairs pressed to the surface. The leaf **blade** is up to 35cm long and 18cm wide, narrowly triangular, 2-pinnate toward the base but becoming 1-pinnate toward the tip, leathery and tough, and dull gray to bluish green, with sparse hairs or hairlike scales on the lower surface. **Pinnae** are in 5–9 pairs, with a distinct stalk in the lower pinnae, while the upper ones are sessile (sit against the rachis). Ultimate segments (pinnules) are more than 4mm wide. **Margins** are smooth but inrolled to form false indusia over the sporangia. **Veins** are obscure. **Sori** are linear and run along the margins, covered by **false indusia**. 2n=87 (triploid).

A. Frond of *Pellaea atropurpurea*.

B. Upper leaf surface.

C. Lower surfaces of fertile pinnae.

D. Uniformly colored stem scales.

Pellaea glabella subsp. *glabella*

COMMON NAME(S) Smooth cliff brake

STATUS Native (endemic to North America), somewhat common

HABITAT/DISTRIBUTION Drier habitats, including rocky outcrops, slopes, and ledges, usually on limestone; range extends into western North America (additional subspecies occur in western North America)

- -

Plants are terrestrial and epipetric. **Stems** are compact and ascending, with uniformly reddish-brown or golden-brown scales. **Leaves** are up to 40cm long, clustered along the stem, and somewhat dimorphic, with the fertile fronds a bit longer and more divided than the sterile ones. **Stipes** are reddish brown to brown, smooth and shiny, and without hairs or scales. The **rachis** is reddish brown to brown throughout, up to 10cm long, and nearly smooth. The leaf **blade** is up to 30cm long and 8cm wide, narrowly triangular to ovate lanceolate, usually 2-pinnate toward the base and becoming 1-pinnate toward the tip, somewhat leathery, and pale bluish or grayish green. The lower surface is smooth except for a few scattered hairlike scales. **Pinnae** are in 4–9 pairs, with a distinct stalk in the lower pinnae, while the upper ones have less of a stalk or are sessile (sit against the rachis). Ultimate segments (pinnules) are more than 4mm wide. **Margins** are smooth but inrolled to form false indusia over the sporangia. **Veins** are obscure. **Sori** are linear and run along the margins, covered by **false indusia**. 2n=116 (tetraploid).

A. Plants of *Pellaea glabella* subsp. *glabella*.

B. Lower pinnae.

C. Lower surface of fertile pinnae.

D. Stipe bases.

Pellaea viridis

COMMON NAME(S) Green cliff brake

NOTABLE SYNONYMS *Cheilanthes viridis*

STATUS Not native, uncommon

HABITAT/DISTRIBUTION Naturalized in a few locations in the southeast, on rocky outcrops in open forests; native to Africa

Plants are terrestrial and epipetric. **Stems** are short creeping, with bicolored scales that have a dark central stripe and pale brown margins. **Leaves** are up to 50cm long and clustered along the stem, and sterile and fertile leaves do not differ in appearance. **Stipes** are dark brown to purplish or black, smooth and shiny, and with scattered scales, especially toward the base. The **rachis** is dark brown to black, up to 20cm long, and usually smooth but with scattered hairlike scales. The leaf **blade** is up to 30cm long and 20cm wide, lanceolate to ovate or triangular, usually 2-pinnate but up to 4-pinnate at the base, and pale bluish to green. **Pinnae** are in 8 or more pairs, with a distinct stalk (though this may be very short in the upper pinnae). Ultimate segments (pinnules) are more than 4mm wide. **Margins** are smooth to somewhat bluntly toothed, and inrolled to form false indusia over the sporangia. **Veins** are obscure. **Sori** are linear and run along the margins, covered by **false indusia**. 2n=unknown.

A. Frond of *Pellaea viridis.*

B. Upper leaf surface.

C. Lower leaf surface with marginal sori.

Pellaea wrightiana

COMMON NAME(S) Wright's cliff brake

STATUS Native (endemic to North America), rare

HABITAT/DISTRIBUTION Known from only 1 site in South Carolina, on a sheer, west-facing cliff wall, where it likely arrived via long-distance dispersal of spores; also occurs in the southwestern U.S. and Mexico

Plants are terrestrial and epipetric. **Stems** are compact and ascending, with bicolored scales that have a dark central stripe and pale brown margins. **Leaves** are up to 40cm long and clustered along the stem, and sterile and fertile leaves do not differ in appearance. **Stipes** are dark brown, smooth and shiny, and without hairs or scales. The **rachis** is dark brown throughout, up to 5cm long, and usually smooth. The leaf **blade** is up to 35cm long and 5cm wide, linear oblong, usually 2-pinnate toward the base and becoming 1-pinnate toward the tip, somewhat leathery, and pale bluish or grayish green. **Pinnae** are in 9 or more pairs, with a distinct stalk in the lower pinnae, while the upper ones are sessile (sit against the rachis); the pinna tips often curve upward, especially when fertile. Ultimate segments (pinnules) are more than 4mm wide. **Margins** are smooth but inrolled to form false indusia over the sporangia. **Veins** are obscure. **Sori** are linear and run along the margins, covered by **false indusia**. 2n=116 (tetraploid).

A. Plants of *Pellaea wrightiana*.

B. Upper surface of a leaf.

C. Lower surface of a leaf.

D. Lower surface of fertile pinnae.

FAMILY: **THELYPTERIDACEAE**

Phegopteris is a genus primarily of temperate regions in the Northern Hemisphere. It includes at least 6 species at present, but more may be added. Several of its species are known to have multiple cytotypes, and in recent years some (but not yet all) of these have been recognized and named as distinct species. In eastern North America, this has so far grown our *Phegopteris* flora from 2 species to 4. *Phegopteris excelsior* is an allotetraploid that used to be included in *P. connectilis* and was recently separated from it. *Phegopteris connectilis* is a widespread species that is thought to be uniformly triploid in North America, but diploid cytotypes are also known (from Asia), which could lead to additional named species in the future. Because of their close relationship, *P. connectilis* and *P. excelsior* can be difficult to tell apart; the final couplet in the key below distinguishes them. *Phegopteris taiwaniana* was introduced to the southeastern U.S. from Asia, but the plants here were originally reported and published as *P. decursive-pinnata*. Several authors have recently shown, however, that *P. taiwaniana* and *P. decursive-pinnata* are in fact a diploid and a tetraploid, respectively, which are distinguishable morphologically. These studies have concluded that only the diploid, *P. taiwaniana*, has naturalized in North America (for now). Base chromosome number (x) = 30.

KEY TO THE SPECIES OF *PHEGOPTERIS* IN OUR FLORA:

1a   The leaf blade is elongate elliptic to lanceolate and widest toward the middle; the lowest pinnae are shortened and reduced in size; pinnae on the fertile fronds are spaced well apart, with a distinct wing of triangular lobes along the rachis between the pinna bases ⋯⋯⋯⋯⋯⋯⋯⋯⋯⋯⋯⋯⋯⋯ *Phegopteris taiwaniana*

1b   The leaf blade is broadly triangular and widest at or just below the base; the lowest pinnae are not substantially reduced in size, though the very lowest pair may be slightly shorter than the second pair; pinnae on the fertile fronds are not spaced well apart, though there is still a wing of tissue along most or all of the rachis ⋯⋯⋯⋯⋯ 2

     2a   The leaf blade is a bit wider than it is long; the wing of tissue along the rachis is present throughout the leaf blade, all the way to the lowest pinna pair; the lowest pinnae are 2–3 times longer than they are wide ⋯⋯⋯⋯ *Phegopteris hexagonoptera*

     2b   The leaf blade is longer than it is wide; the wing of tissue along the rachis does not extend to the lowermost pinnae; the lowest pinnae are 4–5 times longer than they are wide ⋯⋯⋯⋯ 3

         3a   The lowest pinnae are strongly reflexed and point downward; the lowest pinnae are, on average, about 4 times longer than they are wide; the fronds are smaller overall than those of *P. excelsior* ⋯⋯⋯⋯ *Phegopteris connectilis*

         3b   The lowest pinnae are less strongly reflexed and point outward or downward less sharply than in *P. connectilis*; the lowest pinnae are, on average, about 5 times longer than they are wide; the fronds are 10–20% larger overall than those of *P. connectilis* ⋯⋯⋯⋯ *Phegopteris excelsior*

Young plants of
Phegopteris connectilis.

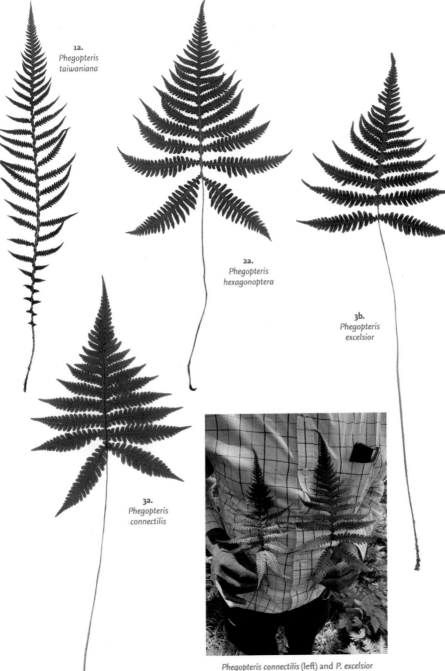

1a.
Phegopteris taiwaniana

2a.
Phegopteris hexagonoptera

3b.
Phegopteris excelsior

3a.
Phegopteris connectilis

Phegopteris connectilis (left) and *P. excelsior* (right), held by Art Gilman, one of the authors of *P. excelsior*.

| F | S | C | N |

Phegopteris connectilis

COMMON NAME(S) Narrow beech fern, northern beech fern

STATUS Native, somewhat common

HABITAT/DISTRIBUTION Shady, moist forests, especially on acidic and/or rocky soils; also occurs in western North America, Greenland, Europe, and Asia

Plants are terrestrial. **Stems** are long creeping, branching, and scaly. **Leaves** are up to 50cm tall and typically emerge from the stem 1–2cm apart, and sterile and fertile leaves do not differ in appearance. **Stipes** are yellowish to green, with brown scales toward the base, and up to 25cm long. The **rachis** is similar in color to the stipe, with small, clear hairs, and a wing of tissue along the sides, between the pinna bases; this wing does *not* continue all the way down to the lowest pinna pair. The leaf **blade** is 1-pinnate-pinnatifid, up to 25cm long and 15cm wide (generally longer than it is wide), narrowly to broadly triangular and widest at or just above the base, and finely hairy on both surfaces. **Pinnae** are up to 12cm long and 3.3cm wide, in 12–15 pairs, with the lowest 1–2 pairs pointing downward and outward, often at a sharp angle. **Margins** are smooth to bluntly toothed or lobed. **Veins** are simple and free or forked. **Sori** are round, without **indusia**, and near the pinna margins. 2n=90 (triploid).

A. A colony of *Phegopteris connectilis*.

B. Fronds

Phegopteris excelsior

COMMON NAME(S) Tall beech fern, tetraploid beech fern

STATUS Native (endemic to eastern North America), rare

HABITAT/DISTRIBUTION Shady, moist forests with generally circumneutral soils; known only from extreme northeastern U.S. and southeastern Canada, including Nova Scotia, New Brunswick, Québec, New England, and eastern New York

Plants are terrestrial. **Stems** are long creeping and branching, with scattered scales. **Leaves** are up to 60 or 70cm tall and typically emerge from the stem 1–2cm apart, and sterile and fertile leaves do not differ in appearance. **Stipes** are dark toward the base but become yellowish to green toward the blade, with pale brown scales toward the base, and are up to 37cm long (or occasionally longer). The **rachis** is similar in color to the stipe, with small, clear hairs and white scales on the lower surface, and a wing of tissue along the sides, between the pinna bases; this wing does *not* continue all the way down to the lowest pinna pair. The leaf **blade** is 1-pinnate-pinnatifid (or occasionally up to 2-pinnate in larger fronds), up to 44cm long and 29cm wide (generally longer than it is wide), broadly triangular and widest at or just above the base, and finely hairy on both surfaces. **Pinnae** are up to 14.5cm long and 3.7cm wide, in 21–39 pairs, with the lowest 1–2 pairs pointing somewhat downward and outward. **Margins** are smooth to bluntly toothed or lobed. **Veins** are simple and free or forked. **Sori** are round to slightly oblong, without **indusia**, and near the pinna margins. 2n=120 (tetraploid).

A. Fronds of *Phegopteris excelsior.*

B. Lowest pinnae.

C. Lower leaf surface with sori.

D. Sori, hairs, and scales.

E. Stipe base.

Phegopteris hexagonoptera

COMMON NAME(S) Broad beech fern, southern beech fern

STATUS Native (endemic to North America), common

HABITAT/DISTRIBUTION Shady, moist forests, on moderately acidic to circumneutral soils; range extends somewhat west of the Mississippi

Plants are terrestrial. **Stems** are long creeping and branching, with scattered brown scales. **Leaves** are up to 75cm tall and typically emerge from the stem 1–2cm apart, and sterile and fertile leaves do not differ in appearance. **Stipes** are up to 45cm long and reddish brown, with tan scales toward the base, but become yellowish to green toward the blade. The **rachis** is similar in color to the stipe, with small, clear hairs and whitish scales and a wing of tissue along the sides, between the pinna bases; this wing *does* continue all the way down to the lowest pinna pair, though it may be very narrow between the first and second pinna pairs. The leaf **blade** is 1-pinnate-pinnatifid (occasionally up to 2-pinnate-pinnatifid in larger fronds), up to 33cm long and 30cm wide (generally wider than it is long, or about as wide as long), broadly triangular and widest at or just above the base, and finely hairy on both surfaces. **Pinnae** are up to 20cm long and 8cm wide, in 12–15 pairs, with the lowest 1–2 pairs spreading outward and pointing only slightly downward. **Margins** are smooth to bluntly toothed or lobed. **Veins** are simple and free or forked. **Sori** are round to slightly oblong, without **indusia**, and near the pinna margins. 2n=60 (diploid).

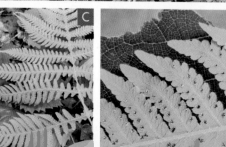

A. A colony of *Phegopteris hexagonoptera*.

B. Fronds.

C. Lowest pinnae.

D. Lower surface of a fertile pinna.

Phegopteris taiwaniana

COMMON NAME(S) None, but "Taiwanese beech fern" seems appropriate

STATUS Not native, uncommon

HABITAT/DISTRIBUTION Naturalized in a few locations in Alabama and Georgia, in shady forests near streams or waterfalls; native to Asia

----

Plants are terrestrial. **Stems** are erect to ascending, with pale brown scales. **Leaves** are up to 84cm tall and clustered along the stem, and sterile and fertile leaves generally do not differ in appearance (though sterile fronds can be somewhat shorter and more compact than fertile ones). **Stipes** are up to 20cm long, yellowish to green, and sparsely scaly. The **rachis** is similar in color to the stipe, with small, clear hairs and a pronounced wing of tissue along the sides that continues all the way to the lowest pinna pair; this wing has the appearance of triangular lobes between the pinna bases. The leaf **blade** is pinnatifid, up to 59cm long and 15cm wide, elongate elliptic to lanceolate and widest at the middle, and finely hairy on both surfaces. **Pinnae** are up to 11cm long and 1.7cm wide, in 26–44 pairs, with the lowest few pairs distinctly shorter and narrower than those above. **Margins** are smooth to shallowly wavy. **Veins** are simple and free or forked. **Sori** are round to slightly oblong, without **indusia**, and near the pinna margins. 2n=unknown.

A. Plants of *Phegopteris taiwaniana.*

B. Fronds.

C. Lowest pinnae, narrowing toward the base.

D. Lower surface of a fertile pinna.

FAMILY: **POLYPODIACEAE**

We have only 1 species of this genus in our flora: *Phlebodium aureum*, which is common throughout Florida. Other species of *Phlebodium* occur in the subtropical and tropical regions of the Americas. *Phlebodium aureum* is easily confused with *Microsorum grossum* (p. 350), an exotic invasive species that it resembles closely, but both species have unique, easily observed features that give them their common names: *M. grossum*, the wart fern, has distinct, deeply impressed sori that stick out of the upper surface of the leaf, while *P. aureum*, the goldfoot fern, has a dense covering of long, reddish-brown to golden scales on the stem and lower stipe. Base chromosome number $(x) = 37$.

*Phlebodium
aureum*

A. *Phlebodium aureum* plants growing on palm trees.

B. Golden stem scales characteristic of this species.

Phlebodium aureum

F S C N

COMMON NAME(S) Golden polypody, goldfoot fern, bear's foot fern

NOTABLE SYNONYMS *Polypodium aureum*

STATUS Native, common

HABITAT/DISTRIBUTION Trees (especially sabal palms, *Sabal palmetto*) and logs in various habitats, especially swamps and hammocks; also occurs in the Caribbean, Mexico, and Central and South America

Plants are epiphytic. **Stems** are long creeping and branched, usually more than 8mm in diameter, and densely covered with long (up to 1cm) reddish-brown to golden scales, from which the species gets its common name. **Leaves** are up to 1.3m long, with long **stipes** (up to 50cm) that are typically brown and smooth, with a few scales near the base. Sterile and fertile leaves do not differ in appearance. The leaf **blade** is up to 50cm wide, pinnatifid and deeply lobed, with rounded sinuses, and is broadly ovate to elliptic, often with slightly wavy margins. Individual **pinna** segments are linear, lanceolate, or elliptic, each 6–20cm long and 1–4cm wide, with a long terminal segment. **Margins** are entire. **Veins** are highly reticulate, forming networks of areoles. **Sori** are round, lack indusia, and occur in 1 line on either side of the midrib and pinna midveins. 2n=148 (tetraploid).

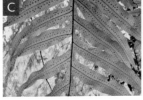

A. A frond of *Phlebodium aureum*.

B. Stem with dense covering of golden scales.

C. Lower leaf surface with sori.

D. Close-up of sori.

FAMILY: **WOODSIACEAE**

The species now recognized in the genus *Physematium* were previously included in a large *Woodsia* genus (p. 486), but DNA-based analyses as well as morphological differences between the 2 groups support their recognition as distinct genera. Globally *Physematium* has about 30 species, which occur throughout Asia, Africa, and the Americas. In both *Woodsia* and *Physematium*, the sorus sits on top of the indusium—which is either multilobed (*Physematium*) or filamentous and hairlike (*Woodsia*)—like a cup on top of a saucer. The lobes or filaments emerge from underneath the sorus and wrap around or stick out from it. Both genera also tend to have veins that end in modified pores called *hydathodes*, which often appear as a slight widening of the vein at its very tip. The 2 groups differ in whether they have articulate stipes (*Woodsia* does, *Physematium* does not) and whether glandular hairs are present on the leaf tissues; *Woodsia* species may have hairs but they will not be glandular, while *Physematium* species will always have at least some glandular hairs. *Physematium oreganum* subsp. *cathcartianum* crosses with *P. scopulinum* subsp. *laurentianum* to form the hybrid *P.* × *maxonii*, and with *Woodsia ilvensis* to form the intergeneric hybrid ×*Woodsimatium abbeae*. Both hybrids are very rare. Base chromosome number (x) = 38.

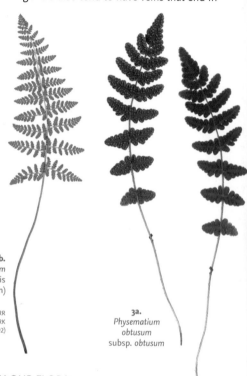

3b.
Physematium oreganum
(subspecies of this
specimen unknown)

3a.
*Physematium
obtusum*
subsp. *obtusum*

KEY TO THE SPECIES OF *PHYSEMATIUM* IN OUR FLORA:

1a The stipe is reddish brown to dark purple at maturity, and very brittle; the pinnae have a dense covering of flat hairs along the midvein, on both leaf surfaces ········· 2

    2a The lobes of the indusia are wide and not filamentous; the scales on the stem and stipe bases are bicolored, with a wide, dark central stripe ·········· *Physematium scopulinum* subsp. *appalachianum*

    2b The lobes of the indusia are narrow and filamentous; the scales on the stem and stipe bases are 1 color or have a discontinuous narrow central stripe ·········· *Physematium scopulinum* subsp. *laurentianum*

1b The stipe is yellowish to light brown at maturity (though it can be dark purplish brown in *P. oreganum*) and pliable and not brittle; the pinnae do not have hairs concentrated along the midveins ········· 3

    3a The indusia are split into wide, shallow lobes ·········· *Physematium obtusum* subsp. *obtusum*

    3b The indusia are split into narrow, deep lobes ·········· *Physematium oreganum* subsp. *cathcartianum*

Physematium obtusum subsp. obtusum

COMMON NAME(S) Blunt-lobed cliff fern

NOTABLE SYNONYMS *Woodsia obtusa* subsp. *obtusa*

STATUS Native (endemic to North America), somewhat common

HABITAT/DISTRIBUTION Rocky slopes and cliffs of a variety of substrates, very occasionally on rocky soils; range extends into western North America

Plants are terrestrial. **Stems** are horizontal and creeping to erect and compact, with a mix of brown and bicolored scales, and usually with a cluster of persistent stipe bases from old fronds. **Leaves** are up to 40cm long, and sterile and fertile leaves do not differ in appearance. **Stipes** are light brown or yellowish at maturity and may be darker toward the base, up to ca. 10cm long, and with brown or bicolored scales. The **rachis** is similar to the stipe, with glandular hairs and scattered scales, and grooved on the upper surface. The leaf **blade** is 2-pinnate to 2-pinnate-pinnatifid at the base, lanceolate to ovate and tapering toward the base, and up to 30cm long and 12cm wide. The leaf surfaces have a moderate covering of glandular hairs. **Pinnae** are ovate triangular to elliptic. The pinna midveins are grooved, and this groove is continuous with the groove on the rachis. **Margins** are toothed and may be deeply lobed. **Veins** are free and simple or forked, usually ending in enlarged vein tips (hydathodes). **Sori** are round and near the pinnule margins. **Indusia** are multilobed, and lobes are wide and shallow. 2n=152 (tetraploid).

A. Plants of *Physematium obtusum* subsp. *obtusum*.

B. Upper leaf surface.

C. Lower surface of a fertile leaf.

D. Close-up of sori.

F	S	C	N

Physematium oreganum subsp. *cathcartianum*

COMMON NAME(S) Oregon cliff fern

NOTABLE SYNONYMS *Woodsia oregana* subsp. *cathcartiana*

STATUS Native (endemic to North America), rare

HABITAT/DISTRIBUTION Rocky slopes and cliffs of a variety of substrates, very occasionally on rocky soils; also occurs in western North America, where it is much more common than in the east

Plants are terrestrial. **Stems** are ascending to erect, with a mix of brown and bicolored scales, and usually with a cluster of persistent stipe bases from old fronds. **Leaves** are up to 25cm long, and sterile and fertile leaves do not differ in appearance. **Stipes** are reddish brown to purplish at maturity and up to ca. 5cm long, with brown scales. The **rachis** is similar to the stipe, with scattered glandular hairs and hairlike scales, and grooved on the upper surface. The leaf **blade** is 1-pinnate-pinnatifid to 2-pinnate at the base, linear to lanceolate ovate, and up to 25cm long and 4cm wide. The leaf surfaces have a sparse to moderate covering of glandular hairs. **Pinnae** are ovate triangular to elliptic. The pinna midveins are grooved, and this groove is continuous with the groove on the rachis. **Margins** are toothed and may be deeply lobed. **Veins** are free and simple or forked, and hydathodes are present but vein tips are only slightly enlarged. **Sori** are round and near the pinnule margins. **Indusia** are multilobed, and lobes are very narrow and deep. 2n=152 (tetraploid).

A. A plant of *Physematium oreganum* subsp. *cathcartianum*.

B. Lower surface of a fertile leaf.

PHOTOGRAPHS BY ALAN CRESSLER

F S C N

Physematium scopulinum subsp. *appalachianum*

COMMON NAME(S) Appalachian cliff fern

NOTABLE SYNONYMS *Woodsia appalachiana, Woodsia scopulina* subsp. *appalachiana*

STATUS Native (endemic to eastern North America), rare

HABITAT/DISTRIBUTION Damp, shaded ledges and cliffs, mostly on mildly acidic shale or sandstone substrates

Plants are terrestrial. **Stems** are ascending to erect, with bicolored scales that have a wide, dark central stripe, and usually with a cluster of persistent stipe bases from old fronds. **Leaves** are up to 35cm long, and sterile and fertile leaves do not differ in appearance. **Stipes** are reddish to purplish brown at maturity and up to ca. 5cm long, with scales at the base similar to those on the stem. The **rachis** is similar to the stipe, with numerous hairs and scales, and grooved on the upper surface. The leaf **blade** is 2-pinnate toward the base, linear to lanceolate, and up to 30cm long and 8cm wide. Both leaf surfaces have a moderate covering of hairs, with a mix of glandular and nonglandular hairs. **Pinnae** are ovate to narrowly triangular, shallowly lobed, and rounded or broadly pointed at the tip. The pinna midveins are grooved, and this groove is continuous with the groove on the rachis. The pinnae have a dense covering of flattened hairs along the midvein, on both surfaces of the leaf. **Margins** are nearly entire or broadly, shallowly lobed and may be hairy. **Veins** are free and simple or forked, ending in vein tips (hydathodes), but these are typically not enlarged or only slightly enlarged. **Sori** are round and near the pinnule margins. **Indusia** lobes are wide and not filamentous. 2n=76 (diploid).

A

B

C

A. A colony of *Physematium scopulinum* subsp. *appalachianum.*

B. Lower surface of a fertile leaf.

C. Close-up of sori.

PHOTOGRAPHS BY ALAN CRESSLER

Physematium scopulinum subsp. *laurentianum*

COMMON NAME(S) Mountain cliff fern, Rocky Mountain cliff fern

NOTABLE SYNONYMS *Woodsia scopulina* subsp. *laurentiana*

STATUS Native (endemic to North America), rare

HABITAT/DISTRIBUTION Rocky slopes and cliffs of a wide range of substrates, from limestone to granite; also occurs in western North America, where it is much more common than in the east

Plants are terrestrial. **Stems** are ascending to erect, with mostly 1-colored scales that may have a darker central stripe, and usually with a cluster of persistent stipe bases from old fronds. **Leaves** are up to 35cm long, and sterile and fertile leaves do not differ in appearance. **Stipes** are reddish to purplish brown at maturity and up to ca. 5cm long, with scales at the base similar to those on the stem. The **rachis** is similar to the stipe, with numerous hairs and scales, and grooved on the upper surface. The leaf **blade** is 2-pinnate toward the base, linear to lanceolate, and up to 30cm long and 8cm wide. Both leaf surfaces have a moderate covering of hairs, with a mix of glandular and nonglandular hairs. **Pinnae** are ovate to narrowly triangular, shallowly lobed, and rounded or broadly pointed at the tip. The pinna midveins are grooved, and this groove is continuous with the groove on the rachis. The pinnae have a dense covering of flattened hairs along the midvein, on both surfaces of the leaf. **Margins** are nearly entire or broadly, shallowly lobed, and may be hairy. **Veins** are free and simple or forked, ending in vein tips (hydathodes), but these are typically not enlarged or only slightly enlarged. **Sori** are round and near the pinnule margins. **Indusia** lobes are narrow and filamentous. 2n=152 (tetraploid).

FAMILY: **MARSILEACEAE**

Pilularia americana is one of the water ferns in our flora, and it is unique in being the only fern in eastern North America that can spend its entire life submerged beneath the water's surface (though it can be emergent and can also survive on mud if the water recedes, but it will dry out if these conditions persist). Other ferns that grow in close association with water bodies belong to the genera *Azolla* (p. 187), *Salvinia* (p. 455), *Marsilea* (p. 335), and *Ceratopteris* (p. 219), but these are all floating or emergent aquatics. The true water ferns, which include *Azolla, Salvinia, Marsilea,* and *Pilularia* (but not *Ceratopteris*), are quite different from all other ferns in that they are heterosporous, meaning that they have separate male and female spores. These megaspores (female) and microspores (male) are produced in separate sporangia, but those sporangia will be mixed within a sporocarp, which is a hardened, globose structure that protects the sporangia and is found in both *Pilularia* and *Marsilea* (members of the family Marsileaceae). These sporocarps are spherical and buried in the substrate in *Pilularia*. Base chromosome number (x) = 10.

Pilularia americana plants dislodged from the substrate and floating on the surface.

PHOTOGRAPH ON PREVIOUS PAGE BY ALAN CRESSLER

Pilularia americana

COMMON NAME(S) American pillwort

STATUS Native (endemic to North America), rare (though it is likely overlooked because of its grasslike appearance and may be more common than is thought)

HABITAT/DISTRIBUTION Shallow water bodies, especially ponds and along the edges of lakes and reservoirs; also occurs in western North America and Mexico

Plants are terrestrial and aquatic, rooted in the substrate, with the plant body entirely submerged. **Stems** creep horizontally, with roots emerging at the same nodes as leaves. **Leaves** are up to 10cm long and reduced to stipes, lacking any expanded blade tissue (though they do still form fiddleheads). **Sporocarps** attach to the stem near the leaf bases and have short stalks (up to 3mm); the sporocarps themselves are hardened and globose or spherical, somewhat resembling seeds, often with a covering of dense, short hairs. 2n=20 (diploid).

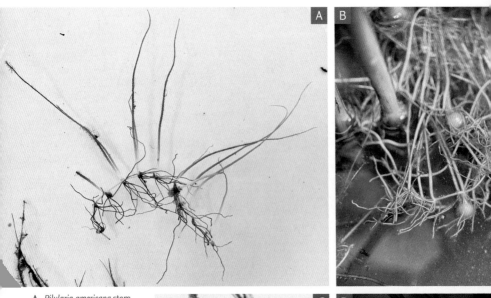

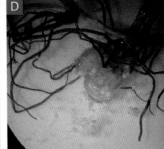

A. *Pilularia americana* stem with leaves, roots, and sporocarps attached.

B. Floating plants, with 2 large sporocarps.

C. Leaf bases, stem, and a sporocarp.

D. A ruptured sporocarp with sporangia.

FAMILY: **PTERIDACEAE**

Pityrogramma is a relatively small genus, with only about 20 species worldwide. We have 2 species in eastern North America, both of which occur only in Florida. One of these is considered native (*P. trifoliata*), while the other (*P. calomelanos* var. *calomelanos*) is not. Both are also relatively widely distributed in Central and South America. In our flora, *Pityrogramma* species are most easily distinguished from all others by having 1) sporangia that are scattered across the lower surface of the leaf (as opposed to well-defined sori), and 2) farina, a waxy or powdery coating on the undersides of the leaves that is distinctly white, silvery, or yellowish. Base chromosome number (x) = 29, 30.

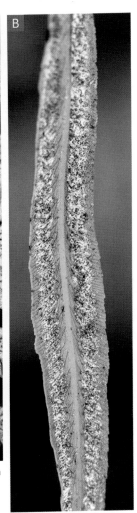

A. Lower leaf surface of *Pityrogramma calomelanos* var. *calomelanos*, showing waxy farina (white) and sporangia (black).

B. Lower leaf surface of *Pityrogramma trifoliata*, showing waxy farina (white) mixed with sporangia (brown).

KEY TO THE SPECIES OF *PITYROGRAMMA* IN OUR FLORA:

1a   Leaf blade is 2-pinnate-pinnatifid toward the base, with typically fernlike leaf division; margins of tip-most pinnae are smooth (though may be lobed); leaf blade is 2-dimensional and flat in profile ⸺⸺⸺⸺ *Pityrogramma calomelanos* var. *calomelanos*

1b   Leaf blade is 2-pinnate toward the base, but pinnae have enlarged, elongated pinnules that are not typically fernlike; margins of tip-most pinnae are serrate; leaf blade is 3-dimensional, with pinnae oriented parallel to the ground and having an almost whorled appearance ⸺⸺⸺⸺ *Pityrogramma trifoliata*

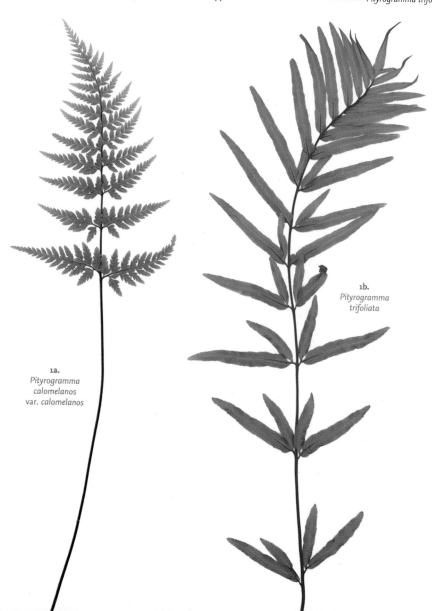

1b.
Pityrogramma
trifoliata

1a.
Pityrogramma
calomelanos
var. *calomelanos*

Pityrogramma calomelanos var. *calomelanos*

COMMON NAME(S) Silverback fern

STATUS Not native, uncommon

HABITAT/DISTRIBUTION Escapes from cultivation in Florida and can become established in ditches and riverbanks, usually in shaded or forested areas; native to the American tropics (additional varieties are also known from the American tropics)

Plants are terrestrial. Stems are ascending to erect, with shiny, dark brown scales. Leaves are clustered along the stem and are up to 1.2m tall; sterile and fertile leaves do not differ in appearance. Stipes are smooth, shiny, black to reddish or purplish, and up to about 60cm long, with a distinct groove running along the upper surface. The rachis is similar to the stipe. The leaf blade is up to 95cm long and 30cm wide, 2-pinnate-pinnatifid or up to 3-pinnate at the base, narrowly triangular to ovate lanceolate, and leathery, with a dense white coating (farina) on the lower surfaces. Pinnae are narrowly triangular, with sharp pinnule lobes or teeth, and lie in the plane of the blade. Margins are lobed to smooth, or occasionally serrate. Veins are free. Sporangia do not form well-defined sori but instead are scattered along the veins and may be obscured by the farina. Indusia are not present. 2n=unknown.

A. A small population of *Pityrogramma calomelanos* var. *calomelanos* along a riverbank.

B. Fronds.

C. Lower surface of fertile leaf with waxy farina and sporangia.

D. Upper surface of a leaf with a groove along the rachis.

E. A fiddlehead covered in farina.

Pityrogramma trifoliata

COMMON NAME(S) Goldenrod fern

STATUS Native, rare

HABITAT/DISTRIBUTION Open and/or disturbed habitats such as ditches, trailsides, and roadsides, often on sandy soils; also occurs in the Caribbean, Mexico, and Central and South America

Plants are terrestrial. **Stems** are ascending to erect, with dark brown scales that may be black in the center. **Leaves** are clustered along the stem and are up to 1.5m tall or occasionally taller; sterile and fertile leaves do not differ in appearance. **Stipes** are up to 35cm long, shiny and reddish or purplish brown, and smooth or with fine, scattered hairs, with a distinct groove running along the upper surface. The **rachis** is similar to the stipe. The leaf **blade** is up to 120cm long and 20cm wide, 2-pinnate at the base and 1-pinnate at the tip, linear to lanceolate, and not leathery, with a dense white to yellowish coating (farina) on the lower surfaces. **Pinnae** at the base of the blade are pinnately or palmately divided into 2 or 3 elongated, linear segments; those at the tip are undivided (1-pinnate) and elongated. Pinnae sit parallel to the ground, not in the plane of the blade. **Margins** are serrulate. **Veins** are free and forked. **Sporangia** do not form well-defined sori but instead are scattered along the veins and may be obscured by the farina. **Indusia** are not present. 2n=116 (tetraploid).

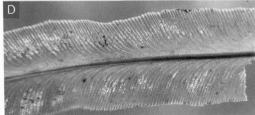

A. Plants of *Pityrogramma trifoliata*.

B. Lower pinnae that are pinnately or palmately divided.

C. A mix of mature (black) and immature (tan) sporangia, with farina.

D. Forking veins.

FAMILY: **POLYPODIACEAE**

The single species of this genus in our flora, *Platycerium bifurcatum*, is an easily recognized epiphytic introduction from the tropics via the horticulture trade. Staghorn ferns are popular house and garden plants and have become naturalized in parts of southern Florida, where they are considered invasive. Their very low tolerance for freezing temperatures likely sets the limit of their distribution and prevents them from moving farther north. Colonies can grow to enormous sizes (up to roughly 2m by 2m) using vegetative production of new "pup" plants, and the species has a unique leaf morphology, with 2 entirely distinct leaf types. The fertile leaves that stick out from the tree give the species its common names, as they roughly resemble the antlers of elk or deer. Base chromosome number (x) = 37.

Platycerium bifurcatum

A. Lower surface of a fertile frond of *Platycerium bifurcatum*.

B. Closeup of acrostichoid sporangia.

F   S   C   N

Platycerium bifurcatum

COMMON NAME(S) Elkhorn fern, common staghorn fern

STATUS Not native (invasive), uncommon

HABITAT/DISTRIBUTION Naturalized in southern Florida, especially in Broward and Miami-Dade Counties, often near homes and along roadsides, particularly in oak and other hardwood trees; native to the Austral-Pacific region

Plants are epiphytic. **Stems** are short creeping, and as the plant matures, the stems become buried under multiple layers of basal leaves, which may provide some protection from cold temperatures. Leaves are of 2 types: the **sterile basal leaves** are round, overlapping, and clasping or flattened against the substrate tree trunk, typically light green and somewhat succulent, and erect when young but becoming brown, papery, and flattened with maturity; the **fertile leaves** are light to medium green, elongated, strap shaped, typically forking (bifurcating) at least once, and up to 50cm long and emerging outward from the substrate, usually at a downward angle. The **stipe** and **rachis** are not differentiated from the blade. The **blade** of the fertile leaves often has a grayish cast because of its small scales, and **sporangia** are acrostichoid and located toward the tips of the fronds. No **indusia** are present. 2n=74 (diploid).

A. *Platycerium bifurcatum* growing on a tree with bromeliads and other ferns.

B. Bifurcating, pendent fronds.

C. Nonbifurcating basal leaves.

D. Lower surface of a fertile frond, with acrostichoid sporangia.

FAMILY: **POLYPODIACEAE**

We have 2 species of *Pleopeltis* in our flora today; historically, 2 additional species were known from Florida—*P. astrolepis* and *P. marginata*—but both are likely now extirpated there. This genus includes one of the most common epiphytic ferns in eastern North America, *P. michauxiana*, which is widespread in the southeast. Historically this species was considered a variety of *P. polypodioides*, but it is now recognized as distinct, and *P. polypodioides* is restricted to extreme southern Florida. Both of our *Pleopeltis* species are most similar in overall appearance to species of *Polypodium* (p. 432), but they can easily be distinguished by the presence in *Pleopeltis* of dense scales on the underside of the leaf blade. These scales are stalked and round or oval to somewhat star shaped, with a darker brown center that lightens toward the edges. *Polypodium* species do not have scales like this. Both of our *Pleopeltis* species have common names that include "resurrection fern," a reference to their ability to dry up when water is scarce, with the leaves curling, turning brown, and appearing fully dead, only to quickly revive and green up when water becomes available again. Base chromosome number (x) = 34, 35, 37.

KEY TO THE SPECIES OF *PLEOPELTIS* IN OUR FLORA:

1a The upper surface of the leaf blade is smooth, without scales; plants are
widespread in the southeast ⸺ *Pleopeltis michauxiana*

1b The upper surface of the leaf blade has distinct small white scales; plants
are present only in southern Florida ⸺ *Pleopeltis polypodioides*

1a.
*Pleopeltis
michauxiana*

Pleopeltis michauxiana dried up
but still alive, waiting for rain.

F   S   C   N

Pleopeltis michauxiana

COMMON NAME(S) Resurrection fern, Gray's polypody, scaly polypody

NOTABLE SYNONYMS *Pleopeltis polypodioides* var. *michauxiana*, *Polypodium polypodioides* var. *michauxianum*

STATUS Native, common

HABITAT/DISTRIBUTION Epiphytic, especially on hardwood tree trunks, in a wide variety of habitats; also occurs in the Caribbean, Mexico, and Central America

Plants are generally epiphytic, though occasionally they may be terrestrial or occur on rocks. **Stems** are long creeping, with scales that are dark brown to black in the center and lighter toward the edges. **Leaves** emerge gradually along the stem and are up to 25cm long, and sterile and fertile fronds do not differ in appearance. **Stipes** are up to 8cm long, densely scaly, and round in cross section but with a groove. The **rachis** is typically somewhat scaly on 1 or both sides. The **blade** is deeply pinnatifid to 1-pinnate, elongate deltate to elliptic, with the widest part toward or at the base, and is up to 17cm long and 5cm wide. The blade is densely scaly on the lower surface; scales are round to oval and golden brown, darker toward the center and lightening toward the edges. Scales are not present on the upper surface, but minute white glands may be present. The **pinnae** are linear to oblong, and rounded or bluntly lobed at the tips. **Margins** are smooth to somewhat hairy. **Sori** are round and may form distinct deep bumps visible on the top surface of the leaf. **Indusia** are absent. 2n=74 (diploid).

A

B

C

D

A. Plants of *Pleopeltis michauxiana* growing in a cypress dome.

B. Fronds.

C. Lower surface of a fertile leaf, with scales and sori.

D. Upper surface of a fertile leaf with scattered scales along the rachis, and deeply impressed sori.

Pleopeltis polypodioides

COMMON NAME(S) Tropical resurrection fern

NOTABLE SYNONYMS *Polypodium polypodioides*

STATUS Native, rare

HABITAT/DISTRIBUTION Epiphytic on tree trunks and old logs; known from a few hammocks in southeastern Florida; also occurs in the Caribbean, Mexico, and Central and South America

Plants are generally epiphytic, though occasionally they may be terrestrial or occur on rocks. **Stems** are long creeping, with scales that are dark brown to black in the center and lighter toward the edges. **Leaves** emerge gradually along the stem and are up to 25cm long, and sterile and fertile fronds do not differ in appearance. **Stipes** are up to 8cm long, densely scaly, and round in cross section but with a groove. The **rachis** is typically somewhat scaly on 1 or both sides. The **blade** is deeply pinnatifid to 1-pinnate, elongate deltate to elliptic, with the widest part toward or at the base, and is up to 17cm long and 5cm wide. The blade is densely scaly on the lower surface; scales are round to oval and golden brown, darker toward the center and lightening toward the edges. In this species only, the blade also has scattered whitish scales on the upper surface. The **pinnae** are linear to oblong, and rounded or bluntly lobed at the tips. **Margins** are smooth to somewhat hairy. **Sori** are round and may form distinct deep bumps visible on the top surface of the leaf. **Indusia** are not present. 2n=74 (diploid).

A. Fronds of *Pleopeltis polypodioides.*

B. Lower surface of a fertile leaf.

C. Upper leaf surface, with whitish scales unique to this species.

FAMILY: **POLYPODIACEAE**

Polypodium species are evergreen ferns that typically form colonies or dense mats on and around rocks and rocky outcrops, though they can sometimes be found growing on the ground, on trees, or on old stumps and logs. In our flora, *P. appalachianum* was formerly recognized as a cytotype within *P. virginianum*, but DNA-based studies have shown that *P. virginianum* is actually a fertile allotetraploid hybrid and *P. appalachianum* is one of its diploid parents. The two are visually quite similar, and they often hybridize to form morphologically intermediate plants (the hybrid is aptly named *P. × incognitum*). Both of our *Polypodium* species have small structures in the sori called *sporangiasters*; these are mixed in with the sporangia and are highly modified sporangia that look like tiny bulbous heads studded with glandular hairs. The number of sporangiasters per sorus can help distinguish our 2 *Polypodium* species. *Polypodium* may also be confused with *Pleopeltis michauxiana* (p. 430) in the southeast, but *Pleopeltis* does not have sporangiasters, and it does have a dense covering of scales on the underside of the leaf blade that is missing in *Polypodium*. Base chromosome number (x) = 37.

KEY TO THE SPECIES OF *POLYPODIUM* IN OUR FLORA:

1a   Stem scales are uniformly golden brown; the leaf blade is narrowly triangular and widest just above the base; pinna lobes are relatively narrow or pointy at the tips; each sorus has more than 40 sporangiasters ··· *Polypodium appalachianum*

1b   Stem scales are bicolored, with light brown margins and a dark central stripe; the leaf blade is oblong to narrowly ovate or lanceolate and widest toward the middle; pinna lobes are rounded at the tips; each sorus has fewer than 40 sporangiasters ··· *Polypodium virginianum*

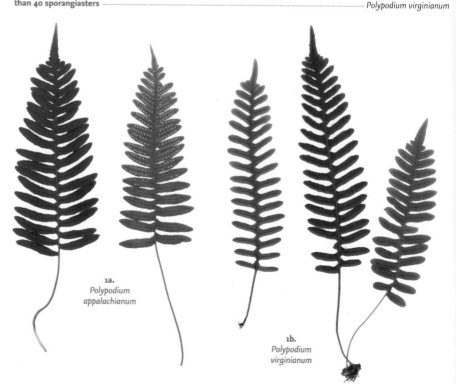

1a.
Polypodium appalachianum

1b.
Polypodium virginianum

Polypodium appalachianum

COMMON NAME(S) Appalachian polypody, rock cap fern

STATUS Native (endemic to eastern North America), somewhat common

HABITAT/DISTRIBUTION Rocky outcroppings and boulder fields of a variety of substrates

----

Plants are terrestrial or occasionally epiphytic, often forming dense colonies. **Stems** are long creeping and branched, with scales that are mostly uniformly golden brown. **Leaves** are up to 40cm long, and sterile and fertile leaves do not differ in appearance. **Stipes** are yellowish to green, often with scattered scales toward the base, and may have a small wing of tissue. The **rachis** is similar to the stipe. The leaf **blade** is deeply pinnatifid, narrowly triangular, and widest at the base. **Pinnae** are linear to oblong, with tips slightly more acute than in *P. virginianum*. **Margins** are smooth to slightly serrate. **Veins** are free and forked. **Sori** are round. **Indusia** are absent. **Sporangia** are typically yellow, turning brown at maturity. **Sporangiasters** are present, typically more than 40 per sorus. 2n=74 (diploid).

A. A plant of *Polypodium appalachianum*.

B. Upper and lower leaf surfaces.

C. Golden stem scales.

D. Lower surface of a fertile leaf, with immature sori.

Polypodium virginianum

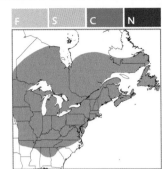

COMMON NAME(S) Rock polypody

STATUS Native, common

HABITAT/DISTRIBUTION Rocky outcroppings and boulder fields; also occurs in Greenland

Plants are terrestrial or occasionally epiphytic, often forming dense colonies. **Stems** are long creeping and branched, with scales that are mostly bicolored (lighter brown around the edges with a dark central stripe), often with golden and light brown scales also mixed in. **Leaves** are up to 40cm long, and sterile and fertile leaves do not differ in appearance. **Stipes** are yellowish to green, often with scattered scales toward the base, and may have a small wing. The **rachis** is similar to the stipe. The leaf **blade** is deeply pinnatifid, oblong to narrowly ovate or lanceolate, and widest toward the middle. **Pinnae** are linear to oblong, with tips that are blunter and more rounded than in *P. appalachianum*. **Margins** are smooth to slightly serrate. **Veins** are free and forked. **Sori** are round. **Indusia** are absent. **Sporangia** are typically yellow, turning brown at maturity. **Sporangiasters** are present, typically fewer than 40 per sorus. 2n=148 (tetraploid).

A. A colony of *Polypodium virginianum*.

B. Fronds.

C. Lower surface of a fertile leaf, with immature sori.

D. Bicolored stem scales.

E. Close-up of sori.

FAMILY: **DRYOPTERIDACEAE**

We have 3 species of *Polystichum* in our flora, including one of the most common ferns of forests in the central and northern parts of the region: *P. acrostichoides*, the Christmas fern. This species is easily recognized by its partly dimorphic leaves, with the tip-most sets of pinnae highly contracted and covered in sporangia on the lower surface. *Polystichum* species are often evergreen, making them very visible in the north in wintertime, where the leaves remain green against the snow. *Polystichum* species are also very prone to hybridization and polyploidy, and the eastern species form several hybrids (see figure below). Only 1 of these is at all common in our region: *P.* × *potteri* (Potter's holly fern). The other 2 are known from only 1 location in Ontario (*P.* × *hagenahii*, Hagenah's holly fern) or are not known to occur in our region at all (*P.* × *meyeri*, Meyer's holly fern, reported only from Alaska and Europe). In addition to these hybrids within the genus, *P. lonchitis* also forms one of the only intergeneric hybrids known in ferns: it crosses with *Dryopteris goldiana* (p. 285) to produce ×*Dryostichum singulare*, which is also known from only from a single location in Ontario. Base chromosome number (x) = 41.

Relationships among *Polystichum* species in eastern North America. Blue circles are fertile diploids (2x), the green square is a fertile allotetraploid (4x), and the gray circle and triangles are a sterile diploid and triploids, respectively. Arrows show the direction of genetic contribution from parental toward offspring taxa. For more information about interpreting these figures, see p. 12.

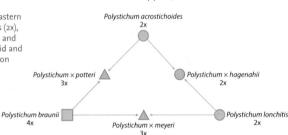

Polystichum acrostichoides
2x

Polystichum × potteri
3x

Polystichum × hagenahii
2x

Polystichum braunii
4x

Polystichum × meyeri
3x

Polystichum lonchitis
2x

KEY TO THE SPECIES OF *POLYSTICHUM* IN OUR FLORA:

1a Leaves are partly dimorphic, with pinnae toward the leaf tip becoming fertile; these fertile pinnae are narrow and contracted relative to the lower, sterile pinnae ⋯⋯⋯ *Polystichum acrostichoides*

1b Leaves are not dimorphic, and fertile and sterile pinnae are alike in size and shape ⋯⋯⋯⋯⋯⋯ 2

2a Leaves are 1-pinnate, and pinnae are close together along the rachis ⋯⋯⋯⋯ *Polystichum lonchitis*

2b Leaves are 2-pinnate, and pinnae are spaced somewhat apart ⋯⋯⋯⋯⋯⋯⋯ 3

3a Leaves are dull green; the leaf blade narrows substantially at the base, with pinnae becoming very short; the lowest pinnules on the upper side of each pinna are only slightly longer than the next pinnules ⋯⋯⋯⋯⋯ *Polystichum braunii*

3b Leaves are shiny green; the leaf blade narrows only somewhat toward the base; the lowest pinnules on the upper side of each pinna are distinctly longer than the next pinnules ⋯⋯⋯⋯⋯⋯⋯⋯⋯ *Polystichum* × *potteri*

1a.
*Polystichum
acrostichoides*

2a.
*Polystichum
lonchitis*

3a.
*Polystichum
braunii*

3b.
*Polystichum
× potteri*

Polystichum acrostichoides

COMMON NAME(S) Christmas fern

STATUS Native (endemic to North America), common

HABITAT/DISTRIBUTION Forests, shaded rocky ravines, and slopes; range extends into western North America and Mexico

Plants are terrestrial. **Stems** are creeping to erect, and old stipe bases typically remain attached. **Fiddleheads** are often bent elaborately backward. **Leaves** are evergreen, up to 80cm long and 12cm wide, and form vaselike clusters. Leaves are partly dimorphic, with fertile leaves held slightly more erect than the arching sterile leaves. On the fertile leaves, the pinnae at the tips of the leaf are highly contracted and bear sporangia on the lower surface, while the lower pinnae are expanded and identical to those on the sterile leaves. **Stipes** are up to 20cm long, green to brownish, and grooved, with dense brown scales at the base that become more scattered toward the blade. The **rachis** is similar to the stipe. The leaf **blade** is 1-pinnate and linear lanceolate, with small scales on the lower surface. **Pinnae** are up to 6cm long and oblong to falcate, with a distinct auricle at the pinna base, on the upper edge. **Margins** are entire or more often serrate. **Veins** are free and forked. **Sori** are round to irregularly shaped and are densely packed together, nearly completely covering the lower surfaces of the fertile pinnae at maturity. **Indusia** are round and peltate (umbrellalike). 2n=82 (diploid).

A. A fertile plant of *Polystichum acrostichoides*.

B. Mostly sterile fronds.

C. Sterile pinnae, with auricles at the bases and serrate margins.

D. Lower surface of contracted, fertile pinnae.

Polystichum braunii

COMMON NAME(S) Braun's holly fern

STATUS Native, uncommon

HABITAT/DISTRIBUTION Moist, shady forests, often on boulders; also occurs in western North America, Europe, and Asia

Plants are terrestrial. **Stems** are erect, and old stipe bases typically remain attached. **Leaves** are evergreen (or nearly so), up to 1m long and 20cm wide, arching, and form vaselike clusters. Sterile and fertile leaves do not differ in appearance, and fertile fronds are not dimorphic. **Stipes** are up to 17cm long, green to brown, and grooved, with dense silvery to light brown scales at the base that become smaller toward the blade. The **rachis** is similar to the stipe. The leaf **blade** is 2-pinnate and broadly lanceolate to ovate, tapering gradually at the base, with small hairlike scales on both surfaces, but denser on the lower surface. **Pinnae** are up to 10cm long, oblong to lanceolate or falcate, with short stalks, and a somewhat auriculate shape at the base, on the upper edge. **Margins** are toothed and bristly. **Veins** are free and forked. **Sori** are round and spaced apart, in a single row between the pinnule midvein and margin. **Indusia** are round and peltate (umbrellalike). 2n=164 (tetraploid).

A. A frond of *Polystichum braunii*.

B. Base of a frond with tapering pinnae.

C. Close-up of scales on the rachis and pinnae.

D. Lower surface of a fertile leaf, with sori.

Polystichum lonchitis

COMMON NAME(S) Holly fern

STATUS Native, uncommon

HABITAT/DISTRIBUTION Mixed hardwood and conifer forests, also in and around ravines and rocky areas; also occurs in western North America and Greenland

Plants are terrestrial. **Stems** are erect, and old stipe bases may be present. **Leaves** are evergreen, up to 60cm long and 12cm wide, erect, and form vaselike clusters. Sterile and fertile leaves do not differ in appearance, and fertile fronds are not dimorphic. **Stipes** are up to 10cm long, green to yellowish, and grooved, with dense light brown scales at the base that become smaller toward the blade. The **rachis** is similar to the stipe. The leaf **blade** is 1-pinnate and linear, often widest above the middle and tapering gradually toward the base, with small scales on the lower surface only. **Pinnae** are up to 3cm long, oblong to lanceolate or falcate (though the lowest pinnae may be almost triangular), with a well-developed auricle at the base of the pinnae, on the upper edge. **Margins** are finely, sharply toothed. **Veins** are free and forked. **Sori** are round and spaced apart, in a single row between the pinnule midvein and margin but often with an extra few in the auricle. Sori are typically present only in the upper half of the blade. **Indusia** are round and peltate (umbrellalike). 2n=82 (diploid).

A. A plant of *Polystichum lonchitis.*

B. Fronds.

C. Lower leaf surface with sori.

D. Pinnules with auricles at the base.

FAMILY: **PSILOTACEAE**

We have 1 species of *Psilotum* in our flora, *P. nudum*. Because of its relatively simple morphology, this plant was long thought to be an anachronism, a direct descendant of the earliest vascular plants, until its placement in the ferns was confirmed by molecular analyses of DNA sequence data in the late 1990s. *Psilotum* is essentially a highly reduced fern: it lacks true leaves and roots and consists of a short horizontal stem with aboveground, dichotomously branching green shoots that lack any true leaves. In our fern flora, *Psilotum* might be confused visually only with *Odontosoria clavata* (p. 371), which also has dichotomously branching aboveground parts that lack large, expanded leaf blades, though in *O. clavata*, these aboveground organs are in fact leaves, as opposed to shoots as in *Psilotum*. Base chromosome number (x) = 52.

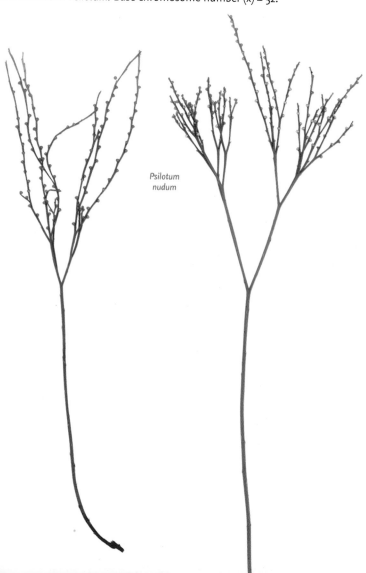

*Psilotum
nudum*

Psilotum nudum

COMMON NAME(S) Whisk fern

STATUS Native, common

HABITAT/DISTRIBUTION A variety of habitats including wet woods, hammocks, swamps, and thickets; occurs in tropical and subtropical regions essentially worldwide

Plants are terrestrial or epiphytic, often on tree bases and in the forks of trunks and branches. **Stems** are short creeping, black, and hairy, without roots. **Aboveground shoots** are erect, green to yellowish, up to 50cm tall and 4mm in diameter at the base, repeatedly dichotomously branched, and may have a distinct groove or furrow running down their length. Yellowish-green scales or bract-like **appendages** up to 2.5mm long may be present periodically along the shoots, near the branching points. Fertile segments end in **synangia**: these globose, distinctly 3-lobed structures are green to yellow or orange and contain the spores. 2n=104 (diploid).

A. *Psilotum nudum* growing on a tree.

B. Plants.

C. Plants with immature (green) and maturing (yellow) synangia.

D. Close-up of nearly mature, yellow synangia.

FAMILY: **DENNSTAEDTIACEAE**

The bracken fern genus, *Pteridium*, includes what is probably the most widespread fern, and one of the most widespread vascular plants, in the world: *P. aquilinum*. This species occurs essentially globally, grows aggressively, and can become obnoxiously weedy. It is frequently encountered in roadside ditches, pastures, open forests, and forest edges, especially in acidic soils. Much taxonomic controversy has surrounded the naming of taxa in *Pteridium*, with some authors recognizing only 1 species, *P. aquilinum*, with multiple varieties, and others raising 1 or more of these varieties to full species status. Three varieties are typically considered to occur in eastern North America; one of these is distinct enough that it is treated here as its own species, *P. caudatum*. The other 2 varieties are included together in the description for *P. aquilinum* (*P. aquilinum* vars. *latiusculum* and *pseudocaudatum*). Base chromosome number (x) = 26.

KEY TO THE SPECIES OF *PTERIDIUM* IN OUR FLORA:

1a Ultimate segments (pinnules) throughout the leaf are not particularly narrow and may touch their neighbors; when fertile, the ultimate segments are generally 3–6mm wide; plants are widespread in eastern North America ⋯⋯⋯⋯⋯⋯⋯⋯⋯⋯ *Pteridium aquilinum* (vars. *latiusculum* and *pseudocaudatum*)

1b Ultimate segments (pinnules) throughout the leaf are quite narrow and separated from one another; when fertile, the ultimate segments are less than 2mm wide; plants occur only in central to southern Florida ⋯⋯⋯⋯⋯⋯⋯⋯⋯⋯ *Pteridium caudatum*

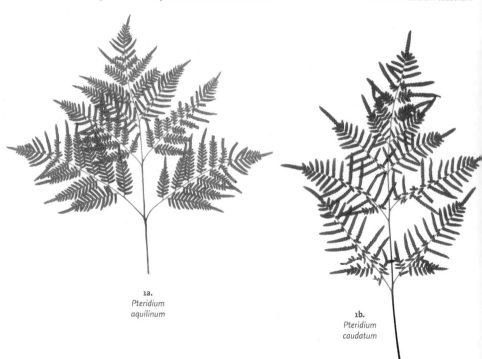

1a.
*Pteridium
aquilinum*

1b.
*Pteridium
caudatum*

Pteridium aquilinum, including varieties *latiusculum* and *pseudocaudatum*

COMMON NAME(S) Bracken, bracken fern, eastern bracken

NOTABLE SYNONYMS Treated here as including *Pteridium aquilinum* var. *latiusculum* and *P. aquilinum* var. *pseudocaudatum*

STATUS Native, common

HABITAT/DISTRIBUTION Open forests, pastures, and disturbed areas such as roadsides, often in acidic or sandy soils; occurs essentially worldwide

Plants are terrestrial and frequently form dense colonies or thickets. **Stems** are long creeping and usually very deep. **Leaves** are erect and up to about 1m tall but can be taller. **Stipes** are up to 1m long, brown to yellow or green, and smooth or with scattered short hairs. The **rachis** is similar to the stipe, often with a groove in the upper surface. The leaf **blade** is soft to more often coarse or leathery, broadly triangular, up to about 1m long and wide, and typically held close to parallel to the ground. The blade is usually divided into 3 parts, each of which is 1–2-pinnate, making the leaf as a whole 3-pinnate to sometimes 3-pinnate-pinnatifid at the base. **Pinnae** are pinnately divided, and the ultimate segments are oblong to linear and 3–6mm wide when fertile; neighboring segments may touch each other. **Margins** are smooth or slightly wavy. **Veins** are free and forked but may join at a vein that runs along the margin. **Sori** are marginal, running in a continuous line under a false **indusium** created by inrolling of the leaf margin. 2n=52 (diploid).

A. A colony of *Pteridium aquilinum.*

B. Plants.

C. Lower surface of pinnae.

D. Lower surface of a pinna showing venation and inrolled leaf margin.

Pteridium caudatum

COMMON NAME(S) Southern bracken, lacy bracken

NOTABLE SYNONYMS *Pteridium aquilinum* var. *caudatum*

STATUS Native, common

HABITAT/DISTRIBUTION Open wooded areas including pinelands and flatlands, often in full sun and in acidic or sandy soils; also occurs in the Caribbean, Mexico, and Central and South America

Plants are terrestrial and frequently form dense colonies or thickets. **Stems** are long creeping and usually very deep. **Leaves** are erect and usually up to about 1m tall but can be much taller in the right conditions. **Stipes** are up to 75cm long, brown to yellow or green, and smooth or with scattered short hairs on the lower surface. The **rachis** is similar to the stipe, often with a groove in the upper surface. The leaf **blade** is coarse or leathery, broadly triangular to elongate triangular, up to about 1m long and wide (or much more), and 3-pinnate to sometimes 3-pinnate-pinnatifid toward the base. **Pinnae** are pinnately divided, and the ultimate segments are narrow, elongated, and less than 2mm wide when fertile; neighboring segments are separated by a space that can be several times their width. **Margins** are smooth or slightly wavy. **Veins** are free and forked but may join at a vein that runs along the margin. **Sori** are marginal, running in a continuous line under a false **indusium** created by inrolling of the leaf margin. 2n=52 (diploid).

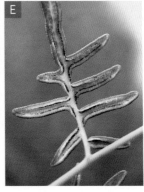

A. A colony of *Pteridium caudatum*.

B. Pinnae.

C. Leaf tip.

D. Lower surfaces of fertile pinnae.

E. Close-up of fertile pinnae.

FAMILY: **PTERIDACEAE**

Pteris is a primarily tropical genus of ferns, and the species in eastern North America are here largely because of introductions from horticulture, although 1 (*P. bahamensis*) is native. All 5 of the species in our flora can be found in Florida, and 2 also extend a bit farther northward (*P. multifida* and *P. vittata*, the latter of which is considered invasive). *Pteris vittata* and *P. bahamensis* also occasionally form a sterile hybrid (*P. × delchampsii*) that can be found in southern Florida and is highly variable, with individual plants more strongly resembling one parent or the other, though most often it looks like a narrower and less scaly version of *P. vittata*. Members of the genus can be most easily recognized by their linear, marginal sori with false indusia, and leaves that are either 1-pinnate or with the lowest pinna pair pedate (palmately divided into 2 or more lobes), which will distinguish them from most other fern species in the south. Members of the genus typically have "brake" in their common names, which means "fern" in Middle English. Base chromosome number $(x) = 29$.

KEY TO THE SPECIES OF *PTERIS* IN OUR FLORA:

1a Leaves are divided at the base of the blade into 3 large primary divisions (pinnae), which are
themselves further divided, with the ultimate divisions appearing pinnate to pinnate-pinnatifid;
veins are anastomosing, forming distinct networks .... *Pteris tripartita*

1b Leaves are either 1-pinnate or pedate at the base and become pinnate farther up; veins are free 2

    2a Leaves are 1-pinnate throughout 3

        3a Petioles are only sparsely scaly; scales are dark brown or blackish; pinnae often sit
directly against the rachis, with no stalk, and pinna tips are typically short pointed .... *Pteris bahamensis*

        3b Petioles are densely scaly; scales are light brown to reddish brown; pinnae may
have short stalks that separate the base from the rachis, and pinna tips are typically
long pointed .... *Pteris vittata*

    2b Leaves are pedate at the base and become pinnate farther up 4

        4a At maturity, a broad wing of tissue is present along the rachis, throughout the
leaf blade .... *Pteris multifida*

        4b At maturity, a wing of tissue along the rachis (if present at all) is present only
just below the terminal pinna, not throughout the leaf blade 5

            5a The leaf blade is solid green .... *Pteris cretica*

            5b The leaf blade is variegated, with the centers of the pinnae white and
the edges green .... *Pteris parkeri*

Fertile pinnae of *Pteris vittata* with the linear, marginal sori typical of the family Pteridaceae.

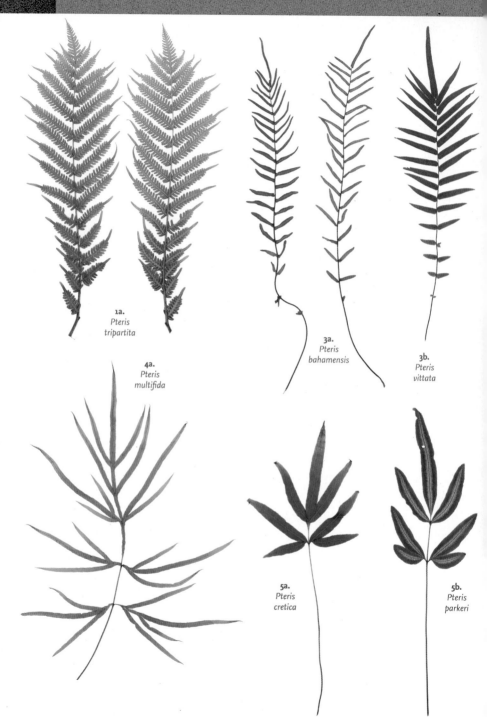

1a.
*Pteris
tripartita*

4a.
*Pteris
multifida*

3a.
*Pteris
bahamensis*

3b.
*Pteris
vittata*

5a.
*Pteris
cretica*

5b.
*Pteris
parkeri*

Pteris bahamensis

COMMON NAME(S) Bahama ladder brake

STATUS Native, uncommon

HABITAT/DISTRIBUTION Limestone hammocks, pinelands, and rocky crevices, often in thin soils over limestone; also occurs in the Caribbean

Plants are terrestrial. **Stems** are short creeping and branched, with scattered dark brown or black scales. **Leaves** are clustered and can be up to 1m tall, and sterile and fertile leaves do not differ in appearance. **Stipes** are up to 45cm long, dark purplish black at the base and becoming yellow or greenish toward the blade, smooth at maturity, and with 2–3 distinct ridges or grooves on the upper surface. The **rachis** is similar to the stipe. The leaf **blade** is 1-pinnate, up to 60cm long and 16cm wide, lanceolate to oblanceolate, and smooth or with a few scattered hairs along the midveins. **Pinnae** are narrow, linear, up to 9cm long and 5mm wide, well separated from one another, and sit against the rachis, and the terminal pinna is often quite elongated. **Margins** are smooth to finely toothed. **Veins** are free and forked. **Sori** are linear and run continuously along the pinna margins, covered by a **false indusium** created by inrolling of the margin. 2n=116 (tetraploid).

A. Plants of *Pteris bahamensis*.

B. Close-up of fertile pinnae, with linear sori and false indusium.

C. A plant growing on limestone.

D. Lower surface of a fertile leaf.

PHOTOGRAPHS A & C BY ALAN CRESSLER

| F | S | C | N |

Pteris cretica

COMMON NAME(S) Cretan brake

STATUS Not native, uncommon

HABITAT/DISTRIBUTION Escapes from cultivation and may become naturalized in the south in hammocks, sinkholes, and other areas with exposed limestone; native to Africa and Asia

Plants are terrestrial. **Stems** are creeping, with scattered dark to chestnut-brown scales. **Leaves** are up to 1m tall and clustered along the stem; sterile and fertile leaves are somewhat dimorphic, with pinnae on the fertile leaves narrower and more elongated than on the sterile leaves. **Stipes** are up to 50cm long, dark reddish brown toward the base and becoming yellow to whitish toward the blade, with sparse scales at the base, and with 2–3 distinct ridges or grooves on the upper surface. The **rachis** is similar to the stipe; a wing of tissue along the rachis (if present at all) is present only just below the terminal pinna, not throughout the leaf blade. The leaf **blade** is ovate, up to 30cm long and 25cm wide, and pedately divided toward the base, with 2 lateral pinnae that have 2 or more elongated pinnules; farther up, there is often 1 additional pinna pair plus a terminal pinna. **Pinnae** are up to about 25cm long and 1.5cm wide, with the fertile pinnae a bit longer and narrower than this. Pinnae are solid green. **Margins** are finely toothed or even spiny in the fertile pinnae, especially toward the leaf apex. **Veins** are free and simple or forked. **Sori** are linear and run continuously along the pinna margins, covered by a **false indusium** created by inrolling of the margin. 2n=58 (diploid).

A. A colony of *Pteris cretica*.

B. Leaves with pedate lowest pinnae.

C. Marginal, linear sori with false indusia.

D. Finely toothed margins and veins that are free and simple or forked.

Pteris multifida

COMMON NAME(S) Spider brake, Huguenot fern

STATUS Not native, somewhat common

HABITAT/DISTRIBUTION Naturalized across the south, especially on limestone and in disturbed habitats, both human made and natural, including riverbanks, rock and masonry walls, and dump sites; native to Asia

Plants are terrestrial. **Stems** are short creeping, with dense, dark brown or reddish-brown scales. **Leaves** are up to 60cm tall and clustered along the stem; sterile and fertile leaves do not differ in appearance. **Stipes** are up to 30cm long, pale green to brownish, with a few scales at the base but becoming smooth farther up, and with 2–3 distinct ridges or grooves on the upper surface. The **rachis** is similar to the stipe but has a conspicuous wing of tissue along both sides, throughout the blade. The leaf **blade** is oblong to narrowly triangular, up to 40cm long and 25cm wide, pedately divided toward the base, and pinnately divided farther up. **Pinnae** are linear, up to about 12cm long and 1.2cm wide, typically in 3–7 pairs spaced widely apart, with an elongated terminal pinna, and may have sparse hairs along the midveins on the lower surface. Fertile pinnae are a bit narrower than sterile pinnae. **Margins** are irregularly and/or finely serrate, especially toward the leaf tip. **Veins** are free and simple or forked. **Sori** are linear and run continuously along the pinna margins, covered by a **false indusium** created by inrolling of the margin. 2n=116 (tetraploid).

A. A colony of *Pteris multifida*.

B. Plants with pedate pinnae.

C. Lower surface of fertile leaf showing marginal sori and serrate tip.

F   S   C   N

Pteris parkeri

COMMON NAME(S) White-lined Cretan brake

NOTABLE SYNONYMS *Pteris cretica* var. *albolineata*

STATUS Not native, uncommon

HABITAT/DISTRIBUTION Escapes from cultivation and may become naturalized in the south in hammocks, sinkholes, and other areas with exposed limestone; native to Africa and Asia

----

Plants are terrestrial. **Stems** are creeping, with scattered dark to chestnut-brown scales. **Leaves** are up to 1m tall and clustered along the stem; sterile and fertile leaves are somewhat dimorphic, with pinnae on the fertile leaves narrower and more elongated than on the sterile leaves. **Stipes** are up to 50cm long, dark reddish brown toward the base and becoming yellow to whitish toward the blade, with sparse scales at the base, and with 2–3 distinct ridges or grooves on the upper surface. The **rachis** is similar to the stipe; a wing of tissue along the rachis (if present at all) is present only just below the terminal pinna, not throughout the leaf blade. The leaf **blade** is ovate, up to 30cm long and 25cm wide, and pedately divided toward the base, with 2 lateral pinnae that have 2 or more elongated pinnules; farther up, there is often 1 additional pinna pair plus a terminal pinna. **Pinnae** are up to about 25cm long and 1.5cm wide, with the fertile pinna a bit longer and narrower than this. Pinnae are variegated, with white centers and green edges. **Margins** are finely toothed or even spiny in the fertile pinnae, especially toward the leaf apex. **Veins** are free and simple or forked. **Sori** are linear and run continuously along the pinna margins, covered by a **false indusium** created by inrolling of the margin. 2n=58 (diploid).

A. Plants of *Pteris parkeri*.

B. Variegated pinnae.

C. Marginal, linear sori with false indusia.

Pteris tripartita

COMMON NAME(S) Giant brake

STATUS Not native, uncommon

HABITAT/DISTRIBUTION Naturalized in southern Florida, especially in damp to wet forested habitats such as cypress glades and pond apple swamps; native to Africa, Asia, and the Austral-Pacific region

Plants are terrestrial. **Stems** are creeping to ascending, with dense, pale brown scales. **Leaves** are up to 3m tall and clustered along the stem. **Stipes** are up to about 1.25m long and yellowish to reddish brown, with scales toward the base but becoming smooth farther up, and with 2–3 distinct ridges or grooves on the upper surface. The **rachis** is similar to the stipe and is not winged. The leaf **blade** is up to 2m long and 2m wide, triangular to pentagonal (5-sided), and divided at the base into 3 large primary divisions (pinnae), which are themselves further divided, with the ultimate divisions appearing pinnate to pinnate-pinnatifid. **Margins** are smooth to finely toothed. Lateral **veins** are anastomosing near the midveins but may become free and forked toward the margins. **Sori** are linear and run continuously along the pinna margins, covered by a **false indusium** created by inrolling of the margin. 2n=58 (diploid).

A. A young frond of *Pteris tripartita*.

B. Base of the blade, showing the first split into 3 large divisions.

C. Close-up of mature sori.

D. Close-up of immature sori.

E. Lower surface of mature fertile pinnae.

Pteris vittata

COMMON NAME(S) Chinese ladder brake

STATUS Not native (invasive), common

HABITAT/DISTRIBUTION Naturalized throughout Florida and into the southeast in a variety of natural and human-made habitats, including ditches, culverts, rock and brick walls, and banks of canals and rivers; native to Asia

Plants are terrestrial and often epipetric. **Stems** are short creeping and densely covered with pale brown scales. **Leaves** are up to 1m tall and clustered along the stem. **Stipes** are up to 30cm long, densely scaly at the base, and green to light brown, with 2–3 distinct ridges or grooves on the upper surface. The **rachis** is similar to the stipe, with scattered to dense scales, and not winged but with a groove in the upper surface. The leaf **blade** is 1-pinnate, up to 80cm long and 35cm wide, and oblanceolate (widest above the middle). **Pinnae** are linear to lanceolate, up to 18cm long and 9mm wide, and separated from one another at the base of the blade but becoming more closely spaced toward the tip. The terminal pinna is often quite elongated. **Margins** are finely toothed, especially toward the pinna tips. **Veins** are free and forked. **Sori** are linear and run continuously along the pinna margins, covered by a **false indusium** created by inrolling of the margin. 2n=116 (diploid).

A. *Pteris vittata* plants growing on limestone masonry.

B. Fertile pinnae.

C. Immature sori.

D. Mature sori.

FAMILY: **DRYOPTERIDACEAE**

Rumohra adiantiformis is the only member of this genus in our flora, and like many nonnative fern species in eastern North America, it is known only from Florida and the southeast, where it escapes from cultivation and becomes naturalized. In addition to being planted for gardening and landscaping purposes, *R. adiantiformis* is also regularly used in floral arrangements, thanks to the hardiness and durability of its leaves; it may look familiar if you have bought cut flowers or a corsage. Base chromosome number $(x) = 41$.

Rumohra adiantiformis

A. *Rumohra adiantiformis* growing in landscaping in Florida.

B. Sori nearing maturity; some are still fully covered by translucent indusia, while in others the indusia have become papery and are retracting to allow spore dispersal.

F   S   C   N

Rumohra adiantiformis

COMMON NAME(S) Leather fern

STATUS Not native, somewhat common

HABITAT/DISTRIBUTION Escapes from cultivation and becomes naturalized throughout peninsular Florida and into the Florida Panhandle and Louisiana in drier wooded habitats, often along roadsides and ditches; native to tropical regions essentially worldwide, but considered introduced in Florida

Plants are terrestrial. **Stems** are long creeping, with large orange-brown to brown scales. **Leaves** are erect and up to about 1.5m long, very stiff and leathery, and spread out along the creeping stems; sterile and fertile leaves do not differ in appearance. The **stipe** is yellowish to dark brown, with scales similar to those on the stem. The **rachis** is up to 40cm long, deeply grooved on the upper surface, with scattered orange-brown scales on the lower surface, and is similar in color to the stipe toward the base but becomes greener throughout the blade. The leaf **blade** is up to 90cm long and 75cm wide, 2–3-pinnate, triangular overall, and widest at the base. **Pinnae** have short stalks and are narrowly triangular to lanceolate, up to 37cm long and 10cm wide. **Margins** are smooth but usually have a few blunt, coarse teeth toward the pinnule tips. **Veins** are inconspicuous. **Sori** are round, with prominent, peltate (umbrellalike) **indusia** that curl up and retract toward the center of the sorus when sporangia are mature and ready to disperse spores. 2n=82 (diploid).

A. A frond of *Rumohra adiantiformis*.

B. Lowest pair of pinnae.

C. Lower surface of a fertile leaf, with sori.

D. Scales at the base of the stipe.

E. Close-up of nearly mature sori still covered by indusia.

FAMILY: **SALVINIACEAE**

Salvinia is one of several genera of true water ferns. These plants belong to the families Salviniaceae and Marsileaceae and spend their entire lives associated with watery habitats. In members of Salviniaceae (*Salvinia*, p. 455; and *Azolla*, p. 187), the plants float on the surface of the water and do not have true roots, while in the Marsileaceae (*Marsilea*, p. 335; *Pilularia*, p. 421; and *Regnellidium*, the last of which does not occur in our flora), the plants are rooted in the substrate.

Salvinia's morphology is quite unique, with 2 types of leaves: a large green ovate type that floats on the surface, and a second type that is finely divided and rootlike and hangs below the plants into the water. Attached to these submerged leaves are hardened, globose structures that contain spores; these are technically highly modified sori but are often called sporocarps (see the section on *Marsilea* for further discussion of sporocarps). The true water ferns are unique among ferns in being heterosporous (having separate male and female spores), and in *Salvinia* the spore-bearing structures contain either megasporangia that produce large female megaspores, or microsporangia that produce numerous, much smaller, male microspores. *Salvinia* may produce spores throughout the growing season, but it is quite rare to find fertile plants. The floating leaves of *Salvinia* are also notable for the upward-pointing, branched hairs that coat their upper surfaces and are thought to assist with shedding water and therefore keeping the leaves afloat. Both of the *Salvinia* species in eastern North America are considered noxious invasives, capable of clogging waterways and altering native ecosystems. Base chromosome number (x) = 9.

A large colony of *Salvinia minima* on a pond surface.

KEY TO THE SPECIES OF *SALVINIA* IN OUR FLORA:

1a Floating leaves are up to 1.5cm long; on the upward-pointing hairs on the upper surface of the floating leaves, the tips of the hairs are spread apart and do not touch ⸳⸳⸳⸳⸳⸳⸳⸳⸳⸳⸳⸳ *Salvinia minima*

1b Floating leaves are up to 2cm long or sometimes longer; on the upward-pointing hairs on the upper surface of the floating leaves, the tips of the hairs bend in to touch one another, resembling tiny eggbeaters ⸳⸳ *Salvinia molesta*

Salvinia minima

COMMON NAME(S) Water spangles, floating fern

NOTABLE SYNONYMS Sometimes incorrectly referred to as *Salvinia rotundifolia* in Florida

STATUS Not native (invasive), somewhat common

HABITAT/DISTRIBUTION Still or slow-moving bodies of water including ponds, swamps, rivers, and canals; native to the American tropics

Plants are floating aquatics (and can also survive for some time on mud if water recedes). **Stems** are up to about 6cm long and hairy. **Leaves** are in sets of 3, with each set including 2 floating and 1 submerged leaf. The **floating leaves** are up to 1.5cm long, elliptic to ovate or almost round, with a distinct midrib that causes the leaf to look as if it is folding in half, and with stiff, upward-facing hairs that are 4-pronged at their tips, the tips not touching but spreading apart from one another. The **submerged leaves** hang downward in the water column and are finely divided, resembling hairlike roots. **Sori** are modified into hard, globose structures that contain either megasporangia producing large female megaspores, or microsporangia producing small male microspores. 2n=18 (diploid).

A. A colony of *Salvinia minima*.

B. Floating leaves.

C. Close-up of hairs, with tips that spread apart from one another.

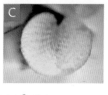

D. Plant with large green floating leaves and rootlike submerged leaves.

Salvinia molesta

COMMON NAME(S) Giant salvinia, Kariba weed
(after an infestation of Lake Kariba in West Africa)

STATUS Not native (invasive), somewhat common

HABITAT/DISTRIBUTION Still or slow-moving bodies of
water including ponds, swamps, rivers, and canals;
native to southeastern Brazil

Plants are floating aquatics (and can also survive for some time on mud if water recedes). **Stems** are up to about 6cm long and hairy. **Leaves** are in sets of 3, with each set including 2 floating and 1 submerged leaf. The **floating leaves** are up to 3cm long, elliptic to ovate or almost round, with a distinct midrib that causes the leaf to look as if it is folding in half, and with stiff, upward-facing hairs that are 4-pronged at their tips, the tips touching and giving the appearance of an eggbeater. The **submerged leaves** hang downward in the water column and are finely divided, resembling hairlike roots. **Sori** are modified into hard, globose structures that contain either megasporangia producing large female megaspores, or microsporangia producing small male microspores. 2n=unknown.

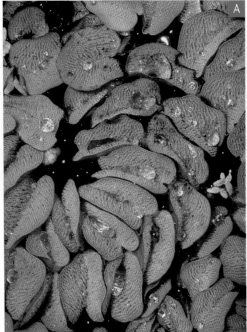

A. Plants of *Salvinia molesta*.

B. Close-up of eggbeater-shaped hairs.

C. & D. Upper leaf surfaces with hairs.

PHOTOGRAPHS BY ROBBIN MORAN

FAMILY: **OPHIOGLOSSACEAE**

Sceptridium is a genus of ferns whose members were traditionally included in a very large *Botrychium* genus. In recent years, studies of morphology augmented by DNA-based analyses of relationships resulted in recognition of several genera for the species formerly included in *Botrychium*; these now belong to *Botrypus* (1 species, p. 213), a smaller *Botrychium* (now with 15 species in our flora, p. 193), and *Sceptridium*, with 7 species in our flora. *Sceptridium* species are commonly called grape ferns, after the resemblance of their sporangial clusters to bunches of grapes. Members of this genus are similar to *Ophioglossum* and *Botrychium* species in their habitat preferences, favoring open, grassy areas such as lawns and roadsides (though many species will often grow happily in open forests without dense undergrowth). All these genera are known for their tendency to inhabit cemeteries, which seem to have the right amount of low-level disturbance (i.e., regular mowing and infrequent foot traffic) to facilitate their growth. In almost all our *Sceptridium* species, the sterile trophophores remain green year-round (or may become browned or bronzed during winter), with the fertile sporophore segment produced seasonally in early to late spring. Base chromosome number $(x) = 45$.

KEY TO THE SPECIES OF *SCEPTRIDIUM* IN OUR FLORA:

1a   The sterile trophophore has a very short stalk, and its blade sits flat against the substrate; 2 sterile blades are usually produced per plant; the main stalk and sporangia-bearing branches of the fertile sporophore are distinctly flattened ·········· *Sceptridium lunarioides*

1b   The sterile trophophore has a stalk several centimeters long, and its blade is held up above the substrate; 1 sterile blade is usually produced per plant; the main stalk and branches of the sporophore are only slightly flattened ·········· 2

    2a   The pinnae in the first (lowest) pair are distantly alternate and themselves have long stalks before the first pinnule division; the pinnules have fanlike venation, with a short midrib ·········· *Sceptridium jenmanii*

    2b   The pinnae in the first pair are alternate to almost opposite and have short stalks before the first pinnules; the pinnules have pinnate venation, usually with a clear midrib ·········· 3

        3a   Pinnae are divided into pinnules all the way to the pinna tip ·········· 4

            4a   The blade and pinnules are nearly flat (planar); pinnules are ovate to rounded; margins are entire to shallowly, bluntly toothed ·········· *Sceptridium multifidum*

            4b   The blade and pinnules are ruffly to wrinkly and usually somewhat curled or curved (not lying flat); pinnules are trowel shaped and widest at the base; margins are finely toothed or coarsely cut into narrow segments ·········· 5

                5a   Pinnae are finely rugulose (wrinkly); margins are finely toothed ·········· *Sceptridium rugulosum*

                5b   Pinnae are ruffly in appearance; margins are deeply cut into narrow, pointy lobes or segments ·········· *Sceptridium dissectum* (more-divided leaf form)

        3b   Pinnae are not divided all the way to the tip but end in a long terminal pinnule ·········· 6

            6a   Terminal pinnules are elongated, have parallel sides, and are roughly the same width throughout ·········· *Sceptridium biternatum*

            6b   Terminal pinnules are wider at the base or toward the middle and are not the same width throughout ·········· 7

                7a   Pinnule tips are rounded; pinnule margins are finely, bluntly to sharply toothed; leaves remain green through the winter ·········· *Sceptridium oneidense*

                7b   Pinnule tips are pointed; pinnule margins are bluntly to coarsely toothed; leaves often turn tan or bronze in the winter ·········· *Sceptridium dissectum* (less-divided leaf form)

1a.
*Sceptridium
lunarioides*

2a.
*Sceptridium
jenmanii*

4a.
*Sceptridium
multifidum*

5a.
*Sceptridium
rugulosum*

5b, 7b.
*Sceptridium
dissectum*

6a.
*Sceptridium
biternatum*

7a.
*Sceptridium
oneidense*

IMAGE COURTESY OF THE C. V. STARR
VIRTUAL HERBARIUM OF THE NEW YORK
BOTANICAL GARDEN (NY 03527673)

F   S   C   N

Sceptridium biternatum

COMMON NAME(S) Southern grape fern, sparse-leaved grape fern

NOTABLE SYNONYMS *Botrychium biternatum*

STATUS Native (endemic to North America), common

HABITAT/DISTRIBUTION Open woods and brushy fields; range extends into Texas

Plants are terrestrial. **Stems** are upright. **Leaves** are 2-parted, with a short common stalk that separates near ground level into a sterile trophophore and fertile sporophore. The **trophophore** is held erect, with the blade above the ground surface, and has a long stalk that is up to 20cm long and ends in a blade that is 2–3-pinnate, broadly triangular, up to 18cm long and 28cm wide, and herbaceous. The blade has up to 7 pairs of **pinnae**, which are usually somewhat spaced out along the rachis and divided into pinnules only at their bases. **Pinnules** are elongated and narrowly lanceolate. **Margins** are finely toothed. **Veins** are free and venation is pinnate. The **sporophore** is 1–2-pinnate and 2–3 times the length of the trophophore (up to ca. 40–50cm long). **Sporangia** may have short stalks or sit directly against the sporophore branchlets. 2n=90 (diploid).

A. A plant of *Sceptridium biternatum*.

B. & C. Sterile trophophore blade.

D. Fertile section of sporophore.

Sceptridium dissectum

COMMON NAME(S) Cut-leaf grape fern, dissected grape fern

NOTABLE SYNONYMS *Botrychium cuneatum, Botrychium dissectum*

STATUS Native, common

HABITAT/DISTRIBUTION A range of habitats, from more open fields and lawns to open woods; range extends somewhat west of the Mississippi; also occurs in the Caribbean

Plants are terrestrial. **Stems** are upright. **Leaves** are 2-parted, with a short common stalk that separates near ground level into a sterile trophophore and fertile sporophore. The **trophophore** is very variable, even within a population, with the blade being either barely dissected or highly dissected, and the pinnules taking on various shapes. The trophophore is held erect, with the blade above the ground surface, and has a long stalk that is up to 15cm long and ends in a blade that is 3–4-pinnate, broadly triangular, up to 20cm long and 30cm wide, and tough and leathery. The blade has up to 10 pairs of **pinnae**, which are variously spread along the rachis and divided into pinnules only at their bases. **Pinnules** are elongate heart shaped or trowel shaped and are either very shallowly lobed or deeply divided into narrow, pointy lobes. **Margins** are toothed to coarsely cut. **Veins** are free and venation is pinnate. The **sporophore** is 2–3-pinnate and 1.5–2.5 times the length of the trophophore (up to ca. 50cm long). **Sporangia** may have short stalks or sit directly against the sporophore branchlets. 2n=90 (diploid).

A. A sterile trophophore blade of *Sceptridium dissectum*, from the nondissected leaf form.

B. A sterile trophophore blade from the dissected leaf form.

C. A fertile plant.

D. Darker leaves later in the season.

Sceptridium jenmanii

COMMON NAME(S) Alabama grape fern

NOTABLE SYNONYMS *Botrychium jenmanii*

STATUS Native, rare

HABITAT/DISTRIBUTION A range of habitats, from grassy areas to open forests; also occurs in the Caribbean

Plants are terrestrial. **Stems** are upright. **Leaves** are 2-parted, with a short common stalk that separates near ground level into a sterile trophophore and fertile sporophore. The **trophophore** is held erect, with the blade above the ground surface, and has a long stalk that is up to 15cm long and ends in a blade that is 3-pinnate, broadly triangular, up to 18cm long and 26cm wide, and herbaceous. The blade has up to 5 pairs of **pinnae**, which are spread out along the rachis and divided into pinnules all the way to the tip. The pinnae in the first (lowest) pair are distantly alternate and have long stalks before the first division into pinnules (the first pinnae in the other species are more closely alternate to almost opposite, with short stalks). **Pinnules** are ovate or fan shaped. **Margins** are finely toothed. **Veins** are free and venation is fanlike, with a short midrib. The **sporophore** is 2-pinnate to 2-pinnate-pinnatifid and 1–2.5 times the length of the trophophore (up to ca. 45cm long). **Sporangia** may have short stalks or sit directly against the sporophore branchlets. 2n=180 (tetraploid).

A. A sterile trophophore blade of *Sceptridium jenmanii*.

B. A fertile plant.

C. Fertile portion of sporophore.

D. Base of the leaf where the trophophore and sporophore stalks meet.

Sceptridium lunarioides

COMMON NAME(S) Winter grape fern, prostrate grape fern

NOTABLE SYNONYMS *Botrychium lunarioides, Holubiella lunarioides*

STATUS Native (endemic to North America), uncommon

HABITAT/DISTRIBUTION Open grassy areas including cemeteries, roadsides, trailsides, and prairies; range extends into Texas

Plants are terrestrial. **Stems** are upright. **Leaves** are 2-parted, with a short common stalk that separates near ground level into a sterile trophophore and fertile sporophore. The **trophophore** is held flat against the ground surface and has a short stalk that is up to 1cm long and ends in a blade that is 2–3-pinnate, broadly triangular, up to 8cm long and 12cm wide (often smaller), and delicate. The blade has up to 5 pairs of **pinnae**, which are spaced out along the rachis and divided into pinnules all the way to the tip. **Pinnules** are fan shaped. **Margins** are finely toothed. **Veins** are free and venation is fanlike, with no midrib. The **sporophore** is 2-pinnate and 1–2 times the length of the trophophore (up to ca. 18cm long). Sporophores are produced in fall, but the fertile segments may not become erect until early spring. **Sporangia** may have short stalks or sit directly against the sporophore branchlets. 2n=90 (diploid).

A. A plant of *Sceptridium lunarioides*.

B. An unfurling sporophore.

C. Close-up of a sporophore.

D. A sporophore after sporangia have released their spores.

Sceptridium multifidum

COMMON NAME(S) Leathery grape fern

NOTABLE SYNONYMS *Botrychium multifidum*

STATUS Native, somewhat common

HABITAT/DISTRIBUTION A variety of open grassy areas such as fields, lawns, and cemeteries; also occurs in western North America, Greenland, Europe, and Asia

Plants are terrestrial. Stems are upright. Leaves are 2-parted, with a short common stalk that separates near ground level into a sterile trophophore and fertile sporophore. The trophophore is held erect, with the blade above the ground surface, and has a long stalk that is up to 15cm long and ends in a blade that is 2–3-pinnate, broadly triangular, up to 25cm long and 35cm wide, and tough and leathery. The blade has up to 10 pairs of pinnae, which are variously spread along the rachis and divided into pinnules all the way to the tip. Pinnules are ovate to round. Margins are shallowly, bluntly to sometimes more finely toothed. Veins are free and venation is pinnate. The sporophore is 2–3-pinnate and typically a little longer than the trophophore (up to ca. 30cm long). Sporangia may have short stalks or sit directly against the sporophore branchlets. 2n=90 (diploid).

A. A plant of *Sceptridium multifidum*.

B. Immature, unfurling sporophore.

C. Sterile trophophore blade.

Sceptridium oneidense

COMMON NAME(S) Blunt-leaved grape fern

NOTABLE SYNONYMS *Botrychium oneidense*

STATUS Native (endemic to eastern North America), uncommon

HABITAT/DISTRIBUTION Damp, shady woods and swamp edges

Plants are terrestrial. **Stems** are upright. **Leaves** are 2-parted, with a short common stalk that separates near ground level into a sterile trophophore and fertile sporophore. The **trophophore** is held erect, with the blade above the ground surface, and has a long stalk that is up to 15cm long and ends in a blade that is 2–3-pinnate, broadly triangular, up to 15cm long and 20cm wide, and tough and leathery. The blade has up to 5 pairs of **pinnae**, which are fairly well separated along the rachis and divided into pinnules only at their bases. **Pinnules** are ovate to oblong. **Margins** are finely, bluntly to sharply toothed. **Veins** are free and venation is pinnate. The **sporophore** is 2–3-pinnate and 1.5–2.5 times the length of the trophophore (up to ca. 45cm long). **Sporangia** may have short stalks or sit directly against the sporophore branchlets. 2n=90 (diploid).

A. Sterile trophophore blade of *Sceptridium oneidense*.

B. Close-up of trophophore blade.

C. Fertile section of sporophore.

PHOTOGRAPHS BY NATE MARTINEAU

Sceptridium rugulosum

COMMON NAME(S) Ternate grape fern, St. Lawrence grape fern

NOTABLE SYNONYMS *Botrychium rugulosum*

STATUS Native (endemic to eastern North America), rare

HABITAT/DISTRIBUTION Grassy areas and open forests

Plants are terrestrial. Stems are upright. Leaves are 2-parted, with a short common stalk that separates near ground level into a sterile trophophore and fertile sporophore. The trophophore is held erect, with the blade above the ground surface, and has a long stalk that is up to 15cm long and ends in a blade that is 2–5-pinnate, broadly triangular, up to 15cm long and 26cm wide, and herbaceous, with the pinna segments cupped and folded rather than lying in a plane, giving the blade a wrinkly appearance. The blade has up to 9 pairs of pinnae, which are fairly close together along the rachis and divided into pinnules all the way to the tip. Pinnules are trowel shaped. Margins are finely toothed. Veins are free and venation is pinnate. The sporophore is 2-pinnate and 1–2 times the length of the trophophore (up to ca. 50cm long). Sporangia may have short stalks or sit directly against the sporophore branchlets. 2n=90 (diploid).

A. A fertile plant of *Sceptridium rugulosum*.

B. Sterile trophophore blade.

C. Fertile section of sporophore.

D. Close-up of trophophore blade.

FAMILY: **SCHIZAEACEAE**

We have only 1 species of this genus in our flora: *Schizaea pusilla*. *Schizaea* is a member of the "curly grass" family, the Schizaeaceae, which has only 2 species in North America, *S. pusilla* and *Actinostachys pennula* (which was formerly treated in *Schizaea*, p. 119). Both of these species have narrow, elongated leaves that give them a somewhat grasslike appearance, though in *Schizaea* the sterile leaves curl up near the ground surface, while in *Actinostachys* they remain erect. *Actinostachys pennula* occurs only in Florida, while *S. pusilla* can be found in the northeastern U.S. and Canada; it is particularly strongly associated, both ecologically and culturally, with the New Jersey Pine Barrens. Base chromosome number (x) = 77, 94, 103.

A. Plants of *Schizaea pusilla*.

B. The curly sterile leaves of the curly grass fern.

IMAGE COURTESY OF THE C. V. STARR VIRTUAL HERBARIUM OF THE NEW YORK BOTANICAL GARDEN (NY 03554337)

Schizaea pusilla

Schizaea pusilla

COMMON NAME(S) Curly grass fern

STATUS Native, rare

HABITAT/DISTRIBUTION Damp, acidic substrates, including bogs, swamp and pond edges, and sandy or grassy depressions and swales; also occurs in South America (though this may be a separate, closely related species)

Plants are terrestrial and can form large colonies. Stems are erect and covered in tiny hairs. Leaves are undivided, extremely narrow, and elongated, up to 12cm long and 1mm wide. The stipe and blade are not clearly distinguished from one another. Sterile and fertile leaves are dimorphic: sterile fronds are slightly shorter but also twisted and curled up, so they appear to reach only ⅓–½ the height of the fertile fronds, which are straight and erect. The fertile fronds terminate in an expanded section where the blade appears to flatten out into several well-defined vertical "digits" or rays. These have a somewhat fan-shaped arrangement and bear sporangia in 2 rows on each digit. When the spores are mature, the digits will dry out, turn brown, and may flare apart from one another to aid spore dispersal. The lower, grasslike portion of the leaf typically remains green. 2n=206 (diploid).

A. Fertile leaves of *Schizaea pusilla* with a lycophyte (*Lycopodiella alopecuroides*) in the background.

B. Curly sterile leaves.

C. Close-up of fertile segments.

D. Two mature fertile segments; the one on the left has already dispersed its spores and dried up.

FAMILY: **TECTARIACEAE**

Tectaria is a mostly tropical genus of ferns with about 200 species globally, 3 of which can be found in eastern North America, all in Florida. Two of these species are considered native to our flora, while the third, *T. incisa*, is a noxious invasive. Members of the genus often have "halberd fern" in their common names, a reference to the medieval weapon that consisted of a long pole capped with a combination ax, spike, and backward-pointing hook. The lowest pinnae of *Tectaria* species somewhat resemble the ax and spike portion of the halberd head, especially in larger fronds. Base chromosome number (x) = 40.

KEY TO THE SPECIES OF *TECTARIA* IN OUR FLORA:

1a At maturity, the leaf blade is less than 15cm long and has at most 1–2 pairs of lateral pinnae ·········· *Tectaria fimbriata*

1b At maturity, the leaf blade is longer than 15cm and has 2 or more lateral pinnae ···································· 2

    2a The leaf blade at maturity is not more than 50cm long and has 3 pinna pairs at most; leaves are shiny green; the lower surface of the rachis is smooth, without hairs; lateral veins are typically not deeply impressed into the leaf surface; indusia are centrally attached ··············· *Tectaria heracleifolia*

    2b The leaf blade at maturity can be up to 1.2m long and have up to 10 pinna pairs; leaves are dull green; the lower surface of the rachis is hairy; lateral veins are often deeply impressed into the leaf surface; indusia are attached along the side ·································· *Tectaria incisa*

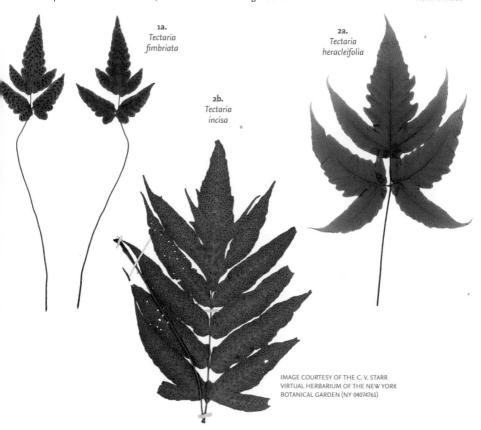

1a.
Tectaria fimbriata

2a.
Tectaria heracleifolia

2b.
Tectaria incisa

IMAGE COURTESY OF THE C. V. STARR
VIRTUAL HERBARIUM OF THE NEW YORK
BOTANICAL GARDEN (NY 04074761)

Tectaria fimbriata

COMMON NAME(S) Least halberd fern

STATUS Native, rare

HABITAT/DISTRIBUTION Rocky habitats such as limestone sinkholes, ledges, and outcrops, usually in shade; also occurs in Mexico and the Caribbean

Plants are terrestrial and epipetric. **Stems** are short creeping. **Leaves** are clustered along the stem, and sterile and fertile leaves do not differ in appearance. **Stipes** are pale brown or yellowish to green, up to 28cm long, with hairs (especially on the upper surface) and scales around the base. The **rachis** is similar to the stipe. The leaf **blade** is up to 11cm long and 10cm wide, triangular to pentagonal, entire and lobed to pinnatifid or bipinnatifid, and hairy on the lower surface, especially along the midveins. **Pinnae,** if present, are in 1–2 pairs, triangular, and up to 7cm long; usually the blade is only lobed to shallowly pinnatifid. **Margins** are smooth to wavy. **Veins** are anastomosing, and the areoles only rarely include free veinlets. **Sori** are round, with peltate (umbrellalike) **indusia.** 2n=80 (diploid).

A. Plants of *Tectaria fimbriata*.

B. Plants growing on limestone.

C. Lower leaf surface with sori.

D. Immature sori.

E. Mature sori.

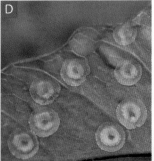
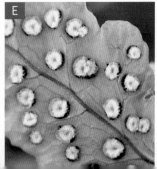

Tectaria heracleifolia

COMMON NAME(S) Broad halberd fern

STATUS Native, somewhat common

HABITAT/DISTRIBUTION Rocky limestone habitats including sinks, outcrops, and hammocks; also occurs in the Caribbean, Mexico, and Central and South America

Plants are terrestrial and epipetric. **Stems** are erect to ascending, and scaly. **Leaves** are clustered along the stem and are shiny and bright to dark green; sterile and fertile leaves do not differ in appearance. **Stipes** are up to 45cm long (usually longer than the blade), pale brown or yellowish toward the blade and darker toward the base, and not hairy. The **rachis** is similar to the stipe. The leaf **blade** is up to 50cm long and 45cm wide, ovate triangular to pentagonal, pinnate pinnatifid (or lobed at the base, if plants are small), and smooth on the lower surface except for minute, scalelike hairs along the veins. Main lateral veins are typically not deeply impressed into the leaf blade. **Pinnae** are usually present and in 1–3 pairs, triangular, and up to 23cm long; the lowermost pinnae have short stalks and are deeply lobed (often appearing to be 2 pinnae each). **Margins** are wavy to lobed or bluntly toothed. **Veins** are anastomosing, and the areoles often include free veinlets. **Sori** are round, with peltate (umbrellalike) **indusia.** 2n=160 (tetraploid).

A. Plants of *Tectaria heracleifolia.*

B. Upper leaf surface.

C. Lower leaf surface with sori.

D. Sori with peltate indusia.

Tectaria incisa

COMMON NAME(S) Incised halberd fern

STATUS Not native (invasive), somewhat common

HABITAT/DISTRIBUTION Rocky limestone habitats such as hammocks, outcrops, and around sinks and swamps; native to the Caribbean, Mexico, and Central America

Plants are terrestrial and epipetric. Stems are erect and woody, with dense, dark brown scales. Leaves are clustered along the stem and are a light, dull green; sterile and fertile leaves do not differ in appearance. Stipes are up to 60cm long (about equal in length to the blade), yellowish to tan or medium brown, scaly at the base, and hairy throughout. The rachis is similar to the stipe. The leaf blade is up to 1.2m long and 0.5m wide, oblong to ovate triangular, 1-pinnate, and hairy along the veins on the lower surface. The main lateral veins are often somewhat deeply impressed into the leaf blade. Pinnae are in 3–10 pairs, up to 25cm long, and elongate triangular, often curving downward toward the tip and with a lobe at the base, on the upper edge. Margins are wavy to lobed or bluntly toothed. Veins are anastomosing, and the areoles often include free veinlets. Sori are round, with indusia that attach along the side. 2n=160 (tetraploid).

A. A frond of *Tectaria incisa*.

B. Lower surface of a frond tip.

C. Fertile pinnae with sori.

D. Close-up of sori.

FAMILY: **BLECHNACEAE**

We have 1 member of the genus *Telmatoblechnum* in our flora: *T. serrulatum*. This genus was historically included in a very large *Blechnum* genus, which has recently been broken up into a number of smaller genera, including *Telmatoblechnum*. This species—*T. serrulatum*—is therefore (unsurprisingly) quite similar in appearance to the single species of *Blechnum* in our flora, *B. appendiculatum* (p. 191). The 2 can be distinguished by their pinna margins, which are quite obviously serrate and sharply toothed in *T. serrulatum* but smooth in *B. appendiculatum*. *Telmatoblechnum serrulatum* also typically has much larger leaves and is much more common than *B. appendiculatum*. Base chromosome number (x) = 36.

Telmatoblechnum serrulatum

A. *Telmatoblechnum serrulatum* growing in a Florida cypress swamp.

B. Reddish young leaves that are characteristic of the family Blechnaceae.

F S C N

Telmatoblechnum serrulatum

COMMON NAME(S) Dentate midsorus fern, marsh fern, swamp fern

NOTABLE SYNONYMS *Blechnum serrulatum*

STATUS Native, common

HABITAT/DISTRIBUTION Moist habitats such as swamps, marshes, hammocks, and wet prairies and pine woods; also occurs in the Caribbean, Mexico, and Central and South America

Plants are terrestrial or can become somewhat epiphytic in brackish or frequently flooded areas, where they begin to climb trees. **Stems** are long creeping and branched, becoming erect at the tips, with brown to black scales. **Leaves** are up to 2m long, stiff and erect in the sun to arching and more supple in the shade. Young leaves may be distinctly reddish (a feature often associated with members of the family Blechnaceae). Fertile and sterile leaves appear similar overall. **Stipes** are up to 55cm long and yellowish to grayish or light brown, with small, narrow scales near the base but becoming smooth and hairless farther up. The **rachis** is grayish green and smooth and may have a groove running down the upper surface. The leaf **blade** is up to 70cm long and 28cm wide, oblong to elliptic lanceolate or narrowly triangular and widest at the base, 1-pinnate throughout, and smooth, but with scales along the pinna midveins on the underside of the blade. **Pinnae** arise alternately along the rachis, are 3–15cm long and 0.5–2cm wide, and linear to lanceolate; the fertile pinnae are often smaller and somewhat contracted. Pinnae may have short stalks, and the pinna bases may be somewhat lobed at the corners. **Margins** are serrulate to serrate, especially toward the tips of the pinnae. **Veins** are free and forked. **Sori** are linear, running in 2 continuous lines on either side of the pinna midveins. **Indusia** are present, and sori open toward the midvein. 2n=72 (diploid).

A. Plants of *Telmatoblechnum serrulatum.*

B. Linear sori on the lower leaf surface.

C. Close-up of linear sori.

D. Reddish young leaves.

FAMILY: **THELYPTERIDACEAE**

The family Thelypteridaceae is one of the largest fern families, with nearly 1,200 species, and the classification of these species into genera has been a circuitous process. At one point nearly all members of the family were included in a single, enormous *Thelypteris* genus, but the most recent classification recognizes 37 genera in the family, based on morphological characters and DNA-based analyses of relationships, among other forms of data. Under this system, 20 of the 21 fern species in eastern North America that were formerly included in the genus *Thelypteris* have now been moved to other genera, leaving only 1 species of "true" *Thelypteris*: *T. palustris*, the marsh fern. The other 20 former *Thelypteris* species are now recognized in these genera: *Amauropelta* (3 species, p. 130), *Amblovenatum* (1 species, p. 134), *Christella* (2 species, p. 225), *Coryphopteris* (1 species, p. 230), *Cyclosorus* (1 species, p. 240), *Goniopteris* (4 species, p. 303), *Leptogramma* (1 species, p. 322), *Meniscium* (2 species, p. 345), and *Pelazoneuron* (5 species, p. 395). Base chromosome number (x) = 36.

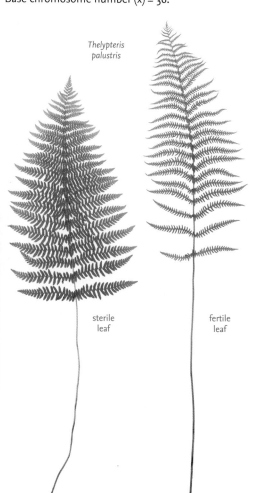

Thelypteris palustris

sterile leaf

fertile leaf

A sterile frond of *Thelypteris palustris*, with fertile fronds in the background.

Thelypteris palustris

COMMON NAME(S) Marsh fern

STATUS Native, common

HABITAT/DISTRIBUTION Wet habitats including swamps, marshes, and other wetlands, and wet wooded areas including riverbanks and streamsides; range extends into western North America; also occurs in the Caribbean

Plants are terrestrial. **Stems** are long creeping. **Leaves** are up to 90cm long and spaced up to 3cm apart along the stem, forming diffuse colonies. Sterile and fertile leaves are similar in appearance, though fertile leaves are often taller, narrower, and more erect and have contracted pinnae because the margins roll inward toward the sori. **Stipes** are brownish toward the base but become yellowish to light green toward the blade, are up to 45cm long or sometimes longer, with scattered tan scales, and have a distinct groove in the upper surface. The **rachis** is similar to the stipe, with hairs present. The leaf **blade** is up to 40cm long or sometimes longer, 20cm wide, 1-pinnate-pinnatifid, narrowly elliptic to lanceolate overall, tapering toward the tip (which becomes pinnatifid), and squared off (truncate) at the base, with the lowest pinnae only slightly shorter than those immediately above them. **Pinnae** are up to 10cm long and 2cm wide and have a sparse to dense covering of hairs along the main veins and pinnule midveins but usually not on the blade surface. The pinna midvein has a distinct narrow groove in the upper surface. **Margins** are smooth and may be somewhat inrolled toward sori on fertile pinnae. **Veins** are free and almost always distinctly forked; the lowest veins of adjacent pinnules do not come together before the sinus but reach the margins of each pinnule above the sinus. **Sori** are round and located midway between the pinnule midvein and the margin. **Indusia** are present and often hairy. 2n=72 (diploid).

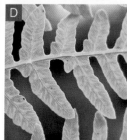

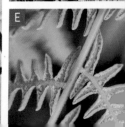

A. A colony of *Thelypteris palustris* in a swamp.

B. Sterile leaves.

C. Fertile leaves.

D. Sterile pinnae with forked veins.

E. Close-up of sori and inrolled margins.

FAMILY: **HYMENOPHYLLACEAE**

The filmy fern family, Hymenophyllaceae, includes 8 species that are part of the eastern North American flora. Historically, all 8 belonged to 2 genera: *Trichomanes* (6 species) and *Hymenophyllum* (2 species, p. 317). Recently, however, many of the species formerly in *Trichomanes* have been moved to other genera, including *Crepidomanes* (1 species, p. 232), *Didymoglossum* (3 species, p. 262), and *Vandenboschia* (1 species, p. 479). *Trichomanes holopterum* is the sole remaining species classified in this genus in eastern North America. All former members of *Trichomanes* have a stiff bristle that bears sporangia and emerges from the trumpet-shaped sori, and this gives *T. holopterum* (as well as the members of *Didymoglossum* and *Vandenboschia*) the common name "bristle fern." This species is extremely rare and known from only a few locations in southern Florida, where it occurs in cypress swamps. Like all members of the primarily tropical Hymenophyllaceae family, it has very thin leaves that are not tolerant of cold temperatures or low humidity. Base chromosome number (x) = 32.

Trichomanes holopterum

Trichomanes holopterum growing on a tree stump.

Trichomanes holopterum

COMMON NAME(S) Entire-winged bristle fern

STATUS Native, rare

HABITAT/DISTRIBUTION Old logs, stumps, and tree bases in cypress swamps; also occurs in the Caribbean and Mexico

Plants are epiphytic and form colonies, usually growing around the bases of living cypress trees or on stumps or fallen logs. **Stems** are erect, with leaves emerging in clusters. **Leaves** are up to 10cm long but usually shorter in Florida. **Stipes** are up to 3.5cm long, and typically winged with tissue that is continuous with the blade. The **rachis** is light to dark green and similar in color to the blade. The leaf **blade** is up to 7cm long and 2cm wide, pinnatifid, light to dark green, and thin and membranous. **Margins** are smooth and wavy. **Veins** are free and forked. **Sori** are marginal, at the ends of veins, and trumpet shaped, with a flaring, conical valve around the lip and a stiff bristle that emerges from the sorus bearing clustered sporangia. 2n=128 (tetraploid).

A. A colony of *Trichomanes holopterum*.

B. Fronds of various sizes.

C. Upper leaf surfaces.

D. A fertile frond with immature, trumpet-shaped sori.

E. A fertile frond with mature sori and emergent bristles.

FAMILY: **HYMENOPHYLLACEAE**

Vandenboschia boschiana is the only member of this genus in eastern North America, and the species was formerly included in *Trichomanes*, as *T. boschianum*. It has a wider range in our region than any other member of the family Hymenophyllaceae, and like its relatives in the genera *Crepidomanes* (p. 232) and *Hymenophyllum* (p. 317), it tolerates a northerly distribution, while the remaining members of the family in our flora (in the genera *Didymoglossum*, p. 262; and *Trichomanes*, p. 477) are found only much farther south, in climates more typical for species belonging to this primarily tropical family. The filmy ferns that do persist in temperate regions of eastern North America, including *V. boschiana*, do so by inhabiting rocky grottoes that maintain warmer and more humid conditions than their surroundings, even in winter. Base chromosome number (x) = 36.

*Vandenboschia
boschiana*

Vandenboschia boschiana

COMMON NAME(S) Appalachian bristle fern, Appalachian filmy fern

NOTABLE SYNONYMS *Trichomanes boschianum*

STATUS Native, uncommon

HABITAT/DISTRIBUTION Outcrops and grottoes of noncalcareous rocks; also occurs in Mexico

Plants are terrestrial and epipetric. **Stems** are long creeping, with dark hairs. **Leaves** are up to 20cm long and widely spaced along the stem, and sterile and fertile leaves do not differ in appearance. **Stipes** are up to 7cm long, dark brown to green, and frequently winged with bladelike tissue. The **rachis** is similar to the stipe. The leaf **blade** is lanceolate, 1–2-pinnate-pinnatifid, up to 13cm long and 4cm wide, and may have scattered hairs along the main veins. **Pinnae** are deeply, irregularly divided. **Margins** are smooth. **Veins** are free and forked. **Sori** are marginal, at the ends of veins, and conical but without a flared valve. A bristlelike structure emerges from the sorus, surrounded by clustered sporangia. **Gametophytes** are branched and ribbonlike. 2n=72, 108, 144 (diploid, triploid, and tetraploid cytotypes are known).

A. A small colony of *Vandenboschia boschiana*.

B. Plants.

C. Upper surfaces of fronds.

D. Fertile fronds with trumpet-shaped sori.

FAMILY: **PTERIDACEAE**

We have 3 species of *Vittaria* (shoestring ferns) in our flora. One of these—*V. appalachiana*, commonly known as the Appalachian gametophyte—is one of only 2 fern species in eastern North America that exists only in the gametophyte phase (see p. 26). These 2 species (the other is *Crepidomanes intricatum*, p. 232) never produce sporophytes but persist in the haploid gametophyte stage and reproduce vegetatively. Of the other 2 *Vittaria* species in our region, 1 (*V. graminifolia*) produces sporophytes very rarely, while the other, *V. lineata*, is a common member of the sporophytic fern flora of Florida. The gametophytes of all *Vittaria* species are ribbon shaped and highly branched, and they produce propagules for vegetative dispersal called gemmae (singular: gemma), which occur in pairs at the ends of small stalks along the edges of the gametophyte body. The number of cells that make up the main body of an individual gemma is a diagnostic feature used to distinguish species of *Vittaria*. A hand lens can be used to observe the gemmae, though a microscope may be necessary to see them well enough to count cells and key them to species. Base chromosome number (x) = 60.

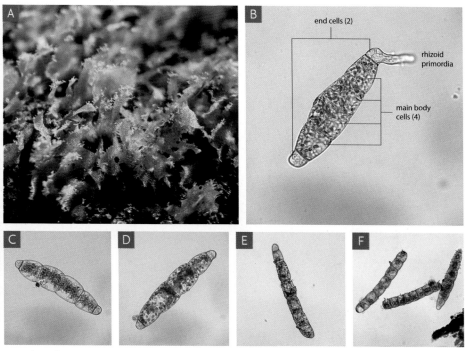

A. A colony of *Vittaria appalachiana* gametophytes. Gemmae are visible as the frilly segments along the edges of the larger gametophyte bodies.

B. Gemma of *V. graminifolia* with cell features labeled. Green structures are individual chloroplasts

C–D. Gemmae of *V. graminifolia*.

E–F. Gemmae of *V. appalachiana*.

PHOTOGRAPHS B–F BY NOAH YAWN; NOT SHOWN TO SCALE

KEY TO THE SPECIES OF *VITTARIA* IN OUR FLORA:

1a Only gametophytes are present ⋯⋯ 2

  2a Gemmae are all the same length, with 4 main body cells and smaller,
  rounded end cells that have rhizoid primordia ⋯⋯⋯⋯⋯⋯⋯⋯⋯⋯⋯⋯⋯⋯⋯⋯⋯⋯⋯⋯⋯⋯⋯⋯ *Vittaria graminifolia*

  2b Gemmae vary in length, with 2–16 main body cells and smaller, rounded
  end cells that may or may not have rhizoid primorida ⋯⋯⋯⋯⋯⋯⋯⋯⋯⋯⋯⋯⋯⋯⋯⋯⋯⋯⋯⋯⋯⋯⋯⋯⋯⋯⋯⋯ 3

    3a Gemmae have 2–12 main body cells (some gemmae with only 2–3 cells
    are usually present); the end cells are enlarged and can be larger than the main
    body cells; rhizoid primordia are often missing from 1 or both end cells and
    are almost never on main body cells; sporophytes are not known ⋯⋯⋯⋯⋯⋯ *Vittaria appalachiana*

    3b Gemmae have 4–16 main body cells; the end cells are equal in size to the main
    body cells, or smaller; rhizoid primordia are usually present on the end cells and
    sometimes on the main body cells; sporophytes are often abundantly produced ⋯⋯⋯⋯⋯ *Vittaria lineata*

1b Sporophytes are present ⋯⋯⋯ 4

  4a Stem scales have an elongated, hairlike tip; leaves are up to 60cm long and 3mm wide ⋯⋯⋯ *Vittaria lineata*

  4b Stem scales do not have an elongated, hairlike tip; leaves are up to 30cm long and
  2mm wide ⋯⋯ *Vittaria graminifolia*

Linear sori of *Vittaria lineata*.

Vittaria appalachiana

COMMON NAME(S) Appalachian gametophyte

STATUS Native (endemic to eastern North America), uncommon

HABITAT/DISTRIBUTION Sandstone and other noncalcareous rocks in caves, crevices, and grottoes

Plants are terrestrial and epipetric. **Sporophytes** are not known. **Gametophytes** are ribbonlike, 1 cell layer thick, up to 1 × 2cm, and often irregularly branched or lobed. **Gemmae** are held at the tips of lobes and are variable in length, from 2 to 12 cells long, and with the cells at the ends often larger than those toward the middle (a hand lens or microscope is needed to observe this). Rhizoid primordia may be present on 1 or both end cells but are often missing, and they almost never occur on main body cells. n=120 (tetraploid; 2n would equal 240, but the 2n sporophyte generation is not known to exist for this species).

Colonies of *Vittaria appalachiana* gametophytes.

Vittaria graminifolia

COMMON NAME(S) Grass fern

STATUS Native, rare

HABITAT/DISTRIBUTION On rocky, damp sandstone outcrops and grottoes, or growing epiphytically in moist hardwood forests; also occurs in the Caribbean, Mexico, and Central and South America

Plants are epiphytic or epipetric and are typically found as gametophytes (sporophytes occur only infrequently in our region). **Stems** are short creeping, branched, densely scaly with dark brown scales, and noticeably hairy. **Leaves** are densely clustered and pendent, up to 30cm long, and lack a well-defined **stipe**. The leaf **blade** is undivided and narrowly linear, up to 2mm wide. Sterile and fertile leaves do not differ in appearance. **Sori** are linear and run the length of the leaf, forming 2 parallel lines that sit in grooves, 1 on either side of the leaf midrib. **Gametophytes** are ribbonlike, 1 cell layer thick, up to 1 × 2cm, and often irregularly branched or lobed. **Gemmae** are uniform in length, each with 4 body cells plus 2 small end cells that have rhizoid primordia. 2n=120, 240 (both diploid and tetraploid cytotypes are known).

A. Sporophytes of *Vittaria graminifolia* with gametophytes present on the rocks in the background.

B. Sporophyte leaves.

C. Linear sori.

D. A gametophyte colony.

F S C N

Vittaria lineata

COMMON NAME(S) Shoestring fern

STATUS Native, somewhat common

HABITAT/DISTRIBUTION Moist woods and hammocks; also occurs in the Caribbean, Mexico, and Central and South America

Plants are epiphytic, especially on palm trunks. **Stems** are short creeping, branched, densely scaly with dark brown scales, and noticeably hairy. **Leaves** are densely clustered and pendent, up to 60cm long, and lack a well-defined **stipe**. The leaf **blade** is undivided and narrowly linear, up to 3mm wide. Sterile and fertile leaves do not differ in appearance. **Sori** are linear and run the length of the leaf, forming 2 parallel lines that sit in grooves, 1 on either side of the leaf midrib. **Gametophytes** are ribbonlike, 1 cell layer thick, up to 1 × 2cm, and often irregularly branched or lobed. **Gemmae** are variable in length, from 4 to 16 cells long, with the cells at the ends often smaller than or equal in size to cells toward the middle. Rhizoid primordia are usually present on the end cells, and sometimes on the main body cells. 2n=240 (tetraploid).

A. Plants of *Vittaria lineata* growing on a palm tree.

B. Leaves and fiddleheads.

C. A small plant.

D. Linear sori.

FAMILY: **WOODSIACEAE**

Woodsia is a genus commonly known as cliff ferns; its members can be found growing on rocky soils or directly on cliffs and ledges. Globally there are about 40 species in the genus, most of which are restricted to the northern temperate and boreal regions. The *Woodsia* species in our flora include 2 diploids and their allotetraploid offspring, plus 2 hybrids, neither of which is common (see figure below). Several additional species in our flora were previously treated in *Woodsia* but are now recognized as belonging to the genus *Physematium* (p. 416), to better align their taxonomy with evolutionary relationships. In both *Woodsia* and *Physematium*, the sorus sits on top of the indusium, which is either filamentous and hairlike (*Woodsia*) or multilobed (*Physematium*), with these lobes or filaments emerging from underneath the sorus and curving up around it, like a cup (the sorus) sitting atop an ill-formed and wobbly-edged saucer (the indusium). In both genera, the veins typically end, before they reach the leaf margin, in modified pores called *hydathodes*, which often appear as a slight widening of the vein at its very tip. *Woodsia ilvensis* also hybridizes with *P. oreganum* subsp. *cathcartianum* to form the intergeneric hybrid ×*Woodsimatium abbeae*. Base chromosome number (x) = 39, 41.

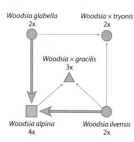

Woodsia glabella
2x

Woodsia × tryonis
2x

Woodsia × gracilis
3x

Woodsia alpina
4x

Woodsia ilvensis
2x

Relationships among *Woodsia* species in eastern North America. Blue circles are fertile diploids (2x), the green square is a fertile allotetraploid (4x), and the gray circle and triangle are a sterile diploid and triploid, respectively. Arrows show the direction of genetic contribution from parental toward offspring taxa, with wide arrows where crosses have produced fertile hybrids, and narrow arrows for sterile hybrids. For more information about interpreting these figures, see p. 12.

KEY TO THE SPECIES OF *WOODSIA* IN OUR FLORA:

1a The rachis and both surfaces of the leaf blade are smooth and without hairs, except for a few very scattered, flat, minute glands; the leaf blade is no more than 1.2cm wide; the stipe is green or yellowish throughout its length .... *Woodsia glabella*

1b The rachis and/or surfaces of the leaf blade have hairs or scales; the leaf blade is wider than 1.2cm, or if the blade is narrower than this, the stipe is dark purplish or reddish brown at the base 2

    2a The lower leaf surface and rachis have no or only a few scattered scales .... *Woodsia alpina*

    2b The lower leaf surface and rachis have numerous scales and hairs .... *Woodsia ilvensis*

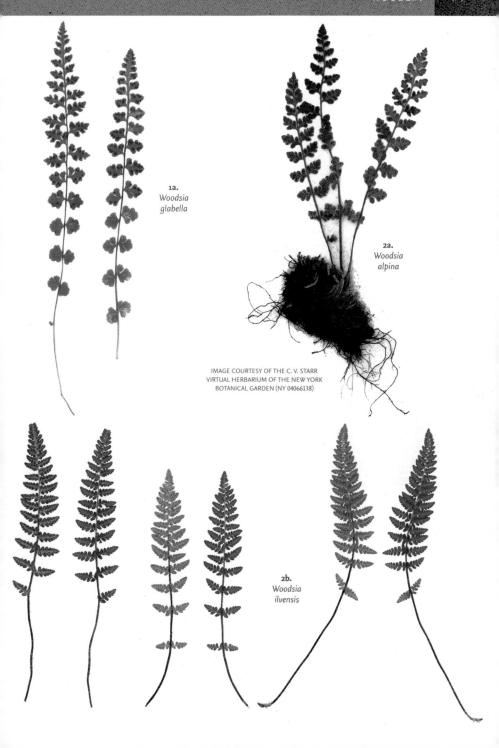

1a.
Woodsia glabella

2a.
Woodsia alpina

IMAGE COURTESY OF THE C. V. STARR
VIRTUAL HERBARIUM OF THE NEW YORK
BOTANICAL GARDEN (NY 04066138)

2b.
Woodsia ilvensis

F S C N

Woodsia alpina

COMMON NAME(S) Alpine cliff fern

STATUS Native, rare

HABITAT/DISTRIBUTION Damp, shaded ledges and crevices in cliffs, usually on calcareous rock; also occurs in western North America, Greenland, Europe, and Asia

Plants are terrestrial. **Stems** are ascending to erect, with brown scales, and usually with a cluster of persistent stipe bases from old fronds. **Leaves** are up to 20cm long, and sterile and fertile leaves do not differ in appearance. **Stipes** are reddish to purplish brown at maturity and up to ca. 4cm long, with reddish-brown scales at the base. The stipe is articulate and distinctly jointed above the base, with a swollen abscission zone where old fronds break off. The **rachis** is similar to the stipe, with scattered hairs and scales, and grooved on the upper surface. The leaf **blade** is 1-pinnate-pinnatifid, linear to lanceolate, and up to 15cm long and 2.5cm wide. The lower leaf surface has only a few scattered hairs and scales, while the upper surface is smooth. **Pinnae** are ovate to deltate, with the smallest ones nearly fan shaped and the largest ones more elongated. The pinna midveins are grooved, and this groove is continuous with the groove on the rachis. **Margins** are nearly entire or broadly, shallowly lobed. **Veins** are free and simple or forked, ending in enlarged vein tips (hydathodes). **Sori** are round and near the pinnule margins. **Indusia** are filamentous and resemble long hairs. 2n=160 (tetraploid).

A. Plants of *Woodsia alpina*.

B. Fronds.

C. Close-up of sori.

Woodsia glabella

COMMON NAME(S) Smooth cliff fern

STATUS Native, uncommon

HABITAT/DISTRIBUTION Somewhat rare, but more common in the northern part of its range. On shaded, damp cliffs and ledges, mostly on calcareous substrates; also occurs in western North America, Greenland, Europe, and Asia

Plants are terrestrial. Stems are ascending to erect, with brown scales, and usually with a cluster of persistent stipe bases from old fronds. Leaves are up to 15cm long, and sterile and fertile leaves do not differ in appearance. Stipes are green or yellowish, up to 3cm long, and have brown scales at the base. The stipe is articulate and distinctly jointed above the base, with a swollen abscission zone where old fronds break off. The rachis is similar to the stipe, smooth and without hairs or scales, and shallowly grooved. The leaf blade is 1-pinnate-pinnatifid, linear to lanceolate, and up to 12cm long and 1.2cm wide. Both surfaces are smooth and without hairs, except for a few very scattered, minute glands. Pinnae at the base of the blade are fan shaped, while pinnae farther up are more elongated. The pinna midveins are grooved, and this groove is continuous with the groove on the rachis. Margins are nearly entire or broadly, shallowly lobed. Veins are free and simple or forked, and hydathodes are present but vein tips are only slightly enlarged. Sori are round and near the pinnule margins. Indusia are filamentous and resemble long hairs. 2n=78 (diploid).

A. A plant of Woodsia glabella.

B. Fronds.

C. Lower surface of a fertile frond.

D. Lowest, fan-shaped pinnae.

Woodsia ilvensis

COMMON NAME(S) Rusty cliff fern

STATUS Native, rare

HABITAT/DISTRIBUTION Exposed or partly shaded slopes, cliffs, and ledges of various substrates (including occasionally serpentine); also occurs in western North America, Greenland, Europe, and Asia

Plants are terrestrial. Stems are ascending to erect, with brown scales, and usually with a cluster of persistent stipe bases from old fronds. Leaves are up to 25cm long, and sterile and fertile leaves do not differ in appearance. Stipes are brown to purplish at maturity, up to ca. 10cm long, and have brown scales. The stipe is articulate and distinctly jointed above the base, with a swollen abscission zone where old fronds break off. The rachis is similar to the stipe, with numerous hairs and scales, and grooved on the upper surface. The leaf blade is 2-pinnate at the base, narrowly lanceolate, and up to 20cm long and 3.5cm wide. The lower leaf surface has dense hairs and scales, while the upper surface has hairs along the pinna midveins. Pinnae are ovate lanceolate to deltate. The pinna midveins are grooved, and this groove is continuous with the groove on the rachis. Margins are nearly entire or broadly, shallowly lobed. Veins are free and simple or forked, ending in enlarged vein tips (hydathodes). Sori are round and near the pinnule margins. Indusia are filamentous and resemble long hairs. 2n=82 (diploid).

A. Plants of *Woodsia ilvensis*.

B. Upper surface of leaf.

C. Lower surface of fertile leaf.

D. Scaly stipe.

E. Close-up of sori and lower leaf surface.

CHECKLISTS OF FERN AND LYCOPHYTE SPECIES IN EASTERN NORTH AMERICA

LYCOPHYTE SPECIES IN EASTERN NORTH AMERICA (61 IN TOTAL)

SPECIES	FLORIDA (16 species)	SOUTH (31 species)	CENTRAL (43 species)	NORTH (29 species)
Dendrolycopodium dendroideum				■
Dendrolycopodium hickeyi				■
Dendrolycopodium obscurum		■		
Diphasiastrum complanatum subsp. complanatum				■
Diphasiastrum digitatum		■		
Diphasiastrum sitchense				■
Diphasiastrum tristachyum				
Huperzia appalachiana				■
Huperzia lucidula		■		
Huperzia porophila				
Huperzia selago				■
Isoetes appalachiana	■			
Isoetes boomii	■			
Isoetes butleri				
Isoetes echinospora subsp. muricata				■
Isoetes engelmannii	■			
Isoetes flaccida (including vars. flaccida and chapmanii)	■			
Isoetes georgiana				
Isoetes graniticola				
Isoetes hyemalis			■	
Isoetes junciformis				
Isoetes laurentiana				■
Isoetes louisianensis				
Isoetes macrospora				■
Isoetes mattaponica			■	
Isoetes melanopoda (including subsp. melanopoda and silvatica)			■	
Isoetes melanospora				
Isoetes microvela				
Isoetes piedmontana			■	
Isoetes prototypus				■
Isoetes riparia (including vars. reticulata and riparia)			■	

SPECIES	FLORIDA (16 species)	SOUTH (31 species)	CENTRAL (43 species)	NORTH (29 species)
Isoetes septentrionalis			■	■
Isoetes tegetiformans			■	
Isoetes tennesseensis			■	
Isoetes tuckermanii (including subsp. acadiensis and tuckermanii)				■
Isoetes valida		■	■	
Isoetes virginica		■		
Isoetes viridimontana			■	■
Lycopodiella alopecuroides	■	■	■	
Lycopodiella appressa	■	■	■	■
Lycopodiella inundata			■	■
Lycopodiella prostrata	■	■		
Lycopodiella subappressa				■
Lycopodium clavatum subsp. clavatum		■	■	■
Lycopodium lagopus			■	■
Palhinhaea cernua	■	■	■	
Pseudolycopodiella caroliniana	■	■	■	
Selaginella acanthonota	■	■		
Selaginella apoda	■	■	■	■
Selaginella arenicola	■	■		
Selaginella braunii		■	■	
Selaginella corallina		■		
Selaginella eatonii	■			
Selaginella eclipes			■	■
Selaginella ludoviciana	■	■		
Selaginella rupestris		■	■	■
Selaginella selaginoides				■
Selaginella tortipila		■	■	
Selaginella uncinata	■		■	
Selaginella willdenowii	■			
Spinulum annotinum			■	■

FERN SPECIES IN EASTERN NORTH AMERICA (244 IN TOTAL)

SPECIES	FLORIDA (129 species)	SOUTH (101 species)	CENTRAL (129 species)	NORTH (105 species)
Acrostichum aureum	●			
Acrostichum danaeifolium	●			
Actinostachys pennula	●			
Adiantum aleuticum			●	●
Adiantum anceps	●			
Adiantum capillus-veneris		●	●	
Adiantum melanoleucum	●			
Adiantum pedatum			●	●
Adiantum tenerum	●			
Adiantum viridimontanum				●
Amauropelta noveboracensis			●	●
Amauropelta resinifera	●			
Amauropelta sancta	●			
Amblovenatum opulentum	●			
Anchistea virginica				●
Anemia adiantifolia	●			
Anemia wrightii	●			
Arachniodes simplicior	●			
Argyrochosma dealbata			●	
Aspidotis densa				●
Asplenium abscissum	●			
Asplenium auritum	●			
Asplenium bradleyi			●	
Asplenium cristatum	●			
Asplenium dentatum subsp. dentatum	●			
Asplenium heterochroum	●			
Asplenium monanthes			●	
Asplenium montanum			●	●
Asplenium pinnatifidum				
Asplenium platyneuron			●	●
Asplenium plenum	●			
Asplenium pumilum	●			
Asplenium resiliens	●		●	
Asplenium rhizophyllum				●

SPECIES	FLORIDA (129 species)	SOUTH (101 species)	CENTRAL (129 species)	NORTH (105 species)
Asplenium ruta-muraria var. cryptolepis				
Asplenium scolopendrium var. americanum				
Asplenium septentrionale subsp. septentrionale				
Asplenium serratum				
Asplenium trichomanes				
Asplenium tutwilerae				
Asplenium verecundum				
Asplenium viride				
Astrolepis integerrima				
Astrolepis sinuata				
Athyrium angustum				
Athyrium asplenioides				
Athyrium niponicum				
Azolla cristata				
Azolla mexicana				
Azolla pinnata subsp. pinnata				
Blechnum appendiculatum				
Botrychium angustisegmentum				
Botrychium ascendens				
Botrychium campestre				
Botrychium crenulatum				
Botrychium gallicomontanum				
Botrychium matricariifolium				
Botrychium michiganense				
Botrychium minganense				
Botrychium mormo				
Botrychium neolunaria				
Botrychium pallidum				
Botrychium simplex var. simplex				
Botrychium spathulatum				
Botrychium tenebrosum				
Botrypus virginianus				
Campyloneurum angustifolium				
Campyloneurum costatum				

SPECIES	FLORIDA (129 species)	SOUTH (101 species)	CENTRAL (129 species)	NORTH (105 species)
Campyloneurum phyllitidis				
Ceratopteris pteridoides				
Ceratopteris richardii				
Ceratopteris thalictroides subsp. *thalictroides*				
Cheiroglossa palmata				
Christella dentata				
Christella hispidula				
Claytosmunda claytoniana				
Coryphopteris simulata				
Crepidomanes intricatum				
Cryptogramma acrostichoides				
Cryptogramma stelleri				
Ctenitis sloanei				
Ctenitis submarginalis				
Cyclosorus interruptus				
Cyrtomium falcatum subsp. *falcatum*				
Cyrtomium fortunei				
Cystopteris bulbifera				
Cystopteris fragilis				
Cystopteris laurentiana				
Cystopteris protrusa				
Cystopteris tennesseensis				
Cystopteris tenuis				
Dennstaedtia bipinnata				
Dennstaedtia punctilobula				
Deparia acrostichoides				
Deparia petersenii				
Dicranopteris flexuosa				
Didymoglossum krausii				
Didymoglossum petersii				
Didymoglossum punctatum subsp. *floridanum*				
Diplazium esculentum				
Diplazium lonchophyllum				
Dryopteris campyloptera				

SPECIES	FLORIDA (129 species)	SOUTH (101 species)	CENTRAL (129 species)	NORTH (105 species)
Dryopteris carthusiana				
Dryopteris celsa				
Dryopteris clintoniana				
Dryopteris cristata				
Dryopteris erythrosora				
Dryopteris expansa				
Dryopteris filix-mas subsp. brittonii				
Dryopteris fragrans				
Dryopteris goldiana				
Dryopteris intermedia subsp. intermedia				
Dryopteris ludoviciana				
Dryopteris marginalis				
Equisetum arvense subsp. arvense				
Equisetum fluviatile				
Equisetum hyemale subsp. affine				
Equisetum laevigatum				
Equisetum palustre				
Equisetum pratense				
Equisetum scirpoides				
Equisetum sylvaticum				
Equisetum variegatum subsp. variegatum				
Goniopteris domingensis				
Goniopteris reptans				
Goniopteris sclerophylla				
Goniopteris tetragona				
Gymnocarpium appalachianum				
Gymnocarpium continentale				
Gymnocarpium dryopteris				
Gymnocarpium robertianum				
Homalosorus pycnocarpos				
Hymenophyllum tayloriae				
Hymenophyllum tunbrigense				
Hypolepis barringtonii				
Leptogramma burksiorum				

SPECIES	FLORIDA (129 species)	SOUTH (101 species)	CENTRAL (129 species)	NORTH (105 species)
Lomariopsis kunzeana				
Lorinseria areolata				
Lygodium japonicum				
Lygodium microphyllum				
Lygodium palmatum				
Macrothelypteris torresiana				
Marsilea hirsuta				
Marsilea macropoda				
Marsilea minuta				
Marsilea mutica				
Marsilea oligospora				
Marsilea quadrifolia				
Marsilea vestita				
Matteuccia struthiopteris var. pensylvanica				
Meniscium reticulatum				
Meniscium serratum				
Microgramma heterophylla				
Microsorum grossum				
Moranopteris nimbata				
Myriopteris alabamensis				
Myriopteris gracilis				
Myriopteris lanosa				
Myriopteris microphylla				
Myriopteris rufa				
Myriopteris tomentosa				
Nephrolepis × averyi				
Nephrolepis biserrata				
Nephrolepis brownii				
Nephrolepis cordifolia				
Nephrolepis exaltata				
Nephrolepis falcata				
Nephrolepis hirsutula				
Odontosoria clavata				
Onoclea sensibilis				

SPECIES	FLORIDA (129 species)	SOUTH (101 species)	CENTRAL (129 species)	NORTH (105 species)
Ophioderma pendulum	■			
Ophioglossum crotalophoroides	■	■	■	
Ophioglossum engelmannii			■	
Ophioglossum nudicaule	■	■	■	
Ophioglossum petiolatum	■	■	■	■
Ophioglossum pusillum				■
Ophioglossum pycnostichum	■			
Osmunda spectabilis	■	■	■	■
Osmundastrum cinnamomeum subsp. *cinnamomeum*	■	■	■	■
Pecluma bourgeauana	■			
Pecluma dispersa	■			
Pecluma plumula	■			
Pelazoneuron abruptum var. *grande*	■			
Pelazoneuron augescens	■			
Pelazoneuron kunthii	■	■	■	
Pelazoneuron ovatum	■	■		
Pelazoneuron patens	■	■		
Pellaea atropurpurea		■	■	■
Pellaea glabella subsp. *glabella*			■	■
Pellaea viridis	■			
Pellaea wrightiana			■	
Phegopteris connectilis			■	■
Phegopteris excelsior			■	
Phegopteris hexagonoptera	■	■	■	■
Phegopteris taiwaniana			■	
Phlebodium aureum	■			
Physematium obtusum subsp. *obtusum*		■	■	■
Physematium oreganum subsp. *cathcartianum*				■
Physematium scopulinum subsp. *appalachianum*			■	■
Physematium scopulinum subsp. *laurentianum*				■
Pilularia americana	■	■	■	
Pityrogramma calomelanos var. *calomelanos*	■			
Pityrogramma trifoliata	■			
Platycerium bifurcatum	■			

SPECIES	FLORIDA (129 species)	SOUTH (101 species)	CENTRAL (129 species)	NORTH (105 species)
Pleopeltis michauxiana				
Pleopeltis polypodioides				
Polypodium appalachianum				
Polypodium virginianum				
Polystichum acrostichoides				
Polystichum braunii				
Polystichum lonchitis				
Psilotum nudum				
Pteridium aquilinum (including vars. latiusculum and pseudocaudatum)				
Pteridium caudatum				
Pteris bahamensis				
Pteris cretica				
Pteris multifida				
Pteris parkeri				
Pteris tripartita				
Pteris vittata				
Rumohra adiantiformis				
Salvinia minima				
Salvinia molesta				
Sceptridium biternatum				
Sceptridium dissectum				
Sceptridium jenmanii				
Sceptridium lunarioides				
Sceptridium multifidum				
Sceptridium oneidense				
Sceptridium rugulosum				
Schizaea pusilla				
Tectaria fimbriata				
Tectaria heracleifolia				
Tectaria incisa				
Telmatoblechnum serrulatum				
Thelypteris palustris				
Trichomanes holopterum				

SPECIES	FLORIDA (129 species)	SOUTH (101 species)	CENTRAL (129 species)	NORTH (105 species)
Vandenboschia boschiana				
Vittaria appalachiana				
Vittaria graminifolia				
Vittaria lineata				
Woodsia alpina				
Woodsia glabella				
Woodsia ilvensis				

ACKNOWLEDGMENTS

I am very grateful to the team at Princeton University Press, including Robert Kirk, Abigail Johnson, Megan Mendonça, Kathleen Cioffi, Laurel Anderton, and David Price-Goodfellow, for the invitation to take on this book project and for guiding me through the process.

This book would not have been possible without the extraordinary generosity of numerous people who helped me locate and visit ferns and lycophytes in the field. Some of them gave me a place to stay or joined me for short trips while others planned and organized extensive outings and spent hours to days in the field with me, searching for ferns and lycophytes. I would not have gotten anywhere (literally!) without them. For the gift of their time, support, and assistance, I am eternally grateful to (in alphabetical order): Wayne Barger, Ric Barnett, Dave Barrington, Rodney Bartgis, Rita and Eric Bauer, Mike Breiding, Tracy Cook, Stan Corwin-Roach, Alan Cressler, Stephen Dickman, Don Farrar, Kim Gaffett, Art Gilman, Emily Guinan, Chris Hoess, Jimmy Lange, Tim Lee, Malcolm and Rosemary MacFarlane, Janie Marlow, Josie Merck, Mike Owen, Jennifer Possley, Tony Reznicek, Carol Rowe, Joey Shaw, Tom Shisler, Bob Simons, Nora Steele, Keith Stokes, Kay Wade, Eddie Watkins, G. R. Welsh, Colleen Werner, Paul Wolf, and Noah Yawn. I am also especially thankful for the help of Keith Bradley, Susan Fawcett, Alan Franck, Donna Ford-Herntz, Trey Hannah, Jordan Metzgar, Janet Novak, Alan Smith, Cynthia Venuti, Alan Weakley, and Steve Woodmansee, who provided advice, information, and/or plant locality data. Special thanks to the Wahkeena Nature Preserve, Huntsville Botanical Garden, Jocassee Lake Tours, and the Bruce family in Miami for providing access to several populations of ferns.

I also benefited hugely from the generosity and collective knowledge of the iNaturalist community. I sent many, many messages to iNat users inquiring about their observations and seeking further information about species and sites, and their assistance was invaluable. Many thanks to those who responded warmly and enthusiastically to my requests for help: Patrick Alexander, Bryan Ames, Derek Anderson, Rod Belshee, Leif Boman, Brian Bowers, Joshua Copen, Brandon Corder, Josh Doby, Jared Gorrell, Robert Gundy, Asher Higgins, Howard Horne, Claire Jarvis, Mary Keim, Joseph Kurtz, Nate Martineau, Damon Moore, Christian Nunes, Evan Raskin, Alyssa Roberts, Annkatrin Rose, Ryne Rutherford, Anastasia Sallen, Josh Sands, Frank Schimkus, Jeff Sommer, MaLisa Spring, Steve Taylor, Julie Tuttle, Kurt Unger, Karen Walter, and Mathew Zappa.

Part of the fun of this project was finding species in the field to photograph, but there were a handful that I could not get to, and I am thankful to the following excellent photographers for allowing me to use their images: Keith Bradley, Dan Brunton, Brandon Corder, Alan Cressler, Nolan Exe, Don Farrar, Malcolm MacFarlane, Nate Martineau, Robbin Moran, Greg Rand, and Noah Yawn.

Particular thanks are due to Dan Brunton and Don Farrar, who allowed me to use numerous images and scans of *Isoetes* and *Botrychium*, respectively, that they have created over the decades they have worked on these genera. They both also provided extensive input on the text and range maps for those groups. Those sections of the book were enhanced immeasurably by their contributions (and any errors remaining are without question my own).

In addition to all those who helped directly with the creation of this book, I am also thankful for the support and encouragement of many friends, family, and colleagues not mentioned above. Bob Holt and Harvey Lillywhite provided early advice about this project and urged me to go for it. Tom Givnish is endlessly enthusiastic about all my endeavors; it was a fern field guide that first drew Tom to plants and ecology, and I am honored and humbled to have come full circle by producing my own field guide to these remarkable plants. The members of my lab at the University of Florida and my many new colleagues and friends at the New York Botanical Garden, where I moved partway through the project, were unflagging in their support. My #botanicalbestie, Rachel Jabaily, was a constant source of laughter and cheerleading. I thank my parents, Janis and Robert Butler, for their excitement about this project, and for a lifetime of encouragement and enthusiasm. My most profound thanks of all are for my husband, Jonathan Sessa, whose love and partnership make all my goals achievable.

FURTHER READING AND REFERENCES

GENERAL REFERENCE BOOKS

Beentje, H. J. 2016. *The Kew Plant Glossary: An Illustrated Dictionary of Plant Terms*. 2nd ed. Rickmond, UK: Royal Botanic Gardens, Kew.

Cobb, B. 2005. *Peterson Field Guide to Ferns: Northeastern and Central North America*. 2nd ed. New York: Houghton Mifflin Harcourt.

Diggs, G. M., and Lipscomb, B. L. 2014. *The Ferns and Lycophytes of Texas*. Fort Worth: Botanical Research Institute of Texas Press.

Fawcett, S., and Smith, A. R. 2021. *A Generic Classification of the Thelypteridaceae*. Fort Worth: Botanical Research Institute of Texas Press.

Flora of China Editorial Committee. 2018. *Flora of China*. Vols. 2–3: *Lycopodiaceae through Polypodiaceae*. Beijing and St. Louis: Science Press and Missouri Botanical Garden Press.

Flora of North America Editorial Committee. 1993. *Flora of North America*. Vol. 2: *Pteridophytes and Gymnosperms*. New York: Oxford University Press (also available online at http://floranorthamerica.org/Main_Page).

Haines, A. 2003. *The Families Huperziaceae and Lycopodiaceae of New England: A Taxonomic and Ecological Reference*. Bar Harbor, ME: V. F. Thomas.

Harris, J. G., and Harris, M. W. 2001. *Plant Identification Terminology: An Illustrated Glossary*. 2nd ed. Payson, UT: Spring Lake Publishing.

Mickel, J., and Smith, A. R. 2004. *The Pteridophytes of Mexico*. Bronx: New York Botanical Garden Press.

Moran, R. C. 2016. Division Polypodiopsida, Ferns. In *New Manual of Vascular Plants of Northeastern United States and Adjacent Canada*, R.F.C. Naczi et al., collaborators. Bronx: New York Botanical Garden Press.

———. 2016. Lycopodiaceae, the Clubmoss Family. In *New Manual of Vascular Plants of Northeastern United States and Adjacent Canada*, R.F.C. Naczi et al., collaborators. Bronx: New York Botanical Garden Press.

Nelson, G. 2000. *The Ferns of Florida: A Reference and Field Guide*. Sarasota, FL: Pineapple Press.

Neyland, R. 2011. *A Field Guide to the Ferns and Lycophytes of Louisiana*. Baton Rouge: Louisiana State University Press.

Palmer, D. D. 2018. *Michigan Ferns and Lycophytes: A Guide to Species of the Great Lakes Region*. Ann Arbor: University of Michigan Press.

Proctor, G. R. 1989. *Ferns of Puerto Rico and the Virgin Islands*. Bronx: New York Botanical Garden Press.

Short, J. W., and Spaulding, D. D. 2012. *Ferns of Alabama*. Tuscaloosa: University of Alabama Press.

Stearn, W. T. 2004. *Botanical Latin*. 4th ed. Portland, OR: Timber Press.

Weakley, A. S. 2022. *Flora of the Southeastern United States*. Chapel Hill: University of North Carolina at Chapel Hill.

Wunderlin, R. P., and Hansen, B. F. 2000. *Flora of Florida*. Vol. 1: *Pteridophytes and Gymnosperms*. Gainesville: University Press of Florida.

———. 2011. *Guide to the Vascular Plants of Florida*. 3rd ed. Gainesville: University Press of Florida.

SCIENTIFIC PAPERS

Assis, F. C., and Zimmer, B. 2014. Notes concerning the nomenclature of *Polypodium ptiloton* and its correct spelling in *Pecluma*. *Taxon* 63(3): 641–642.

Barger, T. W., Cressler, A., Holt, B. D., and Medley, M. 2010. *Asplenium abscissum* Willd. (cutleaf spleenwort) in Alabama. *American Fern Journal* 100(1): 54–57.

Barrington, D. S. 1986. The morphology and cytology of *Polystichum* × *potteri* hybr. nov. (=*P. acrostichoides* × *P. braunii*). *Rhodora* 88(855): 297–313.

Benedict, R. C. 1934. Can anyone readily distinguish the northern and southern lady fern species? *American Fern Journal* 24(4): 117–119.

Bradley, K. A. 2006. *Thelypteris sancta* (L.) Ching, new for Florida and the continental United States. *American Fern Journal* 96(4): 112–114.

Dauphin, B., Grant, J. R., Farrar, D. R., and Rothfels, C. J. 2018. Rapid allopolyploid radiation of moonwort ferns (*Botrychium*; Ophioglossaceae) revealed by PacBio sequencing of homologous and homeologous nuclear regions. *Molecular Phylogenetics and Evolution* 120: 342–353.

De Gasper, A. L., Dittrich, V. A. D. O., Smith, A. R., and Salino, A. 2016. A classification for Blechnaceae (Polypodiales: Polypodiopsida): New genera, resurrected names, and combinations. *Phytotaxa* 275(3): 191–227.

Dubuisson, J. Y., Hennequin, S., Douzery, E. J., Cranfill, R. B., Smith, A. R., and Pryer, K. M. 2003. rbcL phylogeny of the fern genus *Trichomanes* (Hymenophyllaceae), with special reference to Neotropical taxa. *International Journal of Plant Sciences* 164(5): 753–761.

Ebihara, A., Dubuisson, J. Y., Iwatsuki, K., Hennequin, S., and Ito, M. 2006. A taxonomic revision of Hymenophyllaceae. *Blumea– Biodiversity, Evolution and Biogeography of Plants* 51(2): 221–280.

Ebihara, A., Iwatsuki, K., Ito, M., Hennequin, S., and Dubuisson, J. Y. 2007. A global molecular phylogeny of the fern genus *Trichomanes* (Hymenophyllaceae) with special reference to stem anatomy. *Botanical Journal of the Linnean Society* 155(1): 1–27.

Evrard, C., and Van Hove, C. 2004. Taxonomy of the American *Azolla* species (Azollaceae): A critical review. *Systematics and Geography of Plants* 74(2): 301–318.

Florez-Parra, S., and Keener, B. R. 2016. *Phegopteris decursive-pinnata* (Thelypteridaceae), new to the Alabama (USA) flora. *Journal of the Botanical Research Institute of Texas* 10(2): 501–503.

Fujiwara, T., Ogiso, J., Ishii, S., Togo, K., Nakato, N., Serizawa, S., Chao, Y.-S., Im, H.-T., Ebihara, A., and Watano, Y. 2021. Species delimitation in the *Phegopteris decursive-pinnata* polyploid species complex (Thelypteridaceae). *Acta Phytotaxonomica et Geobotanica* 72(3): 205–226.

Gilman, A. V. 2015. Use of gemma characters to identify North American *Huperzia* (Lycopodiaceae). *American Fern Journal* 105(3): 145–161.

Grusz, A. L., and Windham, M. D. 2013. Toward a monophyletic *Cheilanthes*: The resurrection and recircumscription of *Myriopteris* (Pteridaceae). *PhytoKeys* 32: 49–64.

Hauk, W. D., Parks, C. R., and Chase, M. W. 2003. Phylogenetic studies of Ophioglossaceae: Evidence from rbcL and trnL-F plastid DNA sequences and morphology. *Molecular Phylogenetics and Evolution* 28(1): 131–151.

Hirai, R. Y., and Prado, J. 2012. Monograph of *Moranopteris* (Polypodiaceae). *Pteridologia* 4: 1–113.

Hirai, R. Y., Rouhan, G., Labiak, P. H., Ranker, T. A., and Prado, J. 2011. *Moranopteris*: A new Neotropical genus of grammitid ferns (Polypodiaceae) segregated from Asian *Micropolypodium*. *Taxon* 60(4): 1123–1137.

Jacono, C. C., and Johnson, D. M. 2006. Water-clover ferns, *Marsilea*, in the southeastern United States. *Castanea* 71(1): 1–14.

Keener, B. R., and Davenport, L. J. 2007. A new name for the well-known *Asplenium* (Aspleniaceae) from Hale County, Alabama. *Journal of the Botanical Research Institute of Texas* 1(1): 103–108.

Kinosian, S. P., Pearse, W. D., and Wolf, P. G. 2020. Cryptic diversity in the model fern genus *Ceratopteris* (Pteridaceae). *Molecular Phylogenetics and Evolution* 152: 106938.

Lange, J. J., and Angelo, C. L. 2020. *Goniopteris moranii* (syn.: *Thelypteris guadalupensis*; Thelypteridaceae), new to Florida and the continental United States. *American Fern Journal* 110(2): 75–78.

Lu, N. T., Zhou, X. M., Zhang, L., Knapp, R., Li, C. X., Fan, X. P., Zhou, L., Wei, H. J., Lu, J. M., Xu, B., and Peng, Y. L. 2019. A global plastid phylogeny of the cliff fern family Woodsiaceae and a two-genus classification of Woodsiaceae with the description of ×Woodsimatium nothogen. nov. *Taxon* 68(6): 1149–1172.

Metzgar, J. S., Schneider, H., and Pryer, K. M. 2007. Phylogeny and divergence time estimates for the fern genus *Azolla* (Salviniaceae). *International Journal of Plant Sciences* 168(7): 1045–1053.

Montgomery, J. D. 1982. *Dryopteris* in North America. Part II: The hybrids. *Fiddlehead Forum* 9(4): 23–30.

Moran, R. C. 2000. Monograph of the Neotropical species of *Lomariopsis* (Lomariopsidaceae). *Brittonia* 52(1): 55–111.

Nagalingum, N. S., Schneider, H., and Pryer, K. M. 2006. Comparative morphology of reproductive structures in heterosporous water ferns and a reevaluation of the sporocarp. *International Journal of Plant Sciences* 167(4): 805–815.

Patel, N. R., Fawcett, S., and Gilman, A. V. 2019. *Phegopteris excelsior* (Thelypteridaceae): A new species of North American tetraploid beech fern. *Novon: A Journal for Botanical Nomenclature* 27(4): 211–218.

Pemberton, R. W. 2003. The common staghorn fern, *Platycerium bifurcatum*, naturalizes in southern Florida. *American Fern Journal* 93(4): 203–206.

Pinson, J. B., Chambers, S. M., Nitta, J. H., Kuo, L. Y., and Sessa, E. B. 2017. The separation of generations: Biology and biogeography of long-lived sporophyteless fern gametophytes. *International Journal of Plant Sciences* 178(1): 1–18.

Pinson, J. B., Chambers, S. M., and Sessa, E. B. 2017. *Vittaria graminifolia* (Pteridaceae) and *Didymoglossum petersii* (Hymenophyllaceae) in Broxton Rocks, GA. *American Fern Journal* 107(4): 257–264.

Possley, J., and Howell, P. L. 2015. Misidentification of "*Microsorum scolopendria*" in South Florida. *American Fern Journal* 105(2): 127–130.

Pteridophyte Phylogeny Group (PPG) I. 2016. A community-derived classification for extant lycophytes and ferns. *Journal of Systematics and Evolution* 54(6): 563–603.

Rothfels, C. J., Johnson, A. K., Windham, M. D., and Pryer, K. M. 2014. Low-copy nuclear data confirm rampant allopolyploidy in the Cystopteridaceae (Polypodiales). *Taxon* 63(5): 1026–1036.

Schwartsburd, P. B. 2018. Eight new taxa of *Hypolepis* (Dennstaedtiaceae) from the Neotropics. *American Fern Journal* 108(4): 151–169.

Schwartsburd, P. B., Perrie, L. R., Brownsey, P., Shepherd, L. D., Shang, H., Barrington, D. S., and Sundue, M. A. 2020. New insights into the evolution of the fern family Dennstaedtiaceae from an expanded molecular phylogeny and morphological analysis. *Molecular Phylogenetics and Evolution* 150: 106881.

Sessa, E. B., Zimmer, E. A., and Givnish, T. J. 2012. Unraveling reticulate evolution in North American *Dryopteris* (Dryopteridaceae). *BMC Evolutionary Biology* 12: 104.

Sleep, A. 2014. Hybridization in *Polystichum* (Dryopteridaceae: Pteridophyta). *Fern Gazette* 19(8): 319–341.

Smith, A. R., Kreier, H. P., Haufler, C. H., Ranker, T. A., and Schneider, H. 2006. *Serpocaulon* (Polypodiaceae), a new genus segregated from *Polypodium*. *Taxon* 55(4): 919–930.

Smith, A. R., and Tejero-Díez, J. D. 2014. *Pleopeltis* (Polypodiaceae), a redefinition of the genus and nomenclatural novelties. *Botanical Science* 92: 43–58.

Stensvold, M. C., and Farrar, D. R. 2017. Genetic diversity in the worldwide *Botrychium lunaria* (Ophioglossaceae) complex, with new species and new combinations. *Brittonia* 69(2): 148–175.

Sundue, M. A., and Rothfels, C. J. 2014. Stasis and convergence characterize morphological evolution in eupolypod II ferns. *Annals of Botany* 113(1): 35–54.

Tejero-Díez, J. D., and Torres-Díaz, A. N. 2012. *Phymatosorus grossus* (Polypodiaceae) in Mexico and comments on other non-native pteridobionts. *Acta botánica mexicana* 98(98): 111–124.

Triana-Moreno, L. A. 2011. Novedades en *Pecluma* (Polypodiaceae). *Brittonia* 63(1): 62–65.

Triana-Moreno, L. A., Yañez, A., Kuo, L.-Y., Rothfels, C. J., Pena, N. T. L., Schwartsburd, P. B., and Sundue, M. 2022. Phylogenetic revision of Dennstaedtioideae (Dennstaedtiaceae: Polypodiales) with description of *Mucura*, gen. nov. *Taxon* 72(1): 20–46.

Wagner, W. H., Jr., and Nauman, C. E. 1982. *Pteris × delchampsii*, a spontaneous fern hybrid from southern Florida. *American Fern Journal* 72(4): 97–102.

Wagner, W. H., Jr., Wagner, F. S., Miller, C. N., Jr., and Wagner, D. H. 1978. New observations on the royal fern hybrid *Osmunda × ruggii*. *Rhodora* 80(821): 92–106.

Wagner, W. H., Jr., Wagner, F. S., Reznicek, A. A., and Werth, C. R. 1992. *×Dryostichum singulare* (Dryopteridaceae), a new fern nothogenus from Ontario. *Canadian Journal of Botany* 70: 245–253.

Watkins, J. E., and Farrar, D. R. 2002. A new name for an old fern from north Alabama. *American Fern Journal* 92(2): 171–178.

Xu, K. W., Zhang, L., Rothfels, C. J., Smith, A. R., Viane, R., Lorence, D., Wood, K. R., Chen, C.-W., Knapp, R., Zhou, L., Lu, N. T., Zhou, X.-M., Wei, H.-J., Fan, Q., Chen, S.-F., Cicuzza, D., Gao, X.-F., Liao, W.-B., and Zhang, L.-B. 2020. A global plastid phylogeny of the fern genus *Asplenium* (Aspleniaceae). *Cladistics* 36(1): 22–71.

WEB-BASED RESOURCES

Biota of North America Program: http://bonap.org

Canadensys: https://www.canadensys.net

Cornell University Plant Anatomy Collection: http://cupac.bh.cornell.edu

C. V. Starr Virtual Herbarium at the New York Botanical Garden: http://sweetgum.nybg.org/science/vh/

Flora of North America: http://floranorthamerica.org/Main_Page

Global Biodiversity Information Facility: https://www.gbif.org

iNaturalist: https://www.inaturalist.org

Institute for Regional Conservation: https://www.regionalconservation.org/index.html

Integrated Digitized Biocollections (iDigBio): https://www.idigbio.org

Lady Bird Johnson Wildflower Center Plant Database: https://www.wildflower.org/plants/

Michigan Flora: https://michiganflora.net/ferns

Minnesota Department of Natural Resources Rare Species Guide: https://www.dnr.state.mn.us/rsg/index.html

Minnesota Wildflowers: https://www.minnesotawildflowers.info

NameThatPlant.net: http://www.namethatplant.net

Plant Atlas collection of websites: https://plantatlas.usf.edu

Pteridophyte Collections Consortium: https://pteridoportal.org/

World Ferns: https://www.worldplants.de/world-ferns/ferns-and-lycophytes-list

ISOETES IMAGE CREDITS

ISOETES APPALACHIANA
SOURCE: D. M. Britton, University of Guelph, Guelph, ON (1993); Specimen: Huntingdon County, PA; D. F. Brunton & K. L. McIntosh 11171, 6 July 1992 (OAC)

ISOETES BOOMII
SOURCE: D. M. Britton, OAC (1999); Specimen: Clay County, FL; D. F. Brunton & K. L. McIntosh 13997, 31 March 1999 (OAC)

ISOETES BUTLERI
SOURCE: D. M. Britton, University of Guelph, Guelph, ON (1999); Specimen: Rutherford County, TN; D. F. Brunton & K. L. McIntosh 10331, 22 May 1991 (OAC)

ISOETES ECHINOSPORA SUBSP. MURICATA
SOURCE: D. M. Britton, University of Guelph, Guelph, ON (1999); Specimen: Parry Sound District, ON; D. M. Britton 9523, August 1988 (OAC)

ISOETES ENGELMANNII
SOURCE: P. Sokoloff & D. F. Brunton, Canadian Museum of Nature, Ottawa, ON (2018–2023); Specimens: (left) D. F. Brunton & K. L. McIntosh 14184, Gloucester County, VA (DFB); (right) G. Engelmann s.n., September 1842, Jefferson County, MO (P–Isotype)

ISOETES FLACCIDA VAR. CHAPMANII
SOURCE: D. M. Britton, University of Guelph, Guelph, ON (1994); Specimen: R. K. Godfrey 61963, 19 May 1962, Jackson County, FL (VDB)

ISOETES FLACCIDA VAR. FLACCIDA
SOURCE: D. M. Britton, University of Guelph, Guelph, ON (1997); Specimen: Hernando County, FL, R. Kral & M. Kral 6625, 5 June 1958 (FSU)

ISOETES GEORGIANA
SOURCE: D. M. Britton, University of Guelph, Guelph, ON (left: 1993; right: 1994); Specimens: (left) D. F. Brunton & K. L. McIntosh 11550, 7 July 1993, Worth County, GA, (OAC); (right) R. Kral 80949, 19 June 1992, Turner County, GA (VDB)

ISOETES GRANITICOLA
SOURCES: D. M. Britton, University of Guelph, Guelph, ON (1993); Specimen: D. F. Brunton & K. L. McIntosh 11394, 19 March 1993, Randolph County, AL (OAC)

ISOETES HYEMALIS
SOURCES: (left) P. Sokoloff & D. F. Brunton, Canadian Museum of Nature, Ottawa, ON (2018); (right) D. M. Britton, University of Guelph, Guelph, ON (1994); SPECIMENS: (left) D. F. Brunton & K. L. McIntosh 11165, 4 July 1992, Harnett County, NC (DFB); (right) R. Kral 65983, 17 July 1980, Southampton County, VA (VDB)

ISOETES JUNCIFORMIS
SOURCE: D. M. Britton, University of Guelph, Guelph, ON (1995); Specimen: D. F. Brunton & W. J. Crins 11848, 3 May 1994, Tift County, GA (DFB)

ISOETES LAURENTIANA
SOURCE: P. Sokoloff & D. F. Brunton, Canadian Museum of Nature, Ottawa, ON (left: 2019; right: 2018); Specimen: D. F. Brunton & K. L. McIntosh 20092, 20 August 2018 (DFB), Communaute de Québec, QU (DFB)

ISOETES LOUISIANENSIS
SOURCE: D. M. Britton, University of Guelph, Guelph, ON (1993); Specimen: G. Landry, s.n., 21 April 1972, Washington County, LA (MICH)

ISOETES MACROSPORA
SOURCE: P. Sokoloff & D. F. Brunton, Canadian Museum of Nature, Ottawa, ON (2023); Specimen: D. F. Brunton & K. L. McIntosh 13364, 16 August 1997, Pontiac County, QC (DFB)

ISOETES MATTAPONICA
SOURCE: D. M. Britton, University of Guelph, Guelph, ON (1999); Specimen: C. Caplen 96-06, 25 June 1996, New Kent County, VA (OAC)

ISOETES MELANOPODA SUBSP. MELANOPODA
SOURCE: D. M. Britton, University of Guelph, Guelph, ON (1994); Specimen: E. Hall s.n., July 1863, Menard County, IL (NY)

ISOETES MELANOPODA SUBSP. SILVATICA
SOURCE: D. M. Britton, University of Guelph, Guelph, ON (1993); Specimen: J. F. Matthews s.n., 7 May 1993, Mecklenburg County, NC (OAC)

ISOETES MELANOSPORA
SOURCE: D. M. Britton, University of Guelph, Guelph, ON (left: 1994; right: 1990); Specimens: same site, DeKalb County, GA; (left) W. D. Burbanck and F. H. Bormann s.n., 19 April 1956 (GA); (right) D. F. Brunton & K. L. McIntosh 9559, 15 April 1990 (OAC)

ISOETES MICROVELA
SOURCE: D. M. Britton, University of Guelph, Guelph, ON (1990); Specimen: D. F. Brunton & K. L. McIntosh 12213, 23 June 1995, Onslow County, NC (OAC)

ISOETES PIEDMONTANA
SOURCE: D. M. Britton, University of Guelph, Guelph, ON (1994); Specimens: same site, Columbia County, GA; (left) J. H. Pyron and R. McVaugh 1776, 23 May 1937 (GA); (right) R. Kral 57557, 10 April 1976 (VDB)

ISOETES PROTOTYPUS
SOURCE: D. M. Britton, University of Guelph, Guelph, ON (1988); Specimen: D. M. Britton 11910A, 26 September 1988, York County, NB (OAC)

ISOETES RIPARIA VAR. RETICULATA
SOURCE: D. M. Britton, University of Guelph, Guelph, ON (1998); Specimens: both Fairfax County, VA; (left) G. Vasey & F. V. Coville s.n., 22 July 1888 (US); (right) G. H. Shull 252, 22 August 1902 (US)

ISOETES RIPARIA VAR. RIPARIA
SOURCE: D. M. Britton, University of Guelph, Guelph, ON (1997); Specimen: D. F. Brunton, K. L. McIntosh & C. Caplan 13388, 21 August 1997, King William County, VA (OAC)

ISOETES SEPTENTRIONALIS
SOURCE: P. Sokoloff & D. F. Brunton, Canadian Museum of Nature, Ottawa, ON (2023); Specimen: D. F. Brunton 13646, 28 July 1998, Ottawa, ON (DFB–Isotype)

ISOETES TEGETIFORMANS
SOURCE: D. M. Britton, University of Guelph, Guelph, ON (1990); Specimen: D. F. Brunton & K. L. McIntosh 9617, 19 April 1990, Columbia County, GA (OAC)

ISOETES TENNESSEENSIS
SOURCE: D. M. Britton, University of Guelph, Guelph, ON (1994); Specimen: B. E. Wofford 85-55, 1 August 1985, Polk County, TN (VDB)

ISOETES TUCKERMANII SUBSP. ACADIENSIS
SOURCE: D. M. Britton, University of Guelph, Guelph, ON (1984); Specimen: M. L. Fernald, B. Long & D.H. Linder 19626, 4 September 1920, Yarmouth County, NS (NSPM)

ISOETES TUCKERMANII SUBSP. TUCKERMANII
SOURCE: P. Sokoloff & D. F. Brunton, Canadian Museum of Nature, Ottawa, ON (2023); Specimens: (left) D. F. Brunton & K. L. McIntosh 11354, 20 September 1992, Androscoggin County, ME (DFB); (right) D. F. Brunton & K. L. McIntosh 15248, Avalon Peninsula, NL (DFB)

ISOETES VALIDA
SOURCE: P. Sokoloff & D. F. Brunton, Canadian Museum of Nature, Ottawa, ON (2018); Specimen: T. Porter s.n., October 1866, Lancaster County, PA (P)

ISOETES VIRGINICA
SOURCE: D. M. Britton, University of Guelph, Guelph, ON (1994); Specimen: L. W. Carr s.n., 13 June 1936, Augusta County, VA (PH)

ISOETES VIRIDIMONTANA
SOURCE: P. Sokoloff & D. F. Brunton, Canadian Museum of Nature, Ottawa, ON (2018); Specimen: D. F. Brunton, K. L. McIntosh & M. Rosenthal 20065, 4 August 2018 (DFB)

INDEX TO SCIENTIFIC NAMES

Bold italics currently accepted species names
Italics: synonyms of species names
Page numbers in bold: the main entry for that genus or species

A

Acrostichum 36, **114–117**, 345
  Acrostichum aureum 114, 115, **116**, 493
  Acrostichum danaeifolium 114, 115, **117**, 493
Actinostachys 34, **118–119**, 467
  Actinostachys pennula 118, **119**, 467, 493
Adiantum 10, 37, **120–129**
  Adiantum aleuticum 122, **123**, 493
  Adiantum anceps 121, **124**, 493
  Adiantum capillus-veneris 121, **125**, 493
  Adiantum caudatum 10
  Adiantum hispidulum 10
  Adiantum melanoleucum 121, **126**, 493
  Adiantum pedatum 122, **127**, 493
  Adiantum tenerum 121, 122, **128**, 493
  Adiantum trapeziforme 10
  Adiantum villosum 10
  Adiantum viridimontanum 122, **129**, 493
Amauropelta 25, 39, **130–133**, 230, 475
  Amauropelta noveboracensis 130, **131**, 230, 493
  Amauropelta resinifera 130, **132**, 493
  Amauropelta sancta 25, 130, **133**, 493
Amblovenatum 40, **134–135**, 475
  Amblovenatum opulentum 134, **135**, 493
Amphineuron 135
  Amphineuron opulentum (***Amblovenatum opulentum***)
  135
Anchistea 37, **136–137**, 191, 326
  Anchistea virginica 136, **137**, 326, 493
Anemia 34, 35, 36, **138–141**
  Anemia adiantifolia 138, 139, **140**, 493
  Anemia wrightii 36, 138, 139, **141**, 493
Anemiaceae 11, 138
Anisocampium 186
  Anisocampium niponicum (***Athyrium niponicum***) 186
Arachniodes 23, 40, **142–143**
  Arachniodes simplicior 23, 142, **143**, 493

Argyrochosma 37, **144**, 402
  Argyrochosma dealbata **144**, 493
Aspidotis 37, **145**
  Aspidotis densa **145**, 493
Aspleniaceae 11, 146, 315
Asplenium 12, 25, 34, 37, **146–179**
  Asplenium × alternifolium 147, 148, 152, 153
  Asplenium × biscayneanum 147, 148, 155
  Asplenium × boydstoniae 147
  Asplenium × clermontae 147
  Asplenium × curtissii 147, 148, 155, 156
  Asplenium × ebenoides 147, 148, 150, 151
  Asplenium × gravesii 147, 148, 151
  Asplenium × herbwagneri 147
  Asplenium × heteroresiliens 147, 148, 153, 155
  Asplenium × inexpectatum 147
  Asplenium × kentuckiense 147, 149, 151
  Asplenium × morganii 147
  Asplenium × shawneense 147
  Asplenium × trudellii 147, 149, 151
  Asplenium × virginicum 147
  Asplenium × wherryi 147
  Asplenium abscissum 147, 152, 153, **158**, 493
  Asplenium auritum 25, 152, 153, **159**, 493
  Asplenium bradleyi 147, 150, 151, **160**, 493
  Asplenium cristatum 155, 157, **161**, 493
  Asplenium dentatum* subsp. *barbadense 162
  Asplenium dentatum* subsp. *dentatum 147, 152, 153,
    162, 493
  Asplenium erosum (***Asplenium erosum***) 159
  Asplenium heterochroum 147, 153, 154, **163**, 493
  Asplenium monanthes 153, 154, **164**, 493
  Asplenium montanum 147, 155, 156, **165**, 493
  Asplenium nidus 175
  Asplenium pinnatifidum 147, 150, 151, **166**, 493
  Asplenium platyneuron 147, 152, 153, **167**, 493
  Asplenium plenum 147, 155, 157, **168**, 493

Asplenium pumilum 151, **169**, 493

Asplenium quadrivalens (*Asplenium trichomanes* subsp. quadrivalens) 176

Asplenium resiliens 147, 153, 154, **170**, 493

Asplenium rhizophyllum 34, 147, 149, 150, **171**, 493

Asplenium ruta-muraria var. cryptolepis 147, 155, **172**, 494

Asplenium scolopendrium var. americanum 34, 149, 150, **173**, 494

Asplenium septentrionale subsp. caucasicum 174

Asplenium septentrionale subsp. rehmanii 174

Asplenium septentrionale subsp. septentrionale 34, 147, 149, 150, **174**, 494

Asplenium serratum 34, 149, **175**, 494

Asplenium trichomanes 147, 153, 154, **176**, 494

Asplenium trichomanes subsp. quadrivalens 176

Asplenium trichomanes subsp. trichomanes 176

Asplenium trichomanes-dentatum (*Asplenium dentatum* subsp. dentatum) 162

Asplenium trichomanes-ramosum (*Asplenium viride*) 179

Asplenium tutwilerae 147, 150, 151, **177**, 494

Asplenium verecundum 147, 155, 157, **178**, 494

Asplenium viride 153, **179**, 494

Astrolepis 37, **180–182**

Astrolepis cochisensis 180

Astrolepis integerrima 180, **181**, 494

Astrolepis sinuata 180, **182**, 494

Athyriaceae 11, 183, 257, 266, 315

Athyrium 10, 37, 146, **183–186**

Athyrium angustum 183, **184**, 494

Athyrium americanum 10

Athyrium asplenioides 183, **185**, 494

Athyrium filix-femina 184, 185

Athyrium filix-femina var. angustum (**Athyrium angustum**) 184

Athyrium filix-femina var. asplenioides (**Athyrium asplenioides**) 185

Athyrium niponicum 183, **186**, 494

Azolla 32, **187–190**, 219, 335, 421, 455

Azolla caroliniana (**Azolla cristata**) 189

Azolla cristata 187, 188, **189**, 494

Azolla filiculoides 187

Azolla mexicana 187, **189**, 494

Azolla microphylla (**Azolla mexicana**) 189

Azolla pinnata subsp. africana 190

Azolla pinnata subsp. asiatica 190

Azolla pinnata subsp. pinnata 187, **190**, 494

B

Blechnaceae 11, 136, 191, 326, 473

Blechnum 37, **191–192**, 473, 474

Blechnum appendiculatum 191, **192**, 473, 494

Blechnum occidentale var. minus (**Blechnum appendiculatum**) 192

Blechnum serrulatum (**Telmatoblechnum serrulatum**) 474

Botrychium 10, 35, **193–212**, 213, 214, 377, 458, 460, 461, 462, 463, 464, 465, 466, 501

Botrychium acuminatum (**Botrychium matricariifolium**) 204

Botrychium angustisegmentum 194, 195, **199**, 494

Botrychium ascendens 194, 198, **200**, 494

Botrychium biternatum (**Sceptridium biternatum**) 460

Botrychium campestre 194, 196, **201**, 494

Botrychium crenulatum 194, 196, 197, **202**, 494

Botrychium cuneatum (**Sceptridium dissectum**) 461

Botrychium dissectum (**Sceptridium dissectum**) 461

Botrychium farrarii 194

Botrychium gallicomontanum 194, 196, 197, **203**, 494

Botrychium jenmanii (**Sceptridium jenmanii**) 462

Botrychium lanceolatum subsp. angustisegmentum (**Botrychium angustisegmentum**) 199

Botrychium lunaria (**Botrychium neolunaria**) 208

Botrychium lunaria var. crenulatum (**Botrychium crenulatum**) 202

Botrychium lunaria var. matricariifolium (**Botrychium matricariifolium**) 204

Botrychium lunaria var. minganense (**Botrychium minganense**) 206

Botrychium lunarioides (**Sceptridium lunarioides**) 463

Botrychium matricariifolium 194, 195, **204**, 494

Botrychium michiganense 194, 195, **205**, 494

Botrychium minganense 194, 197, 198, **206**, 494

Botrychium mormo 194, 195, **207**, 494

Botrychium multifidum (**Sceptridium multifidum**) 464

Botrychium neolunaria 194, 196, 197, **208**, 494

Botrychium oneidense (**Sceptridium oneidense**) 465

Botrychium pallidum 193, 194, 195, 197, **209**, 494

Botrychium rugulosum (**Sceptridium rugulosum**) 466

Botrychium simplex var. *compositum* 210

Botrychium simplex var. *simplex* 194, 195, **210**, 494

Botrychium simplex var. *tenebrosum* (**Botrychium tenebrosum**) 212

Botrychium spathulatum 194, 198, **211**, 494

Botrychium tenebrosum **212**, 494

Botrychium virginianum (**Botrypus virginianus**) 214

Botrypus 23, 35, 193, **213–214**, 458

Botrypus virginianus 23, 193, 213, **214**, 494

Bryodesma 94, 98, 100, 102, 106, 108

Bryodesma acanthonota (**Selaginella acanthonota**) 98

Bryodesma arenicola subsp. *acanthonota* (**Selaginella acanthonota**) 98

Bryodesma arenicola (**Selaginella arenicola**) 100

Bryodesma arenicola subsp. *riddellii* (**Selaginella corallina**) 102

Bryodesma rupestre (**Selaginella rupestris**) 106

Bryodesma tortipilum (**Selaginella tortipila**) 108

C

Campyloneurum 34, **215–218**

Campyloneurum angustifolium 215, **216**, 494

Campyloneurum costatum 215, **217**, 494

Campyloneurum phyllitidis 215, **218**, 495

Ceratopteris 32, **219–222**, 234, 421

Ceratopteris pteridoides 219, **220**, 495

Ceratopteris richardii 219, **221**, 495

Ceratopteris thalictroides subsp. *thalictroides* 219, **222**, 495

Cheilanthes 181, 182, 353, 355, 356, 357, 358, 359, 360, 406

Cheilanthes alabamensis (**Myriopteris alabamensis**) 355

Cheilanthes eatonii (**Myriopteris rufa**) 359

Cheilanthes feei (**Myriopteris gracilis**) 356

Cheilanthes integerrima (**Astrolepis integerrima**) 181

Cheilanthes lanosa (**Myriopteris lanosa**) 357

Cheilanthes microphylla (**Myriopteris microphylla**) 358

Cheilanthes sinuata (**Astrolepis sinuata**) 182

Cheilanthes tomentosa (**Myriopteris tomentosa**) 360

Cheilanthes viridis (**Pellaea viridis**) 406

Cheiroglossa 35, 193, **223–224**, 375

Cheiroglossa palmata 223, **224**, 375, 495

Christella 39, **225–227**, 395, 475

Christella dentata 225, **226**, 495

Christella hispidula 225, **227**, 495

Christella hispidula var. *versicolor* 227

Cibotiaceae 11

Claytosmunda 36, **228–229**, 386, 388

Claytosmunda claytoniana 386, 388, 228, **229**, 495

Coryphopteris 39, **230–231**, 475

Coryphopteris simulata 230, **231**, 495

Crepidomanes 26, 32, **232–233**, 317, 477, 479, 481

Crepidomanes intricatum 26, 232, **233**, 481, 495

Cryptogramma 35, **234–236**

Cryptogramma acrostichoides 234, **235**, 495

Cryptogramma stelleri 234, **236**, 495

Ctenitis 39, **237–239**

Ctenitis sloanei 39, 237, **238**, 495

Ctenitis submarginalis 39, 237, **239**, 495

Culcitaceae 11

Cyatheaceae 11

Cyclosorus 40, **240–241**, 475

Cyclosorus interruptus 240, **241**, 495

×*Cystocarpium* 245, 309

×*Cystocarpium roskamianum* 245, 309

Cystodiaceae 11

Cyrtomium 23, 25, 40, **242–244**

Cyrtomium falcatum subsp. *australe* 243

Cyrtomium falcatum subsp. *falcatum* 23, 25, 242, **243**, 495

Cyrtomium falcatum subsp. *littorale* 243

Cyrtomium fortunei 242, **244**, 495

Cystopteridaceae 11, 245

Cystopteris 26, 38, **245–253**, 309

Cystopteris × *illinoensis* 245

Cystopteris × *wagneri* 245

Cystopteris bulbifera 245, 246, 247, **248**, 495
Cystopteris fragilis 245, 246, 247, **249**, 309, 495
Cystopteris "*hemifragilis*" 245
Cystopteris laurentiana 245, 246, 247, **250**, 495
Cystopteris protrusa 245, 246, 247, **251**, 495
Cystopteris reevesiana 245
Cystopteris tennesseensis 26, 245, 246, 247, **252**, 495
Cystopteris tenuis 245, 246, 247, **253**, 495

D

Davalliaceae 11
Dendrolycopodium 33, **42–46**, 86, 111
Dendrolycopodium dendroideum 42, 43, **44**, 491
Dendrolycopodium hickeyi 42, 43, **45**, 491
Dendrolycopodium obscurum 42, 43, **46**, 491
Dennstaedtia 36, **254–256**
Dennstaedtia bipinnata 254, **255**, 495
Dennstaedtia punctilobula 254, **256**, 495
Dennstaedtiaceae 11, 254, 320, 442
Deparia 38, 146, **257–259**
Deparia acrostichoides 257, **258**, 495
Deparia petersenii 257, **259**, 495
Desmophlebiaceae 11
Dicksoniaceae 11
Dicranopteris 34, **260–261**
Dicranopteris flexuosa 260, **261**, 495
Didymochlaenaceae 11
Didymoglossum 12, 14, 34, **262–265**, 317, 477, 479
Didymoglossum krausii 262, **263**, 495
Didymoglossum lineolatum 12
Didymoglossum membranaceum 12
Didymoglossum petersii 262, **264**, 495
Didymoglossum punctatum subsp. *floridanum* 262, **265**, 495
Diphasiastrum 10, 18, 33, **47–52**
Diphasiastrum × *habereri* 47
Diphasiastrum × *sabinifolium* 47
Diphasiastrum × *verecundum* 47
Diphasiastrum × *zeilleri* 47
Diphasiastrum alpinum 10
Diphasiastrum complanatum subsp. *complanatum* 47, 48, **49**, 491
Diphasiastrum complanatum subsp. *montellii* 49

Diphasiastrum digitatum 18, 47, 48, **50**, 491
Diphasiastrum sitchense 47, 48, **51**, 491
Diphasiastrum tristachyum 47, 48, **52**, 491
Diplaziopsidaceae 11, 315
Diplaziopsis 316
Diplaziopsis pycnocarpos (**Homalosorus pycnocarpos**) 316
Diplazium 38, 146, **266–268**, 315, 316
Diplazium esculentum 38, 266, **267**, 495
Diplazium lonchophyllum 38, 266, **268**, 495
Diplazium pycnocarpon (**Homalosorus pycnocarpos**) 315, 316
Dipteridaceae 11
Dryopteridaceae 11, 142, 237, 242, 269, 435, 453
Dryopteris 12, 23, 36, 40, **269–288**, 435
Dryopteris × *algonquinensis* 270
Dryopteris × *australis* 269, 270, 271
Dryopteris × *benedictii* 270
Dryopteris × *boottii* 269, 270, 271, 274
Dryopteris × *brathaica* 270
Dryopteris × *burgessii* 270
Dryopteris × *correllii* 270
Dryopteris × *dowellii* 270
Dryopteris × *leedsii* 270, 271
Dryopteris × *mickelii* 270
Dryopteris × *montgomereyi* 270
Dryopteris × *neowherryi* 270, 271
Dryopteris × *pittsfordensis* 271
Dryopteris × *separabilis* 271
Dryopteris × *slossoniae* 271
Dryopteris × *triploidea* 269, 271, 272
Dryopteris × *uliginosa* 269, 271
Dryopteris campyloptera 270, 272, 273, **276**, 495
Dryopteris carthusiana 269, 270, 272, 273, **277**, 496
Dryopteris celsa 270, 274, 275, **278**, 496
Dryopteris clintoniana 36, 269, 270, 274, 275, **279**, 496
Dryopteris cristata 23, 36, 269, 270, 274, **280**, 496
Dryopteris erythrosora 274, 275, **281**, 496
Dryopteris expansa 270, 272, 273, **282**, 496
Dryopteris filix-mas subsp. *brittonii* 270, 272, 274, **283**, 496
Dryopteris filix-mas subsp. *filix-mas* 283

Dryopteris fragrans 269, 270, 272, 273, **284**, 496
Dryopteris goldiana 269, 270, 274, 275, **285**, 435, 496
Dryopteris goldieana (**Dryopteris goldiana**) 285
Dryopteris intermedia subsp. *azorica* 286
Dryopteris intermedia subsp. *intermedia* 269, 270, 272, 273, **286**, 496
Dryopteris intermedia subsp. *maderensis* 286
Dryopteris ludoviciana 36, 269, 270, 272, 274, **287**, 496
Dryopteris marginalis 269, 270, 272, 273, **288**, 496
Dryopteris "semicristata" 270
×*Dryostichum* 269, 435
×*Dryostichum singulare* 269, 435

E

Equisetaceae 11, 289
Equisetum 7, 8, 10, 22, 25, 31, 32, **289–302**
Equisetum × *ferrissii* 289
Equisetum × *litorale* 289
Equisetum × *nelsonii* 289
Equisetum × *trachyodon* 289
Equisetum arvense subsp. *arvense* 289, 290, 291, 292, **294**, 496
Equisetum fluviatile 8, 289, 290, 291, 292, **295**, 496
Equisetum hyemale subsp. *affine* 289, 290, 291, **296**, 496
Equisetum hyemale subsp. *hyemale* 296
Equisetum laevigatum 289, 290, 293, **297**, 496
Equisetum palustre 290, 291, **298**, 496
Equisetum pratense 290, 291, 292, **299**, 496
Equisetum ramosissimum 10
Equisetum scirpoides 290, 291, 293, **300**, 496
Equisetum sylvaticum 290, 291, 292, **301**, 496
Equisetum variegatum subsp. *alaskanum* 302
Equisetum variegatum subsp. *variegatum* 289, 290, 291, 293, **302**, 496

G

Gleicheniaceae 11, 260
Goniopteris 39, **303–308**, 475
Goniopteris domingensis 303, 304, **305**, 496
Goniopteris reptans 303, 304, **306**, 496
Goniopteris sclerophylla 303, 304, **307**, 496

Goniopteris tetragona 303, 304, **308**, 496
Grammitis 352
Grammitis nimbata (**Moranopteris nimbata**) 352
Gymnocarpium 38, 245, **309–314**
Gymnocarpium × *achriosporum* 309
Gymnocarpium × *brittonianum* 309
Gymnocarpium × *heterosporum* 309
Gymnocarpium × *intermedium* 309
Gymnocarpium appalachianum 309, 310, **311**, 496
Gymnocarpium continentale 309, 310, **312**, 496
Gymnocarpium disjunctum 309
Gymnocarpium dryopteris 309, 310, **313**, 496
Gymnocarpium jessoense subsp. *parvulum* (**Gymnocarpium continentale**) 312
Gymnocarpium robertianum 309, 310, **314**, 496

H

Hemidictyaceae 11
Holubiella 463
Holubiella lunarioides (**Sceptridium lunarioides**) 463
Homalosorus 38, 146, **315–316**
Homalosorus pycnocarpos 315, **316**, 496
Huperzia 10, 16, 17, 18, 33, **53–58**, 111
Huperzia × *bartleyi* 53
Huperzia × *buttersii* 53
Huperzia × *josephbeitelii* 53
Huperzia × *protoporophila* 53
Huperzia appalachiana 53, 54, **55**, 491
Huperzia appressa (**Huperzia appalachiana**) 55
Huperzia lucidula 18, 53, 54, **56**, 491
Huperzia miyoshiana 10
Huperzia porophila 17, 53, 54, **57**, 491
Huperzia selago 53, 54, **58**, 491
Huperzia selago subsp. *appressa* (**Huperzia appalachiana**) 55
Hymenophyllaceae 11, 232, 262, 317, 477, 479
Hymenophyllum 25, 34, 232, **317–319**, 477, 479
Hymenophyllum tayloriae 232, 317, **318**, 496
Hymenophyllum tunbrigense 317, **319**, 496
Hypodematiaceae 11
Hypolepis 36, 254, **320–321**
Hypolepis barringtonii 254, 320, **321**, 496
Hypolepis repens (**Hypolepis barringtonii**) 320, 321

I

Isoetaceae 7, 8, 11, 16, 20, 59
Isoetes 8, 10, 12, 20, 21, 32, **59–78**, 501
  Isoetes × *altonharvillii* 60
  Isoetes × *brittonii* 60
  Isoetes × *bruntonii* 60
  Isoetes × *carltaylorii* 60
  Isoetes × *eatonii* 60
  Isoetes × *echtuckeri* 60i
  Isoetes × *fairbrothersii* 60
  Isoetes × *fernaldii* 60
  Isoetes × *foveolata* 60
  Isoetes × *harveyi* 60
  Isoetes × *hickeyi* 60
  Isoetes × *jeffreyi* 60
  Isoetes × *kareniae* 60
  Isoetes × *robusta* 60
  Isoetes appalachiana 60, 64, **65**, 491
  Isoetes boomii 60, 63, **65**, 491
  Isoetes butleri 20, 21, 60, 62, **66**, 491
  Isoetes caroliniana (*Isoetes valida*) 77
  Isoetes echinospora subsp. *echinospora* 66
  Isoetes echinospora subsp. *muricata* 21, 60, 63, **66**, 491
  Isoetes engelmannii 8, 21, 60, 64, 65, **67**, 491
  Isoetes engelmannii var. *georgiana* (*Isoetes appalachiana*) 65
  Isoetes flaccida 20, 21, 60, 63, **67**, 491
  Isoetes flaccida var. *chapmanii* **67**, 491
  Isoetes flaccida var. *flaccida* **67**, 491
  Isoetes georgiana 20, 21, 60, 63, **68**, 491
  Isoetes graniticola 63, **68**, 491
  Isoetes hyemalis 60, 64, **69**, 491
  Isoetes junciformis 62, **69**, 491
  Isoetes lacustris (*Isoetes macrospora*) 71
  Isoetes laurentiana 64, **70**, 491
  Isoetes louisianensis 64, **70**, 491
  Isoetes macrospora 60, 63, **71**, 76, 491
  Isoetes mattaponica 60, 63, **71**, 491
  Isoetes melanopoda 21, 62, **72**, 491
  Isoetes melanopoda subsp. *melanopoda* **72**, 491
  Isoetes melanopoda subsp. *silvatica* 21, **72**, 491
  Isoetes melanospora 62, **72**, 491

  Isoetes microvela 60, 64, **73**, 491
  Isoetes piedmontana 62, 68, **73**, 491
  Isoetes prototypus 63, **74**, 75, 491
  Isoetes riparia 60, 64, **74**, 75, 491
  Isoetes riparia var. *reticulata* **74**, 75, 491
  Isoetes riparia var. *riparia* **74**, 75, 491
  Isoetes saccharata (*Isoetes riparia*) 74
  Isoetes septentrionalis 60, 64, **75**, 492
  Isoetes tegetiformans 21, 62, **75**, 492
  Isoetes tennesseensis 63, **76**, 492
  Isoetes tuckermanii 21, 60, 64, 70, **76**, 77, 492
  Isoetes tuckermanii subsp. *acadiensis* **76**, 77, 492
  Isoetes tuckermanii subsp. *tuckermanii* 21, **76**, 77, 492
  Isoetes valida 60, 63, **77**, 492
  Isoetes virginica 62, 73, **78**, 492
  Isoetes virginica var. *piedmontana* (*Isoetes piedmontana*) 73
  Isoetes viridimontana 63, **78**, 492

L

Leptogramma 39, **322–323**, 475
  Leptogramma burksiorum 322, **323**, 496
Lindsaeaceae 11, 371
Lomariopsidaceae 11, 324
Lomariopsis 34, 36, 232, **324–325**
  Lomariopsis kunzeana 232, 324, **325**, 497
Lonchitidaceae 11
Lorinseria 35, 191, **326–327**
  Lorinseria areolata 326, **327**, 497
Loxsomataceae 11
Lycopodiaceae 7, 8, 11, 16, 17, 18, 42, 47, 53, 79, 86, 90, 92, 111
Lycopodiella 8, 33, **79–85**, 90, 91, 92, 93, 468
  Lycopodiella × *brucei* 79
  Lycopodiella × *copelandii* 79
  Lycopodiella × *gilmanii* 79
  Lycopodiella × *robusta* 79
  Lycopodiella alopecuroides 79, 80, **81**, 468, 492
  Lycopodiella appressa 79, 80, **82**, 492
  Lycopodiella caroliniana (*Pseudolycopodiella caroliniana*) 93
  Lycopodiella cernua (*Palhinhaea cernua*) 91

Lycopodiella inundata 8, 79, 80, **83**, 492

Lycopodiella margueritae 79

Lycopodiella prostrata 79, 80, **84**, 492

Lycopodiella subappressa 79, 80, **85**, 492

Lycopodioides 94, 97, 99, 101, 103, 104, 105, 109, 110

Lycopodioides apodum (*Selaginella apoda*) 99

Lycopodioides braunii (*Selaginella braunii*) 101

Lycopodioides eatonii (*Selaginella eatonii*) 103

Lycopodioides eclipes (*Selaginella eclipes*) 104

Lycopodioides ludovicianum (*Selaginella ludoviciana*) 105

Lycopodioides uncinatum (*Selaginella uncinata*) 109

Lycopodioides willdenowii (*Selaginella willdenowii*) 110

Lycopodium 16, 17, 33, 42, 44, 45, 46, 49, 50, 51, 52, 55, 56, 57, 58, 79, 81, 82, 83, 84, **86–89**, 93, 111, 112

Lycopodium alopecuroides (*Lycopodiella alopecuroides*) 81

Lycopodium annotinum (*Spinulum annotinum*) 112

Lycopodium appressum (*Lycopodiella appressa*) 82

Lycopodium carolinianum (*Pseudolycopodiella caroliniana*) 93

Lycopodium clavatum subsp. clavatum 17, 86, 87, **88**, 492

Lycopodium clavatum subsp. contiguum 88

Lycopodium complanatum (*Diphasiastrum complanatum subsp. complanatum*) 49

Lycopodium dendroideum (*Dendrolycopodium dendroideum*) 44

Lycopodium digitatum (*Diphasiastrum digitatum*) 50

Lycopodium hickeyi (*Dendrolycopodium hickeyi*) 45

Lycopodium inundatum (*Lycopodiella inundata*) 83

Lycopodium inundatum var. *appressum* (*Lycopodiella appressa*) 82

Lycopodium lagopus 86, 87, **89**, 492

Lycopodium lucidulum (*Huperzia lucidula*) 56

Lycopodium obscurum (*Dendrolycopodium obscurum*) 46

Lycopodium porophilum (*Huperzia porophila*) 57

Lycopodium prostratum (*Lycopodiella prostrata*) 84

Lycopodium selago (*Huperzia selago*) 58

Lycopodium selago subsp. *appressum* (*Huperzia appalachiana*) 55

Lycopodium sitchense (*Diphasiastrum sitchense*) 51

Lycopodium tristachyum (*Diphasiastrum tristachyum*) 52

Lygodiaceae 11, 328

Lygodium 34, **328–332**, 348

Lygodium japonicum 328, 329, **330**, 497

Lygodium microphyllum 328, 329, **331**, 497

Lygodium palmatum 328, 329, **332**, 497

M

Macrothelypteris 38, 39, 237, **333–334**

Macrothelypteris torresiana 333, **334**, 497

Marattiaceae 11

Marsilea 28, 31, 32, 187, 219, **335–342**, 421, 455

Marsilea hirsuta 335, 336, **337**, 497

Marsilea macropoda 335, 336, **337**, 497

Marsilea minuta 335, **338**, 497

Marsilea mutica 335, 336, **339**, 497

Marsilea oligospora 335, 336, **340**, 497

Marsilea quadrifolia 335, 336, **340**, 497

Marsilea vestita 335, **342**, 497

Marsileaceae 11, 187, 335, 421, 455

Matoniaceae 11

Matteuccia 35, **343–344**, 388

Matteuccia pensylvanica (**Matteuccia struthiopteris var. pensylvanica**) 344

Matteuccia struthiopteris var. pensylvanica 343, **344**, 388, 497

Matteuccia struthiopteris var. struthiopteris 344

Maxonia 12

Maxonia apiifolila var. apiifolia 12

Meniscium 25, 39, **345–347**, 475

Meniscium reticulatum 25, 345, **346**, 497

Meniscium serratum 345, **347**, 497

Metaxyaceae 11

Microgramma 34, 215, **348–349**

Microgramma heterophylla 348, **349**, 497

Micropolypodium 352

Micropolypodium nimbatum (**Moranopteris nimbata**) 352

Microsorum 39, **350–351**, 414

Microsorum grossum 350, **351**, 414, 497

Microsorum scolopendria (***Microsorum grossum***) 351

Moranopteris 38, 215, 232, **352**

Moranopteris nimbata 232, **352**, 497

Mucura 255

Mucura bipinnata (***Dennstaedtia bipinnata***) 255

Myriopteris 37, **353–360**

Myriopteris alabamensis 353, 354, **355**, 497

Myriopteris gracilis 353, 354, **356**, 497

Myriopteris lanosa 353, 354, **357**, 497

Myriopteris microphylla 353, 354, **358**, 497

Myriopteris rufa 353, 354, **359**, 497

Myriopteris tomentosa 353, 354, **360**, 497

N

Nephrolepidaceae 11

Nephrolepis 40, **361–370**

Nephrolepis × averyi 361, 362, 363, **364**, 497

Nephrolepis biserrata 362, 363, 364, **365**, 497

Nephrolepis brownii 361, 362, **366**, 497

Nephrolepis cordifolia 361, 362, 363, **367**, 497

Nephrolepis exaltata 361, 362, 363, 364, **368**, 497

Nephrolepis falcata 362, **369**, 497

Nephrolepis hirsutula 362, **370**, 497

Nephrolepis multiflora (***Nephrolepis brownii***) 366

Notholaena 181, 182

Notholaena integerrima (***Astrolepis integerrima***) 181

Notholaena sinuata (***Astrolepis sinuata***) 182

O

Odontosoria 36, **371–372**, 440

Odontosoria clavata 371, **372**, 440, 497

Oleandraceae 11

Onoclea 35, 343, **373–374**

Onoclea sensibilis 343, 373, **374**, 497

Onocleaceae 11, 343, 373

Ophioderma 35, 193, 223, 224, **375–376**

Ophioderma palmatum (***Cheiroglossa palmata***) 224

Ophioderma pendulum 223, 375, **376**, 498

Ophioglossaceae 11, 25, 31, 34, 193, 213, 223, 375, 377, 458

Ophioglossum 33, 34, 35, 193, 223, 224, 376, **377–385**, 458

Ophioglossum crotalophoroides 378, 379, **380**, 498

Ophioglossum engelmannii 378, 379, **381**, 498

Ophioglossum nudicaule 378, 379, **382**, 498

Ophioglossum palmatum (***Cheiroglossa palmata***) 224

Ophioglossum pendulum (***Ophioderma pendulum***) 376

Ophioglossum petiolatum 378, 379, **383**, 498

Ophioglossum pusillum 378, 379, **384**, 498

Ophioglossum pycnostichum 378, 379, **385**, 498

Ophioglossum reticulatum (***Ophioglossum petiolatum***) 383

Ophioglossum vulgatum (***Ophioglossum pycnostichum***) 385

Ophioglossum vulgatum var. *pycnostichum* (***Ophioglossum pycnostichum***) 385

Oreopteris 10

Oreopteris quelpartensis 10

Osmunda 36, 228, 229, **386–387**, 388, 389

Osmunda × ruggii (**×Osmunimunda ruggii**) 228, 386

Osmunda cinnamomea (***Osmundastrum cinnamomeum* subsp. *cinnamomeum***) 389

Osmunda claytoniana (***Claytosmunda claytoniana***) 229

Osmunda regalis (***Osmunda spectabilis***) 386, 387

Osmunda regalis var. *spectabilis* (***Osmunda spectabilis***) 387

Osmunda spectabilis 228, 386, **387**, 498

Osmundaceae 11, 228, 386, 388

Osmundastrum 35, 228, 229, 386, **388–389**

Osmundastrum cinnamomeum* subsp. *asiaticum 389

Osmundastrum cinnamomeum* subsp. *cinnamomeum 228, 229, 386, 388, **389**, 498

×*Osmunimunda* 228, 336

×*Osmunimunda ruggii* 228, 336

P

Palhinhaea 33, **90–91**

Palhinhaea cernua 90, **91**, 492

Parathelypteris 131, 231

Parathelypteris noveboracensis (***Amauropelta noveboracensis***) 131

Parathelypteris simulata (***Coryphopteris simulata***) 231

Pecluma 8, 23, 39, **390–394**
  Pecluma bourgeauana 390, 391, **392**, 498
  Pecluma dispersa 8, 390, 391, **393**, 498
  Pecluma plumula 23, 390, 391, **394**, 498
  Pecluma ptilodon var. *caespitosa* (*Pecluma*
    bourgeauana) 392
  Pecluma ptilota var. *bourgeauana* (*Pecluma*
    bourgeauana) 392
  Pecluma ptilota var. *caespitosa* (*Pecluma*
    bourgeauana) 392
  Pecluma ptilotos var. *bourgeauana* (*Pecluma*
    bourgeauana) 392
Pelazoneuron 23, 40, **395–401**, 475
  Pelazoneuron abruptum var. *grande* 395, 396, **397**,
    498
  Pelazoneuron abruptum var. *pallescens* 397
  Pelazoneuron augescens 395, 396, **398**, 498
  Pelazoneuron kunthii 23, 395, 396, **399**, 498
  Pelazoneuron ovatum 395, 396, **400**, 498
  Pelazoneuron patens 395, **401**, 498
Pellaea 37, 144, **402–407**
  Pellaea atropurpurea 402, 403, **404**, 498
  Pellaea glabella subsp. *glabella* 402, 403, **405**, 498
  Pellaea viridis 402, 403, **406**, 498
  Pellaea wrightiana 402, 403, **407**, 498
Phegopteris 39, **408–413**
  Phegopteris connectilis 408, 409, **410**, 498
  Phegopteris excelsior 408, 409, **411**, 498
  Phegopteris hexagonoptera 408, 409, **412**, 498
  Phegopteris taiwaniana 408, 409, **413**, 498
Phlebodium 38, 215, 350, **414–415**
  Phlebodium aureum 350, 414, **415**, 498
Phlegmariurus 12
  Phlegmariurus dichotomous 12
Phyllitis 173
  Phyllitis scolopendrium var. *americanum* (*Asplenium*
    scolopendrium var. *americanum*) 173
Phymatosorus 351
  Phymatosorus grossus (*Microsorum grossum*) 351
Physematium 38, **416–420**, 486
  Physematium × *maxonii* 416
  Physematium obtusum subsp. *obtusum* 416, **417**,
    498

Physematium oreganum 416, 418
  Physematium oreganum subsp. *cathcartianum* 416,
    418, 486, 498
  Physematium scopulinum subsp. *appalachianum*
    416, **419**, 498
  Physematium scopulinum subsp. *laurentianum* 416,
    420, 498
Pilularia 32, 187, 219, 335, **421–422**, 455
  Pilularia americana 421, **422**, 498
Pityrogramma 36, **423–426**
  Pityrogramma calomelanos var. *calomelanos* 423,
    424, **425**, 498
  Pityrogramma trifoliata 423, 424, **426**, 498
Plagiogyriaceae 11
Platycerium 25, 36, **427–428**
  Platycerium bifurcatum 25, 427, **428**, 498
Pleopeltis 12, 22, 38, **429–431**, 432
  Pleopeltis astrolepis 12
  Pleopeltis marginata 12
  Pleopeltis michauxiana 22, 429, **430**, 432, 499
  Pleopeltis polypodioides 429, **431**, 499
  Pleopeltis polypodioides var. *michauxiana* (*Pleopeltis*
    michauxiana) 430
Polypodiaceae 11, 215, 348, 350, 352, 390, 414, 427,
  429, 432
Polypodium 12, 38, 351, 392, 429, 430, 431, **432–434**
  Polypodium × *incognitum* 432
  Polypodium appalachianum 432, **433**, 499
  Polypodium aureum (*Phlebodium aureum*) 415
  Polypodium grossum (*Microsorum grossum*) 351
  Polypodium polypodioides (*Pleopeltis polypodioides*)
    431
  Polypodium polypodioides var. *michauxianum*
    (*Pleopeltis michauxiana*) 430
  Polypodium ptilodon (*Pecluma ptilodon* var.
    bourgeauana) 392
  Polypodium triseriale (*Serpocaulon triseriale*) 12
  Polypodium virginianum 432, **434**, 499
Polystichum 10, 36, 40, 269, **435–439**
  Polystichum × *potteri* 435, 436
  Polystichum × *hagenahii* 435
  Polystichum × *meyeri* 435
  Polystichum acrostichoides 36, 435, 436, **437**, 499

Polystichum braunii 435, 436, **438**, 499
Polystichum lonchitis 269, 435, 436, **439**, 499
Polystichum scopulinum 10
Pseudolycopodiella 33, **92–93**
Pseudolycopodiella caroliniana 92, **93**, 492
Psilotaceae 11, 440
Psilotum 7, 8, 25, 32, 371, **440–441**
Psilotum nudum 7, 8, 25, 371, 440, **441**, 499
Pteridaceae 11, 114, 120, 144, 145, 180, 219, 234, 353,
    402, 423, 445, 481
Pteridium 22, 25, 37, **442–444**
Pteridium aquilinum 22, 442, **443**, 499
Pteridium aquilinum var. *caudatum* (***Pteridium***
    caudatum) 444
Pteridium aquilinum var. *latiusculum* 442, **443**, 499
Pteridium aquilinum var. *pseudocaudatum* 442, **443**,
    499
Pteridium caudatum 25, 442, **444**, 499
Pteris 10, 25, 37, **445–452**
Pteris × *delchampsii* 445
Pteris bahamensis 445, 446, **447**, 499
Pteris cretica 445, 446, **448**, 499
Pteris cretica var. *albolineata* (***Pteris parkeri***) 450
Pteris grandifolia 10
Pteris multifida 445, 446, **449**, 499
Pteris parkeri 445, 446, **450**, 499
Pteris plumula 10
Pteris quadriaurita 10
Pteris tripartita 445, 446, **451**, 499
Pteris vittata 25, 445, 446, **452**, 499

R
Regnellidium 187, 335, 455
Rhachidosoraceae 11
Rumohra 40, **453–454**
Rumohra adiantiformis 453, **454**, 499

S
Saccolomataceae 11
Salvinia 32, 187, 219, 335, 421, **455–457**
Salvinia minima 455, **456**, 499
Salvinia molesta 455, **457**, 499
Salvinia rotundifolia (***Salvinia minima***) 456

Salviniaceae 11, 187, 455
Sceptridium 25, 35, 193, 213, **458–466**
Sceptridium biternatum 458, 459, **460**, 499
Sceptridium dissectum 25, 458, 459, **461**, 499
Sceptridium jenmanii 458, 459, **462**, 499
Sceptridium lunarioides 458, 459, **463**, 499
Sceptridium multifidum 458, 459, **464**, 499
Sceptridium oneidense 458, 459, **465**, 499
Sceptridium rugulosum 458, 459, **466**, 499
Schizaea 34, 118, **467–468**
Schizaea pusilla 118, 467, **468**, 499
Schizaeaceae 11, 118, 467
Selaginella 8, 10, 19, 30, 33, **94–110**
Selaginella acanthonota 19, 95, 97, **98**, 492
Selaginella apoda 96, 97, **99**, 492
Selaginella apoda var. *ludoviciana* (***Selaginella***
    ludoviciana) 105
Selaginella arenicola 95, 97, **100**, 492
Selaginella arenicola subsp. *riddellii* (***Selaginella***
    corallina) 102
Selaginella arenicola var. *riddellii* (***Selaginella***
    corallina) 102
Selaginella armata var. *eatonii* (***Selaginella eatonii***)
    103
Selaginella braunii 96, 97, **101**, 492
Selaginella corallina 95, 97, **102**, 492
Selaginella eatonii 97, **103**, 492
Selaginella eclipes 96, 97, **104**, 492
Selaginella kraussiana 10
Selaginella ludoviciana 96, 97, **105**, 492
Selaginella rupestris 8, 94, 95, **106**, 492
Selaginella selaginoides 94, 95, **107**, 492
Selaginella tortipila 94, 95, **108**, 492
Selaginella uncinata 19, 96, 97, **109**, 492
Selaginella willdenowii 19, 96, 97, **110**, 492
Selaginellaceae 7, 8, 11, 16, 18, 19, 94
Serpocaulon 12
Serpocaulon triseriale 12
Sitobolium 256
Sitobolium punctilobulum (***Dennstaedtia***
    punctilobula) 256
Sphenomeris 372
Sphenomeris clavata (***Odontosoria clavata***) 372

Spinulum 17, 33, 53, 86, **111–112**
  Spinulum annotinum 17, 111, **112**, 492
  Spinulum canadense 111
Stegnogramma 323
  Stegnogramma burksiorum (**Leptogramma burksiorum**) 323
Stenochlaena 10
  Stenochlaena tenuifolia 10

T

Tectaria 12, 40, **469–472**
  Tectaria coriandrifolia 12
  Tectaria fimbriata 469, **470**, 499
  Tectaria heracleifolia 469, **471**, 499
  Tectaria incisa 469, **472**, 499
Tectariaceae 11, 469
Telmatoblechnum 37, 191, **473–474**
  Telmatoblechnum serrulatum 191, 473, **474**, 499
Thelypteridaceae 11, 130, 134, 225, 230, 240, 303, 322, 333, 345, 395, 408, 475
Thelypteris 39, 130, 131, 132, 133, 134, 135, 225, 226, 227, 230, 231, 240, 241, 303, 305, 306, 307, 308, 322, 323, 345, 346, 347, 395, 397, 398, 399, 400, 401, **475–476**
  Thelypteris augescens (**Pelazoneuron augescens**) 398
  Thelypteris dentata (**Christella dentata**) 226
  Thelypteris grandis var. grandis (**Pelazoneuron abruptum var. grande**) 397
  Thelypteris guadalupensis (**Goniopteris domingensis**) 305
  Thelypteris hispidula var. versicolor (**Christella hispidula**) 227
  Thelypteris interrupta (**Cyclosorus interruptus**) 241
  Thelypteris kunthii (**Pelazoneuron kunthii**) 399
  Thelypteris noveboracensis (**Amauropelta noveboracensis**) 131
  Thelypteris opulenta (**Amblovenatum opulentum**) 135
  Thelypteris ovata (**Pelazoneuron ovatum**) 400
  Thelypteris palustris 230, 475, **476**, 499
  Thelypteris patens var. patens (**Pelazoneuron patens**) 401
  Thelypteris pilosa var. alabamensis (**Leptogramma burksiorum**) 323

Thelypteris reptans (**Goniopteris reptans**) 306
Thelypteris resinifera (**Amauropelta resinifera**) 132
Thelypteris reticulata (**Meniscium reticulatum**) 346
Thelypteris sancta (**Amauropelta sancta**) 133
Thelypteris sclerophylla (**Goniopteris sclerophylla**) 307
Thelypteris serrata (**Meniscium serratum**) 347
Thelypteris simulata (**Coryphopteris simulata**) 231
Thelypteris tetragona (**Goniopteris tetragona**) 308
Thyrsopteridaceae 11
Trichomanes 12, 34, 233, 262, 263, 264, 265, 317, **477–478**, 479, 480
  Trichomanes boschianum (**Vandenboschia boschiana**) 479, 480
  Trichomanes holopterum 477, **478**, 499
  Trichomanes intricatum (**Crepidomanes intricatum**) 233
  Trichomanes krausii (**Didymoglossum krausii**) 263
  Trichomanes lineolatum (**Didymoglossum lineolatum**) 12
  Trichomanes membranaceum (**Didymoglossum membranaceum**) 12
  Trichomanes petersii (**Didymoglossum petersii**) 264
  Trichomanes punctatum subsp. floridanum (**Didymoglossum punctatum subsp. floridanum**) 265

V

Vandenboschia 34, 317, 477, **479–480**
  Vandenboschia boschiana 479, **480**, 500
Vittaria 26, 32, 33, 232, 376, **481–485**
  Vittaria appalachiana 26, 32, 232, 481, 482, **483**, 500
  Vittaria graminifolia 481, 482, **484**, 500
  Vittaria lineata 376, 481, 482, **485**, 500

W

Woodsia 38, 416, 417, 418, 419, 420, **486–490**
  Woodsia × abbeae (×**Woodsimatium abbeae**) 486
  Woodsia × gracilis 486
  Woodsia × maxonii (**Physematium × maxonii**) 416, 486
  Woodsia × tryonis 486

Woodsia alpina 486, 487, **488**, 500

Woodsia appalachiana (**Physematium scopulinum**

subsp. appalachianum) 419

Woodsia glabella 486, 487, **489**, 500

Woodsia ilvensis 416, 486, 487, **490**, 500

Woodsia obtusa subsp. obtusa (**Physematium**

obtusum subsp. obtusum) 417

Woodsia oregana subsp. cathcartiana (**Physematium**

oreganum subsp. cathcartianum) 418

Woodsia scopulina subsp. appalachiana

(**Physematium scopulinum subsp. appalachianum**)

419

Woodsia scopulina subsp. laurentiana (**Physematium**

scopulinum subsp. laurentianum) 420

Woodsiaceae 11, 416, 486

×Woodsimatium 416, 486

×Woodsimatium abbeae 416, 486

Woodwardia 136, 137, 326, 327

Woodwardia areolata (**Lorinseria areolata**) 327

Woodwardia virginica (**Anchistea virginica**) 136, 137

INDEX TO COMMON NAMES

A note on common names: Because there are no rules governing the creation or application of common names, they can be extremely confusing, and are not nearly as useful or precise as the Latin binomials that are the "official" names for species. Multiple species can share the same common name, and individual species often have multiple common names, as the index below shows. Especially misleading are the common names for species that reference what were historically assumed to be their relationships or generic affinities, when those species are recognized today as belonging to a different group. For example, the two species of *Deparia* in our flora, *D. acrostichoides* and *D. petersenii*, each have a common name that includes the term "spleenwort". This is a relic of their historical inclusion in *Asplenium*, the genus commonly called the spleenworts. While both of these species are now recognized as belonging to the genus *Deparia*, their old common names persist.

A

Adder's-tongue

Bulbous adder's-tongue (*Ophioglossum crotalophoroides*) 380

Limestone adder's-tongue (*Ophioglossum engelmannii*) 381

Northern adder's-tongue (*Ophioglossum pusillum*) 384

Old World adder's-tongue (*Ophioderma pendulum*) 376

Slender adder's-tongue (*Ophioglossum nudicaule*) 382

Southern adder's-tongue (*Ophioglossum pycnostichum*) 385

Stalked adder's-tongue (*Ophioglossum petiolatum*) 383

Alabama streak-sorus fern (*Leptogramma burksiorum*) 323

American bird's-nest fern (*Asplenium serratum*) 175

American hart's-tongue fern (*Asplenium scolopendrium* var. *americanum*) 173

American pillwort (*Pilularia americana*) 422

American royal fern (*Osmunda spectabilis*) 387

Appalachian gametophyte (*Vittaria appalachiana*) 483

Autumn fern (*Dryopteris erythrosora*) 281

B

Bear's foot fern (*Phlebodium aureum*) 415

Beech fern

Broad beech fern (*Phegopteris hexagonoptera*) 412

Narrow beech fern (*Phegopteris connectilis*) 410

Northern beech fern (*Phegopteris connectilis*) 410

Southern beech fern (*Phegopteris hexagonoptera*) 412

Taiwanese beech fern (*Phegopteris taiwaniana*) 413

Tall beech fern (*Phegopteris excelsior*) 411

Tetraploid beech fern (*Phegopteris excelsior*) 411

Bipinnate cuplet fern (*Dennstaedtia bipinnata*) 255

Bladder fern

Brittle bladder fern (*Cystopteris fragilis*) 249

Bulblet bladder fern (*Cystopteris bulbifera*) 248

Illinois bladderfern (*Cystopteris* × *illinoensis*) 245

Laurentian bladder fern (*Cystopteris laurentiana*) 250

Lowland bladder fern (*Cystopteris protrusa*) 251

Southern bladder fern (*Cystopteris protrusa*) 251

St. Lawrence bladder fern (*Cystopteris laurentiana*) 250

Tennessee bladder fern (*Cystopteris tennesseensis*) 252

Upland brittle bladder fern (*Cystopteris tenuis*) 253

Wagner's bladderfern (*Cystopteris* × *wagneri*) 245

Bog fern (*Coryphopteris simulata*) 231

Bracken

Bracken (*Pteridium aquilinum*) 443

Bracken fern (*Pteridium aquilinum*) 443

Eastern bracken (*Pteridium aquilinum*) 443

Lacy bracken (*Pteridium caudatum*) 444

Southern bracken (*Pteridium caudatum*) 444

Brake/brake fern
Bahama ladder brake (*Pteris bahamensis*) 447
Chinese ladder brake (*Pteris vittata*) 452
Cretan brake (*Pteris cretica*) 448
Delchamps' ladder brake (*Pteris × delchampsii*) 445
Giant brake (*Pteris tripartita*) 451
Spider brake (*Pteris multifida*) 449
White-lined Cretan brake (*Pteris parkeri*) 450
Bristle fern
Appalachian bristle fern (*Vandenboschia boschiana*) 480
Dwarf bristle fern (*Didymoglossum petersii*) 264
Entire-winged bristle fern (*Trichomanes holopterum*) 478
Florida bristle fern (*Didymoglossum punctatum* subsp. *floridanum*) 265
Kraus's bristle fern (*Didymoglossum krausii*) 263
Peters' bristle fern (*Didymoglossum petersii*) 264
Treemoss bristle fern (*Didymoglossum krausii*) 263
Brittle fern (*Cystopteris fragilis*) 249

C

C-Fern (*Ceratopteris richardii*) 221
Christmas fern (*Polystichum acrostichoides*) 437
Cinnamon fern (*Osmundastrum cinnamomeum* subsp. *cinnamomeum*) 389
Cliff brake
Green cliff brake (*Pellaea viridis*) 406
Purple-stem cliff brake (*Pellaea atropurpurea*) 404
Slender cliff brake (*Cryptogramma stelleri*) 236
Smooth cliff brake (*Pellaea glabella* subsp. *glabella*) 405
Wright's cliff brake (*Pellaea wrightiana*) 407
Cliff fern
Alpine cliff fern (*Woodsia alpina*) 488
Appalachian cliff fern (*Physematium scopulinum* subsp. *appalachianum*) 419
Blunt-lobed cliff fern (*Physematium obtusum* subsp. *obtusum*) 417
Mountain cliff fern (*Physematium scopulinum* subsp. *laurentianum*) 420
Oregon cliff fern (*Physematium oreganum* subsp. *cathcartianum*) 418

Rocky Mountain cliff fern (*Physematium scopulinum* subsp. *laurentianum*) 420
Rusty cliff fern (*Woodsia ilvensis*) 490
Smooth cliff fern (*Woodsia glabella*) 489
Climbing fern
American climbing fern (*Lygodium palmatum*) 332
Japanese climbing fern (*Lygodium japonicum*) 330
Old World climbing fern (*Lygodium microphyllum*) 331
Small-Leaved climbing fern (*Lygodium microphyllum*) 331
Climbing vine fern (*Microgramma heterophylla*) 349
Cloak fern
Hybrid cloak fern (*Astrolepis integerrima*) 181
Powdery false cloak fern (*Argyrochosma dealbata*) 144
Wavy climbing fern (*Astrolepis sinuata*) 182
Wavy scaly climbing fern (*Astrolepis sinuata*) 182
Clubmoss 7, 8, 16, 42
Appressed bog clubmoss (*Lycopodiella appressa*) 82
Bog clubmoss (*Pseudolycopodiella caroliniana*) 93
Bristly clubmoss (*Spinulum annotinum*) 111
Bruce's clubmoss (*Lycopodiella × brucei*) 79
Butters' clubmoss (*Huperzia × buttersii*) 53
Common clubmoss (*Lycopodium clavatum* subsp. *clavatum*) 88
Copeland's clubmoss (*Lycopodiella × copelandii*) 79
Flat-branched tree clubmoss (*Dendrolycopodium obscurum*) 46
Foxtail bog clubmoss (*Lycopodiella alopecuroides*) 81
Gilman's bog clubmoss (*Lycopodiella × gilmanii*) 79
Hickey's tree clubmoss (*Dendrolycopodium hickeyi*) 45
Nodding clubmoss (*Palhinhaea cernua*) 91
Northern appressed clubmoss (*Lycopodiella subappressa*) 85
Northern tree clubmoss (*Dendrolycopodium dendroideum*) 44
Northern bog clubmoss (*Lycopodiella inundata*) 83
One-cone clubmoss (*Lycopodium lagopus*) 89

Prickly tree clubmoss (*Dendrolycopodium dendroideum*) 44
Prostrate bog clubmoss (*Lycopodiella prostrata*) 84
Robust clubmoss (*Lycopodiella* × *robusta*) 79
Slender clubmoss (*Pseudolycopodiella caroliniana*) 93
Stag's horn clubmoss (*Lycopodium clavatum* subsp. *clavatum*) 88
Staghorn clubmoss (*Palhinhaea cernua*) 91
Comb fern
Brown-hair comb fern (*Ctenitis submarginalis*) 239
Red-hair comb fern (*Ctenitis sloanei*) 238
Common staghorn fern (*Platycerium bifurcatum*) 428
Creeping bramble fern (*Hypolepis barringtonii*) 321
Cuplet fern (*Dennstaedtia bipinnata*) 255
Curly Grass fern (*Schizaea pusilla*) 468

D
Dense lace fern (*Aspidotis densa*) 145
Dentate midsorus fern (*Telmatoblechnum serrulatum*) 474
Downy shield fern (*Christella dentata*) 226
Dwarf staghorn (*Cheiroglossa palmata*) 224

E
Elkhorn fern (*Platycerium bifurcatum*) 428

F
Flakelet fern (*Hypolepis barringtonii*) 321
Filmy fern
Appalachian filmy fern (*Vandenboschia boschiana*) 480
Taylor's filmy fern (*Hymenophyllum tayloriae*) 318
Tunbridge filmy fern (*Hymenophyllum tunbrigense*) 319
Firmoss 7, 53
Bartley's firmoss (*Huperzia* × *bartleyi*) 53
Beitel's firmoss (*Huperzia* × *josephbeitelii*) 53
Hybrid rock firmoss (*Huperzia* × *protoporophila*) 53
Mountain firmoss (*Huperzia appalachiana*) 55
Northern firmoss (*Huperzia selago*) 58
Rock firmoss (*Huperzia porophila*) 57
Shining firmoss (*Huperzia lucidula*) 56
Floating antler fern (*Ceratopteris pteridoides*) 220

Floating fern (*Salvinia minima*) 456
Florida tree fern (*Ctenitis sloanei*) 238
Forked fern (*Dicranopteris flexuosa*) 261
Fragile fern (*Cystopteris fragilis*) 249

G
Giant salvinia (*Salvinia molesta*) 457
Glade fern
Glade fern (*Homalosorus pycnocarpos*) 316
Narrow-leaved glade fern (*Homalosorus pycnocarpos*) 316
Silvery glade fern (*Deparia acrostichoides*) 258
Goldenrod fern (*Pityrogramma trifoliata*) 426
Goldfoot fern (*Phlebodium aureum*) 415
Grape fern 25
Alabama grape fern (*Sceptridium jenmanii*) 462
Blunt-leaved grape fern (*Sceptridium oneidense*) 465
Common grape fern (*Botrypus virginianus*) 214
Cut-leaf grape fern (*Sceptridium dissectum*) 461
Dissected grape fern (*Sceptridium dissectum*) 461
Leathery grape fern (*Sceptridium multifidum*) 464
Prostrate grape fern (*Sceptridium lunarioides*) 463
Southern grape fern (*Sceptridium biternatum*) 460
Sparse-leaved grape fern (*Sceptridium biternatum*) 460
St. Lawrence grape fern (*Sceptridium rugulosum*) 466
Ternate grape fern (*Sceptridium rugulosum*) 466
Winter grape fern (*Sceptridium lunarioides*) 463
Grass fern (*Vittaria graminifolia*) 484
Ground-cedar 7, 47
Blue ground-cedar (*Diphasiastrum tristachyum*) 52
Haberer's ground-cedar (*Diphasiastrum* × *habereri*) 47
Juniper-leaved ground-cedar (*Diphasiastrum* × *sabinifolium*) 47
Modest ground-cedar (*Diphasiastrum* × *verecundum*) 47
Northern ground-cedar (*Diphasiastrum complanatum* subsp. *complanatum*) 49
Southern ground-cedar (*Diphasiastrum digitatum*) 50
Zeiller's ground-cedar (*Diphasiastrum* × *zeilleri*) 47

H

Halberd fern
  Broad halberd fern (*Tectaria heracleifolia*) 471
  Incised halberd fern (*Tectaria incisa*) 472
  Least halberd fern (*Tectaria fimbriata*) 470
Hammock fern (*Blechnum appendiculatum*) 192
Hand fern (*Cheiroglossa palmata*) 224
Hand tongue (*Cheiroglossa palmata*) 224
Hartford fern (*Lygodium palmatum*) 332
Hay-scented fern (*Dennstaedtia punctilobula*) 256
Holly fern
  Asian holly fern (*Cyrtomium falcatum* subsp.
    falcatum) 243
  Braun's holly fern (*Polystichum braunii*) 438
  Climbing holly fern (*Lomariopsis kunzeana*) 325
  East Indian holly fern (*Arachniodes simplicior*) 143
  Fortune's holly fern (*Cyrtomium fortunei*) 244
  Hagenah's holly fern (*Polystichum* × *hagenahii*)
    435
  Holly fern (*Cyrtomium falcatum* subsp. *falcatum*)
    243
  Holly fern (*Lomariopsis kunzeana*) 325
  Holly fern (*Polystichum lonchitis*) 439
  Meyer's holly fern (*Polystichum* × *meyeri*) 435
  Potter's holly fern (*Polystichum* × *potteri*) 435
Holly vine fern (*Lomariopsis kunzeana*) 325
Horsetail 7, 8, 22, 25
  Common horsetail (*Equisetum arvense* subsp.
    arvense) 294
  Ferriss' horsetail (*Equisetum* × *ferrissii*) 289
  Field horsetail (*Equisetum arvense* subsp. *arvense*)
    294
  Littoral horsetail (*Equisetum* × *litorale*) 289
  Mackay's horsetail (*Equisetum* × *trachyodon*) 289
  Marsh horsetail (*Equisetum palustre*) 298
  Meadow horsetail (*Equisetum pratense*) 299
  Nelson's horsetail (*Equisetum* × *nelsonii*) 289
  River horsetail (*Equisetum fluviatile*) 295
  Woodland horsetail (*Equisetum sylvaticum*) 301
Huguenot fern (*Pteris multifida*) 449

I

Interrupted fern (*Claytosmunda claytoniana*) 229

J

Japanese painted fern (*Athyrium niponicum*) 186

K

Kariba weed (*Salvinia molesta*) 457

L

Lady fern
  Japanese lady fern (*Deparia petersenii*) 259
  Lady fern (Genus *Athyrium*) 183
  Lowland lady fern (*Athyrium asplenioides*) 185
  Narrow lady fern (*Athyrium angustum*) 184
  Northern lady fern (*Athyrium angustum*) 184
  Southern lady fern (*Athyrium asplenioides*) 185
Lance-leaf twin-sorus fern (*Diplazium lonchophyllum*)
  268
Lattice-vein fern
  Dentate lattice-vein fern (*Meniscium serratum*) 347
  Lattice-vein fern (*Meniscium reticulatum*) 346
  Toothed lattice-vein fern (*Meniscium serratum*)
    347
Leather fern
  Coast leather fern (*Acrostichum aureum*) 116
  Giant leather fern (*Acrostichum danaeifolium*) 117
  Golden leather fern (*Acrostichum aureum*) 116
  Inland leather fern (*Acrostichum danaeifolium*) 117
  Leather fern (*Acrostichum aureum*) 116
  Leather fern (*Rumohra adiantiformis*) 454
Lip fern
  Alabama lip fern (*Myriopteris alabamensis*) 355
  Eaton's lip fern (*Myriopteris rufa*) 359
  Hairy lip fern (*Myriopteris lanosa*) 357
  Slender lip fern (*Myriopteris gracilis*) 356
  Smooth lip fern (*Myriopteris alabamensis*) 355
  Southern lip fern (*Myriopteris microphylla*) 358
  Wooly lip fern (*Myriopteris tomentosa*) 360
Log fern (*Dryopteris celsa*) 278

M

Mackay's brittle fern (*Cystopteris tenuis*) 253
Maiden fern
  Abrupt-Tip maiden fern (*Pelazoneuron augescens*)
    398

Alabama maiden fern (*Leptogramma burksiorum*) 323

Caribbean maiden fern (*Amauropelta sancta*) 133

Downy maiden fern (*Christella dentata*) 226

Glandular maiden fern (*Amauropelta resinifera*) 132

Grid-scale maiden fern (*Pelazoneuron patens*) 401

Guadeloupe maiden fern (*Goniopteris domingensis*) 305

Jeweled maiden fern (*Amblovenatum opulentum*) 135

Mariana maiden fern (*Macrothelypteris torresiana*) 334

Rough hairy maiden fern (*Christella hispidula*) 227

Southern maiden fern (*Pelazoneuron kunthii*) 399

Stately maiden fern (*Pelazoneuron abruptum* var. *grande*) 397

Variable maiden fern (*Christella hispidula*) 227

Wax-dot maiden fern (*Amauropelta resinifera*) 132

Widespread maiden fern (*Pelazoneuron kunthii*) 399

Maidenhair

Aleutian maidenhair (*Adiantum aleuticum*) 123

Brittle maidenhair (*Adiantum tenerum*) 128

Common maidenhair (*Adiantum capillus-veneris*) 125

Double-Edge maidenhair (*Adiantum anceps*) 124

Fragrant maidenhair (*Adiantum melanoleucum*) 126

Green Mountain maidenhair (*Adiantum viridimontanum*) 129

Northern maidenhair (*Adiantum pedatum*) 127

Southern maidenhair (*Adiantum capillus-veneris*) 125

Western maidenhair (*Adiantum aleuticum*) 123

Maidenhair pineland fern (*Anemia adiantifolia*) 140

Male fern (*Dryopteris filix-mas* subsp. *brittonii*) 283

Marsh fern

Marsh fern (*Telmatoblechnum serrulatum*) 474

Marsh fern (*Thelypteris palustris*) 476

Ovate marsh fern (*Pelazoneuron ovatum*) 400

Massachusetts fern (*Coryphopteris simulata*) 231

Merlin's grass (*Isoetes*) 59

Mosquito fern

Carolina mosquito fern (*Azolla cristata*) 189

Crested mosquito fern (*Azolla cristata*) 189

Eastern mosquito fern (*Azolla cristata*) 189

Feathered mosquito fern (*Azolla pinnata* subsp. *pinnata*) 190

Mexican mosquito fern (*Azolla mexicana*) 189

Mosquito fern (*Azolla cristata*) 189

Moonwort

American moonwort (*Botrychium neolunaria*) 208

Dainty moonwort (*Botrychium crenulatum*) 202

Daisy-leaf moonwort (*Botrychium matricariifolium*) 204

Frenchman's Bluff moonwort (*Botrychium gallicomontanum*) 203

Least moonwort (*Botrychium simplex* var. *simplex*) 210

Little goblin moonwort (*Botrychium mormo*) 207

Michigan moonwort (*Botrychium michiganense*) 205

Mingan moonwort (*Botrychium minganense*) 206

Mischievous moonwort (*Botrychium tenebrosum*) 212

Narrow triangle moonwort (*Botrychium angustisegmentum*) 199

Pale moonwort (*Botrychium pallidum*) 209

Prairie moonwort (*Botrychium campestre*) 201

Spatulate moonwort (*Botrychium spathulatum*) 211

Upswept moonwort (*Botrychium ascendens*) 200

N

Nardoo (*Marsilea mutica*) 339

Netted chain fern (*Lorinseria areolata*) 327

New World midsorus fern (*Blechnum appendiculatum*) 192

New York fern (*Amauropelta noveboracensis*) 131

O

Oak fern

Appalachian oak fern (*Gymnocarpium appalachianum*) 311

Asian oak fern (*Gymnocarpium continentale*) 312

Britton's oak fern (*Gymnocarpium* × *brittonianum*) 309

Intermediate oak fern (*Gymnocarpium* × *intermedium*) 309

Limestone oak fern (*Gymnocarpium robertianum*) 314

Nahanni oak fern (*Gymnocarpium continentale*) 312

Northern oak fern (*Gymnocarpium dryopteris*) 313

Tetraploid hybrid oak fern (*Gymnocarpium* × *achriosporum*) 309

Ostrich fern (*Matteuccia struthiopteris* var. pensylvanica) 344

P

Pine fern (*Anemia adiantifolia*) 140

Parsley fern

American parsley fern (*Cryptogramma acrostichoides*) 235

Slender parsley fern (*Cryptogramma stelleri*) 236

Polypody

Appalachian polypody (*Polypodium appalachianum*) 433

Comb polypody (*Pecluma bourgeauana*) 392

Dwarf polypody (*Moranopteris nimbata*) 352

Eastern hybrid polypody (*Polypodium* × *incognitum*) 432

Golden polypody (*Phlebodium aureum*) 415

Gray's polypody (*Pleopeltis michauxiana*) 430

Plume polypody (*Pecluma plumula*) 394

Rock polypody (*Polypodium virginianum*) 434

Scaly polypody (*Pleopeltis michauxiana*) 430

Swamp plume polypody (*Pecluma bourgeauana*) 392

West Indian dwarf polypody (*Moranopteris nimbata*) 352

Widespread polypody (*Pecluma dispersa*) 393

Prickly mountain-moss (*Selaginella selaginoides*) 107

Q

Quillwort 7, 8, 13, 16, 20, 28

Appalachian quillwort (*Isoetes appalachiana*) 65

Black-spored quillwort (*Isoetes melanospora*) 72

Boom's quillwort (*Isoetes boomii*) 65

Butler's quillwort (*Isoetes butleri*) 66

Carolina quillwort (*Isoetes valida*) 77

Chesapeake quillwort (*Isoetes mattaponica*) 71

Eastern black-footed quillwort (*Isoetes melanopoda*) 72

Engelmann's quillwort (*Isoetes engelmannii*) 67

Flat rock quillwort (*Isoetes graniticola*) 68

Florida quillwort (*Isoetes flaccida*) 67

Georgia quillwort (*Isoetes georgiana*) 68

Green Mountain quillwort (*Isoetes viridimontana*) 78

Lake quillwort (*Isoetes macrospora*) 71

Limestone quillwort (*Isoetes butleri*) 66

Louisiana quillwort (*Isoetes louisianensis*) 70

Mat-forming quillwort (*Isoetes tegetiformans*) 75

Northern quillwort (*Isoetes septentrionalis*) 75

Piedmont quillwort (*Isoetes piedmontana*) 73

Prototype quillwort (*Isoetes prototypus*) 74

Rush quillwort (*Isoetes junciformis*) 69

Shore quillwort (*Isoetes riparia*) 74

Short-veiled quillwort (*Isoetes microvela*) 73

Spiny-spored quillwort (*Isoetes echinospora* subsp. muricata) 66

St. Lawrence quillwort (*Isoetes laurentiana*) 70

Strong quillwort (*Isoetes valida*) 77

Swamp quillwort (*Isoetes boomii*) 65

Tennessee quillwort (*Isoetes tennesseensis*) 76

True quillwort (*Isoetes valida*) 77

Tuckerman's quillwort (*Isoetes tuckermanii*) 76

Virginia quillwort (*Isoetes virginica*) 78

Winter quillwort (*Isoetes hyemalis*) 69

Woodland quillwort (*Isoetes melanopoda*) 72

R

Rattlesnake fern (*Botrypus virginianus*) 25, 214

Ray fern (*Actinostachys pennula*) 119

Ray spiked fern (*Actinostachys pennula*) 119

Resurrection fern

Resurrection fern (*Pleopeltis michauxiana*) 430

Tropical resurrection fern (*Pleopeltis polypodioides*) 431

Ribbon fern (*Ophioderma pendulum*) 376

Rockbrake

American rockbrake (*Cryptogramma acrostichoides*) 235

Fragile rockbrake (*Cryptogramma stelleri*) 236

Slender rockbrake (*Cryptogramma stelleri*) 236

Steller's rockbrake (*Cryptogramma stelleri*) 236

Rock cap fern (*Polypodium appalachianum*) 433

Royal fern (*Osmunda spectabilis*) 387

Rugg's Osmunda (×*Osmunimunda ruggii*) 228, 336

Running-pine 47

    Northern running-pine (*Diphasiastrum complanatum* subsp. *complanatum*) 49

    Southern running-pine (*Diphasiastrum digitatum*) 50

S

Savinleaf ground-pine (*Diphasiastrum* × *sabinifolium*) 47

Scouring rush

    Common scouring rush (*Equisetum hyemale* subsp. *affine*) 296

    Dwarf scouring rush (*Equisetum scirpoides*) 300

    Smooth scouring rush (*Equisetum laevigatum*) 297

    Variegated scouring rush (*Equisetum variegatum* subsp. *variegatum*) 302

Sensitive fern (*Onoclea sensibilis*) 374

Serpent fern (*Microsorum grossum*) 351

Serpentine fern (*Aspidotis densa*) 145

Shield fern 911

    Southern shield fern (*Dryopteris ludoviciana*) 287

    St. John's shield fern (*Christella hispidula*) 227

    Swamp shield fern (*Cyclosorus interruptus*) 241

Shoestring fern (*Vittaria lineata*) 485

Short-fruit nardoo (*Marsilea hirsuta*) 337

Silverback fern (*Pityrogramma calomelanos* var. *calomelanos*) 425

Single-sorus fern (*Asplenium monanthes*) 164

Sinkhole fern (*Blechnum appendiculatum*) 192

Sitka clubmoss (*Diphasiastrum sitchense*) 51

Spikemoss 7, 8, 16, 94

    Blue spikemoss (*Selaginella uncinata*) 109

    Braun's spikemoss (*Selaginella braunii*) 101

    Buck's meadow spikemoss (*Selaginella eclipes*) 104

    Dwarf spikemoss (*Selaginella rupestris*) 106

    Eaton's spikemoss (*Selaginella eatonii*) 103

    Gulf spikemoss (*Selaginella ludoviciana*) 105

    Hidden spikemoss (*Selaginella eclipes*) 104

    Louisiana spikemoss (*Selaginella ludoviciana*) 105

    Meadow spikemoss (*Selaginella apoda*) 99

    Northern spikemoss (*Selaginella selaginoides*) 107

    Peacock spikemoss (*Selaginella uncinata*) 109

    Riddell's spikemoss (*Selaginella corallina*) 102

    Rock spikemoss (*Selaginella rupestris*) 106

    Sand spikemoss (*Selaginella arenicola*) 100

    Sandy spikemoss (*Selaginella acanthonota*) 98

    Spiny spikemoss (*Selaginella acanthonota*) 98

    Twisted-hair spikemoss (*Selaginella tortipila*) 108

    Vine spikemoss (*Selaginella willdenowii*) 110

Spleenwort 146

    Abscised spleenwort (*Asplenium abscissum*) 158

    Alternate-leaved spleenwort (*Asplenium* × *alternifolium*) 147, 148, 152, 153

    Auricled spleenwort (*Asplenium auritum*) 159

    Biscayne spleenwort (*Asplenium* × *biscayneanum*) 147, 148, 155

    Black-stemmed spleenwort (*Asplenium resiliens*) 170

    Bradley's spleenwort (*Asplenium bradleyi*) 160

    Boydston's spleenwort (*Asplenium* × *boydstoniae*) 147

    Crested spleenwort (*Asplenium cristatum*) 161

    Curtiss's spleenwort (*Asplenium* × *curtissii*) 147, 148, 155, 156

    Cutleaf spleenwort (*Asplenium abscissum*) 158

    Delicate spleenwort (*Asplenium verecundum*) 178

    Eared spleenwort (*Asplenium auritum*) 159

    Ebony spleenwort (*Asplenium platyneuron*) 167

    Forked spleenwort (*Asplenium septentrionale* subsp. *septentrionale*) 174

    Graves's spleenwort (*Asplenium* × *gravesii*) 147, 148, 151

    Green spleenwort (*Asplenium viride*) 179

    Hairy spleenwort (*Asplenium pumilum*) 169

    Hemlock spleenwort (*Asplenium cristatum*) 161

    Herb's spleenwort (*Asplenium* × *herbwagneri*) 147

    Japanese false spleenwort (*Deparia petersenii*) 259

    Kentucky spleenwort (*Asplenium* × *kentuckiense*) 147, 149, 151

    Lobed spleenwort (*Asplenium pinnatifidum*) 166

    Maidenhair spleenwort (*Asplenium trichomanes*) 176

Modest spleenwort (*Asplenium verecundum*) 178

Morgan's spleenwort (*Asplenium × morganii*) 147

Morzenti's spleenwort (*Asplenium × heteroresiliens*) 147, 148, 153, 155

Mountain spleenwort (*Asplenium montanum*) 165

Narrow-leaved spleenwort (*Homalosorus pycnocarpos*) 316

Parsley spleenwort (*Asplenium cristatum*) 161

Ruffled spleenwort (*Asplenium plenum*) 168

Scott's fertile spleenwort (*Asplenium tutwilerae*) 177

Scott's spleenwort (*Asplenium × ebenoides*) 147, 148, 150, 151

Shawnee spleenwort (*Asplenium × shawneense*) 147

Silvery spleenwort (*Deparia acrostichoides*) 258

Toothed spleenwort (*Asplenium dentatum* subsp. *dentatum*) 162

Triangle spleenwort (*Asplenium pumilum*) 169

Trudell's spleenwort (*Asplenium × trudellii*) 147, 149, 151

Tutwiler's spleenwort (*Asplenium tutwilerae*) 177

Varicolored spleenwort (*Asplenium heterochroum*) 163

Virginia spleenwort (*Asplenium × virginicum*) 147

Wherry's spleenwort (*Asplenium × wherryi*) 147

Spready tri-vein fern (*Cyclosorus interruptus*) 241

Star-hair fern

Creeping star-hair fern (*Goniopteris reptans*) 306

Free-tip star-hair fern (*Goniopteris tetragona*) 308

Stiff star-hair fern (*Goniopteris sclerophylla*) 307

Strap fern

Long strap fern (*Campyloneurum phyllitidis*) 218

Narrow strap fern (*Campyloneurum angustifolium*) 216

Tailed strap fern (*Campyloneurum costatum*) 217

Swamp fern (*Telmatoblechnum serrulatum*) 474

Sword fern

Asian sword fern (*Nephrolepis brownii*) 366

Avery's sword fern (*Nephrolepis × averyi*) 364

Fishtail sword fern (*Nephrolepis falcata*) 369

Giant sword fern (*Nephrolepis biserrata*) 365

Rough sword fern (*Nephrolepis hirsutula*) 370

Scaly sword fern (*Nephrolepis hirsutula*) 370

Sword fern (*Nephrolepis exaltata*) 368

Tuberous sword fern (*Nephrolepis cordifolia*) 367

T

Tapering tri-vein fern (*Christella dentata*) 226

Torres's fern (*Macrothelypteris torresiana*) 334

Tropical curly-grass fern (*Actinostachys pennula*) 119

V

Vegetable fern (*Diplazium esculentum*) 267

Venus' hair fern (*Adiantum capillus-veneris*) 125

Virginia chain fern (*Anchistea virginica*) 137

W

Walking fern (*Asplenium rhizophyllum*) 171

Wall rue (*Asplenium ruta-muraria* var. *cryptolepis*) 172

Wart fern (*Microsorum grossum*) 351

Water clover

Bigfoot water clover (*Marsilea macropoda*) 337

Bristly water clover (*Marsilea hirsuta*) 337

European water clover (*Marsilea quadrifolia*) 340

Hairy water clover (*Marsilea vestita*) 342

Small water clover (*Marsilea minuta*) 338

Tropical water clover (*Marsilea oligospora*) 340

Water fern

Floating water fern (*Ceratopteris pteridoides*) 220

Triangle water fern (*Ceratopteris richardii*) 221

Water hornfern (*Ceratopteris thalictroides* subsp. *thalictroides*) 222

Water Spangles (*Salvinia minima*) 456

Water Sprite (*Ceratopteris thalictroides* subsp. *thalictroides*) 222

Water velvet (*Azolla cristata*) 189

Wedgelet fern (*Odontosoria clavata*) 372

Weft fern (*Crepidomanes intricatum*) 233

Whisk fern (*Psilotum nudum*) 7, 8, 25, 371, 441

Wild Boston fern (*Nephrolepis exaltata*) 368

Willdenow's fern (*Cyclosorus interruptus*) 241

Wood fern/woodfern

Algonquin wood fern (*Dryopteris × algonquinensis*) 270

Benedict's wood fern (*Dryopteris × benedictii*) 270

Boott's wood fern (*Dryopteris* × *boottii*) 269, 270, 271, 274

Brathay wood fern (*Dryopteris* × *brathaica*) 270

Burgess' wood fern (*Dryopteris* × *burgessii*) 270

Clinton's wood fern (*Dryopteris clintoniana*) 279

Correll's hybrid wood fern (*Dryopteris* × *correllii*) 270

Crested wood fern (*Dryopteris cristata*) 280

Dixie wood fern (*Dryopteris* × *australis*) 269, 270, 271

Dowell's wood fern (*Dryopteris* × *dowellii*) 270

Evergreen wood fern (*Dryopteris intermedia* subsp. *intermedia*) 286

Fragrant wood fern (*Dryopteris fragrans*) 284

Goldie's wood fern (*Dryopteris goldiana*) 285

Leeds' wood fern (*Dryopteris* × *leedsii*) 270, 271

Marginal wood fern (*Dryopteris marginalis*) 288

Marsh wood fern (*Dryopteris* × *uliginosa*) 269, 271

Mickell's wood fern (*Dryopteris* × *mickelii*) 270

Montgomery's wood fern (*Dryopteris* × *montgomereyi*) 270

Mountain wood fern (*Dryopteris campyloptera*) 276

Northern wood fern (*Dryopteris expansa*) 282

Pittsford's wood fern (*Dryopteris* × *pittsfordensis*) 271

Separate wood fern (*Dryopteris* × *separabilis*) 271

Slosson's wood fern (*Dryopteris* × *slossoniae*) 271

Southern wood fern (*Dryopteris ludoviciana*) 287

Spinulose wood fern (*Dryopteris carthusiana*) 277

Spreading wood fern (*Dryopteris expansa*) 282

Toothed wood fern (*Dryopteris carthusiana*) 277

Triploid wood fern (*Dryopteris* × *triploidea*) 269, 271, 272

Wherry's wood fern (*Dryopteris* × *neowherryi*) 270, 271

Woodsia

Abbe's woodsia (×*Woodsimatium abbeae*) 416, 486

Slender woodsia (*Woodsia* × *gracilis*) 486

Maxon's woodsia (*Physematium* × *maxonii*) 416

Tryon's woodsia (*Woodsia* × *tryonis*) 486

Wright's pineland fern (*Anemia wrightii*) 141